THACKERAY

THE USES OF ADVERSITY

1811 – 1846

BOOKS BY GORDON N. RAY

The Letters and Private Papers of
William Makepeace Thackeray. *Four Volumes. 1945–1946*

The Rose and the Ring Reproduced in Facsimile from the
Author's Original Manuscript in the Pierpont Morgan Library. *1947*

The Buried Life. A Study of the Relation between
Thackeray's Fiction and His Personal History. *1952*

Thackeray's Contributions to the "Morning Chronicle." *1955*

Thackeray. The Uses of Adversity. 1811–1846.

IN PREPARATION

Thackeray. The Age of Wisdom. 1847–1863.

Thackeray in the later 1830s

From an oil painting by Frank Stone

THACKERAY

THE USES OF ADVERSITY

(1811-1846)

GORDON N. RAY

McGraw-Hill Book Company, Inc.
NEW YORK TORONTO LONDON

Library of Congress Catalog Card Number: 55-7282

Published by the McGraw-Hill Book Company, Inc.
Printed in the United States of America

For

HOWARD MUMFORD JONES

Preface

This volume is the first of two designed to provide the comprehensive account of Thackeray's life and writings which I promised in my edition of his *Letters and Private Papers* ten years ago. It is the initial instalment of the only full-length biography ever authorized by his family; and throughout its preparation I have enjoyed the help of his grand-daughter and grandson, Mrs. Richard Fuller and Mr. W. T. D. Ritchie. Thackeray's *Letters* have inevitably served as the foundation of this work, but the existence of my edition has rendered a "life and letters" on the familiar pattern inappropriate. With regard to the several studies of various aspects of Thackeray and his books which I have published since 1945, my usual practice has been to summarize very briefly my conclusions, referring the reader to the studies themselves for fuller information. Thus I have discussed the important and interesting question of Thackeray's "originals" only incidentally, since this was a central subject of my recent volume *The Buried Life: A Study of the Relation between Thackeray's Fiction and His Personal History*. But I have ventured to repeat from this monograph three short passages concerning Major and Mrs. Carmichael-Smyth and Mrs. Butler; and in discussing Thackeray's periodical work in the 1840s, I have drawn on my recent introduction to *Thackeray's Contributions to the "Morning Chronicle."* I have neither new data concerning these subjects, nor a novel perspective from which to view them; and a rewriting of my earlier formulations would be mere elegant variation.

Since the appearance of Thackeray's *Letters,* it has been my good fortune to locate in English archives, both public and private, an abundance of fresh and significant manuscript material. Pride of place among these discoveries belongs to the more than 700 letters written by Thackeray himself. They include nearly the whole of his correspondence with his principal publishers, Bradbury and Evans and George Smith, a correspondence filled with insights into his methods of composition and his habits as editor of the *Cornhill Magazine.* Hardly less absorbing are two shorter series addressed to the families of close friends, Eyre Evans Crowe and Sir Jonathan Frederick Pollock. These letters and many others will eventually add an ample supplementary volume to his published correspondence. Almost as useful to the biographer are the Brookfield papers, some 250 letters written by Mrs. Brookfield and her husband for the most part during the period of their intimacy with Thackeray. Not only are these documents indispensable to any detailed account of Thackeray's relations with the Brookfields; they are also of capital importance for the history of his life in general during the years between *Vanity Fair* and *Esmond.* Examination of the papers of Thackeray's family has proved extremely rewarding. A long series of letters exchanged by his mother, his aunts, and his grandmother has illuminated the obscure early history of the Thackerays in India. The family archives have also supplied hundreds of letters written to Thackeray, the extensive correspondence exchanged by his daughters and mother during his lifetime, and the manuscript diaries and reminiscences of his older daughter, Lady Ritchie. These are all sources of great significance, as is a very different document, Henry Silver's manuscript diary of conversations at the *Punch* table between 1858 and 1870.

I offer most grateful acknowledgment to the following for the use of papers (those just described and many others), drawings, or recollections of family tradition: Mr. E. Arthur Ball, Father Paul Brookfield, the firm of Bradbury Agnew (and Mr. Alan G. Agnew, its Managing Director), Mr. Evelyn Carmichael of Carmichael, the proprietors of the Carnegie Bookshop, Mr. J. A. Waley Cohen, the Marchioness of Crewe (through the good offices of Mr. James Pope-Hennessy), Mrs. Aline Edgcumbe, Mrs. Freshfield, Maggs Brothers, Dr. Eric Millar, Mrs. Tempë Monroe of Auchinbowie, Sir John Murray, Major Anthony Murray-Smith, the late Dr. A. S. W. Rosenbach, the late Mrs. Reginald Smith, the firm of W. T. Spencer, and the late Orlando F. Weber, Jr. I am also much indebted to the officials of the Athenaeum, Garrick, and Reform Clubs, the Berg Collection of the New York Public Library (particularly Dr. John

Gordan), the British Museum (particularly Mr. F. C. Francis), Charterhouse School, the Commonwealth Relations Office, the Genealogical Office at Dublin Castle, the Houghton Library of Harvard University (particularly Professor William A. Jackson), the Huntington Library, the London Museum, the National Library of Scotland, the Pierpont Morgan Library (particularly Mr. Frederick B. Adams, Jr.), Trinity College, Cambridge (particularly J. R. M. Butler, Regius Professor of History), and the War Office. I am thankful as well to my friends Professor Gordon Haight and Dr. Robert Metzdorf of Yale University and Professor G. Blakemore Evans of the University of Illinois, who have read the proofs of this book with attentive scrutiny. But my principal obligation, as always, has been to Mrs. Fuller and Mr. Ritchie, by whose permission, incidentally, I am enabled to quote from the unpublished writings of Thackeray and Lady Ritchie.

I must also record my thanks for timely aid in the form of fellowships or grants to the Guggenheim and Rockefeller Foundations and to the Graduate College Research Board of the University of Illinois. I passed the academic year 1952–1953 as the initial occupant of the Henry W. and Albert A. Berg Professorship of English and American Literature at New York University; and Vice-Chancellor Leroy A. Kimball, Dean Thomas Pollock, and Professors Oscar Cargill, Karl Holzknecht, and William R. Parker did all they could to make my tenure of this position both pleasant and productive. Finally, my work has been greatly furthered at my own university by the unvarying support and assistance of former President George D. Stoddard, Provost Henning Larsen, Director of the Library Robert B. Downs, Professor Robert W. Rogers, and the English Department's Secretary and Librarian, Mrs. Hobart Peer and Miss Eva Faye Benton.

G. N. R.

UNIVERSITY OF ILLINOIS
18 March 1955

Contents

List of Illustrations

(The name of the owner of each illustration taken from the original is noted in parenthesis.)

THACKERAY

THE USES OF ADVERSITY

1811 – 1846

Introduction

I

ONE EVENING IN 1862 Thackeray and Henry Silver walked away together from a *Punch* dinner. Silver had been reading Mary Gordon's life of John Wilson ("Christopher North" of the *Noctes Ambrosianae*), and he told his friend how much he admired the manliness Wilson had displayed in thrashing the tinker, in turning to work after he lost his fortune, and in other exploits recounted by Mrs. Gordon. "Thackeray dissents," Silver noted in his diary. "Says JW did nothing worth record—and the effect of the life upon him, Th^y^, was to make him tell his daughters 'Mind, no biography' of himself." [1] It is easy to understand how Thackeray had come to this decision. Worn out by painful afflictions long endured, he had by 1862 largely lost his earlier buoyancy and resilience. Despite his world-wide fame, he was a modest man, honestly diffident regarding his claims on the attention of posterity; and of recent years he had become depressed about the worth of his writing because he could find nothing new to say. Even if it were granted that posterity had a legitimate interest in him, many difficulties remained. The idea of a mere eulogy, in which the sensitive passages in his character and career would be glossed over, was repellent to him; yet many years must pass before these passages could be candidly dealt with. Moreover, he was acutely conscious of the jealousy and dislike with which he was regarded in certain quarters. Particularly since the "Garrick Club Affair" of 1858, the London literary scene had been marked by something like open warfare between his adherents and those of Dickens. A biography would inevitably lead to widespread discussion in the press, and the thought of what might be contributed to this debate by his enemies could not but be distressing to him. Finally, he was a Victorian gentleman, who treasured his privacy and thoroughly endorsed the maxim *Secretum meum mihi.* So it was that his prohibition against a biography had not been withdrawn when he died late the following year; and Lady Ritchie noted in her heart-broken recollections of her father set down in the winter of 1864–1865: "Papa said when I drop there is to be no life written of me, mind this & consider it as my last testament & desire." [2]

There were many obituary notices of Thackeray, some of considerable biographical significance; and two unauthorized lives appeared during 1864: a slight but interesting *Brief Memoir of the Late Mr. Thackeray* by his friend James Hannay, and a scissors-and-paste compilation called *Thackeray: The Humourist and Man of Letters* by "Theodore Taylor, Esq., Membre de la Société des Gens de Lettres," who was actually the notorious John Camden Hotten. Sensing that Thackeray's edict against a biography could not after all be enforced, Edward FitzGerald proposed to Lady Ritchie that Tom Taylor be commissioned to write his life. But she had determined to abide by her father's command; and on 14 May 1865, FitzGerald withdrew his proposal:

> I think it is much [the] best to have no memoir of your Father: as you say, he is in his Books. I only suggested Tom Taylor in case there *were* any; or to anticipate some stupid Cockney, should any such project such a work.[3]

For fifteen years Lady Ritchie, with the formidable aid of Sir Leslie Stephen, who had married Thackeray's younger daughter, held to this line. If biographical data of value occasionally found their way into print, it was against the family's wishes. Lady Ritchie even took exception to the delightful paper which James T. Fields devoted to Thackeray in the *Atlantic Monthly* during 1871 and afterwards reprinted in *Yesterdays with Au-*

thors.[4] Trollope's appeal for information, when he was asked to contribute the Thackeray volume to the English Men of Letters series in 1879, was neatly parried both by Lady Ritchie and by FitzGerald; [5] and his book is consequently of little biographical importance. Stephen summed up the family's position in a terminal essay written for Smith, Elder's sumptuous *édition de luxe* of Thackeray's *Works* in 1879:

Mr. Thackeray intimated to his daughters during his life that he wished them to have no concern in any biography of their father. His known wishes were necessarily regarded as final by them. The family representatives of an eminent man may often feel it to be not merely a right but a duty to publish his life. But it is a duty for the discharge of which they are responsible to their own consciences and not to the public. The decision must rest upon the particular circumstances of the case, and involves considerations which can be fully known to none but the persons immediately concerned. If they decide upon silence, the same reasons which make silence desirable, may also make it undesirable to publish the grounds of their decision. Their conduct cannot be pronounced upon by a tribunal which is unprovided with the necessary materials for judgment. It is enough, therefore, to say that Mr. Thackeray's representatives not only accept—as they would in any case be bound to accept—but fully approve of his decision. They cannot discuss the question whether it was prompted by a conviction that they would be placed in a false position by biographers; by a sense of the difficulty of writing the life without violating private confidence; or by any more special considerations. This alone may be said; and I say it with the most entire conviction of its truth. Nothing could be told of Mr. Thackeray's private life by those who have the fullest means of knowledge which would not confirm the highest estimate derivable from his writings of the tenderness of his heart and the moral worth of his nature; and all that could be told would tend to justify the profound affection with which they cherish his memory.[6]

The year after this firm and confident pronouncement appeared, Disraeli's posthumous novel *Endymion* was published. The book was a best seller for a time, and the attention of its many readers centred on the novelist St. Barbe, "the vainest, the most envious, the most amusing of men," [7] who was immediately identified with Thackeray. Disraeli's portrait was a malicious reworking with many fictional additions of his sparse and hazy recollections of Thackeray in the early 1840s, but the great public, ignorant of these refinements, was titillated and amused. The novel roused to action Thackeray's old enemy Edmund Yates, whose abuse of him in a minor London weekly had set off the Garrick Club Affair of 1858. Yates took advantage of the appearance of *Endymion,* W. C. Brownell relates, "to recall his early personal attack upon Thackeray, and claim some credit for his perspicacity at a time when it required so much courage to make it that he was expelled from the Garrick Club in consequence, and found it proper to apologize for it long afterwards in public lectures, on the ground of his extreme youth." [8] Not content with a magazine justification of his behaviour towards Thackeray,[9] Yates four years later made a longer and more adroitly organized attack upon him in his *Recollections and Experiences.* Once more, though informed observers discounted Yates's charges on the ground that he was "a literary gutter-scraper" who had recently been sentenced to four months' imprisonment for criminal libel,[10] the great public listened and was impressed. Encouraged by Yates's example, such other old enemies as Serjeant Ballantine, W. P. Frith, and John Cordy Jeaffreson contributed further hostile testimony,[11] and gradually a caricature of Thackeray, utterly unlike the man himself, began to gain general circulation. The upshot of his family's "almost morbid reticence," Sir John Skelton pointed out, had been to create the misconception that Thackeray was "an utterly heartless worldling, curt, cynical, unsympathetic, finding his chief joy in eating and drinking and the assiduous cultivation of social 'swells.' " [12]

However distressing these publications might be, they were at least the work of outsiders. But in 1886 Lady Ritchie had been informed by Mrs. Brookfield, "my father's lifelong friend and mine," [13] that the desperate financial need of her clever but erratic son Charles, later a well-known West End actor, had made it imperative for her to sell publication rights to certain of Thackeray's letters to Charles Scribner's Sons in New York. After Stephen had examined the letters, Lady Ritchie reluctantly let herself be quoted to the effect that she was "very glad to hear" that Mrs. Brookfield had made these arrangements, though she was herself unable by her father's "expressed wish" to do anything of the sort.[14] When the letters had run their course in *Scribner's Magazine* during 1887, it was proposed that they should be brought out as a book simultaneously in England and in the United States. Lady Ritchie was profoundly disturbed by this suggestion. She at last permitted English publication, though without even her reluctant American *imprimatur,* after Stephen had once more examined the material in *Scribner's* serial and assured her that the letters were "absolutely harmless as regards the relationship to Mrs. Brookfield." [15] He would greatly have preferred their suppression, and he was concerned that Mrs. Brookfield of all people should have been involved in the matter, but he felt that under the circumstances, Lady Ritchie had "nothing to do except to do nothing." [16] When the English edition of *A Collection of Letters of Thackeray* appeared, however, it was greatly resented in some quarters. "How any woman could bear to coin a man's heart into filthy lucre passes my comprehension," Lady Stanley of Alderley wrote to Lady Ritchie. "Is it not revolting for a woman to sell the heart's blood of one who gave her his inmost thoughts & love?" [17] And an acrimonious correspondence was printed in the London *Standard* between Charles Brookfield and George Smith, Thackeray's publisher, out of which both Brookfield and his mother emerged somewhat tarnished.[18]

Lady Ritchie regarded these publications of the 1880s as so many intrusions upon the privacy of her family circle. Reflecting on "Thackeray and His Biographers" in an article of 1891, she came as close to bitterness as was possible to a person of her gentle and forgiving spirit:

It is curious to note how feelings change with time. Once the most reverent tribute which people knew how to pay to those who were gone was that which Antigone rendered to her brothers. In these modern days a different feeling exists. Letters are broken open; diaries are scanned; passing emotions and impressions, words hastily spoken, and almost forgotten, are recalled and reprinted, in one, two, three editions, for the edification of those who run, while others are still there to shrink and to suffer unexpected stings, and to feel a lifelong regret for what might perhaps be all explained could the dead speak, and might have been spared had the living been more silent.[19]

She was still unwilling to attempt a biography herself, but she realized that her former position had become untenable. When an old friend of the family, Herman Merivale, concluded an eloquent protest against *A Collection of Letters of Thackeray* by expressing the hope that its publication would at least "lead before too late, to the issue of a full biography, as all must hope it will," [20] she authorized him to attempt such a work. Unhappily Merivale's "mental health" gave way before he had progressed very far with his task, and though Sir Frank T. Marzials was brought in to finish the book, it turned out to be an inconclusive production which satisfied nobody.

Lady Ritchie thereupon determined to provide herself the authoritative biographical tradition that was clearly needed to bulwark her father's reputation.[21] She would observe the letter of his prohibition and write no formal biography, yet she would at the same time supply so full a commentary that such a book would become unnecessary. Her first and best effort in this direction was *Chapters from Some Unwritten Memoirs,* which appeared serially in *Macmillan's Magazine* between 1890 and 1894. In 1898 and 1899 she wrote a series of Introductions for the Biographical Edition of her father's works, and in 1911 she extended these somewhat for the Centenary Biographical Edition of his writings. Mr. Walter De la Mare spoke for most of Thackeray's admirers when he praised "Lady Ritchie's store of memories, gilded with the sunshine of childhood, bringing with such sure and simple touches as her father himself might have envied his very presence before our eyes." [22] Swinburne alluded to the devotion, taste, and tact, even the "exquisite genius," displayed in these papers.[23] No one certainly has succeeded in catching the atmosphere of Thackeray's domestic life so perfectly, in setting down with so delicate a hand the "trivial fond records" of his home existence.

But having said this, one must acknowledge that Lady Ritchie suffered from important deficiencies as a biographer. Her knowledge was limited to one aspect of her father's varied career. Not merely was she unable to present what S. M. Ellis calls "the loose jesting Thackeray of Bohemian Paris, and of the Garrick Club and Evans's," [24] but she was inclined altogether to deny the existence of such a figure. As she studied Thackeray's life, she came to "feel more and more what a courageous tender-hearted father I had, and how proud I am of him." [25] Hence she wrote with "a justifiably pious grace, rather than with a desire to let the utmost be known," [26] "angelicizing" Thackeray, just as he had "angelicized" his stepfather in drawing him as Colonel Newcome. Moreover, Lady Ritchie was often vague and inaccurate. "I can never trust my own impressions of place or time or quantity," she confessed; "only I can feel the essence which is there and which does not vary." Just as she was beginning the Centenary Biographical Introductions, she noted: "My memory is a worry. I remember, but so slowly that it is most provoking and irritating." [27] Finally, she was incapable of arranging her material in a large and inclusive pattern. Though there is more than a touch of animus [28] in Virginia Woolf's picture of Lady Ritchie as Mrs. Hilbery struggling helplessly with her poet-father's biography in Chapter 3 of *Night and Day,* the episode is not altogether without warrant. Hence her essays on her father remain a series of vivid and evocative sketches, that hardly combine to produce a complete and coherent portrait.

Having turned biographer herself, Lady Ritchie was no longer in a position to enforce her father's prohibition very strictly upon others, and accordingly between 1890 and 1930 many books were published concerning Thackeray's life and character. There were volumes of letters, studies of special aspects of his career, collections of reminiscences, and several biographies. The most important work in the last category was *William Makepeace Thackeray: A Biography* by Lewis Benjamin, who wrote under the pen-name of "Lewis Melville." [29] Though this is a compilation rather than a proper book, it is based on long and arduous research and (particularly through its bibliography) retains some usefulness today. Further sections of Thackeray's letters to Mrs. Brookfield found their way into print through the auction-sale catalogues of the Major Lambert (1914) and Goodyear (1927) collections.[30] In 1924 Mrs. Richard Fuller supplemented her mother's account of Thackeray's life at home by drawing anew on family papers in *Thackeray and His Daughter*. But the flood of print of which these were the high points served as much to confuse as to clarify the prevailing conception of Thackeray as a man and a writer.

In 1931 Mr. Michael Sadleir published *Edward and Rosina: 1803–1836* (later entitled *Bulwer and His Wife*), an account of the early life and work of the first Lord Lytton. Partially because he saw Thackeray through the jaundiced eyes of an old antagonist, and partially in an effort to bring into the open information concerning Thackeray which he felt was being unfairly withheld, Mr. Sadleir devoted a section of this brilliant book to summarizing the case against Thackeray the man. His verdict, supported by an impressive array of unfriendly evidence derived from his unrivalled acquaintance with Victorian periodicals and memoirs, was that Thackeray could only be regarded as "both a hypocrite and a snob." [31] As it happened, Mr. Sadleir's book was succeeded in 1932 by Mr. Malcolm Elwin's *Thackeray: A Personality*. This biography, by all odds the most coherent, inclusive, and accurate life which had appeared to that date, presented a very favourable view of its subject. But since Mr. Elwin had depended chiefly on published sources, Mr. Sadleir was able to contend that the truth had still not been fully told, that Mr. Elwin had failed to present "the shadow side of Thackeray," that his book in fact was simply an attempt to cover "the retreat of an already mildewed paragon." [32] When Mr. Simon Nowell-Smith in 1933 presented his convincing, point-by-point defence of Thackeray against Mr. Sadleir's charges, he none the less granted that doubt regarding Thackeray's character would persist until the full facts were known.

> Trollope's eclipse was due to his revelations of himself [wrote Mr. Nowell-Smith]; Thackeray's to his refusal to be revealed. . . . To this day his family have never consented to put their material into the hand of a biographer. . . . He did not foresee that this reticence—his daughters' rather than his own—would be construed as a suppression of "the truth," a deliberate concealment of the discreditable. But there are always commentators ready to think and

insinuate the worst, and such a construction has been put on Lady Ritchie's innocent and pious, but most unhappy, action.[33]

Moved not only by these considerations but also by the reflection that all persons intimately associated with Thackeray had long since died, Mrs. Fuller and Mr. Ritchie decided that the time had come to make all materials bearing on their grandfather's life and character fully available to the public. They accordingly authorized me in 1939 to prepare a comprehensive collection of Thackeray's *Letters and Private Papers*. When the four volumes of this edition appeared in 1945–1946, it soon became plain that they were doing their expected work. Not only were they accepted as a classic of epistolary literature, which constituted as well a fascinating panorama of English nineteenth-century life; they were also taken by most readers as a complete vindication of Thackeray. Mr. Sadleir, for example, was not slow to offer an *amende honorable*. In his review of the book he included

> a humble confession of error from one who thought to read Thackeray aright, but in fact grossly maligned him. In a book about Bulwer Lytton, published fifteen years ago, I drew conclusions as to Thackeray's character from a number of his periodical writings and from reminiscences of hostile or unperceptive contemporaries, which conclusions are now proved to have been mistaken.[34]

Yet sceptics remain. One ingenious writer, indeed, has recently ransacked Thackeray's *Letters and Private Papers* for data to support in a book-length study almost exactly the view of Thackeray advanced and afterwards withdrawn by Mr. Sadleir.[35] It seems clear, then, that an authoritative life of Thackeray is still needed to supplement his *Letters and Private Papers*.

II

The materials for Thackeray's biography are remarkably extensive and interesting. They can be divided into three categories, each of which presents its pitfalls for the biographer. His writing for publication contains much autobiography, some of it quite open, even more disguised. These passages are important evidence, but they must be used with caution. After a course of reading in the novels of Thackeray's maturity, the biographer is tempted to strive in his own narrative for something of the fine balance and nostalgic charm of *The Newcomes* or *Denis Duval.* Yet to mute discords and soften asperities in the manner of these fictions would be to falsify one's picture; it is impossible to be at once "Thackerayan" in this sense and faithful to fact. Consider, for example, the various sketches of Charterhouse in Thackeray's stories, passing from the idyllic "Grey Friars" of *The Newcomes* back through "Dr. Swishtail's Seminary" in *Vanity Fair* to the brutal "Slaughter House" of the early "Mr. and Mrs. Frank Berry." The nearer one approaches to his school-days, the less genial and the more authentic Thackeray's presentation of them becomes; and it is evident from contemporary testimony that even the last of these pictures glosses over certain aspects of life at an unreformed public school. Thackeray's correspondence, which reflects the direct impress of events, does not require this sort of scrutiny. Saintsbury was certainly correct in regarding it as the "one infallible source of biography, a source [which] . . . in the case of a man like Thackeray, with his unconquerable impulsiveness and his horror of publicity, is nearly pellucid." [1] But it has to be complemented by the testimony of his friends and acquaintances. "It was fair to believe that General Beal knew no more about himself than most men," James Gould Cozzens remarks of a character in his *Guard of Honor,* "and, out of his self-knowledge, could tell you, no matter how hard and honestly he tried, less than you could learn from what you saw or heard of his behavior." [2] Thackeray attained to far more self-knowledge than most of us; yet even he did not achieve the impossible feat of seeing himself with entire impartiality and completeness.

In view of the sketch already provided of the Thackerayan biographical tradition, the reader will readily understand that statements concerning him must be carefully assayed for bias. I have excluded altogether anecdotes of the class definitively described by Macaulay as "believed only by idiots and biographers"; and many others, when sifted in the light of their narrator's motives, have survived only in part. A special problem must be noted at this point. During the period of Thackeray's great popularity, he was the subject of an inordinate amount of smoking-room gossip. He testifies himself, for example, to the extreme annoyance caused him by Charlotte Brontë's well-intentioned dedication to him of the second edition of *Jane Eyre*. For years after its appearance there was circulated against him a "story of Jane Eyre, seduction, surreptitious family in the Regent's Park, &c.," which made him "wild" whenever he heard of "poor gentlemen and poor governesses accused of this easy charge." [3] His exasperation is illustrated in the following exchange, reported to have taken place between him and an American lady at a dinner-party in London as late as 1860:

Fair American Visitor: 'Tell me, Mr. Thackeray, is it true, the dreadful story about you and Currer Bell?'

Thackeray: 'Alas, Madam, it is all too true. And the fruits of that unhallowed intimacy were six children. I slew them all with my own hand.' [4]

After his death the printed record occasionally provides portentous hints of "strange stories . . . current in society with regard to his discredit" and revelations which this or that writer could make if he chose.[5] Perhaps Mr. Sadleir had some of these legends in mind when he wrote in 1932 that "the inescapable and recurrent problem of Thackeray as a traditional personality is how to reconcile what we are asked to believe he was with what we know he did." [6] As a conscientious investigator, I have done my best to ascertain whether any of these "strange stories" are grounded in fact. Thackeray admittedly experienced many misfortunes: he lost a substantial inheritance as a young man, he was afflicted from early manhood until death with stricture of the urethra, his wife became mentally ill after a short but most happy marriage, and he later fell in love with the wife of his best friend; but his behaviour throughout each of these trials was exemplary. The result of my researches, indeed, has been to make me confident that one may say of Thackeray, as Tennyson said of the Duke of Wellington,

Whatever record leap to light
He never shall be shamed.

Interest in Thackeray the man derives primarily from interest in his works, and this book deals as fully with his writings as with his life. Contrary to current critical orthodoxy, it is my view that the two mesh inextricably, at least in the case of a novelist like Thackeray, and that biography and criticism should go hand in hand. Thinking, with Mr. Edmund Wilson, that "literary criticism ought to be . . . a history of man's ideas and imaginings in the setting of the conditions which have shaped them," [7] I have made it my primary aim to see Thackeray's work in historical perspective. Hence I have drawn substantially on Victorian criticism for its evidential value, but I have made only incidental use of modern criticism, even of such studies as those of Professor John Dodds [8] and M. Raymond Las Vergnas [9] for which I have real respect. Like everyone else who has dealt with Thackeray during the last fifty years, I am of course much indebted to the various writings of that most learned and devoted of all Thackerayans, George Saintsbury.

The historical approach offers marked advantages in dealing with a major but currently unfashionable author. Since the decade of the First World War, Thackeray's work has been consistently underestimated, because it has been judged by the standards of a narrowly defined modernism. If we try to achieve an approximation of the perspective in which his own age viewed him, if we accept him in something like his own relaxed and tolerant spirit, if we view the society of which he was a part as interesting and even admirable in itself (and Victorian society at its best surely had a dignity and maturity unmatched in our own time), perhaps his importance will once again become clear. T. Earl Welby suggested such an approach when he remarked of Mr. Elwin's *Thackeray* in 1932: "[In this book] there is hardly an attempt to sketch out the intellectual position of Thackeray to his age, and it happens that just there is one of the tasks waiting for Thackerayan criticism." [10] Some modern critics of Thackeray have assumed that he took no significant "intellectual position" regarding Victorian problems. Yet Charlotte Brontë, in dedicating the second edition of *Jane Eyre* to Thackeray, found in him "an intellect profounder and more unique than his contemporaries have yet recognized," and described him as "the first social regenerator of the day." [11] Victorian comment, though generally phrased with less exuberance, confirms Charlotte Brontë's verdict; and Mr. G. M. Young, than whom no higher authority could be cited on such a point, has recently hailed Thackeray as "with Dickens and Carlyle the third great moralist of his time." [12]

I shall urge in the ensuing narrative that Thackeray attained this high position among his contemporaries chiefly by redefining the gentlemanly ideal to fit a middle-class rather than an aristocratic context. An account of the way in which his personality and work developed out of the circumstances that formed them will show how he came to do this. His birth assured him a good social position and an easy fortune. In his home circle, at Charterhouse, and at Cambridge, he was consequently given "the education of a gentleman," as this formula was understood during the Regency and under George IV, and this training taught him much that was valuable. But he was also led to believe for a time that the members of society were arranged in a strict hierarchical order in accordance with their birth, fortune, and employments. He was made familiar with the code of "honour" which allowed a gentleman to play fast and loose with his inferiors, as long as he discharged obligations to his equals. He was brought to admire and imitate the young "bloods" of the day, whose expensive and ostentatious way of life might be largely given over to idling, drinking, gambling, and womanizing, but who at least did not soil their hands with business or contaminate themselves by practising the arts. Thus led astray, not so much by his official mentors as by the prevailing opinions of those among whom he lived, he tried clumsily and half-heartedly to put these lessons into effect, and the result was prolonged unhappiness and ultimate disaster.

As he slowly and painfully made his way back to the main road, he contented himself for a time with demonstrating, like Douglas Jerrold and like Dickens in his later novels, that a society which honoured the gentlemanly ideal must be radically corrupt. But experience also gradually brought home to him the value of the better elements in his education, and he began to free the central and timeless qualities of gentlemanliness from its outmoded aristocratic trappings. By scraping away the meanness, the affectation, and the arrogance that disguised it; by emphasizing its simplicity, urbanity, gentleness, and manliness; he showed it to be as worthy as ever of allegiance. And in *The Book of Snobs* and *Vanity Fair* he gave this message to a reading public that collectively had been through much the same experience that he had individually and was therefore waiting eagerly for the prophet who would explain it to them.

When the modern reader is told by Mr. Van Wyck Brooks that Thackeray "wrote novels in the gentlemanly interest," [13] he envisions Thackeray as a quaint period curiosity. When Mr. De la Mare, having noted that Thackeray, "wrote for the most part books about gentlemen for gentlemen," goes on to remark that this was "a limited source of inspiration," [14] the modern reader wonders only at Mr. De la Mare's moderation of statement. When Mr. Edmund Wilson urges that Thackeray's social preoccupations made him "rather a shallow commentator on life," whose books appealed to "nice people" on both sides of the Atlantic, and who was therefore praised beyond his deserts by such "Old World 'bourgeois' critics as George Saintsbury and H. L. Mencken," [15] the modern reader finds this judgment entirely plausible. Yet we have noted that, in the context of his own age, Thackeray's loyalty to the gentlemanly code as he had redefined it was a hard-won and valid lesson, which performed an immense service in refining Victorian social feeling. Jeaffreson, who was just to Thackeray the writer if unjust to him as a man, spoke for many of his contemporaries when he described Thackeray as "emphatically the true gentleman of our generation, who has appealed to our best and most chivalric sympathies, and raising us from the slough and pollution of the Regency has made us once more 'a nation of gentlemen.' " [16]

Moreover, there is a larger issue involved here. The time has surely come when the irrational compulsion of middle-class writers to discredit middle-class ideals should be called into question. Fifty years ago Chesterton remarked of Thackeray: "He did not know the way things were going: he was too Victorian to understand the Victorian epoch . . . he seemed to take it for granted that the Victorian compromise would last; while Dickens . . . had already guessed that it would not."[17] This comparison, which was picked up by Shaw and developed with his usual persuasiveness, has become a commonplace among subsequent critics. Yet a close study of Thackeray's career suggests a very different way of viewing the matter. He was far more knowledgeable about the past course of history than Dickens and just as sensitive to its future drift. But being convinced with Dr. Johnson—

> How small of all that human hearts endure
> That part which laws or kings can cause or cure—

he gave little thought to the transitoriness or permanence of the Victorian scheme of things. Knowing that the difficulties of the human condition would remain much the same under any social order, he found Dickens's exacerbated rebelliousness towards the Victorian way of life profoundly wrong-headed and unprofitable. His view of his great contemporary's social philosophy was much the same as Walter Bagehot's:

> He began by describing really removeable evils in a style which would induce all persons, however insensible, to remove them if they could; he has ended by describing the natural evils and inevitable pains of the present state of being in such a manner as must tend to excite discontent and repining. . . . Mr. Dickens has not infrequently spoken . . . in what really is . . . a tone of objection to the necessary constitution of human society.[18]

The sagacity that Thackeray displayed in his view of the Victorian social organism was of a piece with his general wisdom, his achieving of which is the main theme of this volume. To study the compelling human drama that was his life is to see how his courageous struggle with long-continued adversity made him the great writer that he was. Indeed, his career affords a classic illustration of Xavier de Maistre's maxim: *"Ce qui gêne l'homme, le fortifie."* A grand defect of the English outlook on life, as it has expressed itself in fiction, has been its relative superficiality. If Thackeray at his finest rises above this tradition, as Trollope and even Fielding never do, it is perhaps because he had survived so searching an ordeal without being broken by it and without hardening into callous indifference. "The men capable of the highest passion," Ruskin observes in *Praeterita,* "are always tossed on fiery waves by [life]; the men who find it smooth water, and not scalding are of another sort. . . . There must be great happiness in the love-matches of the typical English squire. Yet English squires make their happy lives only a portion for foxes." [19] Thackeray's contemporaries thought him a classic above all because of the weight of feeling and experience behind his work. There have been suggestions in the last few years that readers are beginning to reawaken to this surpassing merit in his books.[20]

This is not the place to attempt a final judgment on Thackeray's work, an undertaking which must be deferred until his entire career has been described. I need only remark here that my study of his work in its historical setting has given me a renewed conviction of the greatness of its creator. If he belongs by what Mr. Cyril Connolly has called his "broad human touch" [21] with the great novelists of the world, he remains at the same time an integral part of his native tradition. He represents "in that gigantic parody called genius," as Chesterton pointed out, "the spirit of the Englishman in repose." [22] His kind of accomplishment is not fashionable today. For many years the pattern novelist has been James Joyce, who repudiated his family, his country, and his religion in order to devote himself wholly to his art. Thackeray's way was very different. Knowing the price that must be paid for such repudiations, he was content to work out his literary destiny within the limits imposed by the common life of his age, to share existence as it must be lived under the normal conditions of middle-class society. Certainly Thackeray is an imperfect artist when compared with Joyce. Yet to place a Victorian master like Thackeray or George Eliot side by side with such modern culture heroes as Joyce and Virginia Woolf is to be conscious of the same contrast that Professor Auerbach has noted between Balzac and Stendhal, on the one hand, and Flaubert and the Goncourts on the other. For all their dazzling achievements, the work of the latter betrays the weakness that inevitably accompanies "aesthetic isolation and the treatment of reality exclusively as an object of literary representation." It is marked by "something narrow, something oppressively close. . . . They are full of reality and intellect, but poor in humor and inner poise. The purely literary, even on the highest level of artistic acumen and amid the greatest wealth of impressions, limits the power of judgment, reduces the wealth of life, and at times distorts the outlook upon the world of phenomena." [23]

Nor can Thackeray's full stature as a man be realized until his story is completely told. The groundlessness of charges brought against him by hostile witnesses has already been noted, but a comprehensive estimate of Thackeray the man should not be presented in negative terms. Many great writers have been extremely disagreeable human beings; Mr. Eric Linklater has noted, indeed, that wanting to know a writer because you like his work is like wanting to know a goose because you like *pâté de foie gras*. But Thackeray was a remarkably engaging and admirable person, of whom it was accurately observed that he had "more feeling, more generosity, more manliness, and more shrewd common sense than most men of genius." [24] As a provisional judgment, I cannot do better than cite the words of that lifelong student of Thackeray's personality and work, the late Sir Desmond MacCarthy:

> to have expressed your genius and written beautifully; to have enjoyed life in spite of being extremely sensitive to its ugliness and pain; to have kept faith in goodness in spite of observing that it is usually speckled; to have consumed your own smoke instead of blowing black depression in other people's faces; to have refused to regard yourself as a great exceptional man though half the world proclaimed you; to have been endowed with an epicurean temperament and been stoical when it benefited others and yourself; to have known well the meaning of the word "vanity" without giving yourself airs of spiritual superiority; to have been a lover of idleness, yet to have worked furiously; to have been born touchy, yet to have been often magnanimous; to have been naturally impulsive and reckless and yet to have saved yourself and sheltered those you loved; and lastly, to have made those few singularly happy and kept the respect of every old friend—to have lived thus thoroughly and honorably was an achievement in the art of living which should exempt a man at any rate from the patronage of inexperience.[25]

To adjust the minute events of which literary biography is composed can only be "tedious and troublesome," Dr. Johnson contended long ago; "it requires no great force of understanding, but often depends upon enquiries which there is no opportunity of making, or is to be fetched from books and pamphlets not always at hand." [26] Yet without such painstaking preparations no lasting work of this kind can be done, and I have tried not to shirk them. I have sought to examine and appraise all pertinent material, in order to be able to speak with authority when denying as well as when affirming. I have relied not at all on modern biographies of Thackeray, even on such workmanlike books as those by Mr. Elwin and Professor Lionel Stevenson,[27] since it has been my invariable habit to go back to original sources. For the most part I have declined to take issue with what seem to me the errors of earlier writers, feeling that an authentic narrative implicitly disproves contradictory stories, however elaborately presented. Still less have I set myself to refute the various attempts to sum Thackeray up in a phrase that have at one time or another had some currency. He was not "a domesticated dandy," "a novelist ruined by dining out," "a spoilt artist," or any of the hundred other things that he has been accused of being by critics who know as little about his character as they do of his work. No reader of this book will require to have explained to him the inadequacy of these or other easy generalizations which

> . . . men smatter
> When they throw out and miss the matter.

I have endeavoured in the Notes to provide the reader with the means of checking all significant statements, a particular necessity with Thackeray, who has long suffered from the failure of his biographers to document their assertions. And I should say in conclusion that, far from finding my labours "tedious and troublesome," I have come instead to understand why Saintsbury envied the biographer of Thackeray who in possession of all available material would have the opportunity of trying to "weave the whole, with comment and connection, into a perfect web." [28]

I

The Three Generations That Made a Gentleman

I

IT CAN BE ARGUED that a knowledge of forbears is more essential in understanding William Makepeace Thackeray than any other English novelist. This is not to say that Thackeray's life and character, like Ernest Pontifex's in *The Way of All Flesh,* are best explained in terms of "unconscious memory," although occasional resemblances between generations assert the claims of nature against those of nurture. The significance of Thackeray's family associations lies instead in their shaping of the environment in which he grew up and in his attitude towards them.

Thackeray passed his early years as part of a self-contained Anglo-Indian social group. Except for his friends at school and the university, the intimate associates of his youth were for the most part relatives—Thackerays, Bechers, Shakespears, Carmichael-Smyths, and the families with whom they intermarried. The clannishness developed among these empire-builders by the circumstances of their residence in India was reinforced in England by the prevailing indifference or hostility with which returned "Indians" were regarded; and the Anglo-Indian world of the early nineteenth century was consequently knit close by ties of blood, shared experience, common interest, and like assumptions.

Moreover, the Thackerays and their relations formed a tribe which prided itself on its heritage. Thackeray was taught to feel pleasure in his family tradition and to regard it as a bulwark in life. "It takes three generations to make a gentleman," [1] he used to say; and when later years brought him the opportunity, he visited Hampsthwaite, Harrow, and Hadley Green, the localities where his gentility had thus been distilled. It is told of him, indeed, that finding his great-grandfather's tomb in Harrow Churchyard in disrepair at a time when he had only five sovereigns to his name, he had it tended at his own expense.[2] His preoccupation with origins is illustrated again in the care with which he traced the ancestry of his characters. linking his eighteenth-century with his modern fiction, and contemplating "a novel of the time of Henry V., which would be his *capo d'opera,* in which the ancestors of all his characters, Warringtons, Pendennis's, and the rest would be introduced." [3]

Yet it is important to particularize the aspects of family tradition that fascinated Thackeray. "Heraldry to him had only the quaint interest and prettiness of old China," reports James Hannay. "If you bored him with genealogy, he would begin 'Quantum distet ab Inacho,' which was a quite sufficient hint." [4] Stories of achievement, glimpses of curious old manners, revelations of striking traits of personality were what remained in his memory; and it is these things that will be emphasized in the accounts that follow of his three immediate ancestors, his great-grandfather, Archdeacon Thomas Thackeray; his grandfather, William Makepeace Thackeray; and his father, Richmond Thackeray. Their careers must be recorded in some detail,* even at the risk of seeming to defer unconscionably—like Tristram Shandy's biographer—the appearance of the proper subject of these pages. The reader impatient of ancestral history is of course at liberty to turn at once to Chapter 2.

The compilers of the Thackeray family book found Thakwras, Thackras, and Thackwras farming on the edge of Knaresborough Forest in the West Riding of Yorkshire as early as the

* For genealogies of the Thackeray, Becher, and Shawe families, see pp. 505–509.

fourteenth century.[5] The first holder of this Saxon name as it is now spelled appears to have been one Walter Thackeray, who died in 1618 at the nearby village of Hampsthwaite. The line survived at Hampsthwaite, which Thackeray himself regarded as "the birth place of the Thackerays," [6] until 1804. They were born and with two exceptions remained yeomen, a part of that "bold peasantry" whose decline Goldsmith lamented, content to farm the land they owned without emerging further from obscurity than to serve occasionally as parish clerks. Hampsthwaite, when Thackeray visited it with his daughters in the last year of his life, was "a secluded little village, amongst the low-lying and wooded hills, purple with gleams of heather, on the banks of the river Nidd, over which, near the church is a narrow stone bridge of three arches." [7] The clergyman showed him many entries concerning the Thackerays in parish registers, and he was told of the family house which had only recently been torn down, a building of Elizabethan times on the hillside beyond the bridge.[8]

The first of the Thackerays to break away from Hampsthwaite was Elias, son of Thomas, who was admitted a sizar (or poor student) of Christ's College, Cambridge, in 1682. Having taken the degrees of B.A. and M.A., he was in 1711 presented to the living of Hawkeswell in Yorkshire by Mary, Viscountess Preston. He died there unmarried in 1737 at the age of seventy-one. Concerning his character there has transpired only a Latin tombstone inscription, in which he appears as grave, firm, and pious, respected by his parish, and "a bright example of paternal affection to his family." [9]

If the author of this epitaph was Elias's nephew Thomas, as is supposed, he had good reason to speak of his uncle's "paternal" affection. Presumably it was through Elias's good offices that Thomas, born at Hampsthwaite in 1693, was admitted a King's Scholar at Eton in 1706 and enabled six years later to matriculate at King's College, Cambridge.[10] In 1715 he took his B.A. degree and was elected a Fellow of his college, and he later proceeded to his M.A. and Bachelor of Divinity. Meanwhile, he had returned to Eton as Assistant Master. Being "an ardent and inflexible Whig," devoted to the House of Hanover, he found the Tory and Jacobite leanings of most of his colleagues abhorrent, and in

1728 he withdrew from Eton to accept from Sir Peter Soame the rectories of Heydon and Chisall Parva in Essex.

Early in the morning of 17 January 1743 the fellows of King's College met in their chapel to elect a Provost in succession to the late Dr. Snape. The favoured candidates were Thackeray and Dr. George, like Thackeray a Whig; but the Tory element in the college supported Dr. Chapman, Archdeacon of Surrey. On the first ballot George polled twenty-two votes, Thackeray sixteen, and Chapman ten. Each party remained firm, and since the statutes of the college made no provision for adjournment within the forty-eight hours allowed for the election until a decision was reached, the fellows had to remain overnight in the chapel.

> A friend of mine, a curious man [writes Daniel Wray, a gleeful don of Queens' College], tells me he took a survey of his brothers at the hour of two in the morning, and that never was a more curious, or a more diverting spectacle. Some wrapped in blankets erect in their stalls like mummies, others asleep on cushions, like so many Gothic tombs. Here a red cap over a wig, there a face lost in the cape of a rug. One blowing a chafing-dish with a surplice sleeve, another warming a little negus, or sipping *Coke upon Littleton, i.e.* tent and brandy. Thus did they combat the cold of that frosty night.

At two o'clock the next afternoon Chapman's supporters went over to George,[11] and the fellows were released from their vigil. George had the support of Sir Robert Walpole and was the more moderate Whig of the two. The Tories still harboured "resentment for some severe speeches, many years before, and which were now but too well remembered, made by Mr. Thackeray against their party, which were never to be forgotten or forgiven."

But though extreme Whiggery might be temporarily inconvenient, it was not at this period left for ever unrewarded. In 1729 Thackeray had married Ann Woodward, daughter of the Sub-Prosser of Eton College, who during the next twenty years bore him nine girls and seven boys. When the trustees of Harrow School, taking their cue from the battle of Culloden, offered Thackeray the headmastership in 1746, he accepted it in order "to educate his own and other people's children." He found

Harrow in a deplorable state. His predecessor had absconded, after having for "a great while past lived a disorderly, drunken, idle life," and enrolment had fallen off to forty boys. Thackeray's vigorous restorative measures caused a later headmaster to call him the "second founder of Harrow School." His first concern was to raise the standard of scholarship. His keen eye for ability led him to remark of one pupil, later to become the great orientalist Sir William Jones, "that he was a boy of so active a mind, that if he were left naked and friendless on Salisbury Plain, he would nevertheless find the road to fame and riches." Also trained by him were the learned Dr. Bennet, Bishop of Cloyne, and the famous Dr. Samuel Parr, who wrote that he had reason "to love and revere him as a father as well as a master." Nor did Thackeray neglect to give Harrow the social cachet necessary to a successful public school in the eighteenth century. The favour shown him by Frederick, Prince of Wales, whose Chaplain he became in 1748, and his demonstrated loyalty to the House of Hanover, made Harrow a fashionable school with aristocratic Whigs, particularly the Scottish adherents of the party. Within a few years there were 130 boys in the school.

Thackeray became an honorary Doctor of Divinity of the University of Aberdeen in 1747, and further ecclesiastical preferment came his way in 1753, when Bishop Hoadly made him Archdeacon of Surrey. He resigned his headmastership in August, 1760, expecting to be made a bishop by the son of Prince Frederick, who was shortly to succeed the failing George II; but he died suddenly the following month before this final honour could be bestowed upon him. His contemporaries unite in testifying to his integrity and learning; and one of them adds that he was "a man of very graceful and portly stature, of a most humane and candid disposition, and generally beloved by all his acquaintances." The care of his large family, which included seven unmarried daughters, fell to his widow. So prudent was her management of his inconsiderable fortune that when she died in 1797, she left £10,000 to be divided among her children.[12]

II

Archdeacon Thackeray may properly be called the founder of the Thackerays' fortunes. With him the family rose permanently from yeoman to professional status, for his sons became, and his daughters married, clergymen, college dons, army officers, government officials, and surgeons. "They were tall, thin people," Thackeray used to tell his daughters, "with marked eyebrows, and clear dark eyes, simple, serious." [1] To the Archdeacon's youngest child was reserved a less conventional career, which marked a new departure in the family's history. William Makepeace Thackeray—so named, according to family tradition, after an ancestor "who had been burned for his faith in the days of Queen Mary" [2]—was born at Harrow 20 June 1749 and grew up there among his many brothers and sisters. When he was fourteen, his widowed mother persuaded a director of the Honourable East India Company, "the Grandest Society of Merchants in the Universe," [3] to nominate him as a writer in the Company's service. This was no small achievement, for as Lord Clive told the House of Commons a few years later, "the advantages arising from the Company's service are now generally known; and the great object of every man is to get his son appointed a writer in *Bengal.*" [4] For a year young Thackeray was placed under a writing master, who duly certified in 1765 that he had "gone through a regular set of Merchant's accounts and the practical Rules of Arithmetic." [5] Six months later he set out for India aboard the *Lord Camden,* carrying with him his mother's Bible, in which under the date 3 February 1766 she had inscribed the words: "To my youngest and dear son, William Makepeace Thackeray, I give this Bible which was the gift of my godfather at five years old, and has been my constant companion for upwards of fifty years." [6]

In view of the nature of the enterprise upon which young Thackeray had embarked, his mother's parting gift was somewhat incongruous. To Thackeray, as to each of the twenty-two other newly appointed writers who were his companions, most of them like himself just turned sixteen, it had been reiterated by friends and relatives alike,

> how certain he is of making a fortune: that my Lord such a one, and my Lord such a one, acquired so much money in such a time; and Mr. such a one, and Mr. such a one, so much in such a time. Thus are their principles corrupted at their very setting out [Clive continues] and as they generally go a good many together, they influence one another's expectations to such a degree, in the course of the voyage, that they fix upon a period for their return before their arrival.[7]

On 1 August 1766, after the customary six months' passage of those days, the *Lord Camden* lay to off Kedgeree at the mouth of the Hooghly River,[8] and the new writers proceeded by barge to Calcutta.

Since Clive's victory at Plassey nine years before, the East India Company, without ceasing to be a trading corporation, had become the virtual ruler of a vast and wealthy empire. The Company was operated for the benefit of its proprietors, and its policies were established by the Court of Directors elected by these proprietors. But the policies determined at the East India House in Leadenhall Street, London, were put into effect by the Company's servants in Bengal, an exchange of letters with whom required a whole year. In such circumstances strict supervision was impossible. In order to preserve an appearance of economy, moreover, the Court of Directors paid their servants only nominal salaries and expected them to realize the bulk of their income by private trade. No system more deadening to the sense of duty could have been devised. Burke's famous picture of the Company's servants in India is hardly overcharged:

> animated with all the avarice of age, and all the impetuosity of youth, they roll in one after another; wave after wave; and there is nothing before the eyes of the natives but an endless, hopeless prospect of new flights of birds of prey and passage, with appetites continually renewing for a food that is continually wasting.

So gross was the exploitation which Bengal civilians permitted themselves, and so disastrous the consequence of their peculations, that in 1765 Clive had been returned to India as Governor of Fort William "to cleanse the Augean stable." Clive's measures of reform were bitterly opposed by nearly the whole of the Bengal establishment, and if they made looting more difficult, they still left abundant opportunities for plunder, of which the Company's servants continued to take advantage without scruple. Six months before Thackeray's arrival, Clive pronounced Calcutta to be "one of the most wicked Places in the Universe, Corruption, Licentiousness & a want of Principle seem to have possess'd the minds of all the Civil Servants, by frequent bad Examples they are grown callous, Rapacious & Luxurious beyond Conception." [9]

Clive's superlatives may seem difficult to credit, in view of the extent to which bribery and corruption prevailed in England itself during the early years of George III's reign. Yet if the East India Company's servants did claim a larger licence, they were not without excuse. A young man going out to India was in effect gambling his life against the chance of returning home in a few years with a fortune, and in this wager the odds were by no means in his favour. George Francis Grand, who shared the great cabin of the *Lord Camden* with Thackeray and ten other writers in 1766, noted in 1802 that of this group only he and Thackeray were still alive.[10] James Forbes, who sailed for India with nineteen young writers and cadets in 1765, noted that seventeen of this number had died many years before his departure in 1784.[11] During Warren Hastings's trial, evidence was submitted which showed that of 502 civilians sent out to Bengal between 1762 and 1785, 180 had died, 321 were still in India, and only 37 had returned to England. The point is made even more pungently than by this testimony in the offhand comment of an early writer about Park Street, a fashionable thoroughfare in Calcutta then bluntly called Burial Ground Road. "All funeral processions," he observes, "are concealed as much as possible from the sight of the ladies that the vivacity of their tempers may not be wounded." [12] Even if the Company's servant did return to England with the wealth he had sought, he was more often than not a broken man. There was then no ice to mitigate the overwhelming heat; there were no hill-stations to which to withdraw; an impaired liver and a yellow countenance were the least penalties exacted by the Indian climate.

For details of the temptations that faced Thackeray upon his arrival in Calcutta, we may turn to Clive's picture of a young writer "arrived in Bengal, and not worth a groat."

As soon as he lands, a Banyan [native broker or agent] worth perhaps one hundred thousand pounds, desires he may have the honor of serving this young gentleman, at four shillings and six-pence *per* month. The Company has provided chambers for him, but they are not good enough;—the Banyan finds better. The young man takes a walk about the town, he observes that other writers, arrived only a year before him, live in splendid apartments or have houses of their own, ride upon fine prancing Arabian Horses, and in Palanqueens and Chaises; that they keep Seraglios, make Entertainments, and treat with Champaigne and Claret. When he returns, he tells the Banyan what he has observed. The Banyan assures him that he may soon arrive at the same good fortune; he furnishes him with money; he is then at his mercy. . . . The Banyan . . . lays his bags of silver before him to-day; Gold tomorrow; Jewels the next day; and, if these fail, he then tempts him in the way of his profession, which is Trade. He assures him that Goods may be had cheap, and sold to great advantage up the Country. In this manner is the attack carried on; and the Company's servant has no resource, for he cannot fly. In short, flesh and blood cannot bear it.[13]

If such a Banyan attached himself to Thackeray, he must for some time have had to content himself with a relatively small return upon his investment. In August of 1766 Thackeray was placed in a subordinate post in the office of the Secretary. During the following year Harry Verelst, who had succeeded Clive as Governor of Bengal, made him his Cash Keeper and Assistant, apparently an important promotion, for though these employments brought him an annual salary of only 1,158 rupees (about £145), this trivial sum was nearly twice that received by most of the writers who had come out with him on the *Lord Camden*.[14] John Cartier, who followed Verelst as Governor in 1769, employed Thackeray as his Secretary for two more years.

There is little information concerning Thackeray's life in Calcutta during these years, but as Assistant to the Governor he must have seen the best society that the city had to offer. His position was sufficiently assured, at any rate, that he felt able to bring two of his sisters to Calcutta. His object in arranging this visit was quite candidly to find them husbands. Even at this time Bengal seems to have had its parallel to the "fishing fleet" of English girls who each year explored the matrimonial possibilities of Malta; [15] and in *Vanity Fair* we read of the Indian matron Mrs. Hardyman, who "had out her thirteen sisters, daughters of a country curate, the Rev. Felix Rabbits, and married eleven of them, seven high up in the service." [16] On 2 November 1768 the Court of Directors granted permission to Jane and Henrietta Thackeray to proceed to India upon the invitation of their brother and of John Cartier.[17] Jane was at this time twenty-nine years old, plain in appearance, but "sweet, sensible, and unaffected." She comes to life for a moment in a fragment of family legend. Her sister-in-law Lydia, hearing that, "conscious of her want of personal attractions and devoted to the care of her Sister, she had no thought for herself but of single life," exclaimed indignantly: "If there's a sensible man in India he will find out Jane." [18] Henrietta, on the other hand, was a twenty-two-year-old beauty, described in later life as "a charming person, not at all clever, rather languishing . . . and relying upon others, but sweet-tempered and beloved by all." [19] She was married on 15 January 1771 to James Harris, a senior merchant in the Company's service, who had recently been appointed Chief at Dacca, after nine years in that provincial capital.[20]

Through the influence of his brother and of John Cartier, Thackeray was transferred on 25 August 1771 to Dacca as Fourth in Council, a position of high responsibility in one of India's richest provinces. Presumably Jane accompanied him on the barge journey of 400 miles that was necessary to reach Dacca from Calcutta at this time, and she no doubt returned to Calcutta with her sister the following year, when Harris was made Tenth Member of Council of the Governor of Fort William. Not long after this event Lydia's prophecy was fulfilled, and Jane on 15 October 1772 from Governor Cartier's house in Calcutta married, if not the cleverest, certainly the wisest man in India, Captain James Rennell, the "father of Indian geography." [21]

His sisters handsomely provided for, Thackeray in May of

1772 accepted an appointment as Amin, or supervisor, of Sylhet, a frontier province to the northeast of Dacca. In October of the same year, after the Company had assumed control of Indian revenue, his title was changed to Collector. He remained in Sylhet (despite designation as Third in Council at Dacca in 1774) until he was recalled to Calcutta in 1775. Thus for three years Thackeray was the supreme English authority over a tract of land covering nearly 3,000 square miles, inhabited by some 400,000 natives, and rich in rice, lime, lumber, and elephants.[22] By incurring a heavy debt he procured a large store of goods in Dacca with which to trade privately in Sylhet (a practice not declared illegal until 1773, and even then generally condoned), but he soon found that he had greatly overestimated the opportunities for business in his new province. Casting about him for some way in which to retrieve his position, he hit upon a dubious expedient. As Collector it was his duty to receive the revenue of Sylhet from natives who had purchased from the Company the privilege of "farming" this territory.

> The District was put up to be Farmed for five years [he wrote later in excuse of his conduct]. . . . I delivered in proposals for the Farm in the name of Black Men, which were thought advantageous, and consequently accepted. . . . Had I not delivered in proposals for the Farm, more advantageous than any that were made, It must have fallen into the Hands of Black Men by which I have reason to think the Company could not have been benefitted. When I gave in Proposals for the Farm of Silhet, I had neither sense nor apprehension of either Injustice to my Honble Employers, or the Public.[23]

Despite these protestations Thackeray's action in farming his own district in the names of Indian men of straw was patently a dereliction of duty. In violation of explicit Company regulations he was himself carrying on the operations that he was supposed to supervise and control. Nor was the farm of Sylhet his only source of illicit revenue. Again contrary to Company rule, he exercised a monopoly of the sale of salt in his district. The discontent inevitable under such a regimen was enhanced by Thackeray's inability to control his native subordinates, who were guilty of flagrant rack-renting on their own account. The piteous complaints of the people of his province thus victimized and the accusations of local Indian capitalists angry at having lucrative employments illegally snatched from them resulted eventually in Thackeray's recall.

Meanwhile, in 1774, again in the names of the fictitious farmers of Sylhet, he had offered sixty-six elephants for sale to the Company. His tender was accepted; a price of 1,000 rupees per elephant was set, half of which was paid in advance; and "the farmers of Sylhet" were ordered to deliver the elephants to an agent at Sylhet, who was to transport them to Patna. The agent at Sylhet was appointed by Thackeray himself, and no examination was made of the elephants, now only sixty-two in number, for four had died while still in Thackeray's possession, until their arrival in Patna. They were there found to be "unfit in every respect for service," [24] but were nevertheless accepted by the Council at Patna acting for the Company. On a further march from Dinapore to Belgram (no great distance [25]) all except sixteen of the elephants died. No complaint was made at the time, but here was obviously another rod laid up in pickle for Thackeray.

That Thackeray was allowed to remain at Sylhet for three years, and that he was finally recalled from his province in 1775, are developments that may alike be explained by fluctuations in the fortunes of another servant of the Company with whom as early as 1773 he had formed an alliance. This was the notorious Richard Barwell, born in 1740 and sent out to India as a writer in 1758. His father being William Barwell, a former Governor of Bengal and a Director of the East India Company for nearly fifteen years, he rose rapidly in the service. By 1773 he was not only Ninth Member of Council at Calcutta, but also Chief at Dacca, and thus Thackeray's immediate superior.[26] His letters reveal him to have been greedy, unscrupulous, and cynical,[27] and suggest that, even after allowance has been made for the malignance that Sir Philip Francis habitually displayed to his enemies, much truth remains in the following estimate:

> Mr. Barwell, I think, has all the bad qualities common to this climate and country, of which he is in every sense a native. . . . He is rapacious without industry, and ambitious without any exertion

of his faculties or steady application to affairs. He would be governor-general if money could make him so; and in that station he would soon engross the wealth of the country. He will do whatever can be done by bribery and intrigue. He has no other resource.[28]

Barwell kept a European mistress and pensioned her husband, lost vast sums to Francis and others at cards, and fought a duel with General Clavering, his fellow member of Council. He assumed that every man had his price, whether politicians and directors at home or Company servants in Bengal; and in this assumption, it must be granted, experience rarely contradicted him. Yet at the same time he was a man of good education and wide reading who could quote La Rochefoucauld and Horace to some purpose,[29] and he possessed an extensive knowledge of the Indian world. Like Lord Steyne, he proved to have more "bottom" than most of his contemporaries, outlasted nearly all of them, and carried home a fortune after a quarter of a century in India.

On 29 November 1773 we find Barwell writing to Thackeray on the subject of complaints made to him about the latter's administration of Sylhet.

You must be sensible my inclination leads me to consider your wishes as far as may be consistent with the indispensable duties of my public office; those I must perform and allow a superior claim to my consideration. A reference in all my complaints is my intention, and my intention remains the same; but when it is represented that an obvious interest thwarts or obstructs a repeated application for justice in a cause of *meum* and *tuum,* you are sensible I cannot deny my interposition or refuse to hear it before me. This is . . . the only necessity under which I shall ever interfere; and could I preclude all applications that bring it upon me, it would give me a double pleasure, first by avoiding the trouble occasioned to myself; secondly by answering in the fullest manner your desire that the whole concern, whether publick or private, relating to the Province of Sylhet, or individuals who reside there, be submitted to you.[30]

In other words, Thackeray was to have a free hand in Sylhet, as long as Barwell could refrain from interfering without getting himself into trouble. For this forbearance there was good reason. As we shall see, Barwell was himself a party to the deal in elephants already described and shared in its profits. (He had been Chief at Patna before becoming Chief at Dacca, and it may be assumed that his assistance was essential in securing the Patna Council's acceptance of the moribund elephants.) It will further appear from a letter shortly to be cited that he and another member of Council at Dacca had a financial interest in Thackeray's Sylhet farm.

To understand Thackeray's situation in 1775 as an ally of Barwell, it is necessary to recapitulate briefly Anglo-Indian history during the three previous years. In 1772 Parliamentary investigations of the East India Company had aroused great ill will against its Bengal establishment. "Such a scene of tyranny and plunder has been opened as makes one shudder," wrote Horace Walpole. "We are Spaniards in our lust for gold, and Dutch in our delicacy of obtaining it." [31] As a result of the agitated state of public feeling, the India Act of 1773 was passed to bring the Company to some degree under the government's supervision. Supreme power in Bengal was vested in a Governor General and four Councillors, all named in the act; and in case of disagreement within Council, the vote of the majority was to prevail, though the Governor General had the casting vote in the event of a tie. Warren Hastings was made Governor General, and Richard Barwell was appointed to Council. Both had been in the Company's service for many years and were on the whole content with the prevailing system. The remaining members of Council were Lieutenant-General John Clavering, Colonel George Monson, and Philip Francis. These men were new to India, they entertained the low opinion of the Company's servants that was generally held in England, and they were determined to work a wholesale reform.

Lines of battle were drawn between the two factions in Council as soon as Clavering, Monson, and Francis arrived in India in 1774. Warren Hastings was the object of their most determined attack, as the chief spokesman for the existing system; but as Barwell came more and more to support Hastings, he too fell within their line of fire. By August, 1775, Barwell was writing of

the distracted state of our Councils which has simply for its pursuit the destruction of Mr. Hastings's name and character and the vilifying the Service throughout. . . . The malignant spirit of envy and detraction under the mask of public good, stalks impudently abroad, and the *Fiat Justicia* is called upon not to weigh the merits of men, but to cancell their services.[32]

In their effort to discredit Hastings and the existing customs of the service, "General Clavering and his Junto," [33] as Barwell described his opponents, encouraged natives throughout Bengal to complain against the servants of the Company set over them. "A species of subornation of the most extensive kind is impudently adopted," Barwell contended, "under the flimsy veil of detecting peculation." [34] Abuses of all sorts were brought to light and were punished with greatest energy where they seemed to throw discredit on Hastings or Barwell.

This was the atmosphere, then, in which Thackeray found himself when in August, 1775, he addressed two letters to the Supreme Council in which he sought by a "candid confession" of culpability in regard to the principal charge brought against his administration at Sylhet, that he had himself farmed the province under fictitious names, to obtain pardon for his conduct as after all excusable and permission to return to Sylhet, there to terminate his farm and other business affairs. The verdict of the Council, dictated by Clavering, Monson, and Francis, was hostile to him; but Hastings and Barwell filed a joint minute on 12 September 1775 in which he was more humanely treated. They granted that he had acted improperly in farming Sylhet. And they admitted that his salt monopoly was, strictly speaking, illegal: "The Custom of the Country might encourage, but it could not warrant, an act of that nature." None the less, it was their opinion that Thackeray's

conduct has been moderate and his Collections duly kept up. His crimes are the crimes of a deviation from the public Regulations and a violation of the rigid line of propriety. Crimes productive of no ill consequence in themselves, but of bad Example.[35]

Thackeray was deprived of his farm and of his position as Third in Council at Dacca, but he was allowed to return to Sylhet to wind up his affairs.[36]

Thackeray was again in Calcutta early in 1776, appearing in

the Company's records as a Junior Merchant "without employ." On 24 March, Barwell wrote to John Graham, apparently another partner in Thackeray's Sylhet enterprises:

Poor Thackeray has fallen a victim to the villainous calumnies of lying complaints, in consequence of which I deemed him richly entitled to any benefits he proposed to have divided and have accounted to him for the sums he lodged in my hands during my Chiefship. To have done less, I conceived, would have been no more consistent with your principle of action than mine towards him, who looked up to us with confidence and dependence.[37]

As a final step in settling his Indian business Thackeray a week later boldly applied to the Governor General for payment of the 33,500 rupees due him for elephants supplied to the Company in 1774. His case depended upon his receipt for the delivery at Patna of sixty-two elephants, none of which were at that time "so bad or unhealthy as to be objected to by the Council there in the muster they underwent." [38]

But Thackeray was in bad odour with the Clavering Junto to which the affair of the elephants had a still more disreputable appearance than his suit of the previous year. Colonel Monson summarized their view of the matter:

The proposals for taking [i.e., catching and supplying] the elephants were made in the name of persons who never existed. The order for delivering the elephants was made to Mr. Thackeray who was the proprietor of them and who appointed the agent to receive them on the part of the Company. The elephants arrived in such a state at Patna that they were not in a condition to perform any service and the greatest part of them are now reported dead.[39]

When Thackeray came before the Council on 18 June, moreover, it quickly became evident that General Clavering had got wind of Barwell's silent partnership in his affairs. Thackeray testified that an agent had submitted his proposals for supplying elephants to the Company, received the 33,000 rupees paid in advance, and shared this sum with him.[40] Clavering repeatedly inquired the identity of this agent, but Thackeray steadfastly declined to reveal his name, on the ground that the transaction between them was a private one. Thackeray was at last allowed to withdraw, and the opinions of the Council's members were taken. Only Hastings favoured paying him. Barwell moved that the matter should be decided by a friendly suit against the Company in the Supreme Court. (This was by no means a betrayal of Thackeray's interests, since the Supreme Court had already shown itself favourable to Hastings.) In agreeing with Barwell's proposal Clavering paid him a sarcastic compliment:

I entirely approve of Mr. Barwell's proposition. I don't see how a member of the late administration can give his assent to the payment of a demand which from Mr. Thackeray's last answer a doubt may arise whether he himself had not a concern in it or by his influence had engaged the members of the Council of Patna to agree to take them notwithstanding the bad conditions they were probably in at the time. I therefore second Mr. Barwell's motion which I think does him honor.[41]

On 1 July, Thackeray wrote to the Council again urging his claim and again declining to reveal the name of his agent. He had given his word not to divulge this information; to break his solemn pledge would be "to forfeit the character of a man of principle and honour." [42] Barwell's comment on this communication reveals some agitation of mind:

I think that Mr. Thackeray has given the Board all the satisfaction that was in his power, circumstanced as he describes himself. Nothing but the basest principle of fear can possibly influence him to deviate from the reply he has already made.[43]

He and Hastings opposed the majority's proposal to bring Thackeray again before the Board, but to no avail. Thackeray's second appearance was a repetition of his first. He repelled Clavering's furious attacks, and withdrew without having given Barwell away.

Abandoning hope of moving the Council, Thackeray on 16 August gave notice that he intended to bring suit against the Company to recover the 33,500 rupees owing him. The Council on 2 September directed their Standing Counsel to prepare an opinion on the affair. His verdict was:

In every part of the transaction, from the origin to the close, I perceive such strong marks of a fraudulent misrepresentation and concealment that it seems to be essential to justice to investigate the matters to the bottom by a Bill of Discovery.[44]

But this advice was not followed. On 25 September Monson died. Control of the Council passed to Hastings and Barwell, since the Governor General possessed the casting vote in the case of a deadlock. They directed that Thackeray's suit should remain virtually unopposed; and when the Supreme Court gave him a decree for 29,427 rupees, they ordered the sum paid on 10 December. Clavering and Francis bitterly opposed this line of action to the last, but without result except to elicit from the Court of Directors the following judgment:

When we find it suggested by General Clavering, that the cause was lost by "*a most* shameful desertion" on the part of the defendants, whose duty it certainly was to guard our property; that not a single witness was produced on the Part of the Company, we are induced to think, with the General, that a majority of the Board though they may not chuse to make a formal order on the treasury to satisfy unjust claims, may nevertheless encourage suits to be instituted in the Supreme Court, overrule the opinion of the Company's Counsel, prevent their attornies from adopting the best mode of defence, suffer verdicts to be given against the Company, and shelter themselves under such verdicts, in disposing of our property to individuals.[45]

It would appear that family legend had acquainted Thackeray with his grandfather's ordeal, out of which only his dogged tenacity and a fortunate turn of fate had brought him victorious. How else to explain the fact that in *Pendennis* the reprobate baronet, married to the possessor of an Anglo-Indian fortune, is christened Sir Francis Clavering? Nor had his family failed to acquaint him with Richard Barwell's career.

'A few of the Indians were in society in my time,' . . . says Lady Kew musingly [in *The Newcomes*]. 'My father has often talked to me about Barwell, of Stanstead, and his house in St. James's Square; the man who ordered "more curricles" when there were not carriages enough for his guests.'[46]

And in *The Virginians* that candid opportunist Sir Miles Warrington remarks to George Warrington:

"Why, I have my dear little Miley at a dancing school with Miss Barwell, nabob Barwell's daughter, and I don't disguise my wish that the children may contract an attachment which may endure through their lives. I tell the nabob so. We went from the House of Commons one dancing-day and saw them. 'T was beautiful to see the young things walking a minuet together." [47]

In 1775 Thackeray had applied for permission to return home, his career in the service seemingly terminated by his dismissal from Sylhet and Dacca. But Hastings and Barwell now had the upper hand in Council, and he had demonstrated his loyalty to the latter in particularly trying circumstances. Probably because they feared the censure of the Court of Directors, however, his friends would do nothing for him. Thackeray told Joseph Farrington forty years later that, when he "applied for a place which had become vacant, . . . Mr. Hastings and Barwell put him off with promises which so disgusted him that he left India with abt. £20,000." [48] This was no small sum for a young man of twenty-six, whose official salary during ten years' service had totalled 16,230 rupees (about £2,000), which "might perhaps have sufficed for his necessary expenses during twelve months." [49] In judging Thackeray's career in Bengal it should be kept in mind that his standards were typical of the period. He followed "the custom of the country" at a time when considerations of profit rather than administrative efficiency governed the servants of the East India Company. Neither a scoundrel nor a pattern of rigid virtue, he was simply one of the many young Englishmen in India whom Burke described as "full grown in fortune long before they were ripe in principle," more fortunate than most in that events forced him home in the prime of life with his health unimpaired.[50]

III

Thackeray did not sail alone aboard the *Triton* on 19 January 1777; in Calcutta on 31 January of the previous year he had married Amelia, the second daughter of Lieutenant-Colonel Richmond Webb.[1] There were four Webb girls, each of whom was sent to India at an early age. Sarah had arrived on 25 June 1772, and married Peter Moore, a writer in the Company's service at Patna, on 8 January 1774. Moore was shortly afterwards made Secretary to the Committee on Revenue in Calcutta, and it was no doubt to his home that Amelia was welcomed when she reached Calcutta in the summer of 1774.[2] In 1776, after she in turn had married, her two younger sisters, Charlotte and Augusta, the latter "still in her Frocks with her Hair over her Forehead," [3] joined the Moores in India; but they were not to prosper as had their sisters, for their pursuit of matrimony ended respectively in disaster and in disappointment.[4]

Thackeray himself was inclined to underscore the significance of his grandfather's marriage. He used the Webb crest of arms in preference to his own, finding it "much prettier and more ancient"; [5] he told his daughter Anne that, whereas the Thackerays were "simple, serious" people, through the Webbs "the wits had come into the family"; [6] and he joked, but not without satisfaction, about the Richmond Webbs' claim to trace their line back to Roaldus of Richmond.[7] The earliest ancestor of whom there is knowledge, however, was a Wiltshire gentleman named William Richmond Webb who flourished in the fifteenth century. The ninth in direct descent of his line was General John Richmond Webb, whose military exploits are celebrated in *Esmond.* Thackeray's branch of the family stemmed from a younger son of the sixth Richmond Webb, the father of Amelia, and himself a noted soldier who fought at Culloden and was buried in Westminster Abbey. "We appear to have held greatly to this alliance in our family," Thackeray wrote to a Webb connexion, noting how often the name Richmond had been used by his relatives. "Had I had a son, he would have got the same baptismal name which is certainly prettier than that family one." [8]

The *Triton* brought the Thackerays on 11 July 1777 to an England where returned Bengal civilians were most unpopular. Still vividly remembered from 1772 were the Parliamentary hearings on the East India Company and Samuel Foote's Sir Matthew Mite in *The Nabob.* In 1785 the pungent comments of

Mackenzie's John Homespun on the Mushrooms, arrived from India with a fortune of £100,000, found a delighted audience among the readers of *The Lounger*. The popular conception of the nabob that prevailed at this time is summed up in *The Newcomes:*

the jaundiced monster of romances and comedies, who purchases the estates of broken-down English gentlemen, with rupees tortured out of bleeding rajahs, who smokes a hookah in public, and in private carries about a guilty conscience, diamonds of untold value, and a diseased liver; who has a vulgar wife, with a retinue of black servants whom she maltreats.[9]

The conduct of certain returned Anglo-Indians gave warrant to this caricature. Consider the home-coming of Richard Barwell, "the famous Nabob of Stanstead Park." He arrived in London in 1780 with a fortune reputed to total more than £400,000; and proceeded to display to free-born Englishmen all the arrogance that he had shown in India to a conquered race and to white subordinates dependent on his favour. After he had been roundly rebuked by a committee of the House of Commons for the insolence with which he had replied when asked to testify before them, he retired to the estate of the late Earl of Halifax at Stanstead, Sussex, which he had purchased from the creditors of that nobleman for £90,000. He pointedly neglected to attend a dinner and ball given in his honour at the neighbouring town of Chichester.

Not content with insulting the men of Chichester [William Hickey continues], Mr. Barwell made it his study, as it should seem, to render himself obnoxious to persons of all ranks, shutting up gates and paths through his parks that had, as an indulgence, always been open to the public, preventing the poor from supplying themselves with water from a spring they had long been used to frequent; in short, doing everything that was illiberal, offensive, and ill-natured. His very name from this conduct soon was held in such detestation that men, women, and children hissed and hooted at him as he passed, with all his Oriental state, through the villages.[10]

It is not surprising that the *Calcutta Gazette* of 11 August 1784 should have noted regretfully: "Many private letters mention the great disrespect in which East Indians are held in England, so much so that they are driven to associate almost entirely with each other."[11]

Thackeray probably escaped such ostracism. He had none of Barwell's insolent vanity; nor would his modest competence have allowed him the ostentation that turned the eye of envy and detraction on his friend's vast fortune. He and his wife seem first to have settled at South Mimms, Middlesex, where they were living in 1780.[12] On 10 January 1786 he bought a residence and other property at the nearby village of Hadley,[13] 12 miles northwest of London, where they settled for the quarter of a century of life that remained to them. Mrs. Pryme has described their home and its surroundings as she knew them many years later, when it had come to be called the "Manor House" and belonged to a Mr. Hyde:

> Hadley Green . . . is a delightful place; a 'quiet mead' with here and there fresh pools of water shining beneath clusters of fair lime trees. It is enclosed by woods on one side, and by a few good detached residences on the other. . . . [The Thackerays' home] was a solid well-built white house, entered by a portico. . . . [Its windows opened] on to a far-reaching lawn, smooth, and of an exquisite verdure; adorned by groups of trees on either side. . . . [And in the background was] a charming picture of green sloping fields and distant wooded hills.[14]

As the years passed, an Anglo-Indian colony formed itself about the Thackerays at Hadley Green. Peter Moore returned to England in 1785 to become Lord of the Manor at Hadley, which he used as a base for an active career in politics, associating himself with Francis and Burke in their attacks on Warren Hastings.[15] Mrs. Harris was recruited to the colony after the death of her husband in 1790. The Rennells were near at hand in London; and Mrs. Thackeray, the widow of the Archdeacon, with Thackeray's brother Joseph and his unmarried sisters, lived a few miles away at Harrow.

The picture that emerges of Amelia and William Thackeray during their Hadley years is an altogether pleasant one. Though Amelia had returned to England indolent and a lover of ease, usually to be found dressed in white and reclining upon a sofa, she also brought home with her an Anglo-Indian fondness for dancing, and her "routs" were great events in the Hadley community.[16] She had a reputation for cleverness hardly confirmed by her surviving letters to her son, which are on the pattern of Polonius's precepts to Laertes.[17] The simplicity and bonhomie of her husband appear even in a trivial story told by Mrs. Bayne, who visited him with her cousin as a little girl. Disliking his pepper-and-salt suit, they pertly inquired why he wore it. "My dears," was his reply, "as I do not like the trouble of choosing I tell my tailor to send me at one time this coloured suit, and at another a blue with brass buttons, so that when I write for a new one he looks in his order-book and sees which turn it is." [18] His son Richmond pictures him supervising the construction of gravel paths and "digging with old Anthony" in the garden.[19] He sought no employment during his years at Hadley, but he was active in looking after the affairs of friends and relatives still in India and in acting as guardian to their children.[20]

The main business of Thackeray's later life, however, was the upbringing of his large family. The "spacious entrance halls, wide oaken staircases, and low wainscoted rooms" [21] of the Hadley home were thronged with seven sons and four daughters [22] born between 1778 and 1797. Thackeray provided for his boys by cultivating assiduously his interest with the East India Company. The agents in bestowing patronage upon them were Sir Hugh Inglis, a friend of Thackeray and Cartier in Bengal and of the Rennells in London, who was almost continuously a member of the Court of Directors between 1784 and 1813; Sir William Bensley, a director from 1781 to 1809; and George Woodford Thelluson, a director from 1796 to 1808.[23] No doubt the influence of Peter Moore was also considerable in Leadenhall Street, though he was never in the Direction. Thackeray's five oldest boys were all provided for by the Company. William, Richmond, Webb, and St. John received writerships, worth £3,500 apiece; and Thomas became a cadet, a less valuable but still considerable preferment.[24] Latterly Thackeray's interest seems to have waned, for Francis remained at home, and Charles, the youngest boy, went out to India as a lawyer without Company appointment. Even Thackeray's daughters, as we shall see, profited by his Indian connexion.

Richmond Makepeace Thackeray, his second son, was born at Hadley 10 November 1781.[25] Ten years later he appears as an oppidan in the second form at Eton. He became a King's Scholar in 1794, and he last figures in the school lists as a member of the fifth form in 1796.[26] Having been appointed a writer in that year, he removed from Eton and set to work learning merchants' accounts and arithmetic, as his father had done before him. On 9 June 1798, at the age of sixteen, he sailed from Portsmouth on board the Indiaman *Thetis*.[27]

He never again saw his mother or father, nor did his other brothers who went out to India. All of them died in the East, though William returned briefly to England on furlough in later life. Some hint of the profound affection that united parents and children, despite their early separation, may be gained from a story told by Lady Ritchie.

> At the back of the drawing-room [at Hadley] was a study, with a criss-cross network of wire bookcase along the walls; it was here that Amelia Thackeray was sitting when her husband came in agitated and very pale; he said there was terrible news from India, and as she started, terrified, from her seat, he exclaimed, 'Not William, not William, but Webb.' 'O Webb, my Webb,' cried the poor mother, and dropped senseless on the ground. She never quite recovered the use of her limbs, though she regained consciousness. Until then she had never told anybody that she loved Webb the best of all her children.[28]

Though paralysed, Mrs. Thackeray lingered on until 29 April 1810. Her husband died 11 March 1813 and was buried by her side at Hadley Green.

IV

The *Thetis,* Captain Henry Bullock commanding, sailed from England in company with the Honourable Company's ships *Berrington, Rockingham, Calcutta,* and *Osterly.* Richmond Thackeray's fellow passengers included the wife of a captain in the Bengal Artillery; five young ladies; some thirty officers, writers, cadets, and surgeons; and eighty odd recruits to the Indian army. They had much to talk about, for the *Berrington* brought to Madras the astounding rumour

> that the FRENCH and VENETIAN Fleet, had sailed from Toulon, and that Buonaparte with an army of Forty Thousand Men was embarked upon it. . . . The destination of this Fleet was supposed to be for IRELAND, which we are sorry to announce, was in a state of general, and positive Rebellion. . . . Intelligence that the above fleet had passed the Straits of Gibraltar, had been received by the British Government.[1]

Though the *Thetis* encountered no French men-of-war, it none the less had an eventful voyage. On 29 June the *Calcutta* proceeded alone to St. Helena. The *Berrington* inadvertently parted company with her sister ships "off the Cape, in a hard Gale of wind, on the 19th of August," [2] the day after the *Rockingham* had broken off to make sail for Bombay. What afterwards befell the *Thetis* is related in the single page of Thackeray's journal of the voyage that has been preserved:

> 13th September nothing particular happened untill today when a very dreadful leak has sprung & cannot be found which makes an immazing deal of Water—I suppose tomorrow the passengers will be made to pump The Women do not yet know it I suppose when they do we shall have weeping anow Thank God the Osterly is in Company all the rest of the fleet have left us we have just been making the signal of Distress The people now begin to think of Danger
> 14th to Day all Passengers were obliged to pump indeed it is very hard work The Ladies are now going on board the Osterly which has been speaking to us Cap Piercy says he will never be 50 yards from us to night we are to keep watch
> 15th Things now begin to wear a terrible appearance—I have sent my letters & a little clean linen on board the other ship. Capt Bullock seems very low I now am glad I can swim for I am afraid there will be occasion [3]

It was necessary to throw overboard the guns of the *Thetis* and part of her cargo. The pumps were manned without interruption. The ship's carpenter predicted that the vessel would go down suddenly by the stern. Mutiny threatened; and an allowance of "two pints of grog, one pint of porter and a dram" that Captain Bullock ordered to be distributed daily had the effect of fuddling rather than heartening the crew. The Captain noted in his log-book:

I have made known to Mr. Jupp 3^d Mate that he is no longer to be consider'd an Officer of the Ship. He was so extreme drunk on Sunday and at pains to make the men at the pump in the same state that I sent to desire he would desist and at his peril give liquor to any part of the crew. I was much hurt to hear that many of the ship's company had declared their indifference to endeavoring to save the ship, that they already consider'd her untenable, in consequence had been guilty of many excesses, & that some murmurs had been heard at the pumps.[4]

The ship's treasure chest and wine store were plundered. But the *Thetis* rode out the heavy weather, and by 18 September the crisis had passed. "The passengers exert themselves in an uncommon degree," wrote Captain Bullock. "I am confident without their aid and example we shou'd not succeed in keeping her afloat." [5] Conferring with the captain of the *Osterly,* Captain Bullock determined that the ships should proceed together to the nearest port. On the way he had the satisfaction of noting in the log-book:

Punished Francis Cowling Seaman with 3 dozen lashes, which I deferred till now for reasons beforementioned, he had been detected plundering a half chest of wine and distributing it among the crew on the 17″ instant when the ship was in such imminent danger, the consequence of which was that he was insolent to the Commanding Officer and set such a mutinous example that had immediate punishment taken place, I have no doubt but it would have been followed.[6]

On 28 September the *Thetis* anchored in Trincomallie Harbour, Ceylon, her pumps still going, and 5 feet of water in her hold. Emergency repairs having been made, she proceeded north. Thackeray on 3 October noted, in the final entry of his diary, "I am now thank god arrived at Madras"; and on 23 October the *Thetis* lay to off Kedgeree at the mouth of the Hooghly.

As Thackeray approached Calcutta by barge, there came first into sight Garden Reach, a green expanse dotted with country-houses, "more resembling the palaces of princes than the abodes of private gentlemen." [7] Then, after an abrupt turn in the river, was revealed the great metropolis of England's Indian empire, a prospect that Lord Valentia four years later described as "the finest view I ever beheld." [8] On the bank of the Hooghly, which swarmed with shipping, enormous ghats, or stairs, led to Fort William, a vast edifice begun by Clive after the battle of Plassey, and to the great tract of open land around it known as the Esplanade. To the left of Fort William and overlooking the Esplanade was a spacious street lined with large buildings in the "Grecian" style, to which the new Governor General, Marquess Wellesley, was shortly to add the superb Government House. At right angles to this thoroughfare and looking across the Esplanade towards the river was the mile-long residential district of Chowringhee. Hidden from sight by the European quarter was the Black Town with its 700,000 inhabitants, where the streets were narrow and dirty and the houses built usually of mud, "perfectly resembling the cabins of the poorest class in Ireland." [9] The contrast of grandeur and misery was calculated and necessary. India was a country, as Lord Valentia pointed out, "of splendor, of extravagance, and of outward appearance." [10] It could be governed from a palace, but not from a counting-house.

For the time being, however, Thackeray had little opportunity to become acquainted with Calcutta. The exertions of the voyage and the unfamiliar rigours of the Indian climate had made him ill, and a cruise to Madras was prescribed. He hoped to see his brother William, who had preceded him to India some years before, but the latter's tasks as Commercial Resident at Vizagapatam prevented him from returning to the Presidency. In a moment of loneliness and depression Thackeray wrote to his mother on 17 February 1799:

> I would give anything to be at home: I would even be glad to carry gravel in a basket on my shoulder in the garden. It was this time last year we made the new walk; it will be wonderfully altered when I see it again. I am very much out of spirits at not seeing William here, and if he cannot get leave in a few days, I shall go to him. I hope Emily won't forget her journals, &c., as the greatest pleasure *here* is hearing from our friends.[11]

But Thackeray threw off his homesickness as his health improved. Returning to Bengal he entered upon his duties as Assistant to the Collector of Midnapore, a post to which he had been appointed on 17 December 1798.

Thackeray found that the service had greatly changed since his father's day. Pitt's Charter Act of 1793 had provided decent salaries for Indian civilians. Promotion was by strict seniority; a fixed salary was attached to each office; and more lucrative positions could be held only after achieving minimum periods of service.[12] A careful junior official could save even from his initial salary, and the high rate of interest prevailing in Calcutta enabled him to double his capital in seven years or less.[13] In consequence there gradually had grown up "a race of trained administrators around whom the old commercial tradition did not cling, who had not graduated in chicanery, or grown grey in corruption." [14]

Thackeray throve in this atmosphere. That he gave satisfaction at Midnapore is witnessed by the fact that in 1800 his salary already amounted to £660 a year, somewhat more than the maximum provided for a Company servant of only two years' service. But he wished to be in Calcutta, where further preferment might come his way; and in 1801 he accepted the opportunity offered him by the Marquess Wellesley of enrolling in the newly founded College of Fort William. He was admitted to that institution 5 May 1801.[15] The Governor-General's object in creating this institution was to train young writers in native languages in order that they might be fit to act as "ministers and officers of a powerful sovereign," and to preserve them from the temptations of unsupervised idleness. But the Marquess did not neglect to provide tangible incentives to industry. "After a year of fagging extremely hard at Arabic and Persian," Thackeray had written to his mother on 29 January 1801, "I have no doubt but that I shall immediately receive 4 times my present salary." [16]

He left the college on 1 January 1802 [17] without attaining particular distinction in his studies.[18] On 11 March of that year he was appointed Assistant to the Collector of Dacca, where his father had preceded him thirty years earlier. Other provincial appointments followed during the next six years—at Beerbohm in 1803 and again in 1806, at Jessore in 1805, at Tipperah in 1806, at Ramghur in 1807, and at Midnapore in 1808—but these seem to have been temporary employments, lasting only for brief periods. On the evidence of the *East-India Register* it would seem that his main work between 1802 and 1811 was with the Board of Revenue in Calcutta, of which he became Assistant to the Secretary and to the Persian and Bengallee Translator on 17 August 1802, Sub-Secretary on 1 August 1804, and Secretary on 1 January 1807.[19]

It was probably in 1802 that he became a householder in Calcutta; by that year his salary touched £1,200,[20] and his future prospects were excellent. No doubt William bore part of the expense of his new home, for the brothers had long been desirous of bringing their sisters to India. In a letter of 1801 Thackeray had asked that Emily, the oldest, be sent to him. "Her coming here is I think the most eligible thing in the world," he wrote to his mother, "not only for herself but also for our sisters for girls who are well brought up I think are equally as certain of marrying well as young men of good abilities are of coming on." [21] To Emily herself, with mock formality, he sent a solemn invitation:

> A CARD.
> Mr. Thackeray requests the honour of Miss Thackeray's company at his house in Calcutta.[22]

He proposed that his third sister, Charlotte, be Emily's companion, but his parents preferred to send out Augusta, who was a year older. Their father put the girls aboard the Indiaman *United Kingdom* in March, 1802, and they arrived at Diamond Harbour 28 July.[23]

Their brother's home in the "village of palaces" mentioned by Lord Valentia was one of many mansions arranged in three irregular rows beyond the Esplanade. These houses were built of brick and covered with brilliant and highly polished *chunam,* a white stucco made from the lime of burnt sea-shells. They were three or four storeys in height, had impressive porticos and verandahs, and were surrounded by individual gardens.[24] Tradition identifies Thackeray's residence with a building which later became the Armenian College at 39 Free School Street.[25]

The *grande tenue* that Thackeray and his sisters observed is suggested by a notice of the sale of effects "at his house in Chowringhee," announced to take place 10 January 1806.

Very handsome new Plate and Plated-ware, of the most useful kinds; Persian Scimitars and Poniards, in velvet Scabbards, very richly mounted in silver; dress and other Swords and Fire Arms; an handsome Ebony Portable Desk, richly ornamented and mounted in solid silver; a large Mahogany Box of Reeves's Colors, with silver mountings; an excellent Library of Books; Ackermann's Collection of beautiful Engravings for 1804–5, exquisitely colored and highly finished, in large vellum Portfolios, richly gilt and lettered, imported on one of the last ships, and cost upwards of 100 Guineas; a capital patent Saloon Organ, with fine Barrels, of the latest and most approved Tunes, having the Flageolet, Tabor, Drum, Triangle, Diapason Principal, Twelfth and Flute Stops; very fine Statues in Plaister of Paris; handsome plated mounted double and single branch Wall Shades, and large hanging Vase Lamps, with plated rims, boxes, chains, complete; valuable Paintings, Prints, and Convex Mirrors, in rich burnished gold frames; very fashionable Household Furniture, in white and gold and in Mahogany, Ebony, and other handsome Wood; Carpets; Settringes; and a variety of other articles.

Likewise, his Coach and valuable Carriage and Saddle Horses, viz—

The young very active, and high dressed, light grey Arab Saddle Horse *'Nimble'* 14½ hands high, moves in an elegant style, shows much blood, has a fine generous temper, and is believed perfectly sound, wind and limb.

A young and handsome dark Iron Grey Saddle Horse, half Arab, 1·5 hands high, has good temper, and promises well.

A handsome little Chestnut Mare that has been rode by a lady, and believed to be perfectly sound and quiet.

A pair of strong and very beautiful young Dark Chesnut [*sic*] Carriage Horses, above 15½ hands high, an excellent match, sound and quiet, go in good style, having been trained with the utmost attention and care, and are worthy the attention of any Gentleman in want of a pair of horses of this description.

A handsome European built Coach, body painted a Dark Brown, ornamented with double plated beading and lined with yellow Cloth, lamps in front, and suitable carriage part.[26]

To maintain a household on a scale commensurate with such belongings required two or three score servants, for caste restrictions narrowly limited the functions that the individual Hindu was allowed to perform. A contemporary writer lists the following as "absolutely necessary": a butler, a headbearer or valet, a sircar to superintend accounts, a hookahburdar to care for the master's hookah, waiters, a cook, a water-cooler, a baker, a cow-keeper, a sheep-keeper, a fowl-keeper, a butterman, a fisherman, a bhisti or water-carrier, candle-snuffers, a dogkeeper, a washerman, a gardener, grass-cutters, a tailor, a porter, and linkboys. Two sices, or grooms, attended each of Thackeray's horses. Palanquin-bearers were needed for short trips during the day, since English gentlemen never walked. And for his sisters a whole retinue of female servants was essential.[27]

One wonders what Emily and Augusta thought of a second establishment that Thackeray maintained nearby his Chowringhee mansion.[28] He had urged his mother to send out letters of introduction with his sisters. "To tell the truth," he wrote, "I am very far from a lady's man." [29] Yet beside his tomb in North Park Street Cemetery is a smaller monument on which appears the inscription:

In memory of
Mrs. Sarah Blechynden
lady of the late
James Blechynden Esq.
and only daughter of the late
Richmond Thackeray, Esq., B. C. S.
Died 15th May 1841, aged 35 years.[30]

Sarah was Thackeray's child by Charlotte Sophia Rudd, elsewhere called Radfield and Redfield,[31] his Moslem or possibly—in view of her name—Eurasian mistress. Sarah was born in 1804, despite the evidence of her monumental inscription; [32] she was baptized on 23 September 1815, ten days after her father's death; and she married another illegitimate half-caste, James Blechynden, in Calcutta on 20 July 1820.[33]

In India at the beginning of the nineteenth century concubinage of this sort was still customary among unmarried Europeans.[34] It was assumed that the private soldiers of the Bengal army would form native connexions, and as early as 1782 an Orphan Institution had been founded to provide for the children of such unions. The 4,000 white men of superior social position in Bengal were forbidden by the Company to marry natives or half-castes (as the soldiers could, if they chose); but since only 250 European ladies were as yet to be found in the entire province, no restrictions were placed on extralegal unions.[35] Nor apparently did the ladies of Calcutta society feel abhorrence at the thought of such alliances. They were a subject for amused and tolerant comment, even when the gentlemen in question affected "plurality":

> I have known various instances of two ladies being conjointly domesticated [writes Captain Williamson]; and one, of an elderly military character, who solaced himself with no less than SIXTEEN, of all sorts and sizes! Being interrogated by a friend as to what he did with such a number, 'Oh!' replied he, 'I give them a little rice, and let them run about!'
>
> This same gentleman . . . [paid] his addresses to an elegant young woman lately arrived from Europe, but who was informed by the lady at whose house she was residing of the state of affairs: the description closed with, 'Pray, my dear, how should you like to share a sixteenth of Major —— ?' The courtship was allowed to proceed, merely to make sport of the good man's *foible*.[36]

Nor were irregular unions regarded as disreputable by Moslems (few Hindus engaged in them), if a written contract governing their terms was entered into, and the woman maintained in suitable style. Living "under the protection" of a European gentleman, as the phrase went, was considered quite as proper as marriage to another native.

There was nothing sordid, degrading, or even unusual, then, in Richmond Thackeray's alliance. Speculation as to its success is perhaps idle. The letters and light literature of the time abound in satirical references to the infidelity of native *chères amies,* to the audacities of their black followers, and to the excessive darkness of the children imputed by them to their white protectors.[37] Captain Williamson testifies feelingly to their masterfulness and the uncertainty of their tempers. Yet Thackeray may possibly have achieved the sort of tender union that Kipling was later to describe in "Without Benefit of Clergy." He was certainly most generous to mother and daughter in his will.

The world of which Richmond Thackeray and his sisters formed a part was at once more decorous and more splendid than that which his father had known. "The hearts of the British in this country seem expanded by opulence," wrote Lord Valentia; "they do everything upon a princely scale." [38] The Governor General, it is true, held himself aloof from the society of his "subjects," which he regarded as "so vulgar, ignorant, rude, familiar and stupid, as to be disgusting and intolerable." [39] But most prominent officials gave elaborate receptions each week. Dinner-parties of thirty or forty guests, at which claret and Madeira flowed in profusion, were the rule. Balls were "the grand amusement in the Cold Season." [40] Most important of all was the daily gathering on the Esplanade. "About a quarter of an hour after Sun-set," writes one of Thackeray's contemporaries, "all the Carriages come out until at last all of the City may be said to be assembled; high and low, rich and poor, great and small, all mix promiscuously in this varied scene." [41]

On 28 March 1803, nine months after her appearance in this lively world, Emily Thackeray accomplished the purpose for which she had been sent to India by marrying John Talbot Shakespear.[42] It must have been a love-match, for Shakespear was a writer of nineteen, three years younger than his bride, whose fortune was yet to be achieved. After a year at Beerbohm, where he was Assistant to the Collector, he rejoined Richmond Thackeray at the Board of Revenue in Calcutta. Augusta Thackeray meanwhile remained with her brother. She was to be a fixture in his household until he died.

The prominent role that Richmond Thackeray played in the city's social life is suggested by an account of a masked ball given by him and three other gentlemen on 11 December 1807.[43] Some three hundred guests were invited to the principal rooms of entertainment in Calcutta; the chambers, "overspread with green and flowery foliage, presented to the eye of the spectator a scene of rural beauty"; the band of His Majesty's 67th Regiment performed in the passage to the ball-room. Ample time having been allowed for the preparation of ingenious masks, the result was a tableau of "peculiar splendor, animation, gaiety, and appropriate humor." Among the characters represented were *"a devil,* giving the Company a very accurate and horrible idea of the present costume of the infernal regions"; "*Rhadamanthus* attended by his faithful Cerberus, a most amiable three headed cur"; "*a Nurse,* with a babe in leading strings, measuring about 6 feet high"; and most successful of all, "*a quack doctor* anxious to dispose of his medicines," directing his harangues chiefly to the ladies "whom he professed to cure of their propensity to scandal."

Despite the assiduity with which he cultivated Calcutta society, Richmond Thackeray long remained unmarried. It was not until the winter of 1809–1810 that he fell in love with Anne Becher, a beautiful girl of seventeen who had just arrived from England. Some fifty-five years later, on the night before she died, she recalled to her grand-daughters "what a handsome, noble gentleman Richmond Thackeray was, and how he came courting her on a white horse." [44] They were married in St. John's Church on 13 October 1810. The witnesses included the bride's stepfather, Lieutenant-Colonel E. W. Butler, and Henry Davenport Shakespear, a younger brother of Emily's husband.[45]

V

It now becomes necessary to examine Thackeray's maternal heritage. A family genealogist, cautiously dismissing biblical references to the Becher name [1] as "of interest, but not seriously considered," finds himself on solid ground as early as the sixteenth century. There then flourished one Henry Becher, a haberdasher's merchant, armiger, alderman and sheriff of the City of London, who owned land in Devon and Somerset. From him descended both the Irish and the English branches of the family, the former established by his third son, Phane Becher, who was granted 12,000 acres of land from the forfeited estates of the Earl of Desmond in county Cork. The senior English line was made up chiefly of clergymen and officers. Anne Becher's grandfather was Captain John Becher, Royal Navy, born in 1736. Captain Becher and Anne his wife, who came into the world a year later,[2] settled in Fareham, Hampshire. At least five children were born to them: their eldest son, who lived in Bury St. Edmund's Suffolk; John Harman Becher; Alexander Becher, who like his father became a captain in the Navy; Anne; and another daughter.

John Harman Becher was born 26 March 1764.[3] He was appointed a writer on the East India Company's Bengal establishment in 1779. He appears to have owed his nomination to Richard Becher. This kinsman—it is not clear what degree of relationship obtained—first came out to India in 1743. He, his wife, and his infant daughter were among the English expelled from Calcutta during the uprising of 1756 which culminated in the atrocities of the "Black Hole," and both mother and child eventually died as a result of the hardships that they experienced. Becher lived on to become a senior member of Council during Clive's term as Governor General. He at length returned to England with a "modest independence" after a quarter of a century of honourable service.[4] The calamity that there overtook him is related in the fulsome phrases of his epitaph: "By nature, open, liberal and compassionate; unpractised in guile himself and not suspecting it in others, to prop the declining credit of a friend, he was led to put his all to hazard and fell the victim of his own benevolence." His influence in the East India Company continued, however, and in 1781 he returned to India in the subordinate position of Superintendent of the Mint at Dacca, his two sons accompanying him as writers. "But the vigour of life was past," his epitaph continues, "and seeing thro' the calamity of the times his prospects darken, in the hopeless efforts to re-erect the fortunes of his family, under the pang of disappointment, and the pressure of the climate; a worn mind and a debilitated body, sunk to rest." [5] He left behind him in India a family connexion even more extensive than that founded by William Makepeace Thackeray. Sir William Hunter mentions "a manuscript record of no fewer than fifteen Bechers in India during the half century after . . . 1781."

John Harman Becher arrived in India on 12 November 1779. His rise in the service was slow, but by 25 December 1786 he was sufficiently well established to marry Harriet Cowper at St. John's Church, Calcutta.[6] Of Miss Cowper's lineage nothing definite is known, but according to family tradition she had some Asiatic blood.[7] Certainly Lady Ritchie writes of her as "my brown grandmother." [8] Bengal records list four children from the union: John, baptized 26 September 1788; Harriet, born 30 August 1790; Anne, born 13 October 1792; and Maria, born in 1795.[9] All of them appear to have been sent home to Fareham in early childhood.

After Maria's birth, disaster overtook John Harman Becher, but the absence of any but occasional references to his name in official records makes it difficult to determine exactly what happened to him. In 1793 he was made Registrar of the Provincial Court of Appeal and Circuit, Calcutta Division, and he afterwards became Collector of the Twenty-four Pergunnahs, an appointment that was one of the great prizes of the service and should have made his fortune secure. Yet in 1797 he is described as "out of employ." When he drew up his will on 28 October 1799, he was a broken bankrupt, stripped of his possessions, and in near expectation of death. Indeed, this document includes a pathetic plea to his creditors that he may be allowed to leave a few mementoes to his relations: a family Bible, odd volumes of Shakespeare, and certain plain gold rings in each of which is to be engraved the inscription "This from poor Jack." [10] He was buried in Calcutta on 6 October 1800.[11]

Nowhere in his will does John Harman Becher mention his wife. There is an explanation for this omission in family tradition, which tells us that Mrs. Becher tired of her husband and left him sometime before his death.[12] Whether her departure was the cause or the result of his ruin does not appear. In any event, nothing is known of her between 1795 and 1802. In the latter year she figures as the wife of Captain Charles Christie, in a will which he drew up on 20 October.[13] It should be noted, however, that though Christie's duties kept him continuously in Bengal after his arrival in India in 1781, there is no entry in the Bengal Ecclesiastical Records concerning his marriage to Mrs. Becher. If she lived under Christie's "protection" while her husband survived, she may not have found it convenient to legalize the connexion after his death. Anglo-Indian society took a lenient view of marital irregularities.

In 1802 Christie and his "lady" were living in a bungalow overlooking the Ganges at Fatehgarh. Captain Christie was in the field most of the following year. He took part in the reduction of Kachaura Fort in the "Mud War"; and he was present at the battle of Delhi and the siege of Agra in the Second Mahratta War. In 1804 he rejoined Mrs. Christie at Fatehgarh, where he was directed to form the second battalion of the 25th Native Infantry. His relations with this corps, which was called after him "Cristeen-ki-Paltan," [14] are related by a friend:

Captain Christie had raised, clothed and disciplined the corps with all the tenderness of a parent, and all the solicitude and pride of a soldier; the commander and the men were proud of each other. But he had barely accomplished this first wish of his heart in bringing the corps to maturity, when he was seized with a violent illness. . . . Captain Christie died on the 30th of April, 1805, and was buried at Saintree, on the left bank of the Jumna, between Agra and Muttra. The Native officers of the corps, so contrary to their customs and religious prejudices, solicited permission to carry the corpse of their beloved commander to the grave: the whole corps followed the mournful procession with a general countenance of affliction and grief, presenting one of the most affecting scenes I ever beheld. After the funeral ceremony each sepoy stepped forward to look into the grave, threw a clod of earth on the coffin, and retired in melancholy silence; the whole corps sorrowing in tears.[15]

Mrs. Christie remained for a time at Fatehgarh, where Lieutenant John Pester visited her on 18 June, noting that "my having been in continual habits of friendship with Christie, recalled past events to her remembrance, and she appeared much distressed at first." [16] She was presumably in straitened circumstances, since Christie lamented in his will his "inability to leave her a Sufficience to ensure her a Small but Comfortable independence." Yet she was only thirty-five and possessed considerable personal attractions. By 17 December 1805 she had moved to Barrackpore, a few miles from Calcutta,[17] and on 28 October 1806 she married Captain Edward William Butler of the Bengal Artillery.[18]

By this step Mrs. Butler must have altogether retrieved her position in the easy-going Anglo-Indian world. Captain Butler was an officer of means and position, who had behind him twenty-three years of service in India.[19] Nor was he in a position very forcibly to reproach Mrs. Butler for past peccadilloes. Four natural children had been borne to him by native mistresses, and three of these children survived: Caroline Ann Sophia Butler, born in 1780; Louisa Ann Maria Butler; and Edward William Butler, born 27 May 1806.[20] Caroline had been sent to England to be educated. On 8 February 1807 Captain Butler went on furlough,[21] embarking with Mrs. Butler aboard the Honourable Company's ship *Bengal* to join his daughter at home.[22]

Meanwhile, Mrs. Butler's daughters by John Harman Becher —the son had died while still a boy [23]—were growing up at Fareham under the care of their grandmother, Mrs. John Becher, and her unmarried daughter Anne. "With its tall church spire and its peal of Sunday bells across the cowslip meadows," writes Lady Ritchie, "Fareham was a Miss Austen-like village, peopled by retired naval officers and spirited old ladies who played whist every night of their lives and kept up the traditions of England, not without some asperity." [24] Grandmother Becher was one of these stern and imperious old ladies. Her older daughter she invariably addressed as "Miss Becher," and the children were always "Miss Harriet," "Miss Nancy," and "Miss Maria." Miss Becher made up for Mrs. Becher's aloofness. "This good old lady," Thackeray wrote at the time of her death, "was a mother to my mother in her youth." [25] Despite the formality that prevailed, the girls' lives must have been agreeable enough. The Becher house, Lady Ritchie continues,

> stood in Fareham High Street, with pretty old-fashioned airs and graces, and a high sloping roof and narrow porch. The low front windows looked across a flower garden into the village roadway, the back windows opened into a pleasant fruit garden sloping to the river. . . . The little old house was as pleasant within as without; big blue China pots stood in the corners of the sitting-rooms and of the carved staircase with its low steps. In the low-pitched front parlor hung the pictures (a Sir Joshua Reynolds among them) of earlier generations.[26]

The girls had an upper room with little white beds, pattens to wear when it rained, willow plates of their own, dry bread on week-days—butter being forbidden "as a pernicious luxury for children"—and cherry-pie on Sundays. For excitement there were bulletins concerning the Napoleonic wars, the naval engagements of which in particular were followed with breathless interest. In later life Anne used to tell her grand-daughters of the memorable day on which the news of Nelson's death was received.

Old Mrs. Becher enjoyed company, and in the winter of 1807–1808, she went to Bath, accompanied by Anne, who at fifteen was just entering society. Anne enjoyed great success in Bath; her son later remarked, thinking of this period, that she "began beautiful & brilliant with a world of admirers round about her."[27] At one of the assembly balls to which her grandmother took her, she met Lieutenant Henry Carmichael-Smyth, of the Bengal Engineers,[28] the second son of James Carmichael-Smyth, a well-known London medical practitioner, twice Censor of the Royal College of Physicians and Physician Extraordinary to George III. The Carmichaels were a distinguished Scottish clan, related to the Earls of Hyndford and able to trace an unbroken line of ancestors back to the fourteenth century.[29] Henry had been born in 1780 and educated at Charterhouse School before coming out to the East.

Anne and Henry re-enacted the early history of Desdemona and Othello. He had on 10 October 1807 returned on a medical certificate after ten adventurous years in India, arriving in England on 7 April 1808.[30] He had served with Lord Lake in the Second Mahratta War, being present at the storm and capture of Aligarh, the battle of Delhi, and the battle of Laswari in 1803; at the taking of Rampura, the battle and capture of Deig, in 1804; and at the siege of Bhurtpore in 1805. He later received the India Medal for his services at Bhurtpore, and his work at Deig led Lord Lake to mention his "peculiar merit" in a dispatch to Lord Wellesley of 26 December 1804.[31] In 1806 he participated in the operations against the Rana of Gohad and was present at the capture of Gohad Fort. Thackeray refers to his courtship in an apostrophe to Anne written fifty-five years later, apropos of her fondness for Fanny Burney's *Evelina:*

I suspect that when you read that book which you so love, you read it *à deux*. Did you not yourself pass a winter at Bath, when you were the belle of the assembly? Was there not a Lord Orville in your case too? As you think of him eleven lustres pass away. You look at him with the bright eyes of those days, and your hero stands before you, the brave, the accomplished, the simple, the true gentleman; and he makes the most elegant of bows to one of the most beautiful young women the world ever saw; and he leads you out to the cotillon.[32]

But worldly old Mrs. Becher did not intend that her lovely grand-daughter should marry a younger son of uncertain prospects, and she refused to permit their engagement. Henry followed Anne back to Fareham. What there occurred is related by Mrs. Fuller:

Their secret trysting place was a terrace at the end of the Bechers' garden, past which flowed the broad tidal river which skirts the town. Here Anne was accustomed to wait for the boat that brought her lover. But their meetings were discovered, and Anne was ordered to her room, where she was kept under lock and key until she would give her word of honour that she would not again see Lieutenant Carmichael-Smyth. With this order she refused to comply, and she was supported in her confinement by the letters which the Lieutenant managed to smuggle to her by a maid, and to which she replied by the same agent.

Then suddenly the letters ceased, and one day old Mrs. Becher hobbled into her granddaughter's room and told her to muster all her courage to bear a great blow; the Ensign had died of a sudden fever and on his death-bed had sent her messages of his undying love. Anne pined and mourned in silence. After a time a family council decided that the broken-hearted young woman should be sent out to India as soon as possible.[33]

No doubt Mrs. Butler participated in this family council; for whatever may have been the Bechers' attitude towards her in the years that followed her desertion of her husband, she was welcome as the wife of Captain Butler, a matron of assured position. In any event, on 25 April 1809 there embarked on the Indiaman *Earl Howe,* Captain William Eastfield commanding,

Captain Butler, his daughter Caroline, Mrs. Butler, and Anne and Harriet Becher.[34] Anne was "dressed for the six months' voyage in a long riding habit of dark green cloth and a high hat swathed in veils." They disembarked at Calcutta after an uneventful voyage on 24 October.[35] The purpose for which the girls had been sent to India was soon accomplished. On 16 February Harriet married Captain Allan Graham of the Artillery,[36] and eight months later, as we have seen, Anne married Richmond Thackeray.

2

Calcutta and Home

I

WILLIAM MAKEPEACE THACKERAY, the Richmond Thackerays' only child, was born in Calcutta on 18 July 1811.[1] He was a seven-month baby, and the officiating physician told his mother that "it was happy for her that he was, as otherwise she must have died." [2] She was informed that it would be impossible for her to have other children; and the ordeal through which she had passed in the midst of the hot, rainy season proved so shattering that her health was impaired for many years after.[3] The place of Thackeray's birth is uncertain, though what evidence exists points to Richmond Thackeray's house in Chowringhee.[4] The baby was baptized at St. John's Church by the Chaplain, the Reverend J. Ward, D.D., on 3 January 1812.[5]

Meanwhile, Richmond Thackeray, having completed twelve years of Company service, became qualified to hold positions worth £4,000 or more a year. On 24 December 1811 he was accordingly appointed Collector of the Twenty-four Pergunnahs, a district of nearly 900 square miles immediately to the south of Calcutta, and in 1813 he assumed the additional office of Collector of the House Tax at Calcutta. The first of these was a coveted appointment, for it combined large emoluments with residence in the capital. There is supposed to have been attached to the position as an official residence the large lodge or bungalow at Alipur in which Sir Philip Francis had lived from 1774 to 1780, "a spacious hall and four chambers, surrounded by a verandah and colonnade, and standing in the midst of twenty acres of ground: pleasant to the last degree." [6] It has been assumed that Richmond Thackeray removed with his family to this house not long after he became Collector,[7] an assumption which cannot easily be reconciled with a reference in his will of 3 March 1815 to "the house in Chowringhee in which I reside." [8]

Whatever Richmond Thackeray's place of residence, he must have lived in great state, for he was now one of the first gentlemen of Calcutta. He figures, for example, among the leading citizens entrusted in 1813 with the office of drawing up an address of welcome to the new Governor General, Lord Minto.[9] He commissioned a family group from the most renowned of Calcutta artists, George Chinnery, who was at this time earning 5,000 rupees a month painting the Governor General, the justices of the Supreme Court, and the leading soldiers and civilians of the city.[10] His sister Augusta continued to reside with him, and it is reported of her and of his wife that they "were so beautiful and so dignified that they were treated like two Queens. When they rose to leave the room any gentlemen who were present rose instantly to hand them to the door." [11] When his wife's youngest sister Maria came out to India in 1814, she also may have joined the household. At any rate, in writing of her sister's child she later recalled how she "used to nurse him and play with him all day." [12]

Not that her assistance was indispensable, for young Thackeray possessed the retinue of a little prince. "Every Gentleman's Child in this country," explains a contemporary writer, "has two or three Servants, Men or Women. Babies have their wet-Nurses, for Ladies in India never perform this maternal duty." On fine mornings, he continues, European children go out on the Esplanade "with their black Nurses in neat spring-hung Carriages drawn by Oxen." [13] Thackeray's ayah, or nurse, figures in a note added by his great-aunt Anne to his first letter to his mother from England. She relates how

William drew me your house in Calcutta not omitting his monkey looking out of the window & Black Betty at the top drying her Towells. & told us of the number you collected on his Birth day in that large Room he pointed to us! [14]

In later life Thackeray's recollections of his first years in his "native country" [15] were scanty. He "could just remember" his father, writes Lady Ritchie, "a very tall, thin man, rising out of a bath," and "crocodiles floating on the Ganges." [16] In a letter of 1849 he records another memory, the picture of his grandfather, hanging on the wall, and his "admiring above all how the stick was painted, wh was made to look as if it was polished & shone."

In 1812 a *revenant* disturbed the even tenor of the Richmond Thackerays' married life. Captain Henry Carmichael-Smyth, still very much alive, had left England on 6 June 1810 [17] and arrived in India in 15 December, where he took up his appointment as Garrison Engineer at Agra, a post to which he had been appointed the previous year. In March, 1811, he embarked with an expedition to Java. There he participated in the action at Weltervreden on 10 August and in the reduction of the fortified lines at Cornelist on 26 August. After the surrender of the island on 17 September, he and the other officers received medals from the Prince Regent for their parts in the campaign. On 2–3 February of the following year he was employed as Field Engineer in the reduction of Kalinjar Fort. A proclamation of the Governor General in Council of March, 1812, refers to "the exemplary valour displayed by Capt. Smyth, the directing engineer, on the morning of the 2d ult." [18]

The reunion of this distinguished officer with Anne Thackeray is described by Mrs. Fuller:

Returning from his club in Calcutta one day, Richmond Thackeray said to his wife: 'I have just made the acquaintance of a most delightful and interesting Engineer officer; he only arrived yesterday morning, knows no one, and I have invited him to dine with us to-night so that we can introduce him to our friends.'

The hour of the dinner party arrived, the guests assembled, and the last to come was the stranger. The servant announced in a loud voice, 'Captain Carmichael-Smyth,' and in walked Anne's long-lost lover!

What that dinner was like no words can describe. After what seemed an eternity, Anne and Captain Carmichael-Smyth had a moment to themselves, and in a low trembling voice she exclaimed: 'I was told you had died of a sudden fever.' And with bitter reproach he replied, 'I was informed by your grandmother that you no longer cared for me and had broken our engagement. As a proof, all my letters to you were returned unopened. And when in despair I wrote again and again begging for an interview, you never gave me an answer or a sign.'

After a while the situation became so impossible that Richmond Thackeray had to be told; he listened gravely, said little, but was never the same to Anne again.[19]

Captain Carmichael-Smyth's presence did not long inconvenience Richmond Thackeray, for he shortly repaired to Agra to resume his duties as Garrison Engineer. Nor did his reappearance permanently impair the harmony of the Thackerays' household.

During the rainy season of 1815 Richmond Thackeray fell gravely ill of a lingering fever. To mitigate the oppressive heat his wife and sister had him carried aboard a ship in the Ganges, the customary expedient in the days before there were hill-stations to which to retire. Theirs must have been a moving vigil, for in 1849, when Augusta in turn was mortally afflicted, she fancied herself back on the ship with her stricken brother.[20] He died on 13 September 1815.[21] In a brief obituary paragraph the *Calcutta Gazette* described him as "distinguished for the mildness and benevolence of his nature." [22] The inscription on his tombstone reads in part:

To the best endowments of the understanding and to the purest principles in public life, he united all the social and tender affections. Under the influence of these moral and intellectual qualities he ever maintained the character of an Officer with the highest degree of credit to himself and discharged in a manner not less exemplary the duties which devolved upon him in the several relations of private life.[23]

No more personal tributes than these have transpired, though the respect, at any rate, with which his widow regarded him appears in a letter of 1820. Her son, she then wrote, "is the living image of his father, and God in heaven send he may resemble him in all but his too short life." [24] And when she herself died, nearly fifty years after her husband, her last words to her granddaughters, so Lady Ritchie relates, "were of papa's father coming to see her on his white horse." [25]

Richmond Thackeray's practical abilities and his solicitude for his family are alike illustrated in his will.[26] In this document, which was drawn up on 3 March 1815, he estimated the property of which he then stood possessed to be worth about £15,000. He anticipated that this sum would produce an annual income of about £800, which was to be used to provide the following annuities:

To Mrs. Thackeray	£450
To William Makepeace Thackeray	£100
To Augusta Thackeray	£100
To Sarah Redfield (his illegitimate child)	£100
To Sarah Redfield's mother, 16 sicca rupees per month, and To "the wife of the old Syce who was killed by a horse in my Service," 3 sicca rupees per month, together about	£ 30

Since his monthly savings averaged £300, his fortune at the time of his death totalled £17,000, and it proved possible to raise his son's annuity to £200. In the event of his wife's remarriage, half of her annuity was to go to their son, who was, moreover, residuary legatee to all other annuitants. During his son's minority, all sums not required for his education and maintenance were to accumulate for his use after attaining the age of twenty-one.

A substantial part of Richmond Thackeray's fortune was in the form of his Chowringhee residence. If his widow, sister, and son were indeed living at the Collector's house in Alipur, it was presumably to Chowringhee that they withdrew after his death. The income of £750 of which they together were possessed must have permitted them to live there in entire comfort. On 5 October 1816, however, Augusta married John Elliot,[27] who had been Judge and Magistrate of the Twenty-four Pergunnahs during the years when her brother was Collector.[28] Despite certain drawbacks—Elliot was fifty-three and the father of eight illegitimate children [29]—the marriage was by no means a bad one for an aging spinster. Maria Becher, spurred by Augusta's neglect of her sister-in-law Charlotte Elliot after her husband's death, once remarked: "She seems to have forgotten she was once Miss Thackeray with very [limited] means and that she owed all to Charlotte's brother." [30]

Augusta's departure from the household no doubt reminded Anne of an obligation that could no longer be shirked. At five years of age her son had already overstayed his time in India.

What a strange pathos seems to me to accompany all our Indian story! [Thackeray wrote in *The Newcomes.*] . . . The family must be broken up. Keep the flowers of your home beyond a certain time, and the sickening buds wither and die. In America it is from the breast of a poor slave that a child is taken; in India it is from the wife, and from under the palace, of a splendid proconsul.[31]

Anne could not herself take her son home, for her first loyalty was to Captain Carmichael-Smyth, whom she had promised to marry after eighteen months of mourning. But she made other arrangements. Passage was booked for the boy on the Indiaman *Prince Regent,* where he was well looked after. James Munro MacNabb, Richmond Thackeray's assistant in collecting the revenues of the Twenty-four Pergunnahs during the three years before his death,[32] was returning to England on furlough. Among the native passengers was one Lawrence Barlow, described in the log as "Servant to Master Thackeray." And Emily Shakespear dispatched her son Richmond, a year younger than Thackeray, on the same ship. Nearly half a century later Thackeray recalled the scene: "A ghaut, or river-stair, at Calcutta; and a day when, down those steps, to a boat which was in waiting, came two children, whose mothers remained on shore." [33] On 17 December 1816 the ship got under way from New Anchorage.

The *Prince Regent,* Captain Thomas H. Harris commanding, had been launched in 1811. It was of 953 tons, three decks in height, 149 feet long, and 38 feet wide.[34] In this narrow space were confined for nearly five months more than one hundred passengers, including twenty-one children from one to five years of age, and fifty soldiers. It cannot have been an altogether cheerful voyage, for ten members of this last group died before the *Prince Regent* reached England. Yet presumably the children at least were able to amuse themselves, though it is difficult to form any precise conception of their pursuits. Narratives of life aboard Indiamen come exclusively from adults, most of whom regarded their juvenile companions as nuisances. William Hickey complained bitterly of their "horrid screeches" when crying and their "vociferous mirth" when at play in the steerage.[35] And Sir James Mackintosh tells how he "finished part of Stewart amidst the uproar of the mob of spoiled children on the quarter-deck. It is the severest test to which the power of attention of a student of philosophy was ever subjected. If I can acquire the art of studying metaphysics in the midst of this noise, I must not despair of being able to go through the most intricate reasonings of the 'Principia' on the hustings of Covent Garden." [36] Yet Thackeray found at least one adult friend in John Reid, the ship's purser, whom he described after meeting him again thirty-five years later as "a kind old affectionate gentleman with the curiousest love of children, and faithful memory of old times." [37]

The *Prince Regent* put in at the Cape of Good Hope 17 February 1817, but the great event of the voyage was a visit to St. Helena on 8 March. There his native servant Lawrence Barlow, Thackeray later related, "took me a long walk over rocks and hills until we reached a garden, where we saw a man walking. 'That is he,' said the black man: 'that is Bonaparte! He eats three sheep every day, and all the little children he can lay hands on!' " [38] The *Prince Regent* sailed from St. Helena on 12 March. On 4 May 1812 the passengers were put ashore at Weymouth, and Mr. Reid took Thackeray to the home of his aunt and uncle Ritchie in London.[39]

Thackeray was never to return to India, though he at one time gave thought to such a visit.[40] The direct effect of the years that he spent there was small enough. He departed too young to retain the kind of detailed familiarity with the subcontinent that later enabled Kipling to write *Kim*. Only in *The Tremendous Adventures of Major Goliah Gahagan,* as Lady Ritchie has pointed out, is there "enough meaning and intention in the names and Hindustanee to show that he still retained something of his early impressions." [41] Yet he was raised among Anglo-Indians whose talk was chiefly about the land that they had left. He was brought up on such books as the histories of India of James Mill and Orme, Bishop Heber's *Narrative of a Journey through India,* Southey's *Curse of Kehama,* and Tom Moore's *Lalla Rookh*. India thus continued to be a living force in his imagination. Moreover, the indirect effect of Thackeray's Indian heritage and experience was immense. Belonging as he did to one of those families described by Kipling as serving India "generation after generation as dolphins follow in line across the open sea," [42] he grew up in the compact world that Anglo-Indians made for themselves at home, a world in which the Indian service was regarded as a "sacred college of sons and nephews" and there existed "small sympathy for talent without relations." [43] If Thackeray's sense of family ties was thus greatly strengthened, as has already been noted, he also acquired something of the curious point of view that prevailed in this tight little society. Having devoted their best years to the demanding duties of responsible positions in India, these servants of John Company and of the King returned home proud of their accomplishments and imbued with a proper sense of their importance. The civilians found that their pretensions were treated with small respect, while the soldiers discovered that they were regarded with positive antipathy.[44] The humiliations thus endured by returned "Indians," whom half a lifetime of arduous service had sometimes made into personalities of formidable strength and eccentricity, gave them a detached and critical perspective from which to view the structure and customs of English society. Many of them asked the question that Kipling was to put many years later: "What do they know of England, who only England know?" Finding ignorance, corruption, and frivolity in high places, both in the state and the army, they tended to criticize the social system of their day with unrestrained asperity. Henry

James was surely justified in observing how important in its consequences was the fact that Thackeray's forbears on both sides had been "drops in the great bucket" of the "ravenous, prodigious Service," and had experienced "the huge, hot, horrible century of English pioneership, the wheel that ground the dust for a million early graves." "The Thackerays and the Bechers helped to feed the machine," James concluded, "and the machine turned them out with the big special stamp that sometimes, for variety, didn't crush to death." [45]

II

Mrs. John Ritchie, to whom Mr. Reid brought Thackeray from the *Prince Regent,* was a sister of Richmond Thackeray, who lived with her husband at Chatham Place in London. The Ritchies were not well regarded by the Bechers, possibly because John Ritchie was a Scottish merchant of peasant origin.[1] When Anne returned to England, she took an immediate dislike to her sister-in-law, and sent a frank account of her to India. "I certainly hoped she would have found a sensible affectionate if not elegant woman in Mrs. R.," Maria wrote regretfully to her mother, implying that in Anne's view even the two former qualities were lacking.[2] The boy was less critical and got along famously with his aunt and uncle. What he saw in Mrs. Ritchie may be surmised from his daughter's description of her a quarter of a century later:

> I loved my great-aunt Ritchie, as who did not love that laughing, loving, romantic, handsome, humorous, indolent old lady? Shy, expansive in turn, she was big and sweet-looking, with a great look of my father. Though she was old when I knew her, she would still go off into peals of the most delightful laughter, just as if she were a girl.[3]

Thackeray did not long remain with the Ritchies, however, for his home when not at school was to be with the Bechers at Fareham. The town had changed very little during the thirty years in which his great-grandmother and great-aunt had lived there. In all essentials it was much the same as it had been when his mother was a girl. Thackeray has described it as "the little old town of Fareport in Hampshire," in a cancelled passage written for his last novel:

During and after the Great European War the society was mainly composed of wives, widows, and daughters of officers of his Majesty's navy. Portraits of gentlemen in blue coats and white facings hung in most of the parlours. Pictures of shipwrecks and naval combats were to be seen in almost all drawing rooms. I think the two prints representing the famous action between the Java and the Constitution were the most modern works to be seen at Fareport, and you know that battle was fought in the year before Waterloo. A sedan chair or two still existed in the place, and took out the good ladies to tea on rainy evenings. Dinner was at three or four o'clock. Home-made wines (by some young palates thought delicious) were not uncommonly served at dessert. At six appeared tea; and then came cards, quadrille and whist until eleven, when a neat little supper terminated the evening's mild amusement; Betty and Mary arrived with the shawls, clogs, and lantern; and the good ladies went to rest, to rise the next morning for just such another day's gossip, business, and pleasure. There were scarcely any men in the Fareport society. There were many widows, and elderly spinsters, daughters of deceased commodores and captains. It was not certainly an intellectual society. Very few books were read: indeed, books were not considered fit furniture for ladies' drawing-rooms. I don't know how many families would club together to take in the Portsmouth paper.[4]

In this old-fashioned town—"so like a novel by Jane Austen" that Thackeray later wondered, "was she born and bred there?" —the little boy found much to interest him. He was awed by great-grandmother Becher, who remained the dominant personality in the household, though she was approaching eighty, "a most lovely and picturesque old lady, with a long tortoise-shell cane, with a little puff, or *tour,* of snow white (or was it powdered?) hair under her cap, with the prettiest little black velvet slippers and high heels you ever saw." [5] In the garden behind the Bechers' house on the High Street, he read his first novel, *The Scottish Chiefs.* He could not quite bring himself to finish the account of Wallace's tragic end in the fifth volume, he later recalled, though he "peeped in an alarmed furtive manner at some of the closing pages." "It was as sad . . . as going back to school!" [6] The Bechers had at last to give up their house in Fareham to the gentleman from whom they rented it, but only in July, 1820, the month in which Thackeray's mother and stepfather reached England.[7]

In the autumn of 1817 Thackeray was put into the Arthurs' school at Southampton,[8] "a school of which our deluded parents had heard a favourable report," he later wrote, "but which was governed by a horrible little tyrant, who made our young lives so miserable that I remember kneeling by my little bed of a night, and saying, 'Pray God, I may dream of my mother!' " [9] Elsewhere he exclaims: "What a dreadful place that private school was: cold, chilblains, bad dinners, not enough victuals, and caning awful!" [10] And he tells in the *Roundabout Papers* of an occasion on which "the wiseacre of a master" ordered all the boys "one night, to march into a little garden at the back of the house, and thence to proceed one by one into a tool or hen house, . . . and in that house to put our hands into a sack which stood on a bench, a candle burning beside it. I put my hand into the sack. My hand came out quite black. I went and joined the other boys in the school-room; and all their hands were black too." Thackeray and his companions went bewildered back to bed. Only later was it explained to them that, something having been stolen, the master had thought to detect the thief from his shirking when told to put his hand into this bag of soot.[11] Thackeray's companions in misery under this idiot despot included Richmond and George Trant Shakespear, Richmond's older brother who had preceded him home by several months. "I can remember George coming and flinging himself down upon my bed the first night," Thackeray later told a common relative.[12] A friendship between the two began that was interrupted only when George Shakespear went out to India as a writer twelve years later.

Thackeray spent the summer of 1818 with the Bechers at Fareham. He describes his experiences in a letter to his mother written "to tell how happy I am":

This has been Neptune day with me I call it so because I go into the water & am like Neptune Your old acquaintances are very kind to me & give me a great many Cakes, & great many Kisses but I do not let Charles Becher kiss me I only take those from the Ladies I dont have many from Grandmama. . . . I am three feet 11 inches and a quarter high I have got a nice boat. I learn some poems which you was very fond of such as the Ode on Music &c. I shall go on Monday to Chiswick to see my Aunt Turner & heare the Boys speak. I intend to be one of those heroes in time.[13]

There is no breath of complaint in the three letters from Southampton that survive, only the wistful hint to his aunt Ritchie, "It seems a long time since I saw you." [14] But Thackeray made his feelings about the Arthurs clear during the holidays, and in the autumn of 1818 he was granted his wish of entering the school at Chiswick presided over by his mother's cousin, the Reverend John Turner, D.D. No doubt this establishment was superior to the Arthurs'. But nearly all private schools were bad at this period—consider Thackeray's candid picture of such an institution in *Dr. Birch and His Young Friends*—and it may be surmised that he found his three years with the Turners dreary enough. On one occasion, indeed, he was driven to run away. He was still small for his age (because of his premature birth), and the older boys at school made a pet of him and encouraged him to develop his budding powers of caricature. An unflattering sketch that he had made of an usher was discovered by Dr. Turner, and to escape punishment he took to his heels. But coming to the end of the lane that led to the school, he "was so frightened by the sight of Hammersmith High Road that he ran back again, and no one was the wiser." [15]

Despite his relatives' good-natured patronage, the little boy must have led a dismal life until his mother and stepfather returned from India, a life all the more difficult to bear because of the contrast it afforded to the care and affection lavished upon him in his splendid Indian home. He later looked back at these glum days in describing Harry Esmond's lonely boyhood.

The unhappiness of those days is long forgiven [he wrote], though they cast a shade of melancholy over the child's youth, which will accompany him, no doubt, to the end of his days: as those tender twigs are bent the trees grow afterwards; and he, at least, who has suffered as a child, and is not quite perverted in that early school of unhappiness, learns to be gentle and long-suffering with little children.[16]

Yet Thackeray was a clever, forward child, concerning whom very favourable reports could be sent to India. Early in 1820 his mother writes fondly:

John Turner gives me an instance of his progress in Latin which he said he would not have believed had he not seen it, he construed to my Aunt the Motto to the Becher arms which is *'Bis vivit qui bene'*, (he lives twice who lives well) Henry [Carmichael-Smyth] says it is a beautiful instance because the *first* (vivit) is only once expressed therefore he must have carried on the sense of it in his own mind; & when you think that he is only 8 years old it is even more so; & with all he has so much fun, he tells me he had seen the Prince Regents yacht & the bed in wh his 'Rl Highness breaths his *royal snore.'* [17]

In another letter of the same period she notes that William is "sixth in the school, though out of the twenty-six there are only four that are not older than himself." [18]

When she wrote these letters, Anne had for some time been Mrs. Carmichael-Smyth. Since his dramatic reappearance in her life, Captain Carmichael-Smyth's career had continued to be an active one. He bore his part in the disasters of the Nepal War, being present at the repulse of Kalanga and the unsuccessful attack on Jaithak in October and December of 1814. After two quiet years at Agra, he participated in the investment and capture of Hathras Fort in February and early March of 1817. Returning from this campaign, he married Mrs. Thackeray at Cawnpore 13 March 1817,[19] exactly a year and a half after Richmond Thackeray's death. They settled down together at Agra for three final years in India.

The Indian chapter in the lives of Mrs. Carmichael-Smyth's sisters and mother was also drawing rapidly to a close. In the case of her sisters it was to be the final chapter. Captain Allan Graham had died at Agra on 7 June 1816,[20] leaving his widow with two children, Charles Allen, christened 15 August 1814 at Agra, and

Mary Elliot, born 1 September 1815 at Calcutta.[21] Captain Graham directed in his will that his "house in the Fort of Agra" and other property should be sold and the proceeds invested in the Funds, in order to provide his "very Dear and beloved Wife" with a suitable income.[22] But the expense of sending little Charles and Mary home to their Graham relatives at Harwich was considerable, and when their mother followed them to England towards the end of 1819, the money for her passage had to be supplied by Colonel Alexander Knox. She learned of the death of her son not long before she sailed.[23]

Colonel Knox was Maria Becher's husband. They had married at Rewari on 22 November 1817,[24] and despite the fact that he was fifty-seven and she twenty-two, the match was a successful one. "Polly," as she was called in the family,[25] was a "little fragile child," [26] whom the Indian climate had reduced to semi-invalidism. She was loyal and affectionate to her husband and devoted to her mother and sisters, particularly to Anne, an "Angel," she wrote, who had been to her "in the light of a second conscience." [27] The Colonel was a grizzled veteran of thirty-seven years in India. He had fought in a score of battles, and on two occasions had a horse killed or disabled under him. In the year after his marriage a cavalry brigade under his command captured a native army of 10,000 men.[28]

The Knoxes lived in 1818 at Rajputana, where the Colonel was military commander and Lieutenant-Colonel Butler was one of his subordinates. On 1 August 1819, after the Butlers had removed to Agra, Mrs. Butler was again left a widow.[29] For a while she remained with the Carmichael-Smyths. "I can indeed imagine," Maria wrote to her, "all the anxious and affectionate attendance of our beloved Anne." [30] She thought for a time of going at once to England, but instead, restless as ever, joined the Knoxes early in 1820 at Nusserabad. Though her husband had died insolvent, he was fortunately a participator in two insurance schemes for the families of officers; and with an income of nearly £500 a year, she was very much her own mistress.[31] Tiring of the narrow round of provincial society, the indefatigable lady set off alone later in the year for Barrackpore.[32] She had hardly arrived when the news that Maria expected a child set her off again on "four or five months dreary travelling" back to Nusserabad.[33] Before Mrs. Butler could reach her, however, Maria's doctor became so alarmed at her condition that he started her on the way to Calcutta, in the hope that a sea voyage from that city might recover her.[34] Mother and daughter met at Agra and returned together to the Bengal Presidency.[35] But to no avail, for Maria was buried in Calcutta on 28 May 1822. Mrs. Butler returned to England shortly thereafter.

The Carmichael-Smyths had sometime since departed from India, on a furlough, as the Captain supposed, but actually never to return. During his last years as Garrison Engineer at Agra, the Captain did not extend his record of military exploits, though he served under Lord Hastings as Field Engineer of the Centre Division of the Grand Army during a campaign in which the enemy was not engaged. Anne longed for home, because of the low state of her health—"a poor scraggy thing," she describes herself as being in 1820 [36]—and because of the wonderful reports concerning her boy that reached her from England. On 3 February 1820 she wrote to her mother:

> I have had a delightful letter from my Man . . . the day Charles [Carmichael-Smyth] arrived, he was in high spirits all day, but when he went to bed he could restrain [himself] no longer & burst into tears, the Servant asked him why he cried, he said 'I cant help it, to see one who has so lately seen my dear Mother & to see her picture & the dear Purse she has made for me'!! Is there a Mother in India with such a proof of her Childs affection, never cease to pray for him as you pray for my life. Shall I ever see this treasure? [37]

On 20 February the Carmichael-Smyths went aboard the Indiaman *Fame*.[38] Their trip home, though enlivened by a bitter and protracted quarrel between Captain Remington and his first and second mates into which Captain Carmichael-Smyth may have been drawn,[39] was not otherwise eventful. They disembarked in England on the evening of 5 July.[40]

They repaired at once to "the old Chateau," the home of the Captain's father at Charlton, a few miles outside London. Sad news awaited Anne there; her sister Harriet Graham was dead and little Mary was an orphan. But there was consolation in the sight of her own son, "my Boy my precious Boy," after a three-and-one-half-year separation. Robert Langslow, an uncle who acted as one of his guardians, brought him to Charlton the day after the Carmichael-Smyths' arrival,

for Mrs. Turner [Anne explains] w^{d} not part with him till we came that I might see him in full bloom & truly he is so, dear soul he has a perfect recollection of me he could not speak but kissed me & looked at me again & again, I could almost have said 'Lord now let thou thy servant depart in peace for mine eyes have seen thy salvation.' [41]

For Thackeray too this reunion was a critical experience, which he was later to draw upon in describing Lady Castlewood's appearance to young Harry Esmond. "She had come upon him as a *Dea certè,* and appeared the most charming object he had ever looked upon." "The soul of the boy was full of love, and he had longed . . . for someone on whom he could bestow it." [42]

After eleven years' absence from England there was much for the Carmichael-Smyths to see and do. Anne was delighted with Dr. Carmichael-Smyth, "the good old Father who is exactly what I expected full of good humour firm spirits his conversation replete with elegant wit & strong sense." He made her "quite mistress of the house" [43]—he had long been a widower—and would take nothing from Henry towards the heavy expenses of hospitality at the Chateau. The remaining Carmichael-Smyths Anne found less congenial, except for brother Charles, whom she had known well in India. He learnt of their arrival while travelling in Italy, and set off immediately for England. "Just like Charles," [44] Maria comments.

Anne's letters to her mother and sister were filled with reports of her boy.

Nothing is like my William's affection [she wrote to Maria], he takes my hand & kisses it and looks at me as if he never could look long enough, the other day he said to me 'Mama its a long time since I have seen a Play and I should like to have a treat.' 'Very well dear I said if there's a Theatre at Gosport you shall go, but I can't go with you.' 'Then I'm sure I shan't what's the use of going without you I had rather see you than the play.' . . . Dr Turner says he is one of the cleverest boys in the School that he sees things in a minute which others plod over for hours, but his idleness is almost unconquerable.[45]

Maria's comment is significant. "Does not this great quickness and idleness except when roused, remind you of his poor father?"

On 10 August the Carmichael-Smyths took Thackeray back to Chiswick. With him went Colonel Butler's illegitimate son Edward, "not so good looking as I expected or so fair," Anne remarked, "but still much fairer even than some Europeans." [46] For some time afterwards Thackeray was restless at school.

My Billy Boy dispatched a document to me the day before I was leaving Charlton [his mother wrote] begging that he & Edward might come home at Michaelmas it was without a seal & unknown to the Dr so I could only send him a cake and promises of a holiday when I return. I do find such difficulty in refraining from seeing him but he is so soon unsettled I dont like to do it.[47]

After some weeks at Charlton the Carmichael-Smyths embarked upon a country tour that took them to Windsor, Oxford, Cambridge, Stratford, and Leamington. They lingered for a time in the last-named town, in order that the Captain might drink the waters. Then they proceeded to Harwich to claim Mary Graham from her aunt. And finally they visited Gosport, where the Bechers had settled after their removal from Fareham. Aunt Becher, Maria wrote to her mother, "says she has put all neat [in their new home] and was quite ready for Nannys reception and had got a Cellar large enough to hold the malmsey which had reached them at last and that dear Granny drank a glass every day at 12 o'clock." [48]

Though there was much to see and do, Anne was not entirely content with England. Three months after her arrival she told her mother:

England is very delightful the climate fine, the Country Paradise, but the people! the people are not Indians, they live for themselves, we live for our friends & I dont think in a whole life I should ever make such a friend as a few months in your kinder land has given me; if I had you all here, this wd not strike me, but I feel such a void, no Mother no Charlotte El[l]iot no little Polly no —— .[49]

(The blank was an allusion to Anne's unforgotten sister Harriet). Nor was the reserve of the English all that Anne had to complain of. "The secret is," she wrote, "we live in India as people in this Country do who now spend 3000£ a year and then come home to live upon one." [50] "It's more for Henry than herself," Maria explained. "He of course would feel some degree of mortification to see his Elder Brother living in a style of splendor and himself limited as he must be in almost all his wishes." [51] Altogether the Carmichael-Smyths' return to England was a disappointment; and if they adopted a strongly radical view of the English social order of their day, a view that materially affected their son's outlook, it was in large part because of the experiences of these years.

Anne and her husband continued to make the Chateau their home until the death of Dr. Carmichael-Smyth on 18 June 1821. It meant a great deal to the Captain to have this year at Charlton. "His poor Father has often told me," Anne wrote, " 'Harry is my only Child who never did a thing that I could have wished done otherwise. I believe there is not a happier Father in the world than I am but impartial as my feelings are & proud as I am of them all, there is not one whom I can compare to Harry.' " [52] Though only a second son, his financial position was improved by his father's death; and it began to seem less essential that he return to India, particularly after he received his majority, and a consequent increase in half pay, on 19 July 1821.

A letter which Mrs. Carmichael-Smyth wrote to India in August, 1821, provides a picture of Thackeray in his last months with Dr. Turner at Chiswick:

My poor Billy-Boy was getting better of his cough, and he was going into school when Henry unfortunately went to see him and gave him half-a-crown, with which my little gentleman must buy a lump of cheese, which of all things you know was the very worst, and brought back the enemy. . . . Billy-Man says, 'give my love to them all, *I wish* they would come over.' Here is the little figure he has done in a few minutes of Captain Bobadil; it was a thick pencil and he could not make a good outline. He painted a little theater for young Forrest, or rather a scene with sides entirely from his own imagination, which Mrs. Forrest says was capital. . . . Our time is limited to the 19th, when I must be at Chiswick to hear my little hero hold forth—I don't know how I shall go through with it. They have not selected an interesting speech—Hannibal's address to his soldiers—which you must all read and fancy me and Billy Boy—but you can't fancy such a great fellow.[53]

Much to the Turners' annoyance, Thackeray was removed from Chiswick just before Christmas in order that he might be sent to Charterhouse. The holidays were celebrated in a family party at Shanklin, Isle of Wight, where the Carmichael-Smyths were living. Anne wrote to her sister:

Charles & his Boy [an illegitimate child born in India, who was somewhat younger than Thackeray] & my Boy came down to us on the 18th & we all appear able to eat the Turkey at 4 o'clock, that the young ones may have Christmas pleasures at reasonable hours; my dearest William is very much grown & free from all ills this winter which is a great blessing to me for I had terrible apprehensions last year of confirmed cough, now he is as handsome a boy as you will see; the likeness to his Father at times almost startles me. I can only pray that his mind & heart may preserve as strong a resemblance if it pleases God to spare my dear Henry's life he will form him into what he should be.

My two Boys & Billy Boy are taking a walk & Mary & Charley playing in the verandah. . . . There's my Mary singing the old election ballad how it would gladden your hearts to hear her, she has such a sweet voice. . . . We have quite an Academy of Arts—William takes his by fits but you w^{d} be surprised at his performances. I have seen some portraits from Lord Byron's 'Cain' which are very fine.[54]

After the holidays Thackeray was duly dispatched to his new school. The Carmichael-Smyths had planned an extended trip to Scotland and France, after which they thought of returning to India; but, as we shall see, they had said farewell to the East.

3

The Forest Life of a Public School

I

BY ENTERING CHARTERHOUSE on 15 January 1822, Thackeray began the "education of a gentleman," a process that was to extend over eight and a half years at school and university. He was often discontented and unhappy while he was undergoing this experience, and in early maturity he was inclined to trace most of his misfortunes to the bad habits and false standards that it had taught him. Yet his years at Charterhouse and Cambridge were of capital importance to him in two ways. Coming to see his total experience there in perspective was one of the most enlightening things that ever happened to him; out of his rebellion against certain aspects of the code that had been taught him came the novel perspective that informs such books as *Barry Lyndon, The Book of Snobs,* and *Vanity Fair.* More important still, perhaps, was the continuing influence upon him of certain other aspects of this code which he never seriously questioned; out of his adherence to these came the more traditional but no less interesting perspective that informs his later books.

Considering the nature of the unreformed English public school during the 1820s, one cannot but be surprised that the most privileged class of the richest and most powerful nation in the world entrusted its first-born by free choice to such an institution. Sydney Smith has left the classic account of the doubts concerning it that suggested themselves to acute minds even of that period:

In a forest, or public school for oaks and elms, the trees are left to themselves; the strong plants live, and the weak ones die: the towering oak that remains is admired; the saplings that perish around it are cast into the flames and forgotten. But it is not, surely, to the vegetable struggle of a forest, or the hasty glance of a forester, that a botanist would commit a favourite plant: he would naturally seek for it a situation of less hazard, and a cultivator whose limited occupations would enable him to give it a reasonable share of his time and attention.[1]

For a long time Thackeray seemed to be one of these perishable saplings. Few observers at Charterhouse would have had the temerity to predict his eventual development into a mighty oak.

"Take that boy and his box . . . and make my regards to Mr. Smiler, and tell him the boy knows nothing and will just do for the 'lowest form.' " If Charterhouse tradition may be credited, these were the directions that Headmaster Dr. John Russell bellowed to the porter after his first interview with a timid and bewildered ten-year-old Thackeray.[2] There had been cogent reasons, none the less, for sending Thackeray to Charterhouse. His stepfather had been trained there before joining the Indian army, and the school had since maintained a strong Anglo-Indian connexion.[3] Moreover, its prestige had never been greater. The Duke of Wellington described it in 1820 as "the best school of them all," [4] and Thackeray was one of 161 new boys who entered in 1821–1822.[5]

Though Thackeray began in the twelfth and lowest form, he rose rapidly. The Charterhouse school-lists issued in May of each year place him in the tenth form in 1822, the seventh form in 1823, the fifth form in 1824, and the third form in 1825, his last year in the lower school.[6] At whatever level, his studies were much the same, the classical languages taught in a literal and pedantic fashion. It is perhaps too much to say, indeed, that they were *taught* at all. The lower school possessed only six masters, and they confined their efforts largely to discipline. In "De Juventute" Thackeray conjures up the picture of a boy in a jacket. He is at a desk; he has great books before him, Latin and Greek books and dictionaries. Yes, but behind the great books, which he pretends to read, is a little one, with pictures, which he is really reading. It is—yes, I can read now—it is the *Heart of Mid-Lothian,* by the author of *Waverley*—or, no, it is *Life in London, or the Adventures of Corinthian Tom, Jeremiah Hawthorn, and their friend Bob Logic,* by Pierce Egan; and it has pictures—oh! such funny pictures! As he reads, there comes behind the boy, a man, a dervish, in a black gown, like a woman, and a black square cap, and he has a book in each hand, and he seizes the boy who is reading the picture-book, and lays his head upon one of his books, and smacks it with the other.[7]

To increase enrolment without materially enlarging his staff and expenses, Dr. Russell had introduced a system of pupil-teaching. Instruction in the lower school was chiefly the business of *praepositi.* A "poz," as he was familiarly called, was chosen by Dr. Russell from among the boys in the top half of the second form and set as a teacher above each of the lower forms.[8] The system succeeded only in those rare instances when a "poz" had both the strength to keep his form in order and the intelligence to instruct it. What usually happened is illustrated in a story that Thackeray used to tell of "how once Russell entered a classroom where chaos appeared to be ruling, and there being no sign of a 'praepositus,'—'Where is your praepositus?' cried Russell. 'Please, sir, here he is,' and they fished out, from under the desk, the very small boy who had been set to rule over them. They had placed him there to be out of the way." [9]

Thackeray's preparation in his earlier private schools had been inadequate, and Charterhouse gave him no opportunity of making up lost ground. Having no stimulus to intelligent curiosity, he fell into habits of listlessness and indolence. "A pretty, gentle, and rather timid boy," [10] he shrank both from his masters and their subjects.

I always had my doubts about the classics [he wrote twenty years later]. When I saw a brute of a schoolmaster, whose mind was as coarse-grained as any ploughboy's in Christendom; whose manners were those of the most insufferable of Heaven's creatures, the English snob trying to turn gentleman; whose lips, when they were not mouthing Greek or grammar, were yelling out the most brutal abuse of poor little cowering gentlemen standing before him: when I saw this kind of man (and the instructors of our youth are selected very frequently indeed out of this favoured class) and heard him roar out praises, and pump himself into enthusiasm for, certain Greek poetry, —I say I had my doubts about the genuineness of the article. . . . Fancy the brutality of a man who began a Greek grammar with '*τύπτω*, I thrash!' [11]

The final sentence of this bitter passage serves as a reminder that the discipline of Charterhouse was maintained at the flogging-block.[12] As an "Under" (a member of the lower school) Thackeray more than once submitted to a whipping.[13] "It hurt like h-ll," he confided to Henry Silver.[14] Serious misdeeds were summarily punished. Routine offences were recorded in the "Black Book," and if a boy's name appeared therein three times during a single week, he was "swished." After the last class, offenders were taken to Dr. Russell in the side chapel of the lower school, where stood the dreaded instrument, "shaped something like an executioner's block, with one step to kneel on, and another over which to bend the head." [15] The attending monitor gave the Doctor a 5-foot bunch of birch, "armed with buds as sharp as thorns." [16] The usual punishment was six strokes. "The fourth, fifth, and sixth hurt abominably," it is reported. "Sitting down was not a comfortable process for a whole day afterwards." [17] For gross offences Dr. Russell proceeded to *les grands moyens*. One imagines the fascinated horror with which was received the order reported in "Horae Carthusianae": "Three rods eighteen and most severely." Though the punishment was inflicted privately, it had the attention of the whole school. "Every cut was anxiously listened to by all the boys assembled in Big School, and grimly counted." [18] Thackeray at Charterhouse may be pictured, indeed, in the words of Surrey:

> I saw the little boy in thought how oft that he
> Did wish of God to scape the rod a tall young man to be.

Even the names that he later gives to teachers in his stories (Dr. Birch, Mr. Swishtail, and Miss Tickletoby) show how closely the thought of school was associated in his mind with its peculiar institution.[19]

Apart from the three school-times, which lasted from seven in the morning (eight in winter) until four in the afternoon, with intervals for breakfast and lunch, the boys administered their own affairs. During his first two and a half years at Charterhouse, Thackeray was one of fifty-six boarders who trudged home each afternoon through a tunnel that led to the house of the Reverend Henry Penny, M.A., at 28 and 30 Wilderness Row. Since it was not a large house, the boys had to put up with great overcrowding and entire want of privacy. They ate, played, and studied in the long room, the older boys having cupboards and desks of their own, the younger ones little lockers and places at the common table. Bedrooms were small and packed tight with beds. Lavatory facilities were primitive; the boys "had to wash in a leaden trough, under a cistern, with lumps of fat yellow soap floating about in the ice and water," [20] and used a common towel. The fare was plentiful but coarse, its staple being boiled beef, or "boiled child" as the boys facetiously called it.[21] Thackeray used to supplement his meals, when he had the money, with half-a-crown's worth of pastry and ginger beer.[22] In the last year of his life Thackeray opened one of his old school-books and found in it a packet of brown sugar. "It was the thing to do in those days he said [to his daughter Anne], you put by your store and then you had the gratification of coming on it unexpectedly." [23]

When Thackeray was not in school or at Penny's house, he was on the playground, which consisted of the "Upper Green," covered with gravel, and the "Under Green," paved with stone. The games played on these unyielding surfaces were cricket (at which a boy was killed in Thackeray's time), football, tennis, prisoners' base, and hoops. In later life Thackeray indignantly denied that he and his schoolfellows played marbles. Hoops was an odd pastime.

This came in for a fortnight at the beginning of Oration Quarter [writes H. W. Phillott], and consisted in 'tooling,' i.e. driving two hoops—to tool a single one was low and contemptible—up and down Cloisters and also round Green, but in this last sometimes three were used, and even four by great proficients. . . . To 'tool' a pair of hoops up and down Cloisters in a crowd of other pairs similarly engaged was a performance of no little skill, and to turn at each end a matter of great nicety and neatness of handling. When the hoop fortnight was over, the hoops were all shied up into the trees, and then brought down again by the sticks shied also into them for that purpose.[24]

Another amusement was to repair to the "bog," a remote part of the playground near the wall, where there were " 'coach trees'—climbed to see mail coaches go by." [25] Thackeray was very near-sighted, and since the feeling then prevailed that children had no business with spectacles,[26] he was able to take little part in games. But he could join Dr. Johnson in remarking "how wonderfully well he had contrived to be idle without them." [27]

There was good reason for the name "Slaughter House" by which Thackeray referred to his old school until well into middle life. Left to their own devices in the boarding-houses or on the playground during most hours out of the twenty-four, the boys formed a primitive, Spartan society, in which *force majeure,* mitigated only by a rudimentary and erratic sense of fair play, was the sole authority. The upper school (the two top forms) held the lower school (the remaining forms) in absolute submission; and among the "Uppers," in turn, the "cock of the school" was the boy who could whip all the rest. The prevailing system of fagging, which Dr. Russell had vainly tried to abolish, kept the younger boys in virtual slavery. Any "Under" was duty bound to fetch and carry for any "Upper" and to "fag out" for him at cricket. "Fire fags" maintained blazing fires in the long rooms, and "milk fags" kept milk perpetually warm for coffee. In addition to this general fagging, each Upper had a private fag, who served him as a kind of valet, waking him in the morning, blacking his boots, getting his clothes ready, toasting his rolls, preparing his coffee, and cleaning up after him.[28] Private fagging was not devoid of merit. It discouraged promiscuous bullying, since the master protected his fag from the brutality of other Uppers and caned him, as the phrase went, only so much as was good for him. Often a close friendship developed between master and fag, sealed by the present of a book or a watch upon the former's departure from school. But it remained true, as Thackeray noted, that "torture in a public school is as much licensed as the knout in Russia." [29]

With another feature of "Slaughter House" life, Thackeray became quickly and disastrously acquainted. Even Thomas Hughes, that disciple of Dr. Arnold, asserted that "fighting with fists is the natural and English way for English boys to settle their quarrels." [30] In unreformed Charterhouse, boxing was the chief entertainment, and a boy's position among his fellows depended largely upon his pugilistic strength and skill. Contests were patterned on the famous professional encounters of the day, such as that between the Gasman and Bill Neate which Hazlitt describes in "The Fight"; and they were often long and bloody.[31] In "Mr. and Mrs. Frank Berry," indeed, Thackeray records a "Slaughter House" affray that lasted 102 rounds.[32]

Thackeray was the fag of John Stuart Roupell, a monitor in Penny's house, who late in life told how "on a wet half-holiday" in 1822, a boy named Thomas George Gossip "came and asked leave for Thackeray and George Stovin Venables to fight." "We wanted amusement," Roupell continues, "so I let them fight it out in our long room." Busy himself with Greek iambics, he did not see the battle. It may be assumed that Venables triumphed, for word was later brought to Roupell that "Thackeray's nose was still bleeding," and Thackeray used to recall the "scrunch" with which Venables's damaging blow had landed.[33] Though his nose was permanently flattened by it to the button revealed in his portraits, he and Venables became lifelong friends, and Thackeray in after years used to refer jokingly to him as "my old schoolfellow you know who spoiled my profile." [34]

This sketch of Charterhouse would not be complete without reference to the "system of premature debauchery" that prevailed there and at other public schools. "They only prevent men from being corrupted by the world," wrote Sydney Smith, "by corrupting them before their entry into the world." [35] The masters accepted no responsibility for the boys' moral welfare; "they practically ignored everything out of school, much as a captain knows nothing of his company off duty." [36] Religious services were numerous but perfunctory. Henry George Liddell tells how Dr. Russell in the hour before church every Sunday had each boy read out a single verse from the Bible; if there was a failure in emphasis, "the Doctor roared at him, just as in a lesson from Euripides or Cicero." [37] Such exercises hardly provided effective guidance through the problems of adolescence, particularly since "Holywell Street was suffered to infect Charterhouse with its poison," as Martin Tupper relates, and "books of the vilest character were circulated in the long-room." [38] In later life Thackeray and John Leech used to talk around the *Punch* table of "Charterhouse morality—fresh innocent voices singing b[aw]dy songs without knowing their intent." [39] No doubt the Reverend Thomas Bowdler exaggerated when he thundered, "the Public Schools are the very seats and nurseries of vice." [40] Yet it is evident that Thackeray's school was not a place of light and leading, and that Liddell after three years there had reason for dating a letter to his father "Beastly Charterhouse." [41]

II

But Thackeray's life was not entirely dismal, even during his early years at Charterhouse. There was the pleasure, for example, of going on holiday. Consider his account of the August vacation of 1823.[1] During the last two months of term he had been badgered by "a large and violent boy" named Hawker, from whom he had acquired on credit a silver pencil-case. Since he was perpetually out of money himself and the Carmichael-Smyths were away in Scotland, he was not able to pay Hawker until the day of his departure, and then only out of the sum given him for expenses on his trip. In the coach to Tunbridge Wells, where he was to meet the Carmichael-Smyths, he went hungry except for a fourpenny meal in a coffee-shop, bought from money given him by the Reverend Mr. Penny to reimburse the Major for an overpayment. His mother and stepfather were waiting for him when he arrived. But "I was in such a state of remorse about the fourpence," Thackeray writes, "that I forgot the maternal joy and caresses, the tender paternal voice. . . . 'Here's your money,' I gasp[ed] out, 'which Mr. P[enny] owes you, all but fourpence.' " Once forgiven, Thackeray found the holiday pure delight. There was a library on the Pantiles (or Parade) from which he obtained a supply of novels, among them Pierce Egan's *Life in London,* Jane Porter's *Thaddeus of Warsaw,* and Mrs. Radcliffe's *Mysteries of Udolpho.* As he thought of this holiday forty years later, the paper over which he was bending faded before his eyes.

They are looking backwards [he wrote], back into forty years off, into a dark room, into a little house hard by on the Common here, in the Bartlemy-tide holidays. The parents have gone to town for two days: the house is all his own, his own and a grim old maid-servant's, and a little boy is seated at night in the lonely drawing-room—poring over *Manfroni, or the One-Handed Monk,* so frightened that he scarcely dares to turn round.[2]

We learn of another holiday in Bristol, where he again accompanied his stepfather and "his mother with her diamonds & they went gorgeously to the play." [3] But most of his early vacation time was passed at Addiscombe, near Croydon, where Major Carmichael-Smyth acted as *pro tem.* Resident Superintendent of the East India Company's military seminary from 7 August 1822 until 6 April 1824. This institution had been founded in 1809 to provide training for young men destined to serve in the artillery and engineer corps of the rapidly expanding Indian army. The Major received an annual salary of £600 for directing an establishment of fifteen officers and masters, twelve public servants, and some hundred uniformed students, ranging in age from fourteen to eighteen. Writing on 20 January 1823, Thackeray asked his mother to "tell me all about Addiscombe & the *Gentlemen Cadets* and tell me if Papa has got a *cock hat* that will fit him." [4]

During his visits to Addiscombe, Thackeray lived with the Carmichael-Smyths in an imposing brick pile of three storeys. The house had been built in 1702–1703 for William Draper, son-in-law of John Evelyn, supposedly after a design by Vanbrugh. It was afterwards the residence successively of Lord Chancellor Talbot, Lord Grantham, and Charles Jenkinson, first Earl of

Liverpool. During the tenure of Lord Liverpool, Addiscombe was the haunt of William Pitt. *The Rolliad* tells how Pitt's roistering during an early morning ride back to London caused an alarmed farmer to mistake him for a highwayman and fire upon him:

> Ah! think what danger on debauch attends.
> Let Pitt, once drunk, preach temp'rance to his friends:
> How, as he wandered darkling o'er the plain,
> His reason drown'd in Jenkinson's champagne,
> A rustic's hand, but righteous fate withstood,
> Had shed a Premier's for a robber's blood.

Sixty acres of ground surrounded the mansion, which within was a scene of faded magnificence. The walls and ceiling of the grand staircase and the great saloon into which it led were adorned with mythological paintings, chiefly by Sir James Thornhill. The feast of Bacchus, Pan surprising Syrinx, Diana visiting Endymion, and Danaë and the golden shower were among the subjects portrayed. Over the fire-place was a pompous allegorical design, in which Britannia led the Goddess of Justice towards England's Eastern empire, represented by the bulky shape of an elephant.[5]

No contemporary account of Thackeray's months at Addiscombe survives, but his reflections when he returned there a quarter of a century later may serve in its place.

> The villas dont slacken until you get to Streatham [he wrote in his diary], where I saw the well-remembered church, trees Inn & schools on the common. All sorts of recollections of my youth came back to me: dark and sad and painful with my dear good mother as a gentle angel interposing between me and misery. . . . I went to see our old quarters . . . the chairs in the drawing-room were still ours, and I recognized what I am sure was my mothers bed—it made me feel very queer— My old room is the Generals dressing room—how well I remember the cawing of the rooks there of a morning! they were still talking away in the wilderness w$^{\underline{h}}$ is quite unaltered. . . . after Chapel went to see old Mother Dodd at the hospital a vulgar old harridan flattering & lying: but she was kind to me as a child: and I gave her a sovereign.[6]

Shortly after Thackeray returned to Charterhouse at the end of the long vacation of 1824, he removed from Penny's house and became a day-boy.[7] During his remaining years at school he resided with Mr. and Mrs. Boyes at 9 Charterhouse Square. His fellow boarders included students from the nearby Merchant Taylors school, the Boyeses' son John Frederick among them, and Thackeray found himself in the agreeable position of being able to forget Charterhouse during a good part of each day. That there was an imperfect sympathy between him and Mrs. Boyes [8] counted for little when weighed against the relative comfort and decency of life in a private house.

Thackeray was singularly fortunate, moreover, in his new companions. John Boyes maintains in his penetrating "Memorials of Thackeray's School Days" [9] that "it was a positive intellectual descent from the school set to which Thackeray belonged to the ordinary college level, and a very considerable one." Boyes himself, Joseph Carne, William Withers Ewbank, William Wellwood Stoddart—"perhaps Thackeray's greatest favourite of all" —and James Reynolds Young eagerly read, discussed, and imitated the writing of the day. Stoddart "brought from home anecdotes of the men in whom we were interested," Boyes relates, "of Scott, Coleridge, Wordsworth, Lamb, and Hazlitt, with all of whom his father, Sir John Stoddart, was closely intimate." The lads clubbed together to take in the magazines "*Blackwood,* the *New Monthly,* the *London,* and the *Literary Gazette,*" avoiding only the *Quarterly* and *Edinburgh* as "too high and dry." It may be assumed that they were not above "the *John Bull* newspaper," which Thackeray has Sam Titmarsh and Gus Hoskins read in *The Great Hoggarty Diamond.* "It had one of the Ramsbottom letters [by Theodore Hook] in it," Sam says, ". . . and we nearly killed ourselves with laughing." [10] They organized private theatricals, Thackeray on one occasion playing Fusbos in William Barnes Rhodes's burlesque *Bombastes Furioso,* and they formed a lively speaking society. They well deserve the praise that Boyes gives them as Thackeray's "ripeners."

Stimulated by this atmosphere and indifferent to the Charterhouse curriculum, Thackeray spent much of his time in omnivorous reading. "When I was young," he later wrote, "I read everything I could lay my hands on." [11] He continued to be firmly addicted to romantic fiction, those "tender, kind-hearted, silly books" and the "little silent world of fancy" that they presented.[12] He added to his list most of Scott (*Ivanhoe, Old Mortality,* and *Quentin Durward* were his favourites), Cooper's Leatherstocking Tales, Mrs. Radcliffe's *The Italian; or, The Confessional of the Black Penitent,* Smollett's *Peregrine Pickle* and *Roderick Random,* T. H. Lister's *Granby* and *Herbert Lacy,* and many other romances.[13]

With the "raspberry open-tarts" [14] of fiction, he mixed plainer pabulum; Boyes specifies "memoirs, moralists like Addison and Goldsmith; and . . . poetry from the best hands." [15] The magazines further extended his literary education. The great days of the *London Magazine* were nearly over, though Charles Lamb's essays continued to appear in its pages. Yet the contributors who had replaced De Quincey and Hazlitt managed to maintain a high level of interest.[16] In addition to serious articles, filled with solid information weightily presented, each issue included lighter papers about which hung an aura of bohemianism, not to say genial blackguardism. Plain speaking was the rule, and personalities abounded. (Harriette Wilson's notorious book was described as "the memoirs of a ci-devant prostitute published by a ci-devant member of the Society for the Suppression of Vice.") [17] Any deviation from the downright common-sense point of view was fair game for attack or burlesque. The other magazines to which Thackeray and his friends subscribed provided a similar survey of current topics, though with less wit and distinction.

"Light literature" of this stamp a clever boy could readily imitate. As the *London Magazine* parodied the fashionable high falutin of Disraeli's *Vivian Grey* or Lister's *Granby,* so one of Thackeray's earliest compositions burlesques a silly ditty by L. E. L. called "Violets." Here are the opening stanzas of the two poems:

Violets

Violets!—deep blue violets!
April's loveliest coronets!

There are no flowers grow in the vale,
Kiss'd by the dew, woo'd by the gale,—
None by the dew of the twilight wet,
So sweet as the deep-blue violet! [18]

Cabbages

Cabbages! bright green cabbages!
April's loveliest gifts, I guess,
There's not a plant in the garden laid,
Raised by the dung, dug by the spade,
None by the gardener watered, I ween,
So sweet as the cabbage, the cabbage green.[19]

These verses, or others like them, were written for *The Carthusian,* a projected but never published magazine.[20] Thanks to Boyes's retentive memory, they survive to show how early Thackeray's characteristic manner of satirical imitation was formed.

The urge to parody was dominant as well in Thackeray's drawing, a talent that he cultivated from earliest childhood. Liddell relates how he and Thackeray spent most of their time sketching when they sat next to each other in the second form. "His handiwork was very superior to mine, and his taste for comic scenes at that time exhibited itself in burlesque representations of incidents in Shakespeare. I remember one—Macbeth as a butcher brandishing two blood-reeking knives, and Lady Macbeth as the butcher's wife clapping him on the shoulder to encourage him." [21] There is record also of a series of humorous allegorical drawings: "Painting," a ragamuffin blacking boots; "Carving," a Jew attacking an immense ham with an enormous knife and fork; "Music," an Italian with hurdy-gurdy and monkey; and so forth.[22]

Thackeray and his friends found the chief models for their drawing in the prints of George Cruikshank. In "Knight's, in Sweeting's Alley; Fairburn's, in a court of Ludgate Hill; Hone's, in Fleet Street," they found "bright, enchanted palaces, which George Cruikshank used to people with grinning, fantastical imps, and merry, harmless sprites."

How we used to believe in them [Thackeray later recalled], to stray miles out of the way on holidays, in order to ponder for an hour before that delightful window in Sweeting's Alley! In walks through Fleet Street, to vanish abruptly down Fairburn's passage, and there make one at his charming "gratis" exhibition. There used to be a crowd round the window in those days of grinning, good-natured mechanics, who spelt the songs, and spoke them out for the benefit of the company, and who received the points of humour with a general sympathizing roar.

Thackeray and his friends would carry off prizes from these shops. "Did we not forgo tarts, in order to buy his 'Breaking-up,' or his 'Fashionable Monstrosities,' of the year eighteen hundred and something?" Was not "the admirable 'Illustrations of Phrenology' . . . purchased by a joint-stock company of boys, each drawing lots afterwards for the separate prints, and taking his choice in rotation? The writer of this, too, had the honour of drawing the first lot, and seized immediately upon 'Philoprogenitiveness'— . . . a marvellous print, indeed,—full of ingenuity and fine jovial humour." [23]

Thus Thackeray's real education at school came to him largely outside the class-room, from intercourse with his friends, from reading, and from drawing. Important as well was the sense of the past which a perceptive boy like Thackeray insensibly acquired during six years spent among the ancient buildings and traditional usages of Charterhouse in London. Since 1371, when Sir Walter Manny established the Carthusian monastery from which Charterhouse took its origin, the foundation had held a significant place in English annals. Upon the dissolution of the monasteries it was occupied successively by Lord North, whom Queen Elizabeth twice visited, and by the Duke of Norfolk, executed in 1572 for complicity in the treason of Mary, Queen of Scots. In 1611 it passed from the Howard family to Thomas Sutton, a great banker and merchant prince, who before his death on 12 December of that year arranged for its conversion into a free school and a hospital for unfortunate gentlemen. During the two centuries that followed, Joseph Addison, Sir William Blackstone, Richard Crashaw, George Grote, Richard Lovelace, Sir Richard Steele, Connop Thirlwall, and John Wesley were only a few of the famous Englishmen whom it trained.

Everywhere at Charterhouse Thackeray saw reminders of the

continuity of English life. The original structure of the fourteenth century survived in parts of the chapel wall, and most of the school's notable architectural features—the great staircase, the great chamber, the great hall, and the master's lodge—had been constructed during the next two hundred years. He mingled every day with the recipients of the founder's benefactions, the gown boys in trencher and livery, and the eighty "poor brethren"—fifty years or more of age, and "Gentlemen by Descent, and in Poverty, Souldiers that have born Arms by Sea or Land, Merchants decayed by Pyracy or Shipwrack, or Servants in Household to the King and Queen's Majesty." [24] On the last day of Oration Quarter, as he waited eagerly for the Christmas holidays to begin, he watched the solemn ceremonies with which was celebrated the anniversary of Sutton's death: the head gown boy's Latin oration in Governor's Room (the great chamber), service in chapel, and dinner in the great hall.[25] Scenes like these awoke in Thackeray a feeling for history, much as the Roman road and rudely marked stone of Ecclefechan did in young Carlyle; and a historical novelist was born as Thackeray gazed year after year on the panelled halls, the tapestried chambers, the quadrangles, cloisters, gardens, and greens of his ancient school.

In these years as well Thackeray began to acquire his intimate knowledge of London. The area of the city near the school itself was not a savoury one, for it included Smithfield Market, the chief London *abattoir* (a jocular name for Charterhouse, indeed, was "Smiffle"), where scenes of terrible cruelty to animals still aroused little protest; and Newgate Prison, where the public hanging of criminals and exposure of their bodies was still customary. But on week-ends Thackeray was allowed to visit friends and relatives in remoter parts of the metropolis, a privilege of which he took full advantage, since, among other pleasant things, it meant a visit to the play (where on one occasion he saw George IV) [26] and the chance of a tip.

He went frequently to the Turners at Chiswick, where he was a favourite with the little children. " 'Whackaway' was his school name," his cousin Richard Bedingfield recalls. "I used to hear the boys cry gleefully, 'Here's Old Whackaway!' when, a

Triton among the minnows, he appeared on the playground." [27] This intimacy was interrupted by an unhappy accident. He borrowed a wig from Dr. Turner (who had once been a barrister) to wear in private theatricals, and, losing it, "boy-like, he did not venture to show his face at Chiswick for a considerable time." [28] Another house of call was that of the Ritchies in Southampton Row, where John Ritchie, who had fallen into financial difficulties,[29] was living with his wife and four children above his place of business. Richmond Shakespear, another visitor to the Ritchies at this time, relates that Thackeray "was full of humour and cleverness . . . and used to draw caricatures for us. . . . He used also to act with us sometimes, and I remember him in a wig capitally got up as Dr. Pangloss." [30] "I think that Southampton Row was the only part of my youth wh was decently cheerful," Thackeray wrote many years later to Mrs. Ritchie; "all the rest strikes me to have been as glum as an English Sunday." [31]

At school, meanwhile, Thackeray took his place among the upper classmen and began himself to claim the privileges of seniority. His particular favourite among the younger boys was John Leech, who had entered Charterhouse, aged eight, in 1825. Noting that he had "brought him up," Thackeray had a vivid recollection of Leech, "a small boy . . . in a little blue buttoned-up suit, set up on a form and made to sing 'Home sweet home,' to the others crowding about." [32] Perhaps we come closest to Thackeray during his last years at school in the portrait which Boyes included in his "Memorials":

> He was then a rosy-faced boy with dark curling hair, and a quick, intelligent eye, ever twinkling with humour, and *good* humour. He was stout and broad-set, and gave no promise of the stature which he afterwards reached. . . .
>
> For the usual schoolboy sports and games Thackeray had no taste or passion whatever. . . . But he was by no means what a good many men of genius are said to have been in their youth—disposed to isolation or solitary musing. For a non-playing boy he was wonderfully social, full of vivacity and enjoyment of life. His happy *insouciance* was constant. Never was any lad at once so jovial, so healthy, and so sedentary. . . . We were now and then, indeed, out together in small fishing parties, but it was for the talking, and the change,

and the green fields, and the tea abroad instead of at home—cakes, &c. accompanying (for he was always rather gustative, never greedy) —that Thackeray liked these expeditions. . . .

He was eminently good-tempered to all, especially the younger boys, and nothing of a tyrant or bully. Instead of a blow or a threat, I can just hear him saying to one of them, "Hooky, . . . go up and fetch me a volume of *Ivanhoe* out of my drawer, that's a good fellow; in the same drawer you will, perhaps, find a penny, which you may take for yourself." The penny was, indeed, rather problematical, but still realized sufficiently often to produce excitement in the mind of the youth thus addressed, and to make the service a willing one. When disappointed, it was more than probable that the victim would call Thackeray a "great snob" for misleading him, a title for which the only vengeance would be a humorous and benignant smile.[33]

III

As Thackeray approached the end of his time at Charterhouse, he came under the direct surveillance of Dr. Russell. By May of 1826 he was in the second form, and in his last two years he was a member of the first form, which was taught by the Headmaster himself.[1] Dr. Russell was a very successful instructor with boys of precise, retentive minds, who had been well grounded in the classics by earlier preparation. Venables describes him as "vigorous, unsympathetic, and stern, though not severe," [2] and Phillott, though at first terrified of him, came later to regard him with "warm affection and profound respect." [3] But to diffident or incompetent students he was merciless. Tupper, who attributed to Russell's bullying the persistence into middle life of his habit of stammering, inquires: "What should we think nowadays, of an irate schoolmaster smashing a child's head between two books in his shoulder-of-mutton hands till his nose bled?" [4] Thackeray fared less well even than Tupper, because he attempted resistance. "Russell was rough with Thackeray," writes Thomas Mozley, "not more so perhaps than with many others, but when he saw Thackeray's spirit and humor rising with him, that made matters worse." [5] Thackeray wrote to his mother on 19 February of his last year:

Doctor Russell is treating me every day with such manifest unkindness and injustice, that I really can scarcely bear it: It is so hard when you endeavour to work hard, to find your attempts nipped in the bud—if ever I get a respectable place in my form, he is sure to bring me down again; to day there was such a flagrant instance of it, that it was the general talk of the school. . . . On every possible occasion he shouts out reproaches against me for leaving his precious school forsooth! He has lost a hundred boys within two years, and is of course very angry about [it]— There are but 370 in the school, I wish there were only 369.[6]

Russell's class-room procedure made little concession to human weakness. He was quite content to get through only two or three lines in a school-time, if he felt that his form had mastered them. He first demanded a literal translation of the text, causing "every single Greek or Latin word to be rendered by a single one in English, a process which sometimes resulted in ludicrous exhibitions of bald phraseology." Then followed an effort by the pupils to "exhibit the passage in 'English idiom;' " "a process," Phillott remarks, "which sometimes called forth wondrous specimens of style, which our Doctor did not fail to criticise with unsparing dissection." [7]

What this routine meant in practice to a sensitive, indolent boy like Thackeray, and how damaging it was to his self-confidence, may be judged from "Horae Carthusianae," written by his fellow sufferer Charles Robert Baynes in 1828.[8] Here is one of Dr. Russell's characteristic harangues from this account of a disastrous day at Charterhouse:

Again in school, again the storm begins,
Again I hear my catalogue of sins.
"Sir I scarce think that even now you see,
Why in that passage I prefer the τε,
If you had read your notes you'd then have seen
Why Brunk rejects the τὸν and takes the τὴν,
Now construe on οἴ μοι τι δράσω."
"What shall I do (by Jove I say so)."
"Sir you were prompted and you tried to cheat;
As bad as picking pockets in the street;
Go to the bottom and translate the play,
You'l not put down your name for Saturday.

Now try and scan, now prythee dont assist him,
His nurse has taught him the An[a]paestic system,
If she has not she's very much to blame,
And every man of sense will say the same,
The youngest child in every nursery
Ought to have perfect all his prosody.
Ταλιν Ah! Ah! Ah! What? is that the way
You'l not translate Sir but you'l parse the play,
Tis scarcely one, I think," "yes Sir tis past,"
"Well go in order but dont go too fast,
You've stept across a bench, come back and try
To go again with proper decency." [9]

It is not surprising that Thackeray wrote after two years of these tirades of being "abus⟨ed⟩ into sulkiness and bullied into despair." [10] To the end of his life, indeed, he remembered vividly "the tingling cheeks, burning ears, bursting heart, and passion of desperate tears, with which you looked up, after having performed some blunder, whilst the doctor held you to public scorn before the class, and cracked his great clumsy jokes upon you—helpless, and a prisoner!" [11] Of course, there were mitigating circumstances in Thackeray's ordeal. He had the sympathy of his fellow students, who in their boy-world paid little attention to Dr. Russell's pronouncements from on high. And for Dr. Russell's assistant in the upper school, the Reverend Edward Churton—whom even Tupper describes as a "really excellent teacher and good clergyman"— [12] he conceived a lasting affection.[13] Yet it was certainly without regret that Thackeray said good-bye to Charterhouse in May of 1828.

From his formal training at school Thackeray gained little. Mathematical studies were not emphasized, and in the classics Dr. Russell's method did not encourage wide reading. In six years his best students got through only "four or five Greek plays, with Porson's notes, two or three books of the Iliad, a little Pindar, Cicero's Offices and some of his Orations, . . . the Georgics of Virgil, . . . most of the Satires and Epistles of Horace, . . . and Plato's Apology." [14] It was his custom as well to require his students, before they were admitted to the "Emeriti" (the top division of the second form), "to learn all the Odes and Epodes of Horace by heart, and to be able without book to translate them and answer all questions—grammatical, geographical and historical." [15] But Thackeray was not set this task. Because of dwindling enrolment, he was allowed to pass directly from the lower part of the second form to the first form.[16] Though Major Carmichael-Smyth had given Thackeray his big volume of Horace with an armorial book-plate in 1824,[17] Thackeray's "scholastic knowledge of Latin" [18] in general and Horace in particular was a later acquirement. For a time Dr. Russell's teaching left him with an extreme distaste for exact classical knowledge.

Though scholastic deficiencies were to handicap him at Cambridge, his inattention to lessons need not otherwise be greatly deplored. He was not so much idle as wisely passive, reaping "the harvest of a quiet eye." And what a field for observation "the microcosm of a public school" opened up to him! At Charterhouse Thackeray served an early apprenticeship to life. He learned to recognize the diversity of human character; he charted its complex mixture of good and evil; and he mastered the hard truth that the strong survive and the weak go to the wall. The Charterhouse world displayed in little but without distortion most of the great themes that he was to make his own. Take snobbery as an example. Though personal qualities counted for more than rank or wealth among the boys, they could not entirely resist the example of their elders at home and in school. The masters were accomplished tuft-hunters, who allowed every liberty to scions of noble families. Tupper relates how "lobsters, surreptitiously obtained from out-of-bounds by the big boys were sworn in the *debris* of their smaller claws to be pieces of sealing wax! and nothing else; at least a reckless young aristocrat declared that they were so,—and the mean-spirited Rev. Andrew Irvine, fearful of giving offence in such high quarters, pretended to believe him." [19] No wonder that, glancing back at his days in school, Thackeray wrote in the "Epilogue" to *Dr. Birch and His Young Friends:*

> . . . the griefs, the joys,
> Just hinted in this mimic page,
> The triumphs and defeats of boys,

Are but repeated in our age. . . .
I'd say, we suffer and we strive
Not less nor more as men than boys:
With grizzled beards at forty-five,
As erst at twelve, in corduroys.[20]

The effect upon Thackeray's own character of six years at Charterhouse was by no means so clearly advantageous as his study of the characters of others. No doubt the give and take of communal life prevented him from becoming the "muff and milksop" that private education made of Ruskin.[21] At the same time his sympathies were drastically narrowed. For ever afterwards he took it for granted that class differences were part of the nature of things; despite the broad humanity of his later outlook, he never ceased to ask himself about anyone that he met, is he "a man of kindly nurture," a gentleman by birth and education? [22] His unconscious acceptance of public-school values helps to account as well for other characteristic attitudes of his maturity: his preference for conformity in dress, conduct, and manners; his dislike of the extravagant and exaggerated; his distrust of emotional display; his disproportionately high estimate of animal strength and courage; his conviction that character matters more than intellect.

Charterhouse also made Thackeray excessively conscious of supposed personal deficiencies. His failure in schoolwork increased his diffidence regarding his intellectual ability. Kinder and more attentive masters would have stirred his curiosity and tempted him to explore subjects that he would not allow himself to be driven to study. The strange incapacity for abstract thought that marked him throughout his life might not have developed if his mind had been opened early to ideas. Moreover, the rough handling that he had received destroyed prematurely the generous confidence of childhood. His friendly, outgoing nature was turned in upon itself, and he acquired a cool, even satirical, outer manner which gave him a misleading appearance of reserve and self-sufficiency. "When I knew him better, in later years," Venables observed, "I thought I could recognize the sensitive nature which he had as a boy." [23] But his sensitive nature was no longer displayed in chance encounters.

All this amounts only to saying that if Charterhouse opened some doors to Thackeray, it closed others to him. His own considered judgment on this phase of his life may be found in a review that he wrote in 1844 of Arthur Stanley's *Life of Dr. Arnold:*

Every man whose own school-days are not very distant, and who can remember that strange ordeal of his early life—the foolish old-world superstitions which obtained in the public school; the wretched portion of letters meted out to him there—the misery, vice, and folly, which were taught along with the small share of Greek and Latin imparted to him—the ten years wasted in pursuit of a couple of languages which not one lad in a hundred mastered—the total ignorance upon all other matters of learning, which was almost enjoined by the public school system—will be apt to think, as we imagine, "Why had I not Arnold for a master?" [24]

4

Devon Interludes

I

UPON LEAVING CHARTERHOUSE, Thackeray repaired to what he grandly called "my country seat," [1] Larkbeare House, a mile and a half north of Ottery St. Mary in Devon. He knew it well, for he had already passed four long vacations there. When the Major resigned his superintendency of Addiscombe, the Carmichael-Smyths achieved the common ambition of retired Anglo-Indians by settling down in rural retirement. Early in 1824 they had leased their new home from Sir John Kennaway, the local magnate; and they took up residence there shortly after 5 June of that year.[2]

Ottery St. Mary lies in the valley of the Otter, 6 miles north of Sidmouth. The parish, which extends across the 4 miles between East and West Hills, was populated at this time by 4,000 inhabitants. The buildings of the town are grouped on a small hill on the eastern side of the river. Chief among them is the church, which Bishop Grandison reconstructed between 1337 and 1342 as a small-scale replica of his cathedral at Exeter. Thackeray mentions in *Pendennis* "its great grey towers, of which the sun illuminates the delicate carving, deepening the shadows of the great buttresses, and gilding the glittering windows and flaming vanes." [3] Twelve miles to the west is Exeter, the principal city of the county. In Thackeray's time it was also the "ecclesiastical capital of the West of England," [4] and Thackeray with boyish enthusiasm declared its magnificent cathedral to be finer than Notre Dame.[5]

A frequent visitor to Larkbeare was a little girl of eight named Maria, who afterwards became Mrs. Brotherton. At the request of Lady Ritchie she nearly sixty-five years later wrote out her still vivid recollections of the "Maison Blanche, as Mary Graham called it," [6] in the 1820s:

The road to Larkbeare was a by-road from the great London road, and was partly a beautiful over arching beech avenue. About half way there was a pond that we called a lake—at least I did—so pretty and lonely and mysterious; with trees and shadows all about it, and a little leafy eyot, and a rather old boat that I longed to make voyages of discovery in—but was forbidden ever to get into. This by-path was not a private road to Larkbeare, but ran past it, under the wall of the lawn, to the village of Tallaton, where we went to church behind Prince & Blucher, and sometimes walked to. I have no doubt P. & B. ploughed, for I remember your Grandmother often wanted them, and couldn't have them, so I suppose they were otherwise engaged. There was a yard, with stables & barns round it: this had a gate into the road that made a turn there, and passed the house, under the wall of a raised lawn, which was level with it. There was a green door in the wall of the yard, that opened on the front of the house & the lawn. . . . Larkbeare was just an old grey-white oblong comfortable house, with a good many rooms in it. . . . From the drawing and dining room windows we could only see the heads of people passing on horseback, or in carriages, in the Lane below the wall. . . . There was a walled kitchen garden sloping up behind the house—with some wonderful big yellow egg-plums, crowding the south wall atop. . . . When I think of that rough lawn and its homely beds of stocks & wall-flowers I always see your Grandmother standing there on a "calm summer evening" looking with her wide beautiful grey eyes at the sunset:—tall & stately and graceful,—with perhaps a fur cap of her husband's on her beautiful black hair. . . .

I thought it all very delightful, and not the least dull, though it may have been so to older people. There were no very near neighbors, but some of the nearest ones used to come to dinner parties at which of course I did not 'assist'—and I recollect two elderly ladies called Porter who were literary—*could* one of them have been the famous 'Jane'? They sang, after dinner, and thrilled me through and through with "The Captive Knight," and other pathetic compositions. . . .

I remember, in short, almost everything about Larkbeare,—even the Chupatties (is that the right spelling?) for breakfast, and the delicious homemade brown bread—but I never saw your father there, nor for many years after. He was always an invisible though very important personage in those Larkbeare days. Constantly alluded to by your Grandmother and her husband, as "Bill," and a propos of almost everything talked about. . . . I slept in his room, which I can see now, exactly as it was. Its door was the last in a passage, and opposite the window, which had leaded panes, like all the windows at the back of the house. It was a small room, and the dressing table was beside the window and close to the bed. The drawers of this dressing table were so crammed with scraps of paper that they wouldn't quite shut, and those scraps were covered with pen and ink caricatures. In the early mornings before I was called, I used to pull out these drawers and empty them on the counterpane, and look at their contents over and over again, with inexhaustible delight. Backs of letters, both sides of bills, visiting cards, all available odds and ends, were covered with these pen and inkings. Sometimes there were words in little writing under the figures—Downstairs, in the drawing-room, the drawers of the old fashioned piano were stuffed in the same way.[7]

Mrs. Brotherton's picture of life at Larkbeare may be completed by mentioning the remaining members of the household: little Mary Graham, whom Thackeray had come to regard as a sister since she joined the Carmichael-Smyths in 1820; two faithful family servants, John and Martha Goldsworthy; and for a year or two Mrs. Butler. It is easy to surmise why the old lady did not remain with them longer from the breathless response of Aunt Becher to her initial proposal to return home. She wrote to Mrs. Carmichael-Smyth:

tell your Mother if she comes to England to be as near as she can we will do all we can towards contributing to her comfort, if that could be done by her living with us we would do so, but our house won't allow of it & says dear Granny I could never expect anyone to put up with all my whims.[8]

Thirty-five years of hectic Indian life had made Mrs. Butler an eccentric and difficult companion, and it was found desirable that she should live by herself in a nearby town. In April of 1830 she was at Budleigh Salterton, in June at Sidmouth; and the following winter she was still in the country, for Thackeray regrets not being able to attend the rout to which she had invited local gentry.[9]

Of county society, which may be described in Mr. Micawber's phrase as "a happy admixture of the agricultural and the clerical," the Carmichael-Smyths saw a good deal. They were on friendly terms with Sir John Kennaway, the principal landed proprietor of the parish, who lived at nearby Escot Lodge, situated within an extensive park "pleasantly diversified with wood and water." [10] Born in Exeter, Kennaway had entered the military service of the East India Company at the age of fourteen. He and his older brother Richard, a commercial servant of the Company, had gone out to India together in 1772. They were shipwrecked at the mouth of the Ganges, but both survived to achieve distinction in their respective branches of the service. After an active military career, which included two years as A.D.C. to the Governor General, Marquess Cornwallis, Kennaway was dispatched in 1788 to negotiate a treaty with the Nizam of Hyderabad. So well did he perform this delicate and important mission that he was created a baronet in 1791. When ill health forced him to return to Devon in 1794, he purchased Escot House and its 4,000-acre estate from Sir George Yonge, the lord of the manor, for £110,000. He married the daughter of a Southampton M.P. and by her had seven sons and five daughters. Richard Kennaway, whose employments as Secretary to the Board of Trade and Import Warehouse Keeper at Calcutta were less spectacular but perhaps no less remunerative, remained unmarried after his return to England in 1796.

> But retaining in manhood and old age the warm affection of youth [their common epitaph informs us], they dwelt in the same house, were loved by the same family, and submitted themselves to the same trials. In the decline of life it pleased God to visit them both with the same affliction of blindness.[11]

One of their trials was the destruction by fire of Escot House in 1808. Noting in his journal that it could hardly be replaced for

£25,000, "especially at this time, when the price of timber is so high," Sir John added the prayer that God might "make this worldly loss conducive to my spiritual gain! . . . I am rather doubtful if this house, while it stood, did not daily tempt me to break His Holy Commandment, 'thou shalt not worship any graven image.' "[12]

If the tone of lay affairs was thus set by a gentleman as pious as he was opulent, the Church was equally well served. The Carmichael-Smyths' closest friends were the Reverend Francis Huyshe, rector of Clyst Hydon, and his family.[13] This gentleman, upon whom Thackeray modelled Dr. Portman in *Pendennis,*[14] was descended from an ancient Somerset family, whose seat since 1561 had been the manor-house of Sand, near Sidmouth. Though the manor-house was occupied by the farmers of the estate in his time, Huyshe's contributions to the *Gentleman's Magazine* testify to his keen interest in family history, arms, and quarterings.[15] The Huyshes lived at Talaton, a few miles south of Larkbeare, and there was much intercourse between the two families. Thackeray's particular friend was Wentworth, the Huyshes' son and heir, who was less than a year younger than he. When home from school, they were much together; and after a severe illness made it necessary for Wentworth to seek a warmer climate instead of matriculating at Trinity College with Thackeray, a regular correspondence was exchanged by the two. Wentworth was never to fulfil the brilliant promise he had displayed at Harrow,[16] for he died at Madeira on 28 November 1829. Twenty years later Thackeray wrote to his mother: "I saw Wentworth's tomb-stone over the boys' gallery, at Harrow the other day: and took a walk with him on Tallaton Common—as the parson preached the foolishest sermon."[17]

In the Reverend Francis Huyshe, who was fifty-seven when they first met, Thackeray can hardly have found a familiar friend, but another local clergyman, much nearer his own age, was less dignified and more approachable. Dr. Sidney Cornish, school-master and later vicar of Ottery St. Mary, the son of a poet and lifelong friend of Keble, had himself literary and antiquarian tastes. He told Lord Coleridge how he used to lend Thackeray books, among them Cary's translation of *The Birds* of Aristophanes, which Thackeray adorned with humorous watercolour drawings.[18] He also arranged the appearance of Thackeray's first publication.[19] The Irish politician Richard Lalor Sheil was a leading agitator for Catholic Emancipation, to which the Carmichael-Smyths were strongly opposed. On 24 October 1828 Sheil attended a mass demonstration against this measure at Penenden Heath in Kent. He endeavoured to address the 30,000 assembled voters, but because of constant interruptions, nothing of his speech was heard. It appeared in full in next day's papers, none the less, since he had left copies with editors in London. Thackeray neatly underlined this piquant discrepancy in "Irish Melody," published in *Flindell's Western Luminary and Family Newspaper* on 4 November. He contributed other short poems to the same journal in the next few weeks.[20] Of Thackeray's impressions of Cornish, unless we ungraciously assume that something of him may be found in the Reverend Mr. Smirke of *Pendennis,* there remains only an offhand query of later life: "How's that jovial fellow Cornish?" [21]

Thackeray enjoyed the company of his Devon friends, and a resident of Ottery St. Mary meeting him a quarter of a century later was "astonished at his accurate knowledge of the place and neighbourhood." [22] Yet it may be doubted if he found Devon life very exciting. Though Samuel Taylor Coleridge had been born at Ottery St. Mary, one suspects that Thackeray would have endorsed Peacock's definition of country gentleman as "a generic term applied by courtesy to the profoundly ignorant of all classes." [23] The Major tried to teach him to shoot, in order that they might hunt partridges together, but Thackeray's weak vision rendered him incapable of hitting the outline of a man chalked on the garden wall for him to fire at.[24] And he does not appear to have fished, though the Otter abounded in salmon and trout. Riding was his one athletic pursuit. No doubt he often visited Exeter for the pleasure of a run through picturesque and well-wooded country followed by a stroll to the cathedral and ruined castle, dinner at one of the city's three fine inns, and a visit afterwards to the new theatre with its "air of gaiety and comfort." [25] For the rest, Thackeray's confirmed cockneyism appears in a comical boast with which he concludes a letter written to Boyes a few weeks after his final departure from Charterhouse:

"I have become quite rural since I came down here. I know turnips from potatoes and sheep from carrots, but my chief excellence lies in the strawberry line." [26] He also did full justice to another *spécialité du pays*—Devonshire cream, jam, and brown bread.[27]

During the summer of 1828 Thackeray attained his mature height. He later told Bedingfield "that he was quite a short fellow, being but five feet six at fifteen; but that he had an illness of some months duration, and rose up at his full altitude of six feet three." "People must have looked astonished at you," his cousin remarked; to which Thackeray replied, "I don't know; my coats looked astonished." [28] The nature of his affliction is not known, but it evidently necessitated shaving his head. During convalescence he wrote to Boyes: "I hope you will make allowance for the inconsistency of this my letter by the heat of the weather, and weight of my wig which since my late lamentable illness— As pants the hart for cooling streams— See Hymn Book —I have been compelled to assume." [29]

Once he had recovered, the Major set about preparing him for Cambridge, where he had been admitted pensioner on 23 October 1826,[30] in the expectation that he would matriculate during the Michaelmas term of 1828. Lady Ritchie writes that she was later told by his mentor that "Euclid was like child's play to my father, who went through the first books with absolute ease and facility. Algebra, on the contrary, he always disliked." [31] Another event of these months was a brief visit to Stoddart in Oxford, where Thackeray was entertained by his host at "a brace of wine and supper parties" and "had some tolerably good fun." [32] In these studies and amusements passed the last months of the only prolonged experience that Thackeray had of English country life.

II

"We who have lived before railways were made," Thackeray once wrote, "belong to another world." [1] No account of his Larkbeare days would be complete without mention of the "Defiance" coach, which covered the 160 miles between the Bull Inn, Holborn, and Exeter in little more than twenty hours.[2] Thackeray liked to travel outside, "for economy and pleasure," and his mother told his children that he once "had to be lifted down, so benumbed was he with the cold," [3] after a winter journey from London. However uncomfortable, the trip home was at least redeemed by the prospect of future pleasures; Thackeray experienced "sorrow's crown of sorrow" as he travelled away from Larkbeare.

Don't you remember how that last morning was spent? [he was later to inquire]—how you went about taking leave of the garden, and the old mare and foal, and the paddock, and the pointers in the kennel; and how you went and looked at that confounded trunk which old Martha was packing with the new shirts, and at that heavy cake packed up in the play-box; and how kind "the governor" was all day, and how at dinner he said, "Jack"—or "Tom"—"pass the bottle," in a very cheery voice; and how your mother had got the dishes she knew you liked best; and how you had the wing instead of the leg, which used to be your ordinary share; and how that dear, delightful, hot raspberry roly-poly pudding, good as it was, and fondly beloved by you, yet somehow had the effect of the notorious school stick-jaw, and choked you and stuck in your throat; and how the gig came; and then, how you heard the whirl of mailcoach wheels, and the tooting of the guard's horn as, with an extraordinary punctuality, the mail and the four horses came galloping over the hill? Shake hands, goodbye! God bless everybody! Don't cry, sister; away we go! [4]

This vignette puts vividly before us the three people with whom Thackeray was most intimate in early life—Major and Mrs. Carmichael-Smyth and Mary Graham. The dominant figure among them was his mother. We have seen that in India she had been accounted "one of the most beautiful women of her time"; [5] and she remained "exquisitely handsome" in her country retirement, "fascinating everyone who came her way." [6] "Of the commanding order of women," [7] she continued to cultivate in England the "imperial manner" [8] that she had acquired in Calcutta. There was a style about her that gained her recognition as a personage wherever she went. Thackeray never forgot how, when she took him to Exeter for a concert as a boy, "she came splendidly dressed, in a handsome carriage, and all suitable appurtenances." [9]

Nor was her character less remarkable than her person. Its key, perhaps, was what her grand-daughter described as "her almost romantic passion of feeling." [10] She was incapable of regarding any person or subject dispassionately; her sympathies were always deeply and earnestly engaged. Thackeray once told Bedingfield how, "when he went with his mother to the play, she 'disgraced them all by her tears.' " [11] Though she loved her husband and niece, her affection was lavished chiefly upon Thackeray. She thought him, the only child it would ever be possible for her to have, "the divinest creature in the world." [12] The intensity of her feeling may perhaps be sensed when Thackeray makes Pendennis say, "in his wild way, that he felt sure of going to heaven, for his mother never could be happy there without him." [13] There are many passages in his letters and novels that testify to the tenderness with which he reciprocated her attachment.[14] "If I were to die," he wrote late in life, "I can't bear to think of my Mother living beyond me." [15]

Though by no means a *bas bleu,* Mrs. Carmichael-Smyth was a woman of considerable culture and refinement. She had a decided flair for literature. In her correspondence she adheres to something of the stateliness and formality of an earlier age; and Thackeray noted with only slight exaggeration in 1831: "She can write much better letters & quite as good verses as I." [16] There have survived in manuscript an unfinished novel for children and a sheaf of poems, which testify to her considerable command of language but never attain the level of professional competence.[17] At Larkbeare she read much fiction and poetry with her son, and in later life she followed his literary career with the closest attention.

There is also to be noted in her character an entire absence of humour. "I would die," Thackeray once said, "rather than make a joke to her." [18] And her enthusiasm and energy were such that she could not live without some person or cause to serve as a focus of interest for her. She passionately advocated such forlorn hopes as hydropathy and homoeopathy, and she was rarely without a protégée chosen from among the lamest of lame ducks. Since she could not endure that anyone whom she loved should differ with her about matters concerning which she felt strongly, it was not always easy to preserve the harmony of the household. Unhappily her most persistent crusade was on behalf of evangelical Christianity. From her Indian letters it would appear that, though she was always pious, she did not pay great attention to religious doctrine until her return to England; indeed, on more than one occasion she deplores evangelical excesses. But she was of a melancholy turn of mind; Thackeray noted that he inherited from her his own tendency to glumness and remarked her "favourite propensity to be miserable"; [19] and in the leisure of country retirement it was not long before she adopted the gloomy evangelical creed with her customary fervour. She became, in Thackeray's words, "a dear old Gospel mother who is a good Christian, and who always has chapter and verse to prove everything." [20] Cards were forbidden in the household as a "waste of time"; [21] church attendance and improving works were insisted upon. "When I was of your age," he told his daughter Anne when she was fifteen, "I was accustomed to hear and read a great deal of the Evangelical (so called) doctrine and got an extreme distaste for that sort of composition —for Newton, for Scott, for the preachers I heard & the prayer-meetings I attended." [22] Not unnaturally this process of forced feeding led finally to revulsion on Thackeray's part.

Many other disputes followed. "We differ about a thousand things," he told Bedingfield in mature life. "Those of a past generation can't feel with us." [23] And indeed as Thackeray's knowledge of life increased, he came to regard his mother with new eyes. "When I was a boy at Larkbeare," he wrote in 1852, "I thought her an Angel & worshipped her. I see but a woman now, O so tender so loving so cruel." [24] His severance of the silver cord was hard for Mrs. Carmichael-Smyth to bear. Even after he became famous, so her grand-daughter relates, "she used to make him unhappy by her reproofs & she always treated him as if he was a little boy." When he remonstrated, she had recourse to tears.[25] Considering the history of his relations with his mother, as he was presenting them in *Pendennis,* he wrote:

I. Richmond Thackeray as a young man

From an oil painting

II. John Harman Becher as a young man

From an oil painting

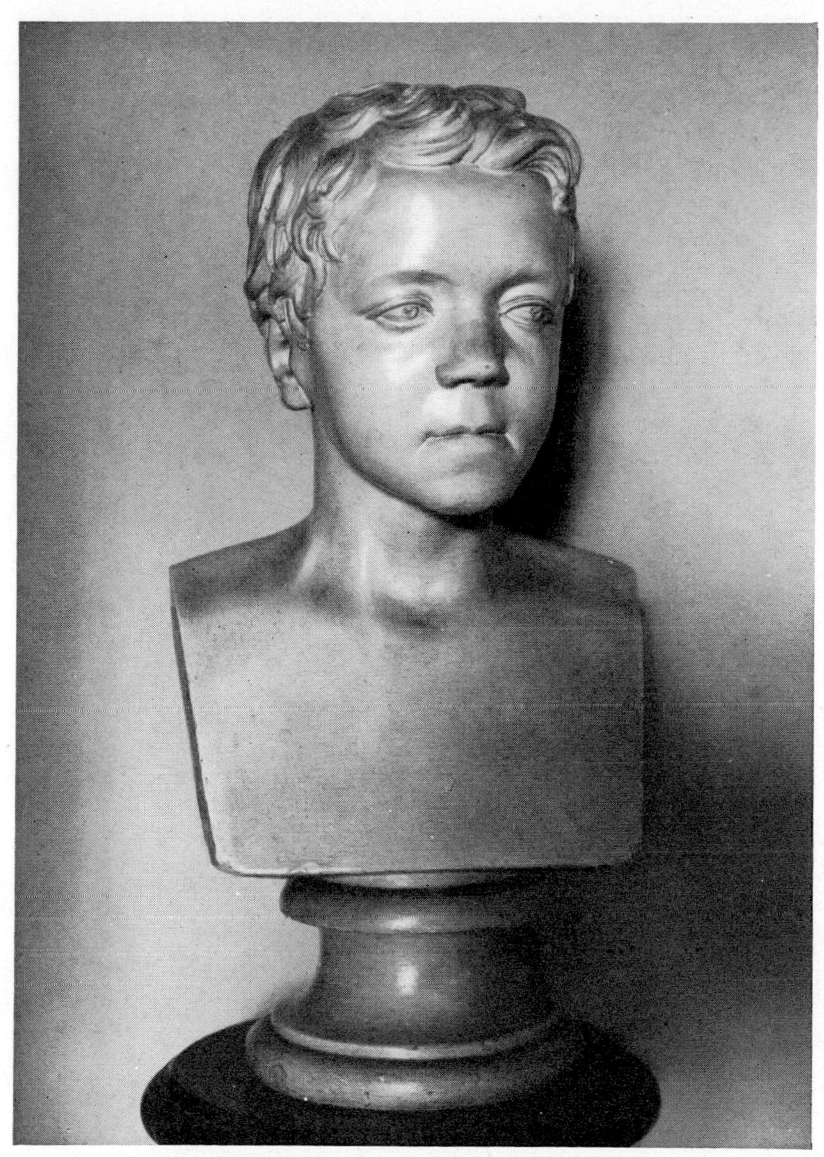

III. Thackeray in 1822

From a bust by Deville

IV. Thackeray in 1829

From a sketch by James Spedding

"I look at her character and go down on my knees as it were with wonder and pity. It is Mater Dolorosa, with a heart bleeding with love." [26]

This insight was an achievement of maturity. During the years of his young manhood, his mother's jealous affection tormented while it comforted him. She was always thinking and worrying about her only child. Exceedingly ambitious for him, she was correspondingly crushed at his long-deferred success, and Thackeray was haunted by her unexpressed disappointment. Not without reason did he acknowledge to Dickens a fondness for Mrs. Steerforth in *David Copperfield* and hint that her relationship to her son was not unlike his mother's with him.[27]

Moreover, Thackeray always remained faithful to certain impressions that he had formed in his early years of untroubled sympathy with his mother. His words upon revisiting Addiscombe in maturity may be recalled: "All sorts of recollections of my youth came back to me: dark and sad and painful with my dear good mother as a gentle angel interposing between me and misery." [28] He saw life permanently henceforth in terms of a dichotomy between the warmth and trust of a happy home circle and the selfish indifference of the outside world. His remembrance of what his mother had been to him in youth fixed once for all his ideal of womanhood, and created in him a permanent need for the society of a woman whom he could love and in whom he could confide on the same terms. He was never quite able to bring himself to recognize the degree to which his ideal was tinged, in George Bernard Shaw's blunt but accurate words, by an "affectionate and admiring love of sentimental stupidity for its own sake." [29]

Major Carmichael-Smyth presented an odd contrast to his brilliant wife. The earliest description of him dates from the 1840s, at which time, Lady Ritchie notes, he was "quite bald with kind blue eyes," habitually dressed in "a short cloak that he called a poncho & a straw hat." [30] After a quarter century of active service in the army, during which he had gained an enviable reputation for intrepidity [31] and professional competence, he wished at forty-five to settle quietly into the uneventful life of a country gentleman. He supported his wife in her enthusiasms, but not from any kindred feeling, for he was quite happy with his garden, his horses, and his newspaper.

One eccentricity he did permit himself. He was an indefatigable projector. His mind ran constantly on mechanical contrivances that were to make the family's fortune. We may assume that he puttered about at Larkbeare, as he did later in Paris, in "a room full of chemical experiments, barrels of beer, bottles, old German dictionaries, and medical works." [32] There is a family tradition that he invented a steam carriage which in some respects anticipated the automobile. But the one invention about which detailed information has survived does not inspire confidence in his methods. Lady Ritchie tells the story in "Across the Peat-fields":

> My granduncle, who was of an ingenious turn of mind, had come to Visy to try a machine he had invented, and to make experiments in the manufacture of peat-fuel. It is certain that with his machine, and the help of an old woman and a boy, he could produce as many little square blocks of firing in a day as M. Mérard, the rival manufacturer, in three, with all his staff, including his cook and his carter's son. It is true that our machine cost about 300£. to start with, and that it was constantly getting out of order and requiring the doctoring of a Paris engineer; but setting that aside, as Monsieur Fontaine proved to us after an elaborate calculation, it was clear that a saving of 35 per cent. was effected by our process.
>
> The engineer from Paris having failed us on two occasions, I believe that my granduncle had at one time serious thoughts of constructing a mechanical engineer, who was to keep the whole thing in order, and only to require an occasional poke himself to continue going. I remember once seeing a wooden foot wrapped up in cotton wool in a box in our workshop, but I believe this being went no further. The Frankenstein's foot alone cost twelve pounds, so that it is easy to reckon how other more complicated organs would have run up the bill.[33]

Though Major Carmichael-Smyth had been educated at Charterhouse, he was not of a literary turn. His reading was chiefly in the reports of Parliamentary debates, concerning which as an extreme radical he took strong views. There is a tradition in the Carmichael family that after his removal to France he displayed his contempt for the Napoleonic tradition, and his resolute John Bullishness, by walking about the streets of Paris with a little dog which he christened "Waterloo" and continually called to heel by that name.[34]

For the rest, he was devoted to his wife. Her first marriage had left him with an uneasy jealousy which he could never entirely suppress. When Maria Knox's many admirers failed to disturb the equanimity of her elderly husband, Charlotte Elliot commented: "Henry Carmichael-Smyth would be in a fever to live in this house a month and see such a swarm about his wife." [35] But there can have been few occasions to cause him alarm in placid Larkbeare society. The Major and Thackeray got along well enough. No doubt the influence of his stolid manliness helped to counteract Mrs. Carmichael-Smyth's maternal dominance. Yet even their relationship was not entirely unaffected by the overcharged emotional atmosphere that clung round Mrs. Carmichael-Smyth's passionate personality. "There's something immodest in the marriage of an elderly woman with children," Thackeray wrote many years afterwards to Mrs. Elliot. "How disgusted I have felt at hearing my old GP snoring in my mother's room." [36]

The remaining member of the household was the orphaned Mary Graham, sometimes called Polly after her aunt Maria. Four years younger than Thackeray, she displayed an attitude to him very like that of little Laura Bell to Pen in the early chapters of *Pendennis*. Mrs. Carmichael-Smyth trained her in all the accomplishments expected of a young lady, and she mastered them so entirely that a visiting governess thought her "the most charming & gifted of women." [37] Thackeray describes Mary in Larkbeare days as "a very simple generous creature." [38] For many years a real affection existed between the two. But here too the demands of Mrs. Carmichael-Smyth's engrossing love took their toll, and Mary could not remain entirely simple and generous within its circle. Even at the family's first reunion at Christmas of 1821, Mrs. Carmichael-Smyth wrote to her sister that little Mary had inquired plaintively, "Is Bill your own boy then?" and "could not conceal her feeling that I should have more to love than her." [39] As Mary grew older, and as her opinion of herself improved, her latent jealousy flared into the open. "The virtues of that girl . . . want independence to bring them out," Thackeray wrote, when she finally left the Carmichael-Smyths to be married in 1841. "Her Devonshire friends flattered Polly & did her no good." [40]

5

Cambridge

I

At the beginning of the last week of February, 1829, Major Carmichael-Smyth took Thackeray to Cambridge,[1] where the Lent term had already begun. They stopped on the way for two days in London, where Thackeray visited old friends and acquaintances (among them Dr. Russell, who "was very gracious"),[2] replenished his wardrobe, and went to the play. On Wednesday they continued by coach to the university. The Major had taken the precaution of sending ahead Thackeray's "respectful compliments" to William Whewell, the tutor of Trinity College on whose "side" Thackeray was entered as a pensioner. Thus propitiated, and given to understand as well that he had to do with a young gentleman of means and position, Whewell did not suggest lodgings in the town (often the fate of freshmen), but at once assigned to Thackeray the desirable set of rooms on the ground floor to the right as one enters Trinity's Great Gate. Sir Isaac Newton and Macaulay had lived on the same staircase, and Thackeray wrote to his mother: "Men will say some day, that Newton & Thackeray kept near one another!" [3] When the Major departed on Saturday, Thackeray began at once to taste the advantages of his new position.

The young man's life is just beginning [he was later to write in *Pendennis*]: the boy's leading-strings are cut, and he has all the novel delights and dignities of freedom. He has no idea of cares yet, or of bad health, or of roguery, or poverty, or tomorrow's disappointment. The play has not been acted so often as to make him tired. Though the after-drink, as we mechanically go on repeating it, is stale and bitter, how pure and brilliant was that first sparkling draught of pleasure!—How the boy rushes at the cup, and with what a wild eagerness he drains it! [4]

Trinity College, like Charterhouse School seven years before, had been selected for Thackeray by the Carmichael-Smyths as the best of available institutions. Nor were the members of the largest, the wealthiest, and the most distinguished of Cambridge colleges at all backward in asserting its superiority. Sir Leslie Stephen records a characteristic remark by one of them about small-college men: "They, too, are God's creatures." [5] The Master of Trinity was Christopher Wordsworth, youngest brother of the poet, who was out of sympathy with Fellows and students alike and lived a retired life in the Lodge. The sight of Trinity Chapel twenty years later recalled to Thackeray's mind "the Master's peculiar lingo in the Litany: 'Have mercy upon us, *meeserable* sinners.' " [6] Thackeray saw almost as little of his tutor as of the Master. Though Whewell had not yet achieved the European reputation that his *History of the Inductive Sciences* was to bring him in 1837, he was already sufficiently unapproachable. The duties of a college tutor did not at this time include intimate association with undergraduates; yet few of his colleagues can have been so aloof as Whewell.[7] It is related of him that

One day he gave his servant a list of names of certain of his pupils whom he wished to see at a wine-party after Hall, a form of entertainment then much in fashion. Among the names was that of an undergraduate who had died some weeks before. 'Mr. Smith, sir; why he died last term sir!' objected the man. 'You ought to tell me when my pupils die,' replied the tutor sternly.[8]

What individual instruction Thackeray received came from his private tutor or coach, a bachelor scholar reading for a fellowship whom the college authorities allowed to support himself by taking a few undergraduate pupils at substantial fees. Thackeray's private tutor, described by him upon first encounter as looking "a decided reading character," [9] was Henry Edward Fawcett, twenty-seventh wrangler and twelfth classic in 1828.

The curriculum which it was Fawcett's task to assist Thackeray in mastering consisted chiefly of mathematics, the "peculiar honour and glory of the university," [10] though some attention was paid to classics and moral philosophy. Since the college measured the success of its instruction in terms of the positions attained by its students in the university's honours examination, principal emphasis was placed on the training of "reading men." If these industrious youths succeeded in the narrow but rigorous intellectual exercises set them, they gained prestige and substantial preferment. Most undergraduates, feeling themselves unequal to so exacting a routine, were content to take pass degrees. For these "poll men" a much easier training was provided.

Despite his lack of talent for mathematics, the inadequacy of his Charterhouse preparation, and the disadvantage of entering the university at mid-year, Thackeray at first set out eagerly in pursuit of an honours degree. A letter to his mother written during his third week in residence describes his stringent schedule.[11] After chapel and breakfast between seven and eight, he spent an hour with his private tutor. Between nine and eleven he attended Trinity's mathematical and classical lectures, and from eleven to twelve he studied the Greek play of the year with another Trinity freshman. An hour and a half of private work accomplished, he was through for the day, except perhaps for another hour of reading in the evening.

This program was designed to leave free nearly the whole of the day after three-o'clock dinner in Hall. Even so, Thackeray did not long follow it, for Cambridge offered many distractions. In the hours before Hall he could hardly refuse friends who asked him to walk to nearby villages or ride to more distant points. The period after Hall was traditionally given to "lounging." Since Thackeray often lounged at wine parties, where the beverages most commonly consumed were port and punch,[12] it was not always feasible to get up for chapel the next morning. There is desperate improbability in his assurance to his mother, after announcing that he intends to ask thirteen men to one of these affairs, that "reading men always have the largest wine-parties." [13] In later years he looked back

> to what was called "a wine-party" with a sort of wonder. Thirty lads round a table covered with bad sweetmeats, drinking bad wines, telling bad stories, singing bad songs over and over again. Milk punch —smoking—ghastly headache—frightful spectacle of dessert table next morning, and smell of tobacco—your guardian, the clergyman, dropping in in the midst of this—expecting to find you deep in algebra, and discovering the gyp administering soda-water.[14]

Another university institution that drew Thackeray's attention from his studies was the Cambridge Union. He joined this undergraduate debating society during his first week of residence, and for some time he faithfully attended its weekly meetings at the Red Lion Inn.

> A Mr Cookesley spoke in the most extraordinary manner [he wrote to his mother on 10 March]—The Hero of the Union retired with diminished head before Cookesley—His name is Sunderland and he is certainly a most delightful speaker—but is too fond of treating us with draughts of Tom Paine—I will work him next term for it.[15]

So eager was he to participate in the debate, however, that he found it impossible to bide his time. On 23 March he wrote:

> I have made a fool of myself!—I have rendered myself a public character, I have exposed myself—how? I spouted at the Union. I do not know what evil star reigns today or what malignant daemon could prompt me to such an act of folly—but however up I got, & blustered & blundered, & retracted, & stuttered upon the character of Napoleon. . . . I went deeper and deeper still, till at last with one desperate sentence to wit that "Napoleon as a Captain, a Lawgiver, and a King merited & received the esteem & gratitude & affection of the French Nation." I rushed out of the quagmire into wh I had so foolishly plunged myself & sat down like Lucifer never to rise again with open mouth in that august assembly.[16]

After this experience, he did indeed keep silent at the Union.

The most serious, because the most constant, interruption to Thackeray's work was his habit of desultory reading of what tough-minded Cambridge mathematicians contemptuously dismissed as "the soft elegant effeminacies" [17] of modern literature.

But Thackeray was not to be diverted from what had already become for him a passion rather than a pastime. At Cambridge he read not only fiction and the magazines, as he had at school, but also standard histories (those of Gibbon, Mitford, Hume, Smollett) and poetry. *The Revolt of Islam* in particular impressed him strongly, and, encouraged by the prospect of a debate on Shelley at the Union, he made the poet an object of special study.[18]

With Thackeray, to read was to write.

> The first literary man I ever met was Croly, [he told Elwin]. I was a lad of seventeen, on the top of a coach, going to Cambridge. I had read Salathiel at sixteen, and thought it divine. I turned back and gazed at him. The person who pointed him out to me said, 'I see that lad is fated!' He knew it by the way I gazed after him as a literary man.[19]

He kept a vigilant eye on undergraduate publications, and at length in *The Snob,* "A Literary and Scientific Journal. Not conducted by members of the University," [20] he found one that caught his fancy. He sent its editor some verses on "Timbuctoo," the subject set for the year's English prize poem (a competition afterwards won by Tennyson), which were duly printed in *The Snob's* fourth number. Thackeray's heroic couplets neatly parody the fading eighteenth-century style of verse-writing which still prevailed among prize poets, just as his elaborate notes effectively burlesque the paraphernalia of erudition by which their effusions were often accompanied. Here are his concluding lines, in which he has endeavoured, so he tells "the Reader," to be "enthusiastic and magnificent":

> Does virtue dwell in whiter breasts alone?
> Oh no, oh no, oh no, oh no, oh no!
> It shall not, must not, cannot, e'er be so.
> The day shall come when Albion's self shall feel
> Stern Afric's wrath, and writhe 'neath Afric's steel.
> I see her tribes the hill of glory mount,
> And sell their sugars on their own account;
> While round her throne the prostrate nations come,
> Sue for her rice, and barter for her rum! [21]

"Timbuctoo received much Laud," he wrote to his mother. "I could not help finding out that I was very fond of this same praise—The men Knew not the Author, but praised the Poem, how eagerly did I suck it in!" [22] In the following issue the editor included among the notes to correspondents, "We shall be glad to hear from 'T.' again," [23] this being the signature that Thackeray had employed. He responded with further contributions, and by 25 May he and the magazine's editor were sitting down together "to write the Snob for the next Thursday." [24] None of his further work for *The Snob* calls for comment, except perhaps his exploitation of the proletarian Mrs. Malaprop whom Hook had christened Mrs. Ramsbottom. Under Thackeray's hands we find this personage congratulating herself on "knowing many extinguished persons" and being "on terms of the greatest contumacy with the Court of Aldermen." [25]

It has usually been assumed that *The Snob* was edited by William Garrow Lettsom of Jesus College, and indeed Lettsom seems to have had a hand in the magazine.[26] But its chief projector was William Williams of Corpus Christi College, who for the next six months was to play an important role in Thackeray's life. Williams was seven years older than Thackeray and in his last undergraduate term. At first Thackeray did not take to him. "The Editor of the Snob," he wrote, ". . . doth not much delight me." [27] As he grew accustomed to Williams's combination of learning and eccentric humour, however, the two became firm friends. Thackeray's other associates during his first year at Cambridge were chiefly men he had known at Charterhouse or the Boyeses'. Among them Joseph Carne was his closest intimate. It was with him that he attended wine and supper parties, visited the Union (where Carne was a most successful orator), rode to Wimpole Hall and Newmarket, and walked to Grantchester.

Thackeray was also warmly received by his relatives in Cambridge. King's College was almost a family monopoly, for his cousins George and Martin Thackeray were respectively Provost and Vice-Provost, and there were two other Thackerays among the fellows. Martin was to be a lifelong acquaintance, though Thackeray never became intimate with him. Another cousin, Dr. Frederic Thackeray, was his physician. "He will take no fee," Thackeray noted, after an application of leeches to relieve a troublesome headache. "What do you think me a Cannibal? quoth he, on my offer." [28] Thackeray attended the lectures of George Pryme, professor of political economy, who had married Jane Towneley Thackeray, later (with her daughter Mrs. Bayne) to be the family historian. But the sober and sedate society of elderly relations was soon deserted for the company of young men of his own age. "The Dons parties are most desperately stupid," [29] he told his mother.

One afternoon early in May, when Thackeray was dozing in his rooms, he was visited by the Reverend Francis Huyshe. "Much was I astonished and greatly was I rejoiced," he writes to his mother.[30] They strolled together for an hour, Huyshe telling him the news from home and displaying considerable knowledge of Cambridge ways. "We . . . saw the new St. Johns buildings near wh there is a tall iron gate," Thackeray continued. "That is a gate wh men get over late at night Said Mr Huyshe— Did you ever do such a thing Sir?" Huyshe then went off to see Peacock, the tutor on whose side Wentworth was entered, a sad errand in view of what the future held in store.

As the end of the Easter term approached, Thackeray consulted Martin about his progress. The cautious Vice-Provost advised him to "keep nonens" [31] (i.e., not to count the months he had been at Cambridge towards the residence requirements for his degree), and thus avoid the "May examinations." Since this course would have forced him to spend an extra year at Cambridge, Thackeray did not adopt it. Luck was against him, however, for he was sick during the fortnight preceding examination week and had little opportunity to study. From 1 to 5 June he sat in Hall eight hours every day answering questions on Euclid, algebra, plane trigonometry, and the classical authors set for the year. He was not sanguine about his success. "I cannot possibly be anything but low," he wrote on 3 June; ". . . next year my name will I trust stand a hundred places higher than it does this." [32] When the results were posted, Thackeray found himself in the fourth class, "where clever 'non-reading' men were put, as in a limbo." [33] Though undistinguished, this position at the top of the poll (the honours men formed the first three classes) was at least not discreditable.

II

Martin Thackeray had told his cousin that "every young man sh^{d} go abroad after he had taken his degree." [1] Impatient to see the world, Thackeray persuaded his parents to dispense with the suggested preliminary. Soon after examination week he departed for France accompanied by Williams, who had been engaged on the strength of his newly acquired bachelor's degree to coach Thackeray in mathematics.[2] Having begun to learn French years before in the *Ami des enfans,* Thackeray eagerly drank in everything that he saw. Thirty years later he remembered vividly

> that first day at Calais; the voices of the women crying out at night, as the vessel came alongside the pier; the supper at Quillacq's and the flavour of the cutlets and the wine; the red-calico canopy under which I slept; the tiled floor, and the fresh smell of the sheets; the wonderful postilion in his jack-boots and pigtail . . . [all the impressions] of a time . . . when the little French soldiers wore white cockades in their shakos—when the diligence was forty hours going to Paris; and the great-booted postilion, as surveyed by youthful eyes from the coupé, with his *jurons,* his ends of rope for the harness, and his clubbed pigtail, was a wonderful being, and productive of endless amusement.[3]

After a few days in a hotel, the two young men moved into a boarding-house recommended by a Cambridge friend. Kept by a Baronne de Vaude, the authenticity of whose title seems more than suspect, this establishment first introduced Thackeray to the raffish Continental society that he was later to describe *ab experto.* "There are about a dozen people in the house . . . of all Nations," he wrote. "They are most inordinate card players here, & I am told play rather high." [4] Among these new acquaintances he took particular interest in a dubious Mrs. Twigg, who explained the absence of her husband by a pathetic story of ill-treatment and desertion.[5] Before his alarmed mother could enjoin him to quit such unsavoury surroundings, he and Williams themselves decided that "the boarding house was an idle, dissipated ecarte-playing boarding house," [6] and took lodgings at 54 Rue Neuve St. Augustin, where they remained for the duration of their visit.

Meantime, Thackeray was familiarizing himself with Paris. He visited the art galleries and recorded his impressions.

I am greatly very greatly disappointed in the pictures here—I hardly see a tolerable one. The odious French style predominates, Even in Versailles where one might expect better things there are a number of pictures if not by David, at least in the manner of that paltry god of French adoration.[7]

If he found French painting artificial, however, the Parisian theatre seemed to him wholly natural and delightful. He took particular pleasure in the performances of Mlle. Mars in the new romantic drama. When his mother rebuked him for his devotion to the boards, he pointed out that the lessons in French thus acquired were of more use to him than those of the master he employed. He cared little for Rossini's most recent operas, *Le Comte Ory* and *William Tell,* but he was enchanted with Marie Taglioni, the celebrated ballet dancer. For the rest, he browsed among the books and prints displayed in shops and stalls; he learned to dance from the famous Coulon ("a little creature of four feet high with a pigtail" [8]); and he walked about the city, familiarizing himself with its buildings and prospects. He had ample leisure as well for reading. He did not like *Devereux,* "altho' it is in the time of Swift & Bolingbroke," [9] already his favourite historical period; and he asserted confidently that he could write as good a novel himself. Yet Bulwer's story at least gave him a motto for the essay on Shelley on which he was working.

Williams's instruction in mathematics, meanwhile, was proving somewhat perfunctory. Far more subject to the lovely Twigg than Thackeray himself while they remained in the Baroness's boarding-house, he afterwards left his pupil largely to his own devices. At first this neglect led Thackeray to feel "rather low

& lonely," [10] but he shortly found an amusement that was to develop into an ungovernable mania.

We went a party of four of us to Frascatis the other night [he wrote to his mother]—had I stopped at one time I should have come away a winner of 200 Francs as it was I neither won nor lost. . . . The interest in the game Rouge et Noir is so powerful that I could not tear myself away until I had lost my last piece—I dreamed of it all night—& thought of nothing else for several days, but thank God I did not *return* The excitement has passed away now, but I hope I shall never be thrown in the way of the thing again, for I fear I could not resist.[11]

Ominous words, particularly since later letters reveal that écarté was the chief amusement among the young men with whom he associated in Paris. It is not too much to say that by the time Thackeray left France he was a confirmed gambler.

The Carmichael-Smyths were understandably disturbed by their son's candid communications and instructed him to return to England. By 22 October he was in London, where he saw Fanny Kemble in *Romeo and Juliet,*[12] and four days later he had arrived in Cambridge.[13] But the experiences of the summer had given Thackeray a glimpse of a world outside college walls which he found irresistible; he was drawn back to Paris like a moth to the flame. Looking ahead a few months, we may appropriately consider here the surreptitious visit that he paid to the French capital during the Easter vacation of 1830.

A windfall of £20 having come his way, he told Whewell that he would spend the holiday with his "friend Slingsby, in Huntingdonshire," [14] and set off to join Edward FitzGerald in Paris. On this visit he had to husband his resources more carefully than during the previous summer, and serious gambling must have been out of the question. But he soon found himself in still deeper water.[15] On Shrove Tuesday, together with other "great raw young English lads," he determined to take part in the masked balls which mark that occasion. Mingling with the young men and maidens ("the latter word is used from pure politeness") that these festivities brought forth, Thackeray was "so frightened and wonder-stricken by the demoniacal frantic yells and antics of the frequenters of the place," as to be about "to slink home perfectly dumb and miserable," when a lady tapped me on my shoulder, saluted me by name, and was good enough to put her arm into mine quite uninvited, and to walk once or twice with me up and down the room. This lovely creature appeared to be about five-and-thirty years of age;—she was dressed like a man, in a blouse and pair of very dirty-white trousers—had an oilskin hat, ornamented with a huge quantity of various-coloured ribbons, and under it an enormous wig with three tails, that dangled down the lady's back; it was of the fashion of the time of Louis XV, and so old and dirty that I have no doubt it had been worn at Carnivals any time since the death of that monarch.—'Don't you know me?' said she, after a moment, seeing my wonder, and at [my] confessing my forgetfulness, she told me who she was.

Indeed, I recollect her a governess in a very sober, worthy family in England, where she brought up the daughters, and had been selected especially because she was a *Protestant*. I believe the woman did her duty perfectly well in her station, but, upon my word, she told me she had pawned her gown to get this disgusting old dress, and dance at this disgusting masquerade. She was not very young, as has been seen, and had never been pretty. Squalid poverty had not increased her charms; but here she was, as mad after the Carnival as the rest, and enjoying herself along with the other mad men and women. In her private capacity she was a workwoman; she lived in the Rue Neuve St. Augustin, and I found her a few days afterwards eating garlic soup in a foul porter's lodge, from which she conducted me up a damp, mouldy staircase to her own apartment, on the seventh floor, with the air and politeness of a duchess.

Thackeray goes on to explain to the readers of the *Britannia,* to whom he eleven years later recounted this experience, that he visited Mlle. Pauline's apartment "upon the subject of a half-dozen of shirts which the lady made for me." Yet he came to know her well enough to hear most of the secrets of her life, which she told him "with the utmost simplicity, and without the slightest appearance of confusion." In the censored version which Thackeray prepared for his English readers, her story was as follows:

Before she turned Protestant, and instructed that respectable English family in whose bosom she found a home, where she became acquainted with all the elegances of life, and habituated to the luxuries of refinement, where she had a comfortable hot joint every day with the children, in the nursery, at one, and passed the evening deliciously in the drawing-room, listening to the conversation of the ladies, making tea, mayhap, for the gentlemen as they came up from their wine, or playing quadrilles and waltzes when her lady desired her to do so—before this period of her genteel existence, it is probable that Mademoiselle Pauline was a grisette. When she quitted Sir John's family she had his recommendation, and an offer of another place equally eligible; more children to bring up, more walks in the park or the square, more legs of mutton at one. She might have laid by a competence if she had been thrifty, or have seized upon a promise of marriage from young Master Tom, at college, if she had been artful; or, better still, from a respectable governess have become a respectable step-mother, as many women with half her good looks have done. But no. A grisette she was, and a grisette she would be; and left the milords and miladies, and *cette triste ville de Londres, où l'on ne danse pas seulement le dimanche,* for her old quarters, habits, and companions, and that dear gutter in the Rue du Bac, which Madame de Stael has spoken of so fondly.

Thackeray conceived a considerable admiration for this little adventuress; and we can be sure, not only from his account of her but also from certain points of resemblance between her career and character and those of Becky Sharp, that she long remained a living figure in his memory.

It might certainly be thought that this excursion to Paris had shown Thackeray as much of "life" as a respectable English youth of eighteen was ready to absorb, but his adventures were not over yet. Thirty years later the circumstances of his trip home were still fixed vividly in his mind.

I remember as a boy, at the 'Ship' at Dover (imperante Carlo Decimo), when, my place to London being paid, I had but 12*s.* left after a certain little Paris excursion (about which my benighted parents never knew anything), ordering for dinner a whiting, a beef-steak, and a glass of negus, and the bill was, dinner 7*s.*, glass of negus 2*s.*, waiter 6*d.*, and only half a crown left, as I was a sinner, for the guard and coachman on the way to London! [16]

After this excitement, the Cambridge round must have seemed tamer than ever.

III

Thackeray's course during his second and final year at Cambridge is not easily charted. Only two of his letters home during this period have survived, and these are neither as long nor as frank as those which he wrote in the Lent and Easter terms of 1829. Nevertheless, a reasonably coherent if somewhat tentative account of his experiences as a Junior Soph can be assembled from other sources.

The curriculum prescribed for Junior Sophs at Trinity College emphasized mathematics and moral philosophy, but also included classics as represented by one of the Gospels in Greek.[1] Thackeray assured his mother at the beginning of Michaelmas term that his "days have passed in a very equable routine Mathematics & Classics, Classics & Mathematics." [2] Three weeks later, however, he wrote: "Dismiss your visions of wranglers, my dear Mother, if I am a Senior Optime you should be very well content." [3] And finally, tiring of his struggle with an uncongenial and what seemed to him profitless course of study, he grew content to drift, like Wordsworth forty years earlier,

. . . with the shoal
Of more unthinking natures, easy minds
And pillowy.

Thackeray's abandonment of serious pretensions to academic achievement left him time for many other activities. Williams had revived *The Snob* under a new title, *The Gownsman,* "A Literary and Scientific Journal, now conducted by Members of the University," and to its seventeen issues between 5 November 1829 and 25 February 1830 Thackeray made several contributions.[4] He was not enough of a celebrity to belong to the "Apostles." He regarded the members of that famous society with some awe, indeed, and he afterwards told his daughter "that in his early days at Cambridge it was considered a distinction by the young men to be seen out walking with Mr. Brookfield," [5] who, though not himself an Apostle, was the close friend of several. But he did join a debating society of Trinity undergraduates formed late in October in imitation of the "Apostles." Its members, Henry Alford, John Allen, Henry Nicholson Burrows, Charles Christie, William Hepworth Thompson, and John Hailstone, were pillars of the academic community, and several of them afterwards achieved distinction in the Church. "There are amongst them 3 1st Class Men, who are very nice fellows," Thackeray assured his mother; but he could not help adding, "only they smell a little of the shop." [6] That they in turn had reservations about Thackeray may be surmised from the recollections of one of their number, Thompson, who, when Master of Trinity, recalled that Thackeray had been

> a tall thin large-eyed, full and ruddy faced man with an eye glass fixed *en permanence*. . . . We [of the Debating Society] did not see in him even the germ of those literary powers which . . . he afterwards developed. . . . He led a somewhat lazy but pleasant and "gentlemanlike" life in a set mixed of old schoolfellows and such men as . . . [Allen and Robert Groome]; with them . . . he no doubt had much literary talk, but not on "University Subjects." . . . But though careless of University distinction, he had a vivid appreciation of English poetry, and chanted the praises of the old English novelists —especially his model, Fielding. He had always a flow of humour and pleasantry, and was made much of by his friends. At supper parties, though not talkative—rather observant—he enjoyed the humours of the hour, and sang one or two old songs with great applause. "Old King Cole" I well remember to have heard from him at the supper I gave to celebrate my election as Scholar. It made me laugh excessively—not from the novelty of the song—but from the humour with which it was given.[7]

The Debating Society convened in the rooms of each member in turn on Friday evenings from 6:15 until 9:00. Some of the topics discussed, and the positions that Thackeray took with regard to them, have been preserved:

27 November 1829	Has woman, since the Fall, been the cause of more good or evil to to mankind?	Good
4 December	Are works of fiction prejudicial to the moral character?	Good

11 December	Has the institution of Duelling been of benefit to mankind?	Affirmative
5 February	Was the Elizabethan age deservedly called the golden age of English Literature?	Negative
19 February	Which exerts the greater moral influence, the poetry of intellect or that of passion?	Passion
7 March	Whether a change of politics in a public character is in any case justifiable.	Negative
12 March	Is a Feudal System of Government calculated to promote the happiness of the People?	Affirmative

The subject for 11 December was proposed by Thackeray. If an amendment passed by the Society on 27 November was observed, he began this meeting by reading an essay on duelling.[8] But by late March Thackeray had tired of the Society, and Burrows was complaining to John Allen that he had fallen into the habit of cutting its debates.[9]

Thackeray's closest friends during his second year at Cambridge were Edward FitzGerald and John Allen. When Thackeray met FitzGerald, the latter was in his tenth and last term at the university. The introduction took place in late October at the rooms of Williams, who was coaching FitzGerald for his approaching examinations.[10] It was a lucky chance that thus brought the two young men together, for FitzGerald lived in lodgings and ordinarily saw little of other undergraduates. During the eight weeks that remained of Michaelmas term, the acquaintance between Thackeray and FitzGerald rapidly ripened into intimacy.

FitzGerald was one of the several sons of a respected but eccentric Anglo-Irish clan. He called it the "Ballyblunder family," admitting freely that he was its "legitimate offspring." "The FitzGeralds are all mad," he once said, "but my brother John is the only one who doesn't know it." Lucy Barton, whom FitzGerald later married, describes his father as "an inefficient, kindly man, big of body and hale of cheek, . . . [possessing] a kind of dumb distinction." His mother, she continues, was "an elegantly ostentatious woman of the scentless-rose sort." If FitzGerald was allowed to grow up "untrammelled intellectually and a mental freeman," it was not because of any parental theory of education, but because of "a vacuum in the matter of common sense" in his home.[11]

FitzGerald's odd upbringing had made him shy, and Thackeray found him "a very good fellow but of very retired habits." [12] Since he could look forward to an assured income, he was not forced out of his shell through the process of having to earn his living. As a young man his lack of ambition and his penchant for contemplative idleness made him uneasy, but gradually he became content with a spectator's role. Congratulating Edward Byles Cowell on an academic triumph in 1848, he remarked that ten years earlier he might have been vexed at his friend's success. "But now," he continued, "I am glad to see any man do anything well; and I know that it is my vocation to stand and wait, and to know within myself whether it *is* done well." [13] He became the amateur *par excellence,* eager only to cultivate his taste. "His life and conversation," said William Bodham Donne, "are the most perfectly philosophic of any I know. They approach in grand quiescence to some of the marvels of contentment in Plutarch. He is Diogenes without his dirt." [14]

But FitzGerald's withdrawal from the world was not to be ascribed to a lack of interest in it or an inability to understand and get along with people. He had a firm grasp of the realities of life, and he was an acute judge of human nature. "The vineyard of morality," he once observed, should be "the chief object of our cultivation." [15] His own very real ability attracted other men of talent to him; it was through FitzGerald, indeed, that Thackeray came to know John Mitchell Kemble, James Spedding, and Tennyson. Without such associations life would have been empty to FitzGerald. "I am an idle fellow, of a very ladylike turn of sentiment," he told John Allen; "and my friendships are more like loves I think." [16]

Thackeray and FitzGerald were united in their dislike for the narrow program of studies provided at Cambridge and for the spirit in which these studies were pursued. They saw clearly enough, what Leslie Stephen was later to point out, that the

Cambridge system at this time was "not to teach anyone anything, but to offer heavy prizes for competition in certain well-defined intellectual contests."[17] In his Cambridge dialogue *Euphranor,* FitzGerald deplored

> the present rage for *intellect,* . . . not for its own sake only, but for advancement in the peaceful professions, now so thronged since war has been quiet. Jack and Tom, you know, must not only shine at the literary tea-table, they must get fellowships, livings, silk gowns at the bar,—they cannot be crammed too fast,—and to this end the order of Nature is reversed, to get early at faculties which come last in the order of growth.[18]

Thackeray and FitzGerald preferred to loaf and invite their souls, to pass their time discussing books, music, and the theatre, or the vicissitudes of the human condition. Out of these long conversations, indeed, many of Thackeray's distinctive ideas about art and life first began to take definite shape.

Thackeray and FitzGerald also had much the same taste in humour, extravagant, yet solidly anchored in reality. Here again they were indebted to Williams, who had himself been to school to that strange Cambridge fantast Edward William Clarke.[19] Their common vein may be briefly illustrated from FitzGerald's comments to Frederick Tennyson about a portrait of Spedding by Samuel Laurence:

> Not swords, nor cannon, nor all the Bulls of Bashan butting at it, could, I feel sure, discompose that venerable forehead. No wonder that no hair can grow at such an altitude: no wonder his view of Bacon's virtue is so rareified that the common consciences of men cannot endure it. Thackeray and I occasionally amuse ourselves with the idea of Spedding's forehead: we find it somehow or other in all things, just peering out of all things: you see it in a milestone, Thackeray says. He also draws the forehead rising with a sober light over Mont Blanc, and reflected in the lake of Geneva. We have great laughing over this.[20]

When Thackeray and FitzGerald were not enjoying such fancies as these, their conversation often turned to the topic of religion. We have seen that Thackeray had received so thorough a grounding in evangelical Christianity that he grew rebellious and uneasy with this narrow faith. In FitzGerald he found a companion much farther gone in doubt, who was later to write in the *Rubáiyát:*

> Myself when young did eagerly frequent
> Doctor and Saint, and heard great argument
>   About it and about: but evermore
> Came out by the same door where in I went.

The demonstrations which FitzGerald drew from the arsenal of scepticism very quickly destroyed Thackeray's feeble defences and left him for some time in a state of restless bewilderment concerning religion.

Here John Allen, Thackeray's other great friend of his second Cambridge year, proved a counterbalancing influence. Allen was the son of a clergyman, and he was himself destined for the Church. His manuscript diary of 1830–1831 shows how seriously he took his vocation. His life was a constant struggle with the temptations of the world; and since he regarded the smallest concession to comfort or enjoyment as giving in to the Devil, he suffered many defeats. But despite his preoccupation with his spiritual welfare, he was anything but sanctimonious; and his character was otherwise a mixture of goodness and simplicity that made him irresistibly attractive. Thackeray liked and admired him from the first.

When FitzGerald departed from Cambridge, Allen felt that his opportunity was at hand, for he regarded Thackeray as a brand to be snatched from the burning. On 3 February he wrote in his diary: "Thackeray came in, we had some serious conversation when I affected him to tears he went away with a determination tomorrow to lead a new life, Prayed for him Fitzgerald & myself afterwards in tears." Four days later he wrote: "Thackeray came up—expressed some doubts of Xt being = with God, read over St. Matthew together & he was convinced thank God for it." [21] But Thackeray shortly slipped back into doubt; and soon more pressing matters left him little freedom for religious speculation.

It was unlucky for Thackeray that FitzGerald left Cambridge at the end of Michaelmas term. We have seen that he was by no means content with the company of the estimable young men who made up his debating society, and John Allen, though a dear fellow, shared few of his interests. Inevitably he came to mix more and more in the fast life of the university which persisted with almost eighteenth-century vigour. Even at this time an occasional don still provided an exemplar for the "varmint men" among the undergraduates. "You will remember," Macaulay wrote to Whewell, "two reverend gentlemen who were high in college office when I was an undergraduate. One of them never opened his mouth without an oath, and the other had killed his man." [22] But aristocratic undergraduates were quite capable of blazing a trail for themselves. Great deference was still paid to rank and wealth at Cambridge. Noblemen in residence had their toadies and hangers-on, just as in the great world.[23] And no matter what his birth, for a substantial fee a young man could wear the gilded gown of a fellow commoner, and as a "Licensed Son of Ignorance" [24] could obtain his degree after a minimum expenditure of time and energy. As a freshman Thackeray had written to his mother about Henry Stuart Burton, a fellow undergraduate later immortalized as the "Carrigaholt" of *Eōthen:*

> Do you recollect a boy by the name of Burton with whom I used to cronyize at Tunbridge Wells? He is here a gay fellow-commoner, cutting me of course, he had a supper for 30 last night, & the young heroes kept it up till five this morning.[25]

As a Junior Soph, Thackeray sought in the company of these heroes what a severe contemporary moralist dismissed as "the withering contact of opulent folly and titled ignorance." [26] He became a connoisseur of wines and cigars, fine clothes and jewelry, books and prints without counting the cost; and he later complained with reason of "the expensive habits, wh that blessed University Cambridge has taught me." [27] If he was too fastidious to fuddle himself nightly and seek amusement afterwards in "the Finish," a sally into the streets in search of "snobs" with whom to fight, he none the less acquired a thoroughly aristocratic outlook on life, the absurdity of which for a young man so circumstanced as himself he was as yet too inexperienced to see.

This outlook explains his interest in duelling already mentioned, and another preoccupation that was to have more serious consequences. The gambling virus with which Thackeray had become infected in Paris did not long remain dormant after his return to Cambridge. He played first with college acquaintances, but eventually he was marked down as a "pigeon" ready for plucking by professional gamblers, one of whom was the decayed gentleman who later served as his model for Deuceace.[28] These rascals found Thackeray an easy mark. He lamented his curious "greenness" as a young man; and it was of himself as well as of Pendennis that he wrote:

> It had not as yet entered into the boy's head to disbelieve any statement that was made to him; and being of a candid nature himself, he took naturally for truth what other people told him.[29]

At any rate, the sharpers who were pursuing him "took lodgings opposite to Trinity, made his acquaintance, and invited him to their rooms to dinner and écarté. At first he was allowed to win and the stakes were raised, then luck changed and he lost and lost and lost."[30] Before their departure they obtained Thackeray's promise to pay £1,500 when he came into his fortune in 1832.[31]

Varied and costly as were the diversions that Cambridge afforded, Thackeray's resources were by no means limited to them. He was absent from college three entire weeks spaced through the Lent term of 1830.[32] No doubt they were spent in London, the usual destination of "gay men" in unauthorized absences. At any rate, Henry Silver wrote in his diary many years later how:

> Thackeray tells of his asking Sloman [the Jewish improvisatore of the Cider Cellars] to dine with him & feeling hurt,—at ye great man's refusal on the plea of a previous engagement. This was when T. used to come up to ye Bedford from Cambridge—no such champagne since![33]

His trip to Paris in the Easter vacation of 1830 has already been described.

Though Thackeray in the Oxbridge chapters of *Pendennis* carries Pen through the various dissipations that have thus far been described, he "declines to go through Pen's young academical career very minutely." "Alas," he continues, "the life of such boys does not bear telling altogether." [34] And in fact the "gay men" among the undergraduates had it in their power to live sufficiently disorderly lives.[35] A charter granted by Queen Elizabeth authorized the proctors to search the houses of Cambridge for prostitutes and to bring them before the Vice-Chancellor for sentence. But in practice the authorities sought to control rather than to suppress this traffic. If a "Cyprian" were quiet and well behaved, there was little likelihood of her being removed from Barnwell or Castle End to the university's Spinning House; and undergraduates apprehended *in flagrante delicto* often escaped with light penalties. An acute American who studied at Cambridge from 1840 to 1845 noted how this system turned many undergraduates—a large proportion of them destined for the church—into profligates and gave the sexual ethics of nearly all a class bias.

> That shop-girls, work-women, domestic servants, and all females in similar positions, were expressly designed for the amusement of gentlemen, and generally serve that purpose, is a proposition assented to by a large proportion of Englishmen, even when they do not act upon the idea themselves. . . . Once as I was walking in the outskirts of Cambridge with a friend, a man strictly moral in his life, we came upon a group of children at play, mostly girls ten or twelve years old. "Poor things!" said he, "there go the prostitutes for the next generation." It was the first thought that occurred to him on seeing these daughters of the people.[36]

It is by no means certain that Thackeray himself participated actively in this side of undergraduate life. Indeed, the contrary is perhaps implied in an observation to Mrs. Brookfield about FitzGerald: "Quand notre amitié a commencé, je n'avais pas encore appris à aimer une femme." [37] But he had ample opportunities to observe more enterprising friends. There was Harry Matthew, for example, Thackeray's "idol of youth," of whom he wrote in 1849, "I used to think [him] 20 years ago the most fascinating accomplished witty and delightful of men." [38] Matthew was four years older than Thackeray, and his history was already a varied one. The son of a Somersetshire minister, he was sent in 1825 to Balliol College, Oxford, where his father had been before him. He very shortly left, or was required to leave, Oxford; but a place was found for him in 1825 at Trinity

College, Cambridge. Within a year he had worn out his welcome at Trinity College as well, and he migrated to tiny Sidney Sussex College, where he remained until he took his degree in 1832.[39]

Matthew commanded undergraduate admiration as a sort of Byronic hero, equally remarkable for talent and for viciousness. A Cambridge celebrity by virtue of his presidency of the Union in 1830,[40] he was a thorough rake "in mind, & appearance." FitzGerald, "always right about men," warned Thackeray from the first that "this was a bad one and a sham"; [41] and it appears, indeed, that Matthew patronized Thackeray for the same reason that Iago does Roderigo.[42] Yet even a year later, when Thackeray's youthful idolatry had subsided, he was still capable of wondering admiringly at Matthew's "incomprehensible recklessness & quiet with things hanging over him, wh if discovered might leave him a beggar & an outcast." [43]

If we assume that Matthew was the original of Bloundell in *Pendennis,* an identification for which there is strong evidence,[44] this sketch of his character can be elaborated further. Bloundell, a one-time dragoon officer, enters little Boniface College, Oxbridge, "after St. George's and one or two other Colleges had refused to receive him," because there is a living in his family for which he wishes to qualify. He had previously been at Camford, "which he had quitted on account of some differences with the tutors and authorities there." At Oxbridge he soon becomes "the most popular man of the University," a great favourite with his fellow undergraduates. "A man who has seen the world," Thackeray explains, "or can speak of it with a knowing air—a *roué,* or Lovelace, who has his adventures to relate, is sure of an admiring audience among boys." But Bloundell's general influence is bad. "One such diseased creature as this is enough to infect a whole colony, and the tutors of Boniface began to find the moral tone of their college lowered and their young men growing unruly, and almost ungentlemanlike, soon after Mr. Bloundell's arrival at Oxbridge." Nor does Major Pendennis fail to warn Pen to keep clear of him. "That man is a tiger, mark my words—a low man," he tells his nephew. "There is the unmistakeable look of slang, and bad habits, about this Mr.

Bloundell. He frequents low gambling-houses and billiard hells, sir—he haunts third-rate clubs—I know he does. I know by his style." [45] Pen fails to take the Major's advice, just as Thackeray failed to take FitzGerald's, and in both cases the result was a heavy toll in money squandered and in time wasted.

Thackeray remained at Cambridge until the end of the Easter term in 1830.[46] During the Lent term he had taken the Previous Examination, or "Little Go," which at this time covered "one of the four Gospels, or the Acts of the Apostles, in the Original Greek; Paley's Evidences of Christianity; and one of the Greek, and one of the Latin Classics." [47] When results were posted, his name appeared in alphabetical order in the second class—anything but a distinguished position, since 229 men (including most of Thackeray's friends) figured in the first class.[48] He could now hope for nothing better than a pass degree. Deciding that this was not sufficient reward for two further years of residence and anxious to quit the temptations of Cambridge life, he left the university after having kept five terms.

It is not easy to weigh exactly the effect upon Thackeray of his two years at the university. His was not the idealized Cambridge of FitzGerald's *Euphranor* or Tennyson's poetry. The undergraduates of *The Princess,* for example, live a charmed life:

They talk'd
At wine, in clubs, of art, of politics;
They lost their weeks; they vext the souls of dreams;
They rode; they bett'd; made a hundred friends,
And caught the blossom of the flying terms.

Thackeray did all these things, and no doubt he enjoyed himself greatly in the process; but at the same time he was haunted by misgivings over his idleness, the bad habits into which he was falling, and his failure to achieve the success that was expected of him. Looking back a decade later at his experience of school and college, he inquired:

I should like to know . . . how much ruin has been caused by that accursed system, which is called in England 'the education of a gentleman.' Go, my son, for ten years to a public school, that 'world in miniature'; learn 'to fight for yourself' against the time when your real struggles shall begin. Begin to be selfish at ten years of age; study for other ten years; get a competent knowledge of boxing, swimming, rowing, and cricket, with a pretty knack of Latin hexameters, and a decent smattering of Greek plays,—do this and a fond father shall bless you—bless the two thousand pounds which he has spent in acquiring all these benefits for you. And, besides, what else have you not learned? You have been many hundreds of times to chapel, and have learned to consider the religious service performed there as the vainest parade in the world. If your father is a grocer, you have been beaten for his sake, and have learned to be ashamed of him. You have learned to forget (as how should you remember, being separated from them for three-fourths of your time?) the ties and natural affections of home. You have learned, if you have a kindly heart and an open hand, to compete with associates much more wealthy than yourself; and to consider money as not much, but honour—the honour of dining and consorting with your betters—as a great deal. All this does the public school and college boy learn; and woe be to his knowledge! [49]

But this should not be the reader's final judgment, nor was it Thackeray's, as the affectionate "Oxbridge" chapters of *Pendennis* sufficiently show. Thackeray's time at Cambridge had not been wasted. The experience of living at Trinity College helped to deepen his attachment to the English past, without making him an antiquarian or a pedant. He acquired the prevailing tone of "quiet good sense," which in Leslie Stephen's view so markedly distinguished the Cambridge of this period from Oxford.[50] Though he laid the foundations for a broad culture, he learned not to attack his fellows in the name of that goddess as Philistines, an epithet which is sometimes best defined, Stephen notes, as "that which a prig bestows on the rest of the species." [51] And, once and for all, as Sir Richmond Ritchie pointed out, "Cambridge fixed his social status. Though afterwards he was to consort with Bohemians and other strange acquaintances into whose company a man is forced by adversity, he was never a Bohemian, and always faithful to the traditions of the class in which he was born and bred." [52] In the life that was in store for Thackeray, he had need of such an anchor.

6

The Spirit of an Heir

I

After leaving Cambridge during the second week of June, 1830, Thackeray's first obligation was to return home to the Carmichael-Smyths to justify his abandonment of his university career. No record of this family council has survived, but it can be reconstructed from one of Thackeray's later letters:

> You seem to take it so much to heart, that I gave up trying for Academical honors [he wrote at the end of the year]—perhaps Mother I was too young to form opinions but I did form them—& these told me that there was little use in studying what could after a certain point be of no earthly use to me—they told me that subtle reasonings & deep meditations on angles & parallelograms might be much better employed on other subjects—that three years industrious waste of time might obtain for me mediocre honors wh I did not value a straw.

To Thackeray his Cambridge experience was the culminating disappointment in a ten-year scheme of education which his parents had devised without regard for his real abilities and tastes. He had to assert his independence, even at the risk of seeming "idle & ungrateful." [1]

No doubt the Carmichael-Smyths found these arguments singularly naïve and irrelevant. Wishing their son to win in the race for success, they saw public school and university merely as two hurdles to be cleared along the way, and they were naturally disturbed when their entry refused even to jump. But they loved the boy, and they were willing to humour him. It was agreed he should shape his own course during the next few months. After this period of grace, however, he must heed the dictates of worldly wisdom and prepare himself for a profession, perhaps for the law, which he considered the least objectionable of gentlemanly employments.

Since Thackeray's greatest desire was to see the world, mid-July found him in London busy with preparations for a prolonged tour of Germany. After some days passed in studying German and sampling the pleasures of the town, he embarked on the Rotterdam packet with a sheaf of letters of introduction to the English colony in Dresden, whose picture galleries he was eager to visit. From Rotterdam he set off on a steamer up the Rhine. The legends of the country-side fascinated him; he was absorbed with the new acquaintances that he made, both natives and fellow travellers; and his artist's interest in the picturesque led him to fill his sketch-book and letters with drawings. But these pleasures palled, and he was soon assuring his mother scornfully that "the Rhine is almost equal to the Thames." [2]

Falling in at Frankfurt with Franz Anton Schulte, a German student whom he had known in Cambridge, he was glad to join Schulte's reading party and retrace his path to Godesberg. Schulte took him to the University of Bonn nearby, where he was introduced to the student clubs and saw something of their drinking and duelling. It is possible to infer from one of Thackeray's later stories that he became involved in a passing flirtation with a beautiful Jewish girl during these days at Bonn and Godesberg, but no definite information concerning this episode has survived.[3] In any event, he and Schulte soon set off together towards Dresden, and Thackeray found his friend very helpful along the way in learning to read and speak German. Parting with Schulte at Kassel, Thackeray went on alone to Weimar. By the end of September he was writing to his mother for permission to substitute this little city for Dresden as his winter headquarters.

Weimar was the capital of the Grand Duchy of Saxe-Weimar-Eisenach, and a good deal of pomp and formality marked its public life. Uniforms were *de rigueur* on all emergent occasions, and the table of precedence was carefully observed. Society was cosmopolitan, conversation polyglot. But under Grand Duke Karl Friedrich, who had succeeded the renowned Karl August in 1828, Weimar retained little of the intellectual distinction that had made it famous throughout Europe a quarter of a century earlier. Schiller and Wieland were long since dead, and though Goethe still remained in residence, he lived largely in retirement, an old man of eighty-one drawing near his long home. Karl Friedrich's chief amusement was drilling his miniature army of "400 men & nearly as many officers." [4] Far from welcoming free discussion of burning issues, as had his predecessor, he was hostile to new ideas. So strict a censorship was imposed upon the local theatre, indeed, that residents had to withdraw to Erfurt to see so harmless a drama as Schiller's *Die Raüber*.[5] The social atmosphere was comfortable and welcoming to visitors, particularly if they were English and hence presumed to be well-to-do, but in the long run somewhat stodgy and oppressive. It was characteristic of the town that doors were locked each night by ten.

At George Henry Lewes's request Thackeray twenty five years later set down the following recollections of his winter:

At least a score of young English lads used to live at Weimar for study, or sport, or society; all of which were to be had in the friendly little Saxon capital. The Grand Duke and Duchess received us with the kindliest hospitality. The Court was splendid, but yet most pleasant and homely. We were invited in our turns to dinners, balls, and assemblies there. Such young men as had a right, appeared in uniforms, diplomatic and military. Some, I remember, invented gorgeous clothing: the kind old Hof Marschall of those days, M. de Spiegel (who had two of the most lovely daughters eyes ever looked on), being in no wise difficult as to the admission of these young Englanders. Of the winter nights we used to charter sedan chairs, in which we were carried through the snow to those pleasant Court entertainments. . . .

We knew the whole society of the little city, and but that the young ladies one and all, spoke admirable English, we surely might have learned the very best German. The society met constantly. The ladies of the Court had their evenings. The theatre was open twice or thrice in the week, where we assembled, a large family party. . . . In every one of those kind salons the talk was still of Art and letters. The theatre, though possessing no very extraordinary actors, was still conducted with a noble intelligence and order. The actors read books, and were men of letters and gentlemen, holding a not unkindly relationship with the *Adel.* At Court the conversation was exceedingly friendly, simple and polished. The Grand Duchess . . . , a lady of very remarkable endowments, would kindly borrow our books from us, lend us her own, and graciously talk to us young men about our literary tastes and pursuits.[6]

Thackeray's English friends included his Cambridge crony William Garrow Lettsom, whose recommendations first decided him to settle in Weimar; [7] Norman MacLeod, later chaplain to Queen Victoria; Samuel Naylor, who was afterwards to translate Goethe's *Reineke Fuchs* into English; [8] a former guards officer named Caledon George du Pre, who became the town's most eligible bachelor; and half a dozen others.[9] The great patroness of this group was Goethe's daughter-in-law and companion, Ottilie von Goethe, whom Thackeray accordingly described as "his Britannic Majesty's Consul in Weimar." [10] This "crazy angel," as Goethe used to call her, sought consolation for her separation from her husband in the attentions of young and sentimental visitors. Nor was the British contingent behindhand in responding to her overtures, despite the fact that Ottilie was in her middle forties.

Thackeray never joined the group of her favourites, but he did make himself attractive to the younger ladies of the Weimar court. He had Major Carmichael-Smyth procure a cornetcy for him in Sir John Kennaway's Devon yeomanry and send him its uniform decked out in pink and sky-blue.[11] He made rapid progress in "gallopading" at court dances, and he assiduously frequented the parquet of the little Weimar theatre, where general conversation was the rule during intermissions. With such opportunities it is not surprising that he shortly fell in love with Melanie von Spiegel, a Junoesque beauty whom Thackeray described to his mother as "the prettiest woman I ever saw in my life." [12] At first Melanie encouraged Thackeray's suit. Indeed, Weimar was in its small way quite as much of a marriage-mart as

A plain statement of
a most unhappy case –

In re Thackeray }
a lunatic }. Hilary Term. 2 Wm. IV.

Last Sunday night at nine, unhappy Thack-
-eray in velvet vest & breeches black
Sat sweetly musing in his easy chair
With a snug fire & half an hour to spare
Now he surveyed his handsome Sunday clo'es
Now he the bellows blew & now his nose –
He thought how blest in half an hour he'd be
Hearing sweet music drinking sweeter tea
When lo! oblivion on his senses crept
He dozed, he snoozed, he dreamt, he snored, he slept.
~~Boom the loud bell his placid slumber broke~~
Ponderous & brazen tongued the bell then broke
His placid sleep – the lovely youth awoke! –
With startled ears & fears he hears, O Grimes!
Half past eleven by the Temple chimes!!! –

V. An apology

From a letter to John Kemble, January, 1832

VI. Thackeray in 1833

From a sketch by Daniel Maclise

VII. Thackeray about 1834

From a self-portrait

VIII. Isabella Shawe about 1836

From a sketch by Thackeray

the London world, and the local matrons approved of Thackeray as a lively and amusing young man whose fortune by German standards was substantial. But when he gave no sign of proposing, Melanie's favour rapidly diminished. Thackeray next succumbed to Jenny von Pappenheim, another beauty of the court, who in her memoirs classes Thackeray among the "best-loved Englishmen" of her time in Weimar, recalling particularly his imposing figure, his humour, and the rapidity and adroitness with which he sketched caricatures.[13] The infatuation lasted nearly three weeks. Then Du Pre appeared, handsome and an earl's cousin as well as prosperous, and Jenny transferred her affections to him. Thackeray took these defections philosophically. Quoting Constant's *Adolphe,* "Malheur à l'homme qui, dans les premiers moments d'une liaison d'amour, ne croit pas que cette liaison doit être éternelle!" he remarked, "My two first are over, I hope I may be yet allowed a few more before I have done." [14]

In Thackeray's letters to his mother, Weimar seems as innocent as Eden before the advent of the serpent, but other evidence suggests that Thackeray was as usual exercising some censorship in his correspondence. Consider the history of the von Pappenheims.[15] Jenny's mother had married Herr von Pappenheim in 1806, and the couple lived in Weimar after their marriage. The husband was a sick man, suffering from a nervous complaint, and Diana was a young girl of great charm and attractiveness. She became the mistress of Prince Jerome Napoleon, but without separating from her husband, and when their daughter Jenny was born in 1811, Herr von Pappenheim accepted the child as his own. Later the von Pappenheims quarrelled; the husband took their son from his "sinful" mother; and when Diana returned to Weimar with her daughter in middle life, her husband was living elsewhere. Nevertheless, the von Pappenheim ladies received a warm welcome both from her family and from Grand Duchess Maria Paulowna. The easy-going morality of Weimar society readily accommodated itself to such a love-tangle; indeed, it was interested rather than shocked by irregular affairs. A generation brought up on the German romantic drama was fascinated by real-life examples of that branch of morality defined in *The Rovers* as *"the reciprocal duties of one or more husbands to one or more wives, and to the children who may happen to arise out of this complicated and endearing connexion."* [16] A shrewd observer, such as Thackeray despite his acknowledged "greenness" had already become, cannot have missed such overtones in the social atmosphere; and there are touches in the Pumpernickel chapters of *Vanity Fair* which suggest that the cruder immoralities of the city also came under his attentive scrutiny.

But Thackeray's life at Weimar was not entirely, or even largely, devoted to society. He lived first in a boarding-house kept by Mme. Melos, where there were other English lodgers, and latterly at the court cooper's. Much of his time was passed at his lodgings, smoking twenty pipes a day and studying under the tutelage of Dr. Friedrich August Wilhelm Weissenborn, the particular coach and protector of young Englishmen in Weimar. Norman Macleod wrote of Dr. Weissenborn:

> He was a cultivated scholar, and combined the strangest eccentricities of character and belief with the gentlest and most unselfish of natures. He was a confirmed valetudinarian. "My side" had become a distinct personality to him, whose demands were discussed as if it were an exacting member of his household rather than a part of his body, yet Weimar would have lost half its charm but for old Weissenborn, with his weak side, his dog Waltina, his chameleon (fruitful source of many a theory on the "Kosmos"), his collection of eggs, and innumerable oddities of mind and body.[17]

Thackeray found him "a curiosity" and described his regimen to Mrs. Carmichael-Smyth with some wonder: "He rises at six & drinks coffee at nine he eats a mash made of rice & roses, dines at twelve, & sups at six off soup." [18] Yet Thackeray soon became very fond of the Doctor, borrowed money from him, and corresponded with him long after leaving Weimar, while Weissenborn in turn was delighted by his pupil's liveliness, particularly as evidenced in his caricatures.

Under Weissenborn's direction Thackeray read Goethe, Schiller, and other romantic dramatists and poets. Thackeray granted that Goethe was "the Glory of Weimar & of Germany," [19] and in after-life he could "fancy nothing more serene, majestic, and *healthy* looking than the grand old Goethe." His first audience with the poet took place, he recalled,

> in a little ante-chamber of his private apartments, covered all round with antique casts and bas-reliefs. He was habited in a long grey or drab redingot, with a white neck-cloth and a red ribbon in his buttonhole. He kept his hands behind his back, just as in Rauch's statuette. His complexion was very bright, clear and rosy. His eyes extraordinarily dark, piercing and brilliant. I felt quite afraid before them, and recollect comparing them to the eyes of the hero of a certain romance called *Melmoth the Wanderer,* which used to alarm us boys thirty years ago; eyes of an individual who had made a bargain with a Certain Person, and at an extreme old age retained these eyes in all their awful splendour. I fancied Goethe must have been still more handsome as an old man than even in the days of his youth. His voice was very rich and sweet. He asked me questions about myself, which I answered as best I could. I recollect I was at first astonished, and then somewhat relieved, when I found he spoke French with not a good accent.[20]

If Thackeray found Goethe's personality slightly oppressive and his ideas disturbing, he felt for Schiller, on the other hand, a wholehearted admiration and love. He translated Schiller's verses, and wrote of his hero to Mrs. Carmichael-Smyth: "I am in possession of his handwriting and his veritable court-sword—and I do believe him to be after Shakespeare The Poet." [21] This sword remained in Thackeray's possession until he gave it late in life to Bayard Taylor.

Though Thackeray thought that for "deeper subjects—Metaphysics or Theology for instance, the German modern literature affords resources much greater than that of any other language," [22] and though he respected the achievements of German erudition, he confined his studies to *belles lettres* and history. In these subjects, however, he applied himself with a will, as manuscript translations of Kotzebue's *Poor Poet* and Konrad Mannert's *Kompendium der deutschen Reichsgeschichte* survive in the Pierpont Morgan Library to testify. He continued to read French and English books as well, and he conceived many projects for his own literary future. Though he was unsuccessful in placing any of his contributions in Ottilie von Goethe's multilingual magazine *Das Chaos* until after he had left Weimar,[23] this check did not prevent him from dreaming of concocting, "with a sketch-book & a note-book, & I fear still a Dictionary," a volume about Germany "wh would pay me for my trouble & wh would be a novelty in England." [24]

When Thackeray left Weimar in March, 1831, he had gained a good command of the language and considerable insight into German character and literature. He found the old-fashioned German society of this mediaeval city "simple, charitable, courteous, gentlemanlike," [25] but perhaps a bit slow and heavy. In his disparaging allusions to Karl Friedrich,[26] indeed, one may see in germ the attitudes that were later to make him the severest critic of the House of Hanover. The philosophical ferment of the time was beyond his ken, though there is some evidence that he became sufficiently acquainted with German higher criticism to sink further into the religious doubt that FitzGerald had first instilled in him. He liked the unworldliness, the nobility of much German romantic literature, and he enjoyed its excursions into "happy, harmless fable land"; but he was as thorough a John Bull as the wits of the *Anti-Jacobin* in his contempt for romantic sentiment. Except for its literary polish his parody of Goethe's *Werther* might have been written in 1831 instead of two decades later. It was Thackeray's open distaste for *"Schwärmerei,"* indeed, that led Samuel Naylor, in whom German romanticism found an enthusiastic convert, to assure Ottilie von Goethe that "Thackeray and I . . . were never 'Du und Du' with each other, you know. His mind was low-born, and his standard of wit coarse and unsuited to my habits." [27]

Thackeray called his six months at Weimar his "days of youth the most kindly and delightful." [28] They gave him a breathing-space, a period of rest in which the constant pressure to make something of himself was for a time relaxed, and in the hectic years that followed he always thought gratefully of them. Weimar was also a notably broadening experience which helped him to widen his horizon and to define his allegiances; it served to mitigate the provinciality of his English upbringing by showing him new manners and people in a sympathetic light, but it also reinforced his conviction that in a good many matters English ways were best. Thackeray was to return several times to this half year in his later work, most notably in the Kalbsbraten episodes of *The Fitz-Boodle Papers* and in the Pumpernickel chapters of *Vanity Fair,* and always in an affectionate if gently satiric spirit.

II

After some weeks at Larkbeare, Thackeray came to London late in May, 1831, to begin his legal studies. Dismissing the Church, medicine, and the army, Thackeray had settled on the law as "the best among the positive professions," but from the beginning he regarded his new pursuit with extreme distaste. "I must drudge up poor & miserable the first part of my life," he told his mother, "& just reach the pinnacle (or somewhere near it I trust), when my eyes will hardly be able to see the prospect I have been striving all my life to arrive at— These are the pleasures of the law." [1]

None the less, he applied himself at first with some determination. Entering the Middle Temple during Trinity term, he took chambers at 5 Essex Court on 3 June.[2] On the advice of one Mr. Elliot, a Devon barrister of his acquaintance, he made engagements to read with William Taprell, a special pleader whose chambers were at 1 Hare Court. Thackeray undertook to sit with Taprell from twelve to five every week-day during eight months of the year, studying the standard works on special pleading and helping his master with his current cases. He adhered to this routine more or less faithfully for some months, and he even achieved a certain adeptness at his task. But his heart was never in his work. In January, 1832, he was assuring his mother that "this lawyers preparatory education is certainly one of the most cold blooded prejudiced pieces of invention that ever a man was slave to," [3] and by April his attendance at Taprell's had become sporadic and uncertain. Within a year after commencing his legal studies, he had abandoned all pretence of pursuing them, though he continued to keep his Temple chambers as a useful London *pied à terre* and to dine in Hall occasionally.[4]

In these developments there is reason for surprise only in the persistence that Thackeray initially displayed in pursuing his legal training. The Inns of Court in his day offered a bewildering aspect to the novice. They were, indeed, "Clubs of Court," [5] organized for the convenience of the benchers. There were no lectures or examinations. Students were merely provided at an inconvenient hour with dinners for which they paid substantial fees. Their real instruction was obtained by private treaty with a working conveyancer, equity draftsman, or special pleader. Of the three, the special pleader in some ways offered the most interesting work.

> The documents to be prepared were usually short [writes Walter Bagehot], so that the pupil got a good variety. They were all based on the mistakes of life, and each showed how easily business went wrong, and how difficult it was to keep it right. . . . And the mode of tuition was not cold and formal. It consisted in discussing with your fellow-pupils and your teacher the actual points as they turn upon actual living cases.[6]

So we find Thackeray writing to Edward FitzGerald:

> Here am I on my high stool with an action agst Noah Thornley for debauching Martha Dewsnap whereby she became big & sick with child & whereby her father lost the services of her his daughter & servant so that you see Law is not altogether so dry a study as you w^{d} imagine it to be.[7]

But in this system of training there was a fatal want of connexion. No "central doctrine," binding together disparate individual instances, was supplied. A brilliant but impatient young man like Thackeray could have little stomach for

> Mastering the lawless science of our law,
> That codeless myriad of precedent,
> That wilderness of single instances; [8]

and he inevitably tired of what seemed to him a wearisome and pointless routine.

To many visitors the Temple presented a scene quite as dismal as the studies pursued there, but for Thackeray the "brawling courts and dusty purlieus of the law" had an inexhaustible interest, not only because of the curious human beings that he found in them, but also because of their historical associations. Few writers on the Inns of Court have neglected to quote the classic passage which Thackeray devotes to their peculiar charm in *Pendennis:*

those venerable Inns which have the Lamb and Flag and the Winged Horse for their ensigns, have attractions for persons who inhabit them, and a share of rough comforts and freedom, which men always remember with pleasure. I don't know whether the student of law permits himself the refreshment of enthusiasm, or indulges in poetical reminiscences as he passes by historical chambers and says, 'Yonder Eldon lived—upon this site Coke mused upon Lyttleton—here Chitty toiled—here Barnwell and Alderson joined in their famous labours —here Byles composed his great work upon bills, and Smith compiled his immortal leading cases—here Gustavus still toils, with Solomon to aid him': but the man of letters can't but love the place which has been inhabited by so many of his brethren, or peopled by their creations as real to us at this day as the authors whose children they were—and Sir Roger de Coverley walking in the Temple Garden, and discoursing with Mr. Spectator about the beauties in hoops and patches who are sauntering over the grass, is just as lively a figure to me as old Samuel Johnson rolling through the fog with the Scotch gentleman at his heels on their way to Dr. Goldsmith's chambers in Brick Court; or Harry Fielding, with inked ruffles and a wet towel round his head, dashing off articles at midnight for the *Covent Garden Journal,* while the printer's boy is asleep in the passage.[9]

Thus, if Thackeray quickly gave up any serious intention of becoming a practising barrister,[10] he yet continued to find life in the Middle Temple congenial enough. For him and many like him the Inns of Court provided a setting for an existence of gentlemanly idleness. They housed many conscientious and serious students, but they also provided a base of operations from which young blades could explore the amusements of London. Thackeray soon came to belong to the latter group. "His acquaintance," like Philip Firmin's, "lay amongst the Temple Bohemians." [11]

III

It takes time to find the road even to Bohemia, however, and Thackeray's first months in the Temple were a lonely period for a young man of his sociable nature. Luckily he had Edward FitzGerald to help him through it. On the rare occasions when FitzGerald was able to visit him in London, Thackeray was perfectly content. The two roamed the streets, attended the opening of each new play, patronized the "cigar Divans" to read the current periodicals, explored the popular taverns and restaurants, and talked with entire unrestraint about every topic under the sun. When they had to part, "Ned" and "Willy" continued their conversation through the post, so voluminously, indeed, that 1831 henceforth stood out in FitzGerald's mind for its "immortal summer of foolscap." [1] Only a small part of the correspondence that they exchanged has survived. Thackeray was always careless about keeping the letters that he received, and after *Vanity Fair* had made his friend famous, FitzGerald "burned some 50 letters of his written near 20 years ago," [2] his reason being Thackeray's "repeated, and magnanimously blind over-estimate of myself." [3] "I was really ashamed of their kindness," he remarked of "those old foolscap letters." [4] That Thackeray's affection was fully returned may be seen from some verses that FitzGerald addressed to him in October, 1831. They begin:

I cared not for life: for true friend I had none
I had heard 'twas a blessing not under the sun:
Some figures called friends, hollow, proud, or cold-hearted
Came to me like shadows—like shadows departed:
But a day came that turned all my sorrow to glee
When first I saw Willy, and Willy saw me!

The thought of my Willy is always a cheerer;
My wine has new flavour—the fire burns clearer:
The sun ever shines—I am pleased with all things—
And this crazy old world seems to go with new springs;—
And when we're together, (Oh! soon may it be!)
The world may go kissing of comets for me! [5]

For many years FitzGerald remained Thackeray's closest friend. Numerous were the days that they passed together, entirely "happy & idle." Even when circumstances kept them apart in later life, they continued to be united in spirit by remembrance of "the noble & brotherly love" [6] which they had felt for each other as young men.

When FitzGerald left him alone in London, Thackeray had one great resource. Though he wrote to his friend that "when I am alone & thinking about you I get quite wretched," [7] he could always recruit his spirits by a visit to the theatre, for which he had a lifelong passion. "Like all good and unspoiled souls," Herman Merivale relates, "he loved 'the play.' Asking a listless friend one day if he liked it, he got the usual answer, 'Ye-es—I like a good play.' 'Oh! get out,' said Thackeray, 'I said *the* play; you don't even understand what I mean.' " [8] What Thackeray meant may be seen in a letter that he wrote to FitzGerald during a holiday at Larkbeare in the autumn of 1831:

> How I long for the sight of a dear green curtain again—after going 3 times a week to the play for a year one misses it so, O the delight of seeing the baize slowly ascending—the spangled shoes wh first appear then as it gradually Draws up legs stomachs heads till finally it ends in all the glories of a party of 'musqueteers' drinking—a dance—an inn with an infinity of bells jingling or a couple of gay dogs in cocked hats with pieces of silk dangling out of their pockets for handkerchiefs—Yet another month. & all this paradise will be in my reach—really London is to me only the place where the Theatres are.[9]

When Thackeray returned to London, he made up for lost time by seeing all the current attractions twice, and the approach of Twelfth-night brought from him the exclamation, "in a few days come the Pantomimes huzza." [10]

If there was nothing new on the boards, Thackeray turned to novel-reading. Though he did not neglect his study of German light literature, and though he read what French novels came his way, he satisfied his appetite chiefly with English fiction of the past twenty years. Bulwer's *Eugene Aram* and *Pelham,* Maria Edgeworth's *Harrington* and *Tales of Fashionable Life,* Susan Ferrier's *Destiny,* John Galt's *Stanley Buxton,* Thomas Hope's *Anastasius,* Captain Marryat's *The King's Own* and *Newton*

Forster, William Pitt Scargill's *Rank and Talent,* and Scott's *Castle Dangerous* and *Quentin Durward* were a few among the many books that he devoured. He read each with a critical eye and passed judgment upon it. Of *Eugene Aram* he remarked, "The book is in fact humbug, when my novel is written it will be something better I trust." [11] But for some time yet his ambition to make himself a writer was to be no more than an undisciplined urge.

The Carmichael-Smyths did what they could to provide Thackeray with society; and relatives, Devon neighbours passing the season in London, and retired Anglo-Indian intimates all were persuaded to proffer their hospitality. If Thackeray had been content with a constant round of dinners in staid, middle-class households, his needs would have been readily satisfied. And he did take pleasure in visiting certain of these homes. There was that of his uncle, the Reverend Francis Thackeray, for example, a man of learning, integrity, and blameless life. He was the author of a *History of William Pitt,* published in 1827, which had been the occasion of one of Macaulay's finest contributions to the *Edinburgh Review;* and from him Thackeray learned much about family annals in particular and about eighteenth-century history in general. As one of the executors of his brother Richmond's will, Francis felt responsible for his nephew's welfare; and though Thackeray was fond of him, he sometimes found his attentions excessive. "Uncle F[k] . . . is very kind," Thackeray told his mother early in 1832, "but asks me to dinner too often—three times a week." [12] That he was received very cordially in the home of the famous actor Charles Kemble is testified by the amusing note of apology for a missed engagement reproduced as Plate V.[13] Thackeray was also made welcome by the Charles Bullers, an eccentric, but amiable and enlightened family known to the Carmichael-Smyths in Calcutta. Harriet Martineau supplies a piquant picture of one of their parties.

> Mrs. Buller did not excel in tact, and her party was singularly arranged at the dinner table, I was placed at the bottom of the table, at its square end, with an empty chair on the one hand, and Mr. Buller on the other,—he being so excessively deaf that no trumpet was of

much use to him. There we sat with our trumpets [Miss Martineau was also deaf],—an empty chair on the one hand, and on the other, Mr. J. S. Mill, whose singularly feeble voice cut us off from conversation in that direction. As if to make another pair, Mrs. Buller placed on either side of her a gentleman with a flattened nose,—Mr. Thackeray on her right, and her son Charles on the left.[14]

Thackeray became a close friend of the two Buller sons, but he could regard the society offered by the older generation with only the very mildest interest. Long-expected one-and-twenty inevitably sought livelier ways of showing the spirit of an heir.

IV

Leisure-class bachelor life in London, though soberer than in the 1820s, still took its pattern from the dandies of the day, a group intent, in Mrs. Gore's phrase, "on promoting the greatest happiness of the smallest number." [1] Their grand amusement was gambling; and whether in sumptuous rooms at Crockford's, on the turf, by the cockpit, or at meetings of the "Fancy," the pleasure of the occasion came from the wagers laid. Profligacy they took for granted. "Madam, I never make love," Quin said to a pretty glove-maker; "I always buy it ready made." [2] Since the dandies assumed that they were entitled to the best of everything a great city could provide, no stigma attached to owing money, as long as "debts of honor" were promptly paid. When quarrels arose from their exercise of general egoism, recourse was had to a duel if the enemy was a social equal, to a horsewhip if he was not.[3]

Thackeray had no entrée into the world of d'Orsay and Lord Chesterfield. His people were mere country gentry, his fortune was moderate, and his talents were as yet unformed and unproductive. But like many young men of the upper middle class enjoying entire freedom in London while ostensibly acquiring professional training, he was seduced by the glamour of fashionable life into an inept and uneasy imitation of it. A young aristocrat had no reason to be disturbed if his frivolous existence seemed to lead to nothing. Like the lilies of the field, he toiled not, neither did he spin; it was his proper role to live in decorative idleness; his niche in the world was already secure. For Thackeray, who had his way to make, no pattern could have been less appropriate.

Yet by 1832 Thackeray had largely drifted away from friends like FitzGerald and from the sober households to which his anxious parents had commended him. He had fallen in with

> . . . a compaignye
> Of yonge folke that haunteden folie,

and he passed most of his time with would-be dandies who frittered away their days in idleness and dissipation. On most of these cronies the curtains of time have mercifully fallen for ever, but they part briefly to disclose one representative figure. Henry Kemble, younger son of the actor Charles Kemble, was nineteen when Thackeray first came to know him through FitzGerald in the autumn of 1831.[4] The one mediocrity in a brilliant family, he was remarkable only for his startling good looks. He had been spoilt from the first by a doting mother, and his character was fixed at an early age. "When he was quite a child and was asked what profession he intended to embrace," his sister Fanny relates, "he replied that he would be *'a gentleman and wear leather breeches.'* "[5] To this resolve he remained faithful. Having managed to get through Westminster School, he refused to go to Cambridge because the studies pursued there were too strenuous. He established himself instead in London, haunting the theatres, getting himself involved in one "love scrape" after another, and running up a bill at his tailor's, while his fond father and sister racked their brains to provide for him. The Kembles had suffered severe financial reverses, but at length Fanny contrived to buy her brother an army commission with the money that John Murray had given her for her tragedy *Francis the First*. She hoped fervently that he would soon be called to service with his regiment. "Henry is too young and handsome to be doing nothing but lounging about the streets of London," she wrote in December, 1831, "and even if he should be ordered to the Indies it is something to feel that he is no longer aimless and objectless in life—a mere squanderer of time, without interest, stake, or duty in this existence." [6] But the expected call did not come until spring, and it was with this "dear fellow" [7] and others like him that Thackeray passed his time in 1832.

A typical evening would begin innocently enough at one of the taverns of the period. Thackeray's haunts ranged from the sumptuous Sabloniere to the low Spotted Dog, but the most interesting of them all was the Cider Cellars at 20 Maiden Lane, which had included among its earlier patrons such dignitaries as Professor Porson and Dr. Raine, Master of Charterhouse. "Sham cyder casks, ranged against the walls, gave the place its name," Henry Vizetelly relates, "and at the tables, filling the centre of the room, some good glee singers carolled, whilst the guests supped off devilled kidneys and welsh rabbits, accompanied by beakers of unsophisticated stout, with endless 'goes' of something hot and strong to follow." [8] At the Cider Cellars Thackeray acquired his fondness for what he was later to describe as "the British Brandy-and-Water School of Song." [9] In the first chapter of *The Newcomes* he drew a famous picture of this establishment as it was in the early 1830s,[10] not omitting his acquaintance Sloman, the little Jewish *improvisatore,* a picture which amply confirms Vizetelly's comment that by the time "the small hours of the morning were reached, and guests and singers had imbibed more than was good for them, the songs became decidedly equivocal in character." [11]

If the songs sung at the Cider Cellars aroused appetites to which that house of entertainment did not cater, they could easily be satisfied elsewhere.

> The streets at night [writes Serjeant Ballantine of the London of this period], exhibited scenes of disorder and unchecked profligacy. The south end of Regent Street, called the Quadrant, was a covered way, and nearly every other house was devoted to open and public gambling. The same may be said of Leicester Square. There was no limitation as to the hours of closing places of entertainment, and in many of these were exhibited the coarsest description of vice.[12]

Not so many years later it was customary in the licensed conversation that followed the weekly *Punch* dinners to refer to the Haymarket as the "A. Market." [13]

That Thackeray saw a good deal of this aspect of London life is sufficiently evident from the diary that he kept in 1832. He may be there observed, for example, recoiling from its coarser manifestations.

Maginn [he wrote on 17 June 1832] . . . took me to a common brothel where I left him, very much disgusted & sickened to see a clever & good man disgrace himself in that way. . . . Thank God that idle & vicious as I am, I have no taste for scenes such as that of last night—There was an old bawd & a young whore both of them with child—The old woman seemed au reste a good natured beast enough with a countenance almost amiable—The young one was very repulsive in manner & face—Came home sickened & fell asleep instead of going to Kembles.[14]

Yet there are hints in his diary that he was not always so repelled.[15] Moreover, a number of passages were cut from this document by Lady Ritchie, and Thackeray's surviving letters to FitzGerald, in which he also spoke with entire freedom, were carefully pruned by their recipient. We know from many sources that Thackeray liked to talk and write bawdy to congenial company; this habit alone may account for the censorship exercised by his daughter and his friend. But there is clearly another explanation. Henry Silver notes that one evening in 1861 Thackeray was forced to leave the *Punch* table "in pain—had it 30 years he says." It is not explained what his trouble was, but from the context one assumes that it was his stricture of the urethra. Certainly by 1843 he was referring to this condition as his "old complaint." [16]

In any event, gambling was Thackeray's besetting vice, and gambling for him meant, not the turf, the cockpit, or the ring, but cards and dice. In December of 1831 he persuaded Francis Thackeray and Robert Langslow to sell out enough stock to enable him to cover a loss at play of one hundred guineas.[17] If his guardians' restraint was removed when he came of age the following year, he was reminded of the disastrous consequences of his mania by the necessity of settling the gambling debt of £1,500 which he had contracted as an undergraduate.[18] Yet even this painful transaction did not prevent him from frequenting the "hells" of Regent's Quadrant and the private games of his Temple acquaintances throughout 1832 and 1833.[19] Most of his losses were small, but in February of the latter year he was relieved of £668 in one engagement.[20] He derived little pleasure from his protracted folly, and because of it his diary is filled with self-reproaches. But however earnestly he might assure himself that he had visited Regent's Quadrant *"for the last time, so help me God";* [21] however candidly he might describe a long encounter at chicken hazard with casual visitors to Essex Court as "one of the most disgraceful days I ever spent"; [22] until he lost his fortune, he was totally unable to overcome his compulsion to gamble. Even then the old urge remained. He tells, for example, of his response a few years later on learning that a friend to whom he had lent a few francs had turned it into a small fortune in a Parisian hell: "The passion of envy entered my soul: . . . I hated Attwood for *cheating* me out of all this wealth." [23] And some of the most eloquent passages in the books of his maturity deal with the compelling attraction that gambling has for its devotees.[24]

V

But the story of Thackeray's life in 1832 and 1833 need not be entirely a chronicle of idleness and dissipation. He was profoundly interested in the events that led up to the passage of the great Reform Bill in the spring of 1832. Thackeray's sympathies were divided during this critical period of English history. His personal allegiance was to the Tory leader, the Duke of Wellington, and he noted indignantly in his diary the popular demonstrations against this "hero." [1] But seeing clearly at the same time how close the country was to violence, he thought the Whigs were right in urging the necessity of reform, and even on one occasion went canvassing for them.[2] His loyalty remained with the upper class, however; and when he was convinced at a critical moment in May that the House of Commons would soon be replaced by a revolutionary "house of delegates," he "bought a big stick wherewithal to resist all parties in case of attack." [3]

After the Reform Bill became law in June, Thackeray allowed Charles and Arthur Buller to persuade him to join in the former's campaign to get himself returned from Liskeard to the reformed Parliament. Thackeray passed two exciting weeks in Cornwall helping Buller to defeat his wealthy Tory antagonist, Lord Eliot; but he could not bring himself to regard this enterprise with entire seriousness.

> We canvassed for Charles very assiduously & successfully [Thackeray wrote to FitzGerald] pledging him to reforms in politicks & religion of wh we knew nothing ourselves. but nevertheless the farmers were highly impressed with our sagacity & eloquence. Then we published addresses in the name of Charles Buller promising to lessen taxes & provide for the agricultural and commercial interests, & deprecating that infamous traffic, wh at present legalizes the misery of the West Indian slave—Then we wrote songs awfully satirical songs . . . in fact except—"The other day to our town a captain of dragoons came down" &c I know nothing in the language so severe.[4]

None the less, "Parliamentary visions" with a characteristic class bias began to form in Thackeray's head. He told himself that what Parliament needed was a young "Tory knight with his country as his mistress," who would "eternally descant on old times & old glories" and "enlist all the romance of the nation on his side." [5] This program does not reveal much practical political sense, despite its anticipations of Young England; and, indeed, Thackeray was all his life to remain an amateur in political matters. Yet his Cornish experiences at least implanted in him a seed of political ambition which flowered unexpectedly many years later.

Thackeray turned twenty-one on 18 July 1832. "Here is the day for wh I have been panting so long," he wrote in his diary. "I am a man now & must deal with men." [6] Some weeks earlier he had promised his mother that from this time forth he would "take a regular monthly income wh I will never exceed." [7] But there clearly had to be a celebration first, and Thackeray accordingly set off for France at the end of the month. By this time an "old Paris hand," he settled down quickly to a routine that did not differ greatly from his life in London. He read widely in French literature, visited the theatres and art galleries, and frequented the best restaurants. There were plenty of young English idlers to keep him company in these and less innocent amusements. Thackeray gambled even more frequently than at home; his thoughts ran often on "debauchery & its consequences"; [8] and by the end of September he was noting that he did not "feel inclined to mention the expences or the occurrences of these days." [9] Revulsion and repentance followed as usual, and late in November Thackeray returned to his Essex Court chambers, resolved, so he told FitzGerald, to become a model "young gentleman of small fortune; sought by my acquaintance, ⟨hon⟩oured by my tradesmen, & beloved by the poor,—so that mothers when they know me & my character shall prefer me to spendthrifts even tho' they are rich, & shall say to their daughters: better is economy with 500 a year than extravagance with five thousand." [10]

A model young gentleman clearly needed some regular employment. Hence Thackeray cast about for a pursuit in which working capital might be offered in place of special training. By January of 1833 he had associated himself with a bill-discounting firm in Birchin Lane. Thackeray must have acquired a considerable knowledge of the London half-world from this connexion. But concerning the whole society of dandies down on their luck, shady practitioners in dubious enterprises, agents, bailiffs, and money-lenders which must have revealed itself to him, we have only the laconic record of an account-book kept during the early months of 1833.[11] On the surface the enterprise seemed promising enough, since short-term bills were discounted at what amounted to an annual interest rate of 20 to 40 per cent. But in practice there proved to be complications, and after one of his bills was protested in March, Thackeray extricated himself from the undertaking as rapidly as he could. In later life any reference to this venture, which had been both usurious and unsuccessful, touched Thackeray on the raw. When a colleague on the staff of *Fraser's Magazine* referred in 1843 to a "Bill Crackaway," who might be presumed to know all about shady financial transactions because of his part in "the business of a bill-broker in the City," [12] Thackeray protested vigorously to the editor.[13] Yet the rumour persisted, and as late as 1854 an allusion by a jealous hack named William North to "that admired old ex-note-shaver" Thackeray is recorded.[14]

Thackeray's next investment was in a weekly paper. If journalism was in closer harmony with Thackeray's tastes than bill-discounting, it was at this time hardly more respectable.[15] Even so, urged on by a dubious friend named Gunnell, Thackeray had given some thought to buying a paper in the spring of 1832. He had not been able to raise the capital needed for this enterprise, but the negotiations connected with it made him acquainted with Dr. William Maginn, the most brilliant and erudite London pressman of the day. The two quickly became friends, and in the weeks that followed their meeting, Maginn showed Thackeray "the mysteries of printing & writing leading articles" and gave him much other useful information about London journalism. Thackeray grew eager to try his own hand at these employments, though he did not care for the "low literary men" like F. W. N. ("Alphabet") Bayley with whom he found himself associating.[16] After Thackeray came into his fortune, Maginn borrowed £500 from him, for "deck-clearing" (according to Francis Sylvester Mahony),[17] and afterwards gave him some assistance in editing the obscure twopenny paper called the *National Standard* which he had purchased from Bayley.

The National Standard and Journal of Literature, Science, Music, Theatricals and the Fine Arts, to give this publication its imposing full title, had commenced publication on 1 January 1833. On 11 May, Thackeray announced Bayley's withdrawal as editor and proprietor. "We have got free of the Old Bailey, and changed the Governor," was his pleasant way of putting the matter. With disarming candour he granted that publishers did not regard the paper as sufficiently important to warrant their sending "early copies" to its editor, but he urged that this circumstance was really an advantage, because it ensured critical independence. Readers would discover, he concluded, that "the sort of Paper we shall give them for twopence is not to be despised." [18] Though Thackeray boasted of "the assistance of a host of literary talent," he and his subeditor James Hume seem to have been responsible for most of the paper's contents, particularly in its later months. Their task was not as arduous as it might at first glance appear. Despite Thackeray's brave opening pronouncement, much of the *National Standard's* contents was puffery and scissors-and-paste work. Otherwise, Thackeray could remark with Mr. Batchelor of *Lovel the Widower,* speaking of his paper the *Museum:*

I dare say I gave myself airs as editor of that confounded *Museum,* and proposed to educate the public taste, to diffuse morality and sound literature throughout the nation, and to pocket a liberal salary in return for my services. . . . I dare say I wrote satirical articles, in which I piqued myself upon the fineness of my wit, and criticisms, got up for the nonce, out of encyclopaedias and biographical dictionaries; so that I would be actually astounded at my own knowledge. I dare say I made a gaby of myself to the world.[19]

The *National Standard* seemed at first to be "growing in repute"; yet Thackeray knew in his heart that it was "poor stuff"; [20] and though he struggled manfully to make something of it, he was on the verge of giving it up by November, and was glad to terminate its publication the following February.

Unsuccessful as it was, this excursion into journalism had its value to Thackeray. Through his paper he came to know the London literary scene from the inside. The rough-and-ready hack writers of the day may have regarded this ingenuous, gentlemanly amateur with private amusement. They may not have been above taking financial advantage of his "greenness." But they liked him and came to regard him as one of themselves. As late as January, 1835, though Thackeray had by that time been concerning himself with painting rather than writing for nearly a year, the "Fraserians" saw fit to include him in their group portrait by Daniel Maclise.[21] Moreover, through long practice Thackeray was gaining facility in periodical writing. In November, 1833, indeed, he was offered the post of Madrid correspondent of the London *Standard* at £300 a year.[22] In a word, he had at last found an occupation in which he could make his way, even if he was not yet inclined to pursue it.

VI

Until the last months of 1833 Thackeray was a young gentleman of substantial prospects, whose failure to find gainful employment might be regretted but could hardly be regarded as disastrous. It will be remembered that Richmond Thackeray had left an estate worth about £17,000 at his death in 1815.[1] The income from this estate was encumbered by various annuities, but Thackeray was residuary legatee to all other annuitants. Moreover, the Carmichael-Smyths had used only a part of the substantial sum paid to them each year for Thackeray's education and upbringing (£200 until Mrs. Thackeray's remarriage, £425 thereafter); and the residue, which had been allowed to accumulate at compound interest, was Thackeray's by the terms of his father's will when he reached twenty-one. This appears to have been the source of the £4,000 administered by his uncle Francis Thackeray and his cousin Robert Langslow, which Thackeray expected to receive in the summer of 1832.[2] Altogether Thackeray had warrant to think of himself, even after he had paid his debts, as worth between £15,000 and £20,000.

Yet by late December, 1833, Thackeray was ruefully finding reason to "thank heaven for making me poor." [3] Though the nature of the catastrophe that overtook him is not altogether clear, it seems reasonable to suppose that the bulk of Richmond Thackeray's estate was lost in the collapse of the great Indian agency-houses that took place at this period. The cycle began with the failure of Palmer and Company for £5,000,000 in 1830, and ended with the failure of Cruttenden and Company for £1,350,000, in 1834.[4] Both Thackeray and Major Carmichael-Smyth were particularly interested in Cruttenden and Company,[5] and it may have been the Major's obstinate adherence to this firm, like the loyalty of Colonel Newcome to the Bundelcund Bank in *The Newcomes,* which brought Thackeray to disaster. A hint in a letter to his mother suggests that the sum which he lost totalled £11,325.[6] Certainly there is real bitterness in Thackeray's reference in *Vanity Fair* to "the great Calcutta house of Fogle, Fake, and Cracksman," which "failed for a million, and plunged half the Indian public into misery and ruin." [7]

A passage in a draft of a letter from Thackeray to Charles Carmichael relates how he met the difficulties into which he was thrown:

> At the time when my own embarassments occurred I sold out all my funded property in this country: received a sum of money from my Grandmother as a gift: and Borrowed a farther sum from father to set me free. My estate in India was remitted to England. There was more than sufficient to repay my father and replace the stock from wh Mrs Blechynden derived her annuity.

His estate, Thackeray continues, amounted "to nearly £7000. This sum wh was *mine*—in the hands of my mother as guardian—was saddled with a further annuity to her." [8] Now the annuity owed to Mrs. Carmichael-Smyth was £225, that to Thackeray's natural sister Mrs. Blechynden, £52,[9] and after these demands were satisfied, there was clearly little income left for Thackeray himself. By July, 1835, we accordingly find him living on quarterly payments of £25 from Francis Thackeray, beyond which he had no resource except to dip into his "poor little capital." [10]

Yet, as has been noted, Thackeray was inclined to "thank heaven for making me poor." This apparent paradox is not difficult to explain. Connop Thirlwall observed of the England of this period: "Society possesses two or three strong, stiff frames, in which all persons of liberal education who need or desire a fixed place and specific designation must consent to be set." [11] While he possessed a substantial fortune, Thackeray was expected to seek a niche within these frames. He tried public school, the university, and the law; and he was constantly ill at ease, because these institutions clashed both with his tastes and his temperament. Rebelling, he tried work with which English gentlemen were not expected to concern themselves; but he was still uneasy because he seemed to his parents, his friends, and even to himself, to be failing in his plain duty. What is the respectable Englishman's hell? "The terror of 'Not succeeding,' " Sauerteig was to reply a few years later, "of not making money, fame, or some other figure in the world." [12]

No wonder, then, that Thackeray's letters and diary of 1831 to 1833 are filled with self-reproach. He constantly deplored his idleness and irresolution, his dissipations and lavish expenditures. On the eve of his twentieth birthday he confided to FitzGerald: "I cannot find a single day in the course of my life which has been properly employed." [13] Six months later he told his mother: "I have kept a Journal now for six weeks . . . this is the only piece of resolution I ever atchieved." [14] And in April, 1832, he noted in his diary: "Was not at Taprell's, & have not read a syllable of anything for 3 days. I must mend, or else I shall be poor idle & wicked most likely in a couple more years." [15] Nor did abandoning law for journalism help matters; his state of mind remained hopeless and unproductive. We can imagine Thackeray saying to himself: "Unstable as water, thou shalt not excell."

What might easily have happened to him if he had not been forced to give up the aimless, idle life that he was leading, and thus to arrest the paralysis of will and the atrophy of moral feeling that threatened him, may be suggested by a brief view of the later history of his friend Henry Kemble. As a boy Kemble had wished to be a sailor, and when maternal fondness had denied him this career, he became indifferent to what happened to him. "They may put me at a plough-tail," he said, "if they like." [16] We have noted his existence as a gentlemanly idler until his sister Fanny made a soldier of him. After he joined his regiment in 1832, his military duties for some years kept him out of England. By 1841, however, he had returned to London, "very handsome . . . , but very luxurious and selfish, and without a penny to his name." Seeking a rich wife, in order that he might "live at his ease and pursue his pleasures," he laid siege to Thackeray's distant relative Mary Ann Thackeray, "a dull, plain, commonplace girl" but heiress and only daughter of the elderly, ailing, and wealthy George Thackeray, Provost of King's College, Cambridge. Mary Ann Thackeray fell passionately in love with Kemble, but he begged off from the match when her father told him that he would leave his money elsewhere if Kemble married his daughter. More than ten years later, Kemble again returned to England, "still a handsome, selfish, impecunious soldier." George Thackeray had died in the interval; and Miss Thackeray was worth £6,000 a year. But when Kemble again proposed to her, she refused him; his "selfishness had over-reached itself and this was the retribution of time." [17] Thackeray encountered his old friend not long thereafter. "Henry Kemble is better off than some imbeciles," he wrote to Mrs. Proctor. "He is quite happy, tells immense long bow stories all day—now is the bravest man, the handsomest the best rider, the most fortunate in finding favor with your charming sex. Ha—and he fancies himself staying at a gentleman's country seat: and is happy." [18] A wasted life; and Thackeray's might have turned out no better if he had persisted on the path that he was following before he lost his fortune, a path strewn with "dead skulls and bones of men whose life had gone astray."

But in adversity, Thackeray found consolation and reassurance not granted him in prosperity. We have seen how his grandmother and stepfather came to his aid. Later he had to appeal to Francis Thackeray, who had become responsible through the misconduct of Robert Langslow for somewhat more than £700, the remaining portion of the £4,000 held jointly by the two for Thackeray.[19] His uncle replied on 2 July 1834:

Y^r^ letter has come upon me like a thunderstroke. How is it possible you can have incur'd such ruin? My grief at y^r^ losses in increas'd by the consideration that I sh^d^ be in the least degree concern'd in withholding from you any part of y^r^ property.

Mr Langslow's infamous conduct having occasion'd an utter breach between us I have had no communication with him excepting on subjects connected with the claims of George & Richmond Shakespear, & suppos'd that y^r^ own claim had been satisfactorily adjusted.

With respect to myself—I have sustain'd such very heavy losses both thro' him & thro' other channels that it is utterly impossible for me *at once* to pay the sum due to you by Mr Langslow. But everything, I possibly can, I will do—On the 20th instant I will pay you £150; and endeavour (by augmenting our Income by taking a few pupils—a mode to w'h I resort with the greatest unwillingness, as my own health & that of my wife has been extremely impair'd by illness) to pay you the same sum in July 1835, & so on every following July until the whole be defray'd either by Mr Langslow or myself—

If this does not satisfy you—you must proceed by Law as you please—for I have nothing else to offer but a body worn down by grief, pain & anxiety— [20]

Such a letter explains why Thackeray many years later apostrophized "saintly Francis, lying at rest under the turf." [21] For Thackeray, sobered and made sensitive by misfortune, the affection and loyalty that he experienced from his relatives became crucial in defining his allegiances; and around these allegiances the firm standards by which he was to judge character and conduct in maturity began to form.

7

Golden Time

I

BY THE SUMMER OF 1833 Thackeray was thinking of turning artist.[1] Friends and casual acquaintances alike praised his facility in drawing, and he had earned some small reward from London print-sellers for caricatures that he had sketched.[2] "At twenty you know," he later reminded his mother, "we all thought I was a genius at drawing." [3] For a young man of Thackeray's class, the choice of this career was not an easy one, for the artist's social position was still very inferior. "He is *but* a landscape-painter," Tennyson sings in "The Lord of Burleigh," unconscious of any condescension; and Major Pendennis exclaims, upon learning that Colonel Newcome is going to make his son a painter: "I don't know what the dooce the world is coming to. An artist! By gad, in my time a fellow would as soon have thought of making his son a hairdresser, or a pastry-cook, by gad!" [4] In announcing his decision to his mother, Thackeray was careful to specify that he was embarking upon his new profession as "an independent man who is not obliged to look to his brush for his livelihood." Yet even so he had to suffer slights and snubs that put him on the defensive. Consequently he assured his mother that in Paris an artist was "by far a more distinguished personage than a lawyer & a great deal more so than a clergyman." [5] And when business brought him to London, he joined the Garrick Club on 22 June primarily to enjoy the company "of artistes of all kinds, & gentlemen who drop their absurd English aristocratical notions." [6] By October, at any rate, he was happily at work in a Parisian *atelier*.

Then came the collapse of Thackeray's fortune, which has already been described. He returned to London, and by December he was "comfortably installed" in the Carmichael-Smyths' new residence at 18 Albion Street (bought in anticipation of a removal from Larkbeare which did not take place until 1835), where he much liked his "little study, & airy bed-room." [7] He lived there until September, 1834, and after the *National Standard* ceased publication, he seems to have devoted most of his time to the study of painting. The scenes in Mr. Gandish's school of art in Chapters 17 and 18 of *The Newcomes* were no doubt sketched with more or less fidelity from Thackeray's recollections of these months. They appear to describe the establishment at the corner of Charlotte and Streatham Streets in Bloomsbury where Henry Sass offered training to young artists who wished to prepare themselves for the schools of the Royal Academy.[8]

Sass was a curious figure.[9] As a young man he had exhibited elaborate classical and historical paintings without success. When the demands of a numerous family forced him to devote himself to teaching, he remained faithful to "High Art" and sought to inculcate a reverence for it in his pupils. On the wall of his gallery hung the motto: "Those models which have passed through the approbation of ages are intended for your imitation, and not your criticism." [10] His students were first set to copying "outlines from the antique, beginning with Juno's eye and ending with Apollo—hands, feet, mouths, faces, in various positions, all in severely correct outline"; then "a huge white plaster ball standing on a pedestal"; and finally "a gigantic bunch of plaster grapes." [11] Only when Sass regarded a pupil as perfect in these exercises was he allowed to proceed to the entire figure.

Though Sass was of a kindly nature, his disappointment as a painter preyed upon his mind and made him touchy and irritable. In his fits of anger, which irreverent pupils found it amusing to encourage, he quickly grew ungrammatical and incoherent. So unsettled and peculiar did his conduct become in his last years that he had to give up his school and live in retirement. Yet in his prime he was an excellent teacher; his students included Millais and Frith; and he numbered among his faithful friends Constable, Etty, Landseer, Martin, Turner, and Wilkie, whom his pupils met at the *conversazioni* held by Mrs. Sass.

During this period of apprenticeship, Thackeray gained the friendship of several rising artists of the day. He knew Daniel Maclise well. His already noted inclusion in Maclise's 1835 group-portrait of the "Fraserians," indeed, should be regarded as a testimony to his friendship with the artist and Maginn rather than to his services to *Fraser's Magazine*. He also knew George Cattermole and John Frederick Lewis, but the artists of whom he felt fondest were Frank Stone and George Cruikshank. After he was introduced to Stone in Maclise's studio, he used to visit his irregular *ménage* [12] and go walking with him in Kensington Gardens.[13] Cruikshank, with whom Maginn had made him acquainted, served as Thackeray's teacher for a time,[14] and the two were soon on the easiest possible terms.

II

Throughout these months Thackeray was eager to return to Paris. Life in London seemed intolerably dismal to him, when he recalled the carefree days passed in his Parisian *atelier* in 1833.[1] He was persuaded, moreover, that the French capital provided the budding artist with his natural setting.

> The painter's trade, in France, is a very good one [he wrote in *The Paris Sketch Book*]; better appreciated, better understood, and . . . far better paid than with us. There are a dozen excellent schools in which a lad may enter here, and, under the eye of a practised master, learn the apprenticeship of his art at an expense of about ten pounds a-year. In England there is no school except the Academy, unless the student can afford to pay a very large sum, and place himself under

the tuition of some particular artist. Here, a young man, for his ten pounds, has all sorts of accessory instruction, models, &c.; and has further, and for nothing, numberless incitements to study his profession which are not to be found in England; the streets are filled with picture-shops, the people themselves are pictures walking about; the churches, theatres, eating-houses, concert-rooms, are covered with pictures; Nature itself is inclined more kindly to him, for the sky is a thousand times more bright and beautiful, and the sun shines for the greater part of the year.[2]

Thackeray's opportunity to secure these benefits for himself came in September, 1834, when the restless Mrs. Butler decided to settle for a time in Paris. Thackeray went with her as companion and general factotum, and after a month at a boarding-house, the two moved to "very pretty furnished rooms in the Rue de Provence. Nº 22." He lived with his grandmother at this address, and later at 68 Grande Rue de Chaillot, until the following June. His position was anything but a sinecure, however, for the old lady's uncertain temper found its vent on the nearest victim; and Thackeray more than once describes himself as "writhing under the stripes of her satire, & the public expression of her wrath." [3]

Nevertheless, this was, at least initially, a happy period for Thackeray. Freed from the restraints that had bound him when he had to live up to the position of an English gentleman of fortune, he might have said, with Mosby of *Arden of Feversham,* "My golden time was when I had no gold." His empty pockets did not disturb him. Mary Graham told Bedingfield how Thackeray at this time "used to come to her and say, 'Polly can you lend me a franc? I want some cigars.' " [4] Fifteen years later he looked back at these months, when he "came to Paris . . . and made believe to be a painter." "It was a very jolly time," he told Mrs. Brookfield. "I was as poor as Job: and sketched away most abominably, but pretty contented: and we used to meet in each others little rooms and talk about Art and smoke pipes and drink bad brandy & water." [5] This picture is elaborated in *The Paris Sketch Book:*

The life of the young artist here is the easiest, merriest, dirtiest existence possible. He comes to Paris, probably at sixteen, from his province; his parents settle forty pounds a-year on him, and pay his master: he establishes himself in the Pays Latin, or in the new quarter of Nôtre Dame de Lorette (which is quite peopled with painters); he arrives at his atelier at a tolerably early hour, and labours among a score of companions as merry and poor as himself. Each gentleman has his favourite tobacco-pipe; and the pictures are painted in the midst of a cloud of smoke, and a din of puns and choice French slang, and a roar of choruses, of which no one can form an idea that has not been present at such an assembly.[6]

Thackeray's diary reveals that this is a censored version of the *vie de bohème* as he knew it. He tells of one occasion on which "the model, a pretty little woman, . . . w[d] not pose but instead sung songs & cut capers; [and] the men from sixty to sixteen seemed to be in habits of perfect familiarity with the model." [7] And a few months later we find him complaining to his friend Henry Reeve of "the jargon of a corrupt life" which French artists admitted to their studios.[8]

These reservations perhaps explain why there was always an element of detachment in the interest which Thackeray took in Parisian Bohemia. The French friends that he made were certainly from other circles. Among his "old comrades," for example, was the poet and dandy Roger de Beauvoir. It was through him that the "Countess Dash" at this time met Thackeray, whom she described as "un jeune homme assez fantasque, rempli d'esprit et d'humour." "Il causait par boutade," she continues, "mais quand il était en verve, il avait des drôleries tout à fait françaises qu'il débitait avec le flegme de sa nature." [9] Yet despite talents which commanded admiration, Thackeray formed few lasting friendships with the French; not long before his death he told an American acquaintance that "he had never in his life been intimate in a single French family." [10]

Thackeray began his studies by copying old masters in the Louvre. He much preferred their work to the paintings of the new romantic school, even though, as he told his mother, "studying these great old painters puts one sadly out of conceit with one's mean little efforts." [11] He also sketched at the Life Academy, and occasionally he attempted an original watercolour, having an open commission from Edward FitzGerald for these productions. In this fashion he passed the last months of 1834 cheerfully and industriously enough; but early in the new year he became aware how unsatisfactory his progress had been. On 11 April 1835 he sent to Frank Stone a letter whose humorous exaggeration only accentuates its underlying hopelessness:

> As for myself—I am in a state of despair—I have got enough torn-up pictures to roast an ox by—the sun riseth upon my efforts and goeth down on my failures, and I have become latterly so disgusted with myself and art and everything belonging to it, that for a month past I have been lying on sofas reading novels, and never touching a pencil.
>
> In these six months, I have not done a thing worth looking at. O God, when will Thy light enable my fingers to work, and my colours to shine—if in another six months, I can do no better, I will arise and go out and hang myself.[12]

Though he continued to think of painting as his profession and to assure his mother that he had "the stuff to make as good a painter as the very best of them," [13] he gradually came to realize that in painting, as in so many other things that he had attempted, he would never make his name. "He had not the patience to be an artist with pencil or brush," George Cruikshank once explained. "I used to tell him that to be an artist was to burrow along like a mole, heaving up a little mound here and there for a long distance. He said he thought he would presently break out into another element and stay there." [14] Thackeray never lost the facility in drawing that he had acquired in early boyhood, but neither did he progress much beyond the effects that he was able to achieve almost at once. "Don't exaggerate the faces, pray," FitzGerald urged him, "but get them near to Nature." [15] Thackeray was unable to follow this excellent advice, and it is only his comic drawings that rise above insipidity.

Thackeray's state of mind after it became apparent to him that he was destined to fail in painting is nowhere better revealed than in the narrative of an incident of February, 1835, which appears in *The Paris Sketch Book* as "A Gambler's Death." [16] Idling with a group of aimless fellow expatriates, sharing with them *"l'ozio lungo d'uomini ignoranti,"* Thackeray encountered a Charterhouse schoolfellow of ten years before, "a dark-looking, thick-set man, in a greasy well-cut coat, with a shabby hat cocked on one side of his dirty face." [17] Attwood, as Thackeray calls his old acquaintance, was a professional gambler down on his luck. Playing with a five-pound note borrowed from Thackeray, he rocketed to prosperity, and for a time enjoyed all the dubious pleasures that the Parisian *demi-monde* affords. But his luck broke, and rather than face penury again, he cut his throat. "I dare not think of his fate," Thackeray wrote, "for except in the fact of his poverty and desperation was he worse than any of us, his companions, who had shared his debauches, and marched with him up to the very brink of the grave?" [18]

The tale ends with an account of Attwood's early-morning funeral, at which the sole mourners were Thackeray and two other former cronies (all three nearly drunk from the potations consumed during the night to fortify themselves). " 'When we turned out in our great coats,' said one of them afterwards, 'reeking of cigars and brandy-and-water, d——e, sir, we quite frightened the old buck of a parson; he did not much like our company.' After the ceremony was concluded, these gentlemen were very happy to get home to a warm and comfortable breakfast, and finished the day royally at Frascati's." [19] This final reference to one of Paris's principal gambling-houses is heavy with foreboding. Thackeray was telling himself, as he wrote this story: There, but for the grace of God, go I. One sees how intimate was his association for a time with the English raffs who infested the Continent, an association that later led him to exclaim: "There is on the face of this world no scamp like our English one, no blackguard like one of these half-gentlemen, so mean, so low, so vulgar,—so ludicrously ignorant and conceited, so desperately heartless and depraved." [20] One sees how close he came at this time to abandoning the struggle to make something of his own life.

Thus sunk in depression, Thackeray found it impossible to go on living with his grandmother, who overwhelmed him with almost daily reproaches. On 11 June he gave up his rooms in the Rue de Chaillot, much to the distress of Mrs. Butler, and went to live in a "little den in the Rue des Beaux Arts." [21] This was a bold decision, for his grandmother's help was almost indispensable to him. No doubt it was after this separation that Thackeray, as he used to tell his daughters, "lived at Paris for a whole month upon five pounds & bought a waistcoat out of it." [22] Even so, he had to inform his mother in July, "after a bitter & fruitless day's work, such as is every day's work now," that he would shortly have to draw on his tiny capital.[23] The prospect was dismal enough, but Thackeray's despair did not last long. During the summer of 1835 he fell in love.

III

Thackeray met the girl of his choice, not in the Bohemian circles where we have thus far observed him during his visits to France, but in the staid and sober world that the English middle class had made for itself in Paris. The English invasion of France had begun immediately after Waterloo. Regency bucks and fashionable hostesses dominated Parisian society while Wellington and Castlereagh remained in France, and Thackeray's life there while he was still a young man of fortune was a pale reflection of the existence led by the gambling, heavy-drinking, opera-going dandies of the Regency. Gradually this splendour faded, although French Anglomania remained intense under Louis Philippe; and English expatriates of a different sort established themselves in Paris. Men whose creditors made England uncomfortable to them found it convenient to settle in the French capital. Paris had its share of English blacklegs; and decayed gentlemen and dishonoured ladies went there to finish their lives in decent obscurity. The *nouveaux riches* of England came to Paris in the hope of making fashionable connexions that would be useful to them in London. But for the most part the English colony in Paris by the middle 1830s consisted of respectable folk who found it possible to live far more economically in France than at home.[1] Thackeray has left a memorable description of this tight little society, which regarded things French almost with the disdain of Mr. Podsnap and lived entirely to itself, in the pages of *Philip:*

> do not British Trojans, who emigrate to the continent of Europe, take their Troy with them? You all know the quarters of Paris which swarm with us Trojans. From Peace Street to the Arch of the Star are collected thousands of refugees from our Ilium. Under the arcades of the Rue de Rivoli you meet, at certain hours, as many of our Trojans as of the natives. In the Trojan inns of Meurice, the Louvre, &c., we swarm. We have numerous Anglo-Trojan doctors and apothecaries, who give us the dear pills and doses of Pergamus. We go to Mrs. Guerre or kind Mrs. Colombin, and can purchase the sandwiches of Troy, the pale ale and sherry of Troy, and the dear, dear muffins of home. We live for years, never speaking any language but our native Trojan; except to our servants, whom we instruct in the Trojan way of preparing toast for breakfast; Trojan bread-sauce for fowls and partridges; Trojan corned beef, &c. We have temples where we worship according to the Trojan rites. A kindly sight is that which one beholds of a Sunday in the Elysian fields and the St. Honoré quarter, of processions of English grown people and children, stalwart, red-cheeked, marching to their churches, their gilded prayer-books in hand, to sing in a stranger's land the sacred songs of their Zion.[2]

Prominent among Thackeray's houses of call was the home of his aunt and uncle Ritchie, who had moved from London to Paris in 1830. There he acted as big brother to their oldest child, William, now a young man of eighteen about to leave Eton for Cambridge. To him Thackeray gave sound counsel regarding his conduct at the university: "Keep yrself out of DEBT—and to do this you must avoid the dinner parties and rowing (boating) men—however, you will see John Kemble who (particularly when he is drunk) will give you the finest advice on these and other moral and religious points." [3] The home of Eyre Evans Crowe, Paris correspondent of the *Morning Chronicle,* was another of Thackeray's haunts. He was accustomed to go to the Crowes' apartment on the Rue de 29 Juillet every Saturday afternoon and evening, arriving early in order to draw caricatures for the Crowe children before dinner. After the meal Mrs. Crowe would play and the assembled company would sing, "the supreme enjoyment being a song from Thackeray." [4]

Conversation at the Crowes centred on art, literature, and the drama; and in their domestic circle Thackeray met a variety of English artists and writers dwelling temporarily in France. There was John Brine, for example, an eccentric Scottish artist, whom Thackeray later put into *A Shabby Genteel Story* as Andrea Fitch.[5] Thackeray also spent an occasional evening with Douglas Jerrold, the pressing attentions of whose creditors sometimes forced him to withdraw temporarily from London to the Continent, and John F. Barnett, a musician whose *Mountain Sylph* of 1834 won for him the title of "Father of English Opera." [6]

But by the summer of 1835 Thackeray's attentions were concentrated on one family of British Trojans, and on one member of this family.

> I am arrived at such a pitch of sentimentality (for a plain girl without a penny in the world) [he told William Ritchie] that my whole seyn, être, or being, is boulversé or capsized—I sleep not neither do I eat, only smoke a little and build castles in the clouds; thinking all the day of the propriety of a sixieme, boiled beef and soup for dinner, and the possession of the gal of my art.[7]

This was Isabella Shawe, daughter of the late Colonel Matthew Shawe, who was living with her mother, sister, and brothers in a boarding-house near the Champs Élysées.

IV

The Shawes had come to Ireland from Chester in the seventeenth century. Quickly attaining a respectable position among the Anglo-Irish ruling class, the clan for 150 years supplied the professions, particularly the Church and the army, with a series of capable, if undistinguished, recruits. Isabella's grandfather, a barrister named Matthew Shawe, married twice. By his first wife he had one son, Merrick; by his second, four boys and four girls, among them Isabella's father. This extensive brood grew up contentedly together at Lodge, county Galway, the father acting as tutor, and Merrick caring affectionately for the younger children.[1] Merrick entered the Indian army in 1790, thus embarking on a distinguished career that within fifteen years saw him established as private secretary to the Marquess Wellesley, Governor General of India.[2] But he did not forget his half-brothers and half-sisters at home in Ireland; indeed, he made himself responsible for placing them, one after another, in comfortable niches in life.

Matthew Shawe, the third of Merrick Shawe's four half-brothers, appears to have been born at Lodge early in the 1780s. He was educated at home by his father, after whose death Merrick undertook to provide for him. A commission was found for him on 7 May 1799 in the 12th Foot.[3] On 15 November 1801 he exchanged into the 74th Foot (Highlanders), no doubt through the good offices of his uncle Robert Shawe, who was lieutenant colonel of the regiment.[4] Merrick was delighted with the young man. "An excellent tractable good lad," he wrote to Mrs. Shawe in 1803. "I am much pleased with his humour and the readiness he shows to observe any advice that is given him." [5] And Matthew was fortunate in the regiment to which he had been assigned. A fellow officer writes of the "chivalrous spirit and noble emulation" [6] which pervaded the 74th, then in its twelfth year in India; and certainly its record during Matthew Shawe's long and hazardous service was most brilliant.

In 1803 the 74th became part of the army with which Major-General Arthur Wellesley fought the First Mahratta War. Shawe's first major action was the capture of the town and fort of Ahmedruggur on 8 and 12 August. Assaye followed on 23 September.

> The conduct of the SEVENTY-FOURTH, in this memorable battle, was most gallant and distinguished [the regimental historian relates]; but from having been prematurely led against the village of Assaye, on the left of the enemy's line, the regiment was exposed, unsupported, to a most terrible cannonade, and being afterwards charged by cavalry, sustained a tremendous loss.

Eleven of the regiment's eighteen officers were killed, and the rest, with one exception, were severely wounded. For its gallant conduct the 74th subsequently received royal authority to bear on the regimental colours and appointments an elephant with ASSAYE superscribed.[7]

Later in the year Merrick wrote to Matthew's younger brother Charles, for whom a commission in the 74th Foot had also been found, though he was still in Chester concluding his education:

> I have the satisfaction to congratulate you on your promotion to a Lieutenancy in the gallant 74th Regiment—the losses which that gallant corps sustained in the late battle of Assaye made way for your advancement and have made your brother Matt one of the oldest Lts. in the Regt he has been so fortunate as to have seen some glorious & severe service in the course of this war and to acquire experience which must be highly useful to him in the remainder of his Military Career he has purchased it at the expense of a severe wound of which however he is happily recovered a musquet shot passed through above the right wrist & broke one of the bones.[8]

So rapid was Matthew's convalescence that he was able to take part in the battle of Argaum on 15 November and the siege and storming of Gawilghur on 15 December. After further distinguished service in 1804, during the course of which Shawe succeeded to a captaincy, the 74th Foot was ordered to England in September, 1805.

After four years of recruiting in Scotland and Ireland, the 74th embarked early in 1810 for the Peninsula. There they fought once more under their old commander, now Viscount Wellington, who told their colonel that if "the Seventy-Fourth would behave in that country as they had done in India he ought to be proud to command such a regiment." [9] The corps became part of Wellington's Third Division ("the Fighting Division," as it was called), and Shawe was present at most of the major battles during the next three years, including the battle of Busaco on 27 September 1810, the attacks on Redinha and Foz d'Aronce of 12 and 15 March 1811, and the siege and storming of Ciudad Rodrigo in January of 1812. On 5 May 1811 he was wounded during the capture of Fuentes d'Onor, and he received his brevet of major later the same month.

Shawe's most notable exploit, however, came during the siege of Badajoz in 1812. On the night of 25 March he was given command of 200 of the 500 men detached to take Fort Picurina.

> This strong and important outwork [writes the regimental historian] is in the form of a bastion of nearly two hundred feet faces and seventy feet flanks, the rear being closed by a front of fortification; there were seven pieces of ordnance mounted on the ramparts; and the garrison, of nearly three hundred men, was commanded by a colonel of the staff. The detachments advanced to the attack at ten o'clock, and immediately alarms were sounded in the town, rockets thrown up, and a fire opened on them from all the ramparts on the work. The obstacles to an escalade were great, and the resistance of the garrison most determined; but after a hot and doubtful contest, in which the assailants lost four officers and fifty men killed, and fifteen officers and two hundred and fifty men wounded, the work was carried.[10]

Shawe was again dangerously wounded, but he recovered to receive the brevet of lieutenant colonel, Wellington's thanks in general orders, a medal, and nomination as Companion of the Bath.

On 4 June 1813 Shawe transferred to the 59th Foot.[11] While serving in that regiment, he married Isabella Gethin Creagh at Doneraile in Ireland on 9 December 1813.[12] The Creaghs were "an old and wealthy merchant family in Cork," [13] who traced their lineage back to a fifteenth-century mayor of Cork named Christopher Creagh.[14] A branch of the family in Limerick was long prominent in the Irish Church.[15] By the time of Isabella's birth her people had become landed gentry. She was one of ten children of Arthur Creagh and his wife Isabella, daughter of William Bagwell, M.P., and grew up at Laurentinum House, a substantial three-storeyed mansion with extensive grounds located a mile and three-quarters east of Doneraile.[16]

Shawe's regiment was ordered to the East shortly after his marriage, and the couple's first child, christened Merrick Arthur Gethin Shawe, was born to them at Walter Vreedun, Batavia, Java, on 28 November 1814.[17] On 5 December 1816 their second child, Isabella Gethin Shawe, was born in India.[18] Shawe became lieutenant colonel of the 84th Foot on 15 April 1817. He joined the regiment at Cawnpore and, having settled his family there, marched in October with the Grand Army under Lord Hastings in the Pindaree campaign. In 1820 the 84th was ordered from Cawnpore to Fort William, where it remained until 1822. Two years at Ghazeepore followed, during which (in May, 1823) Shawe succeeded to the command of the regiment. After a short period at Berhampore, the 84th returned to Fort William early in 1825. Shawe commanded the garrison there for nine months. By this time he and Mrs. Shawe had five children, including Arthur, born in 1818; [19] Jane; and Henry, born in 1823.[20]

In October, 1825, Shawe took the 87th Foot to Ava in Burma, leaving his family behind in Calcutta. He commanded his regiment in the field until 24 February 1826, when the war against the Burmese was successfully concluded, and then retired to Rangoon to repair his shattered constitution. But he had pressed himself too hard, and he died aboard His Majesty's sloop *Slaney* within a day's sail of Penang, where he was buried with full military honours. "He was much regretted as an excellent man, and an officer of conspicuous gallantry," it is related in the regimental history. "His life was sacrificed to his zeal for active service, for such was the state of his health, on leaving Calcutta, that his military advisers used every endeavour to dissuade him from proceeding to Ava." [21] His will, which he made *in extremis* and did not live to sign, follows:

In the name of God Amen I, Matthew Shawe Lieutenant Colonel in the army and of His Majesty's 87th Regiment being in possession of my faculties, but ignorant to the moment when it may please God to terminate my existence do ordain and constitute this my last Will and testament in the manner following (that is to say) First I recommend my Soul to God that gave it and my Body I commit to the Earth or Sea as it shall please God to order and as for and concerning all my worldly Estate I give bequeath and dispose thereof as followeth. To my beloved wife Isabella G. Shawe I do give devise and bequeath the *interest* of the whole of my property during her life time, and at her death, I bequeath the whole of my property to be equally divided amongst my beloved Children and I do desire that the whole of my property in the East Indies, Viz: my House and Grounds at Ghazeepoor such furniture as I have left at Calcutta and Rangoon be forthwith sold and the proceeds remitted to my agents in England Messrs. Greenwood & Cox for the benefit of my beloved wife and family as well as all arrears due to me in the hands of the Paymaster of the Kings Troops at Calcutta or elsewhere & I do also bequeath to my eldest son my Gold Watch and further I do hereby Constitute and appoint Captain James Thomas Moore & Lieutenant and Adjutant John Hassard of his Majesty's 87th Regiment Sole Executors of this my only Will and Testament.

In witness whereof I hereby subscribe my name and affix my Seal on Board His Majesty's Sloop Slaney off Pulo Penang this eleventh day of April in the year of our Lord one thousand eight hundred and twenty-six.[22]

Thus twelve years after her marriage Mrs. Shawe was left alone in India with sole responsibility for a family of five children. Her husband had left her all his possessions; but even a colonel could save little at this time from army pay, and Mrs. Shawe found herself chiefly dependent upon her pension. Not only was she reduced abruptly from careless affluence to stringent economy, but also she suffered an equally abrupt drop in social position. She was no longer the Colonel's lady, the wife of a distinguished officer on important service; she became instead simply one more unit in the great horde of army widows that spread over England and the Continent in the second and third decades of the nineteenth century.

The years that intervened between Colonel Shawe's death and Thackeray's first meeting with his daughter were not an easy period for the family. Mrs. Shawe had to support her five children on the interest of her husband's estate and her widow's pension of £80 per annum.[23] She could expect little help from the Creaghs, for she was one of ten children, and in any event the family no longer lived in the grand style of her youth.[24] Her chief prop was presumably her brother-in-law. It was no doubt through him that his namesake Merrick was appointed a writer in the East India Company's service in 1834 and sent out to Bengal the following year.[25] And he must also have procured for Arthur the ensign's commission which that young man received on 1 April 1836.[26] Despite Merrick's help, however, financial pressure ultimately forced Mrs. Shawe to settle in Paris, a city in which a little English money went a long way. There she and her children lived the obscure and monotonous boarding-house existence that was the lot of most British expatriates.

When Thackeray first met Mrs. Shawe, she was to outward appearances a very worthy and respectable woman. Her presence and manner were imposing. She was a good manager for her family, economical, efficient, and self-denying. A devout evangelical, she had brought up her children to be godfearing and well-behaved. But even in prosperity she had been dull and narrow, and the trials that she had to undergo after her husband's death had soured her disposition and warped her mind. She compensated for the respect and notice that she no longer received from the outside world by engrossing to herself the love and attention of her children, particularly of her daughters. Her faith sank into bigotry, and her God became the jealous and angry God of the Old Testament. Worst of all, as she lost all control over her temper, she became unable any longer to accept her destiny in silence. Her conversation, expressed more and more in biblical language, became an endless tirade of righteous self-justification. Wherever she went, "storms, whirlwinds, cataracts, tornadoes" [27] accompanied her.

Isabella Shawe, Mrs. Shawe's oldest daughter, bore little resemblance to her mother, either in person or character. She was petite, red-haired, and, if not pretty, yet decidedly attractive. Henry Reeve, who met her early in 1836, thought her "a nice, simple, girlish girl." [28] Innocence of an almost childish kind was her most characteristic feature. Despite their inappropriateness for a young lady of eighteen, she kept her nicknames of "Puss" and "Tobey." Her great pleasure was to play the piano and to sing—indeed, she had mastered a considerable repertoire of songs drawn chiefly from Italian opera; but she also greatly enjoyed gossiping with her dearly loved sister Jane and with friendly girls in her boarding-house. Yet Isabella had suffered from her upbringing. Mrs. Shawe had pampered her from earliest childhood, demanding little from her except unquestioning adoration, and she was hardly capable of independent action. Outside her home circle, consequently, she was unsure of herself, timorous, and retiring. Even so, she seemed to have escaped lightly, for she was warm-hearted, affectionate, and loyal, and on subjects within her range of interest she could form sensible opinions and sound judgments.

V

As we have seen, the early summer of 1835 was a dreary period for Thackeray. If his "little den in the Rue des Beaux Arts" was like the "crib" in the Rue Poussin where Philip Firmin was living when he first met Charlotte Baynes,[1] Thackeray must at times have been sufficiently depressed by his surroundings. Even the company of his intimate friends—John Bowes Bowes, the wealthy illegitimate son of the tenth Earl of Strathmore,[2] who had been attracted to Paris by an intense passion for the theatre; Tom Fraser, Paris correspondent of the London *Morning Chronicle;* and Augustus Stevens, a jovial dentist—must occasionally have irked him because of the contrast between their prosperity and his misfortunes. At the suggestion of Eyre Evans Crowe, he had applied in April for the post of Constantinople correspondent of the *Morning Chronicle.* He read all the books about the East that he could find; he dreamed of the adventures that would come his way; he planned to make his fortune by writing and drawing a *Picturesque Annual* for Charles Heath; but by July this scheme had come to nothing. The only employment that he could find for himself, indeed, was hack-work for *Galignani's Messenger,* a paper in which Bowes had an interest. Moreover, he had the bad luck during the course of a donkey-ride at Montmorency to be pitched over the head of his mount onto a pile of stones, with the result that his nose was broken a second time.[3]

Thackeray's meeting with Isabella Shawe raised him out of his despondency and gave him a new interest in life. He was profoundly dissatisfied with the furtive amours that his school and college training had suggested as a suitable way of alleviating the discomforts incident to the exercise of Malthus's "preventive check," and for years he had been eager to make himself a home.

"I want to settle," he told his mother in 1833, ". . . to marry somebody with some money, & then to live in the little house in Albion Street. going to Church regularly, rising early, & walking in the Park with Mrs T. & the children." [4] Isabella was in no sense an heiress, but Thackeray was too far gone to be prudent. "God knows how it will end," he told William Ritchie. "I will, if I can, bolt before I have committed myself for better or for worser. But I don't think that I shall have the power." [5]

During the winter of 1835–1836, however, Thackeray had to mark time in his courtship. Though Mrs. Shawe disapproved of him as a suitor, she did not at first try actively to discourage his attentions to Isabella. Since Thackeray had no fortune and no settled employment, immediate marriage was in any case out of the question; and no doubt Mrs. Shawe hoped that the affair would prove merely a passing infatuation. Meanwhile, Thackeray set to work manfully to achieve a steady income. During a visit to Paris in January, 1836, Henry Reeve noted that Thackeray was "editing an English paper here, in opposition to Galignani's." [6] With the financial backing of Bowes, he arranged for the publication of *Flore et Zéphyr,* a series of lithographs caricaturing Taglioni's famous ballet "La Sylphide" (but not the dancer herself, whom Thackeray greatly admired), by John Mitchell, librarian and print-seller of Old Bond Street, London. But the paper did not survive, and *Flore et Zéphyr* seems to have attracted little notice.[7]

Thackeray's mother and stepfather had thus far made no effort to help him. They were not themselves enthusiastic about the prospect of his marrying a girl with no money and no very obvious personal attractions, who was tied, moreover, to a termagant Irish mother. But when they saw that in his passion for Isabella, as in almost nothing else in his life, Thackeray was entirely in earnest, they decided to put him in the way of employment. In April, 1836, Major Carmichael-Smyth accordingly interested himself in a joint-stock enterprise called the Metropolitan Newspaper Company, which had been formed to publish a radical newspaper.[8] Subscriptions were opened for 6,000 shares of stock worth £10 each. Though funds were slow in accumulating, enough money was soon in hand to buy a moribund paper called the *Public Ledger,* and it was determined that the new journal should be named the *Constitutional and Public Ledger.* The Major was to be chairman of the company, Laman Blanchard its editor, Douglas Jerrold its dramatic critic, and Thackeray its Paris correspondent. Thackeray's salary was set at eight guineas a week, a very generous stipend which had been made possible by the Major's refusal to take any remuneration for his own services.[9]

On 14 April Thackeray, who had gone to London to participate in conferences concerning the new paper, wrote in high spirits to Isabella:

My father says I could not do better than to marry, my mother says the same. I need not say that I agree with the opinion of my parents—so, dearest, make the little shifts ready, and the pretty night caps; and we will in a few few months, go & hear Bishop Luscombe read, and be married, and have children, & be happy ever after, as they are in the Story books—Does this news please you as it does me? Are you ready and willing to give up your home, & your bedfellow, and your kind mother, to share the fate of a sulky grey headed old fellow with a small income, & a broken nose? [10]

For ten days there was an ominous silence on Isabella's part. Mrs. Shawe had taken alarm at Thackeray's abrupt proposal, and the jealous possessiveness that she felt towards her children was reflected in Isabella's reply of 24 April. Thackeray wrote back in dismay:

what in God's name have I been saying to hurt you (for I see you are hurt) and your Mother?—What a scoundrel should I be were I to endeavour to weaken such a tie as exists between you two—The separation to wh I alluded did not go farther than the bedroom. . . . If you are my wife you must sleep in my bed and live in my house—voila tout—I have no latent plans.[11]

Yet he went on to urge Isabella to consider whether or not she had quite attained a wifely state of mind, to "see whether you who have mastered the mysteries of stocking mending, who have penetrated the depths of the Rule of Three, who have attained the very acmè of pickling, and arrived at the perfectability of pie crust, have not some other little conjugal duties to perform,

one of w^h (& not the most easy) is the duty of affection." [12] Isabella's home experience had been such, indeed, that throughout his courtship Thackeray treated her as a child who had everything to learn about love except love for her own family.

From April through June, Thackeray and Isabella regarded themselves as formally engaged, apparently with Mrs. Shawe's reluctant approval. It had originally been intended to issue the first number of the *Constitutional* on 23 May; but capital continued to come in very slowly, and there was a delay in putting into effect an expected reduction of stamp duties on newspapers. For the time being, therefore, Thackeray could only hover aimlessly around the Shawe boarding-house at 10 Rue Ponthieu, Faubourg Saint Honoré, growing daily more lovesick.

In July Mrs. Shawe took advantage of these circumstances to make a second and more determined effort to break off her daughter's engagement. From Thackeray's letters and Chapters 23 to 28 of *Philip,* whose hero, so he told George Smith, follows "pretty much the career of WMT in the first year of his ruin and absurdly imprudent marriage," [13] it would appear that she was decidedly unscrupulous in her tactics. She insisted that Thackeray stop seeing Isabella, and in his absence she abused him roundly to her daughter. She interpreted his warm and demonstrative affection as licentiousness; she held that his appearance was unprepossessing, his manner arrogant and supercilious; she insisted that his abilities were poor and his prospects uncertain. When Isabella appeared to yield to her endless arguments, she told Thackeray that she and her daughter had agreed that the marriage must not take place.

Bitterly offended by what he regarded as Isabella's betrayal, Thackeray at first withdrew without attempting to see her. But love quickly overcame pride, and he smuggled to her, through a friendly boarding-house servant named Augustine, an impassioned letter urging her to assert her independence.

My love for you is greater than I thought, for it has withstood this terrible three days trial. I have tried to leave you, & you will hardly credit me that I felt obliged to return—for I do not believe in spite of all this heartlessness on your part, that you ever can be other than my wife—You may recollect, that after our second quarrel, we made a kind of vow that, happen what would—you & I were bound together & married before God, & that I told you but a few nights since, that I had prayed to Him to give me aid in quelling any improper desires wh might create your disgust or lessen me in yr esteem.

If you feel that after our three months' marriage for I can call it no less, you are sick of me & my love, *tell me so with your own lips.*[14]

Keyed up by this letter, Isabella found within herself the strength to revolt against her mother's authority. Like Charlotte Baynes in *Philip,* she seems to have asserted her unalterable devotion to Thackeray, and then, exhausted and broken by this effort, to have fallen ill. Frightened at what she had done to her daughter, whom she loved deeply in her own way, Mrs. Shawe gave up the battle. Thackeray was restored to his position of accepted lover, though from this time forth even the appearance of cordiality between him and Mrs. Shawe could be maintained only with difficulty; and active preparations for his wedding to Isabella were entered upon.

This event took place on 20 August in the British Embassy in Paris. Bishop H. M. Luscombe, the Embassy chaplain, performed the ceremony, and Mrs. Shawe signed the register as a witness.[15] The honeymoon began at Versailles, where Thackeray five days later wrote to his aunt Ritchie, a close confidante during the period of trouble that he and Isabella had just gone through:

Mrs Shawe who has just come to pay us a visit of condolence, brings a kind of message from you, wh Mrs Mills in a conference of four hours imparted to her.

WE, (does it not sound very magnificent?) shall be delighted to come and occupy your pretty little rooms, and stay with you a few or a great many days—, for this place has a certain dulness, in spite of my peculiar situation, and I shall be too glad to pass a little time in your pleasant country villa.

So that, on Saturday, my dear Aunt, I hope you will receive me & that diminutive individual, who bears the name of your affte. Nephew.[16]

To *"les Thermes"* the pair duly proceeded, where they remained until mid-September, when they returned to Paris in order that Thackeray might begin his work for the *Constitutional.*

VI

The Thackerays settled in a small apartment at 15 bis Rue Neuve St. Augustin, where they lived an almost blissful existence during the following fall and winter. On 7 October Thackeray described his state of mind to FitzGerald, who with his usual generosity had sent a handsome check as a wedding present:

As for the little wife it does not change one in the least it is only a new quality that one discovers in ones' self, a new happiness if you will, for my dear old friend, any thing so happy, so quiet, so calm you can't fancy; at this moment I am smoking a segar (wh my little woman has got for me) in the very drawing room—the state apartment of the race of Tackeray! I intend with your money to buy chairs and tables, to decorate this chamber, for as yet I have only hired them; and I have got your portrait and further more as the comble of sentiment I shall make Mrs Tack write to you on this very sheet of paper.[1]

To his mother he enlarged on the perfections of "the best little wife in the world." "I never knew a purer mind or a better temper, or a warmer heart (for me & mine)." [2]

Thackeray's days followed a very agreeable routine, under which he grew "strangely fat" and was regarded as "the happiest man in the neighbourhood." [3] His sole duty being the dispatch of a *Constitutional* article once or twice a week, he was accustomed to lie abed until eleven. Then he sallied forth in search of news, returning in time for dinner with Isabella and "pleasant long nights lolling on sofas smoking & making merry." [4] A favourite haunt was Terré's Tavern in the nearby Rue Neuve des Petits Champs. This was a tiny restaurant, where a red-cheeked oyster-opener sat by the lamp-lit door and the proprietor took a smiling interest in the guests' welfare. Having long frequented the establishment in the company of such friends as

Fraser and Stevens to enjoy its *bouillabaisse* and "Chambertin with yellow seal," Thackeray now took particular pleasure in sharing with Isabella his "old accustom'd corner-place" and the good things there provided.[5]

For the rest, they saw much of their Parisian English circle, including Mrs. Shawe and her friends. Though Thackeray continued to regard his mother-in-law as "a singular old deevil" and to deplore her tendency to talk "as big as St. Paul's," he had to admit that she had "become quite civil of late." [6] The proposition which in later life he never tired of repeating, that "every man naturally will, must, and should dislike his mother-in-law," had not yet thoroughly established itself in his mind. Luckily Isabella entertained no such reservations about Mrs. Carmichael-Smyth, whom she regarded from the first with entire trust and affection.[7] She pressed the Carmichael-Smyths to come to Paris and, while awaiting their visit, wrote long letters to Thackeray's mother filled with domestic gossip. In December Mrs. Shawe and Mrs. Carmichael-Smyth were alike pleased to learn that Isabella was expecting a child the following June.

This development awakened Thackeray to a livelier sense of his responsibilities. Knowing that the prospects of the *Constitutional* were uncertain at best, he cast about for other work. Many years later he told how he had tried about this time to persuade Dickens to employ him as illustrator of *The Pickwick Papers,* then just beginning to appear in monthly parts. He made a number of sample sketches, "which strange to say, [Dickens] did not find suitable." [8] It is presumably one of these, a front-wrapper design for *Sketches by Boz,* which is reproduced as Plate IX. He endeavoured with the help of "Father Prout" to obtain a similar commission for Ainsworth's *Crichton.* Though Ainsworth was willing, Thackeray became too preoccupied with courtship and marriage to produce the needed drawings. He applied again early in 1837, but this time his sketches were so badly done as to be unacceptable, and *Crichton* appeared a little later in the year without illustrations.[9] Thackeray also implored John Kemble to commission him to write an article for his *British and Foreign Review* ("we want lightness to my thinking," he told his friend); and he asked the publisher John Macrone to advance him £20 for "a book in 2 Wollums. with 20 drawings. entitled Rambles & Sketches in old & new Paris," adding "I have not of course written a word of it." [10] But these projects bore no immediate fruit.

Early in March, 1837, the Thackerays moved to London, where they lived for a time with the Carmichael-Smyths at 18 Albion Street. For reasons that will shortly be outlined, the *Constitutional* could no longer afford to maintain a Paris correspondent; and in any event Thackeray desired to make London his headquarters. More work would come his way there, and Isabella would have the attendance of Mrs. Carmichael-Smyth during her coming confinement. Thus ended what was perhaps the happiest period of Thackeray's life, the "dear old times" that he later celebrated in "The Ballad of Bouillabaisse."

VII

The *Constitutional* had been created to revive the waning fortunes of the Radical party in the House of Commons by giving it a voice in the daily press; and Charles Buller, George Grote, Joseph Hume, and Sir William Molesworth had promised to support the paper. Their collaboration was sufficient assurance that readers would not be offended by the violence and blackguardism of the usual popular journal. It was hoped that this note of gentlemanliness, together with a substantial reduction of the stamp duty, would ensure the paper's prosperity.

A circulation of 1,500 would have given the Metropolitan Newspaper Company a weekly profit of £44. This total did not seem too much to expect from the patronage of those who would either buy the *Constitutional* for themselves or insist that it be taken in by the proprietors of the taverns that they frequented. (Optimistic references to orders from the thousand members of "the united body of Coffee & Eating-House Keepers" punctuated discussions of the paper's prospects.) In the event, however, the *Constitutional* never had more than 550 subscribers, and it lost money from the first.[1] As it turned out, indeed, a worse period for its establishment could hardly have been chosen. The Radicals' influence in Parliament diminished daily. Mrs. Grote noted in her diary at the end of 1836:

> Mr. Grote, and about five others, find themselves left to sustain the Radical opinions of the House of Commons. One evening, after all other guests had departed, Sir W. Molesworth and Charles Buller remained late at our house, talking of the present aspect of affairs. "I see what we are coming to, Grote," said Charles Buller; "in no very long time from this, you and I shall be left to 'tell' Molesworth!"

During the early months of 1837, moreover, there was a general depression; "the commercial world . . . fell into difficulties; many joint-stock banks failed, confidence was shaken, and a real 'panic' ensued." [2] There is reason for surprise in the fact, not that the *Constitutional* went under, but that it kept afloat as long as it did.

Nevertheless, Thackeray did his best to believe in the paper and to follow the editorial line laid down for him. As "T. T.," the *Constitutional's* Paris correspondent from 17 September until 18 February,[3] it was his cue to present himself as an isolated spokesman for liberty in a land of despotism, even to suggest from time to time that he stood in some personal danger. He expressed his utter abhorrence of Louis Philippe, without whom the revolution of 1830 "would have spread throughout the world"; [4] he denounced July Monarchy France, "this hollow humbug of a representative government, this monstrous satire upon freedom"; [5] he poured unmeasured invective on French policy in Spain, where Louis Philippe had abandoned Queen Christina and the liberal party in favour of the reactionary forces of Don Carlos. Yet it was with great difficulty that Thackeray maintained his attitude of perpetual moral indignation in dealing with questions about which he cared very little, and one cannot but notice a factitious note in his diatribes. "I am afraid I am growing a Tory, in France that is, or rather a Tiers-parti man," he told his mother in confidence; "the Republican party is the most despicable I ever knew: They are bigoted and despotic." [6]

More interesting than Thackeray's views of Continental politics, a subject which he did not really understand, are his occasional references to home affairs. One notices here a paradox which was to mark his point of view throughout his life. He thought of himself as a spokesman for "the people." [7] He dismissed the Whigs as trimmers. He looked forward to the introduction of "a new political code," which was in effect the full Radical program: abolition of the corn-laws, reform of the House of Lords, reduction of bishops' salaries, penny stamps for newspapers, and so on. Episodes illustrating aristocratic arrogance and privilege stirred him to eloquent protest. When Louis Bonaparte was lightly reprimanded for attempting to foment a revolution, while a French workman was executed for the same offence; or when Grantley Berkeley's quality caused his flogging of the publisher James Fraser to be overlooked; Thackeray grew indignant.[8] But if he belonged intellectually to the party of the "genuine radicals," his tastes and inclinations led him the other way. "People in their battles about public matters," he told his mother, "forget the greatest good of all, social-good, I mean fine arts, and civilization, dandyism as you call it: we owe this to the aristocracy, and we must keep an aristocracy (pure & modified as you wish) in order to retain it." [9] One of Thackeray's distinctive contributions to Victorian thought and feeling was to be his reconciliation of the conflicting claims upon society of equality and culture, of human dignity and "civilization," but he was not destined fully to work out this reconciliation for another decade.

When Thackeray returned to England in March, 1837, he found the *Constitutional's* office in Fleet Street in a parlous state. The long delay attendant on the beginning of the paper had caused most of its original staff to desert it. Neither Jerrold nor Blanchard supported the journal for long, and it came in consequence to depend chiefly on the contributions of Irish hacks like Jack Sheehan and Dudley Costello. In the spring a desperate effort was made to save the *Constitutional* by increasing its size. Encouraged by the flurry of new subscriptions that resulted, Major Carmichael-Smyth, who by this time was bearing nearly the whole cost of the paper, late in April made Thackeray its managing director; and Thackeray at once asked the other shareholders for £1,000, urging that, with this support, "in three months the paper would be at a paying point; & in a year, would yield a very large dividend." [10] When three months had passed, however, the fortunes of the *Constitutional* showed no improvement, and publication accordingly ceased on 1 July. Thackeray's final contribution was a dignified account of the paper's unhappy history, which included a tribute to the "chivalrous devotion" which Major Carmichael-Smyth had displayed in supporting it to the end.[11]

8

Great Coram Street

I

THE CESSATION of the *Constitutional* made Thackeray a free-lance writer, dependent for his livelihood upon the commissions that he received from magazines and newspapers. During the next decade he earned his living as a contributor to the "periodical press," an unenviable destiny at this time for a young man of good education and gentle upbringing. Journalism was still anonymous and fiercely partisan, a combination that at best made for licence and irresponsibility, at worst for dishonesty and blackmail. Only in its uppermost reaches, notably the *Edinburgh* and *Quarterly Reviews,* could magazine writing be regarded as a dignified pursuit. Elsewhere its respectability shelved off sharply. "Magazine work is below street sweeping as a trade," Carlyle wrote in 1831; "even I who have no other am determined to try by all methods whether it is not possible to abandon it." [1] Newspaper work ranked still lower in public estimation. When Lockhart was invited to become editor of the London *Representative* in 1825, Scott advised him to decline the offer, thinking it "rash for any young man of whatever talent, to sacrifice, nominally at least, a considerable proportion of his respectability in society in hopes of being submitted as an exception to a rule which is at present pretty general." [2] In 1829 Scott was equally positive concerning the "disgrace and degradation" involved in newspaper writing. "I would rather sell gin to the poor people," he remarked, "and poison them that way." [3]

By the middle 1830s journalism was coming to be regarded in a somewhat more favourable light. Since it was obviously true, as Macaulay had pointed out, that "the gallery in which the reporters sit has become a fourth estate of the realm," [4] there was an increasing disposition on the part of the public to think better of the periodical writers who amused and enlightened them. Certain recruits to the profession, among them Charles Dickens and John Forster, were labouring earnestly to raise its status. But by and large it was still a precarious trade which drew its rank and file from the forlorn hacks who haunted the taverns of literary Bohemia. Scott's maxim, that "nothing but a thorough-going blackguard ought to attempt the daily press," [5] was not forgotten. Nor was Carlyle's description of his magazine associates—"such a scandalous set of dogs out of Tophet I should be puzzled to meet with" [6]—altogether unwarranted. Looking back on this period, Ernest Vizetelly was later able to recall many "journalists and magazine writers who were accustomed to spend a fair portion of their lives within the high walls of the Fleet or King's Bench prisons." [7] Society's attitude in general was that a periodical pressman must be regarded as an outcast, until he produced good evidence to redeem his character.

Thackeray was never himself intimate with the blackguardly element among his colleagues of the fourth estate. The world of *John Bull,* the *Age,* and the *Satirist* was not his, and he was civil rather than friendly with the various nondescript Irishmen who performed much of the hackwork for the magazines and newspapers that employed him. But the taint of periodical writing clung to him. In England, he noted with some feeling in *The Paris Sketch Book,*

> a literary man (in spite of all we can say against it) ranks below that class of gentry composed of the apothecary, the attorney, the wine-merchant, whose positions, in country towns at least, are so equivocal. As for instance, my friend, the Rev. James Asterisk [i.e., James White], who has an undeniable pedigree, a paternal estate, and a living to boot, once dined in Warwickshire, in company with several squires and parsons of that enlightened county. Asterisk, as usual, made himself extraordinarily agreeable at dinner, and delighted all present

with his learning and wit. 'Who is that monstrous pleasant fellow?' said one of the squires. 'Don't you know?' replied another: 'It's Asterisk, the author of so-and-so, and a famous contributor to such-and-such a magazine.' 'Good heavens!' said the squire, quite horrified; 'a literary man! I thought he had been a gentleman!' [8]

Thackeray's consciousness of this widespread prejudice helps to explain why, as late as 1838, he described his occupation in official documents as "student at law," [9] and why he wrote over a series of *noms de plume* until the appearance of the first monthly parts of *Vanity Fair* in 1847.[10] He may possibly have been led to retell the curious anecdote that forms the basis of "Miss Shum's Husband" by reflecting that his own occupation would not be much more favourably regarded by many of his friends of early life than that of the mysterious Mr. Frederick Altamont, who (it turns out) sweeps the crossing from the Bank to Cornhill.[11] If he persisted in following what he called "a bad trade at best," a trade in which the prizes were "fewer and worse than in any other professional lottery," it was because he knew that he was the kind of "man who will be an author whether or no—men are doomed, as it were, to the calling." [12]

When Thackeray embarked upon his career as a free-lance in July, 1837, his needs were in any event far too pressing to permit him to think much about the effect of this step upon his social position. To the jaundiced editorial eye, moreover, he had little enough to offer. His undergraduate work for *The Snob* and *The Gownsman* had been insignificant, his papers for the *National Standard* amateurish, and his political contributions to the *Constitutional* mediocre. He was a writer of small experience, unusual among his fellow aspirants only in his command of French and German, who had not as yet found a "specialty" with which he could identify himself. So circumstanced, his sole recourse was to seek help from his friends; but they responded nobly, and by September he was in "full employment." [13]

Thanks to the interest of Maginn, the columns of *Fraser's Magazine* were opened to him, and until 1844, when he transferred his primary loyalty to *Punch,* most of his writing was done with a view to publication in this periodical. Since its establishment in 1830 under Maginn's editorship, *Fraser's Magazine* had made a distinctive place for itself in the London literary scene. Initially an avowed imitation of the famous *Blackwood's Magazine* (Fraserian nights were presided over by "Nol Yorke," just as the "Noctes Ambrosianae" were governed by "Christopher North"), it soon developed its own line of "bold slapdash." [14] Though many of its contributors were rough-and-ready literary adventurers, who confused wit with brutality and criticism with personal abuse, the voices of Carlyle and of Maginn himself made the magazine a serious if eccentric commentator on the contemporary scene.[15]

By 1837 Maginn's hand had grown slack on the editorial reins, and the affairs of the magazine were largely managed by its publisher, James Fraser, "an honest, ignorant simpleton of a creature," according to Carlyle, "knowing little but that one and one are two." [16] Thackeray had a contemptuous affection for this worthy man, though he sometimes resented his dependence upon him. He addressed him, as a rule, in terms of offhand jocularity. Needing money and uncertain about the state of his account, he would dispatch an "Impromptu":

In case you owe send what you owe
In case you don't dont send you know.[17]

If he sometimes exploded verbally at what he considered Fraser's shabby treatment of him, he always thought better of his anger and was eager for a reconciliation. And, indeed, *Fraser's Magazine* had much to offer Thackeray. He was not required to write on topics that would have necessitated his paying lip-service to the magazine's uncongenial political conservatism. And his publisher's almost total want of literary intelligence allowed Thackeray liberty to treat the subjects that interested him as his whimsical fancy might dictate. When Fraser was driven to timid remonstrance, he was roundly rebuked by Thackeray. "Your friend knows nothing about it," Thackeray assured him on one occasion. "That paper will make a sensation, or I am a Dutchman. Why *should* there be any connection between the Title and the Article?" [18]

Between 1837 and 1840 Thackeray provided *Fraser's Magazine* with three fictional serials, *The Yellowplush Papers*

(1837–1838),[19] *Catherine* (1839–1840), and *A Shabby Genteel Story* (1840), together with much criticism of current art and literature. In the process he added two famous figures to the Fraserian gallery. Asked in October of 1837 to review *My Book; or, The Anatomy of Conduct,* a pretentious manual of "silver fork" etiquette by John Henry Skelton, he created Charles James Yellowplush, "sometime footman in many genteel families," who holds that "to describ fashnabble life, ONE OF US must do the thing, to do it well." [20] Commissioned the following spring to review the annual exhibitions of paintings at the National Gallery and elsewhere, he contributed "Strictures on Pictures" to *Fraser's Magazine* for June, 1838, under the name of Michael Angelo Titmarsh. He seems to have picked up the name Titmarsh from a seventeenth-century tract in his library which had been "Printed for Samuel Tidmarsh at the King's Head in Cornhill near the Royal Exchange." [21] The given names were chosen, not only because Titmarsh is represented as a painter (his historical canvas of "Heliogabalus in the ruins of Carthage" has never been esteemed at its true value),[22] but also because Michelangelo, like Thackeray, had a broken nose. The alias thus adopted turned out to be the most lasting of Thackeray's *noms de plume.* At first, like Yellowplush, a figure of fun and the butt of Nol Yorke's humour, Michael Angelo Titmarsh gradually came more and more to resemble Thackeray himself, until by the middle 1840s he was practically Thackeray's alter ego.

Thackeray's steadiest income in these years was from *Fraser's Magazine.* For his early *Yellowplush Papers* he was paid ten pounds a sheet [23] (sixteen magazine pages). This was not an unfair rate, since little-known writers at this time received only six to eight guineas a sheet.[24] But in March, 1838, Thackeray determined to strike for higher wages. "You pay more to others, I find, than to me," he told Fraser. "Bad as he is, Mr. Yellowplush is the most popular contributor to your magazine, and ought to be paid accordingly." [25] Fraser acceded to his demands, and Thackeray henceforth received twelve guineas a sheet and two guineas for each of the drawings that he supplied to illustrate his text. But this was not enough to support him and his family, and he had to look elsewhere for supplementary employment.

Personal influence also gained Thackeray an entrée to the *Times*. Lieutenant-Colonel Merrick Shawe was the intimate friend of Edward Sterling, a principal writer for this great paper since 1812. Through Shawe, Thackeray came to know and like Sterling, "a stout broad gentleman, perpendicular in attitude, rather showily dressed, and of gracious, ingenious and slightly elaborate manners," [26] who in turn introduced him to the fat and asthmatic Thomas Barnes, editor of the "Thunderer." Though Sterling and Barnes were not on the best of terms, Thackeray received sporadic reviewing assignments from the latter between August, 1837, when he noticed Carlyle's *French Revolution*, and August, 1840. This connexion came to an abrupt end when Sterling left the *Times's* staff in November of that year.[27] Though Thackeray was paid about two pounds each for his contributions,[28] on which he expended far less labour than on his papers for *Fraser's*, he was not sorry to give up the *Times*. Barnes's political policies seemed to him so deeply and unscrupulously reactionary that he was several times moved to denounce "the bigotry and wicked lies of that abominable old Times," [29] and he grew tired of explaining to his friends that he was not the author of offensive articles by the *Times's* other book-reviewers.[30]

This exasperation with the *Times* reflected a chronic dissatisfaction on Thackeray's part with the conservative opinions of the periodicals for which he chiefly wrote. Many years later he reminded his mother that in 1837 he "was offered do you remember to be Editor of the Carlisle Patriot, . . . & refused I think because it was too Tory for me (it was in the Lonsdale interest)." [31] Particularly towards the end of 1839 he gave some thought to his chances of finding employment with one of the organs of the liberal press. He wrote occasionally for the *Globe*,[32] and he sent the *Morning Chronicle* an article on the "Bedchamber Crisis," which that paper declined to use.[33] In December, Albany Fonblanque, the editor of the *Examiner*, approached him concerning a vacant position on his staff. "It w^d^ be great labor & no pay," Thackeray reflected, "but if I had the courage to keep it for 3 years I should have a good smattering of politics, and might so hope to maintain myself in a comfortable dishonesty for the rest of my days." [34] Thus brought to the point of decision, however, he found that he could not persuade himself to enter upon a career of avowedly political journalism.

Meanwhile, he was accepting whatever non-political assignments he could find. He continually pestered his friend John Kemble for commissions to write for the latter's *British and Foreign Review*. "Do not turn away better pens for mine," he wrote on 5 July 1839, "but my dear fellow try and give me all the work you can—for not to mention the marvellous goodness of the pay, and my own want of it the work is so pleasant improving and gentlemanlike that I long for as much as ever I can get hold of." [35] Richard Bentley published "The Professor," Thackeray's story about Dando the oyster-eater, in *Bentley's Miscellany* of September, 1837; and the following year Henry Colburn, Bentley's bitter rival, retaliated by securing Thackeray's narrative of Major Gahagan's adventures for his *New Monthly Magazine*. In the summer of 1839 Thackeray fell in with the American journalist Nathaniel P. Willis, who had come to England to secure matter for his new magazine, the *Corsair*. As the title of this publication candidly asserts, Willis relied chiefly on piracy for his materials. But he had been much struck by Yellowplush and Gahagan, and when he found that Thackeray was willing to work "for a guinea a *close column* of the 'Corsair,'" he ventured to engage him for original contributions. This was "cheaper than I ever did anything in my life," he told his colleague Dr. T. O. Porter. "I will see that he is paid for a while to see how you like him. For myself, I think him the very best periodical writer alive. He is a royal, daring, fine creature too." [36] Between July and October, Thackeray wrote eight letters to the *Corsair*. If they ceased because Willis proved an uncertain paymaster, as seems likely, Thackeray later exacted ample compensation in his satirical sketches of Willis as a kind "of Sly or Bottom introduced to splendors quite unknown to him." [37] But this does not by any means complete the tale of Thackeray's contributions between 1837 and 1840. In 1840 he wrote a long article on his friend George Cruikshank for the *Westminster Review;* he provided text for Victorian picture-books (notably for Cruikshank's *Comic Almanacks* of 1839 and 1840); he wrote for obscure journals like the *Torch* and the *Parthenon;* [38] as the opportunity occurred, he eked out his journalistic earnings by illustrating the text of other writers; and he even executed for a week or two the humble scissors-and-paste duties of a subeditor for *Galignani's Messenger.*[39]

The pressure of necessity was so sharp, indeed, that he had to take any employment which offered, without much thought of what he would like to do or what would help him to build a reputation. "I am as poor as a rat," he told Kemble, "and my spending runs so deucedly close to my earnings that if the payment of these is delayed I and an amiable family run the risk of intermediate starvation." [40] It was by these circumstances that Thackeray was led to reflect in his essay on Fielding, that "indiscriminate literary labour, which obliges a man to scatter his intellect upon so many trifles, and to provide weekly varieties as set-offs against the inevitable butcher's bills, has been the ruin of many a man of talent." [41] Yet life on such terms took on an intensity almost equal to that of his early gambling days. Surtees relates how in 1850 he visited the Trafalgar, Greenwich, with Thackeray, who told him: "I remember dining at this table with my wife when a sovereign was all I had in the world, and I spent 17s. of it. I wanted to nerve and excite myself up to writing." [42] These frantic early years, indeed, fixed once for all Thackeray's working habits. In later life he could say with Scott: "I love to have the press thumping, clattering and banging in my rear; it creates the necessity which almost always makes me work best." [43]

II

Until the first months of 1838 the Thackerays resided with the Carmichael-Smyths at 18 Albion Street. But the failure of the *Constitutional* and a series of ensuing financial misadventures reduced the old people's income to a point where they could no longer afford to live in London. They accordingly removed to Paris, where the Major alarmed his wife by talking of returning to active Indian service; and the Thackerays had to go house-hunting. Twenty-five years later Thackeray recalled how they "looked at [a] house by Brunswick Sq. & found it too dear—£80." [1] But by early March they had discovered a cheaper home at 13 Great Coram Street, which also adjoined Brunswick Square. Bloomsbury at this time was anything but a fashionable location. It was only a few years earlier, indeed, that John Wilson Croker had asked to be told where Bloomsbury Square was. Thackeray used to joke with his friends about his humble address. We find him assuring Bryan Waller Procter, for example, that "Brunswick Square ought to be respectable being only accessible to the gig-keepers." [2] The topic even entered his fiction. In *The Bedford-Row Conspiracy* Lady Gorgon, "always remarkable for her size and insolence of demeanour," persists in misreading the name of nearby Mecklenburgh Square. "I presume that persons in my rank of life are not expected to know everybody's name in Magdeburg-square?" she inquires. And Thackeray comments, with some feeling: "Lady Gorgon had a house in Baker-street, and a dismal house it was." [3]

Though the Thackerays' establishment was unpretentious, it attained a decent minimum of comfort. Their furniture was supplied from the Albion Street house,[4] since the Carmichael-Smyths took little with them for their Parisian apartment. Isabella was even provided with a piano for her modest drawing-room. "Dont you recollect her singing and her sweet sweet voice?" Thackeray wrote many years later to her sister Jane.[5] The servants included (at various times) old John Goldsworthy, who was subsequently joined by his wife; a cook; and a pair of maids.[6] Early in 1839 the household gained an invaluable recruit in Jessie Brodie, a sturdy young nurse who talked broad Scots. She was "tall and erect with red hair and blue eyes," we are informed, "and knitted holding one of her needles to her hip." [7] His servants were uniformly devoted to Thackeray, who unlike many Victorian masters treated them as human beings and made friends of them. He told Bedingfield, for example, that he always wrote to Goldsworthy as "Dear John." [8]

The Thackerays' first child, Anne, had been born on 9 June 1837 at 18 Albion Street. Mrs. Carmichael-Smyth, after whom the child was named, believed fervently in homoeopathy, and she insisted upon calling in her favourite physician for Isabella's confinement. Thackeray later told his daughter that "he knew nothing about it and the homeopathic doctor nearly killed her, and he (Papa) sent out and brought in another who was only just in time to save her life." [9] Certainly her birth was a "bad business," and the health of both child and mother continued to be uncertain for some time thereafter, in part perhaps because of the rival attentions lavished on them by Mrs. Carmichael-Smyth and Mrs. Shawe.[10]

The Thackerays' second child, Jane (named for Isabella's sister), was born on 9 July 1838 at 13 Great Coram Street.[11] Her birth occurred so suddenly that there was no time to secure aid from a doctor or midwife, though the attendance of a competent *accoucheur* was shortly provided. On this occasion, however, Isabella suffered not at all. "She produces children with a remarkable facility," Thackeray assured Mrs. Shawe. "She is as happy and as comfortable as any woman can be." Isabella was attended during her convalescence by Mary Graham, "a most excellent, watchful, tender nurse," and FitzGerald brought her *The Pickwick Papers* to read.[12] But Jane did not thrive, as Anny eventually had, and on 14 March 1839, aged eight months and six days, she died of an "inflammation in the chest." Brodie attended her during her last days and registered her death.[13] Both parents were deeply affected by this event. Thackeray wrote to his mother, in an unaccustomed burst of tenderness:

> What shall I say to you about our little darling who is gone?—I don't feel sorrow for her, and think of her only as something charming that for a season we were allowed to enjoy: when Anny was very ill dying as I almost thought, it seemed to me wrong to pray for her life, . . . and now I would be almost sorry—no that is not true—but I would not ask to have the dear little Jane back again and subject her to the degradation of life and pain.[14]

For some years thereafter Thackeray noted the anniversary of Jane's death in his diaries and letters. Anny relates that he "always expected to find his little Janie somewhere," and that when his death was near a quarter of a century later, he was comforted by the thought that he would not be "left without a child." [15] On 25 March Isabella asked her mother-in-law:

How can you reproach yourself for having done nothing for that sweet one? Did she not wear all the night dresses of your making? the little white frocks of your making As long as she was spared me she was attended to with all the care I had *learnt* from *you* in watching Annie. . . . You know William like most men did not take great delight in very young ones, but she never saw him but she would try to get to him and would call him "Pa," "Pa." Her little heart seemed full of love for every body and such a gentle sweet-tempered Lamb that it seems almost merciful that she should not have had to struggle with this world. I sometimes grieve to think that she was so quickly taken, but how foolish, would I have had her pine and fade because it was a sudden shock to me to have her suddenly removed. A child's death is dreadful but a child's suffering is ten thousand times worse.[16]

Later in this letter Isabella confessed that she felt "rather sluggish for writing brings on such an acute train of recollection," and she was, indeed, profoundly distressed by the loss of her child. Henceforth her life more and more "slipped by . . . quietly reading or *sleeping* or musing." [17]

Meanwhile, Anny's precocity was a delight to her father and a solace to her mother. They collaborated with the little girl in such notes to Mrs. Carmichael-Smyth as the following: "Granny, Here is a letter. I wish my love some day to her. I been Zoologilan gardens, see eflums, and camels leopards, and monkeys and ostriches, & every thing." [18] And their letters abounded in stories about her. When Anny was not yet two, Isabella wrote:

She knows not only the names of animals but the noise they make so that when William called her a little donkey today she began hee haw, hee haw. And one day when she had done something improper on the floor and the Nurse told her it was not like "a young lady but a little pig" she looked up and gave one grunt, which quite upset our gravity.[19]

A few months later Isabella took Anny along with her on a visit to the Kembles, who had a little girl her age.

Miss Gertrude . . . seemed very jealous of her [Isabella wrote to Mrs. Carmichael-Smyth] and at last gave her two *hard* smacks on the head to which looking great astonishment she merely replied "Why you spoil my pretty bonnet." Mrs Kemble then taking her daughter behind the door did what she was correcting the child for doing & Annie in the generosity of her heart forgetting her *head* rushed after her saying "Don't hurt *poor lickle girl.*" [20]

Thackeray's references to his daughter are no less fond than Isabella's, though most of them are not without a saving note of scepticism. "Kemble's child can sing twelve tunes but is as ugly as sin in revenge," he told his mother on one occasion. "However we must n't brag: for every body who comes into the house remarks Missy's squint that strange to say has grown quite imperceptible to me." [21] And we find him observing of Anny's behaviour at a party: "the little wretch went through all her tricks, & danced and sang and giggled just as she used to do before admiring Grannies." [22] To Thackeray, indeed, Anny was an endlessly interesting subject for study. "What are the mysteries of children?" he inquired as he watched her about the house; "how are they moved I wonder? . . . There is a grand power of imagination about these little creatures, and a creative fancy and belief that is very curious to watch: it fades away in the light of common day." [23] Elsewhere he told how "John Allen sent her the other day a great book of scripture prints, those from Mant's Bible, but a great scene took place when she came to Abraham sacrificing Isaac: she cried and screamed and said, 'No, he should not kill poor little boy,' and tried to pull Isaac off the altar." On which Thackeray commented: "Truly out of the mouths of babes and sucklings comes wisdom." [24]

For some time after their removal to England the Thackerays saw relatively little company apart from their relatives and close friends. After the Carmichael-Smyths settled in Paris, Thackeray visited them with some regularity, taking Isabella and Anny along on a trip in November of 1839, but for the most part travelling alone. Mary Graham was a frequent caller, and cordial relations were resumed with the Ritchies after they removed from Paris to London in 1839. Mrs. Shawe and Jane were in London at the time Anny was born and passed some weeks at Great Coram Street in May, 1839; Arthur was a house guest in 1840; and Lieutenant-Colonel Merrick Shawe was a welcome visitor throughout this period. Otherwise the Thackerays depended for companionship chiefly upon other couples on the fringes of the literary world: the John Allens, the Bullers, the Carlyles, the Kembles, the Procters, and the Anthony Sterlings. In this society, manners were simple and unpretentious, dinners were inexpensive repasts in the plain English style, and conversation was largely on literary or domestic topics. It was a *Kleinleben,* certainly, but a *Kleinleben* of a comfortable and cosy kind. Thackeray was thoroughly at home in such company, and Isabella, though she contributed little to the talk, came to feel at ease with such kind and understanding friends.

Thackeray and his wife presented a strange contrast in appearance, as Bedingfield noted, "for he was six feet three, and she was below the middle height; so that she could barely reach his arm." [25] Even stranger were their differences in character and taste, and some of his associates no doubt asked themselves what their friend saw in his quiet little wife. But to Thackeray, who thought that the story of Cinderella was "the sweetest of all stories," [26] there were qualities in Isabella to which the world in general was blind. Her letters reveal that among those whom she loved and trusted Isabella was a loyal, warm-hearted, unaffected young woman. To Thackeray she was a great deal more; he found in her a "nobleness and simplicity" [27] that was hidden from those who knew her less intimately. Moreover, if Isabella could not contribute much to conversation on "grave subjects," this was not always a disadvantage. Thackeray once assured Bedingfield "that it was quite 'refreshing' to escape to his wife sometimes—she was not political." [28] At the time of his first long absence from her in 1838, he wrote: "I feel as if I had left one of my legs in Coram Street, and get on very lamely without it —all this serves to show one how closely a wife gets about the heart, and how ill one can do without her." "It is almost a blessing that I came away, for I see now more strongly than ever, how much I love her, and how my whole heart & bowels go with her. Here have we been nearly 2 years married & not a single unhappy day." [29]

III

The Thackerays' marriage was a successful one, then, by any standard; yet there was a worm in the bud of their happiness. When Isabella first became engaged to Thackeray, he bought her an engagement ring in which a diamond was set between two opals. His grand-daughter tells an ominous story about this ring. "Thackeray, delighted with his purchase, showed it with beaming pride to a friend, who exclaimed in dismay, 'But, William, see what you have done, this is a mourning ring, not an engagement ring.' And sure enough, the setting of the opals was black enamel." [1] As the years passed and the first glamour of happiness faded, Thackeray's awareness that marriage had pains as well as pleasures became increasingly acute. It was brought home to him that Isabella was in some respects woefully unprepared for married life, and though he was too loyal to admit this fact even to himself, there are hints enough in his letters and elsewhere to allow us to see her deficiencies clearly.

She was certainly a lamentably inefficient housewife. Mrs. Carmichael-Smyth did what she could to train her, and Isabella exerted herself to learn, but the effect of these efforts was negligible. Her attempts to keep the family accounts were defeated by what Thackeray called her "noble want of the organ of number." [2] She was hardly an effective disciplinarian. Though she promised Mrs. Carmichael-Smyth that the family would rise at eight, they somehow persisted in getting up at ten. Her mother-in-law, trained with the utmost severity by the stern Mrs. Becher, was appalled at the want of order and cleanliness in her household. Thackeray was later to confess the justice of this criticism in a wry comment that he made about Charles and Mary Carmichael in 1842: "They are fine housekeepers—worse than we were I think such dirt & cobwebs on the walls, suffered so calmly." [3] Isabella's direction of the kitchen left much to be desired. Thackeray once asked his mother whether she could suggest anything "to put into a hash to give it a flavour that was not onions and water." [4] And, crime of crimes in Victorian domestic economy, Isabella even permitted the smoking of cigars in the drawing-room.[5] Thackeray had broken her emotional dependence upon her mother, but neither he nor Mrs. Carmichael-Smyth could compensate for the wasted years that she had passed with Mrs. Shawe. Despite her struggle to improve herself, she remained a child wife, playing at housekeeping, a fact that Thackeray himself tacitly recognized, indeed, by his habit of referring to her by such pet names as "Little Trot" and "Isabinda."

If the Thackerays' circumstances had been easy, Isabella's domestic inadequacies would have mattered less. But unhappily Carlyle's description of Thackeray in 1837 as "writing for his life" [6] was strictly accurate. When Major Carmichael-Smyth found himself in financial straits after the failure of the *Constitutional,* Thackeray told him "that he was welcome to the use of all the money that I had or had a right to *except the sum for Mrs Blechynden's annuity,*" [7] and the Major took advantage of his stepson's offer. Thackeray thus lost for some years all income from the residue of his patrimony, and was rendered altogether dependent on his earnings as a writer. Following the promptings of Mrs. Carmichael-Smyth, various economies were debated: renting a cheaper house, giving up their servants (even the faithful John and the indispensable Brodie), or taking a lodger. Though it did not prove necessary to adopt any of these expedients, Thackeray found himself in a state of chronic insolvency. He was reduced to shifts that a few years back he would have found excruciatingly humiliating, among them the acceptance of a 1,000-franc loan from a French tailor, an event quaintly recorded in the dedication of *The Paris Sketch Book.*[8] He remained cheerful enough under these irritations, but he could not refrain from an occasional whimsical protest against Isabella's incompetent management, and Mrs. Carmichael-Smyth was less restrained in her criticisms. The upshot was that Isabella became still more firmly persuaded of her unworthiness.

Another fruitful source of annoyance was the intense dislike that Mrs. Carmichael-Smyth and Mrs. Shawe conceived for each other. Thackeray must certainly have had in mind the weeks at Albion Street which followed Anny's birth, when he wrote in *A Shabby Genteel Story* that "a house with a wife is often warm enough; a house with a wife and her mother is rather warmer than any spot on the known globe; a house with two mothers-in-law is so excessively hot, that it can be likened to no place on earth at all, but one must go lower for a simile." [9] Mrs. Shawe was particularly angry because she sensed the love and respect that her daughter had come to feel for Mrs. Carmichael-Smyth. Knowing that her pre-eminence in Isabella's affections was doubly lost, she allowed her suspicion of Thackeray and his family to deepen into hatred. For his part, Thackeray detested Mrs. Shawe and found it difficult to remain long in her company without losing his temper. Visiting her in Paris in 1838, he claimed credit from Isabella for bringing off the interview without "the shadow of a row." [10] When Mrs. Shawe came to stay at Great Coram Street the following year, he contrived to be out of the house even more than usual. Thackeray particularly resented her treatment of her second daughter Jane, in whom he no doubt saw what Isabella might have become but for his intervention. When he saw Jane in Paris, he told his wife, she

> began to talk about you, and burst out crying, in a kind of agony. . . . Part of her grief is love for you, part is exquisite wretchedness I do believe—She has no one to love or to speak to: and your mothers solicitude only makes matters worse. . . . Let us see what can be done to comfort her, and give her a little something to pour her heart into: for it is dammed up as it were, & must take all sorts of unnatural channels to give itself vent.[11]

Jane had a suitor who had proposed to her on many occasions.[12] But he did not satisfy Mrs. Shawe's impossibly high standards, which she had persuaded Jane to share; and he lacked the courage to carry off his virgin from her dragon mother, as Thackeray had done. Isabella's brother Arthur, who like the other boys of the family had lived much away from Mrs. Shawe, seemed at first to be "a merry pleasant gentlemanlike fellow without a particle of brogue," [13] relatively free from the usual Shawe failings; but upon prolonged acquaintance Thackeray found him tiresome as well. If Thackeray's nerves were constantly rasped by enforced association with this alien clan, for which he could summon up little sympathy, he was at least storing away a wealth of observation for two of his fictional specialties, the Irish and mothers-in-law. For Isabella, torn as she was between old and new loyalties, renewed association with her family served only to increase the tension under which she lived.

But the Thackerays' difficulties were not limited to external circumstances. Profoundly as they loved each other, there were still causes for friction between them. Though Thackeray hated *Don Juan,* he would have admitted the applicability to his own case of Byron's famous lines:

> Man's love is of man's life a thing apart,
> 'T is woman's whole existence.

As professional demands upon his time multiplied, he found it increasingly difficult to work at home, where "Isabella comes to pay me a visit every 1/2 minute or so, and I'm not as angry as I ought to be." [14] In half-humorous distress he reported to Mrs. Carmichael-Smyth that "Miss Thackeray and her mother are at this moment dragging carts round the room, and yelling Taytoes in a way that precludes all possibility of grammar." [15] Though she made "the prettiest excuses in the world," Thackeray "in the pains of labor" would grow "dreadfully cross" with her; [16] and to spare her and to get on with his task he would withdraw to one of his clubs, or even on occasion farther afield, to Ramsgate with his friend Lettsom, for example, or to Leatherhead to visit the Bullers.[17] Moreover, though Isabella could express herself easily and pleasantly on the small concerns of domestic life, her opinions on general topics were mere echoes of Thackeray's own.[18] When he needed intellectual companionship, she could only cling to him affectionately. Confessing that "without my favorite talk about pictures or books I am good for nothing," [19] Thackeray came more and more to seek elsewhere what his home could not provide.

And if Thackeray left home to work, or to get himself into the mood for work, he often remained to play. Though he wrote that he could not bear to think of Isabella's meeting with neglect, he added the qualification, "any positive neglect I mean —as for jollifying after a day's work I cant help that, and sh^{d} be good for nothing without it." [20] The habits of his bachelor days began to reassert themselves. He was seen more often at the Garrick Club. In 1840 he joined the Reform Club, despite the fact that he could ill afford its twenty-guinea entrance fee.[21] He was the stalwart supporter of several "tavern clubs," including the "Rationals," which met on Saturday afternoons at the Wrekin in Broad Court, Drury Lane, and numbered Cruikshank, Douglas Jerrold, Clarkson Stanfield, Mark Lemon, and Henry Mayhew among its members; [22] the Eccentric Society, among the supporters of which were Percival Banks, George Morland Crawford, William John O'Connell, and Major Renell; [23] and the Shakespeare, which had been established by Jerrold and carried Dickens, Maclise, Macready, and Talfourd on its roll.[24] Even when he stayed away from his clubs, there were friends at hand to entice him away from home. Isabella wrote in 1839 that she was "half cross with Fitz and his tail (Mr Morton forms part of it) They seem as if they could not breathe without William." [25] A night on the town with FitzGerald, Saville Morton, or some of his painter friends, "guttling and gorging," visiting the theatre, the Cider Cellars, or a boxing match, and talking afterwards till two or three in the morning, had irresistible attractions for Thackeray. And though he was by this time sufficiently inured to deep potations to rally his friends upon their inability to keep pace with him,[26] he was at least once seen the worse for drink. In a curious letter of 24 January 1840 he expressed to John Murray, head of the celebrated publishing house, his "shame and contrition" for the insulting behaviour into which he had been led by an "extraordinary quantity of wine" at a dinner given by James Fraser.[27]

Thackeray invariably regretted these excesses the following morning. His letters are dotted with good resolutions. But though he swore to follow a regimen of "breakfast at 8 walk at 2 with Mrs Thack: no club, and a light dinner," [28] he was utterly unable to adhere to this plan. When Becky Sharp reflects that "it isn't difficult to be a country gentleman's wife. . . . I think I could be a good woman if I had five thousand a year," [29] she is merely echoing a thought that occurred to Thackeray in 1839. Praising FitzGerald's brother John Kerrich as a "virtuous man —So good, sober and religious such a fine English squire," he added: "If I had 3000 a year I think I'd be so too." [30] But like Becky, Thackeray was "on the make," and, living under the pressure that he did, he could not do without the excitement that mild dissipation provided.

It was a maxim of Sir Morgan O'Doherty, Maginn's alter ego when he wrote for *Blackwood's Magazine,* that "a husband should be very attentive to his wife until the first child is born. After that she can amuse herself at home, while he resumes his jolly habits." [31] While Thackeray did not subscribe to this heartless counsel, it could none the less be said of him (as Meredith said of Victorian men generally), that if he had rounded Seraglio Point, he had not yet doubled Cape Turk. As Isabella found herself left more and more alone, she grew sick at heart. She tried to persuade herself that her husband's "time was so precious" that she could not expect to engross it. "I see nothing of William," she told Mrs. Carmichael-Smyth, "but this is all for the best I suppose." [32] Even when Thackeray was with her, he was often absorbed in speculations concerning his chances of success, and this too upset Isabella. When Thackeray finished *Vanity Fair,* it occurred to him how Isabella's "anxious little soul would have been alarmed at my prosperities such as they are." [33] She saw the *Kleinleben* into which she fitted so comfortably giving way to a new kind of life with limitless possibilities in which there was no obvious place for her. At the very time when her health was seriously affected, she brooded incessantly over the prospect that she might become an encumbrance to her husband. Her state of mind was an ominous one, but Thackeray was preoccupied and did not sense the dangers it foreboded. It was too late when he finally resolved: "I must learn to love home more, and do my duty at the fireside as well as in my writing-room." [34]

IV

What was Thackeray like within himself during his early years of marriage? It should first be noted that he was sharing the common lot of men approaching thirty; he was experiencing the flight of youth, the advent of middle age. By 1840 his hair was grey,[1] and the long, leisurely days of young manhood, given over to friendship, to the arts, to pleasure, were irrevocably gone. "The horrible glazed eyes of Necessity are always fixed upon you," he reflected; "fly away as you will, black Care sits behind you, and with his ceaseless gloomy croaking drowns the voice of all more cheerful companions." One by one, Thackeray's illusions dropped from him, leaving a world that seemed to him drab and depressing enough:

> Damp and chill the shades of the prison-house begin to close round us, and that 'vision splendid' which has accompanied our steps in our journey daily farther from the east, fades away and dies into the light of common day.
>
> And what a common day! what a foggy, dull, shivering apology for light is this kind of muddy twilight through which we are about to tramp and flounder for the rest of our existence, wandering farther and farther from the beauty and freshness and from the kindly gushing springs of clear gladness that made all around us green in our youth! [2]

If years had not yet brought Thackeray the philosophic mind to which Wordsworth attained even in the gloom of the prison-house, his farewell to youth at any rate inspired in him his first real effort to understand and come to terms with his world.

He made this effort under difficult circumstances. He had long since been jolted out of the comfortable groove along which English gentlemen of comfortable fortune moved. In the eyes of society he had dropped farther and farther down the social ladder as he lost his fortune, married a penniless girl, and entered an almost disreputable profession. Since Thackeray's own estimate of his proper rank in life had not been altered by these events, the contrast between the treatment that he expected from society and the treatment that he received was often painful. He had to endure a series of rebuffs, slights, and humiliations which made him acutely sensitive to the whole subject of social relationships as they were organized in Victorian England.[3]

Under these pressures Thackeray's political and social views shifted appreciably to the left. But he remained as he had been in early years, far more conservative than were the Carmichael-Smyths. His mother admired the Chartist leader Feargus O'Connor,[4] while Thackeray, even at his most exacerbated, wrote to her that he was "not a Chartist, only a Republican." And though he expressed a devout wish to see Whigs and Tories alike disappear, "all men equal, and this bloated artistocracy blasted to the wings of all the winds," [5] he was never an equalitarian. For Thackeray, indeed, the world of the poor was a *terra incognita.* He knew that the educated classes of England were merely the narrow apex of a broad pyramid, that there was "a tremendous society moving around us, and unknown to us—a vast mass of active, stirring life, in which the upper and middling classes form an insignificant speck." But though he admitted that "an English gentleman knows as much about the people of Lapland or California as he does of the aborigines of the Seven Dials or the natives of Wapping," [6] he saw no pressing reason why this situation should be changed. He wished the populace well, he saw much in it that was good, but he had no sense of identification with it.[7] And when revolution seemed to threaten, as it did during the Chartist agitations of 1840, he grew "very much alarmed about the state of the country," even while he asked himself if his alarm was not unnecessary, "for what can I lose?" [8]

If Thackeray's attitude towards the lower classes was one of casual and withdrawn goodwill, he was profoundly resentful of aristocratic privilege. The great past of the English aristocracy, which he was later to celebrate so eloquently in *Esmond,* had not yet caught his imagination. Indeed, he was inclined to inquire, in defiance of Burke, "whether the age of chivalry was cheap or dear, and whether, in the time of the unbought grace of life, there was not more bribery, robbery, villainy, tyranny, and corruption, than exists even in our own happy days?" [9] Towards the parody of the aristocratic code that had survived into the uncongenial atmosphere of the nineteenth century, he was altogether merciless. For George IV and dandyism; for fashionable life, its representative institutions like Almack's, and the "silver-fork" novels in which it was described; for the aristocratic notion of "honour," Thackeray felt a scorn which exceeded even that of Carlyle in his attack on the "Dandiacal Body" in *Sartor Resartus*. The prevailing "Lordolatry" appalled him, and his early fiction is dotted with onslaughts upon it. "We *like* being insulted by noablemen—it shows they're familiar with us," he makes Yellowplush observe. "If Sattn himself were a Lord, I do beleave there's many vurtuous English mothers would be glad to have him for a son-in-law." [10] In *Catherine* he adds: "There is about a free-born Briton a cringing baseness, and lick-spittle awe of rank, which does not exist under any tyranny in Europe, and is only to be found here and in America." [11] Where social position was used to palliate offences against the moral code, Thackeray was particularly severe. "If he had been a common man," said Yellowplush of Deuceace, "you'd have said he was no better than a swinler. It's only rank and buth that can warrant such singularities as my master show'd." [12]

Yet despite his resentment of aristocratic privilege, Thackeray continued to pride himself upon being a gentleman. He was groping towards a redefinition of gentlemanliness which would adapt it to an age of middle-class dominance. Only when this was accomplished, could he feel confident about the grounds for his own position. In the mean time, much accumulated bitterness, deriving from his uncertain status, found its way into his writing. So he avers in *A Shabby Genteel Story* that "it is one good test of gentility to be . . . looked down on by vulgar people." [13] So he makes sure in his fiction, sometimes with an unpleasant vindictiveness, that lower-middle-class men who assume gentlemanly airs get an emphatic come-uppance.[14] In fact, Thackeray's attitude towards social class at this period had something of the inconsistency of George Orwell's when a scholarship boy at Eton, passing "half the time in denouncing the capitalist system and the other half in raging over the insolence of bus-conductors." [15]

It was characteristic of Thackeray to see political issues primarily in their social aspect. But his apathy towards politics and his indifference to what Carlyle called the "Condition-of-England Question" were not the result of callousness. These attitudes derived instead from the fact that his real and absorbing interests lay elsewhere. He had a remarkable capacity for enjoying the good things of life in all their manifestations, and his wide general culture rendered him impatient with any attempt to make literature serve predominantly political and humanitarian ends. At the same time, he believed firmly in the social utility of literature, painting, and music; and he was fond of quoting (from the Latin Grammar, he disarmingly assured his readers) Ovid's tribute to the "ingenuous arts, which prevent the ferocity of the manners, and act upon them as an emollient." [16] Such an essay as the admirable "Caricatures and Lithography in Paris" gains much of its value from Thackeray's demonstration of how the cultivation of art and the encouragement of harmless amusement in France had helped to make the working classes of that country happy and cheerful, while on the other side of the Channel philistinism and puritanism had united to make the English proletariat gloomy and embittered.[17]

By 1840 there was also beginning to emerge in Thackeray's mind, as he came more and more to look before and after—to weigh the limited possibilities of human life—a view of the human condition which gradually became the fixed and settled basis of his mature outlook. If the illusions of youth had disappeared, he felt their absence all the more because he had once believed in them so entirely. Like Molière's Alceste, he was experiencing that most acute form of misanthropy which comes from disenchantment. In his black moods he came to regard the ordinary amenities of social intercourse as revealing only "that kind of cordiality that we see in Sir Harry and my lady in a comedy—a couple of painted, grinning fools, talking parts that they have learned out of a book." [18] The anger which coloured his view of the world, as an acute French critic pointed out, was "la réaction d'une nature tendre, furieuse d'avoir été désapointée." [19] The weakness and evil which he saw about him bewildered and appalled him. Writing to his mother at the end of 1839, when he was greatly distressed by the shipwreck which his friend Salt had made of life, he reflected:

I feel ashamed of my own comfort and happiness in thinking of this dreadful groveling misery—it seems like a reflection upon God who has bestowed his gifts so partially. Look at these unequal lots in the fortunes of men, and see how completely circumstance (of personal disposition or outward fortune) masters all—and one begins to think of Vice and Virtue as here practised, with profound scorn or else with bitter humiliation and debasement.[20]

From this perspective the conventional moral judgments of society seemed hollow and Pharisaical. He reserved his profoundest contempt for those who "have a marvellous respect for prosperity, and a corresponding scorn for ill-fortune." [21] Visiting Saint-Lazare prison in Paris, he saw "a grown woman with a placid face, who had her arm around the neck of a young girl; they were both singing together off the same music-book, and in the intervals seemed to be fond and affectionate towards each other." And he inquired of his reader: "I wonder whether you or I, madam, are a whit better than this couple of choristers in their dingy prison-dresses; or whether, when we, at church, out of gilt prayer-books with gold clasps, follow the clerk and sing the Old Hundredth very gingerly and genteelly—I wonder, I say, whose music is, in reality, the best?" [22] In a world where such questions could be asked, success was surely the emptiest of all illusions. "One wanders and gropes in a slough of stock-jobbing, one sinks or rises in a storm of politics, and in either case it is as good to fall as to rise—to mount a bubble on the crest of the wave, as to sink a stone to the bottom." [23]

It followed inevitably that the heroes of the world were not heroes in Thackeray's eyes. His famous "historical study" of Louis XIV in *The Paris Sketch Book* sums up his views on this subject. Louis in his wig, his flowing robes, and his high shoes is every inch a king. Without them, he is nothing more than a "little, lean, shrivelled, paunchy old man." "Thus do barbers and cobblers make the gods that we worship." [24]

My dear sir [he assures his reader in *Catherine*], when you have well studied the world, how supremely great the meanest thing in this world is, and how infinitely mean the greatest, I am mistaken if you do not make a strange and proper jumble of the sublime and the ridiculous, the lofty and the low. I have looked at the world for my part, and come to the conclusion that I know not which is which.[25]

The upshot of the whole matter to Thackeray was an enigma, an inexplicable mystery.

Who has not felt how he works, the dreadful, conquering Spirit of Ill? Who cannot see, in the circle of his own society, the fated and foredoomed to woe and evil? Some call the doctrine of destiny a dark creed; but, for me, I would fain try and think it a consolatory one. It is better, with all one's sins upon one's head, to deem oneself in the hands of Fate than to think, with our fierce passions and weak repentances, with our resolves so loud, so vain, so ludicrously, despicably weak and frail, with our dim, wavering, wretched conceits about virtue, and our irresistible propensity to wrong, that we are the workers of our future sorrow or happiness.[26]

From life so conceived, the best that man could hope was the sort of golden mediocrity possible in an obscure and contented domestic life.

Still, it must be granted, that for the most part his melancholy view of things enforced itself upon Thackeray only when he sat down at his desk. In active life he was too much engrossed with the business of getting on to have leisure for viewing the world philosophically. He had himself in mind when he wrote in his essay on "George Cruikshank," that

a man who is ceaselessly engaged in . . . [the] trouble and turmoil [of this wicked world], borne hither and thither upon the fierce waves of the crowd, bustling, shifting, struggling to keep himself somewhat above water—fighting for reputation, or more likely for bread, and ceaselessly occupied to-day with plans for appeasing the eternal appetite of inevitable hunger to-morrow—a man in such straits has hardly time to think of anything but himself, and, as in a sinking ship, must make his own rush for the boats, and fight, struggle, and trample for safety.[27]

Yet by the early months of 1840, his motto no longer needed to be *Sauve qui peut.* His reputation as a magazine writer was good and improving. *The Paris Sketch Book* was soon to appear, and he planned to follow it with a collection of his comic tales. He was perfectly justified in asserting, "One good hit and I am made." [28] Moreover, he had come to enjoy the battle in which he was engaged.

> You must not go for to alarm yourself about my infinite struggles hardships & labours [he told his mother]; every one of them do good —and a man's mind would get flaccid and inert if he were always to have others caring for him, and providing his meat & drink. . . . [London] has a tough work-day appearance—and so much the better —look how every body is pushing forward and looking onward, and anxiously struggling—amen by God's help we will push on too: have we not long legs (I mean of mind and body) and why should we lag behind? . . .[29]
>
> O this London is a grand place for scheming, and rare fun for a man with broad shoulders who can push through the crowd.[30]

To the casual onlooker of this period Thackeray must have seemed less like the slim, reserved, and faintly dandified Pendennis, with whom later readers have tended to identify him, than like the burly and companionable Philip. Immersed in life, glorying in his strength, inclined to pass judgment summarily on inadequate evidence, he possessed as yet neither the polished outer manner that later made him welcome in society, nor the subtle understanding that afterwards enabled him to sense human relationships with such exquisite tact. The chastening action of experience was still much needed to cut a gem out of this rough diamond.

9

Apprentice Writer

I

WE HAVE SEEN that Thackeray in the later 1830s was an energetic and downright young man, dissatisfied with the world and his place in it and not inclined to remain silent about his discontent. Detesting pretentiousness, incompetence, and venality, he was confronted by a literary scene of which these were the leading features; and his response was a series of verbal explosions. To understand why he reacted as he did, we must first comprehend what provoked him.

The 1830s were a painful interregnum in the history of English literature. The success of Byron in poetry and Scott in fiction had created a new mass reading public. When these great men died, they left behind them no obvious successors. Yet the appetite for print that they had aroused offered commercial opportunities too tempting to be ignored, and enterprising publishers were quick to take advantage of them. Thus a generation of naïve and half-educated readers came to be exploited by a generation of business men who were hardly better trained. The primitive and uncertain taste of these recruits to literacy was best satisfied by crude and garish effects. A "philosophy of exaggeration" prevailed, which Thackeray illustrated by the following story:

Mr. —— was once behind the scenes at the Opera when the scene-shifters were preparing for the ballet. Flora was to sleep under a bush, whereon were growing a number of roses, and amidst which was fluttering a gay covey of butterflies. In size the roses exceeded the most expansive sunflowers, and the butterflies were as large as cocked-hats;—the scene-shifter explained to Mr. ——, who asked the reason why everything was so magnified, that the galleries could never see the objects unless they were enormously exaggerated. How many of our writers and designers work for the galleries? [1]

So crude was the taste of the age that literary quality became a consideration far less important to publishers and readers than such irrelevant matters as the social rank of a writer. Indeed, the asking price for a manuscript might be doubled or trebled, if its author were titled.

The novel, being of all literary forms the most sensitive to popular taste, suffered particularly under such conditions. Jane Austen had protested in *Northanger Abbey* against a tendency to regard novel-reading as a frivolous amusement. To the disparaging comment "only a novel," she had replied: "Only some work in which the greatest powers of the mind are displayed, in which the most thorough knowledge of human nature, the happiest delineation of its varieties, the liveliest effusions of wit and humour, are conveyed to the world in the best chosen language." [2] But these phrases could be applied to few novels of the 1830s. To sate the appetite of the untutored and semi-literate audience of that day, quantity rather than quality was needed. Mass production was accompanied as always by standardization. Fiction was written to fit certain established categories; there were historical novels, fashionable novels, comic novels, adventure novels, military novels, naval novels, criminal novels, Eastern novels, and religious novels.[3] That these products were for the most part monotonous and repetitive hack-work seemed to matter little to those who read them.

Nor did the situation differ materially with regard to poetry. Here the field was dominated by the annuals, illustrated gift-books published for the Christmas season, which were in many ways the most characteristic productions of the period.[4] Writing in 1837, Thackeray noted:

There have been, as we take it, since the first fashion for Annuals came up, some hundred and fifty volumes of the kind; and such a display of miserable mediocrity, such a collection of feeble verse, such a gathering of small wit, is hardly to be found in any other series.

All these books followed the same pattern.

A large weak plate done in what we believe is called the stipple style of engraving, a woman badly drawn, with enormous eyes—a tear, perhaps, upon each cheek, and an exceedingly low-cut dress—pats a greyhound, or weeps into a flower-pot, or delivers a letter to a bandy-legged, curly-headed page. . . . Miss Landon, Miss Mitford, or my Lady Blessington, writes a song upon the opposite page, about water-lily, chilly, stilly, shivering beside a streamlet, plighted, blighted, love-benighted, falsehood sharper than a gimlet, lost affection, recollection, cut connexion, tears in torrents, true-love token, spoken, broken, sighing, dying, girl of Florence, and so on. The poetry is quite worthy of the picture, and a little sham sentiment is employed to illustrate a little sham art.[5]

If such work flourished in fiction and poetry, criticism was clearly not in a healthy state. When the decade began, severity was the rule in critical judgment, but it was a severity motivated by political partisanship rather than by literary discrimination. After agitation over the Reform Bill had subsided, a work was often puffed or damned according to the degree of cordiality existing between its publisher and the owner of the periodical in which it was reviewed; and since the principle of reciprocity was generally adopted, puffery predominated. Henry Fothergill Chorley noted that in 1834 the *Literary Gazette* under Jerdan was entirely venal, its editor being merely the "puppet" of the booksellers; and when the critics of the *Athenaeum* aimed at impartiality in their criticisms, they were charged in the *Literary Gazette* with "defamation and envy." [6] Hence Thackeray's just complaint that, despite the badness of contemporary writing, "the critical rod . . . is, for the most part, thrown aside, . . . and praise, monstrous, indiscriminate, wholesale, is the fashion of the day." [7]

II

Thackeray was at this time still very much a novice in writing. Disgusted with the prevailing style, he looked for example to those who had spoken out against it most strongly. In 1837 Maginn and Carlyle were outstanding in this small group, and Thackeray for a time regarded these two men as his masters.

We have seen that Thackeray first met Maginn in 1832. It has been argued that the association of the two men remained close during the five years that elapsed before Thackeray became a regular and acknowledged contributor to *Fraser's Magazine*. Indeed, many articles in "Regina" during these years have been assigned more or less confidently to Thackeray, writing alone or in collaboration with his mentor.[1] Though these attributions are for the most part the merest speculation, supported by little or no external evidence, it is none the less clear that Thackeray picked up many ideas and techniques from his friend.

Maginn had himself been to school under "Christopher North" in *Blackwood's Magazine*, "the Great Professor, who, in fun, merely seizes on an unlucky devil, and flogs every morsel of skin off his back, so that he shall not be able to sit, lie, or walk, for months to come." [2] He learnt there to aim at riotous comedy, to lay about him with abandon, making sure only that his target was a political or literary enemy. Convinced that "he whose friendship is worth having, must hate and be hated," [3] Maginn specialized in the "slashing article" and sometimes descended in writing it to the most brutal personalities. But there were redeeming elements in his work: hearty good feeling and sound common sense; profound learning and wide knowledge of the world; and an honest desire to tell the truth as he saw it, where political partisanship or pressure from his publishers did not blur his vision. Even when Maginn's star was rapidly dropping out of sight in 1839, Thackeray could still propose the toast: "THE DOCTOR . . . and long life to him!—the man who reads, writes, and knows everything, and adorns everything of which he writes—even Homer." [4]

Although Thackeray was nearly eighteen years Maginn's junior, he thought of the Doctor as a boon companion. Towards Carlyle, on the other hand, his attitude was almost one of reverence. At this time Carlyle, as Mrs. Lynn Linton remarked, was "the yeast plant, fermenting the whole literary brew." [5] Certainly to Thackeray the author of *Sartor Resartus, The French Revolution,* and *Critical and Miscellaneous Essays* became for a time a "prophet" whose "words were manna to the Israelites." [6] It was primarily Carlyle's campaign against humbug as the besetting sin of the age which led Thackeray to enlist among his disciples; in him alone could he find a teacher who pierced to the heart of the shams of the period and exposed them mercilessly. Despite his reservations concerning the extraordinary style of *The French Revolution,* he thought it a great work, because "It has no CANT." And Carlyle's *Critical and Miscellaneous Essays* of 1840 impressed him as one of the noblest books in the language, because of its detachment from partisan prejudices. "Criticism has been a party matter with us till now," he told his mother, "and literature a poor political lackey—please God we shall begin ere long to love art for art's sake. It is Carlyle who has worked more than any other to give it its independence." [7] Thackeray's friendship with the Carlyles meant a great deal to him in these years; and his confidence in his own abilities was sustained by Carlyle, who said that his earlier performances showed " 'something Hogarthian' to be in him," [8] at a time when praise was rare.

Far less tangible than the influence of Maginn and Carlyle was that of a third writer, now almost altogether forgotten. This was Edward William Clarke, who published the first and only part of his *Library of Useless Knowledge* in 1837.[9] This pamphlet, for it is hardly more, reinforced the penchant towards fantastic nonsense that had helped to bring FitzGerald and Thackeray together at Cambridge. The identifying mark of this peculiar and illusive brand of humour is perhaps its air of specious plausibility. So grave and circumstantial are the terms in which an absurd proposition is advanced that, for one wild instant before common sense reasserts itself, the statement seems almost credible. Its distinctive note is heard, for example, in the speculations that Thackeray and FitzGerald exchanged about Spedding's forehead, or in the undeniable assertion in the passage quoted below from *The Tremendous Adventures of Major Gahagan* (a story full of this sort of humor) that there are no bones in an elephant's trunk.[10] No doubt we can also refer to the tradition of humor that Clarke represents Thackeray's delight in coining odd words like "protemporaneous" and "duelsome" and the almost talismanic significance that he attached to such comic names as "Boogleywallah" and "Bungay." [11]

The writer whose example was most useful to Thackeray in discovering the true bent of his talent, however, was none of these contemporaries but an older master, Henry Fielding.[12] Thackeray began his reading of Fielding as a boy with *Joseph Andrews;* by the time he went to Cambridge he knew Fielding's works well enough to sing their praises to his fellow undergraduates.[13] The first extended body of writing that we have from his pen, his contributions to the *Constitutional* in 1836–1837, is dotted with allusions to Fielding and his books.[14] And from this time until he contributed his famous essay to the *Times* on Thomas Roscoe's edition of *The Works of Henry Fielding,*[15] he lived on intimate terms with Fielding's novels. He regarded the kind of "grotesque humour" in which he specialized as being very much in the style of Fielding.[16] Writing in 1854 to a correspondent in whose work he had detected an imitation of his own *Dr. Birch and His Young Friends,* he remarked: "I daresay you are no more aware of the resemblance, than I was, years ago, that I imitated Fielding: but on looking back lately at some of those early papers I saw whose the original manner was." [17]

Thackeray was attracted to Fielding because his books were "full of benevolence, practical wisdom, and generous sympathy with mankind." They presented "a strong, real picture of human life," which could not but be moral in its total effect, even though it might offend the squeamish in detail.[18] Thus *Jonathan Wild* was a "great comic epic," which gave "a more curious picture of the manners of those times than any recognized history of them." Indeed, Thackeray continued, thanks to the "wondrous power of genius, Fielding's men and women are alive, though History's are not. . . . Is not Amelia preparing her husband's little supper? Is not Miss Snap chastely preventing the crime of Mr. Firebrand? Is not Parson Adams in the midst of his family, and Mr. Wild taking his last bowl of punch with the Newgate Ordinary? Is not every one of them a real substantial *have*-been personage now?" [19] What contrast to the artificiality, the feebleness, the mawkish sentiment of contemporary fiction! Even Dickens, the one authentic new voice of the 1830s, could not compare with Fielding. *Tom Jones* is "immeasurably superior" to *The Pickwick Papers,*[20] and "Fielding's men . . . are Dickens's, . . . drawn with ten times more skill and force." [21]

So much did Thackeray admire Fielding's books, so congenial did he find the attitude of mind displayed therein, that he came to identify himself with their author. It is enlightening to compare Roscoe's prefatory account of "The Life and Works of Henry Fielding" [22] with what Thackeray made of it in his *Times* review; for one quickly sees that Thackeray's unhistorical additions to Roscoe's portrait, such as his picture of "Harry Fielding in his tavern chair, carousing with Heaven knows whom," [23] have autobiographical implications. No wonder he later inquired of Mrs. Brookfield: "Doesn't the apology for Fielding read like an apology for somebody else too?" [24] It was because of this unconscious self-identification with Fielding that Thackeray "misunderstood and mis-stated the Man," as W. E. Henley accurately noted, despite his "absolute sympathy with the Writer." [25]

III

In 1837 Thackeray's real career as a writer began. His previous work had been negligible, but in his contributions to *Fraser's* and his other "magazinery" of the years 1837–1840 he at last achieved a distinctive style and point of view. He was himself inclined to think poorly of this part of his production in later life. We find him insisting, for example, that "when I was young . . . what I wrote was bad and poor stuff for many years." And again: "I look upon my first efforts as jokes and schoolboy exercises." Indeed, he was contemptuous of some of his early work not long after he finished it. Of *The Yellowplush Papers* he said to Bedingfield: "They are horrid rubbish; but I get well paid for them. A man must live." [1] Yet inferior as they are to his mature writing, many of these early stories and articles well repay reading.

Today we think of Thackeray as a realist. In an age when this term had not yet been invented, he preferred to describe himself as a follower of truth and nature. His essential aim was precisely that recommended by Dr. Johnson:

> . . . to bid the Reign commence
> Of rescu'd Nature, and reviving Sense.

Since the popular writers of the time tended to see life in terms of certain established conventions, of what their chief theorist Bulwer called "idealization," Thackeray's emphasis was a novel one. He states it most clearly in his criticism of art. Rejecting French painting of the classical school, he writes:

> Now, as Nature made every man with a nose and eyes of his own, she gave him a character of his own too; and yet we, O foolish race! must try our very best to ape some one or two of our neighbours, whose ideas fit us no more than their breeches! It is the study of Nature, surely, that profits us, and not of these imitations of her.[2]

Again, he adjures the English artists who provided drawings for the annuals: "Look at Nature and blush! See how much nobler she is than your pettifogging art!—how much more beautiful Truth is than your miserable tricked-up lies."

But Thackeray's conception of nature and truth was at this time a very narrow and exclusive one. A sensitive youth of excessive innocence or "greenness," he had met with a series of misadventures that had profoundly disillusioned him; and his long immersion in a world where vulgarity, selfishness, and deception were the rule had made him wonder if these were not the predominant traits in human nature. Halifax contends that "many men can *swallow* the being cheated, but no man could ever endure to chew it." Yet Thackeray in his early stories does exactly this. He was goaded into writing them by the sting of "remembered folly." He believed what the Comtesse de Beauséant tries to persuade young Rastignac in *Le Père Goriot,* that the world is "une réunion de dupes et de fripons." [3] For creative purposes, at any rate, his vision was for some time effectively limited to a single segment of experience. As he later told Dr. John Brown, his misfortunes had developed in him a "sense of the ugly, the odd, of the meanly false, of the desperately wicked"; exacerbated but undefeated, "he laid them bare: them under all disguises he hunted to the death." [4] Regarding society as a general fraud, he made his fiction a means of analysing "greatness," in the sense that Fielding employs the term in *Jonathan Wild,* now as it appeared disguised by humbug and cant in the respectable world, now as it was flaunted by the admitted blackguards of the criminal world. He adopted as his own the motto of Daumier's Robert Macaire: "Les badauds ne passeront pas, occuperons-nous de ce qui est éternel." [5] And he was convinced that his readers would profit by the kind of story that resulted, that there was in it "some grotesque good for the spectator,—a kind of *Beggars' Opera* moral." [6]

Hence nearly all of Thackeray's early narratives deal either with rogues and their victims or with rogues at war with one another. As his stories became more complex, he passed from the rook-and-pigeon theme to the more rewarding one of the biter bit. Though he had himself been only a pigeon, it was the rook who chiefly interested him. Apparently feeling that if his life had taken the wrong turning, he too might have become one of these conscious rogues who make rascality a career, he studied their behaviour with the minutest care. He was fascinated by the lives they led, their state of mind, the rejections and deprivations that their way of existence forced upon them. But if he was persuaded that they belonged morally "to the legion of the lost ones, to the cohort of the damned," he did not for that reason always present them as "dropping down the ladder rung by rung." In his stories inexpert rogues sometimes end badly; but the past masters of the profession succeed gloriously. Such is the way of the world, Thackeray implies.

Thackeray's first extended essay in fiction, *The Yellowplush*

Papers, grew out of his offer to Fraser, after creating his footman-narrator to review Skelton's *My Book,* to "make half a dozen stories by the same author." [7] Thackeray's portrait of Yellowplush has its points of interest. Though Thackeray never conceived of his footman as a Figaro, morally superior to his corrupt masters, he is initially presented as a shrewd and not ill-natured young Cockney, who differs from Sam Weller chiefly by being in rather than out of livery. But he is rapidly coloured by the malignancy of the Deuceace family, just as Sam is coloured by the benevolence of Mr. Pickwick, and he soon prides himself on being "tolerably downy," which means, simply, unprincipled. He explains how he came to take so naturally to rascality:

> my ma wrapped up my buth in a mistry. I may be illygitmit, I may have been changed at nuss; but I've always had genlmnly tastes through life, and have no doubt that I come of a genlmnly origin.[8]

It is as a gentleman's gentleman, he argues, that he takes as a matter of course to eavesdropping, thievery, and betrayal. Yellowplush's unconscious self-revelation through his way of telling his story is the first instance in Thackeray's work of a technique that he was afterwards to elaborate greatly. It fails here because Thackeray's interest in Yellowplush as a character quickly faded; and little individuality is imparted to him in his later contributions.

In any case, Yellowplush's language was regarded as the great feature of his papers. "The elegance of their style," Thackeray ironically observes in his preface to *Comic Tales and Sketches* where they were reprinted, "made them excessively popular in America." [9] Thackeray had a keen ear for the "Cocknaic dialect," [10] which he reproduces with some fidelity; and Yellowplush's character and history being what they are, his speech has a good deal of crude vigour. So old Mrs. Shum is described as being "as fat and as fierce as an old sow at feedin time," and the waves in the Channel are "black and frothy, like fresh drawn porter." [11] But Yellowplush's chief peculiarity (like that of Mrs. Ramsbottom in *The Snob*) is his penchant for malapropisms. If his conceits sometimes have a comic ingenuity that looks forward to *Finnegans Wake* ("Mrs. Siddums in the Tragic Mews," *"O trumpery! O morris!,*" "Shandeleasies," "M'Inations," etc.),[12] they more often bring to mind the faded farce of Milt Gross. Very much to the taste of Thackeray's age, they constitute for modern readers a boring and pointless distraction.[13]

The interest of *The Yellowplush Papers* today is largely confined to "The Amours of Mr. Deuceace: Dimond Cut Dimond" and "Mr. Deuceace at Paris," in neither of which is there much display of footman's English.[14] The former is a well-contrived and economically related short story, the latter a *nouvelle* of considerable power. Thackeray already has a Balzacian appetite for any sort of information that illuminates character. He can suggest a whole way of life in a few biting paragraphs, as in his account of how the Honourable Algernon Deuceace anticipates Becky Sharp in living on "nothink a-year." [15] He can bring home in a brief set-portrait, which seems to have been written in a cold rage, the essential lines of a personality, as in his vignette of Lady Griffin.[16] But once Thackeray has to set his characters in motion, his unpractised hand is revealed. They move through a series of melodramatic tableaux; their language becomes that of the theatre; and the illusion of life is dispelled.

In his next story for *Fraser's Magazine* Thackeray adopted that classic form of youthful protest against entrenched mediocrity, the parody. Just as Fielding had set out to burlesque the shoddy ethics of *Pamela* in *Joseph Andrews,* and Jane Austen the sensational excesses of Gothic romance in *Northanger Abbey,* so Thackeray sought to expose the absurdity of the currently popular "Newgate novel" in *Catherine.* Bulwer had established the "School of Criminal Romance," as he did so many others, in two early tales, *Paul Clifford* of 1830 and *Eugene Aram* of 1832, to which he added *Ernest Maltravers* in 1837. Ainsworth entered the list with *Rookwood,* a story about Dick Turpin, in 1834; and Dickens published *Oliver Twist* in 1837–1838. In January, 1839, Ainsworth's *Jack Sheppard,* the most popular of all criminal romances, began to appear in *Bentley's Miscellany.* By autumn eight dramatic versions of *Jack Sheppard* had reached the London boards; and it was rumoured that Ainsworth intended to back his luck by writing a novel about a third famous highwayman, Claude Duval.[17]

The peculiarity of these stories is that the celebrated criminals with whom they deal are invariably depicted with considerable sympathy. They are presented as engaging and good-hearted young men, harassed by misfortune and persecuted by an uncomprehending and prejudiced society. Bulwer even went so far as to conceive a theory of fiction in terms of which the criminal hero was the only possible choice of a writer who aimed at "High Art." According to his views, the crime of Eugene Aram, for example,

> belongs to those startling paradoxes which the poetry of all countries, and especially of our own, has always delighted to contemplate and examine. Whenever crime appears the aberration and monstrous product of a great intellect, or of a nature ordinarily virtuous, it becomes not only the subject for genius, which deals with the passions, to describe; but a problem for philosophy, which deals with actions, to investigate and solve:—hence the Macbeths and Richards, the Iagos and Othellos.[18]

Thackeray would have none of these sophistical reasonings. He took the common-sense view that a rascal is a rascal and should be presented as such. If the public demands stories about rogues,

> the only way in which poor authors, who must live, can act honestly by the public and themselves, is to paint such thieves as they are; not dandy, poetical, rose-water thieves, but real downright scoundrels, leading scoundrelly lives, drunken, profligate, dissolute, low, as scoundrels will be. They don't quote Plato like Eugene Aram; or live like gentlemen, and sing the pleasantest ballads in the world, like jolly Dick Turpin; or prate eternally about *το καλον*, like that precious canting Maltravers, whom we all of us have read about and pitied; or die white-washed saints, like poor Biss Dadsy, in *Oliver Twist*. No, my dear Madam, you and your daughters have no right to admire and sympathize with any such persons, fictitious or real: you ought to be made cordially to detest, scorn, loathe, abhor, and abominate all persons of this kidney.[19]

Thackeray consequently set about preparing what he called his "*Catherine* cathartic." The public having been "dosed and poisoned by the prevailing style of literary practice," a medicine was needed "that would produce a wholesome nausea, and afterwards bring about a more healthy habit." He made it his aim to produce a story that would "make readers so horribly horrified as to cause them to give up or rather throw up the book and all of its kind." [20]

He accordingly read through *The Newgate Calendar, or The Malefactors' Bloody Register* in search of a history in which victim and murderers alike were creatures unrelievedly sordid and depraved and the crime one of sensational brutality. He found what he wanted in the account of Catherine Hayes, "burnt alive at Tyburn May 9, 1726, for the murder of her husband," which tells briefly and baldly how a turbulent and dissipated wife caused her miserly pawnbroker husband to be killed and dismembered by two lodgers, one of whom was supposed to be her illegitimate son.[21] From this primitive source Thackeray spun out a short novel, most of which was sheer invention. *The Newgate Calendar* mentions in passing, for example, Catherine's youthful connexion with "some officers in the army," with whom she "remained a considerable time" before her marriage to Hayes.[22] Out of this meagre hint Thackeray created that remarkable group of military scoundrels, Count Galgenstein, Corporal Brock, and Ensign Macshane, who certainly constitute the triumph of the book. The Hayeses' domestic life was also of Thackeray's devising. Indeed, only in describing the circumstances of the crime and its discovery did he make detailed use of his source.

Moreover, as Thackeray's story developed, he found it impossible to adhere to his original intention of inducing disgust and nothing else in his readers. If *Catherine* began as a parody, it grew to have an intrinsic interest for Thackeray, just as *Joseph Andrews* and *Northanger Abbey* grew to have for their authors. As Galgenstein and Brock came to life under his hands, they were far from being figures of unredeemed wickedness.[23] Catherine is by no means so ingratiating, but even for her Thackeray conceived "a sneaking kindness . . . , and did not like to make her utterly worthless." [24] So she is allowed to muse eloquently over her past love for Galgenstein, and Thackeray even makes her try ineffectually to prevent the execution of the murder that she helped to plan.[25] It is only in the scenes of violence that conclude the story that Thackeray's parodic intent is substantially preserved. Ainsworth's typical manner is neatly hit off in Thackeray's account of the "THAMES AT MIDNIGHT," while the meeting that follows between Catherine and Galgenstein in St. Margaret's churchyard mimics adroitly Bulwer's habit of climaxing a scene of sentiment with a *coup de théâtre*. A little later Thackeray is obliging enough to provide producers "at a loss for theatrical novelties" with a program of *grands tableaux* into which his story might be arranged. It concludes:

Grand Tableau. Finale. Blue Lights. Green Lights.
The whole strength of the Band.

CATHERINE BURNING AT THE STAKE! BILLINGS HANGED IN THE BACKGROUND!! THE THREE SCREAMS OF THE VICTIM!!!

The Executioner dashes her brains out with a billet.

The Curtain falls to slow Music.

God save the Queen — No money returned.

Children in arms encouraged, rather than otherwise.[26]

These bursts of burlesque are good rough fun, at least for readers who comprehend their topical application; but they destroy the story as a coherent and unified work of fiction. *Catherine* fails, in fact, because Thackeray tried in it to do several incompatible things; the terrible consistency of *Jonathan Wild*, his avowed model, was quite beyond his grasp at this time. Yet one understands why Thackeray was able to report that "Carlyle says Catherine is wonderful, and many more laud it highly." [27] It contains the best character-drawing that Thackeray had yet encompassed. The picture of eighteenth-century life that it provides is a remarkable achievement. And there are many small felicities along the way, such as the expert fashion in which the magistrate entraps Ensign Macshane, or the sketch of Captain Popjoy which opens Chapter 9, a passage worthy of *The Book of Snobs* at its best.[28]

For *A Shabby Genteel Story*, his last fictional contribution to *Fraser's Magazine* during this period, Thackeray once more took his *donnée* where he found it. In the last year of his life he told his friends at the *Punch* table of "Frank Stone having married a woman he'd lived with—his history forming The Shabby Genteel Story. 'Give me your story,' said WMT to him, & used it." [29] But though Thackery took his plot from Stone's domestic history, *A Shabby Genteel Story* is actually much closer to his own experience than either *The Yellowplush Papers* or *Catherine*. The narrative throughout is coloured by his current preoccupations; and its chief characters derive from his intimate life. George Brandon is sketched from the dissipated dandy Harry Matthew, who had been Thackeray's "idol of youth," rather than from the brusque and hearty Stone. Caroline Gann, whom Brandon inveigles into a sham marriage, is drawn from Isabella, rather than from Mrs. Stone. And Thackeray took Andrea Fitch, the cockney artist, from his "old friend Brine" of Paris years, who had recently returned to London from Spain when Thackeray began *A Shabby Genteel Story* in May of 1840. "He sports a wig with ringlets," Thackeray told his mother, "and is just the full blown donkey of former days." [30]

Seduction, rather than gambling or murder, is Thackeray's subject in *A Shabby Genteel Story,* but his absorption in scoundrelism persists. Even so, Brandon is a new type in Thackeray's rogues' gallery. He is a man of some innate intelligence and good feeling, spoiled by "the education of a gentleman," but not so far gone in rascality that he cannot still feel an occasional twinge of remorse. Accordingly Thackeray's portrait of him, though sufficiently severe, is not altogether devoid of sympathy. Towards Caroline, Thackeray's attitude is tender and protective, an understandable circumstance, since she is the first of the series of fictional portraits of Isabella that mark his long narratives, from *A Shabby Genteel Story* through *Vanity Fair*.[31] When Thackeray defends Caroline against the "scornful compassion" of her neighbours, one catches an echo of his defence of Isabella against similar criticism. " 'A poor half-witted thing,' they said, 'who could not say bo! to a goose'; and I think it is one good test of gentility to be thus looked down on by vulgar people." One hears the same echo, perhaps, in the reflection: "There are some meannesses which are too mean even for man—woman, lovely woman alone, can venture to commit them." [32]

Like *The Yellowplush Papers* and *Catherine, A Shabby Genteel Story* is more impressive in its parts than as a whole. Its first chapter was Thackeray's strongest work thus far. The flow of relevant and authentic detail that throughout the story unfailingly supports Thackeray's exposure of the vulgarity and meanness lying beneath the Ganns' pretensions to shabby gentility shows the hand of a master. If it is difficult today to share the attitude of condescending amusement at the odd behaviour of social inferiors which informs Thackeray's portrait of Andrea Fitch, he remains a striking though broadly drawn farcical portrait.[33] But these threads and others become hopelessly entangled in the later chapters, written at a time when domestic troubles were distracting Thackeray's attention from his work; and the story's huddled and abortive conclusion leaves many knots untied. Once again Thackeray had produced a fragment rather than a rounded work of art.

Chapter 9 of *A Shabby Genteel Story,* which brought the tale to an end in *Fraser's Magazine* of October, 1840, has the valedictory: "God bless thee, poor Caroline! Thou art happy now, for some short space at least; and here, therefore, let us leave thee." [34] Early in December Thackeray wrote to Fraser: "I left purposely the Shabby Genteel Story in such a state that it might be continued in the Magazine or not as you and I liked best." He proposed to finish it in four sheets (sixty-four magazine pages), with a view to publishing afterwards "the whole tale w^h^ has a very moral ending in a volume with illustrations." [35] Fraser failed to close with this offer; other projects intervened; and he was not reminded of the story until December, 1852, when he bought a copy of the just-released Appleton reprint on a train between Boston and New York.[36] In republishing the fourth volume of his *Miscellanies* in 1857, he gave some thought to finishing *A Shabby Genteel Story.* But, he reflected,

> The colours are long since dry; the artist's hand is changed. It is best to leave the sketch, as it was when first designed seventeen years ago. The memory of the past is renewed as he looks at it—
>
> *die Bilder froher Tage,*
> *Und manche liebe Schatten steigen auf.*[37]

Yet Thackeray kept a warm spot for the story in his heart. When Shirley Brooks at a *Punch* dinner quoted his observation that Brandon, in a fit of temper while dining with the Ganns, "was so very sarcastic, that not a single soul at table understood him," Thackeray fervently replied: "Bless you Brooks!" [38] And in 1861–1862 he finally published the long-delayed conclusion as *Philip,* his last completed novel.

Of the non-Fraserian fiction of these early years, only a few stories call for comment. *The Tremendous Adventures of Major Gahagan* (to give the story the title assigned it by Thackeray in his *Miscellanies*) appeared in the *New Monthly Magazine* between February, 1838, and February, 1839. In this hilarious extravaganza, laid in the India of Wellesley's day, Thackeray exacts good-natured revenge for long hours spent listening to the tales of military adventure related by such Eastern veterans as Major Carmichael-Smyth and Lieutenant-Colonel Shawe. He takes as his hero an Irish Munchausen named Goliah Gahagan, whose exploits in war are matched only by his disappointments in love, and traces his career from his arrival in India as a raw cornet to his culminating achievements as major of John Company's Ahmednuggar Irregulars.[39] The humour is undeniably very broad. And to readers whose acquaintance with Indian language and geography and with old-time Anglo-Indian usages is limited, Thackeray's burlesque sometimes assumes the aspect of a private joke. But everyone can enjoy such episodes as that in which the redoubtable Major saves the garrison at Futtyghur from the hordes of the abominable Holkar by incapacitating the latter's force of elephants with a single cannon shot. This feat (illustrated with diagrams, after the accepted manner of military historians) is achieved by waiting until the elephants are drawn up in line at right angles to the garrison and firing at their trunks.

> Suppose I had been a common man [the Major remarks], and contented myself with firing bang at the head of the first animal? An ass would have done it, prided himself had he hit his mark, and what would have been the consequence? Why, that the ball might have killed two elephants and wounded a third; but here, probably, it would have stopped, and done no further mischief. The *trunk* was

the place at which to aim; there are no bones there; and away, consequently, went the bullet, shearing, as I have said, through one hundred and thirty-five probosces.[40]

This story is the best early example of Thackeray's mock-heroic vein, which was to culminate so delightfully fifteen years later in *The Rose and the Ring.*

Knowing Thackeray's need of money, his old friend George Cruikshank asked him in May, 1838, to provide the text for twelve plates which he was to contribute to the *Comic Almanac* of 1839. This annual venture had been initiated in 1835; and such was Cruikshank's popularity that it eventually attained a sale of nearly 20,000 copies.[41] Thackeray's payment for the twenty-four pages of *Stubbs's Calendar; or, The Fatal Boots* was modest enough, however, since it amounted to no more than twenty guineas.[42] Thackeray does not seem to have taken undue pains either with *Stubbs's Calendar* or with its successor *Cox's Diary,* perhaps because the Procrustean frame of twelve episodes, each of equal length, was not congenial to his essentially discursive mind. In any event, *Stubbs's Diary* is dreary enough. The reader is so disgusted by Stubbs's unrelieved meanness that he can bring himself to take little interest in the fashion in which his stupid selfishness causes him to overreach himself in each of his predatory campaigns. Thackeray stubbornly contended that Stubbs had "great merit, although his adventures were somewhat of too tragical a description to provoke pure laughter." [43] Nevertheless, he made his text for Cruikshank's plates in the *Comic Almanac* of 1840 a good deal more cheerful. *Barber Cox and the Cutting of His Comb* (retitled *Cox's Diary* in the *Miscellanies*) tells how a barber's family unexpectedly inherits the fortune of a nabob relative who has died intestate. Impelled by the vanity of Mrs. Cox, the family tries to take the place in the fashionable world to which she conceives their money entitles them. They give a ball, go hunting, frequent the opera, hold a tournament, and travel abroad; and in each of these adventures they fall into ludicrous mistakes which culminate in a farcical tableau suited to Cruikshank's pencil. Barber Cox is profoundly relieved when a will is found, the true heir given possession of the estate, and the Cox family restored to its proper position in life. *Cox's*

Diary is less painful than *Stubbs's Calendar,* in that it is a study of awkward vulgarity rather than petty evil; but it is not much more interesting.

The Bedford-Row Conspiracy, which appeared in the *New Monthly Magazine* between January and April, 1840, seems at first glance no more than a delightful trifle; Thackeray himself admitted that it was "stolen" from a *nouvelle* by Charles de Bernard called *Le Pied d'Argile.*[44] Yet this story has its importance as a transitional work that helped to guide Thackeray towards his proper subject-matter. Of all contemporary French authors he liked Charles de Bernard most, because in "a sparkling, gentlemanlike way," Bernard presented "men and women of genteel society—rascals enough, but living in no state of convulsive crimes." [45] In 1843, indeed, he boasted that Bernard "was first discovered by one Michael Angelo Titmarsh, who . . . pilfered one of his stories." [46] Having executed this coup triumphantly, Thackeray may well have asked himself whether he could not devise a comparable original story dealing with English life. *The Great Hoggarty Diamond* of 1841 was perhaps his answer to such a question.

IV

Apart from his fiction, Thackeray's writing in these early years was chiefly critical journalism, his customary topics being painting, literature, and manners. In this field as well he continued to be guided by what he understood by "nature" and "truth." If his critical perspective was thereby drastically narrowed, it still allowed him to perform a useful service in denouncing the artificiality and pretentiousness that vitiated the taste of the age. Unlike most of his fellow journalists, moreover, he did not colour his writing to harmonize with the political views or the commercial interests of his employers. "The critic does not value rightly," he admitted, ". . . once in a thousand times; but if he do not deal *honestly,* woe be to him! The hulks are too pleasant for him, transportation too light." [1]

IX. Design of front-wrapper for *Sketches by Boz*

From a pencil sketch by Thackeray

X. Thackeray and his wife in early married life

From a caricature by Thackeray

XI. Mrs. Thackeray and Anny about 1838

From a sketch by Thackeray

XII. "Rex—Ludovicus—Ludovicus Rex. An Historical Study"

From a water-colour by Thackeray

Much of Thackeray's work was devoted to painting, whether pompously displayed on the walls of the Royal Academy or modestly reproduced in the steel engravings of the annuals. Looking as always for the natural and truthful, he found his demands best satisfied by those *genre* scenes of the day in which realism was agreeably enhanced by sentiment or comedy. He cheerfully passed by Haydon's attempts to render the "Ideal" in accordance with the canons of "High Art" and Turner's experiments in reproducing light on canvas, in order to praise the latest variations by Hunt, Leslie, and Wilkie on their usual themes. "Why, in painting," he inquired, "are we to have monstrous, flaring, Drury Lane tricks and claptraps put in practice, when a quieter style is, as I fancy, so infinitely more charming?" [2]

It will be seen that by modern standards Thackeray's writings on art hardly qualify as criticism at all. Yet they have their excellences. If his point of view was avowedly literary, this was an advantage rather than otherwise when he wrote of such artists as Daumier or Cruikshank. Moreover, he was devoted to art, and the gusto with which he communicated his pleasure in the canvases that he liked was remarkable. Consider, for example, his account of Turner's "The Fighting Téméraire":

> The old Téméraire is dragged to her last home by a little, spiteful, diabolical steamer. A mighty red sun, amidst a host of flaring clouds, sinks to rest on one side of the picture, and illumines a river that seems interminable, and a countless navy that fades away into such a wonderful distance as never was painted before. The little demon of a steamer is belching out a volume (why do I say a volume? not a hundred volumes could express it) of foul, lurid, red-hot, malignant smoke, paddling furiously, and lashing up the water round about it; while behind it (a cold gray moon looking down on it), slow, sad, and majestic, follows the brave old ship, with death, as it were, written on her.[3]

And often Thackeray's downright common sense was valuable in deflating the false sublime (see his description of Girodet's "Deluge") [4] or bringing home defects of execution. He once asked his favourite Leslie, for example, concerning the latter's portrait of Lord Cottenham: "Are not the learned lord's arms somewhat short and fin-like? This is a query which we put humbly, having never had occasion to remark that part of his person." [5]

Thackeray's literary criticism during this period is scattered through *Fraser's Magazine* and the *Times*.[6] Since it deals for the most part with novels, volumes of history, books of travel, memoirs, and diaries that have long since been forgotten, it is now read chiefly by close students of Thackeray's work who are interested in noting how his characteristic attitudes gradually emerged in this commentary on his reading. Occasionally one comes upon an eloquent and memorable passage of praise, when he discusses the work of an author, like Fielding or Dickens,[7] whom he admires. But in general Thackeray's literary journalism in the later 1830s forms a relatively pedestrian chronicle, varied only by flashes of "the old, wild satiric spirit" [8] that was then dying out. In 1844 he was to apologize for the Fraserian "press-Mohawks" of this time, whose high spirits had led them

> to belabour with unmerciful ridicule almost all the writers of this country of England, to sneer at their scholarship, to question their talents, to shout with fierce laughter over their faults, historical, poetical, grammatical, and sentimental; and thence to leave the reader to deduce our (the critic's) own immense superiority in all the points which we questioned in all the world beside. I say *our* [Thackeray went on], because the undersigned Michael Angelo has handled the tomahawk as well as another, and has a scalp or two drying in his lodge.[9]

This vein of boisterous abuse is most consistently mined in his campaign against Bulwer, who for Thackeray was an irresistible target, embodying the worst literary vices of the day in their most extreme form.

Thackeray's attacks on Bulwer would demand our attention, in any event, because they have been made a principal ground for reprobation by writers who have in turn attacked Thackeray. Bulwer himself gave these gentlemen their cue by asserting in his fragmentary autobiography that, beginning with his Cambridge prize poem "Sculpture," *Fraser's Magazine* "under the auspices of Dr. Maginn and Mr. Thackeray, long continued to assail me, not in any form that can fairly be called criticism, but with a kind of ribald impertinence offered, so far as I can remember, to no other author of my time." [10] Attributing

Thackeray's "persecution" of Bulwer to "the malignity of a jealous failure," Mr. Michael Sadleir some years ago arrived at a most unfavourable view of Thackeray's character,[11] and other commentators have followed his lead.[12] What is the truth of the matter?

If Mr. Sadleir demonstrates that Bulwer was in fact a chief butt of *Fraser's Magazine* during its early years,[13] his insistence that Maginn's "vendetta" was inspired primarily by political and personal motives is not convincing. Miss Thrall shows, on the contrary, that Maginn and his associates consistently upheld a clear-cut critical standard, by which Bulwer's books were tried and found wanting, just as were the works of many other authors which gave similar offence.[14] It was the combination of Bulwer's great popular success with his inflated style, his gratuitous ostentation of learning, the pompous egoism of his personal confidences, and the dubious moral implications of his novels that brought down upon his head the Fraserians' particular wrath. And when Bulwer was stung by these critical barbs into abuse of his tormentors, Maginn was not slow to find in this abuse ample reason for attacking his victim personally as well as professionally.

Thackeray began to read Bulwer at least as early as 1829, but his disapproval of Bulwer's novels did not crystallize until May, 1832, when he went through a course of them at the time of his first intimacy with Maginn. His response to *Eugene Aram* established the pattern for all of his later judgments on Bulwer.

> It is a very forced & absurd taste [he wrote in his diary] to elevate a murderer for money into a hero—The sentiments are very eloquent clap-trap. There is no new character (except perhaps the Corporal) & no incident at all—Aram's confession is disgusting, it would have been better, more romantick at least, to have made him actuated by revenge hatred jealousy or any passion except avarice, w[h] is at more variance with the character given him in the Novel, than w[d] have been a hotter & (as we suppose) a nobler passion—The book is in fact humbug, when my novel is written it will be something better I trust.[15]

Though the impress of Maginn's opinions is evident in this passage, it also reflects Thackeray's spontaneous revulsion from Bulwer's artificiality, pretentiousness, and morbidity. When he became a full-fledged Fraserian in 1837, it was natural that he should take a principal part in carrying on the anti-Bulwerian tradition that Maginn had established.

Thackeray began his onslaught upon Bulwer with reviews of the latter's current novels, *Ernest Maltravers* and its sequel *Alice,* in late 1837 and early 1838.[16] Though sufficiently harsh, these reviews are not entirely hostile. Thackeray admits his admiration for *Pelham,* and he shows that he is not blind to Bulwer's imaginative power, his wide knowledge of life, and his intermittent command of witty dialogue. But the attacks that caught the public eye by their brilliance and personality were the concluding Yellowplush papers in *Fraser's Magazine:* "Mr. Yellowplush's Ajew," in August, 1838; and "Epistles to the Literati. No. XIII" in January, 1840. The former tells of an imaginary dinner-party at the home of Yellowplush's employer where "Bullwig" and another favourite Fraserian target, Dr. Dionysius Lardner (editor of *Lardner's Cabinet Cyclopedia*), are confronted with their footman rival.[17] The latter consists of letters from Yellowplush and a friend (not under the necessity of writing footman's English) about Bulwer's play *The Sea-captain.* Both articles take Bulwer to task for his literary sins, in the first through a parody of his style, in the second through a minute analysis of "Bulwerese," following the pattern of Macaulay's examination of Robert Montgomery's poems. These strokes are fair enough, as is the account of Yellowplush's discovery of Bulwer's identity:

> My neas trembled under me, my i's fild with tiers, my voice shook, as I past up the venrabble name to the other footman, and saw this fust of English writers go up to the drawing-room! [18]

It is in footmen like Yellowplush, Thackeray implies, that Bulwer finds his true public.

But when Thackeray goes on to provide a portrait of Bulwer as a vain and feeble dandy, "slim, with a hook nose, a pail fase, a small waist, a pare of falling shoulders, a tight coat, and a catarack of black satting tumbling out of his busm, and falling into a gilt velvet weskit," to suggest that his pronunciation is so genteel that he is totally incapable of pronouncing the letter *r*, and to hint that, though he pretends to like claret, brandy is really more in his line,[19] the reader's sympathies go out to the victim of this crude abuse. Dr. Lardner is made to say of *Fraser's Magazine* and Bulwer, in "Mr. Yellowplush's Ajew," that "the boys about that magazine baste him as if he was a sack of oatmale." [20] This is exactly what Thackeray himself is doing, and we are disappointed, since we expect him to rise above the level of "the boys."

Still, we should remember that personality was a generally accepted weapon in the rough-and-ready literary scene of the 1830s. Barham recalls how Thackeray once drew an unpopular member out of the Garrick Club, so ludicrous and persistent were his caricatures; nor is there any implication in Barham's remarks that Thackeray had acted otherwise than in the public interest.[21] There is abundant contemporary evidence, moreover, to show that Bulwer aroused general resentment and irritation, that he was the Dr. Fell of a large part of the literary world. Lockhart in 1825 thought him a "horrid puppy." H. F. Chorley, hardly himself a robust type, was struck in 1836 by the fashion in which Bulwer's egoism and vanity were

> *all* thrown up to the surface. Yes, he is a thoroughly *satin* character; but then it is the *richest* satin. Whether it will wear as well as other less glossy material remains to be seen. There was something inconceivably strange to me in his dwelling, with a sort of hankering, upon the Count d'Orsay's physical advantages; something beneath the dignity of an author, my fastidiousness fancied, in the manner in which he spoke of his own works, saying that the new ones only interested him as far as they were experiments.

Carlyle in 1840 noted that "his appearance, adding the long nose and open mouth, the dandiacal apparel, weak padded figure, and adventitious renown, is tragic-gawkey." [22] In his eyes Bulwer was not gold, but "scoured brass." Sharing this irrepressible distaste, Thackeray could not resist the opportunities put in his way to express it. "Why, when I used to lampoon a certain Bulwer," he assured John Blackwood in extenuation many years later, "I had never seen him but in a public place, and had no kind of animosity to him. If I had I should never have attacked him." [23]

As we shall see, Thackeray's jokes at Bulwer's expense were to continue for some years. But his later satire in *Punch* was far less crude and personal than his lampoons in *Fraser's Magazine.* Thackeray came ultimately to regret the excesses into which he had been carried by youthful exuberance. Taking young James Hannay to task in 1849 for being "too savage" in his fiction, Thackeray remarked: "I suppose we all begin so—I know one who did: and who is sorry now for pelting at that poor old Bulwer & others, but it was in the days of hot youth." [24] When D. Appleton & Company of New York reprinted *The Yellowplush Papers* in 1852 as part of an unauthorized edition of his works, Thackeray inquired in a preface which the publisher asked him to write for a subsequent volume: "Why were some of the little brats brought out of their obscurity?" And he went on publicly to apologize to Bulwer for "these wild performances of early years," which he had once been misguided enough to regard as mere "harmless jocularity." [25] As was noted in the Introduction, Mr. Sadleir radically revised his general conception of Thackeray's character after reading his *Letters and Private Papers*. Similarly, in the specific case of Thackeray's attitude towards Bulwer, what he had earlier regarded as the "malignity of a jealous failure" he came to see as the "automatic expression of an uncontrollable hatred of Bulwer's kind of writing. The castigation was cruel, too persistent and more wounding than Thackeray ever stopped to realize. But it was a genuine critical reaction and not embittered disgruntlement." [26] With this impartial appraisal, the considered judgment of Bulwer's chief modern champion, we can rest content.

In 1840 Thackeray collected certain of his periodical contributions on French subjects to make up his first book, *The Paris Sketch Book*.[27] It was in extenuation of the miscellaneous and disconnected contents of these two volumes that he devised this unpretentious name for them. He had originally intended, indeed, that his title-page should further state that the "sketchbook" was made up of "copies" (stories adapted from French originals, like "Cartouche," "Mary Ancel," and "Poisinet") and "compositions" (original accounts of his own experiences and observations).[28] Certainly the book is held together chiefly by the personality of its author. From the whimsical frontispiece and dedicatory letter to the famous "historical study" of Louis XIV which illustrates the final paper, the reader is at least conscious that Michael Angelo Titmarsh is an ingenious, idiosyncratic, and entertaining guide to things French.

The stories retold and the artistic and literary criticism that make up much of *The Paris Sketch Book* require no further comment. But a word may be said about the essays on French manners which complete the book. This was a literary form which Thackeray was later to use with great expertness in *Punch* and the *Cornhill Magazine*. In the late 1830s, however, he lacked the humanity and understanding to do it justice. To excuse the brashness and inflexibility of *The Paris Sketch Book,* we must imagine Thackeray in France as a tall, burly young man, constantly looking *down* at the natives as they hurried by him in the streets, almost as if he were Gulliver in Lilliput. How could he respect these scrawny little fellows? When he went to a French dramatization of *Nicholas Nickleby,* he was disgusted with "Prospectus," who should have been a plump and healthy child, a living testimonial to Squeers's generosity and kindness to his flock at Dotheboys Hall:

> By way of a fat specimen, never was one more unsatisfactory than this [he wrote]. Such a poor shrivelled creature I never saw; it is like a French pig, as lanky as a greyhound! Both animals give one a thorough contempt for the nation.[29]

Hence Thackeray at times seems a pattern John Bull, almost rivalling Mr. Podsnap in his insularity, when he denounces French militarism, irreverence, and immorality in *The Paris Sketch Book.* "Thank God that, in England, things are not managed so,"[30] is his constant refrain. Even to the qualities that he admired in French life—the love of the arts, the freedom from snobbishness, and the politeness displayed by the French people—he hardly does justice in these early essays.

V

The interest of Thackeray's writing from *The Yellowplush Papers* to *The Paris Sketch Book* is substantial and varied. Yet he did not himself think highly of it, nor did it bring him success. A balanced estimate of his early work will perhaps resolve these apparent discrepancies of evaluation.

One notes first the freshness and boldness of his writing in this period. His inventive faculty never fails him. Though he deals with recurring character-types and situations in his fiction, he varies them so successfully that the reader does not complain of repetitiveness or monotony. The same resourcefulness appears in his artistic and literary essays. He was particularly fertile in creating spokesmen for himself; Yellowplush, Gahagan, Michael Angelo Titmarsh, and Ikey Solomons, Jr., pleasantly reveal his talent as a ventriloquist. Yet all alike speak with the heartiness, energy, and ingenuousness that constitute Thackeray's trade mark at this period.

In his early fiction there are things that mark him out specifically as a born novelist. He was a rapid and accurate observer with an immense appetite for information about people and the way they live. The awkward doubts concerning the authenticity of what is related which destroy the illusion of probability in most fiction, never arise in Thackeray's case. His mastery of his material seems complete, so saturated is he in the subjects with which he deals. His expertness in the idiosyncrasies of conversation is also notable. When Swigby in *A Shabby Genteel Story* talks about taking "his whack" of pleasure at the public house; when Catherine, proud of the maturity she has achieved at sixteen, tells Galgenstein scornfully that "there's a many girl in the village that, at my age, is quite chits"; [1] the keenness of Thackeray's ear for the vagrant phrase that places its speaker once for all is brought home. And one sees evidence as well of the emergence of another gift, rarer than authenticity of background and accuracy of dialogue. As Thackeray's knowledge of life grew, he became increasingly able to sum up in his characters whole categories of society. The reader gains from each of such portraits, not only knowledge of the individual described, but also insight into the pattern of social relations to which he belongs.

No less notable is the stylistic promise of Thackeray's early writing. From the first he operated on the bold assumption that his readers were alert, intelligent, and literate; he claimed the right to be subtle, extravagant, or allusive as he saw fit. He expected his readers to join in the delight which he took in such absurd yet plausible names as "the Baronne de Florval-Delval, née de Melval-Norval." [2] He expected his readers to recognize the blank verse printed as prose which affords so agreeable a contrast to the commonplace setting of *A Shabby Genteel Story:* "At High Street's corner, near to Hawley Square, they passed the house of Mr. Fincham, chemist, who doth not only healthful drugs supply, but likewise sells cigars—the worst cigars that ever mortal man gave threepence for." [3] He expected his readers to appreciate the wicked fidelity with which he parodied the fiction and poetry of the day. So the purest "Bulwerese" cascades from the mouth of "Bullwig" in *The Yellowplush Papers:*

> Look at me. I am the first novelist in Europe. I have ranged with eagle wing over the wide regions of literature, and perched on every eminence in its turn. I have gazed with eagle eyes on the sun of philosophy, and fathomed the mysterious depths of the human mind. All languages are familiar to me, all thoughts are known to me, all men understood by me. I have gathered wisdom from the honeyed lips of Plato, as we wandered in the gardens of Acadames—wisdom, too, from the mouth of Job Johnson, as we smoked our 'backy in Seven Dials. Such must be the studies, and such is the mission, in this world, of the Poet-Philosopher.[4]

Elsewhere the popular poetry of the time is mocked in a version of the famous old song "Wapping Old Stairs" as T. H. Bayly or W. M. Praed might have rewritten it. Here are the first stanzas of the two sets of verses:

WAPPING OLD STAIRS

Your Molly has never been false, she declares,
Since the last time we parted at Wapping Old Stairs;

When I vowed I would ever continue the same,
And gave you the 'BACCO-BOX marked with your name.
When I passed a whole fortnight between decks with you,
Did I e'er give a kiss, Tom, to one of the crew?
To be useful and kind with my Thomas I stayed,—
For his trousers I washed, and his grog too I made.

THE ALMACK'S ADIEU

Your Fanny was never false-hearted,
And this she protests and she vows,
From the *triste moment* when we parted
On the staircase at Devonshire House!
I blushed when you asked me to marry,
I vowed I would never forget;
And at parting I gave my dear Harry
A beautiful *vinegarette!* [5]

It may be argued that these are pyrotechnical displays; but the staple of Thackeray's prose is quite as admirable as his set-pieces. Consider, for example, this vignette of Captain Gorgon's career in *The Bedford-Row Conspiracy:*

The captain being of noble connexions, younger son of a baronet, cousin to Lord X. and related to the Y. family, had angered all his relatives, by marrying a very silly, pretty young woman, who kept a ladies' school at Canterbury. She had six hundred pounds to her fortune, which the captain laid out in the purchase of a sweet travelling-carriage and dressing-case for himself; and going abroad with his lady, spent several years in the principal prisons of Europe, in one of which he died.[6]

The efficiency of that final clause neatly caps the irony of the whole passage. By 1840 Thackeray was an accomplished stylist.

The qualities thus far described were calculated to attract the acute and discerning, however much they might baffle and irritate the average reader. But other aspects of his early work are more clearly imperfections. It is extraordinarily uneven. Carlyle quite properly noted that Thackeray at this time could not write a *book;* [7] each of his longer efforts starts well, and then falls off badly. Moreover, Thackeray's youth and inexperience often vitiated his judgment. His emphasis on common sense as an antidote to cant blinded him to the ways in which life can be enriched by the imagination. His brash impatience with the inevitable imperfections of humanity often made him seem raw and callow. "He wrote many cynical things in those early days," his daughter wisely observed in palliation, "as young people do when they are very young and happy and their spirits carry them along." [8]

But there was a bitterness beyond youthful cynicism in Thackeray's early work. The fierce pleasure that he took in dissecting his rogues alienated his readers. It was a cardinal principle of Victorian fiction-writing, Dickens later told Percy Fitzgerald, "that if you do not administer a disagreeable character carefully, the public have a decided tendency to think that the *story* is disagreeable, and not merely the fictitious person." [9] Even after Thackeray became famous, many of his admirers could not stomach "those dreadful early works in which every stroke is full of venom." [10] Basing their opinions on these tales, Louis Blanc noted, "Beaucoup jugèrent que c'était un talent sans entrailles que celui d'un homme qui avait au service des ses antipathies tant de flèches empoissonées. Ceux dont il flagellait sans pitié les prétentions le denoncèrent comme un cynique, l'appelèrent Diogène, lui refusèrent le don de la bonté." [11] It is perhaps fair to say that Thackeray's early work, despite the talent to which it intermittently testified, attained as much success as it deserved.

10

"A Year of Pain and Hope"

I

On the last day of 1839 Thackeray wrote to his mother:

> And now God bless you in the new ten years that are about to begin. I think they will be more lucky for us than the last 10: though God knows I have had luck enough for my latter share: and you have only a right to complain because it is the fashion to say that people are unfortunate who have lost their money. Dearest Mammy we know better than that, and so God bless all we love and make us sober humble cheerful whatever luck betide us.[1]

From the trials with which he had thus far been visited, Thackeray had emerged a stronger and wiser man; but his hope for happiness and security in the future was to prove a mirage. A far more severe ordeal lay ahead of him.

By May of 1840 the Great Coram Street household was busy with preparations for Isabella's third lying-in. Chiefly in order to be able to say that there was no room for Mrs. Shawe, Thackeray invited Mrs. Butler to London for a visit. But because he was "afraid of GM. and the nurses rowing," [2] he also asked Mrs. Carmichael-Smyth. Unluckily his mother was at this time very lame and could not leave Paris. One of her intimates, a Mrs. Parker, came to London on another errand, however; and Mrs. Carmichael-Smyth asked her to take an interest in Isabella. Thackeray at first found Mrs. Parker "an excellent hearty creature," [3] but he soon grew tired of her endless gossip about the Parisian English colony.

Isabella's state of mind as she waited for her third child was not a healthy one. Remembrances of the difficulties attendant on Anny's birth oppressed her, and the thought of Jane's early death still caused her pain. She was disturbed by her husband's aversion to her mother, though she could understand the grounds for it. She was more despondent than ever about her inability to run the household economically and efficiently. Mrs. Carmichael-Smyth's letters became so weighty with admonitions (for which there was some warrant, it must be granted, since the Thackerays managed to spend £200 during the first four months of 1840), that Thackeray protested against their severity.[4] Yet Thackeray himself, driven by the need for money and eager for success, allowed his work to occupy nearly all his attention. "I am in a ceaseless whirl and whizz from morning to night," he told his mother, "now with the book, now with the drawings, now with articles for Times, Fraser." [5] In late May, indeed, he became so desperate for quiet surroundings that he withdrew for a few days to Leamington Spa and Warwick.

He returned to Great Coram Street in time for Isabella's confinement on 27 May. The child was a third girl, later christened Harriet Marian Thackeray. Her birth was easy, and Isabella seemed to convalesce rapidly, even though she was attended only by a nurse sent to her by Mrs. John Allen and by the faithful Brodie. But she was not her old self. Anxious to give no trouble, she was outwardly cheerful; but inwardly she felt isolated and uneasy. "The little baby is very like the dear little one we lost—strangely like in voice," [6] Thackeray noted, and in this resemblance also Isabella found a cause for foreboding. Mrs. Butler had been duly installed in the state apartment, and though Thackeray wrote in July that "in the course of her whole visit [she] has not heard or used a rough word," [7] relations between her and Isabella were strained. Moreover, Thackeray himself, reassured by his wife's apparent recovery, quickly slipped back into preoccupation with his work.

The Paris Sketch Book was finished on 1 June and appeared in mid-July. For a work by an almost unknown author, it had considerable success. Thackeray's publisher, Hugh Cunningham, had sold nearly 400 copies by the end of the month.[8] The reviews (some of them solicited from friends) were numerous and favourable. An expedition under the leadership of Richard Monckton Milnes to see the murderer Courvoisier executed on 6 July had left Thackeray dismal and melancholy for a time. The experience weighed upon him, he told his mother, "like cold plum pudding on the stomach." [9] But he quickly threw off his depression and sought to take advantage of the opportunities that *The Paris Sketch Book* had brought him. *Blackwood's Magazine,* which had declined an offered series of London essays only a few weeks earlier, evinced interest in a travel narrative. The great publishing houses of Longman and Chapman and Hall talked about contracts for travel books. Thackeray grew increasingly hopeful "that something good will come out of it all—something better than that odious magazine-work w^h^ w^d^ kill any writer in 6 years." [10]

At length Thackeray decided that, though his next full-length book would deal with Ireland, he could not do better for the present than visit Belgium, where there was a notable exhibition of paintings on display in Antwerp.

> He says he will make a series of articles for Blackwoods [Isabella wrote to Mrs. Carmichael-Smyth after his departure] that it was necessary for his health and that he is sure that Titmarsh in Belgium will take as Titmarsh in Paris. I tried to persuade him not to go but it seems as if I was always to damp him, and that I am to go a round of old saws such as "It is the tortoise and not the hare wins the race" mais enfin il ne m'écoute pas and I must e'en let him make his fortune his own way. I do mind my own business as much as possible but one cannot but be interested.[11]

Failing to detect the loneliness and anxiety behind Isabella's pathetic arguments, Thackeray had set off alone for the Continent about 1 August. He attached no significance at the time to a fact noted remorsefully in a later letter, that "on the day I went to Belgium she began to laugh as I went away." [12]

Thackeray returned from the Continent on 16 August, delighted with his fortnight's vacation. He told his mother, by way of apology for not having written to her:

> with sightseeing and sketching and having good dinners and sleeping on benches of afternoons and writing between times the day was completely spent. Indeed it was a delightful trip, pleasure & sunshine the whole way—& more absence of care than I have enjoyed for many a long day—not that I am very careful. But it seemed a sin to be unhappy in that wonderful blue sky, and so I was as virtuous as possible I mean as jovial.[13]

Impressed by the manuscript that he brought back with him, Chapman and Hall agreed to commission a little guide-book on Belgium and the Rhine for which he was to have £70. This was to be followed by a more substantial work on Ireland, for which the remuneration would be proportionately greater.

But Thackeray's pleasure in these arrangements disappeared in his alarm at the "extraordinary state of languor and depression" in which he found Isabella. It had been a mistake to leave her in the company of Mrs. Butler, "a sad pestering old body," and Mrs. Parker, a prodigy of indiscretion.

> G.M. is angry with her for not answering when spoken to [Thackeray wrote to his mother]—the ⟨poor⟩ thing did not do this from sulkiness but from sheer absence & depression. You & Polly must not in the future be so open in your talk to Mrs Parker, Mrs P. repeated to Isabella just before her confinement every word you said, about her faults not doing her duty & so on, & in the course of her depression the poor thing had worked up these charges so as to fancy herself a perfect demon of wickedness—God abandoned & the juice knows what.

Isabella had herself ventured a timid remonstrance to Mrs. Carmichael-Smyth against Mrs. Parker's *"injudicious repetitions,"* but in his letter there is also an ominous reference to her utter inability to face up to the picture of herself thus provided. "My head flies away with me," she wrote, "as if it were a balloon." [14]

Isabella was examined by the family physician, who told Thackeray "that nothing was the matter with her, that a change of air w^{d} cure her." On 20 August, the fourth anniversary of their marriage, he accordingly took his wife, the children, and Brodie to Margate, where they remained until 7 September.

We have got a charming green little lodging here [he told his mother], but very dear 2½ guineas a week, every body else asked 3 or 4 for rooms not so good. All our windows look to the sea, if you call this sea. A queer little sitting-room with a glass door that walks straight into the street and two neat smart bed rooms 1 on the top of the other.

Thackeray had brought with him to Margate his essay on Fielding for the *Times* and what proved to be the concluding instalment of *A Shabby Genteel Story;* but he found it difficult to apply himself to his task, "now that my poor little woman is so low."

Indeed it is a hard matter to resist catching the infection for I am always with her: nor can I get much work done with the pitiful looks always fixed on me—and I am so unused to living alone keeping back perforce a great fund of animal spirits that want to break out in the shape of argument or jollification that the bottling of them in is annoying to me.

His only relief came from the antics of Anny, "the life & soul of the house with her tantrums," the devotion of Brodie, and occasional visits to "a little quiet Inn two miles off, where I have quiet, & a tea-garden to myself." There alone could he get on with his necessary writing.[15] But he could not often allow himself even this resource, since close watch had to be kept on the children. Years later Anny told him

of walking on the sea shore with Mama & she held me by the hand & once pushed me in a little way, & then her love struggled with her madness & so we came back safe.[16]

Margate having brought about no improvement in Isabella's condition after nearly three weeks, Thackeray returned to London. He had spent £32 in this period, and his financial position was critical. The rebuffs that he encountered in trying to put together a little purse to make up for this disastrous expense —Fraser "refusing me 15£ who owes me £13.10 and the Times to which I apply for a little more than 5 guineas for a week's work, refusing to give me more"—made so profound an impression upon him that he could recall them in detail more than twenty years later.[17] When Brodie asked him for money to pay the household bills, he told Anny many years afterwards, "he changed the last five pounds he had to give her." "We children were in one room crying," his daughter adds, "and Mamma was raving in the other." [18] He asked Mrs. Butler for £100, a request that was indignantly refused; nor were his immediate needs relieved until Mary Graham came to his assistance. With her bond as surety, Chapman and Hall advanced him £120, insisting, however, that he also leave his plate-chest with them, as a "kind of genteel pawn"; and Thackeray found himself once more free from immediate want. If he could not forbear to inquire at this juncture, "O Titmarsh Titmarsh why did you marry?" he had the courage to reply manfully, "why for better or for worse. Let us pray God to enable us to bear either." [19]

After three days at Great Coram Street, Thackeray decided to leave at once for Ireland. London depressed Isabella; Mrs. Shawe, "who had not heard from her daughter for a month, threatened unless she were answered by return of Post to set off from Ireland and come to see her"; and Thackeray wished to begin work *sur les lieux* on "Titmarsh in Ireland," for which he signed an agreement on 8 September with Chapman and Hall. He was to receive £350 for a first edition of 1,250 copies, and unless prevented by "illness or domestic calamity," he undertook to deliver his manuscript by 31 December. He proposed first to visit his mother-in-law in Cork, where "I shall leave the little part of the family and go wandering about as best I may." John Goldsworthy remained behind to "garrison" 13 Great Coram Street, which Thackeray made "an absurd kind of attempt at letting," while he, Isabella, the children, and Brodie sailed on the *Jupiter,* a steamer plying between London and Cork, on Saturday, 12 September.[20]

II

There ensued "a long horrible journey of three days and four nights" that Thackeray could not think of afterwards without shuddering. On Sunday, Thackeray afterwards told his mother, as the *Jupiter* made its way through "the great calm sunshiny sea off the Isle of Wight," Isabella

> flung herself into the water (from the water-closet) & was twenty minutes floating in the sea, before the ship's boat even *saw* her. O my God what a dream it is! I hardly believe it now I write. She was found floating on her back, paddling with her hands, and had never sunk at all. . . . In the next night she made fresh attempts at destruction and the first week here was always attempting to quit the bed: You may fancy what rest I had. I had a riband round her waist, & to my waist, and this always woke me if she moved.

Only at this time did Thackeray fully realize that Isabella was suffering, not from passing melancholia, but from "absolute insanity." And if he deplored his previous blindness to her state, he yet thanked God for His mercy in preventing her suicide.[1]

The party at last reached Cork on 15 September, where Thackeray took lodgings on Grattan's Hill, in a house opposite to that in which Mrs. Shawe and Jane were living.[2] Grattan's Hill was "a pretty little height," commanding a view of "the shining river with the craft along the quays, and the busy city in the distance, the active little steamers puffing away towards Cove, the farther bank crowned with rich woods, and pleasant-looking country-houses." Though the people were in rags and their houses in ruins, Thackeray found "a strange air of forlorn gaiety" about the place.

> Little fat, ragged, smiling children are clambering about the rocks, and sitting on mossy door-steps, tending other children yet smaller, fatter, and more dirty. . . . Two wenches with large purple feet are flapping some carpets in the air. It is a wonder the carpets will bear this kind of treatment at all, and do not be off at once to mingle with the elements. I never saw things that hung to life by such a frail thread.

Thackeray took the drawing-room apartment in one of these "tenements," despite its "pullyless windows, and lockless doors," and he soon found that the warmth of his welcome made up for the deficiencies of his accommodation. His landlady was a young widow who lived elsewhere in the house with her three little children, her cousins, and her uncle. The family quickly took Anny and Harriet to its bosom, the former acquiring within a month "as fine a Munster brogue as ever trolled over the lips of any born Corkagian." Coming home one day Thackeray found Anny in the street

> talking confidentially with a tall old gentleman in a great-coat. 'Who's your friend?' [he inquired] . . . 'Don't you know him, papa?' said the child in the purest brogue. 'Don't you know him?—THAT'S UNCLE JAMES!' And so it was: in this kind, poor, generous, bare-backed house, the English child found a set of new relations; little rosy brothers and sisters to play with, kind women to take the place of the almost dying mother, a good old Uncle James to bring her home apples and care for her—one and all ready to share their little pittance with her, and to give her a place in their simple friendly hearts.[3]

Before Thackeray left London, he had appealed to Mrs. Shawe for help with Isabella. "Do what he will a man is but a bad nurse," he wrote, "and you & Jane must look to the little woman and get her back to spirits again." At first Mrs. Shawe was sympathetic and considerate enough. She told him how "she was herself affected with melancholy when she nursed," and she prayed heartily for Isabella's recovery. If Thackeray had to grant that she "brags bustles bothers prates incessantly of her great merits & sacrifices," he yet tried to excuse her by noting that she "is good in the main—one must not judge too hardly a woman who is really & truly demented." Jane was far more helpful. "Jane has sense talent and feeling—," Thackeray remarked; "poor thing poor thing that she sh^{d} be condemned to live ceaselessly with such a woman, or such a whirlwind." [4]

But as the days passed, Mrs. Shawe became once more the unrestrained termagant that Thackeray had known in Paris. On 22 September he wrote to his mother:

> I don't like to tell you of the conduct of Mrs Shawe: so unmotherly has it been. As far as bringing her daughter tea and dinner & sitting by her bedside she is well enough: but she has a spare room in her house and refused to receive her on account of her nerves (she has been very ill that's certain) & those of her darling Jane. She abused me for bringing her away from London, said her daughter had been denied to her in time of health to be thrown on her in sickness, and so on. She tried to pump out from Brodie whether I had been ill-

treating her or not, and I scarcely get a meal at her home but I am obliged to swallow an insult with it.—but why talk of it? the woman is mad, more desperately self-deceived than any I ever knew. . . . It would do you good to hear Brodie <express her scorn &> hatred of her.[5]

Brodie, indeed, was Thackeray's chief support during these weeks. Though she was very ill, her attention to the children on board the *Jupiter* and afterwards had been unfailing. Thackeray made a friend of her, reflecting that "her steadfastness and affection for the little ones deserves the best feelings I can give her. The poor thing has been very unwell, but never flinched for a minute, and without her I don't know what would have become of us all." Brodie had intended "to be married to a man very well to do in the world," after Isabella's convalescence from the birth of Harriet; but when Thackeray's troubles overtook him, she gave up her engagement rather than leave his children unattended at such a time. Luckily the girls themselves continued to be healthy and happy. "I wish you could see Missy in the bath," Thackeray wrote to his mother, "such a picture of health and beauty, and our dear dear little Harriet, that I love more than the last even—the sweetest tempered little thing God ever made surely." [6]

Thackeray had need of all the comfort he could derive from his children. The passage just quoted concludes: "The mother notices them but seldom." Isabella's condition had improved slightly after her reunion with her mother and sister, but this revival proved transitory and illusory. Brooding on "her own unworthiness," she was more than ever persuaded "that she was never fit to be a wife," and though she grew remorseful over her attempts at suicide, she sank further and further into apathy and melancholy.[7] Taxed by the constant strain of being with Isabella, even Thackeray's robust spirits began to give way.

My wife won't sit still [he wrote to his mother on 5 October], wont employ herself, wont do anything that she is asked & vice versâ. Mong Jew what a time of it, from four o'clock till nine this morning—as soon as ever I was asleep my lady woke me.[8]

Such unremitting attendance made it impossible for him, of course, to do the travelling necessary for "Titmarsh in Ireland."

He employed himself instead on a comedy for Charles Mathews at Covent Garden; and he managed to arrive at the fourth act of this unlikely project, before he abandoned it.[9] How he could have contrived "good lively stuff" for such an undertaking remains a mystery, for his mind ran constantly on past mistakes and future resolutions.

When my little woman gets well—as she will please God [he told his mother], It must be your task to *keep* her so: to put her mind into healthful train and make her able to perform the duties wh. she will be called on to fulfil. We have both of us avoided them as yet, and not met them honestly as we should. I must learn to love home more, and do my duty at the fire side as well as in my writing-room: and I do see how out of all this dreadful trial profit will come to us, if it shall please God to let us have the chance.[10]

Not until almost four weeks had passed did the futility of remaining longer in Cork become clear to Thackeray. On Sunday, 11 October, he wrote to his mother from Clifton:

That woman at Cork became so odious to me . . . that on Friday morning lying in bed awake with my poor Isabella really worse than she had been for some time, worried by the howling of Anny, by the paw-pawing of her mother, & the discomforts of the place—that I say lying awake for 4 hours I said to myself why am I to stay longer here? —and this bright thought having occurred to me, I instantly felt myself happier, got up, walked to the Doctor who advised me to go by all means, and so came off at 2 o'clock by the Queen Steamer, giving Mrs Shawe no hint of my departure until 1: when she was advising me to put Isabella into a mad-house.[11]

He had spent £58 on his Irish trip, and once again a shortage of money threatened. There was only one resource remaining to him, to fall back upon his mother. And since she could not come to England, he made arrangements to take his family to Paris. They had a cabin to themselves for the channel crossing; but Thackeray could not afford a private coach to Paris, and a final trial remained before they were safe in the Carmichael-Smyths' old home at 4 Avenue Sainte Marie, just off the Champs Élysées. Anny, though she was only three at the time, never forgot this last leg of their journey:

I can remember my father punishing me as we travelled to Paris all night in the creaking diligence. I wanted to get out and walk, and they wouldn't let me, and I cried on and on. There was a man in a cap I didn't like, with his nose against the window. He frowned at me when I looked at him. My father was in the corner of the diligence opposite to me and the nurse and the baby, and he struck a match, and lit up a little lantern, which he held up to amuse me. But I only cried the louder. Then he said gravely, 'If you go on crying you will wake the baby, and I shall put out the candle'; so I went on crying, and I woke the baby, who began to cry too; then the man in the corner scolded again, and my father blew out the lantern, and suddenly all was dark. I could not believe it, never before had I been so severely punished. 'Light it, light it,' I screamed. 'No,' said my father's voice in the dark, 'I told you I should put the light out if you cried.' All the time the man in the corner kept on moaning and complaining, and the diligence jogged on, and I suppose I went to sleep on my father's knee at last. I remember hearing him long afterwards speak of that dreadful night, and of the angry Frenchman, who kept saying, 'J'ai la fièvre, mon Dieu. J'ai la fièvre.' The next thing I remember is arriving quite cheerful at Paris, and my grandmother and my grandfather coming down the curling stairs to meet us in the early morning and opening their arms to us all.[12]

III

The relief and gratitude that Thackeray felt at finding himself once more at home, among people who would give him affectionate and unquestioning help, can hardly be exaggerated. In Ireland and on the way to Paris, he had himself been nearer the breaking point than he ever cared to admit. Now his mother and Mary Graham took charge of Anny and Harriet; he was relieved of immediate concern about his shrinking financial resources; and he could turn his mind to the problem of how best to cope with Isabella's affliction.

At the end of November Thackeray decided to send his wife to Jeanne Esquirol's celebrated Maison de Santé at Ivry, "the very best place," for a period of six or seven months. Though Esquirol died shortly after Isabella's admission, Thackeray had the assurance that she was receiving the most enlightened treatment that the medical science of the period could provide. Visiting her for the first time six weeks later, he was assured by Esquirol's nephew, "likewise a famous man in his profession," that *"elle doit guérir."*

At first she was in a fever and violent [he told FitzGerald], then she was indifferent, now she is melancholy & silent and we are glad of it. She bemoans her condition and that is a great step to cure. She knows everybody and recollects things but in a stunned confused sort of way. She kissed me at first very warmly and with tears in her eyes, then she went away from me, as if she felt she was unworthy of having such a God of a husband. God help her.[1]

Freed from constant preoccupation with Isabella, Thackeray began to pick up the broken pieces of his career. His first need was for money. In desperation he called even upon the creditors of his young manhood, John Ritchie and Maginn, for repayment of loans that they had long since found it convenient to forget.[2] But he knew that this was a fruitless gesture and that he must depend upon his own exertions for his salvation. Hence we find him embarking early in December on a period of determined application to his work that did not end until the following summer, when two substantial sums unexpectedly came his way. His first thought was to write a continuation of *A Shabby Genteel Story,* which would have been almost as long again as the narrative already printed, but we have seen that Fraser did not take kindly to this suggestion. Later in December he wrote *The Second Funeral of Napoleon* and "The Chronicle of the Drum"; in January and February *The Great Hoggarty Diamond;* [3] between January and April eight chapters of a never-completed novel called "The Knights of Borsellen"; and between February and May a dozen magazine articles and stories. He had never before laboured so steadily and devotedly or to such excellent purpose. No wonder he wrote to Mrs. Carlyle: "When Titmarsh works this way, be sure there is a reason for it." [4]

Meanwhile, Thackeray was deeply touched by the care and affection that his family lavished on him and his children.

Since my calamity [he told FitzGerald], I have learned to love all these people a great deal more—my mother especially God bless her who has such a tender yearning big heart that I begin to cry when I think of her: and when I see her with the children, cleaving to them, am obliged to walk off for the sight is too much for me.[5]

The English family that sets out to view the Parisian celebrations of 15 December in *The Second Funeral of Napoleon* is the Carmichael-Smyth household pictured with a minimum of fictional adjustment. It was made up, Thackeray writes, of

1. a great-grandmother [Mrs. Butler], a hale, handsome old lady of seventy, the very best dressed and neatest old lady in Paris; 2. a grandfather and grandmother, tolerably young to bear that title; 3. a daughter [Mary Graham]; and 4. two little great-grand, or grandchildren, that may be of the age of three and one, and belong to a son and daughter who are in India.

The grandfather, who is as proud of his wife as he was thirty years ago when he married, and pays her compliments still twice or thrice in a day, and when he leads her into a room, looks round at the persons assembled, and says in his heart, 'Here, gentlemen, here is my wife; show me such another woman in England!' this gentleman had hired a room on the Champs Élysées, for he would not have his wife catch cold by exposing her to the balconies in the open air.

When I came to the street I found the family assembled in the following order of march:—

No. 1. The great-grandmother, walking daintily along, supported by No. 3, her granddaughter.

A nurse, carrying No. 4, junior, who was sound asleep; and a huge basket, containing saucepans, bottles of milk, parcels of infant's food, certain dimity napkins, &c., a child's coral, and a little horse belonging to No. 4, senior.

A servant, bearing a basket of condiments.

No. 2. Grandfather, spick and span, clean shaved, hat brushed, white-buckskin gloves, bamboo cane, brown greatcoat, walking as upright and solemn as may be, having his lady on his arm.

No. 4, senior with mottled legs and a tartan costume, who was frisking about between his grandfather's legs, who heartily wished him at home.

'My dear,' his face seemed to say to his lady, 'I think you might have left the little things in the nursery, for we shall have to squeeze through a terrible crowd in the Champs Élysées.'

The lady was going out for a day's pleasure, and her face was full of care: she had to look first after her old mother, who was walking ahead, then after No. 4, junior, with the nurse,—he might fall into all sorts of danger, wake up, cry, catch cold, nurse might slip down, or Heaven knows what; then she had to look her husband in the face, who had gone to such expense and been so kind for her sake, and make that gentleman believe she was thoroughly happy; and finally, she had to keep an eye upon No. 4, senior, who, as she was perfectly certain, was about in two minutes to be lost for ever, or trampled to pieces in the crowd.

These events took place in a quiet little street leading into the Champs Élysées, the entry of which we had almost reached by this time. The four detachments above described, which had been straggling a little in their passage down the street, closed up at the end of it, and stood for a moment huddled together. No. 3, Miss X——, began speaking to her companion the great-grandmother.

'Hush, my dear,' said that old lady, looking round alarmed at her daughter; '*speak French!*'—and she straightway began nervously to make a speech which she supposed to be in that language, but which was as much like French as Iroquois. The whole secret was out; you could read it in the grandmother's face, who was doing all she could to keep from crying, and looked as frightened as she dared to look. The two elder ladies had settled between them that there was going to be a general English slaughter that day, and had brought the children with them, so that they might all be murdered in company.[6]

This autobiographical passage is by far the most appealing part of *The Second Funeral of Napoleon,* which is otherwise chiefly a workmanlike account of the transportation of the Emperor's remains from St. Helena to France and their burial in Paris. Thackeray required only four days to compose this "important work." To it he added "as an after-thought" a ballad called "The Chronicle of the Drum," which took him all of a week.[7] He wrote *The Second Funeral of Napoleon* primarily to demonstrate how "the great HUMBUG-PLANT" continued to flourish in 1840,[8] and the ballad is likewise a development of the not very novel reflection that domestic happiness should be placed above "greatness" of any sort, since the paths of glory lead but to the grave. Yet both works derive a real poignancy from their many reflections of Thackeray's state of mind at this time, and one understands why four years later he still sturdily referred to the little volume in which they were published during January of 1841 as "the best book I ever wrote." [9]

Thackeray's conviction that family affection is supremely important, a theme that appears only obliquely and sporadically in *The Second Funeral of Napoleon* and "The Chronicle of the Drum," lies at the very heart of his next story, *The Great Hoggarty Diamond*. He had discovered, he told Mrs. Carlyle, that "I am a great deal more unhappy without [Isabella], than ever I thought it was in my nature to be." And he urged marriage upon FitzGerald by contending that, "in spite of all the woes and troubles attendant on it: . . . it completes a man's faculties somehow, and lets him into secrets unknown to bachelors, especially that fine one of loving children." [10] What he had lost through his wife's break-down, indeed, now seemed to him the most important thing in life. In telling the story of Samuel Titmarsh's involvement with the pious swindler Brough and his Independent West Diddlesex Fire and Life Insurance Company, a story which a year before he would have made into still another rogue tale, Thackeray consequently centred his attention upon the dupe rather than the scoundrel, in order to give expression to his faith that, however much rascality may flourish in the world, the central human values exist in a sphere above worldly success or failure.

Sam Titmarsh, an obscure clerk in the West Diddlesex offices, is in love with a simple country girl, Mary Smith, and loved in turn by her; but he sees no prospect of earning enough to marry. Then his aunt Hoggarty gives him a diamond pin, which operates as a kind of charm. Fashionable ladies take Sam under their protection, Brough advances him over the heads of his fellow clerks, a brilliant future seems to be ahead of him. Sam marries and at first all goes well in the new household; but when he attempts under Aunt Hoggarty's tutelage to live up to his new position, he is led into excessive expenses; and because he is increasingly engaged by business affairs, he grows less attentive to his wife. The West Diddlesex bubble bursts, Brough takes refuge on the Continent, and Sam, as an accessible officer of the company, is arrested for its debts. In this extremity he pawns his diamond pin. Immediately he begins to experience "a different and a better sort of luck," and at last, fully reunited with Mary, he realizes that "a good wife is the best diamond a man can wear in his bosom." [11]

There is clearly much veiled autobiography in this story. Mary is drawn, as Thackeray acknowledged, from "that poor little wife of mine." [12] The Titmarshes' life in Lamb's Conduit Street and later in Barnard Street, Russell Square, parallels in many particulars the Thackerays' life in Great Coram Street. The loss of their baby girl directly reflects the death of Jane Thackeray in 1838.[13] Mrs. Hoggarty was suggested by Mrs. Butler; and her persecution of Mary owes something to Mrs. Butler's mistreatment of Isabella. The pecuniary difficulties in which Sam finds himself after his fall from prosperity resemble Thackeray's in the later months of 1840. The profound gratitude that Sam expresses when he and Mary are reunited [14] poignantly reflects Thackeray's trust that a similar destiny lay ahead for Isabella and himself. More significant still than these specific parallels is the peculiar tenderness and openness with which the story is told. Thackeray wrote it at "a time of great affliction," when his "heart was very soft and humble," when he was only "a poor devil, looking wistfully at the few Napoleons in his *gousset,* and giving himself no airs at all." [15] This new-found charity and humility effectively banished from *The Great Hoggarty Diamond* the echo of sounding brass and tinkling cymbal that sometimes falls so disturbingly on the reader's ear in his earlier work, even though the story presents no more cheerful a picture of life than had *The Yellowplush Papers* or *Catherine.* "I don't believe Titmarsh has a bit higher opinion of himself than he has of the rest of the world," Thackeray told Mrs. Procter when he was writing it; "nor does he much conceal his opinion of the one or the other." [16]

It is not surprising, then, that *The Great Hoggarty Diamond* remained "a favourite with its author," despite its "sobriety and melancholy." [17] With regard to characterization, Thackeray's hand had never been surer or more economical. Even Sam Titmarsh, though he is entrusted with the notoriously difficult task of telling his own story, emerges as an interesting portrait of a "green" and trusting youth, whose naïveté is saved from insipidity by a native pawkiness and whose subacid humour gives an edge to his reflections upon the anomalies of life. In Brough Thackeray attempted a character that had long interested him, that of "the getting-and-keeping scoundrel," who stays within the law and is regarded with envy and respect by society.[18] He treats this whited sepulchre, not with the implacable scorn that informs the companion portraits of self-confessed rascals in *The Yellowplush Papers* and *Catherine*, but with the sympathetic understanding that is the right of a brother sinner; and the resulting portrait gains proportionately in subtlety and fidelity. *The Great Hoggarty Diamond* is remarkable, above all, because Thackeray contrived in it to write his first unified and coherent long narrative.[19] It is easily the best of his early stories. No wonder then that Thackeray's friend John Sterling, who read it with "extreme delight" in *Fraser's Magazine,* where it appeared between September and December, 1841, should have inquired: "What is there better in Fielding or Goldsmith? The man is a true genius; and, with quiet and comfort, might produce masterpieces that would last as long as any we have, and delight millions of unborn readers. There is more truth and nature in one of these papers than in all ——'s Novels together." [20]

IV

In the latter part of January the Carmichael-Smyths and Mary Graham left for Italy, where they were to meet the Major's younger brother Colonel Charles Carmichael, who was returning to Europe *via* the "overland route" after twenty years in India. Despite the quarter of a century separating them in age, Charles and Mary had fallen in love by correspondence, and the high point of the Italian excursion was to be their marriage. Thackeray remained behind with Mrs. Butler, Brodie, and the children. The arrangement worked out well enough. Thackeray got along "famously" with the old lady, who kept house, and described himself as being "in clover." [1]

Yet this was a very dismal time for him. He was depressed about his professional prospects. *The Second Funeral of Napoleon,* though it was well reviewed, sold only 140 copies when it appeared in January. "So your poor Titmarsh has made another fiasco," Thackeray wrote to a friend. "How are we to take this great stupid public by the ears?" [2] Nor did *Comic Tales and Sketches* fare much better when it was issued three months later. It began to seem to Thackeray that he was condemned to trudge for ever on the treadmill of magazinery. Isabella's progress at Ivry was slow and doubtful; word still came occasionally of the slanderous abuse of him that Mrs. Shawe poured into the ears of any one who would listen. But for a man of his convivial temperament, the severest trial was the sense of overpowering loneliness which began to oppress him after the Carmichael-Smyths' departure. He had a few friends in Paris. John Bowes Bowes from time to time invited him to a magnificent dinner. Milnes, whom Thackeray found simple, clever, and kind-hearted, was a real resource during his brief visit in January. The amiable dentist Augustus Stevens could be relied on for an occasional evening of "carousing." Yet Thackeray had only one real intimate, a ne'er-do-well Irish journalist named O'Donnell, who cannot have been an altogether agreeable companion. Though he was a survival from the old carefree days at Terré's Tavern whom Thackeray introduced to the Procters and the Carlyles as "one of the best friends I have," Thackeray had to admit that he was "a heavy man," "extremely uncouth and matter-of-factish." [3] In England the Garrick or the Reform would have made up for the absence of friends, but at the one Parisian club to which he belonged Thackeray found only "bawling Frenchmen," smoking and playing billiards; and knowing no one, he soon tired of noting the difference between their conduct and the sedate and reserved behaviour of English clubmen.[4]

Even the theatre, which had never failed to amuse him in the past, proved unbearable to him. He fell into the habit of walking about Paris alone, observing the incidents of common life with a keen interest and encountering here and there "noble characters . . . in little nooks of this great world." He struck up a friendship, for example, with the artist Louis Marvy, who engraved his drawings for *Comic Tales and Sketches.*

> I wish you could see him [Thackeray wrote to his mother]. He is abt 28 has not a spark of genius: works 14 hours a day, never breakfasts except off cheese & bread in his atelier, dines in the same way, never goes out, makes about 3000 francs a year, has a wife & child & is happy the whole day long—the whole house is like a cage of canaries, nothing but singing from night till morning. It goes to my heart to hear his little wife singing at her work.[5]

In the Marvy household Thackeray found an affecting reminder of his own lost happiness; many years later he was to write to Isabella's sister Jane: "Nest ce pas mourir tous les jours—dont you recollect her singing and her sweet sweet voice?" [6]

Meanwhile, Thackeray sought to act on his conviction that he could attain a higher grade in his profession only by producing a successful full-length novel. When Barham late in 1840 urged him to write a romance on the pattern of Joseph Strutt's *Queen-Hoo Hall,* a tale of fifteenth-century life which had been completed by Scott, Thackeray thought well of the project, particularly since Bentley had shown an interest in publishing such a work. During the early weeks of 1841 he read widely in the chroniclers of the period; but before he could begin his story, the necessity of producing in short order "stuff enough to keep my dear little woman where she is for 2 months to come," forced him to "put the novel aside" and to turn to less ambitious undertakings. In April he turned again to "The Knights of Borsellen," as he tentatively entitled his tale, but his attention was soon distracted once more by further periodical writing. The eight chapters that he had written by this time carry the story as far as it was destined to go, though he never gave up hope of eventually completing it.[7] The Middle Ages were hardly Thackeray's spiritual home, and we need not regret his failure to complete "The Knights of Borsellen." There are good things, nevertheless, in this fragmentary story. His picture of mediaeval life, far from being softened and rectified in the usual Victorian fashion, reproduces something of the violence, grossness, and cruelty that he had found in Brantôme, Froissart, and Monstrelet. He was, indeed, endeavouring to answer by anticipation a question which he was later to ask at Rhodes in *Notes of a Journey from Cornhill to Grand Cairo:* "When shall we have a real account of those times and heroes—no good-humored pageant, like those of the Scott romances—but a real authentic story to instruct and frighten honest people of the present day, and make them thankful that the baker governs the world now in place of the baron?" [8] His study of family relations among the Borsellens anticipates in its closely packed acuteness his treatment of the same subject in the early chapters of *Esmond.* And his sketch of the shrewd old courtier Castel-Sarrasin introduces a new character to English fiction, a character which he was later to develop into a finished portrait in creating Major Pendennis.

Of his other work after *The Great Hoggarty Diamond* we need only note that the confiding openness of that story and *The Second Funeral of Napoleon* soon became an occasional rather than a constant feature of his manner. The literary scene of the early 1840s did not encourage confidences between writer and reader, and Thackeray's guard went up as he became able to see once more beyond the range of his personal troubles. Looking back at the early months of 1841 ten years later, he reflected that he had then been "a boy . . . bleating out my simple griefs in the Great Hoggarty Diamond." [9] The callousness and venality of many of his professional associates moved him, indeed, to satirical pictures as harsh as anything he had written before his tragedy. "Reading a Poem," which appeared in the *Britannia* on 1–8 May 1841, seems to suggest that the literary world is made up entirely of toadying or bullying hacks, vapid titled dilettantes, and ignorant publishers.[10] But the staple manner that Thackeray developed during this period was neither that of *The Great Hoggarty Diamond* nor that of "Reading a Poem." He tried instead to "chasten and otherwise popularize" the style in which he composed his "comicalities," to write "in a certain agreeable jocose sneering good-humored scandalous sentimental sort of way." [11]

Meanwhile Thackeray's visits to Ivry during these months made him increasingly despondent; on each occasion the doctors seemed less confident of Isabella's eventual recovery. Thackeray was appalled by glimpses of "wild fierce women rambling about in the garden," and as Isabella began to recover somewhat from the apathy into which she had fallen, he "saw the difference between Pussy & them . . . [and] felt how wrong it was to keep her in such company." [12] Late in March he determined to see whether champagne, "the medicine that is administered in the Opera of the Eliseri d'Amore," might not be more effective than the doctors' remedies.

Off I took the little woman [he told Mrs. Procter] a pleasant walk across the fields to a pleasant little gudgeon house on the river, where we had a dinner and she took two glasses of the elixir which I devoted myself to finish. It did her a great deal of good and made her eyes sparkle, and actually for the first time these six months the poor little woman flung herself into my arms with all her heart and gave me a kiss, at which moment of course the waiter burst in. This only served to mend matters for the lady went off in a peal of laughter, the first these six months again.[13]

Isabella begged Thackeray to take her to the play. Afterwards she pleaded not to be returned to the Maison de Santé, and Thackeray could only yield to her appeal. "The little woman put on such a pitiful look when I talked of sending her away from me: & is so happy and so really affectionate with me, that leave her I will not." [14]

For the next six weeks Thackeray was Isabella's "sole attendant" in the Carmichael-Smyths' house on the Avenue Sainte Marie, and he "almost broke down under the slavery." Then he hired a trustworthy nurse who looked after her very efficiently for ten francs a week. He still tried to persuade himself that her sanity would be fully restored.

There is nothing the matter with her [he told Mrs. Procter] except perfect indifference, silence and sluggishness. She cares for nothing, except for me a little, her general health has greatly improved: her ideas are quite distinct when she chooses to wake from her lethargy. She is not unhappy and looks fresh, smiling and about sixteen years old. Today is her little baby's birthday. She kissed the child when I told her of the circumstance, but does not care for it.[15]

There was clearly nothing that he could do for her for the time being, and he accordingly set off in June for England.

XIII. Yellowplush, Titmarsh, and Gahagan

From the frontispiece to
"Comic Tales and Sketches"

XIV. "The Two Celebrated Literary Characters at Sir John's"
(Dr. Lardner and Bulwer)

From an etching by Thackeray in "Comic Tales and Sketches"

XV. Frontispiece to *The Paris Sketch Book*

XVI. Brodie in later life

From a photograph

After a few days in London, passed in renewing friendships and interviewing publishers, he left for Streatlam Castle, John Bowes's country residence in Durham, where he stayed from 25 June until 13 July. He arrived just in time for the general election of 1841. John Bowes recalled this visit to Thackeray in a letter of 1858:

You don't mean to say it's seventeen years since you came down, & helped a distressed Country Gentleman with his Election; since you were introduced to his B——d & C——le Committee as the Gent who had just voted for Lord John Russell in the City of London, & had hurried to the North to aid the right *cause* in S—th Durham, since enfin the famous Firebrand Correspondence was circulated thro' the Land— 'It's a vast o'taime'—as they say down there, but it has not effaced from my memory the kind aid you then lent me, nor that between us then the little matter you now mention was considered une affaire liquidée.[16]

It must have been a substantial relief to Thackeray when Bowes came so cordially to his financial assistance. Certainly the pleasure that he took in the luxurious life of this great country-house, and the excitement with which he participated in his friend's riotous but successful campaign to represent South Durham in the Whig interest [17] are admirably communicated in one of the best of his unreprinted articles, "Notes on the North What-D-Ye-Callem Election, Being the Personal Narrative of Napoleon Putnam Wiggins, of Passimaquoddy," which appeared in *Fraser's Magazine* for September and October, 1841. As its title suggests, this narrative saw the accomplishment of Thackeray's long-promised burlesque of N. P. Willis, and, indeed, his mimicry of Yankee prejudice and naïveté adds a good deal to the liveliness of the performance.

From Streatlam Castle Thackeray turned south again to York, where he fell in with his friend the London barrister William Frederick Pollock. The two proceeded together to Fryston Hall, where Milnes was expecting them.

As we walked up on a fine summer morning to the then front of the house [Pollock relates], Milnes and his father were standing at the door, the latter in a dressing-gown and smoking a cigar. He at once, after a hospitable greeting, gave one to each of us, and added: 'You may smoke anywhere in this house—in your bedrooms, if you please—and Mrs. Milnes does not mind it in her drawing-room. Only you must not smoke in Richard's room, for he doesn't like it.' Thackeray turned to Milnes and said, 'What a father is thrown away upon you!'

Thackeray enjoyed both Fryston's genial hospitality and its admirable library. When he departed a week later, he said to the older Milnes, after thanking him heartily, "Your house, sir, combines the freedom of the tavern with the elegance of the chateau." [18]

By the end of July Thackeray was in Paris again, where he found Isabella "very glad to see me, and the dear little ones very well & happy." [19] The Carmichael-Smyths and Carmichaels were by this time in Germany, where, Thackeray's mother suggested, the effects of the water-cure might well be tried on Isabella. Thackeray began hydropathic treatments in Paris almost at once, and by 11 August he and Isabella were on their way to join the family party at a sanatorium located in the former Convent of Marienburg near Boppard on the Rhine. There a very exacting regimen prevailed:

At five o'clock in the morning [he told FitzGerald] M[rs] Thack begins to sweat in blankets, at eight they pour buckets of water over her, at twelve she takes an enormous douche for five minutes, at five sweating again, and more buckets of ice-cold water. . . . The first days she would not stand the immense sluicing of the water-pipe, and I was obliged to go in with her. It would have made a fine picture—M[rs] Thack in the condition of our first parins, before they took to eating apples, and the great Titmarsh with nothing on but a petticoat lent him by his mother, and far too scanty to cover that immense posterior protuberance with w[h] nature has furnished him.[20]

For a month Isabella's progress was steady, and Thackeray thought her "all but well." Then it became evident that this treatment, like all the others he had tried, was destined to come to nothing. Late in October he headed back to Paris for "another long weary winter." [21]

Yet despite the gloomy view that he took of the future, these months in Germany effectively ended his frenzied "year of pain and hope." Much of the anxiety that he had experienced since his wife's break-down the previous August had come from his constant effort to keep ahead of his creditors. He had borrowed wherever he could; he had written with a pertinacity which he had never achieved before. In Paris, however, he learned of the death of Mrs. Blechynden, Richmond Thackeray's illegitimate daughter, an occurrence which put him in possession of £500 from his father's estate; and at Boppard, Charles and Mary Carmichael had given him another £500. This happy combination of events, he told Mrs. Ritchie, "puts me out of the reach of fortune for some years to come, and removes the horrible care and fear of want wh has been hanging over me in the past year since my wife's affliction." [22]

V

It can be argued that Thackeray's experiences between August of 1840 and August of 1841 affected his character and work more profoundly than those of any other part of his life. During the first months of this period he was "a very miserable fellow who was quite unaccustomed to that kind of mood," and hence utterly overwhelmed by it. Gradually he learned to endure his griefs "more composedly," though without feeling any real relief.[1] Perhaps the heaviest burden he had to bear was the sense that he was himself responsible for his misfortunes:

> O Lord God [he wrote in his diary on 27 July 1841]—there is not one of the sorrows or disappointments of my life, that as I fancy I cannot trace to some error crime or weakness of my disposition. Strengthen me then with your help, to maintain my good resolutions—not to yield to lust or sloth that besets me: or at least to combat with them & overcome them sometimes.
>
> Above all O Gracious Father, please to have mercy upon those whose well-being depends upon me. O empower me to give them good and honest example: keep them out of misfortunes wh result from my fault: and towards them enable me to discharge the private duties of life—to be interested in their ways & amusements, to be cheerful & constant at home: frugal & orderly if possible. O give me your

help strenuously to work out the vices of character wh have born such bitter fruit already.[2]

Yet in the depths of his despondency, he never wallowed in self-pity, and he never lost the ability to laugh at himself. If he complained to the Procters about being in "the slough of despair," he added: "Despair, Madam, is the word—Byronish—I hate mankind, and wear my shirt collars turned down." If he asked himself, "Ah Yellowplush! where are the days when you lived & laughed?" he replied: "If I don't mind I shall be setting up for an unacknowledged genius, & turn as morbid as Bulwer." [3] He was always capable of a joking return upon himself that effectively preserved his balance and sanity.

The ordeal of Thackeray's "year of pain and hope . . . and bitter bitter tears" [4] fortified his character, deepened his understanding, and matured his talent. Even of the domestic happiness that he had once enjoyed, it may be said that he understood it better and felt it more profoundly for having lost it. Nearly twenty years later, writing to a young friend who had made what his family considered an "imprudent marriage," Thackeray recalled his own marital venture, in which he had "undergone disaster, grief, and immense joys and consolations." His conclusion was to say, "Laus Deo with a very humble grateful heart." [5] No doubt tragedy had overtaken him, leaving him permanently disappointed, suffering, in that sad phrase from *The Virginians*, "some bankruptcy of his heart." [6] But at least he did not have to reproach himself with the reflections that haunt the lady in Browning's "Youth and Art," when she considers her empty success:

> Each life's unfulfilled, you see;
>   It hangs still, patchy and scrappy:
> We have not sighed deep, laughed free,
>   Starved, feasted, despaired,—been happy.[7]

Hence the peculiar bitter-sweet flavour of Thackeray's mature personality and work. Though his own happiness had been shattered, his belief in the possibility of happiness for others remained unimpaired. If he said, in effect, "my dreams have all come true to other men," he did not therefore underestimate the value of these dreams.

The events of this crucial year affected Thackeray in another way, imparting to his work a perspective that has seemed to some readers the height of wisdom, to others the depth of bathos. The pain that he had felt in watching over and cherishing Isabella, the joy that he had experienced when his family came to his aid, made an indelible impression upon him. "It's worth while to be unhappy for a time," he told FitzGerald "—to find how such admirable creatures tend and suffer with one." [8] Affection, which he had earlier taken for granted, came to seem to him life's chief justification. His shift in attitude is perhaps best summed up in a letter which he wrote to James Hannay in 1854:

> I hate Juvenal, I mean I think him a truculent brute, and I love Horace better than you do, and rate Churchill much lower; and as for Swift, you haven't made me alter my opinion. I admire, or rather admit, his power as much as you do; but I don't admire that kind of power so much as I did fifteen years ago, or twenty shall we say. Love is a higher intellectual exercise than Hatred; and when you get one or two more of those young ones you write so pleasantly about, you'll come over to the side of the kind wags, I think, rather than the cruel ones.[9]

He became expert in exploring what Chesterton has described as "the paradox of charity or chivalry that the weaker a thing is the more it should be respected, that the more indefensible a thing is the more it should appeal to us for a certain kind of defense." [10] This paradox lies at the root of Thackeray's so-called sentimentalism. If it sometimes led him to rhetorical outbursts that appear excessive, it remains the key with which he unlocked his heart.[11]

Charity was his guide as well to a deeper comprehension of the complexities of human motivation and conduct. Thackeray's state of mind before Isabella's break-down had often been marked by the brashness of ignorance and inexperience. In his *Life of Johnson* Boswell tells how he once endeavoured to apologize to the great man for Lady Diana Beauclerk, who had married Johnson's friend Beauclerk two days after her divorce from her first husband. Johnson replied, "My dear Sir, never accustom your mind to mingle virtue and vice. The woman's a whore, and there's an end on't." [12] Johnson's positiveness was deliberate, of course; but the immature Thackeray, without a tithe of Johnson's knowledge of life, was sometimes equally dogmatic in dealing with cases of conscience. The difficulties of his tragic year taught him to pause and consider before passing judgment, and the gain to him as a novelist was immense.

Thackeray's new point of view also had the effect of tempering the religious scepticism which he had come to entertain as a young man. His intellectual doubts were not resolved; indeed, they were to return to him with undiminished force at several periods in his later life. But at this time he had a profound emotional need for a deity with whom he could share his burden:

> I find myself growing much more sentimental as I grow older [he told his mother]. The world is not near such a bad one as some of your orthodox pretend. We are not desperately wicked but good & loving many of us: our arms reach up to heaven, though the Devil to be sure is tugging at our heels. My dearest old Mammy I think of you often & always indeed I do: and know I shall never go to Hell for if I went you in Heaven w^{d} be miserable, & there you know people must be happy.[13]

His experience was the common one that Clough was to describe a few years later in "Dipsychus": that, however careless we may be in prosperity about religion,

> . . . almost every one when age,
> Disease, or sorrows strike him,
> Inclines to think there is a God,
> Or something very like Him.

Finally, Thackeray's change in attitude brought with it a new willingness to speak out in his own person as he would not have done earlier in his career. It is true that, not long after he brought *Catherine* to its unsatisfactory conclusion, he told his mother, "I fail by sneering too much," and referred her to "some remarks against myself" in his essay on Cruikshank.[14] There he recorded his discovery that

To be greatly successful as a professional humourist, as in any other calling, a man must be quite honest, and show that his heart is in his work. A bad preacher will get admiration and a hearing with this point in his favour, where a man of three times his acquirements will only find indifference and coldness.[15]

But it was not until after his troubles that he began naturally and easily to take his readers into his confidence, to alleviate his loneliness by talking to them as he would to the intimates who were no longer at hand. And though he was not yet thirty, he fell into the habit of presenting himself as a man fifteen or twenty years older, who had become an observer of the battle of life, rather than a participant in it.[16] He began to look back, to compare, to reflect in the manner of advanced middle age, as if the past were more important to him than the present. And his writing came thereby to be enriched by more and more of those "flashes of unforeseen remembrance" which are so characteristic and significant a part of his mature work.

II

Bachelor Life

I

THACKERAY PASSED THE WINTER of 1841–1842 caring for his wife in Paris. But her malady took a turn for the worse in February, and he had to admit at last that "she was past my management." He accordingly placed her with a Dr. Puzin in nearby Chaillot, in whose care she remained until October, 1845.[1] At first these new surroundings seemed to induce an improvement in her condition. "The poor little woman is getting better & better," he told FitzGerald, ". . . perfectly happy, obedient and reasonable." [2] But there was the usual relapse; and Thackeray never again had the courage to bring her back to his home. FitzGerald relates how much Thackeray admired Charles Lamb for the unwavering fidelity with which, towards the end of his life, he devoted himself to his sister Mary. " 'Saint Charles,' . . . Thackeray once called him, while looking at one of his half-mad Letters, and remember[ing] his Devotion to that quite mad Sister." [3] But Thackeray was still a young man with his way to make in the world, and he had other claims on his loyalty. After eighteen months of almost constant attendance, he had to relinquish the task of looking after Isabella to others.

Though all those he loved best were in Paris, the demands of his profession made it imperative that he live in London. He accordingly returned to England in the spring, and though his visits to France continued to be frequent, London was henceforth his headquarters. The question of where to live proved difficult to resolve. He wanted his own household with his mother in charge, but there proved to be insuperable difficulties in the way of this plan. For four years Thackeray worked towards carrying it out, however, contenting himself with a series of unsatisfactory makeshifts in the mean time.

From the spring of 1842 until his lease expired in May of 1843, he lived at 13 Great Coram Street when he was in London. Charles and Mary Carmichael kept house for him until June, 1842, an arrangement that gave rise to much friction, and after his return from Ireland and Paris early in 1843 Brodie for several months looked after his establishment. But modest as 13 Great Coram Street was, it proved too roomy and expensive for a man living alone, and Thackeray at last released Brodie to other work (she was later employed by Charles Darwin), stored his furniture, and moved to the Hummums Hotel in Covent Garden.

After a protracted Continental visit, Thackeray found lodgings at 27 Jermyn Street, which he rented from December, 1843, until April, 1845. "They are very good to me," he wrote to Isabella. "I have 3 rooms, the use of a footman, a Surgeon below to purge physic sweat bleed &c. and all for the small charge of 25/ per week."[4] Henry Vizetelly, who was at this period editor of the *Pictorial Times*, has left a circumstantial account of a visit to Thackeray in these chambers:

On calling at the address given me—a shop in Jermyn-street, eight or ten doors from Regent-street, and within a few doors of the present Museum of Geology—and knocking at the private entrance, a young lodging-house slavey in answer to my inquiries bade me follow her upstairs. I did so, to the very top of the house and after my card had been handed in, I was asked to enter the front apartment, where a tall slim individual between thirty and thirty-five years of age, with a pleasant smiling countenance and a bridgeless nose, and clad in a dressing gown of decided Parisian cut, rose from a small table standing close to the near window to receive me. When he stood up, the low pitch of the room caused him to look even taller than he really was, and his actual height was well over six feet. . . . The apartment was an exceedingly plainly furnished bedroom, with common rush seated chairs and painted French bedstead, and with neither looking-glass nor prints on the bare, cold, cheerless-looking walls. On the table from which Mr. Thackeray had risen, a white cloth was spread, on which was a frugal breakfast tray—a cup of chocolate and some dry toast—and huddled together at the other end were writing materials, two or three numbers of "Fraser's Magazine," and a few slips of manuscript.[5]

This is a sufficiently dismal picture, but if the "suite of rooms in St. James's Street, looking down on Pall Mall—for 30£ a quarter on the 4 floor" [6] to which Thackeray moved in April, 1845, was "the snug little kingdom up four pair of stair" described in "The Cane-bottomed Chair," [7] he fared better in his new lodgings. He remained at 88 St. James's Street until June, 1846.

Thackeray's appearance during these years of London bachelor life did not altogether coincide with Vizetelly's description, which was written, after all, half a century later. Though he was 6 feet 3 inches in height, he said disparagingly, "after six feet, it all runs to seed." And he was massive rather than slim. He "weighed very heavy" at this time of his life, between 15 and 18 stone, it would seem; [8] hence his choice of the sobriquet "the Fat Contributor" for some of his *Punch* contributions. His hair was grey, his face round and full, and his spectacles were perched precariously on his button nose. He took little exercise, since he disliked walking, and at this time had no opportunity for the horseback riding that he enjoyed. When Bedingfield asked him if he was strong, he replied, "No, . . . I should be; but I don't give the muscles fair play." [9] Still, his formidable appearance kept him out of trouble, and he was ready enough to fight when he found himself in a tight corner. He once described to Bedingfield the narrow margin by which he had escaped an encounter with an enraged costermonger coming back from the Derby.[10]

Thackeray soon settled into a routine, which he followed with little variation while he was in London. He rose about ten, had a simple breakfast, and spent the remainder of what the Victorians called the "morning" (the portion of the day before the fashionable dinner-hour) in "working and dawdling about." [11] About five o'clock he would "take a little trudge as far as Pall-

Mall or possibly the Garrick." [12] At seven-thirty came dinner, a long and elaborate meal, eaten usually at the home of a friend or acquaintance. During the season his calendar was full; he noted with pride, indeed, that, having to spend Christmas of 1843 in London, he had "ELEVEN invitations to Dinner." [13] But when this resource failed, there was always a club or a tavern. Afterwards he occasionally went to the theatre or opera, or attended a *soirée* or ball; but for the most part he was content to drink, smoke, and talk with his friends at the Garrick, the Reform, or one of the taverns that he patronized. He rarely retired before one or two in the morning.

This seems a strenuous schedule, but Thackeray throve on it. "I could not go on with this [work]," he noted, "unless I had the fun in the evening, and the quantum of wine." [14] To allay the fears of his mother, who was constantly protesting against his excesses, Thackeray assured her during a fortnight in 1843 when he had dinner engagements every night, that "this racket agrees better with me than a quieter life and I have managed to write a good deal." [15] Most of his material was in fact drawn from these constant opportunities for observation and discussion. Dining with "a young Cambridge cousin" in 1844, he noted in his diary: "These boys are intolerable. But it would be good to study them. I recalled many of the flippancies and opinions of my own 22." [16] Everywhere he found incidents and characters, themes and anecdotes that he could put to use. FitzGerald did not exaggerate when he assured Frederick Tennyson in 1845 that

> old Thackeray . . . goes on in his way; writing hard for half a dozen Reviews and newspapers all the morning; dining, drinking, and talking of a night; managing to preserve a fresh colour, and perpetual flow of spirits under a wear-and-tear of thinking and feeding that would have knocked up any other man I know two years ago, at least.[17]

Thackeray's attention to business during these years, indeed, was matched only by his devotion to pleasure. If he could not have the domestic affection that he valued more than anything else in life, he proposed to solace himself with the smaller enjoyments that remained. Like Alice, he had always taken "a great interest in questions of eating and drinking," and after his loss of Isabella, he set out consciously to make himself an expert on these topics. To this preoccupation we owe a delightful series of papers which includes "Memorials of Gormandizing," Fitz-Boodle's "Second Profession," Lancelot Wagstaff's "Greenwich—Whitebait," and "Barmecide Banquets." The first and most interesting of these essays had been written in the spring of 1841 with a view to the compilation of a small book called *Dinner Reminiscences: or, The Young Gormandizer's Guide at Paris.* Thackeray's immediate purpose was to provide a "brief dinner-journal," and he does give a most succulent description of dinners at the Café Foy, the Trois Frères Provençaux, the Rocher de Cancale, and elsewhere. But the article has a larger place in Thackeray's work as the first statement of what may be called his philosophy of discriminating enjoyment. "All a man's senses are worthy of employment, and should be cultivated as a duty," he urged. "RESPECT YOUR DINNER; idolize it, enjoy it properly. You will be by many hours in the week, many weeks in the year, and many years in your life, the happier if you do." But tact, connoisseurship, and the play of fancy are essential, if the charge of mere grossness and greediness is to be avoided; and these qualities Thackeray proceeds to supply in his discussion of the pleasures of food, wine, and tobacco. He sums up his position in the course of some reflections on Shakespeare's later years:

> In the queer old pleasant novel of the *Spiritual Quixote,* honest Tugwell, the Sancho of the story, relates a Warwickshire legend, which at the time Graves wrote was not much more than a hundred years old; and by which it appears that the owner of New Place was a famous jesting gentleman, and used to sit at his gate of summer evenings, cutting the queerest, merriest jokes with all the passers-by. I have heard from a Warwickshire clergyman that the legend still exists in the country; and Ward's *Diary* says that Master Shakespeare died of a surfeit, brought on by carousing with a literary friend who had come to visit him from London. And wherefore not? Better to die of good wine and good company than of slow disease and doctors' doses.[18]

Into the more intimate aspects of Thackeray's life at this time, it is perhaps futile to inquire. That he was perfectly continent after his separation from his wife seems unlikely. In his diary of *Punch* table conversations Henry Silver tells of a "Jaw on the necessity of women" in which Thackeray participated during 1859. When Percival Leigh suggested that desire "may be combated by physic," Thackeray commented: "That's unnatural." And when Leigh then argued for subduing the flesh and thinking of better things, Shirley Brooks, F. M. Evans, and Thackeray chorused: "But we don't want better things." [19] Bedingfield relates that Thackeray "would shake hands with many an outcast and an outlaw, male and female; and he once told me that a class to whom one can only refer by a glance at the 'woman' forgiven by a great authority many centuries ago, he believed to be 'very good people'." [20] Speaking many years later of a projected "tour on the Incontinent," Thackeray recalled that he "used to have an ex-Governess there—gave her a Nap[oleo]n & one for herself." [21] We know that he was troubled by a recurrence of his stricture in the spring of 1843.[22] But it is profitless to draw deductions from such hints as these.

II

Thackeray saw many kinds of society during these years in London. That which meant most to him, perhaps, was the company of old college friends and acquaintances, now encountered again in middle life. FitzGerald was by all odds the most intimate of these. During 1843, from February to May and again in November and December, Thackeray had the "great comfort" of his companionship in London. They breakfasted together. Then Thackeray tried to get through his work, though with FitzGerald by his side to "talk nonsense . . . the best of talk," this was sometimes difficult. Later came "a cozy smoke at night over the fire." But at last Thackeray was constrained to deny himself these pleasures. "It is delightful to have him in the house," Thackeray told his mother, in May, 1843, "but I'm afraid his society makes me idle we sit and talk too much about books & pictures and smoke too many cigars." And when FitzGerald proposed another visit in 1844, Thackeray resolved: "I shant live with him, he makes me too idle." [1]

Other Cantabrigian friendships were with Saville Morton, Alfred Tennyson, James Spedding, and the Reverend W. H. Brookfield. Morton was a young Irishman of good family, who had begun his Cambridge career just as Thackeray's was ending. A linguist of real accomplishments and a gifted amateur of the arts, he loafed about London with plenty of money in his pockets, displaying a "genius for scrapes such as no man out of Ireland ever can hope for: & . . . always in some feminine mischief." [2] Thackeray found him a congenial comrade because of his gentlemanliness, his humour, and his enthusiasm for painting.[3] Thackeray saw Tennyson less frequently, since the poet came only occasionally to London. But he greatly liked and admired the "manliness and simplicity of manner" which lay behind Tennyson's "great big yellow face and growling voice." "He seems to me to have the cachet of a great man," Thackeray told Mrs. Procter as early as 1841. "His conversation is often delightful, I think, full of breadth manliness and humour: he reads all sorts of things, swallows them and digests them like a great poetical boa-constrictor as he is." [4] Spedding was too immersed in his Baconian studies often to join Thackeray and his friends for a convivial evening, but even in his absence he added unwittingly to the gaiety of the occasion. The flights to which his friends rose, recalling his confirmed bachelorhood and incorrigible sobriety of manner, as

> . . . softly thro' a vinous mist
> Their college friendships glimmered,

are illustrated by the following set of verses (no doubt only one among many) from Thackeray's hand:

> I would have you know, my dear Spedding
> In case you are thinking of wedding
> That a babe at the breast, disturbs the night's rest
> And occasionally moistens the bedding.

The story of Thackeray's intimacy with Brookfield must be reserved for the sequel to this volume. It need only be mentioned here that there was no one whom Thackeray saw more frequently or liked better than Brookfield, after this lively and unconventional parson received his London preferment in 1842. Brookfield had many a note on the following pattern from Thackeray:

If you like two or three
Of your cronies to see
  There's a swarry
  To-morry
At Mitre court B.[5]

And his diary for July and August, 1845 (representative months, one assumes), records half a dozen evenings in Thackeray's rooms when he stayed up until half past one or two, drinking Schiedam and smoking cigars in the company of such worthies as Morton and "Father Prout." [6]

The mention of Francis Sylvester Mahony (who wrote over the name of "Father Prout") brings us to another range of Thackeray's intimates. He knew well most of his "brothers of the press" at this time, and was perhaps "the most popular man in the craft." [7] Ainsworth, Barham, Robert Bell,[8] Laman Blanchard, Carlyle, George Morland Crawford, Dickens, Fonblanque, Forster, William Jerdan, Mahony, Procter, and Jack Sheehan were among his friends, as were such hangers-on of the literary world as Andrew Arcedeckne, Henry Glyn, Morgan John O'Connell, and James Emerson Tennent. Of all these associations, the one that most demands consideration, both for its significance at this time and its consequences for the future, was that with Dickens and Forster.

Since Thackeray and Dickens first met in 1836, they had been on excellent terms. Thackeray greeted Dickens's astonishing series of books with such eloquent cordiality, both in conversation and in print, that he was sometimes mistakenly considered by other writers to be part of a clique supporting the great man. Dickens was duly grateful for these favours, and during the early and middle 1840s, the two frequently exchanged hospitalities. Yet there were hints of trouble to come even at this time. Thackeray could not hide from himself the conviction that by his standards Dickens was not a gentleman. The spontaneous distaste that certain aspects of Dickens's personality aroused in him appears, for example, in the following offhand reference in a letter to his wife in 1843: "Did I write to you about Mrs Procter's grand ball, and how splendid Mrs Dickens was in pink satin and Mr Dickens in geranium & ringlets?" [9] Dickens for his part disliked some of Thackeray's "comicalities," because they did not display proper earnestness in adhering to the truth, and he felt that Thackeray was not sufficiently loyal to the literary calling. But until the success of *Vanity Fair,* there was no open clash between the two men.

Thackeray was on terms of still closer intimacy during these years with Forster, Dickens's chief friend and lieutenant. Forster was even less of a gentleman, in the Victorian understanding of the term, than Dickens himself. He was born in Newcastle, one of the eight children of an impecunious butcher; but a well-to-do uncle in 1828 had sent him to study law at University College, London.[10] Through his remarkable energy and business ability, which were linked with respectable literary talents, he soon made a central place for himself in the London publishing world; and he numbered Bulwer, Carlyle, Dickens, Fonblanque, Macready, Procter, and Talfourd among his close friends and allies. Yet his pomposity and self-assertiveness made his rise to prominence the subject of much resentful comment. Westmacott attacked him in the *Spy;* Lady Bulwer put him into *Cheveley* as "lick-dust" Fuzboz; Poole caricatured him in *Little Pedlington and the Pedlingtonians.* In private conversation the judgment of Victorian gentlemen was even more severe. Barham's notes opposite Forster's name in his list of Garrick Club members are scurrilously abusive:

A low scribbler without an atom of talent and totally unused to the society of gentlemen. He narrowly escaped expulsion, from publishing an account of a dinner at the Garrick in a newspaper to which he was a reporter. The Committee wrote him a letter on the occasion expressive of their disgust, which would have caused any other man to retire. About a year after he got beastly drunk at the anniversary Club dinner, and was sick in Serjeant Talfourd's pocket. Tom Duncombe got drunk at the same time, but behaved so differently that Poole observed one was the real gentleman drunk, the other the "spewrious" gentleman drunk.[11]

Leech's opinion of him may be gathered from a fragment of *Punch* table conversation:

JF a snob—never at ease among gentlemen, says JL. Jupiter Tonans. JL would like to show him beside butcher's block crying Buy buy! At Newcastle he shrank into far corner of bus & hid himself. Every where else had been blatant.[12]

To this testimony may be added the well-known observation of a London cabby, who pointed him out to a fare with the inquiry: "Do you know that gentleman's name? I drive him very often. He's a harbitrary cove." [13]

Forster lived in chambers on the ground floor of 58 Lincoln's Inn Fields, where he entertained with a magnificence in keeping with his self-esteem. He had a famous servant, known simply as Henry, who fully identified himself with his master's interests. Espinasse relates how he arrived one evening for a dinner, not having received word that the party had been deferred, only to be greeted by Henry, who "surveyed me with an air of dignified surprise, [and] said in a tone slightly reproachful: '*We* wrote you this morning!' " [14] Tennyson used to tell of an occasion on which he dined with the gloriously attired Count d'Orsay at Forster's, when his host was "so carried away by d'Orsay's splendour . . . that he was heard shouting out above the hubbub of voices to his servant Henry: 'Good heavens, sir, butter for the Count's flounders!' " [15] And Thackeray himself wrote to a friend concerning an evening in 1846 on which he had dropped in on Forster unexpectedly:

he and another gent were dining: they had begun with 2 platefulls of mulgatawney s⟨oup⟩ & says I I'll have no soup. But the Ineffable said HENRY BRING SOUP—and there was soup—and my basin was bigger than the other basins. He had some champagne very good for 5/ a bottle on trial. This is very good said the Great One—actually as good as my own—(wh as everybody knows is excellent) How much do you pay for your Champagne? some one asked. HENRY how much do I pay for my Champagne? said the Supreme One—(knowing full well, but willing to try Henry's faith) 'Alf a guinea a bottle said Henry with great gravity. And perhaps its true but the miracle of the soup I cant explain.[16]

When such idiosyncrasies were combined with an appearance which earned Forster the nickname of "the hippopotamus" and a manner and habit of speech closely imitated from the tragic graces of Macready,[17] the cumulative effect was sufficiently ludicrous. Even Dickens on occasion made gentle fun of his friend's peculiarities, as when he had Mrs. Gamp picture Forster on a provincial theatrical tour as a "resolute gent, . . . aperrently going to take the railways by storm—him with the tight legs, and his weskit very much buttoned, and his mouth very much shut, and his coat a flying open, and his heels a giving it to the platform." [18] To Thackeray, Forster cried out for verbal and pictorial caricature. We accordingly find him writing the following "nonsense & stuff" to Tennent:

> Forster is the greatest man I know. Great and Beneficent like a Superior Power—He is the Chief of the Daily News and conducts it with great ability I think and whenever anybody is in a scrape we all fly to him for refuge. He is omniscient and works miracles. . . . His bath is a miracle too—he gets into it every morning he is so stout and the bath not much bigger than a Biddy (excuse the expression). We are going to have him in a statue at Madame Tussauds.[19]

And his letters to friends often contained sketches of Forster's round, plethoric face and bulky person, examples of which appear as Plates XVIII and XIX. By these caricatures Thackeray meant no harm. To him they were perfectly compatible with the real respect and liking that he felt for Forster. But when their victim learnt of them, he flew into a towering rage and denounced Thackeray for what he called, in his best Macready manner, "the private pleasantries of your pen and pencil with me for their theme." [20]

This tempest in a tea-pot brings out a trait in Thackeray's character without which his portrait would be incomplete. He was full of "madcap humour" [21] of an almost boyish kind, and if he saw fun in prospect, he was "very apt to be cajoled into doing what the world calls foolish things." [22] The best-known examples of this foible come from a little later in his career: his assuring Jules Janin, as he shepherded this French critic around London, "that all the statues he saw represented the Duke of Wellington," for instance, or his proposal to Macaulay that they exchange identities at a dinner given by Sir Charles Napier and so bewilder an American lady, "whose great desire in life was to meet the Author of Wanaty Fair and Author of the Lays of A. Rome." [23] Indeed, his high spirits were always sweeping him into jokes, without the preliminary consideration that a more cautious man would have given to the question of whether his proposed target was himself sufficiently lively and amiable to take the jest in good part.

If this habit made for trouble, so did the explosions of "vivacity" (to use Arnold's term) which punctuate his writing. "A Box of Novels," which appeared in *Fraser's Magazine* for February, 1844, is one of the best of his critical articles. It remains today almost as fresh and brilliant as when it first appeared; and the reader is still astonished by the justice of perception and the fertility of invention that inform it. The chief books dealt with in this paper are Lever's *Tom Burke of "Ours"* and Dickens's *Christmas Carol*. Lever and Dickens were at this time close competitors for popular favour. A more deliberate and calculating man, who was like Thackeray the friend of both, would have been careful to hold the scales even between them. Thackeray instead set down exactly what came to his mind. In Lever's case this included a series of witty objections "to the pugnacious and horse-racious parts of the Lorrequer novels" and an allusion to an "admirable parody" of these novels in a recent issue of *Tait's Magazine*. For Dickens, on the other hand, Thackeray had nothing but praise. "There is but one book left in the box," he began, "the smallest one, but oh! how much the best of all. It is the work of the master of all the English humourists now alive; the young man who came and took his place calmly at the head of the whole tribe, and who has kept it." And he went on in the same vein to write the words that have remained the classic appreciation of this famous book.[24] When Lever read this article, he regarded Thackeray's performance as simple treachery. On 7 April 1844, he wrote to Ainsworth (another member of the "tribe" that Dickens had out-distanced):

> There is a decided set among Londoners—who are in any way supposed to interfere with the undivided allegiance of the public to Dickens. I have reason to believe this and do believe it—of course I

expect no mercy from the clique, nor even fairness. Thackeray's rascality first opened my eyes, but they are pretty much accustomed to the sight of such blackguardism now.[25]

Again, Thackeray derived an almost naïve satisfaction from the position which his annual reviews of the exhibitions had gained him in the London art world. He began his "Picture Gossip" for *Fraser's Magazine* in June, 1845, with a ludicrously exaggerated account of the sensation among London painters caused by the unexpected return of Titmarsh from the East early in this year.

You should have seen the consternation of the fellows at my arrival! —of our dear brethren who thought I was safe at Rome for the season, and that their works, exhibited in May, would be spared the dreadful ordeal of my ferocious eye. When I entered the club-room in St. Martin's Lane, and called for a glass of brandy-and-water like a bombshell, you should have seen the terror of some of the artists assembled! They knew that the frightful projectile just launched into their club-room must *burst* in the natural course of things. Who would be struck down by the explosion? was the thought of every one. Some of the hypocrites welcomed me meanly back, some of the timid trembled, some of the savage and guilty muttered curses at my arrival.[26]

This passage is simply a comic extravaganza. But at least one of Thackeray's friends among the painters regarded it almost as a declaration of war. Writing to Frederick Tennyson about this article, FitzGerald remarked:

I met Stone in the street the other day: he took me by the button, and told me in perfect sincerity, and with increasing warmth, how, though he loved old Thackeray, yet these yearly out-speakings of his sorely tried him; not on account of himself (Stone), but on account of some of his friends, Charles Landseer, Maclise, etc. Stone worked himself up to such a pitch under the pressure of forced calmness that he at last said Thackeray would get himself horse-whipped one day by one of these infuriated Apelleses. At this I, who had partly agreed with Stone that ridicule, though true, needs not always to be spoken, began to laugh: and told him two could play at that game.[27]

Once again Thackeray's careless liveliness had got him into hot water with a literal-minded friend. No wonder he complained the following year: "Say that this picture is bad, or that poem poor, or that article stupid, and there are certain authors and artists among us who set you down as an enemy forthwith, or look upon you as a *faux-frère*." [28]

Thackeray's irresistible propensity for joking was a weakness, no doubt, though most observers found it an endearing one. But it is a gross mistake to regard it, as do certain writers who view Thackeray chiefly through the eyes of Dickens and Forster, as an evidence of "the bungling and artlessness of his social contacts." [29] When Thackeray was on his best behaviour, the polish of his outer manner was irreproachable, and there are innumerable stories to illustrate the tact and kindness of his everyday conduct. The sometimes misguided playfulness that has here been illustrated was for the most part an expression of camaraderie, which only touchy people, who were unsure of themselves and hence insistent on their dignity, or dull people, who were baffled by jokes, could misinterpret.

During these years Thackeray was also a welcome visitor in many middle-class homes. He frequented the houses of attorneys, business men and financiers from the City, publishers, and returned Anglo-Indians, but he was friendliest with such literary families as the Brookfields, the Carlyles, the Crowes, the Dickenses, the Pollocks, the Procters, and the Sartorises. Of them all he was perhaps closest to the Procters, who had known him during his years with Isabella, and to whom he turned for consolation during his troubles. Procter, who had attained some reputation as a poet under the pen-name "Barry Cornwall," was passing his declining years in the comfortable post of metropolitan commissioner in lunacy. Thackeray was fond of this easy-going, good-natured, modest man, but he reserved his real admiration for his wife. "Our Lady of Bitterness," as Kinglake called Mrs. Procter in *Eōthen,* was a very remarkable woman. For seventy years her outspokenness, her biting sarcasm, and her talent for assembling about her as close an approximation to a *salon* as Victorian London could provide made her a force in English intellectual life. Thackeray found her an understanding and sympathetic listener to many opinions that he kept silent about in duller and more rigidly respectable company, and he valued her accordingly. But, indeed, few of the homes in which Thackeray was a constant visitor belonged whole-heartedly to the great Victorian *bourgeoisie*. Mrs. Carlyle suggests their spirit in a remark about a party in 1843 for Mrs. Macready, which Thackeray also attended: "I question if there was as much witty speech uttered in all the aristocratic conventional drawing rooms thro' London that night as among us little knot of blackguardist literary people, who felt ourselves above all rules and independent of the universe." [30] When Thackeray's growing reputation as a writer caused him to be invited to dinner occasionally by members of the aristocracy who made a point of patronizing literature, something of the same proud spirit caused him at first to regard these overtures with suspicion.[31]

III

But if London was Thackeray's headquarters during the years 1842 to 1846, he continued to travel widely. In addition to his many visits with his family in Paris, which will be dealt with later, he made three more ambitious excursions: to Ireland in 1842, to the Low Countries in 1843, and around the Mediterranean in the fall and winter of 1844–1845.

Since Thackeray still owed Chapman and Hall £120 for a book on Ireland which he had never written, he reluctantly made plans to return to that country in May of 1842. He tried to persuade FitzGerald to accompany him, but though his friend was "lying idle & moping in the country," [1] he could not summon up the energy to make the trip. No doubt this deprivation enabled Thackeray to form a closer acquaintance with Ireland than he would have achieved in FitzGerald's company. "When a man travels alone," he noted, "it is wonderful how little he cares to select his society; how indifferent company pleases him; how a good fellow delights him; how sorry he is when the time for parting comes, and he has to walk off alone, and begin the friendship-hunt over again." [2]

Thackeray set off late in June, approaching Dublin by way of Wales and Liverpool. In the Irish capital he encountered a lively literary society. Charles Lever, who had by this time given up medical practice and established himself at "his mansion of Templeogue" four miles outside of Dublin as editor of the *Dublin University Magazine,* was one of the first of the Irish wits to welcome him. Major Frank Dwyer has left a detailed account of their initial meeting at Templeogue:

Thackeray's . . . manner was at first reserved, earnest, and quiet; . . . he was . . . carefully observing and desirous of not being drawn out, at least, not prematurely. Conversation languished, as usual during the *mauvais quart d'heure,* but revived after the soup had been disposed of. . . . Thackeray praised some *fricandeau de veau,* of which he had partaken, a thing rarely seen on Irish tables, and the *chef-d'oeuvre* of Lever's German servant, who was cook and butler rolled up into one; which led to mention being made of the artistical arrangements of the kitchen at the Reform Club. This was just what was wanted: we then knew of course what Thackeray's politics were . . . [that] he adopted the liberal ideas of that period to their fullest extent. . . . Lever's politics at this time were of a very different character. . . .

As dinner proceeded, and after the ladies had retired, the two protagonists began to skirmish, endeavouring to draw each other out. . . . The conversation had been led by Lever to the subject of the battle of Waterloo. . . . Thackeray soon joined in; he did not pretend to know anything about the great battle, but he evidently wished to spur on Lever to identify himself with Charles O'Malley. . . . Lever . . . quickly perceiving his antagonist's game, . . . met his feints with very quiet, but perfectly efficacious parries. . . .

French and German literature next came on the *tapis.* Thackeray seemed to value the last named more highly than the other. . . . Thackeray . . . paid Lever the very handsome compliment of saying, that he would rather have written Lorrequer's English version of the Student song, 'The Pope he leads a happy life,' &c., than anything he had himself hitherto done in literature. . . . Passing on to French authors, full justice was done to the celebrities of the day: Dumas, Alphonse Karr, Balzac, George Sand, &c. Thackeray criticised the

French theatre very sharply, and came out with a strong bit of humorous representation, which convulsed us with laughter. It had reference to some drama or opera, I forget what, in which the principal male character comes on the stage with a pirouette, and waving his hand in a majestic manner to a chorus representing Jews in exile at Babylon, says, 'Chantez nous une chanson de Jérusalem.' Thackeray rose from his seat and did the thing, pirouette and all, most inimitably: by the way, he was fond of exhibiting his French pronunciation, also of caricaturing very cleverly that of his own countrymen.[3]

The ice thus broken, Thackeray and Lever became very cordial friends. Nearly twenty years later, when Thackeray was a great man and Lever almost forgotten, he prefaced the offer of a "loankin" to his old acquaintance by inquiring: "Do you remember one night as 'me cyar' drove out of Templeogue gate, your asking me if I were in want of—&c &c—?" [4]

Thackeray soon found it necessary to set out on a tour of the provinces, though he abandoned Lever's kind hospitality and excellent claret with real reluctance. In mid-July he went south to Cork, where he revived bitter memories of 1840,[5] then west to Killarney, and north to Galway. From Galway he returned to Dublin for the month of September. After several weeks in northern Ireland during October, he returned once more to Dublin for a brief final visit. Just as FitzGerald had predicted, Thackeray found "lots of companions in Ireland." [6] His friend's uncle, Peter Purcell of Halverstown, gave him a hearty welcome.[7] With this fat, jolly man who lived with his immense family in a pleasant, snug house surrounded by a trim, prosperous farm of 400 acres, Thackeray passed three happy days. In Cork he met that gentle fanatic, the temperance agitator Father Theobald Mathew. To Émile Forgues, who later attacked *The Irish Sketch Book* as cynical, Thackeray replied:

Vous avez tort, Old Nick de dire que je ne respecte rien—Je respecte le coeur droit et sincère, l'âme simple, la parole vraie sans forfanterie et sans prétension—De tout mon coeur je respecte le Père Mathew, qui n'a pas le moindre esprit, qui n'est plus amusant que n'étoit Washington, mais qui mène une vie grande pure et *manly,* ne cherchant qu'à faire du bien, ne faisant pas de phrases, ni de politique incendiaire.[8]

Back in Dublin he had dinner one evening with Merrick Shawe, a great benefactor of his early married life, who was living almost forgotten with his Irish relatives. Thackeray particularly disliked his host George Corsellis, retired from the East India Company's civil service, "an odious conceited vulgar little wretch"; and it distressed him to think of "the poor old Colonel who has been used to refined and educated gentlemen all his life . . . obliged to put up with such a snob for constant society and with the old ladies that form good old Miss Shawe's twaddling old circle." [9] But his spirits revived when he visited his cousin, the Reverend Elias Thackeray, at Louth Rectory near Dundalk. This admirable gentleman of seventy-one was celebrated for his good works, among which his visitor was most impressed by an infant-school. It contained eighty little people, Thackeray wrote,

> healthy, clean, and rosy, some in smart gowns and shoes and stockings, some with patched pinafores and little bare pink feet, [who] sat upon a half-dozen low benches, and were singing, at the top of their fourscore fresh voices, a song when we entered. All the voices were hushed as the vicar came in, and a great bobbing and curtsying took place; whilst a hundred and sixty innocent eyes turned awfully towards the clergyman, who tried to look as unconcerned as possible, and began to make his little ones a speech. 'I have brought,' says he, 'a gentleman from England, who has heard of my little children and their school, and hopes he will carry away a good account of it. Now, you know, we must all do our best to be kind and civil to strangers: what can we do here for this gentleman that he would like?—do you think he would like a song?'
>
> (*All the children*)—'We'll sing to him!'
>
> Then the schoolmistress, coming forward, sang the first words of a hymn, which at once eighty little voices took up, or near eighty—for some of the little things were too young to sing yet, and all they could do was to beat the measure with little red hands as the others sang. . . . I think I will never, while I live, forget that little chorus, nor would any man who has ever loved a child or lost one.[10]

Such scenes made Thackeray all the more eager to return to his own family, and he was glad to depart from Dublin on 1 November.

In August of the following year Thackeray again went touring. This time he joined forces with his Parisian friend Augustus Stevens in a four-week visit to Belgium and Holland. Thackeray's object was to collect impressions for another sketch-book, while Stevens, who conducted a thriving trade in old paintings in addition to the practice of dentistry, had £150 to spend on pictures. Though Thackeray enjoyed the sights of Brussels, Rotterdam, and the Hague, he found that he could see nothing properly in the company of his "jolly old man of the sea," [11] who insisted on breakfasting at seven in the morning, joining him on all his strolls, and going out "to see a fourth-rate company of Singers do a fourth-rate opera (a sixteenth-rate performance therefrom)." [12] Though he was dependent on his friend for money (having had £20 stolen from him early in the trip), he at last persuaded Stevens that they should take their separate ways, counting on remittances from Chapman and Hall or his family to see him through the trip. For several days neither responded, however, and at last Thackeray found himself in Lille utterly without resources. The anxieties of this period are amusingly recounted in "Titmarsh's Carmen Lilliense":

My heart is weary, my peace is gone,
  How shall I e'er my woes reveal?
I have no cash, I lie in pawn,
  A stranger in the town of Lille.

To stealing I can never come,
  To pawn my watch I'm too genteel,
Besides, I left my watch at home,
  How could I pawn it, then, at Lille?

'La note,' at times the guests will say:
  I turn as white as cold boil'd veal;
I turn and look another way,
  I dare not ask the bill at Lille.

But he is rescued at last, in a fashion which he veraciously describes in his concluding stanzas:

Say, shall I to yon Flemish church,
  And at a Popish altar kneel?
Oh, do not leave me in the lurch,
  I'll cry, ye patron saints of Lille!

Ye virgins dressed in satin hoops,
  Ye martyrs slain for mortal weal,
Look kindly down! before you stoops
  The miserablest man in Lille.

And lo! as I beheld with awe
  A pictured saint (I swear 'tis real),
It smiled, and turn'd to grandmamma!—
  It did! and I had hope in Lille!

'Twas five o'clock, and I could eat,
  Although I could not pay, my meal:
I hasten back into the street
  Where lies my inn, the best in Lille.

What see I on my table stand,—
  A letter with a well-known seal?
'Tis grandmamma's! I know her hand,—
  'To Mr. M. A. Titmarsh, Lille.'

I feel a choking in my throat,
  I pant and stagger, faint and reel!
It is—it is—a ten-pound note,
  And I'm no more in pawn at Lille!

[He goes off by the diligence that evening, and is restored to the bosom of his happy family.] [13]

By far the most ambitious of Thackeray's travels during this period was his Mediterranean trip. He determined upon this excursion so suddenly and unexpectedly that he provided the book that resulted from it with a circumstantial preface, in order "to convince some incredulous friends—who insist still that the writer never went abroad at all, and wrote the following pages, out of pure fancy, in retirement at Putney." [14] On 19 August 1844 Thackeray attended a farewell dinner at the Reform Club given by William Bevan to James Emerson Tennent, who was setting out on a voyage to the East. Tennent invited Thackeray to join his family party, offering, to clinch his argument, a promise that "his friends, the Directors of the Peninsular and Oriental Company, would make Mr. Titmarsh the present of a berth for the voyage." Three days later Thackeray found himself aboard the *Lady Mary Wood* bound for the Bay of Biscay.[15]

Though Thackeray was very seasick, he enjoyed excursions ashore at Vigo and Cadiz before shifting from the *Lady Mary Wood* to the *Tagus* at Gibraltar. Since the Mediterranean was at first little calmer than the Atlantic, Thackeray asked himself in exasperation, "Que diable allait il faire dans cette galère?" But soon the sights of Malta, Athens, Smyrna, and Constantinople took his mind off his troubles. At the last of these cities he moved aboard still another ship, the *Iberia,* to whose captain, Samuel Lewis, Thackeray later dedicated his *Notes of a Journey from Cornhill to Grand Cairo*. Early in October the *Iberia* put into Jaffa, from which city Thackeray set out to Jerusalem. His final port of call was Alexandria, and from there he penetrated to Cairo and the Great Pyramid, leading "3 cheers for Punch on the top" of the latter.[16]

Because he understood that the Carmichael-Smyths were at Nice, because he could not contemplate the Bay of Biscay in November, and perhaps because he wanted "an excuse to take one peep at Italy," Thackeray left the *Iberia* at Malta on 27 October. Fifteen days of quarantine and ten days at Naples followed before he settled in Rome for what was to be an extended visit. At first Thackeray derived great pleasure from walking about the city to observe its splendours and "spending the night smoking with the Artist banditti." [17] William Bevan's brother Samuel, who was at this time living in Rome, noted in a volume called *Sand and Canvas* that

> Of the great men who visited Rome during this winter, M. A. Titmarsh was among the most popular. Himself an artist, he dropped down among us on his way from Cairo, no one knowing when he came or how he went away. Installed in a quiet bedroom at Franz's, in the Condotti, he appeared to amuse himself like Asmodeus, with peering into the studios of his countrymen, and while he rummaged over their dusty portfolios, or critically scanned their pictures on the wall, would unconsciously read their secret thoughts, and penetrate, as it were, the arcana of their pockets, without allowing them for a moment to imagine that he intended aught save a mere friendly visit. Many, however, were the poor devils who managed to push through the winter on the strength of the timely fillip administered by Titmarsh.[18]

Thackeray spent his evenings at the modest parties organized by these impecunious artists. Bevan tells how one night, after a mediocre dinner at Bertini's, Thackeray was voted into the chair for a "round of song and sentiment." He declined to sing, but he did offer "to make amends by getting up a recitation, if some one in the mean time would make a beginning." Thus was engendered Thackeray's most celebrated improvisation; for in due course he composed "The Three Sailors," a free adaptation —it appears—of a Breton original, which he delivered in "a fittingly lugubrious tone of voice":

There were three sailors in Bristol City,
Who took a boat and went to sea.

But first with beef and captains' biscuit,
And pickled pork they loaded she.

There was guzzling Jack and gorging Jimmy
And the youngest he was little Bil-*ly*.

Now very soon they were so greedy,
They didn't leave not one split pea.

Says guzzling Jack to gorging Jimmy,
I am confounded hung-*ery*.

Says gorging Jim to guzzling Jacky,
We have no wittles, so we must eat *we*.

Says guzzling Jack to gorging Jimmy,
Oh! gorging Jim, what a fool you be.

There's little Bill as is young and tender,
We're old and tough—so let's eat *he*.

Oh! Bill, we're going to kill and eat you,
So undo the collar of your chemie.

When Bill he heard this information,
He used his pocket-handkerchee.

Oh! let me say my Catechism,
As my poor mammy taught to me.

Make haste, make haste, says guzzling Jacky,
Whilst Jim pulled out his snicker-snee.

So Bill went up the main top-gallant mast,
When down he fell on his bended knee.

He scarce had said his catechism,
When up he jumps; there's land I see!

There's Jerusalem and Madagascar,
And North and South Ameri-*key*.

There's the British fleet a riding at anchor,
With Admiral Napier, K. C. B.

So when they came to the Admiral's Vessel,
He hanged fat Jack and flogged Jim-*my*.

But as for little Bill, he made him
The captain of a Seventy-three.[19]

But mounting financial anxiety soon caused such pleasures to lose their savour. If Bevan was correctly informed concerning Thackeray's displays of benevolence, they must have occurred early in his stay, for he soon found himself trapped in Rome, as he had been earlier in Lille. There were no remittances from Bradbury and Evans, to whom he wrote on 6 December imploring immediate help and painting a dismal picture of himself, "a man alone, unhappy, in the hotbed of Popery and in pawn." [20] Only after seven weeks and thirty-five visits to the post-office did his captivity end.

> It appears [he explained to Bradbury and Evans] the letters were stowed away under the name of *Jackeray* instead of the other celebrated one: and though the credits were at Tortonia's: and I went to that bank meekly requesting them to cash a bill on my London bankers, the brutes declined, and I should have gone to gaol but for another banker more easy of belief . . . my mind is quite upset at this moment between rage and satisfaction fury at not having gotten the letters till now and pleasure at hearing at last. It wasn't the money, I found a sweet Xtian of a banker here who supplied everything I wanted, but the sentiment.[21]

Thackeray left Rome shortly after receiving these funds and made his way up the peninsula to Leghorn, passing two weeks in Florence *en route*. He travelled by ship to Marseilles, and thence proceeded for a time to Paris before returning to London.

With all its inconveniences, Thackeray's Eastern tour was still a notable success. Yet it had the unexpected effect of causing a coolness between him and Carlyle. When *Notes of a Journey from Cornhill to Grand Cairo* was published in January, 1846, Carlyle compared Thackeray's acceptance of the Peninsular and Oriental Company's hospitality with "the practice of a blind fiddler going to and fro on a penny ferry-boat in Scotland, and playing tunes to the passengers for halfpence." [22] Somehow this comparison found its way into a review of the book in the March issue of *Tait's Edinburgh Magazine*.[23] Thackeray wittily refuted the assumption that he had "made a book of travels for the P. & O. Company," on which Carlyle's sour criticism was based, in an article for *Punch* entitled "Titmarsh v. Tait," published on 14 March.[24] This incident dissipated the last remnants of the profound admiration and awe in which he had once held his friend, though they did not long remain personally estranged.

IV

During these years Thackeray considered Paris his "home," and when he was in London, he used to refer to himself jokingly as an "exile." [1] He visited the Carmichael-Smyths as frequently as business permitted, which was a good many weeks in each year. Even when he was away from his children, he thought about them constantly. The sight of other little girls of their age stirred him deeply. He wrote to his mother from Dublin in September, 1842:

> To day a little child in its nurse's arms in Sackville Street, saw me and began shouting out 'Papa Papa' wh gave me such a turn of the stomach as never was—its a long long time since I have been away from the little people, but pray God the long time will soon be over now.[2]

It affected him even to write to them,[3] but he managed none the less to adjust his letters very accurately to their comprehension. Here, for example, are the final paragraphs of a note to Anny written in 1843:

The other night as I was coming home I met in the street two little girls: and what do you think they were doing?—

Although one was no bigger than you, and the other not so big as Baby, they were singing little songs in the street, in hopes that some one would give them money: they said their mother was at home (that is the elder one said so, the younger was so little that she could not speak plain—only sing)—their mother was ill at home with three more children, and they had no bread to eat!

So I thought of my two dear little girls and how comfortable they were and how their Granny gave them good meals and their Grandmamma a nice house to live in: and I brought the little girls to Mr Hill the baker in Coram Street, and gave them a loaf and some money, and hope soon to give them some more. And this is all I have to say except God bless my dearest Nanny: and that I always say.

Papa.[4]

He debated anxiously with his mother the characters of his two children, and when both exceptional ability and exceptional wilfulness manifested themselves in Anny, he remarked:

I am afraid very much she is going to be a man of genius: I would far sooner have had her an amiable & affectionate woman— But little Minny will be that, please God.—and the Sisters love each other admirably.[5]

The life lived by Anny and Minny, and occasionally shared by Thackeray, at 81 Champs Élysées and on holiday was described with wonderful simplicity and vividness by Lady Ritchie for Minny's daughter, little Laura Stephen, thirty-five years later:

Grandmama was quite young . . . & very beautiful & tall & kind & we called her Grannie & her Mother also came to live with us. She had a brown face & bright dark eyes I used to go out walking with my little sister who still wore her green veil & who used to wake me up at night & in the morning by crying piteously. Our Papa went away & we stayed with our Grandmothers. Grannie was very kind & Grandmama was very unkind & always scolded me: but she could not help loving the poor darling little baby. One night I dreamt somebody had cut the babys two little feet off & I scrambled out of bed &

went to look at her & O I was so glad to see her warm & sound asleep. I had never loved her till then but then I loved her. We went into the Country that year & we used to spend the day in a big forest under the trees & pick tiny little blue deep flowers that I made into wreaths & y^r^ Mommee used to wear a tiny little pink frock. One day when we had just done luncheon someone said look look at Baby, & baby was beginning to walk & holding on to the chairs. I was very naughty that day & I had refused to say Grace, but my Grannie was so pleased with Baby for beginning to walk that I was forgiven I used to be naughty every day like naughty Lucy. Once I picked some cherries off a tree once I kicked a gentleman's legs once I was shut up in a cupboard. I also ran away three times.

Margie & Annies mama was a little girl in those days [6] but she was much older than I & their Uncle George was a baby & they were all in this country place. They lived in a delightful old house with a *round hole* in the wall through wh I could climb backwards & forwards. There was also a boy called Frank Hankey who used to twist my arm round & round. One summers day a little girl in the house died & all the little children came dressed in white & carried her away. When we went back to Paris our Grannie bought a nice little green cart for Minnie to go out in. Sometimes as a great treat I was allowed to get in too. We used to have big bits of bread given to us & a penny each & our nurse used to drag us to a little shop where they sold milk & used to breakfast in the little shop & then go on to a green shady terrace & spend long mornings out of doors. Minnie drank her milk but never would eat much. She used to run away from the table & sometimes my Grannie used to give her her dinner under the table She never liked Rhubarb or vegetables or puddings. Our good old Brodie had gone away to England & was living with Mr and Mrs Darwin who had a little girl of my own age called Annie too. We had a new nurse a funny little short long nosed punch like woman called Justine who was very very fond of yr Mommee & took great care of her. Our Aunt Mary was married by this time & we were all living in the Champs Elysées in a big house called the Maison Valin. One day Aunt Mary went to India, but about a week after she left our Grandmama told us to go upstairs one morning & when we went up with the maid she took us into a room we had never seen before & there was a little boy in his bath. It was our little cousin, Aunt Mary's little boy [Charles or "Chéri" Carmichael] who had fallen ill on the way to Marseilles & had been sent back to live with us. We were so enchanted we thought he would melt away & become a dream. Our

Papa used to come & see us from time to time & I thought he was Jesus Christ. Once he went to Jerusalem & when he came back he had funny little mustachios & y^{r} mommee cried & would only kiss him through a newspaper so he went into his room & shaved them off & came out quite smooth & gave her a kiss. I liked seeing him shave very much he used to go so quick & so straight. Sometimes when he was dressing & we were there he would tear out long paper pictures with little pigs all trotting after one another. We always went away in the summers. One year [1843] we went to Montmorency where I was very unhappy & naughty & shut up in my room for a long time & I was whipped Another year [1844] we went to Chaudfontaine in Belgium & then y^{r} mommee was a little girl about four years old. She & I used to dance together & little Charles Carmichael used to sit & kick on the floor. . . .

[Next year] I . . . went to do my lessons every morning with a little girl called Laura Colmache & Mommee & I used to go & play round & round the statues in the Tuillieries in the afternoon & then Aunt Mary came back f^{m} India & in the summer we all went to [Luc sur Mer, Calvados, in] Normandy, and I used to read the books Papa had brought us, at my bed room window & look out & see all the Normandy men & women dancing on the green.

And mommee liked finding pretty little shells & sea-weeds & we made friends with a little boy called O'Farrell & his sister Fanny & we used to dig deep holes in the sand & line them with oyster shells & sit in them & look at the sea.

One of the nicest things that ever happened to us when we were children at Paris was the arrival of a huge parcel, w^{h} my Grannie cut open and inside there were piles & piles of the most beautiful delightful wonderful fairy tale books all painted with pictures—I thought they would never come to an end but alas! in a week we had read them all. They were called the Felix Summerly Series & on the first page was written—To my three daughters Laetitia Henrietta & Mary I dedicate these volumes. I used to think that they must be the happiest little girls in the world but I never thought we should ever know them.[7] We had some other books—The one about little Willy & his Mama was y^{r} mommees favourite Years afterwards she found it in a shop & asked me to buy it for Margie & Annie & now it is you who read out of it.[8]

At first Thackeray had enjoined Mrs. Carmichael-Smyth, "Mind let the little ones go often to their mother" at Dr. Puzin's in Chaillot.[9] So Lady Ritchie told Laura Stephen:

Our Mama was ill & she used to live with a Doctor in a big house with a great garden full of little paths & we used to go & spend the day with her & run after her down the long slopes of the garden. She was quite young with beautiful red-golden hair, one day when we came we found her sitting on the terrace with all her hair tumbling about her shoulders & somebody combing it out. Then the Doctors said it was better we should not go & see her anymore.[10]

Isabella's behaviour had become so erratic, indeed, that Thackeray was forced to abandon his fond scheme of entirely reuniting his family. He brought her to England in October, 1845, where she was henceforth looked after by Mrs. Bakewell, "an excellent worthy woman," [11] at Camberwell.

But he still wanted his daughters with him, and early in June, 1845, he persuaded Mrs. Carmichael-Smyth to bring Anny and Minny across the channel for a short visit.

All night long we were sick in a ship [Lady Ritchie related to Laura Stephen] & in the morning it was England & we went to a dear little village called Fareham nr Southhampton to an old aunt [Miss Becher] in an old house with blue china pots & old pictures. One of them was the gentleman in the red coat [John Harman Becher] . . . he was our grannees papa & the husband of the old brown lady & he was the brother of Aunt Becher with whom we went to stay. It was very rainy weather when we were at Fareham & our Grannie bought us each a little pair of pattens. There was a little girl there of my own age called Mariana & her aunt Miss Pooke & mommee went to see some of the old ladies & I went to see some of the others & then we paid a visit to some friends in a country house on a hill & we put on our best india frocks & blue sashes every day. Magdelene [Brookfield] will show you the picture of Mrs Barlow the lady with whom we stayed. Then we went off to London Our father was living in London in chambers opposite St James Palace & he came to meet us at the station & immediately gave us each 2 wax dolls, & at breakfast he gave us bigger helps of jam than we had ever had in our lives & after breakfast he took us to feed the ducks in St James Park, & then he bought us picture books the Arabian Nights & Grimms Fairy Tales & then he took us to a diorama & to the Colosseum. I thought he would spend all the money he had in the world when I saw how much he had to pay for us. One day he took us in our flapping straw hats to see Aunt Job [Mrs. Brookfield] who was quite a young lady with curls & who gave us a book.[12]

Thackeray himself lists some of the other events of this week: excursions to Westminster Abbey, the Chinese Exhibition, the Tower of London, and Richmond Park, and much hospitality from "friends old and new." "The evening generally ends," he told Charlotte Ritchie, "by both the children falling asleep in the carriage, and they are borne up like a pair of bundles to the bedroom." [13]

When Mrs. Carmichael-Smyth and the children returned to Paris on 12 June, they left Thackeray profoundly discontented with his bachelor existence, which now appeared to him selfish and epicurean, rootless and trivial. He wrote to his mother later in the month:

> I wish you had never come that's the truth—for I fancied myself perfectly happy until then—now I see the difference: and what a deal of the best sort of happiness it is God's will that I should lose. White-bait dinners are all very well but—hang the buts—it is those we are always sighing after.

His letters henceforth were dotted with such complaints. A few months later he told his wife: "I'm getting weary of being alone, and want some other companions besides those over the bottle." And in the following year he assured Jane Shawe: "As for me I am child-sick, and when I see in Kensington Gardens or my friends' houses a pair of little girls at all resembling my own, become quite maudlin over them." [14]

By this time Thackeray's heart was set on bringing his family to London, but he had many obstacles to surmount. Though he was earning £1,200 a year, he had lost £500 in ill-advised speculations during the railway mania of 1845, and house-agents thought poorly of him as a prospective tenant. Major Carmichael-Smyth's creditors had writs for substantial sums out against him; and though these could have been settled for a few shillings in the pound, the old gentleman refused to take the necessary steps. Moreover, the Carmichaels had returned to London from India in dire financial straits, and Charles was making quite unreasonable charges of mismanagement, and even actual dishonesty, against his brother.[15] Under these circumstances Major Carmichael-Smyth judged it wise to go on living safely and inexpensively in Paris.

In June of 1846 Thackeray at last rented "a house big enough for the whole family" at 13 Young Street, Kensington.

There are 2 capital bed-rooms & a little sitting room for you & GP [Thackeray told his mother]—a famous bed room for G. M. on the first floor—2 rooms for the children on second very airy & comfortable; a couple of rooms big enough for Servants, & 2 little ones quite large enough for me— There's a good study for me down stairs & a dining room & drawing room, and a little court yard or garden and a little green house: and Kensington Gardens at the gate, and omnibuses every 2 minutes.

"What can mortal want more?" Thackeray inquired, but the Major refused to budge. "And so I lose mother and my children too for some time at least," Thackeray wrote in July. "It would break her heart to part with them: and I can't bear that she should be alone and separated from us all." [16]

Not until late autumn did Mrs. Carmichael-Smyth bring Anny and Minny to Thackeray's comfortable bow-windowed house, while the Major, still a "Robin Hood," awaited her return at Boulogne, deploring "the loss of their merry faces." [17]

It was a dark wintry evening [Lady Ritchie recalled fifty years later]. The fires were lighted, the servants were engaged, Eliza—what family would be complete without its Eliza?—was in waiting to show us our rooms. He was away; he had not expected us so early. We saw the drawing-room, the empty study; there was the feeling of London—London smelt of tobacco, we thought; we stared out through the uncurtained windows at the dark garden behind; and then climbing the stairs, we looked in at his bedroom door, and came to our own rooms above it. There were pictures ready hung on the walls of the schoolroom, and of the adjoining fire-lit nursery—the Thorwaldsen prints, Hunt's delightful sleepy boy yawning at us over the chimney-piece, all of which he had caused to be put up; and the picture of himself as a child he had hung up with his own hands, Eliza told us.

Once more, after his first happy married years, my father had a home and a family—if a house, two young children, three servants, and a little black cat can be called a family.[18]

The effect of his altered way of life upon Thackeray was profound. He summed it up in a letter which he wrote on 4

December 1846 to his "dearest old Mother [as] a consolation in her bereavement." He was no longer a bachelor, he pointed out, but an active father to his children.

Continual thoughts of them chase I don't know how many wickednesses out of my mind: Their society makes many of my old amusements seem trivial & shameful. . . . Remember the children are in their natural place: with their nearest friend working their natural influence: getting and giving the good let us hope, wh the Divine Benevolence appointed to result from the union between parents & children. May I hold fast by it I pray to God our Father.[19]

This new perspective was to have the most far-reaching influence on his work, as we shall see when we consider *The Book of Snobs* and *Vanity Fair.*

12

Free-lance

I

BETWEEN 1841 AND 1846 Thackeray was one of the busiest of London's free-lance journalists. He contributed to a dozen magazines and newspapers, his principal outlets being the *Foreign Quarterly Review, Fraser's Magazine,* the *Morning Chronicle,* and *Punch.* If he published only two books during this period, he yet wrote enough to fill several volumes each year. Despite the occasional nature of most of this writing, and the hurried and uncongenial circumstances under which it was done, it has more than an ephemeral interest. Indeed, its subsequent publication in book form (during 1852–1853 in the United States, and during 1856–1857 in England) did much to consolidate Thackeray's reputation; and it remains a significant part of his total achievement.

Thackeray's travel narratives offer the obvious starting point for a survey of his work during this period. They include a variety of contributions to *Fraser's Magazine* and *Punch,* as well as his two published books; but we may reasonably confine our attention to *The Irish Sketch Book* and *Notes of a Journey from Cornhill to Grand Cairo.*[1] These books purport to be written by "Mr. M. A. Titmarsh," but in them for the first time Thackeray signed his own name to the prefaces. This was his way of hinting that the Titmarsh of these works was to be substantially identified with him; and, indeed, each narrative is relatively sober and reflective in tone and almost entirely purged of the caricature and exaggeration that mark his "comicalities."

It is proper that this point be emphasized, for the reader of these books is far more interested in the narrator than in what the narrator sees. A thoroughgoing impressionist, Thackeray had scant faith in verbal description and preferred instead to relate what thoughts each new scene gave rise to in his mind, knowing that this method would somehow convey a sense of place not to be achieved by any orderly listing of characteristics. So, we find him remarking after a brilliantly successful account of the Giant's Causeway written to this formula that "this is not a description of the Giant's Causeway . . . but of a Londoner there." [2] It follows that the reader must be made thoroughly acquainted with the idiosyncrasy of the narrator; and Thackeray consequently presents himself at length as a relaxed, unambitious observer, not readily excited or moved to excessive exertion. In a foot-note he quotes approvingly a *bon mot* of Richard Brinsley Sheridan: " 'I want to go into a coal-mine,' says Tom Sheridan, 'in order to say I have been there.' 'Well, then, say so,' replied the admirable father." [3] His concern for creature comforts may seem excessive to the strenuous and austere, but arm-chair travellers of a less heroic mould find it pleasant to participate vicariously in his adventures, to share his distaste for a dirty inn, his annoyance with an inefficient coachman or an insolent boots, and his delight in a good dinner. Never was a traveller more entirely urban in his point of view. He told his friends, indeed, that *The Irish Sketch Book* "was to have been called 'The Cockney in Ireland,' but for the pathetic remonstrances of the publishers." [4] Dublin, Belfast, Athens, Jerusalem, and Cairo are in turn tried by West End standards—and usually found wanting.

Thackeray's utter honesty in these books has left them defenceless before hostile criticism. It is easy to convict him on his own showing of ignorance and laziness, of narrowness and complacency. Charles Lever's caricature of him as Elias Howle in *Roland Cashel,* the Cockney author of *Snooks in the Holy Land,* is quite comprehensible. Yet such criticism is beside the mark; for Thackeray himself is thoroughly alive to the incompleteness of his point of view. He inquires in Egypt:

Are we so blasés of the world that the greatest marvels in it do not succeed in moving us? Have society, Pall Mall clubs, and a habit of sneering, so withered up our organs of veneration that we can admire no more? My sensation with regard to the Pyramids was that I had seen them before: then came a feeling of shame that the view of them should awaken no respect.[5]

Moreover, this attitude of *nil admirari* is quickly dropped when he encounters a situation which appeals to his humanity. Then the real kindliness of his nature quickly appears, though usually not for long. Thackeray does not propose to bore his readers with sentiment, and he is shortly crying *"Vive la bagatelle"* once more. The candid and complete self-portrait that results from these methods is oddly endearing, and the narrator's deficiencies are readily forgiven.

Thackeray's plan of establishing himself firmly in the centre of the picture adds immensely to the authenticity of what he has to report. The hundreds of small *traits de moeurs* of which his narrative is chiefly made up gain substantially from being seen by *him*. And since Thackeray's overmastering interest is in "the *moral* aspect" [6] of what he sees, he is able to make far clearer to his readers the human condition of the places that he visits than are most writers of systematic and impersonal studies. Thus Thackeray's narratives promise to retain a permanent value in the literature of travel. They should not entirely lose currency so long as interest either in him or in the places that he visited persists.

The Irish Sketch Book is the earlier and more substantial of these volumes. Thackeray's view of Ireland changed rapidly during his four months there in 1842. The assurance with which he had at first passed judgment gradually disappeared.

I am beginning to find out now [he told his mother on 25 September], that a man ought to be forty years in the country instead of 3 months, and *then* he wouldn't be able to write about it. I wonder who *does* understand the place? not the natives certainly, for the two parties so hate each other, that neither can view the simplest proceeding of the other without distrusting falsifying & abusing it. And where in the midst of all the lies that all tell, is a stranger to seek for truth? [7]

The book was written as Thackeray travelled,[8] and its pages reflect his growing bewilderment. By the end of October, when it was "near done," Thackeray observed that it was "a clever book too, but beside the point. If it will amuse people, however, that is all I ask." [9]

This verdict is too severe. The Irish question in the years before the great famine was beyond human solution. The quarrel of Ireland with England had proved absolutely irreconcilable, and within both the Irish and the English parties there were many shades of clashing opinion. In the decade before Thackeray's visit many shrewd travellers had attempted the country, only to retire baffled by its complexities. Thackeray's tentative and unsystematic approach gave him the real advantage of presenting what he had seen as nothing more than one individual's observations. "The puzzle which has perplexed the gravest and the wisest," he remarked in his concluding paragraphs, "may be confessed by a humble writer of light literature, whose aim it only was to look at the manners and the scenery of the country, and who does not venture to meddle with questions of more serious import." [10]

So Thackeray omitted from his book the staple of previous works on Ireland, a detailed description of its desperate political and economic state. He supplied only occasional glimpses of the feature of the country which gave it an awful interest throughout Europe, what a French observer had termed the *"grande misère,"* [11] noting simply that "the epicurean, and traveller for pleasure, had better travel anywhere than here; where there are miseries that one does not dare to think of." [12] For these weighty subjects Thackeray substituted "the chronicling of small-beer," which is, however, as he was careful to point out, "the main business of life." [13] And as Thackeray described these seemingly trivial episodes, they are seen to have their own importance, because they nearly always are so presented as to show what it is that makes people good or bad, decent and self-respecting or the reverse. One moonlight evening in Lismore, for example, Thackeray encountered "a company of ragged boys," poaching in the salmon-fishery of Blackwater. Near by stood the mother of one of them cursing her son for breaking his indentures to join this band of rascals. Tiring at last of futile reproaches, she went away.

> The son [Thackeray continues], a lad of fourteen, evidently the fag of the big bullies round about him, stood dismally away from them, his head sunk down. I went up and asked him, 'Was that his mother?' He said 'Yes.' 'Was she good and kind to him when he was at home?' He said, 'O yes.' 'Why not come back to her?' I asked him; but he said, 'he couldn't.' Whereupon, I took his arm, and tried to lead him away by main force; but he said, 'Thank you, sir, but I can't go back,' and released his arm. We stood on the bridge some minutes longer, looking at the view, but the boy, though he kept away from his comrades, would not come. I wonder what they had done together, that the poor boy is past going home? The place seemed so quiet and beautiful, and far away from London, that I thought crime couldn't have reached it; and yet, here it lurks somewhere among six boys of sixteen, each with a stain in his heart, and some black history to tell.[14]

Thackeray made no attempt to achieve an impossible impartiality in *The Irish Sketch Book.* When he saw evidence of good sense and practical benevolence on the part of the governing English, he said heartily: "Well done our side!" [15] He did not conceal his dislike of Irish shiftlessness and grandiloquence, dirtiness and savagery. He expressed his prejudices with regard to a celibate clergy, nunneries, the presence of a Catholic hierarchy in Ireland, and similar topics with Protestant vigour. Sometimes, indeed, he was led by these prejudices into quite absurd generalizations. So he inquires at one point: "Whence comes that general scowl which darkens the faces of the Irish priesthood?" And elsewhere he launches into a tirade against Catholic Maynooth College, because within its walls "smiling good-humoured faces will come out with a scowl, and downcast eyes that seem afraid to look the world in the face." [16] Yet it can at least be said that he is quite as severe with English complacency as with Irish superstition. Some of his most biting comment is reserved for an Anglo-Irish nobleman expressing his pleasure in seeing landlords associating with their tenants *"on proper occasions,"* a fat college cook from Cambridge demanding to be treated as a gentleman because he *"pays his way,"* and an English reader deriding Irish poverty to his wife as he chokes on his port.[17]

The organization of *The Irish Sketch Book* is characterized by a premeditated casualness. The initial chapter, for example, has been dismissed as a mere grab-bag of passing impressions of Dublin and *faits divers* from the local papers. Actually it was carefully composed in Paris after Thackeray had finished the rest of the book. He wrote it to provide the reader with a preliminary survey of what was to follow; "un petit tableau d'Irlande," Thackeray described it to his friend Émile Forgues, "laissant au lecteur le soin d'y trouver la morale." Hence his plan of touching, in turn, upon the Church in its various manifestations,

le monde Irlandais—la côté triste sale ruinée desertée, la campagne avec ses meurtres, sa misère barbare et hideuse—Viennent les jeunes seigneurs qui s'amusent à parler courses et chevaux: à s'enivrer, a railler les mendiants et les filles—il y a cinquante mille gentlemen de cette espèce dans le pays—hommes grossiers hautains gais ignorans vilaine petite noblesse, avec laquelle nous avons doué ce pays, ne s'amusant que de la vie animale, ne connoissant de livre que le Racing Calendar. Depuis je n'ai plus vu [qu'] un suite de ces gens —parmi mes courses dans le pays j'ai vu des centaines de leurs pareils.[18]

In the details of its writing, *The Irish Sketch Book* is one of the most agreeable of Thackeray's works. One notes many small felicities, as when Thackeray describes the little town of Kilcullen, which "tumbles down a hill and struggles up another," or denominates a greedy diner who gobbles up three wings at a Galway table d'hôte a "turkiphagus." One admires the circumspection with which Thackeray pays an Irish serving-girl a kind of compliment rarely encountered in Victorian writing:

Married if she were,
  Blest would be the daddy
Of the children fair
  Of Peg of Limavaddy.

The pompous memorials of George IV's visit to Ireland call forth Thackeray's best vein of satire; and he is quick to note down other passing examples of bathos that catch his eye. In "the moralizing strain" which is equally prominent throughout the book, Thackeray sometimes rises to passages worthy of *Esmond*. Summing up his account of how in a "little distant Irish village the blood of life is running," he observes:

Here goes a happy party to a marriage, and the parson prays a 'God bless you!' upon them, and the world begins for them. Yonder lies a stall-fed rector in his tomb, flaunting, over his nothingness, his pompous heraldic motto: and yonder lie the fresh fragments of a nameless deal coffin, which any foot may kick over. Presently you hear the clear voices of little children praising God: and here comes a mother wringing her hands and asking for succour for her lad, who was a child but the other day. Such *motus animorum atque haec certamina tanta,* are going on in an hour of an October day in a little pinch of clay in the county Louth.[19]

The subdued and thoughtful melancholy of these sentences is typical of the work as a whole and gives it a unity of tone that Thackeray had achieved before only in *The Great Hoggarty Diamond.*

The Irish Sketch Book was very well received; indeed, it was the first of Thackeray's books to go into a second edition. Its success may be attributed in part to its substantial merits, in part to the lively interest that Ireland then had for the reading public. The book was widely and favourably reviewed in England; and if a few of the English reviews were written by personal friends —Laman Blanchard in *Ainsworth's Magazine,* for example, and Percival Leigh in *Fraser's Magazine* [20]—most were spontaneous tributes.[21] Irish and Catholic reaction to the book was inevitably less cordial. Charles Lever, to whom it was dedicated, praised it eloquently in the *Dublin University Magazine,*[22] which he edited. But the opinion of the *Tablet's* reviewer, that it reflected a regrettable English bias where it was not altogether trivial, has been followed by most Irish and Catholic writers to the present day. Yet even these commentators have generally conceived a grudging affection for Thackeray as he presents himself in this book, however strongly they may deplore his views.[23] Altogether Thackeray had good reason to be pleased by the reception accorded *The Irish Sketch Book;* certainly he needed such reassurance after seeing his earlier works remaindered at a tenth of their original cost in the shop of a Cork bookseller.[24]

In writing *Notes of a Journey from Cornhill to Grand Cairo* Thackeray attempted a subject quite as hackneyed as Ireland, though hardly as controversial. A passage in *Our Street* shows how familiar a figure in London drawing-rooms was the Eastern traveller who had published his book. "Hang it," Titmarsh there remarks in disparagement of one Clarence Bulbul, "has not everybody written an Eastern book? I should like to meet anybody in society now who has not been up to the second cataract."[25] Moreover, the literary quality of works about the East was in general much superior to that of those dealing with Ireland. In 1845, indeed, there appeared two minor classics in this field, both, as it happened, by friends of Thackeray: A. W. Kinglake's *Eōthen,* which was published anonymously, and Eliot Warburton's *The Crescent and the Cross.* Thackeray read "Eothen, a clever book of Cambridge extraction," at sea between Malta and Athens, and immediately guessed its authorship.[26] Though he was content to meet this strenuous competition with the same strategy that he had employed in writing *The Irish Sketch Book,* by filtering his impressions through the consciousness of an idiosyncratic traveller, he was careful to maintain a high pitch of interest by making *Cornhill to Cairo* much more closely knit and compact than his earlier volume had been. The book also charms by its harmoniousness. As Saintsbury has pointed out, Thackeray's penchant for farce found an outlet during his Eastern voyage in the Fat Contributor's papers for *Punch,* just as his reflections on the seamy side of life were drawn off into *Barry Lyndon.*[27] What remains is a light-hearted narrative, which testifies to Thackeray's having contrived to remain on good terms with everyone, even with himself, during the whole of the voyage out. His difficulties in returning to England, which put an end to his holiday mood, were luckily not a part of his subject.

There are many brilliant passages in *Cornhill to Cairo,* among which Thackeray's first glimpse of the East at Smyrna and his picture of the Bay of Glaucus and the ruins of Telmessus stand out.[28] But perhaps the reader remembers even more clearly Thackeray's whimsical accounts of trivial incidents of travel: his hurried half hour at Vigo, where his bulky person was cheerfully carried ashore from the ship's boat by a "living sedan," an "exceedingly small and meagre" Gallego whose whiskers Thackeray clutched for dear life; his first Turkish bath, in which he came to feel "a sort of pleasure . . . in a soft boiling simmer, which, no doubt, potatoes feel when they are steaming"; and his ascent of the Great Pyramid, up which he was pushed by a team of six Arabs.[29] Equally engaging is Thackeray's account of "The White Squall" through which his ship passed at dawn on 28 October. The ballad begins quietly with an account of "the cabin snoring with universal nose." Then the turmoil occasioned by the storm is described in rushing double rhyme and three-stress metre. And, calm and peace having returned at last, Thackeray concludes:

I thought as day was breaking,
My little girls were waking,
And smiling, and making
  A prayer at home for me.[30]

Cornhill to Cairo was even more cordially welcomed than *The Irish Sketch Book* had been. In the second edition, which followed a few months after the first, Thackeray thanked "a score of critics" for receiving his book "with such extraordinary kindliness and favour." [31] There were the familiar complaints of superficiality and irreverence, particularly in religious periodicals like the *Guardian* and the *Tablet;* [32] but such was his "contagious geniality," [33] such was the "delightful diversity of entertainment" which he provided,[34] that he was readily forgiven for his want of earnestness even by these reviewers. Perhaps the keenest review that the book elicited was a four-column article in the *Daily News,* at this time still under Dickens's editorship. Not only did the reviewer pay eloquent tribute to Thackeray's stylistic mastery; he also saw in *Cornhill to Cairo* the emergence of that rare phenomenon, a true humorist. Noting Coleridge's distinction between wit and humour, that the former is impersonal, while the latter "is essentially the *character* or *humour* of a particular person," he showed that Thackeray's best effects, and those of Carlyle, Pepys, Sir Thomas Browne, and others, came from these authors' ability to "let the public into the secret of their own peculiar characters." [35] Thus did this anonymous critic penetrate to the heart of Thackeray's method; and it may be surmised that Thackeray himself had not forgotten this article when he some years later composed his lectures on *The English Humourists.*

II

Thackeray's critical journalism during these years was to a certain degree an extension of the work that he had done in the same line between 1837 and 1841.[1] His principal topics continued to be books and pictures, and on these subjects his opinions had not radically changed. Yet it would be a mistake to hurry over this part of his work. Even though it is largely unread today—much of it, indeed, has never been reprinted—it counted heavily in his development as a writer, and it has substantial intrinsic interest. It will be worth while to examine in turn each of his important periodical connexions—with *Fraser's Magazine,* with the *Foreign Quarterly Review,* and with the *Morning Chronicle.*

The death of James Fraser in October, 1841, did not interrupt Thackeray's association with *Fraser's Magazine.* He continued to work steadily for the new editor, George William Nickisson, though this gentleman never became the personal friend that Fraser had been. Comparing Thackeray's Fraserian papers of the 1840s with those which he wrote in the 1830s, one is first struck by a decided change in tone. Like the rest of the Fraserians, he had by this period "imbibed much of that sweet and wholesome milk of human kindness, at which in youth we are ready to sneer as a vapid and unprofitable potion." [2] Between 1837 and 1839 Thackeray had written a series of "Annual Executions," in which he "pitilessly trampled on *Forget-me-nots,* and massacred whole galleries of *Books of Beauty.*" [3] How different are the parallel series of articles on "Christmas stories, those fireside Christmas pantomimes," [4] which he wrote between 1844 and 1847. As he read these stories and thought of the enjoyment that they would bring to children like Anny and Minny,[5] he fancied himself once more on his way home to Larkbeare, contemplating the pleasures of a boyhood Christmas holiday:

> Can you ever forget the glories of the beefsteak at the Bull and Mouth previous to going home; and the majestic way in which we ordered the port and pronounced it to be 'ropy' or 'fruity'; and criticized the

steak, as if we had been Joseph Bregion, cook to Prince Rasumousky? At twenty-five minutes past four precisely, the greys were in the coach; and the guard comes in, and says, 'Now, gentlemen!' We lighted cigars magnanimously. . . . We take up the insides at the office in the Quadrant; and go bowling down Piccadilly on the road to Hounslow, Snow the guard playing 'Home, Sweet Home,' on the bugle. How clear it twangs on the ear even now! Can you ever forget the cold veal pies at Bagshot, and the stout waiter with black tights, on the lookout for the coach as it came in to a minute? . . . Why, the whole road is a ghost since then. . . . Where are the jolly turn-pike-men who used to come out as the lamps lighted up the white bars of the gates, and the horses were in a halo of smoke? How they used to go over the six miles between Honiton and Escot Lodge! and there—there on Fair Mile Hill is the little carriage waiting, and HOME in it, looking out with sweet eyes—eyes, oh, how steadfast, and loving, and tender.[6]

Thackeray himself calls this passage "sentimental," but it may more fairly be read as one more evidence of that new-found ability to see the past in perspective which gives promise of the "delicious maturity" of his great novels.

Thackeray continued to visit the galleries for *Fraser's*, even though he now performed this service for other periodicals as well. "At the May season and period of the exhibitions," he makes Oliver Yorke comment, "our eccentric correspondent Titmarsh seems to be seized with a double fit of eccentricity, and to break out into such violent fantastical gambols as might cause us to be alarmed did we not know him to be harmless." [7] The season excited Thackeray, not only because it revived his own youthful ambitions to be a painter, but also because for him the viewing of beautiful pictures was one of the most exquisite of life's pleasures. In reporting on these visits he continued to favour *genre* pictures, made agreeable by comedy and sentiment, and to oppose "High Art" and the "Ideal." Yet his sympathies were wider than his theories, and he could praise eloquently, even where he did not fully understand. Here is his account, for example, of another of Turner's great canvases, when it was first exhibited in 1844:

Mr. Turner . . . has out-prodigied almost all former prodigies. He has made a picture with real rain, behind which is real sunshine, and you expect a rainbow every minute. Meanwhile, there comes a train down upon you, really moving at the rate of fifty miles an hour, and which the reader had best make haste to see, lest it should dash out of the picture, and be away up Charing Cross through the wall opposite. All these wonders are performed with means not less wonderful than the effects are. The rain, in the astounding picture called 'Rain—Steam—Speed,' is composed of dabs of dirty putty *slapped* on to the canvas with a trowel; the sunshine scintillates out of very thick smeary lumps of chrome yellow. The shadows are produced by cool tones of crimson lake, and quiet glazings of vermilion. Although the fire in the steam-engine *looks* as if it were red, I am not prepared to say that it is not painted with cobalt and pea-green. And as for the manner in which the *'Speed'* is done, of that the less said the better, —only it is a positive fact that there is a steam-coach going fifty miles an hour. The world has never seen anything like this picture.[8]

There is much else of interest in Thackeray's work for *Fraser's* of this period. "Men and Coats" is an agreeable set of reflections on things in general; "Dickens in France" provides a hilarious account of "Nicholas Nickleby, ou Les Voleurs de Londres" as performed at the Ambigu-Comique in Paris (the "ambiguously comic theatre," Thackeray calls it); "Grant in Paris" reveals that Thackeray could still summon up something of the old "satirical frenzy" when he encountered egregious dulness and ignorance; "A Box of Novels," in addition to the merits already noted, includes a subtle disquisition on the *fond* of melancholy that underlies even the most rollicking of Irish books; and Thackeray's reflections on "the chances of the literary profession" in his memorial article for Laman Blanchard anticipate the view of worldly success to which he was to give definitive expression in *Vanity Fair*. Altogether the record of his labours for *Fraser's* is impressive enough, even though consideration of the fiction which he wrote for the magazine has been deferred until later in this chapter.

Between October, 1841, and January, 1842, the *Foreign Quarterly Review* was acquired by Chapman and Hall. Inevitably they called on Thackeray, an established specialist in foreign matters who was under contract to them to write a book about Ireland, for support in their new venture. Being in Paris, he set to work on an account of French history during the past quarter of a century; and on 25 February, after "6 weeks labor, & the reading of many scores of books," he sent Chapman and Hall a long paper on "The Last Fifteen Years of the Bourbons," which he proposed to follow with a second article on the July Monarchy.[9] This weighty and learned contribution, from which his usual whimsical peculiarities as a writer have been carefully excluded, was clearly intended as a bid for the magazine's editorship. He wrote on 15 March:

If you have a new editor as you will no doubt, and unless you have a great man like Carlyle at the head of your undertaking please to remember your humble servant. . . . I have a couple of languages, French and German, and could have Italian in another month, having already a smattering; and if your intention is not to have a pompous review, but a smart and lively one, I believe I should make as good an editor as another.[10]

To this position, however, Chapman and Hall appointed John Forster, then their chief literary adviser, rather than Thackeray. But they encouraged him to remain a principal contributor; and between April, 1842, and the summer of 1844, when he left for the East, ten papers appeared in the *Foreign Quarterly Review,* including four in one number, which can be ascribed to him with certainty, and there are others which have been attributed to him with some confidence.[11] If he was not entirely pleased at being passed over for the editorship, he yet contrived to remain on cordial if bantering terms with his new chief. We find him sending to Forster, for example, the following progress report concerning his article on the July Monarchy, which was fated to remain incomplete:

Le Général Comte Titmarsh commandant le corps d'armée agissant contre S M. Louis Philippe à l'honneur de prevenir V. Excellence, des succes importans qu'il a eus dans les journées du 6, 7, 8 courant.

L'ennemi a d'abord montré un courage tellement opiniâtre des forces si imposantes que le Général de Titmarsh a failli plusieurs fois commander la retraite. Grace a la valeur indomptable de ses troupes, il a fini néamoins par se rendre maitre d'une grande partie du terrain occupé par l'ennemi, qui en ce moment hésite, fléchit s'ébranle. Jusqu'à la fin de l'attaque, Le Prince de Titmarsh montrera la même bravoure persévérante—il ne doute point que le succès lui soit assuré. Qu'aucun accident funeste ne vienne détruire ces belles espérances!

Le 18 du mois il espère opérer sa jonction complète avec le Commandant en Chef—En conduisant ses colonnes triomphantes auprès de votre Excellence, il n'a guère besoin de demander des récompenses généreuses pour ces soldats qui ont tant souffert! Que votre Excellence fasse seulement entendre sa voix puissant au ministère de Finances: la justice, la générosité de la Nation y répondra. Désormais le soldat n'aura qu'un cri Vive la Patrie, Vive le *Foring-Quatérly!* Courage, et esperance!—Que Dieu preserve votre Excellence!—

Signé. Le Feld Maréchal Prince Titmarsh.[12]

No doubt the *"récompenses généreuses"* that he received from Chapman and Hall reconciled him to his subordinate position with the magazine. In 1842 he accepted £40 as partial remuneration for two articles, and Mrs. Carlyle the following year reported that £50 was paid for a single contribution, though not to Thackeray.[13]

Thackeray's articles for the *Foreign Quarterly Review* were of several kinds. The solid historical narrative that he provided in "The Last Fifteen Years of the Bourbons" was not really his *métier,* and he may have failed to finish its sequel out of sheer boredom. He confined himself chiefly to "pleasant German or French books that may be reviewed without trouble or consultation of other works." [14] In dealing with the recent works of Balzac, Dumas, Hugo, Jules Janin, Scribe, and Eugène Sue, he as a rule summarized the volume under discussion in an unsystematic, joking way, which allowed him to digress to other topics as the spirit moved him. He made a specialty of travel books, in describing which his good-natured fun sometimes contracted to a cutting edge. As he exposes the ignorance and self-importance of Victor Hugo or Alexandre Dumas, indeed, one can see the resolution forming itself in his mind that his own travel narratives will at least not be marred by these faults. If an examination of Thackeray's contributions to the *Foreign Quarterly Review* can only leave the reader with the impression that they were task work, protracted to unnecessary length because he was paid so much a sheet; he yet executed these assignments so easily and pleasantly that his papers remain readable even today.

Thackeray's last identified contribution to the *Foreign Quarterly Review* appeared in April, 1844. No doubt he gave up writing for that magazine because he had in March through the intervention of Eyre Evans Crowe and John Doyle secured a "floating connexion" with the *Morning Chronicle* worth £300 a year.[15] He wrote regularly for this paper until he left for the East in August, and when he returned to London in February, 1845, he resumed his contributions. Only when *Vanity Fair* began to appear in January, 1847, did he relinquish his post, which he regarded in these years as being after *Punch* his chief periodical resource. Even after he became famous, indeed, he resumed work with the paper for a time in 1848, attracted by a fee of five guineas an article.[16]

The *Morning Chronicle* was at this time the chief rival of the *Times* for the title of London's principal newspaper. Its liberal political position made it a far more congenial outlet to Thackeray than the *Times* had been. But though he at first tried his hand at political articles (on 1 June 1844 we find him looking forward to "a day's work at the Emperor of Russia about whose visit all the towns agog"), he had shortly to admit: "I cant write the politics." This was a pity, since "the literary part is badly paid," but Thackeray could at any rate console himself with the reflection that his "Chronicle articles are very well liked—they relieve the dullness of the estimable paper." Though he continued from time to time to attempt political pieces, they invariably missed fire, and his real service to the paper was in providing "outside articles" (book reviews and art criticism) and "occasional jeux d'esprit." [17] Thackeray's readers may be profoundly grateful that he thus failed to "get within the guard of the Chronicle" in political matters.[18] Articles on this subject from his hand would have been tedious even if identifiable, while his lively "outside articles" stand out like plums in a pudding.[19]

If Thackeray hardly rivalled Sainte-Beuve in his stint as the *Morning Chronicle's* regular reviewer, he yet displayed the same knowledge of books and the world, the same unfailing resourcefulness, and the same ability to make a wide variety of topics humanly interesting that the readers of today find in the articles of Mr. V. S. Pritchett for the *New Statesman* or the contributions of Mr. Edmund Wilson to the *New Yorker.* Thackeray's *Morning Chronicle* papers are not merely the culmination of his work as a periodical critic (a specialty with him since 1837); at their best they also anticipate *The English Humourists* and *The Four Georges.* Thackeray's equipment in these articles includes a penetrating insight into character, an ability to present in a few phrases the whole *ambiance* of a subject, a fine irony playing over the incongruities of life, a keen eye for the devastating anecdote, and a felicity in quotation which makes an asset even of this obligatory part of the Victorian reviewer's task. The result is critical journalism of a high order, which has substantial permanent value.

Among the most interesting of Thackeray's *Morning Chronicle* papers are those dealing with such Victorian classics as Dickens's *Cricket on the Hearth,* Disraeli's *Coningsby* and *Sybil,* Jerrold's *Mrs. Caudle's Curtain Lectures,* and Stanley's *Life of Dr. Arnold.* He is particularly expert in revealing where the appeal of these books lay for himself and his contemporaries, as in the following ironical dirge over Mrs. Caudle:

> Though Mrs. Caudle had her faults, perhaps there was no woman who died more universally lamented than she. The want of her weekly discourses was felt all over the kingdom. . . . In *Punch's Almanac* we find Caudle married again. It seems a wrong to the departed woman. We feel personally angry that her memory should be so slighted; but the virtues of the sainted deceased appear more clearly, now that her emancipated husband is indulging in vices which were checked by the anxious prescience of the first and best Mrs. Caudle. She and Mrs. Nickleby ought to take their places among the "Women of England," when Mrs. Ellis brings out a new edition of that work. They are both types of English matrons so excellent that it is hard to say which of the two should have the *pas.* Mrs. Nickleby's maundering and amiable vacuity endear her to all her acquaintance; Mrs. Caudle's admirable dulness, envy, and uncharitableness, her fondness for her mamma, brother, and family, and her jealous regard of her

Caudle, make her an object of incessant sympathy with her numerous friends, and they regret, now she is no more, that amiable British matron and beldam.[20]

Here Thackeray was altogether in sympathy with his subject, but even where he has serious reservations about a book, he contrives to praise with infectious enthusiasm the aspects of it that he is able to admire. The chief effect upon him of *The Cricket on the Hearth,* for example, was to make him long for "the artist's early and simple manner." Yet he paid ungrudging tribute to Dickens's pre-eminence as "literary master of ceremonies for Christmas"; and he granted that if one takes the book "in a Christmas point of view, . . . it and Dot, and the kettle and Gruff and Tackleton become a sort of half-recognized realities which charm and fascinate you, and over which you may laugh or weep according to your mood." [21]

Even better than these papers, however, are those in which Thackeray resuscitates for a moment a vanished society, or sketches a remarkable character of history. As he reviews biographies of Beau Brummell and David Hume, as he notices Mme. d'Arblay's diary and letters, as Horne's *New Spirit of the Age* recalls to his mind his boyhood admiration for Hazlitt and *The Spirit of the Age,* his historical imagination awakes; and the past lives again in his mind. Here, for example, is his response to the sixth volume of Mme. d'Arblay's memoirs:

Six lovely princesses wept over her immortal novel of 'Camilla,' read it hastily in their apartments at Windsor, or 'comfortably' together at Weymouth. The august eyes of Queen Charlotte moistened with tears over those dingy and now forgotten pages. The King himself had a copy and read in it, and was good-natured to the hysterically loyal Fanny d'Arblay—always ready to gush with tears at the feet of her royal master—always plunging from the embraces of one soft and kind-hearted princess into the closet and arms of another. Peace to their honest big-wigged shades! There is something queer, pleasant, and affecting in the picture which Fanny d'Arblay draws of this primitive and kindly female family of George III.; of the princesses so simple, so tender, so handsome, blooming in powder and pomatum; of the old Queen herself, that just and spotless, that economical but charitable lady.[22]

But not all the books that came Thackeray's way were potential classics or dealt with famous figures of the past. Perhaps he shows his greatest ingenuity in making tedious books amusing, in transforming sows' ears into silk purses. In his last complete novel he writes: "And yet egotism is good talk. Even dull autobiographies are pleasant to read: . . . Can't you like a man at whom you laugh a little?" [23] Thackeray could, at any rate. He was fond enough of *originals* to take sincere delight in books that ordinary readers found dull or objectionable. Like Democritus brought back to earth, it was his pleasure to

> See motley life in modern trappings dress'd,
> And feed with varied fools th' eternal jest.

So he remarks of Dr. Carus's *Travels in England:*

> There seems something prodigious in the prosiness of the book. The staleness, and dulness of the author's reflections amount almost to a marvel. The gravity and self-content with which the Doctor lays down the law—the pomp with which he serves out his small-beer—the happy, blundering skill which leads him to miss the great points and occupy him[self] laboriously with the small—all these considerations may deter many readers, at first, from a book which appears quite unexampled for drivelling stupidity. . . . it is only after study and labour that you penetrate the outer dulness, and see what a magnificent treasure is before you.[24]

A brilliant exercise in irony follows in which Carus's ponderous commonplaces and elephantine pleasantries are neatly displayed for the reader's entertainment. Bulwer's *The New Timon,* James Fenimore Cooper's *Ravensnest,* Haydon's *Lectures on Painting,* Horne's *New Spirit of the Age,* and Alexis Soyer's *Gastronomic Regenerator* [25] afford him further "victims to be gently immolated," though he treats none of these as severely as he does poor Carus.

We have thus far been concerned with noting the interest as criticism of Thackeray's *Morning Chronicle* articles. To the student of his work they have the further value of revealing his developing views as to what fiction ought to be. Nowhere else does he speak so explicitly or at such length on this subject. In a significant series of articles he deals with a growing inclination on the part of such writers as Dickens, Disraeli, Lever, and Mrs. Trollope, to make political, economic, or religious manifestos out of their novels.[26]

> If we want instruction [he argues] we prefer to take it from fact rather than from fiction. We like to hear sermons from his reverence at church; to get our notions of trade, crime, politics, and other national statistics, from the proper papers and figures; but when suddenly, out of the gilt pages of a pretty picture book, a comic moralist rushes forward, and takes occasion to tell us that society is diseased, the laws unjust, the rich ruthless, the poor martyrs, the world lop sided, and *vice versa,* persons who wish to lead an easy life are inclined to remonstrate against this literary ambuscadoe.[27]

Indeed, Thackeray continued in a subsequent article:

> Morals and manners we believe to be the novelist's best themes; and hence prefer romances which do not treat of algebra, religion, political economy, or any other abstract science.[28]

In illustration of these opinions he proceeds to deride Disraeli's "comic philosophy" and "sentimental politics" in his articles on *Coningsby* and *Sybil,* and to provide a burlesque plot for a proletarian novel in reviewing Lever's *St. Patrick's Eve.*

The dictum that the novelist should never attempt a subject concerning which he is not thoroughly informed implies a realistic aesthetic. And, indeed, fidelity to personal experience in fiction is a first principle with Thackeray. Hence one finds him asserting that the proletarian novel is "a magnificent and untrodden field," but "to describe it well, a man should be born to it. We want a Boz from among the miners or the manufactories to detail their ways of work and pleasure—to describe their feelings, interests, and lives, public and private." [29] Hence he makes his chief ground of praise for *Mrs. Caudle's Curtain Lectures* that Caudle and his wife "have become real living personages in history, like Queen Elizabeth, or Sancho Panza, or any other past character, who, false or real once, is only imaginary now, and for whose existence we have only the word of a book. And surely to create these realities is the greatest triumph of the fictitious writer." [30] Hence his reservation, already noted, concerning *The Cricket on the Hearth,* that its characters and dialogue "are no more like nature than the talk of Tityrus and Meliboeus are like the real talk of Bumpkin and Hodge over a stile." [31] Hence finally his objection to the fashionable novel, whether written by Disraeli or by Mrs. Gore.

Not an unremarkable characteristic of our society-novelists [he writes] is that ardour of imagination which sets them so often to work in describing grand company for us. They like to disport themselves in inventing fine people, as we to sit in this imaginary society. There is something *naif* in this credulity on both sides: in these cheap Barmecide entertainments, to which author and reader are content to sit down.[32]

"Novels by Eminent Hands" constitutes an extension of the views expressed in these and similar passages, just as *Vanity Fair* is an attempt to show what can be done in fiction if the author does limit himself to the aspects of life that he knows intimately.

Indeed, Thackeray's *Morning Chronicle* articles include many significant anticipations of his later work, forming, as they do, an annotated diary of his reading in the three crucial years before *Vanity Fair* began to appear. We see Thackeray discovering in *Coningsby,* for example, what treasures lay open to the hand of the novelist in the available printed records concerning the third Marquess of Hertford and his circle. Disraeli had made from them a series of "amusing, bitter sketches, . . . of which the likenesses were irresistible, and the malice tickled everybody." [33] Might not another novelist use them to even better purpose? It is of absorbing interest to the admirer of *Vanity Fair* to witness emerging from Thackeray's reflections on his reading that profound disgust with the frivolity and corruption of well-to-do England which supplies the unifying theme of his great novel. His brilliant essay on Beau Brummell is informed by the most scathing contempt for fashionable Regency society, the leadership of which was contended for by "the Prince of Wales (august shade of sixteen stone!)" and "young Brummell, the footman's descendant." As between the two antagonists, Thackeray greatly prefers the latter:

All the profligate splendours of Carlton House could not compete with the Beau's small tenement in Chesterfield-street; there was a tawdry magnificence about George IV., which must have been felt to be bad taste if not acknowledged. . . . Brummell overcame him by simplicity, elegance, and neat impudence and presence of mind. There seems to have been a calmness about him which flustered and intolerably annoyed the unwieldy antagonist with whom he contended for the first place in a certain society.

But what a light this struggle throws on high life of that day! "Let us respect the world which elevated to honour this respectable man!" is Thackeray's sardonic valedictory to Brummell; "and not be too hard upon him, because he was heartless, and a swindler, a fool, a glutton, and a liar." [34] Nor did fashionable society of his own time, as depicted in Mrs. Gore's *Sketches of English Character,* offer a worthier picture:

Supposing that Pall-mall were the world, and human life finished with the season, and Heaven were truffled turkies and the Opera, and duty and ambition were bounded in dressing well and getting tickets to Lady Londonderry's dancing teas, Mrs. Gore's 'Sketches of Character' might be a good guide book. And we are wrong in saying it has no moral: the moral is that which very likely the author intended —that entire weariness, contempt, and dislike which the reader must undergo after this introduction to what is called the world. If it be as here represented, the world is the most hollow, heartless, vulgar, brazen world, and those are luckiest who are out of it.[35]

It has been possible to suggest only faintly in this brief survey the interest of Thackeray's *Morning Chronicle* essays. He has his word, and it is usually an epigram, on most of the leading issues of the day. Tractarianism and evangelicalism as well as Young England and Young Ireland are passed in review. There are delightful glimpses of early Victorian life, as in the account of Christmas preparations that prefaces his review of holiday books.[36] The reports of exhibitions of the Royal Academy and the Water Colour Societies include some brilliantly realized word-painting, ranging in subject from Hunt's comic boys and Maclise's costume melodramas to Turner's most daring experiments.[37] These essays were written just as Thackeray attained maturity as a writer; none of them is negligible; and the best display that wonderful fulness, freshness, and gusto that mark the first productions of a master who has ended his apprenticeship. What he says of Hazlitt applies equally well to his own articles for this paper:

With partialities and prejudices innumerable, he had a wit so keen, a sensibility so exquisite, an appreciation of humor, or pathos, or even of the greatest art, so lively, quick, and cultivated, that it was always good to know what were the impressions made by books, or man, or pictures on such a mind.[38]

Thackeray contributed to a number of other periodicals during the early and middle 1840s. Between March, 1843 and August, 1844, he wrote a long letter each month for the *Calcutta Star,* a newspaper established by his old associate James Hume, who had gone out to India in 1842. Though Hume was able to pay him only about three pounds a letter, friendship kept Thackeray faithful to his task, and he seems to have resumed his contributions for a time after he returned from the East in 1845.[39] In the early months of 1844 he wrote several letters for the adventurer Henry Wikoff's New York *Republic,* a connexion which he terminated when prompt payment was not forthcoming.[40] In March, 1845, his friend Albany Fonblanque added him to the staff of the *Examiner,* though only in the humble capacity of subeditor. "It takes a great deal more time than I bargained for," he told his mother, "and I don't do it as well as many a worse man w^{d} but I shall stay on for it helps me in various ways to get news knowledge of a certain sort, means of pleasantry for Punch, matter to talk of to India &c." Yet by the end of July he had resigned, commenting: "it took more time than I could afford to give for four sovereigns: and I was too clever a fellow to do it well; making omissions blunders &c. w^{h} an honest plodding clerk w^{d} never have fallen into." [41] Thackeray also wrote for *Ainsworth's Magazine,* for the *Pictorial Times,* and for the *Edinburgh Review,* but only the last of these connexions calls for comment.

The reader will not have failed to note how much wider was the range of Thackeray's critical journalism in the 1840s than it had been in the 1830s. In regard to history and literature, at least, he had become a learned man in his easy-going, unsystematic way. In part this was owing to a process of conscious self-education. Proposing a contribution to Chapman and Hall in 1842, he had written: "though the Louis Philippe article will take much time, & bring no profit, I want to do it, for reputation's sake." [42] And later in the year he was gratified by an offer, which he did not in the event accept, "of good & constant work in London (to write a history of England)." [43] In a *Fraser's* paper of 1844 he noted "how astonishingly Sir Walter Scott has influenced the world; how he changed the character of novelists, then of historians, whom he brought from their philosophy to the study of pageantry and costume." [44] By his articles for the *Foreign Quarterly Review* and for the *Morning Chronicle,* he was preparing himself to write, not only Scott's kind of historical fiction, but also the kind of colourful and popular history that Macaulay (whom he admired beyond all other contemporary writers) [45] was supplying in his essays.

Conscious that his work was far more solidly grounded and substantial than it had been earlier in his career, Thackeray was eager to associate himself with the highest level of the periodical press, the dignified and old-established quarterlies. He must have been pleased when Thomas Longman, proprietor of the *Edinburgh Review,* asked him in April, 1845, to describe his specialties as a periodical writer, even though one surmises from the ironical self-depreciation of his reply that Longman's communication had been marked by a good deal of unconscious condescension:

> I hardly know what subjects to point out as suited to my capacity —light matters connected with Art, humorous reviews, critiques of novels—French subjects, memoirs, poetry, history from Louis XV. downwards and of an earlier period—that of Froissart and Monstrelet. German light literature and poetry—though of these I know but little beyond what I learned in a years residence in the Country fourteen years ago: finally subjects relating to society in general where a writer may be allowed to display the humorous *ego,* or a victim is to be gently immolated. But I am better able to follow than to lead and should hope to give satisfaction in my small way.[46]

Longman thereupon recommended Thackeray to his editor, Professor Macvey Napier, as "a good hand for light articles." But Napier, desiring further reassurance, inquired about Thackeray's status of Abraham Hayward. "One requires to be very much on one's guard in engaging with mere strangers," he wrote. "In a Journal like the *Edinbro'*, it is always of importance to keep up in respect of names." [47] Hayward's report was favourable, and it was arranged in July that Thackeray should write an article on N. P. Willis's *Dashes at Life*. He told his mother when he dispatched it two months later: "I rather expect to see it come back on my hands: for the Editor though a learned man and Editor of the Encyclopaedia Britannica as well is evidently a dull personage; and two to one won't relish what I've sent him." [48] Thackeray's doubts were only too well founded. He had to explain his jokes to Napier, and even after this had been done, some of them were omitted from the printed version of the article. He observed in a rueful letter acknowledging the receipt of £21 in October: "From your liberal payment I can't but conclude that you reward me not only for labouring but for being mutilated in your service. . . . O to think of my pet passages gone for ever." [49] He wrote no more for the *Edinburgh Review*. But the experience was at least useful in showing him that he must command success on his own terms. His distinctive and unconventional talent could not be effectively adapted to the standards of the grave and ponderous quarterlies; and if he was to communicate the living understanding of history that he had acquired from the varied reading of which his critical journalism during the years 1841 to 1846 is the chronicle, it would have to be in lectures like those on the English humorists and the four Georges and in novels like *Esmond*.

III

Nearly all of Thackeray's fiction of this period, apart from his work for *Punch*, which will be discussed in the next chapter, was written for *Fraser's Magazine* under the pseudonym of George Savage Fitz-Boodle.[1] Fitz-Boodle was introduced in a "confession" of June, 1842, which made "a sort of hit." [2] Between July, 1842, and November of the following year, he contributed to

Fraser's three "Professions," three further "Confessions," and a series of four stories entitled "Men's Wives." Throughout 1844 *The Luck of Barry Lyndon* appeared over his name. Thus for a time Fitz-Boodle achieved a prominence among Thackeray's alter egos exceeded only by Michael Angelo Titmarsh, whose own activities continued, however, almost unabated.

We possess no likeness of Fitz-Boodle, such as Thackeray has provided of Titmarsh, but it is not difficult to piece together his portrait. A tall, heavy, sedentary man in his forties, he is maladroit both on horseback and the dance-floor. By 1842 he has become a confirmed bachelor, though on his own showing he was singularly susceptible to feminine charm earlier in life. Contrary to Dr. Johnson's maxim, celibacy has not left him without pleasures. He is portrayed, indeed, as a reasonably contented hedonist, "alone and merry at forty year." Not under the necessity of working, he lives in lodgings on his limited allowance, frequenting his clubs, and cultivating the minor pleasures of life. He is a connoisseur of food, wine, cigars, and gossip, and he claims to be the "third-best whist-player in Europe." As the younger son of a noble family, he insists that "with the *plebs*, of course, Fitz-Boodle, in whose veins flows the blood of a thousand kings, can have nothing to do," and he carefully points out that he is not a "reading man" or "a literary character." Indeed, he condescends quite insufferably to the other Fraserians. He concludes a communication to Oliver Yorke by remarking:

> I have said in my letter that I found *all* literary persons vulgar and dull. Permit me to contradict this with regard to yourself. I met you once at Blackwall, I think it was, and really did not remark anything offensive in your accent or appearance.

And elsewhere he mentions "a person by the name of Tidmarsh, who may be a worthy man for aught I know to the contrary; but has, with permission be it spoken, shown the most lamentable vulgarity and ignorance in his writing." [3]

The usefulness of such a *porte-parole* to Thackeray will be sufficiently evident. On the one hand, Fitz-Boodle was sufficiently like his creator in circumstances and tastes to serve as a spokesman for Thackeray's own views suitably heightened and coloured.

On the other hand, his aristocratic assumptions made him the proper object of a gentle but damaging satire that touches not only Fitz-Boodle himself but also the whole of the selfish West End club-life that he represents. In his first "Confession," a comic love-affair brought to nothing by his ungovernable passion for tobacco, and in the three "Professions," the exploration of Fitz-Boodle's character is perhaps Thackeray's central purpose. Afterwards, as we shall see, the focus of interest shifts.

In his "Professions" Fitz-Boodle proposes to make good a "social deficit" by suggesting new lines of endeavour to "younger sons of the nobility." Thackeray had not overlooked the recent auction of Horace Walpole's effects at Strawberry Hill; and he consequently has Fitz-Boodle mention a sale "which made some noise in the world, . . . the late Lord Gimcrack's, at Dilberry Hill," adding his regret that "Horace Waddlepoodle's . . . gentle accumulation of bric-à-brac" should have been auctioned off by a vulgar upstart.[4] Thus Fitz-Boodle's first profession emerges, that of the gentlemanly auctioneer, a conception developed with much ingenuity. But it pales beside the next, that of "dinner-master," which requires for its exercise a complete understanding of the arcana of the "gormandizing science" and the dining resources of London. Fitz-Boodle writes with immense enthusiasm concerning notable instances of culinary *grandeur d'âme,* and he cannot reprobate too severely botched middle-class imitations of fashionable dinners. He has names at hand for his "gastronomic agents," the Hon. George Gormand Gobbleton and Sir Augustus Carver Cramley Cramley; and he even describes the appearance appropriate to them: "You will be yourself a portly grave man, with your hair a little bald and grey. In fact, in this as in all other professions, you had best try to look as like Canning as you can." [5] After these flights, the third paper, dealing with the possibilities latent in being a professional foreigner on the pattern of N. P. Willis, is a distinct anticlimax.

In the next three "Confessions," which deal with Fitz-Boodle's love-passages as a young man in Germany, he is much more closely identified with Thackeray himself. Though these stories are farcical extravaganzas, they none the less came so close to autobiography that Thackeray was unwilling to reprint them in

XVII. "The Common Lot"

From an etching by Thackeray in "The Great Hoggarty Diamond"

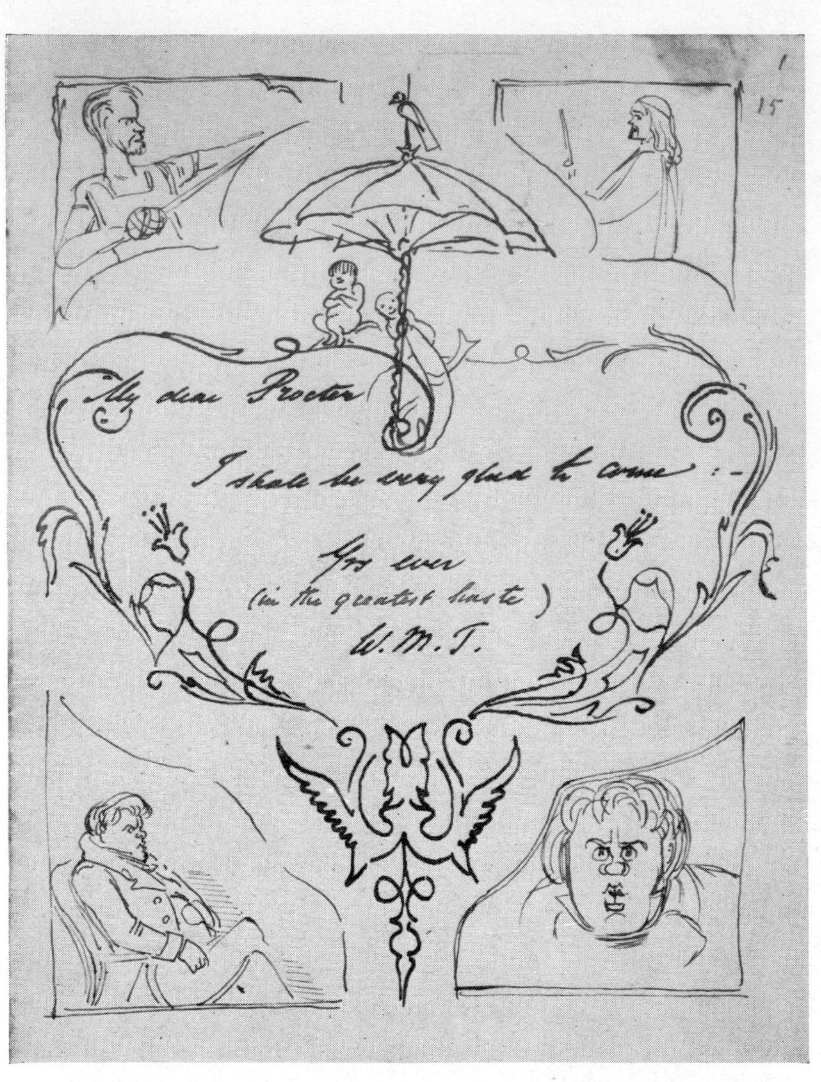
My dear Procter

I shall be very glad to come :-

Yrs ever
(in the greatest haste)
W.M.T.

XVIII–XIX. Caricatures of John Forster in letters to the Procters

Pen-and-ink drawings by Thackeray

NOTES OF A JOURNEY

FROM

CORNHILL TO GRAND CAIRO.

XX. Thackeray on his Eastern trip

From a pen-and-ink self-portrait

his *Miscellanies* of 1857.[6] When Thackeray writes of Fitz-Boodle's adoration of Minna Löwe at Godesberg and of his tender interest in Dorothea and Ottilia at Kalbsbraten (Weimar), he is clearly reflecting his own youthful indiscretions, though the slapstick mishaps that dog Fitz-Boodle were no doubt invented out of whole cloth. Again, as he made Fitz-Boodle describe his own behaviour, he no doubt thought with understandable chagrin of the superior airs that he had himself affected in Germany twelve years earlier:

There is about a young Englishman of twenty a degree of easy self-confidence, hardly possessed even by a Frenchman. . . . The bragging of the Frenchman is not so conceited or intolerable as that calm, silent, contemptuous conceit of us young Britons, who think our superiority so well established that it is really not worth arguing upon, and who take upon us to despise thoroughly the whole world through which we pass. . . . Now when I went abroad I fancied myself one of the finest fellows under the sun. I patronized a banker's dinners as if I did him honour in eating them; I took my place before grave professors and celebrated men, and talked vapid nonsense to them in infamous French, laughing heartily in return at their own manner of pronouncing that language. I set down as a point beyond question that their customs were inferior to our own, and would not in the least scruple, in a calm way, to let my opinion be known. What an agreeable young fellow I must have been! [7]

These three stories are trifles, no doubt, but agreeable trifles which possess the added interest of anticipating the Pumpernickel scenes of *Vanity Fair*.

If Fitz-Boodle's "Professions" show that celibacy after all is not without its pleasures, the series "Men's Wives" can be regarded as a demonstration that marriage has many pains. These tales describe a series of misalliances, each more disastrous than the one which goes before. This is a subject on which the bachelor Fitz-Boodle could hardly pose as an authority, and in these tales he does in fact recede into the background. Except for "Mr. and Mrs. Frank Berry," his connexion with them is purely nominal, nor is the manner in which they are narrated marked by his usual idiosyncrasies. The first and last of these stories are relatively slight performances. "Mr. and Mrs. Frank Berry" is interesting chiefly because it includes Thackeray's first fictional use, a relatively severe and unsparing one, of his boyhood years at Charterhouse, while "The ——'s Wife," is an extravaganza, which testifies once more to Thackeray's odd preoccupation with executions. Not so the remaining tales.

"The Ravenswing" is one of the most substantial, if least attractive, of Thackeray's middle-length narratives. Saintsbury thought that it was written "at least as early as *A Shabby Genteel Story.*"[8] If his arguments on this point do not bear close scrutiny,[9] one must grant at least that "The Ravenswing" does have many points of resemblance to the earlier tale. It deals chiefly with lower-middle-class and Bohemian characters, and Thackeray's account of how the flashy attractions of "Captain" Howard Walker lure away the beautiful Morgiana Crump from the honest love of the barber Eglantine and the tailor Woolsey recalls Brandon's carrying off of Caroline Gann from Andrea Fitch. Each of these four characters is developed with easy mastery. Walker is a lively addition to Thackeray's gallery of English blacklegs, brought to life by the very contempt with which he is described. Morgiana, with the "flood of shining, waving, heavy, glossy, jetty hair" which earns her the name of "Ravenswing" and her eyes "as big as billiard balls," is a worthy first sketch for the Fotheringay. The reader sympathizes with Eglantine, for all his flabbiness and oiliness, as the barber trudges round "his little circle of loves, fears, and vanities," while he comes, like Thackeray himself, to regard the sturdy Woolsey as a man and a brother, despite the torments occasioned this worthy tailor by his red hair.[10] When the Ravenswing becomes a professional singer, Thackeray is enabled to present a series of portraits from the early Victorian musical world, which are no less authentic, if more succinct, than those of his principal characters. But if "The Ravenswing" testifies to the remarkable knowledge that Thackeray had by this time attained of many odd and unlikely nooks and corners of West End London, its total effect is still somewhat cheerless and depressing.

A very different impression is made by "Denis Haggarty's Wife," to which belongs the singular distinction of having commanded admiration from both Strindberg and Saintsbury. Strindberg applauded its devastating exploration of female perversity. Saintsbury thought that Thackeray had nowhere "exhibited better the dreadful irony of fate," that he "never did a maturer thing." [11] Certainly the story is the bitterest of all Thackeray's shorter narratives. Though not autobiographical in the sense that *The Great Hoggarty Diamond* is, it yet remains a profound if oblique commentary on Thackeray's painful relationship with his wife's family. Since his break with the Shawes after his unhappy visit to Cork in the autumn of 1840, good-natured friends had from time to time brought him word of the unreasonable abuse that his mother-in-law was in the habit of pouring out upon him.[12] Against these attacks he had no defence, for Mrs. Shawe's impenetrable self-righteousness made her impervious alike to fact and to argument. Thackeray had to school himself to accept her attitude as part of the nature of things, to reflect glumly that "if a man's character is to be abused, say what you will, there's nobody like a relation to do the business." [13]

His only recourse was to write a story that would give him the relief of expressing something of what he felt. He accordingly begins "Denis Haggarty's Wife" by sketching in Mrs. Major Gam and Miss Jemima Gam, an "odious Irishwoman and her daughter who used to frequent the Royal Hotel at Leamington," a pair of figures that might well be Mrs. Shawe and Jane on their travels after leaving Paris in 1837. Certainly Mrs. Gam's habit of "talking largely . . . of the wonders of her paternal mansion, Molloyville, County of Mayo" [14] suggests what we know of Mrs. Shawe's boasting about Laurentinum House, county of Cork; and Jemima Gam's refusal of her persistent suitor, Surgeon Haggarty, calls to mind Jane's rejection of an equally determined admirer.[15] The awful calamity that overtakes Jemima is an invention, of course, as are her marriage to and final abandonment of poor Haggarty. But these events leave the Surgeon, who otherwise resembles Thackeray not at all, completely unprotected against his mother-in-law's irresponsible and malicious tongue. The personal application that Thackeray made of Haggarty's imagined experience is brought home in two heartfelt passages:

There is a quality in certain people which is above all advice, exposure, or correction. Only let a man or woman have DULLNESS sufficient, and they need bow to no extant authority. A dullard recognizes no betters; a dullard can't see that he is in the wrong; a dullard has no scruples of conscience, no doubts of pleasing, or succeeding, or doing right, no qualms for other people's feelings, no respect but for the fool himself. How can you make a fool perceive that he is a fool? Such a personage can no more see his own folly than he can see his own ears. And the great quality of Dullness is to be unalterably contented with itself. What myriads of souls are there of this admirable sort, —selfish, stingy, ignorant, passionate, brutal, bad sons, mothers, fathers, never known to do kind actions!

The two fools who caused [Haggarty's] misery will never read this history of him; *they* never read godless stories in magazines. . . . They are too dull to understand humility; too blind to see a tender and simple heart under a rough ungainly bosom. They are sure that all their conduct towards my poor friend here has been perfectly righteous, and that they have given proofs of the most Christian virtue. Haggarty's wife is considered by her friends as a martyr to her savage husband, and her mother is the angel that has come to rescue her. All they did was to cheat him and desert him. And safe in that wonderful self-complacency with which the fools of this earth are endowed, they have not a single pang of conscience for their villainy towards him, and consider their heartlessness as a proof and consequence of their spotless piety and virtue.[16]

Before we turn to *Barry Lyndon,* one further tale, written for *Fraser's Magazine* but published elsewhere, deserves mention. In January, 1844, Thackeray read a slight mediaeval novel called *Othon l'Archer,* which Dumas had published in 1840. In the weeks that followed, as a relaxation from the strain of *Barry Lyndon,* he wrote a "nonsensical story" out of this book, in which he showed the preposterous aspects of romantic mediaevalism through burlesque, just as in "The Knights of Borsellen" he had exposed them by portraying fifteenth-century life as it actually was. When the "absurdity" was finished, he offered it to Nickisson under the title of "The Childe of Godesberg." Though Nickisson paid for the story, he did not use it; and it achieved publication only when George Cruikshank selected it as a serial in his *Table Book* for June to December, 1845.[17]

Thackeray follows Dumas' simple plot fairly closely (except for the omission of a long, interpolated story of the Crusades [18]), occasionally translating word for word; yet he contrives to transform Dumas' naïve narrative into a hilarious parody. He does this in two ways. The already improbable incidents recounted by Dumas are exaggerated Gahagan-fashion. Othon swims a few hundred yards under water in the Rhine; Otto, a new Beowulf, swims 25 to 30 miles. Othon brings down a heron just as it is flying out of bowshot; Otto holds back his arrow until the bird seems no bigger than a flea and then shoots it through the right eye. And under Thackeray's hand Dumas' figures behave no longer like figures of romance, but like Thackerayan human beings. Othon's parents are altogether conventional characters; Otto's mother and father fight like cat and dog. Dumas' heroine is the usual milk-and-water figure of romance, while Thackeray's Princess Helen is a jealous and sarcastic creature. Numerous anachronisms add to the fun. Count Ludwig wears a small *horloge* in his waistcoat pocket; the villainous Sir Gottfried calls for a notary when he wishes to confess his sins; and when Otto disappears, advertisements concerning him are placed in the *Journal of Francfort* and the *Allgemeine Zeitung*. The joke is elementary, no doubt, but enhanced by Cruikshank's illustrations, it is pleasant enough.

IV

Thackeray's only long work of fiction during these years was *The Luck of Barry Lyndon*. The idea for this novel had come his way during his visit with John Bowes at Streatlam Castle in June and July, 1841. "I have in my trip to the country," he told Fraser, "found materials (rather a character) for a story, that I'm sure must be amusing. . . . You see how Harry Lorrequer succeeds both in the Dublin Magazine & out of it, why should not my story of BARRY-LYNN (or by what name so ever it may be called) answer in as well as out of Regina?" [1] These "materials" came from the annals of the Strathmore family, of which Bowes was an illegitimate descendant. They are embodied in Jesse Foot's *Lives of Andrew Robinson Bowes and the Countess of*

Strathmore,[2] of which Bowes had an annotated copy in his possession,[3] though it is not clear whether Thackeray read this work or got his information directly from his friend. In any event, the "character" that fascinated him was that of Andrew Robinson Bowes.

This sinister adventurer was born Andrew Robinson Stoney of Cold Pig Hill, county Durham, and King's County, Ireland, in 1745.[4] According to Foot, his family were people of "wealth, respectability, and honourable connexion." By 1763 Stoney had become a lieutenant in the 13th Regiment of Foot through the influence of a relative who held high military rank. On half pay after the disbanding of his regiment, he laid siege to Hannah Newton, the ugly heiress to a Newcastle coal fortune amounting to £20,000 or more. Since his appearance (despite a hook-nose) was pleasing, his wit ready, and his address captivating, he succeeded in his campaign. But his victory was Miss Newton's undoing.

> He behaved like a brute and a savage to his wife [relates an acquaintance], and in a short time broke her heart. He knew secret ways of provoking her before company and then if she looked displeased, or said any thing tart, he appealed to the company—HE TOOK PAINS TO PLEASE HER, BUT COULD NOT.[5]

After his wife's death, Stoney repaired to London. There he fell in with the shabby dandies of the metropolis.

> His associations [writes Foot] were all of that sort, which idle and uneducated men of pleasure pick up at the gaming houses, clubs, horse races, watering places, &c. In such a society, all are much upon a level in point of morals. They carry on a traffic amongst each other, exchange their horses, their dogs, and their mistresses, for the capricious accommodation of one another; and they keep a sharp look out for the opportunity of obtaining money, and improving their fortunes, from heir or heiress, by play or marriage, no matter which.[6]

Among Stoney's acquaintances was another county Durham heiress, Mary Eleanor, daughter of George Bowes of Streatlam Castle and Gibside Park. She was born in 1749 and in 1767 had married the ninth Earl of Strathmore. The match was not a happy one, for this unintellectual and convivial gentleman was as much bewildered by his *bas bleu* wife's linguistic and scientific accomplishments as by her taste for poetry and sentiment. Indeed, the odd admirers whom she gathered around her caused her house in Grosvenor Square to be known as the Temple of Folly. When the Earl died unexpectedly on 7 March 1776, he left his widow with a large if embarrassed estate.

It was clear that Lady Strathmore would not long remain unmarried. Though she had several children, she was still young and of a warm and susceptible temperament. For a time a certain Mr. Gray appeared to be the favoured suitor, but soon Stoney began to show the form that had earlier won him Miss Newton. He sent Lady Strathmore letters purporting to come from one of his forsaken mistresses, which she was led to believe were inspired by the malice of Gray. He bribed the people around Lady Strathmore to promote his interest with her. But his master-stroke was to get himself wounded in a duel with the Reverend Mr. Bate, editor of the *Morning Post,* in the columns of which had appeared letters from "HAMLET" comparing Lady Strathmore's faithlessness and ungovernable appetites to those of Claudius's Gertrude.

This affair delighted Lady Strathmore's romantic imagination. "She blessed even the sword that was used by [Stoney] in the duel, took it home with her, and slept with it constantly at the head of her bed." She wrote a poem entitled "On the Nuptials," in which she proclaimed:

> Unmov'd, MARIA saw the splendid SUITE
> Of rival captives sighing at her feet,
> 'Till in her cause, his sword young S–n-y drew,
> And to revenge, the gallant wooer flew!
> Bravest among the brave!—and first to prove,
> By death! or conquest! WHO best knew to love!
> But pale, and faint, the wounded lover lies,
> While more than pity fills MARIA's eyes!
> In her soft breast! where passion long had strove,
> Resistless sorrow fix'd the reign of LOVE!
> "Dear youth," she cries, "we meet no more to part!
> "Then take thy honour's due,—my BLEEDING heart!" [7]

And on 17 January 1777, four days after the duel, she married Stoney—his rival Gray, who might otherwise have made trouble, being silenced by a substantial bribe.

For a time Bowes (as he was now called, for he had assumed his wife's family name) tried to make a place for himself in respectable society. He served as sheriff of Durham, was Member of Parliament from Newcastle from 1780 to 1784, and even aspired to an Irish peerage. But his natural propensities could not long be restrained, and he was shortly leading a life of unbridled licence, for which he paid by realizing whatever he could from his wife's estate. Lady Strathmore's infatuation with Bowes, reinforced by her love for the son whom she bore him in 1782, led her to consent to these depredations, to overlook his series of mistresses, and to bear cheerfully the loss of the comforts and dignities to which she was accustomed. But his brutality at last proved more than she could bear. He displayed "a miserable sort of energy . . . without any common and fair defined motive," Foot relates, which found its outlet in "beating, scratching, biting, pinching, whipping, kicking, imprisoning, insulting, provoking, tormenting, mortifying, degrading, tyrannizing, cajoling, deceiving, lying, starving, forcing, compelling, and a new torment, wringing of the heart." [8]

Early in 1785 Lady Strathmore escaped from her torturer, and within three months she "exhibited articles of the peace in the Court of King's Bench, against her husband . . . for ill treatment of her person." [9] It was revealed that she had executed an antenuptial deed of trust that invalidated all of his business transactions. Bowes was hard put to counter these proceedings. He could only produce certain "confessions" of misconduct which he had forced his wife to write; but these were of little use, since they dealt with her behaviour before her second marriage. On 10 November 1786 he adopted the desperate expedient of abducting Lady Strathmore and carrying her off to Durham, where he endeavoured by further brutality to make her sign a paper agreeing to return to him and to abandon her lawsuit. After eleven days she was rescued, and abduction was added to the charges against her husband.

In 1787 Bowes was sentenced to three years' imprisonment for this offence; and when Lady Strathmore was granted a decree of separation and divorce two years later, he was kept on in prison for indebtedness. Legal action and appeals to his wife alike proved ineffectual, though when Lady Strathmore died, she was buried at Westminster Abbey in her bridal dress; and Bowes remained within King's Bench Prison and its rules until his own death in 1810. Even there his way of life did not alter. "Bowes considered all females as natural game," Foot comments, "and hunted them down as so many FERAE NATURAE." [10] In the leisure left him by law affairs, he pursued his career of seduction. One of his victims, a Miss S——, became his *maîtresse en titre,* bore him five children, and looked after him in his declining years. In his *Autobiography* Leigh Hunt provides a glimpse of Bowes in his last scene: "a tall thin man, in a cocked hat, [who] had an aquiline nose, and altogether appeared to my childish eyes a strangely inconsistent-looking person for a man of his character, and much of a gentleman." [11]

Bowes's appalling personality and career excited Thackeray's interest because he found in them the supreme example of what had been his main subject throughout his early fiction: the scoundrel-gentleman. As with Deuceace, Crabs, Galgenstein, Brandon, Brough, and Captain Walker, but on a far grander scale, he could by anatomizing Bowes as Barry Lyndon exercise his "sense of the meanly false, of the desperately wicked"; for as Foot pointed out, Bowes's story was "a masterpiece of villainy," beside which even Lovelace's paled in comparison. "Who can say, after this," he inquired, "that fictitious characters, as they are drawn by the novelist, can be ever overstrained?" [12]

Though as late as October, 1841, Thackeray still hoped to devote the winter to *Barry Lyndon,* other tasks intervened, and he did not begin his novel until October, 1843.[13] "The Luck of Barry Lyndon; A Romance of the Last Century. By Fitz-Boodle" began its course in *Fraser's Magazine* in January, 1844, and continued until the end of the year. During this period Thackeray kept only a chapter or two ahead of the printer; indeed, Nickisson had to omit the October instalment for want of copy. From the first he experienced "a great deal of dullness unwillingness & labor" in writing his novel. It required far more reading than he had anticipated, and he found its subject increasingly uncongenial. By August he was complaining that it lay "like a night-mare" on his mind, and during his Eastern tour he found it a veritable old man of the sea, hanging round his neck and preventing him from enjoying the sights. He finished the story at last on 3 November 1844, though "slowly & with great difficulty" and "after great throes," in time to get his manuscript to Nickisson for the December issue of *Fraser's*.[14]

In the more than two years that intervened between Thackeray's learning of Bowes's history and his beginning *Barry Lyndon,* his conception of his subject had been greatly elaborated. His visit to Ireland suggested the setting for Barry's early years, a period not treated by Foot. What could be more appropriate than to present Barry as part of the *"vilain petite noblesse"* which he had seen in that country, as a young man "gross, arrogant, frivolous and ignorant," absorbed in a purely animal life, and knowing no book but the *Racing Calendar?*[15] Thackeray's extensive reading for his magazine articles bore fruit in his account of Barry's young manhood on the Continent. Casanova's *Memoirs* proved useful in describing the gambling campaigns of Barry and the Chevalier his uncle; and he took "The Tragical History of the Princess of X——" from an obscure work by Baron de la Mothe-Langon, *L'Empire, ou dix ans sous Napoléon*.[16] So extensively did these accretions bulk out his story, indeed, that two-thirds of the novel deals with Barry's early life, and only one-third with the episodes drawn from Bowes's career. No doubt Thackeray would have held the balance more nearly even, if *Barry Lyndon* had been less coolly received and if he himself had not tired of his novel long before he finished it.

Still, Barry's character remained firmly anchored to that of Bowes, and Thackeray's idea of using a rascal as the protagonist of a substantial novel remained the leading feature of his story. This conception associates *Barry Lyndon* with the extensive literature of roguery;[17] yet the novel really has little in common with such earlier rogue tales as Smollett's *Ferdinand Count Fathom*. Among antecedent works it is closest in spirit to *Castle Rackrent* and to Captain Freeny's autobiography on the one hand, and to *Jonathan Wild* on the other. The monstrous complacency with which Barry recounts his adventures—a crucial aspect of Thackeray's method, incidentally, since the effect of the book derives from the constant disparity between Barry's point of view and the reader's—brings to mind the simple Thady Quirk in Maria Edgeworth's story, who so loyally upholds the deplorable behaviour of his successive masters. There too, as Brander Matthews has pointed out, "the tale . . . is put in the mouth of one who is forever praising those whom we despise at once, although all our information about them comes to us from the self-appointed eulogist." [18] Equally relevant is the threepenny chap-book purporting to be the autobiography of the Irish highwayman Captain James Freeny which Thackeray read one rainy evening in Galway. Taken by "the noble *naïveté* and simplicity" displayed by this desperado in recounting his own adventures and by his untroubled confidence in his own excellence and high deserts, Thackeray had inquired whether there might not be much profit in "an historical work of which our champion should be the hero." [19] Yet Thackeray had much more to communicate in *Barry Lyndon* than the rather elementary formula suggested by these two works would permit. He wanted Barry's career to illustrate the fallaciousness of the world's estimate of "luck" or success. Hence he showed how completely Barry's prosperity failed to bring him happiness. And he desired to bring out the terrible change worked on the as yet plastic character of a young man by adherence to false standards of gentlemanliness. Hence he showed Barry, led astray by a mistaken conception of honour, turning from the not "ungenerous scapegrace of the early chapters, and the not altogether hateful *picaro* of the middle . . . into the unmitigated and even cowardly scoundrel of the end." [20] In these more searching purposes Thackeray found the example of *Jonathan Wild* invaluable. Since 1836 he had been meditating on the "greatness" of Fielding's antihero,[21] and the complex and sophisticated irony with which worldly and humanly reasonable standards are contrasted in this book helped him to arrive at his mode of treatment in *Barry Lyndon*.

In character portrayal, style, the imaginative realization of a past age, and the powerful communication of a coherent view of life, *Barry Lyndon* was by far the strongest work in fiction that Thackeray had done. It also revealed an unexpected gift for adventure narrative, which was later to attain its full development in *Esmond* and *Denis Duval.* During his Irish visit Thackeray had noted that in "Hibernian novels . . . the heroes pass through a thousand wild extravagant dangers, such as could only have been invented when art was young and faith was large." [22] It was Thackeray's distinctive achievement in *Barry Lyndon* to render plausible by realistic treatment a careful selection from such episodes without thereby depriving them of their interest as stirring adventures. Yet despite these merits the book has never been a favourite with Thackeray's admirers. It is too severe and impersonal for a taste in harmony with his later books. It has appealed most strongly, indeed, to readers who do not particularly care for Thackeray and are pleased to discover, as Saintsbury puts it, a book by him "less sentimental, less English, more profitably provided with gloom and grime" [23] than his major novels.

Certainly *Barry Lyndon* did not succeed as a serial. Thackeray's motives for telling the story were misunderstood and his irony taken literally. To put obtuse readers on the right track, indeed, he had finally to resort to the inartistic device of explanatory editorial asides.[24] When Bedingfield expressed his admiration for the novel, Thackeray replied that "he *meant* it to be good; but he had cut it short, because he was afraid of the public." [25] Though he had proposed *Barry Lyndon* to Fraser in 1841 with a view to making "a handsome saleable volume" out of it at the conclusion of its serial appearance,[26] by December of 1844, this plan was clearly impracticable. The novel was not destined to be issued in book form until D. Appleton & Company of New York published a pirated edition of it in 1852. Its first English book appearance was in the third volume of Thackeray's *Miscellanies* in 1856.

Thus *Barry Lyndon* neatly illustrates Thackeray's dilemma as a professional writer in the years before *Vanity Fair.* He anxiously desired a success which continually evaded his grasp. This explains the extravagant glee with which he reported to his mother, while travelling in Ireland during 1842, that "a man on the coach, quoted *by heart* a passage out of Titmarsh! . . . It was all I could do not to embrace him, and say the Great

Titmarsh is at this moment by your side." [27] He had tried his best to "chasten and otherwise popularize" his style; [28] he even brought himself to take seriously the preposterous accusation of "vulgarity" that excessively genteel critics had brought against his early work.[29] The upshot of his efforts was merely to strengthen his position as a periodical writer. "I can suit the magazines," he wrote in June, 1845, "but I can't hit the public, be hanged to them." [30] No wonder that he racked his brains for an answer to his question: "How are we to take this great stupid public by the ears?" [31] No wonder that he complained again and again of the irresponsiveness of "that most cold-blooded and precise of all personages, the respectable and respected English reader." [32] As he later told Bedingfield, he had "fought fiercely" for popularity,[33] and thus far his fight had been to little avail. But his troubles were nearly over. Within three years his work for another periodical was to give him the secure position that long and devoted service to *Fraser's Magazine* had left well beyond his grasp.

13

The "Punch" Connexion

I

PUNCH, OR THE "LONDON CHARIVARI," was founded early in 1841 in imitation of Philipon's famous Parisian journal.[1] Mark Lemon used to tell how "he was at the sea side when Henry Mayhew wrote—'Come to town—here's a man [presumably Ebenezer Landells, the engraver] with a notion for a comic paper, & he has £2000 to lose.' "[2] The first number appeared, with Lemon and Mayhew as coeditors and at the modest price of threepence, on 17 July 1841. Apart from the editors, the chief contributors were Douglas Jerrold and Gilbert à Beckett. "Jerrold was paid £2 a week," Lemon recollected, "the rest £1."[3]

The magazine's prospects were initially very bleak. A circulation of 10,000 was needed to make it succeed, and for months no issue sold more than 6,000 copies. *Punch's* contributors were men of education and intelligence who sought to appeal to literate and well-informed readers, but unhappily this audience was suspicious of comic papers. At the magazine's coming-of-age dinner in 1862, "Pater" Evans recalled that "Punch met with obloquy at its start, as its printer & Engraver were those of 'The Town,' & other ribald comic papers. Ribaldry & dirt were inseparable from comicality until Punch came."[4] Yet gradually *Punch* made its way. The first *Punch Almanac* was a hit. The responsible firm of Bradbury and Evans became its printers and then its proprietors. By the end of 1842 *Punch* was firmly established.

Thackeray first began to write for *Punch* in June of 1842 against the advice of Edward FitzGerald, who urged a common friend on 22 May of that year: "Tell Thackeray not to go to *Punch* yet." [5] His own doubts are reflected in a letter of 11 June, in which he told his mother that it was "a very low paper . . . —only its good pay, and a great opportunity for unrestrained laughing sneering kicking and gambadoing." [6] His principal contribution during this year was the series "Miss Tickletoby's Lectures on English History," which made no impression. Thackeray withdrew in good humour, pleading that he had done his best, "just as much as if I had been writing for any more dignified periodical," and warning that he would soon "make another attempt upon 'Punch'." [7] During 1843 he contributed drawings and occasional articles, but it was not until 1844 that he established a firm connexion with the magazine.

During the first three years of its existence, Albert Smith had been one of *Punch's* most regular writers. But he was disliked by both Jerrold and Lemon, and when the latter heard that Smith was accustomed "to show his [*Punch*] proofs at the Cheshire Cheese," [8] he procured Smith's dismissal. By 18 December 1843 Thackeray had evidently been assured that Smith's place was to be his, for he wrote to his mother that he was to have his own way "with the worthy Mr Punch, whose pay is more than double of that I get anywhere else." [9] And in June of 1844 he told his mother that he was relying for his income on "the mighty Punch above all," that "Mr Punch is the great card." [10] From 1844 until 1851 he remained a regular contributor, though he never wrote nearly as much for the magazine as did its two work-horses, Jerrold and à Beckett.[11]

Thackeray's accession to *Punch* in 1844 was the step that put him at last on the high road to fame and fortune, as he himself later freely admitted. "If it had not been for *Punch*," he once remarked to the engraver Joseph Swain, "I wonder where I should be!" [12] Yet real success on the magazine came slowly. At first he contributed chiefly short articles and "fillers" on subjects considered to fall within his particular province, notably national peculiarities and the arts. Thackeray was adroit at underlining the points of Irish, French, American, and Jewish behaviour that John Bull found absurd, and since *Punch* at this time was defiantly British and insular, these reaffirmations of national prejudice were very welcome. He enjoyed signalizing Irish chuckle-headedness, as illustrated in "bulls." And though he was genuinely sympathetic with Irish suffering, he was opposed to violence as a remedy for it. His irrational but profound dislike of certain characteristics that he regarded as peculiarly Gallic—bloodthirstiness, braggadocio, and lubricity—led him to join enthusiastically in *Punch's* ridicule of the French. The violence of American public life, the illegitimate curiosity concerning the personal habits of celebrities displayed by American reporters, and the peculiarities of American English caught Thackeray's eye. And he shared what Spielmann calls the magazine's "merry prejudice" against the Jews, "directed against manners rather than against men," [13] of which even Mark Lemon approved.

Thackeray had a free hand in attacking the absurdities of current writing and painting. His first contribution in 1842 had been a good-natured satirical extravaganza concerning John Abraham Heraud and his bad poetry.[14] The flimsy fiction of Ainsworth, Lady Blessington, and Bulwer drew his fire. And the gross puffery that accompanied new and unnecessary works by such booksellers' hacks as James Grant he considered fair game. Thackeray said relatively little about the fine arts in *Punch,* because he was already dealing with them at length in *Fraser's Magazine.* But he could not resist occasional *jeux d'esprit* such as the following mock catalogue entries for the "Academy Exhibition" of 1844 under the name "Trundler, R. A.":

34. A Typhoon bursting in a simoon over the whirlpool of Malestrom, Norway, with a ship on fire, an eclipse, and the effect of a lunar rainbow.

> O Art, how vast thy misty wonders are,
> To those who roam upon the extraordinary deep;
> Malestrom thy hand is here.
>
> *From an unpublished Poem.*

4. (Great Room). HIPPOPOTAMUSES at play in the river Scamander.
1311. The Duke of Wellington and the Shrimp (Seringapatam, early Suarin).

> And it can be, thou hideous imp,
> That life is ah! how brief, and glory but a shrimp!
> *From an unpublished Poem.*

We must protest against the Duke's likeness here; for though his grace is short, his face is not of an emerald-green colour; and it is his coat, not his boots, which are vermillion; nor is it fair to make the shrimp (a blue one) taller than the conqueror of Assaye; with this trifling difference of opinion, we are bound to express our highest admiration of this work. It is the greatest that the English school of quiet landscape has produced. The comet just rising in the foreground, and the conflagration of TIPPOO's widow in the Banyan forest by the seashore, are in the great artist's happiest manner.[15]

The eccentricities of J. M. W. Turner's later style fare no better here than does that artist's *Fallacies of Hope;* yet Thackeray's jollity is so infectious that most of the sting is removed.

But *Punch* reputations were made by series, not by occasional articles. Thackeray's first success in this line was with the travel narratives of the "Fat Contributor," begun 3 August 1844. He here transferred to *Punch* what he had already begun in *Fraser's Magazine,* that frank exploitation of certain aspects of his private personality which led him four years later to confess to Edward Chapman: "I have pushed the caricaturing of myself almost to affectation." [16] When *Punch* introduces "the fattest of our contributors," he is about to leave London on the advice of his physician, for he is "as white as a sheet—as puffy as a bolster," [17] and there are eleven more dinners in his invitation book. The papers that follow tell of his visits to Brighton, Dover, and France, and even of his penetration to the Mediterranean and the Near East; but wherever he goes, the reader's interest remains firmly centred in him, not in what he sees. The Fat Contributor is a great gormandizer (at the table d'hôte of the Hotel de Suède in Brussels he eats fifty-four dishes in three days), devoted to all creature comforts, and very lazy. A discontented bachelor, he has a comic weakness for pretty women; a traveller who prides himself on his *savoir faire,* he is constantly making the most obvious blunders. And so the reader quickly comes to tolerate, even to like him, because of the ludicrous fashion in which his assumptions of superiority are contradicted by hard reality.

More interesting than the Fat Contributor's adventures, which are chiefly of the farcical sort, is the *blasé* and superior attitude of mind that he displays. Everything is brought to the bar of London standards. At Athens, for example, he finds the ruins of little interest, since they may all be paralleled by the Greek revival buildings of London, which are, moreover, "in much better preservation." The Temple of Theseus, he discovers, is "of the exact colour and mouldiness of a ripe Stilton cheese." [18] When he visits Egypt, his great achievement is to post a bill advertising *Punch* on the Pyramid of Cheops. "I suggest this scene, this moment, this attitude," he writes, "to the committee of the Fine Arts as a proper subject for the Houses of Parliament—*Punch* pointing to the Pyramids, and introducing civilization to Egypt—I merely throw it out as a suggestion." [19]

It need hardly be said that Thackeray's target here is the pretensions of the English abroad, not the short-comings of the lands that they visit. Hence James Hannay's regret that Thackeray should have stooped "to a little cockneyism . . . in these travelling sketches in which he attempted to diminish the veneration inspired by the Pyramids" [20] is itself rather absurd. But Hannay's further charge that Thackeray "spoke lightly of the sacred recollections belonging to the scenes of classical antiquity," though oddly phrased, is more solidly grounded. Here Thackeray drops the mask of the Fat Contributor and speaks for himself in a passage that underlines the unresolved bitterness of his mind at this period. Ever since he was thrashed by a "brute of a schoolmaster" for not mastering Greek grammar, he writes, he had entertained "doubts about the classics."

When then I came to Athens, and saw that it was a humbug, I hailed the fact with a sort of gloomy joy. I stood in the Royal Square and cursed the country which has made thousands of little boys miserable. They have blue stripes on the New Greek flag; I thought bitterly of my own. I wished that my schoolmaster had been in the place, that we might have fought there for the right; and that I might have immolated him as a sacrifice to the manes of little boys flogged into premature Hades, or pining away and sickening under the destiny of that infernal Greek grammar. I have often thought that those little cherubs who are carved on tombstones and are represented as possessing a head and wings only, are designed to console little children—usher- and beadle-belaboured—and say 'There is no flogging where we are.' From their conformation, it is impossible. Woe to the man who has harshly treated one of them! [21]

But this is a rare moment of acerbity. For the most part the Fat Contributor is content to amuse, and modest popularity was Thackeray's reward.

Thackeray's next *Punch* series, "The Diary of C. Jeames de la Pluche, Esq.," began on 2 August 1845. He here took as his subject the mania for speculating in railway shares, by which he had himself, along with most of the rest of well-to-do England, recently been touched; and his story of a footman who made and lost a fortune by his paper-operations scored a notable topical hit. It was piratically dramatized, indeed, and performed at the Princess's Theatre.[22] But except for its contemporary application, the series is substantially a combination of *The Yellowplush Papers* and *The Great Hoggarty Diamond.* The former gave Thackeray his footman's English, and from the second he took the contrast of world and domestic standards on which his plot turns. In his ingenuousness and good feeling Jeames resembles Sam Titmarsh rather than Yellowplush; and in his abandonment of Mary Hann Oggins, his pursuit of Lady Hangelina, and his ultimate marriage with Mary Hann and their establishment at the Wheel of Fortune public house, he follows, at a lower level, much the same spiral through the social scale that Sam had traced. The story is a trifle with little novelty to recommend it, then, but slight as it is, Thackeray's execution has such verve and inventiveness that the piece remains amusing today.

"Jeames's Diary" ended as a connected narrative on 7 February 1846, though Thackeray on several later occasions resuscitated Jeames as a commentator on current events. "The Snobs of England," by far the most significant of Thackeray's *Punch* series, began three weeks later. But fully to understand the Snob papers, we must inquire into Thackeray's relations with the *Punch* circle, a group that among his literary friends exceeds even the Fraserians in importance, and trace the process by which his political and social views were modified during the course of his early association with this magazine.

II

By enlisting as a "*Punch* man" Thackeray joined forces with a remarkably able and interesting group of writers and artists. Mark Lemon, who became sole editor after Bradbury and Evans bought *Punch* in 1842, was a shrewd, jovial, and warm-hearted Jew—fat, even roly-poly, in figure, and merry in manner. His father having died when he was a child, Lemon was brought up by a grandfather, who put him into the family hop business when he was fifteen. Employment followed as a clerk in Verey's brewery, Kentish Town, and as the manager of the Shakespeare Head Tavern in Wych Street. But Lemon had early fallen in love with literature, and in 1835 he began his long career as a playwright with a farce for the Strand Theatre. For some years he and his wife (whom he is supposed to have married on a borrowed five-pound note) eked out a scanty living from his plays and magazine writings, but he was on the point of going under as a journalist when Henry Mayhew threw him *Punch* as a lifeline. He proved an admirable editor. "His system," Henry Silver reported after a conversation with him many years later, "is to let each man write what he likes, subject to ML's supervision. 'All cleverer fellows than I am'—says he." [1] He soon gave up his own writing in order to devote all his ingenuity to guiding the policies of *Punch* and minimizing clashes of personality among its contributors. Fellow staff members affectionately called him "Uncle Mark," but they respected him as much as they liked him. He could take a firm stand when the need arose, and on one occasion he even faced down John Forster, who was then supposed to be all-powerful with Bradbury and Evans as their literary adviser.[2]

In 1844 Douglas Jerrold was far and away *Punch's* best-known man. The contrast between his very short, slender, and slightly stooping figure and his massive head was sufficiently striking. His sharp features, bright blue eyes, bushy eyebrows, and above all his "long, light, falling hair, which, in moments of great excitement, he tossed about as a lion does its mane," [3] made his appearance unforgettable. Though he was a simple and unaffected man, his fiery temper (exacerbated by the almost constant pain that he suffered from recurrent rheumatism) made him ready to resent any fancied injury, and his impulsiveness sometimes led him to say severe things even to his friends. Since Jerrold was an authentic wit, after Sydney Smith the most notable of his age, these personal epigrams often became firmly fixed in the general memory. His treatment of casual acquaintances is exampled in his remarks to John Abraham Heraud, the minor versifier whom we have mentioned as the butt of Thackeray's satire. Heraud having inquired if Jerrold had seen his *Descent into Hell* (an epic poem), Jerrold answered: "No, but I should dearly like to." When a friend asked why Heraud always had dirty hands, Jerrold's explanation was, "From his habit of constantly putting them up to his face." But so irrepressible was Jerrold's sarcasm that he was scarcely less trenchant in speaking of his own wife. When she had reached middle age, he jokingly told her "that he wished wives were like bank notes, so that one of forty could be changed into two of twenty." Asked on another occasion who was dancing with her, he replied, "Some member of the Humane society." [4]

Jerrold's acerbity was in part the result of a particularly difficult early life. He was born in 1803, the son of an itinerant actor, and while very young he twice appeared on the stage himself— "when he was carried on by Edmund Kean in *Rolla;* and when he appeared as the child in *The Stranger."* [5] His education was scanty and brief. "Self-helped and self-guided," he later recalled, "I began the world at an age when, as a general rule, boys have not laid down their primers; . . . the cockpit of a man-of-war was at thirteen exchanged for the struggle of London." [6] During his two years as a midshipman Jerrold contracted from the floggings that he had to witness a lifelong hatred of authority tyrannically exercised; and in the years that followed as a working printer he came to know London poverty at first hand. He wrote his first play in 1821; and during the ensuing decade his chief occupation was the production of farces and melodramas for the managers of the despised transpontine theatres, for Davidge of the Royal Cobourg and Elliston of the Surrey. He remained permanently indignant with these worthies for their niggardly rate of payment (his average remuneration was £20 a play) at a time when the needs of his growing family (he had married in 1824) were particularly acute. Only with the success of his nautical melodrama *Black-eyed Susan* in 1829 did he receive an invitation to write for the patent houses Drury Lane and Covent Garden, and even then his financial troubles were not over. He still lived in a world of duns, bailiffs, sponging-houses, and occasional flights to the Continent. The effect of this long experience of poverty and injustice upon Jerrold's fiery temper and independent mind was to turn him into a convinced radical. He read Cobbett and Leigh Hunt eagerly and was converted to their political creed. Though as sensitive to the beauty of the poetry of Wordsworth and Coleridge as to that of Burns and Shelley, he considered Wordsworth "a snob or a scoundrel" and Coleridge "a sot and a tyrant." [7] Indeed, after *Black-eyed Susan* earned him a measure of freedom of expression, he made a major theme of the dramas that followed, the exposure of the defects in English society as they appeared to the radicals of the age.[8]

The reputation that Jerrold achieved as a dramatist launched him on a new career as a journalist. In 1832 he edited for nearly four months a paper called *Punch in London,* notable for its "attacks on the triple giants, snobbery, toadyism and humbug." [9] In his subsequent contributions to such periodicals as the *Examiner,* the *New Monthly Magazine,* and *Blackwood's,* he necessarily had to moderate the expression of his radical views. But in *Heads of the People* (1840), which he himself edited, he enjoyed a freer hand. A characteristic sketch of John Bull in the preface trenchantly hits off English deference to wealth, to position, and to old institutions and customs simply because they are old:

Does John value titles? [Jerrold inquires] Hear the contemptuous roar with which, in the parlour of "The King's Head," he talks of them. "What's a title?" he will ask; "it's the man, eh?" And next week Lord Bubblebrain puts up for the county; and, condescending to ask John Bull for his vote, John stands almost awe-struck at his porch, smooths his hair, smiles, smirks, bows, and feels that there is a sort of white magic in the looks and words of a lord. He stammers out a promise of a plumper, bows his lordship to the gate, and then declares to his neighbours that "It warn't for the title he gave his vote—he should hope not; no, he wouldn't sell his country in that way. But Lord Bubblebrain *is* a gentleman, and knows what's right for the people." And then, John's wife remarks, how affable his lordship was to the children, and especially to the sick baby; which John receives as a matter of course; shortly observing, that "no gentleman could do less; not that he gave his vote for any such doings." [10]

In *Punch* Jerrold for some years had the prevailing voice on political questions, with results that will shortly be set forth.

Henry Mayhew, who married Jerrold's daughter, was, after his father-in-law, the most notable of *Punch's* writers at the time that Thackeray joined the staff. He was an indolent and irresponsible man who loved conversation as much as he hated writing, and though he made a good living, his improvidence kept him almost always in debt. His demotion from the coeditorship of *Punch* was a logical step, though it left him somewhat resentful. He remained for a time "Suggestor-in-Chief," a post for which his unfailing flow of ingenious ideas particularly qualified him, but he withdrew as a writer in 1845, and in the following year he ceased even to attend the *Punch* dinners. He was responsible, it appears, for *Punch's* most famous joke: "Advice to persons about to marry,—don't"; but few of his other contributions attracted much attention. His friends used to contend that his real gift was for systematic thought, and that given proper opportunities he might have rivalled John Stuart Mill or Herbert Spencer. As it was, of all his grandiose schemes only *Punch* and the celebrated *London Labour and the London Poor* came to fruition.[11]

Gilbert à Beckett [12] was as methodical as Henry Mayhew was erratic. The son of a barrister of some standing, he had received the education of a gentleman at Westminster School; but he quarrelled with his father when the latter refused to support his protest to the school authorities against bullying, and took to journalism to support himself. During the 1830s he wrote many plays and edited a variety of cheap papers, of which only *Figaro in London* achieved success. The precarious nature of this employment is suggested by the story John Leech used to tell of "Gil a Beckett being locked up with a deal table, pen & ink & a gin bottle, when Figaro was short of 'copy.' " [13] Before joining *Punch* he had been called to the bar, and he made his first hits in that magazine with his contributions by "Mr. Briefless" and his "Comic Blackstone." He went on from the latter to *The Comic History of England* and *The Comic History of Rome,* which remained his best-known works. In 1849 his legal training gained him an appointment as police-magistrate, which he held until his death. Vizetelly describes him as "the quietest and most diffident of men, singularly retiring in manner." [14] Though he and Thackeray were never close friends, they saw eye to eye on most social and political questions. Thackeray's references to "à Beckett the beak" are uniformly cordial.

Punch's other writers in 1844 were less important. Percival Leigh, who had been a medical student with Leech and Albert Smith, practised for some time as a surgeon before he turned to journalism. He was known on the staff as "The Professor," because of his accurate knowledge of Shakespeare and the Latin poets, and Spielmann holds that he was largely responsible for introducing into *Punch* "the assumption of scholarship in its readers." [15] He was a kindly and reserved man of gentlemanly manners, in whom Thackeray found a firm friend. A reliable but not a brilliant worker, he scored no remarkable success in *Punch.* Horace ("Pony") Mayhew, younger brother of Henry, owed his nickname to the fact that he had first joined the staff as a subeditor or "pony." He was never a well-known or fertile contributor. An extremely handsome and aristocratic-looking man, he became bald early in life; and in the later 1850s Thackeray sometimes greeted him at Evans's with "Ah, here comes Colonel Newcome!" [16] This greeting was not altogether appropriate. As is suggested by his other nickname, "the wicked old Marquis," he was a great *coureur de filles,* and some twenty years later Du Maurier noted that "all his handsome models say of HM 'C'est mon pere!' " [17] When he was married, Mark Lemon joked about "the Haymarket night houses being closed in consequence." [18] Mention may finally be made of Tom Taylor, just recruited to the staff in 1844, who had recently come to London from the University of Cambridge to study for the bar. A man of considerable taste and learning, very well regarded by his colleagues, he was neither witty nor inventive; and though he later became editor of *Punch,* he did his best work for the stage rather than for that magazine.

Towards all of these men except Jerrold, Thackeray's feelings were cordial; but his closest friends on the *Punch* staff were its two artists John Leech and Richard Doyle. Thackeray had known Leech [19] as a boy, it will be remembered, and when they were reunited, he used to remark that it was "curious how Charterh^e has eventuated in Punch." [20] In the intervening years Leech's experience had been almost as exhausting as Thackeray's. John Leech senior had an uncle who made a fortune as owner of the London Coffee-House, Ludgate Hill. When this gentleman retired, he left his nephew in charge. But though the elder Leech is described as "an Irishman, a man of fine culture, a profound Shakespearian scholar, and a thorough gentleman," [21] he had no business sense; and the London Coffee-House went rapidly downhill under his management. Financial disaster overtook him shortly after 1833, when his son left Charterhouse. His father's embarrassments caused Leech to be held in sponging-houses on two occasions,[22] and in later years the old man's expensive habits prevented Leech from saving money,[23] despite the fact that he earned more than £40,000 during his association with *Punch.*

For a brief period before his father's bankruptcy Leech studied at Bartholomew's Hospital and under two well-known London surgeons. Then his family's need for money led him to abandon medicine for drawing, a talent of which he had early given evidence and from which he could expect quicker financial returns. He was entirely self-taught in art, and success did not come quickly. But in 1840 he supplied three plates for the first series of *Ingoldsby Legends* and began his long connexion with *Bentley's Miscellany,* and in the following year his accession to the staff of *Punch* ensured his future prosperity.

In 1843 Leech saw Ann Eaton in a London street. "Following her home," Kitton relates, "he noted the number of the house, looked out the name, obtained an introduction, and married the lady." [24] He quickly became domesticated, and his preoccupation with family life was henceforth reflected in his drawings for *Punch*. The "plump young beauties" of *Punch's* "pictorial harem" he drew from Mrs. Leech; and his children, when they came, also served as models. He and his wife delighted in entertaining his *Punch* colleagues at their simple home, Rose Cottage. After Leech's death Mark Lemon lamented "those dear old days when Leech first married & what a pleasant little unaffected wife he had & how delightful were the little homely banquets of mutton & gin & water to which she invited his friends." [25]

Leech was "tall, strongly but delicately made, graceful, long-limbed, with a grave, handsome face, a sensitive gentle mouth —but a mouth that could be 'set'—deep, penetrating eyes, an open, high, and broad forehead, finely modelled." [26] He was quiet, unassertive, and considerate in manner, but abnormally sensitive to noise and given to melancholy. His chief contribution to the gaiety of convivial occasions, which he greatly enjoyed, was to sing Procter's "King Death" in his fine bass voice. With increasing prosperity he was able to return to the gentlemanly ways in which he had been trained at home and at Charterhouse. He became passionately devoted to fishing, riding, and hunting to hounds; and he developed a fine palate for wine. "I'm a man of extremely simple tastes," he used to say with characteristically gentle irony. "Give me my claret & my hunter & I ask not for more." [27]

Hardly less dear to Thackeray than Leech was Richard ("Dicky") Doyle, who had joined *Punch* in 1843 at the age of nineteen. Doyle was the son of "H. B.," the famous political caricaturist, who between 1829 and 1851 produced portraits of most public figures of the age. Thackeray greatly admired

"H. B." 's lithographs for the novel gentility and distinction that they had brought to English popular art, remarking in 1840 the "polite points of wit [in his pictures], which strike one as exceedingly clever and pretty, and cause one to smile in a quiet, gentlemanlike kind of way." His son, whose mastery of drawing was quite precocious, joined to his father's gentlemanliness a charm and fancy that were altogether his own. His quaint and individual manner caused his *Punch* colleagues to call him the "Professor of Mediaeval Design." Young Doyle was small, shy, and ill at ease among the *Punch* writers (some of whom distrusted him because he was Irish and a Catholic), and Thackeray from the first took him under his protection, praising his work as the opportunity offered in *Fraser's Magazine* [28] and the *Morning Chronicle*.[29]

On the occasion of *Punch's* attaining its fiftieth volume, Mark Lemon remarked at the *Punch* table that "the Punch Brotherhood has been one of the most extraordinary literary brotherhoods the world has ever seen. . . . And in our working together, proprietors & contributors, lies the secret of our great success." [30] This team-work was particularly promoted by the weekly staff dinners, held on Wednesday evenings at six o'clock on the first floor of Bradbury and Evans's place of business at 11 Bouverie Street. The proprietors sat at the head and foot of the table (which was made of deal, though Thackeray's "Mahogany Tree" is often supposed to refer to it), with the principal contributors in their regular places between them. Thackeray sat at first between Gilbert à Beckett and Jerrold but subsequently moved to the other side of the table.[31] Food was sent in, ample drink was provided, and cigars followed the meal. Conversation at first bore chiefly on the next issue of the magazine, but after the subject of the "Big Cut" was decided upon, talk would become general. Songs were a regular feature of the evening, Thackeray's favourite being "Little Billee," John Leech's "King Death," and Horace Mayhew's "The Mahogany Tree." [32]

III

Yet harmony did not always prevail at the *Punch* table or on the *Punch* staff. We have seen how diverse were the backgrounds of the magazine's principal contributors; inevitably the resulting discrepancies in manners and social tone made for uneasiness. To Thackeray and Leech, Mark Lemon's affability often seemed somewhat greasy; and they could not altogether overlook the marks left upon him by his years as mine host at the Shakespeare Head Tavern.[1] Thackeray disliked Jerrold's habit of engrossing the conversation at the *Punch* table, where he was not only the readiest but also the loudest talker,[2] and according to Mark Lemon Thackeray once quarrelled with Jerrold because he "ate peas with a knife & therefore was not fit company for him." [3] Indeed, Vizetelly notes that "unquestionably there was an utter want of sympathy between the two men." [4] Leech, too, was distressed by Jerrold's "low breeding" and used to "imitate D. Jerrold at Rose Cottage throwing his hair back & sprinkling salt with gusto over gooseberry tart." [5] Jerrold and Lemon, for their part, could not but resent the presumed superiority of Thackeray and Leech; and soon other contributors as well took sides in this clash between gentlemanly and Bohemian standards which was importantly to affect *Punch's* future.

These differences gradually came to centre in a protracted duel for supremacy between Jerrold and Thackeray. Vizetelly reports that Jerrold was "the one literary man of whom Thackeray, when in his prime, seemed to be seriously jealous. I was sometimes present when the early number of 'Punch' reached Young Street, and well remember how, as Thackeray nervously tore off the wrapper, he would exclaim, 'Now let's see what young Douglas has to say this week.' " [6] According to Bedingfield, Thackeray considered Jerrold the wittiest man he had ever known.[7] Each man said sharp things about the other. Thackeray, for example, used to tell how, when the *Punch* men one wet night were "at a little oyster-shop then facing the Strand Theatre, the barmaid Jane, thoroughly out of humour at Jerrold's chaff, slapped down before the little man the liquor he had ordered, with the words, 'There's your grog and take care you don't drown yourself.' "[8] Jerrold's jokes about Thackeray have become encrusted with a good many unhistorical additions,[9] but at least one is certainly authentic. Writing to Charles Wentworth Dilke, he remarked, "Lady —— is trying to convert Thackeray to Romanism. She had better begin at his nose."[10] This *mot* Thackeray himself used to repeat with enjoyment.[11] With such sparring in progress, mutual tolerance was the friendliest feeling that could be hoped for between the two men. So we find Thackeray remarking of Jerrold, "What is the use of quarrelling with a man if you have to meet him every Wednesday at dinner?"[12] And Dr. James Hutchinson Stirling records of a conversation with Jerrold of April, 1847, that "In answer to the inquiry 'What like was Thackeray?' he said: 'He's just a big fellow with a broken nose, and, though I meet him weekly at the *Punch* dinner, I don't know him so well as I know you.' "[13]

If this ill feeling had been simply a personal matter, it would hardly deserve detailed description. But behind it lay a profound disagreement in principle, which demands exploration. When Thackeray first joined *Punch's* staff, the magazine was by no means the comfortable conservative organ it has since become. It was still in Thackeray's phrase a "universal railer,"[14] and its staff's high spirits often found expression in unmeasured buffoonery and in personal abuse of such favourite butts as Lord Aberdeen, Lord Brougham, Sir James Graham, Joseph Hume, and even the blameless Prince Albert. During these years, as Spielmann observes, *Punch* was often "strong in the sense in which an onion is strong."[15] Along with its irresponsibility went a decided penchant for the radical view of politics and society. What Carlyle called the "Condition-of-England Question" was a subject for constant comment, and not alone in the famous political articles by Jerrold signed "Q." Other contributors added their voices, and Lemon published Tom Hood's "The Song of the Shirt" in the magazine.[16] The pages of *Punch* abounded in such squibs as "Needles and Coronets.—Great Meeting of the

Duchesses," in which Jerrold described an imaginary meeting of duchesses at Almack's where resolutions in aid of milliners and dressmakers were passed "to limit the hours of work to eight per day" and "to abolish all Sunday work, and to afford the sick early medical advice, change of air, and other necessary comforts." [17] Neither of the existing political parties had *Punch's* support. In 1842 Jerrold asked of the Whigs and Tories: "Will they call a rat-hole a rat-hole; or will they, as they have ever done, swear the hole to be a useful, healthful ventilator?" Knowing that he would get no answer, he went on to assert that "a third party—vindicating the sympathies, affections, and common rights of humanity—is rising, and must be paramount." [18]

Thackeray took little part in this aspect of *Punch's* radical campaign, but he contributed substantially to *Punch's* persistent ridicule of the snobbish veneration with which the middle classes regarded the court and the aristocracy. For *Punch* no divinity hedged a prince consort, though Queen Victoria was left largely undisturbed; and the nobility had to stand and be judged at the bar of common sense like everyone else. Thackeray joined with enthusiasm in the magazine's campaign against Prince Albert. He cheerfully poked fun at Albert's excessive fondness for his native Germany, his *de haut en bas* attitude towards his English subjects, his thriftiness, and even his behaviour while hunting—sometimes, as in the loyal Jeames de la Pluche's "Sonnick Sejested by Prince Halbert Gratiously Killing the Staggs at Sacks-Cobug-Gothy," [19] with devastating effect. Thackeray also took the lead in abusing the Court Circular, in which the trivial details of life at court were minutely set down, and in burlesquing the fashionable intelligence provided by "Jenkins," as Jerrold had christened the conservative *Morning Post*. Any suggestion, indeed, that the aristocracy should be regarded as a specially privileged class was enough to elicit sarcastic comment from Thackeray. When Lady Londonderry's absurd "Journal of a Visit to Foreign Courts" appeared in the *New Monthly Magazine*, Thackeray guyed its pomposity and callousness unmercifully. Lady Londonderry had complained that few things annoy one more "than the appearance of one's maid by one's bedside at four o'clock in the morning." Having expressed his gratification at this truly aristocratic mastery of English ("one only finds people of fashion ever use one's language in the proper way—does one?"), Thackeray pointed out that the maid who had to rise at three must have been even more annoyed.[20] When the Court Circular announced that "the Bishop of London held a confirmation on Maunday Thursday of the *juvenile nobility and gentry,*" Thackeray inquired, "Who can say the church is in danger after this?" [21] Perhaps his attitude is best summed up in a little "filler" entitled "Promotion for Brougham," which contained the announcement that this *bête noire* of *Punch* had just made "so entirely foolish and unreasonable" a speech in the House of Lords "that it is said he is to be made a Duke." [22]

The political and social views of *Punch* gave the magazine a bad reputation among the well-to-do. Harriet Martineau notes in her *Autobiography* that Jerrold was a "dreaded and unpopular man" in many circles.[23] Thackeray shared this disfavour to a certain extent. A sixpenny pamphlet of 1847 called *Anti-Punch; or, The Toy Shop in Fleet Street,* after abusing "Diddleus Jackal" (Douglas Jerrold) unmercifully, goes on to attack Thackeray as "Correggio Rafaello Snob Swamper, the most audacious biped (Benjamin Sidonia and Diddleus Jackal always excepted) in the British Empire." [24] Even after *Punch's* tone had decisively changed, largely because of Thackeray's influence, it retained among conservative readers something of its first reputation as a radical and infidel journal. There is some wryness in Thackeray's "Author's Misery" of 1848 in which he and Jerrold overhear the following conversation in a railway carriage:

OLD GENTLEMAN. 'I am sorry to see you occupied, my dear Miss Wiggets, with that trivial paper *Punch.* A railway is not a place, in my opinion, for jokes. I never joke—never.'
MISS W. 'So I should think, sir.'
OLD GENTLEMAN. 'And besides, are you aware who are the conductors of that paper, and that they are Chartists, Deists, Anarchists, and Socialists to a man? I have it from the best authority, that they meet together once a week in a tavern in St. Giles's, where they concoct their infamous Print. The chief part of their income is derived from

Threatening Letters which they send to the Nobility and Gentry. The principal Writer is a returned Convict. Two have been tried at the Old Bailey; and their Artist—as for their Artist. . . .
GUARD. 'Swin-dun! Sta-tion!'

[*Exeunt two Authors.*[25]

Though public opinion did not sharply distinguish between Thackeray and Jerrold, their political and social views were in fact very different. Jerrold's discontent with the basic organization of Victorian society was an obsession. His characteristic mood, a friendly critic admits, had become one "of righteous, but rather indiscriminate and unpractical indignation against shams, abuses, and inequalities." [26] For him *Punch's* justification lay in its role as a spokesman for "the people," in the exposure its columns provided of the misery that underlay the splendid Victorian upper world, in its assertion of the "rights of poverty" against the "rights of property," and in its reiterated insistence that the oppressed lower classes might not always submit to unfeeling authority. Sometimes his fiery indignation led him to formulations of this point of view as telling as any contrived by Carlyle. Consider, for example, the following apologue devised to illustrate the mammonism of the age:

One day, wandering near this open space [the burial ground at Reculver, then exposed to the sea], we met a boy, carrying away with exulting looks, a skull in very perfect preservation.

He was a London boy, and looked rich indeed with his treasure.

'What have you there?' we asked.

'A man's head—a skull,' was the answer.

'And what can you possibly do with a skull?'

'Take it to London.'

'And when you have it in London, what then will you do with it?'

'I know.'

'No doubt. But what will you do with it?'

And to this thrice-repeated question, the boy three times answered, 'I know.'

'Come, here's sixpence. Now, what will you do with it?'

The boy took the coin—grinned—hugged himself, hugging the skull the closer, and said very briskly, 'Make a money-box of it!'

A strange thought for a child. And yet, mused we as we strolled along, how many of us, with nature beneficent and smiling on all

XXI. Sketch in the copy of *Vanity Fair* presented by Thackeray to George Cruikshank

XXII. Sketch in the copy of *Vanity Fair* presented by Thackeray to Lady Normanby

The Grand Master took a long and earnest glance at the distant Squadron — The clouds are gathering said the brave old man — "I love not that my people should be abroad on such a night — Enguerrand de Umfraville" — he added after a pause — "I would our galleys were back from Sicily!"

"I would they would bring us a few butts of wine" said Raoul the page — "that our butler gives us is as sour as verjuice"

Peace boy! cried Sir Enguerrand severely — This Turkish Dog hath good eyes, Zammit! be yon ships the Sicilian gallies?

"Long prison has dimmed your slave's sight, replied Zammit — "My lord knows his own vessels" — and the Slave's head fell again and he relapsed into his usual moody silence.

I ~~wish~~ like not yon Infidel hound muttered the Stout Sir Enguerrand in his beard — "Tomorrow I will have another cannon ball riven to his chain."

Zammit the slave had recognized the galleys of El Iskender!

From Mr. James's Novel of
'The Orphan of Gozo.'
Vol II. 143.

XXIII. A scene from "Mr. James's Novel of 'The Orphan of Gozo.'"

From a water-colour by Thackeray

XXIV. Tailpiece to *Vanity Fair*

From a pencil sketch by Thackeray

sides—how many of us think of nothing so much as hoarding sixpences—yea, hoarding them even in the very jaws of Death! [27]

It was Jerrold's kind of radicalism that first made *Punch* an important force in moulding English opinion. Even when Alfred Bunn assailed Jerrold as "Wronghead" in *A Word with Punch* of 1845, he conceded: "It is to Jerrold's pen you are indebted, Punch, for the fame you once enjoyed." [28]

Yet, if Jerrold's political passion enabled him to say trenchantly many things that needed saying, it also immensely narrowed his view of life. He was, indeed, an example of the classical radical type, so intent upon his humanitarian purposes as to be blinded to the myriad interests that life possesses for those who do not see it primarily in political terms. His was a dog-in-the-manger attitude; if society did not regard the basic issues of his time as he did, he could have no faith in or liking for society. It is not surprising that Thackeray once called him "a savage little Robespierre." [29] Jerrold's customary mood finds typical expression in a letter of 22 February 1850 to Mrs. Cowden Clark calling attention to the first instalments of Henry Mayhew's *London Labour and the London Poor:*

> Do you read the Morning Chronicle? Do you devour those marvellous revelations of the inferno of misery, of wretchedness, that is smouldering under our feet? We live in a mockery of Christianity that, with the thought of this hypocrisy, makes me sick. We know nothing of the terrible life that is about us,—us, in our smug respectability. To read of the sufferings of one class, and of the avarice, the tyranny, the pocket cannibalism of the other, makes one almost wonder that the world should go on, that the misery and wretchedness of the earth are not, by an Almighty fiat, ended. And when we see the spires of pleasant churches pointing to Heaven, and are told—paying thousands to Bishops for the glad intelligence—that we are Christians! The cant of this country is enough to poison the atmosphere.[30]

Thackeray came to see in Jerrold a living warning of the dangers into which ungoverned radicalism could lead. Lacking the personal experience of poverty which had ingrained in Jerrold the conviction that the "Condition-of-England Question" was of such paramount importance as to overshadow all other concerns, Thackeray had never indulged in the attacks upon property and threats to constituted authority which were essential parts of Jerrold's stock-in-trade. But Jerrold's shrill indignation seemed in other respects almost a parody of his own unmeasured language in moments of exacerbation. He became ashamed of the occasionally intemperate outbursts into which he had fallen in denouncing the privileges claimed by the aristocracy, and he determined henceforth to attack such assumptions jokingly and without losing his temper. This was in any event the attitude natural to him, since his dislike of the inequities of English life derived ultimately from his vision of what England might be if freed from their incubus. This vision is presented, with affecting simplicity, through verses in which Thackeray imagines the land under "Punch's Regency":

At home the cottier coursed his hare,
  Beside the Duke his neighbour;
The weaver got his living fair
  For his ten hours of labour.
And every man without employ
  Got beef—not bones—to feed on,
And every little working boy
  His page of *Punch* could read on. . . .

Then gentlemen might earn their bread,
  And think there was no shame in't;
And at my court might hold their head
  Like any Duke or Dame in't;
A Duchess and her governess
  The same quadrille I clapt in;
I asked old WELLINGTON to mess,
  And meet a half-pay Captain.[31]

Thus, despite the residue of bitterness left by the experiences of his early life, Thackeray was quick to observe that Jerrold's point of view was an unbalanced one. Its exclusively humanitarian emphasis was foreign to his temperament. His fundamental disposition was to observe and to enjoy, and he had a largeness of mind that enabled him to see things in proportion, to weigh accurately competing claims, and to avoid unprofitable extremes. In temperament anything but a revolutionary, he became conscious through his opposition to Jerrold of his true role as a writer, to describe with wit, urbanity, and healthy feeling the life that he knew best, the life of middle- and upper-class England. It was not for him to attempt to shake the foundations of Victorian society, particularly through squibs in a comic paper; but by the proper exercise of his talents he could at least help to raise the level of cultivation and feeling among those who read him. Thackeray's response to the first instalments of *London Labour and the London Poor* was accordingly entirely free from Jerrold's destructive animus:

> What a confession it is that we have almost all of us been obliged to make! A clever and earnest-minded writer gets a commission from the *Morning Chronicle* newspaper, and reports upon the state of our poor in London; he goes amongst labouring people and poor of all kinds—and brings back what? A picture of human life so wonderful, so awful, so piteous and pathetic, so exciting and terrible, that readers of romances own they never read anything like to it; and that the griefs, struggles, strange adventures here depicted exceed anything that any of us could imagine. . . . We have hitherto had no community with the poor. We never speak a word to the servant who waits on us for twenty years; we condescend to employ a tradesman, keeping him at a proper distance—mind, of course, at a proper distance—we laugh at his young men if they dance, jig, and amuse themselves like their betters, and call them counter-jumpers, snobs, and what not; of his workmen we know nothing, how pitilessly they are ground down, how they live and die, here close by us at the backs of our houses; until some poet like Hood wakes and sings that dreadful 'Song of the Shirt'; some prophet like Carlyle rises up and denounces woe; some clear-sighted, energetic man like the writer of the *Chronicle* travels into the poor man's country for us, and comes back with his tale of terror and wonder.[32]

The inevitable battle for supremacy between Thackeray and Jerrold took place in 1846. When the year began, Jerrold was still *Punch's* principal writer. But significantly his greatest success, "Mrs. Caudle's Curtain Lectures" of 1845, which brought him almost as many admirers as Dickens himself, was entirely non-political in nature. To a "wit with a mission," the triumph of Mrs. Caudle seemed a defeat. "He was ashamed of the immense success of the Caudle Lectures," James Hannay recalls. "He did not like to be talked of as a funny man." It depressed him to reflect that "the public will always pay to be amused, but they will never pay to be instructed." [33] The heart went out of his *Punch* contributions, and "Mrs. Bib's Baby" and "The Life and Adventures of Miss Robinson Crusoe," his two series for 1846, were relative failures. We have seen that Thackeray's reputation, on the other hand, was rapidly increasing in these years. And "The Snobs of England," which he began on 28 February 1846, immediately became *Punch's* most popular series.

The issue between Thackeray and Jerrold was resolved at the *Punch* table. There Thackeray's chief ally was Leech, who hated Jerrold's radicalism as much as his "low breeding." [34] But Thackeray also had the support of Gilbert à Beckett, Percival Leigh, Dicky Doyle, and Tom Taylor, all of whom adhered to the gentlemanly code. Mark Lemon himself was shrewd enough to see that the point of view which Thackeray urged upon *Punch* should be adopted for the good of the magazine. Though Thackeray usually avoided expressing unfavourable opinions concerning his fellow *Punch* contributors, Vizetelly recollects that at this time he took no pains "to disguise his contempt for Jerrold's democratic professions." [35] On one occasion his impatience found its way into the magazine itself. On 18 February 1847 Thackeray told John Allen: "Two years ago I used only to make a passive opposition agst the Anti-church and Bishop sneers [in *Punch*]—last year I made an active one (Jerrold & I had a sort of war & I came off conqueror)." [36] This was in what Thackeray called "the Parson-Snob Controversy," [37] which may be studied in his paper called "On Clerical Snobs" of 16 May 1846.

> I know this [Thackeray wrote] that if there are some Clerics who do wrong, there are straightway a thousand newspapers to haul up those unfortunates, and cry, Fie upon them, fie upon them! while, though the press is always ready to yell and bellow excommunication against these stray delinquent parsons, it somehow takes very little count of the many good ones. . . . Let me whisper my belief, *entre nous,* that of those eminent philosophers who cry out against parsons the loudest, there are not many who have got their knowledge of the church by going thither often. . . . When old Father Noah was overtaken in

> his cups, there was only one of his sons that dared to make merry at his disaster, and he was not the most virtuous of the family. Let us too turn away silently, nor huzza like a parcel of schoolboys, because some big young rebel suddenly starts up and whops the schoolmaster.

After denying clerical greed, so overemphasized in "the works of some modern writers of repute," Thackeray concludes with a mock apology for not " 'showing up' the parsons," but instead "indulging in maudlin praises of that monstrous black-coated race." [38] Jerrold resented the obvious allusions to himself in these lines; but sentiment at the *Punch* table was on Thackeray's side, and Jerrold had henceforth to be more respectful in his comments on the Church.

This incident was symptomatic of a far-reaching change that was taking place in *Punch*. Henceforth it was to see the world from the point of view of Thackeray and Leech. Thackeray sympathetically recorded the humours of English social life in print, just as Leech did in line. Both worked in the same spirit, emphasizing the kindly and urbane notation of oddity, the good-humoured and manly exposure of affectation and meanness. Both were "natural truth tellers," [39] untiring in their affectionate study of the world around them. By November, 1847, when Shirley Brooks in "Our Flight with Punch" called upon the magazine to abandon its radical tirades in favour of

> . . . the truthful, social sketch, drawn by Titmarshian skill,
> With colour bright as Dickens's, and pencil keener still,[40]

his appeal was hardly necessary. *Punch* was already in the process of sharply revising its social and political views.[41] When Joe Hume died in 1855, the magazine apologized for its abuse of him by admitting that "at this early date Mr. Punch in his exuberance wrote much that he would now hesitate to commit to paper." And by the 1860s Ruskin could observe:

> You must be clear about Punch's politics. He is a polite Whig, with a sentimental respect for the Crown, and a practical respect for property. He steadily flatters Lord Palmerston, from his heart admires Mr. Gladstone. Steadily, but not virulently, caricatures Mr. D'Israeli; violently castigates assaults upon property in any kind, and holds up for the general idea of perfection, to be aimed at by all the children

of heaven and earth, the British Hunting Squire, the British Colonel, and the British sailor.[42]

But however much a social prophet like Ruskin might deplore *Punch's* growing respectability, this was precisely the factor that made it the favourite with the middle classes which it has remained down to the present, a family jester to which they listen affectionately, not an outsider railing at them.

The effect upon Jerrold of his defeat is revealed in Henry Silver's account of a conversation at the *Punch* table on 26 January 1859:

JL still agst Jerrold WMT says he talked treason at the table & ML charged him with it & for once made him blush. Was about setting up a rival to Punch while he drew his Salary & dined & did no work. At same time was writing Dickens his disapproval of Punch. Evans says they debated whether his salary sh^{d} continue & resolved it sh^{d} [43]

The drift of Jerrold's "disapproval" may be gathered from a letter which he wrote to Dickens in October of 1846:

Punch, I believe holds his course. Nevertheless, I do not very cordially agree with its new spirit. I am convinced that the world will get tired (at least I hope so) of this eternal guffaw at all things. After all, life has something serious in it. It cannot all be a comic history of humanity. Some men would, I believe, write the Comic Sermon on the Mount. . . . Unless *Punch* goes a little back to his occasional gravities, he'll be sure to suffer.[44]

Dickens replied on the twenty-fourth:

This day week I finished my little Christmas Book (writing towards the close the exact words of a passage in your affectionate letter, received this morning: to wit "after all, life has something serious in it"). . . . Anent the Comic History of England and similar comicalities (Snobs in general included) I feel exactly as you do. Their effect upon me is very disagreeable. Such joking is like the sorrow of an undertaker's mute, reversed, and is applied to serious things with the like propriety and force.[45]

The harmony of opinion that united Jerrold and Dickens on this subject is of great significance. Though Thackeray had won his battle with Jerrold against radicalism in *Punch,* he was to be engaged for the rest of his life in an indecisive and far-ranging battle with Dickens against the same doctrine. But this is a theme that must be reserved for the story of Thackeray's later years.

IV

The social outlook crystallized in Thackeray through his quarrel with Jerrold finds its best illustration in his most celebrated *Punch* series, "The Snobs of England, by one of themselves," which appeared in fifty-three weekly instalments between 28 February 1846 and 27 February 1847.[1] Though *The Book of Snobs,* to give these papers their later name, was immediately successful, though it brought Thackeray his first widespread recognition from the general public; it has had few wholehearted admirers. We have seen that his radical fellow writers deplored the facetiousness and frivolity that in their opinion marked Thackeray's attitude in these essays.[2] His conservative critics, on the other hand, have been distressed by the taint of radicalism that for them still clings about the book. So Charles Whibley thought that "*The Snob Papers* betray a lack of humour, an inability to look at things in their right proportion, which it is not easy to condone." [3] Saintsbury, who found *Punch's* politics in general at this period "acridly partisan on the 'popular side,' and so dangerously likely to put fire to those of Thackeray's culverins which were loaded with powder of that sort," dismissed the political pages of the series as "worthless and rather worse," because of their "incoherence and absence of principle." [4]

In a sense the general dissatisfaction that has been expressed with *The Book of Snobs* is a testimony to the accuracy of Thackeray's reporting. Constituting as it does his one consecutive and comprehensive survey of the civilization of which he was a part, it brings out very clearly the inconsistencies of the Victorian social order. Between the battle of Waterloo in 1815 and Germany's triumph in the Franco-Prussian War of 1870, England was by far the greatest and most powerful country in the world.

A kind of "Pax Britannica" prevailed throughout Europe. Even Continental monarchs were Anglophiles. Napoleon III averred, for example, that he began to learn how to govern an empire during "his intercourse with the calm, self-possessed men of the English turf." [5] The exhibition of 1851 at the Crystal Palace affirmed English dominance, which such writers on England as Emerson in *English Traits* and Taine in *Notes sur l'Angleterre* were quick to emphasize as the key to a proper understanding of the country. The court and the aristocracy were tangible symbols of England's position in the world, and their magnificence consequently seemed justifiable, heavy though its cost might be. "Of what use are the lords?" Emerson inquired, and went on to reply, "They have been a social church proper to inspire sentiments mutually inspiring the lover and loved. . . . 'Tis a romance adorning English life with a wider horizon; a midway heaven fulfilling to their sense their fairy tales and poetry." [6] So it was that even after the Reform Bill of 1832, English society consisted of a hierarchy of classes, which was allowed to continue by common consent although it bore increasingly less correspondence to the actual distribution of wealth and power, because of a general disposition on the part of the populace to imitate their "betters" rather than to dislodge them. The nation was largely organized and governed for the benefit of the aristocracy and the upper middle class, and those in authority were tenacious of their privileges and blind to arguments against the ascendancy of birth and good connexions.

Burke's famous description of the virtues attendant upon chivalry, "that generous loyalty to rank and sex, that proud submission, that dignified obedience, that subordination of the heart, which kept alive even in servitude itself, the spirit of exalted freedom," [7] illustrates the admirable aspect of the Victorians' acceptance of the principle of deference as decisive in social behaviour. So too does the prevailing exaltation of the true gentleman, the embodiment of that "unbought grace of life" of which Burke wrote, a man not necessarily clever, nor endowed with practical ability, nor expert in making money, yet somehow, through breeding and training, different from and superior to his fellows in the ordinary, workaday world. Since, as Bulwer has remarked, "Ideas travel upwards, *manners* downwards," [8] the effect upon English manners of the deferential principle was in many ways a happy one. In a classic passage Walter Bagehot has described how subservience to birth and rank mitigated the regard that might otherwise have been paid to mere affluence. "There is no country where a 'poor devil of a millionaire' is so ill off as in England," he wrote. "The experiment is tried every day, and every day it is proved that money alone . . . will not buy 'London Society.' Money is kept down, and so to say, cowed, by the predominant authority of a different power." [9]

To a degree then the phrase "beneficent snobbery," which G. M. Trevelyan has applied to the operation of the deferential principle, may be accepted as appropriate. But it is obvious that deference has its disagreeable side. Imitation of the classes above, an effort constantly to rise in the social scale, an avoidance of contaminating contact with the classes below—these activities do not bring out the nobler aspects of human nature. "Fashion is gentility running away from vulgarity, and afraid of being overtaken by it," Hazlitt has observed. "It is a sign the two things are not very far apart." [10] Everywhere in the Victorian record one finds examples of the sort of snobbery that Thackeray defined as "the mean admiration of mean things." It may be seen in the following stanza from a blatant popular ballad:

And now she is the lawyer's wife
  And dearly does he love her:
And she lives in a happy condition of life,
  And well in the station above her.[11]

It may be seen in *Mrs. Caudle's Curtain Lectures,* when the London merchant Caudle is forced to reject his wife's suggestion that they settle in Clapham after he gives up his business, because "the retired wholesales never visit the retired retails in Clapham." [12] It may be seen in a dialogue between Miss Tox and Mrs. Chick in *Dombey and Son* on the subject of a suitable school for little Paul. "It is not a preparatory school by any means," urges Miss Tox. "Should I express my meaning . . . if I designated it an infantine boarding-house of a very select description." "On an exceedingly limited and particular scale," inquires Mrs. Chick. "Oh! Exclusion itself!" is Miss Tox's reassuring reply.[13] Clearly a marriage that is considered successful because the bride lives "well in the station above her," a community that organizes its visiting in accordance with whether or not residents have been in the wholesale or the retail trade, and a school that is esteemed because of the number of students it excludes do not reflect a very high state of social feeling.

Moreover, by the middle 1840s the deferential principle no longer claimed the unquestioning acceptance that it enjoyed even a quarter of a century earlier. The social cadres still held, but they had been seriously shaken; and the result was a prevailing malaise in social relations—a tendency on the part of those in the superior classes to insist too much on their accustomed privileges, because they could not always be sure that their claim to those privileges would be recognized, and a corresponding tendency to resentment and rebellion among those in the inferior classes. Hence the omnipresence of snobbery, of an uneasy because insecurely grounded pride in position, was perhaps the most striking feature of this period of English social life.[14]

Thus Thackeray was simply bearing witness to the existing condition of English society, not unconsciously revealing a blemish in his own moral nature, when he took snobbery as his guide in surveying English life. A few years later David Masson had this to say on the subject:

> Anti-Snobbism, it may indeed be admitted, is not a perfect summary of the whole decalogue; but, in the present day, and especially in and about London, it is that which most nearly passes for such a summary.[15]

Similarly, Leslie Stephen held that "snobbishness in Thackeray's sense is a special manifestation of an evil tendency much more easily underrated than exaggerated." [16] Not till the contemporary context of the Snob papers had been effectively lost did critics of Thackeray begin to find in them evidence that their author was in any reprehensible sense a snob himself.

So Septimus Berdmore, writing just after Thackeray's death, inquired:

Are we unjust when we say that it was because Thackeray had something of the British flunkey in his disposition that he was enabled to trace out the habits of that noxious animal? That it was because he had in younger days grasped at many little pieces of dignity now become valueless to the well-known author, that he was able to sneer at his followers in the same track? [17]

As the years passed, this kind of objection multiplied, even Trollope contributing mildly to it,[18] until Charles Whibley in 1903 allowed himself the astonishing comment that "there is a touch of wounded pride in every page of this *Book of Snobs,* which Thackeray should never have betrayed." [19]

Such an opinion can be maintained only by taking literally Thackeray's irony ("I am of a savage and envious nature" [20]), and by forgetting his repeated assertion that, in a society so constituted as Victorian England, everyone must be tainted by snobbery.[21] Surely Chesterton proposes a fairer and more acute view of the matter when he writes:

The one supreme and even sacred quality in Thackeray's work is that he felt the weakness of all flesh. Wherever he sneers it is at his own potential self. When he rebukes, he knows it is self-rebuke; when he indulges, he knows it is self-indulgence. This makes him less effective for a fierce war against exceptional and definable abuses; but it secures his special value in the ethics of the age. When Dickens makes game of Major Bagstock we feel that the game (however desirable) is a very long way off. But when Thackeray makes game of Major Ponto, we feel that the vain, worried, worldly little man is very close to us; it is not impossible that he is even inside of us. Here, then, was his special contribution to that chaos of morality which the nineteenth century muddled through: he stood for the remains of Christian humility, as Dickens stood for the remains of Christian charity. Dickens, or Douglas Jerrold, or many others might have planned a Book of Snobs; it was Thackeray, and Thackeray alone, who wrote the great subtitle, 'By One of Themselves.' [22]

It may be admitted that Thackeray's earlier discontent with society occasionally breaks out in *The Book of Snobs.* He is impatient with vestiges of England's feudal heritage,[23] the usages of the older universities annoy him, and he describes the army as "the most enormous Job of all our political institutions." [24] Lordolatry sometimes infuriates him through its intrinsic absurdity. The sight of a footman, "a glorified flunkey in lace, plush, aiguillettes, wearing a bouquet that nobody wears, a powdered head that nobody wears, a gilt cocked hat only fit for a baboon" exasperates him as much as it did when he wrote *The Yellowplush Papers.* "We have abolished negro slavery," he urges. "John must now be *emancipated from plush.*" [25] But there are only two or three passages in the book which the severest critic would describe as rabid, and in these Thackeray has been pushed into fanaticism by his acute awareness of the harm done by snobbery. Hence his examination of the inconveniences of a hereditary aristocracy, his remark after describing the absurd results of trying to introduce fashionable usages into a middle-class household that he is "ready to order a general *battue* of peacocks," and his tirade against "this diabolical invention of gentility which kills natural kindliness and honest friendship." [26]

These are minor details in Thackeray's total picture. For the most part he wrote with moderation and good humour, pulling himself up short when he grew "too savage," because he had learned that radicalism impedes social enlightenment quite as much as does extreme reaction.[27] He holds that, "Society having ordained certain customs, men are bound to obey the law of Society, and conform to its harmless orders." [28] His restraint, his limited objectives, his position as an insider calling attention to shared faults, rather than as an outsider thundering destruction, made him a force with middle-class readers that Jerrold could never hope to be. The message for which he thus gained a hearing was, not that class distinctions should be eliminated, but that the middle class to which he belonged and for which he wrote should free itself of what Hannay calls "social servility,—with the consequent insolence to 'inferiors' by which servility recoups itself, and endeavours to save its *amour propre*"; [29] not that there is no place in the Victorian world for the gentleman, but that the middle class did not as yet properly understand the gentleman's true qualities; not that success, position, and money are worthless, but that they are valuable primarily as means to the true ends of human existence, "the gratification of the domestic affections, of intellectual or artistic impulses, of any of the deepest instincts of our nature." [30]

To bring about this change in attitude Thackeray hit upon a brilliant expedient; he would take a short, pungent, familiar word which was a valued weapon in the armory of false gentility, and change its meaning by the sheer authority of his pen. When Thackeray wrote for *The Snob* at Cambridge, that term was "applied indiscriminately to all who have not the honour of being Members of the University; but in a more particular manner to the *'profanum Vulgus,'* the Tag-rag and Bobtail." [31] To the British public of 1846, snobs still existed "among the lower classes merely." Thackeray contended that, on the contrary, "an immense percentage of Snobs I believe is to be found in every rank of this mortal life." [32] He boldly redefined the word in terms of moral qualities rather than of class; a snob was *"he who meanly admires mean things."* [33] His middle-class readers were sufficiently startled to find this contemptuous term applied to themselves and to the aristocracy; but a further shock was in store for them. In his second chapter Thackeray proceeded to the very "fountain of honour" itself. Having exhibited the deficiencies of the English court in the person of that "Snob Royal," George IV, he charged his readers in a telling climax:

> If you want to moralize upon the mutability of human affairs, go and see the figure of Gorgius in his real, identical robes, at the waxwork. —Admittance one shilling. Children and flunkeys sixpence. Go, and pay sixpence.[34]

But Thackeray would destroy the false only to make way for the true; he felt that "love and simplicity, and natural kindness," [35] given fair play, would bring about the change in social feeling that was needed. The spirit in which he writes, indeed, is fairly summed up in the hope of his final paragraph that *Punch* may "laugh honestly, hit no foul blow, and tell the truth when at his very broadest grin—never forgetting that if Fun is good, Truth is still better, and Love best of all." [36]

In its contemporary context, then, *The Book of Snobs* was a moderate statement, consciously devised to set bounds to *Punch's* radicalism. What are we to make, it may be asked, of Thackeray's often-quoted denunciation of the volume to Motley in 1858: "He told me that he hated the 'Book of Snobs,' and could not read a word of it"? [37] In this conversation Thackeray was discussing his historical fiction, of which Motley notes, he "evidently considers that kind of thing his forte." Thackeray really disowned, not his general position with regard to snobbery, which did not substantially change in later life,[38] but his unmeasured denunciation of "old-world institutions," "feudal Middle-Age superstitions," and the "brutal and odious relic[s] . . . of the wicked torturing old times." [39] In the intervening years he had acquired a profound feeling for the past and the lives that had been lived out in it, a reverence for old institutions and traditions which was not to be shaken by the unworthiness of their current representatives, and he was pained by the recollection of his earlier naïveté.

The Book of Snobs has many kinds of interest apart from its statement of Thackeray's attitude towards his age. His masterly conspectus of Victorian social life is dotted with brilliant character sketches: figures half-way between such types as "Bobus Higgins, Sausage-Maker on the grand scale," in *Past and Present* and the fully drawn portraits of Thackeray's fiction. Whether one looks at Lord Buckram, Lady Susan Scraper, Sir Alured de Mogyns (who began as simple Muggins but now boasts an entry in *Fluke's Peerage* and the motto "*Ung Roy ung Mogyns*"), General Tufto, Crump of St. Boniface, or, best of all, Major Ponto, one finds each prepared, as Hannay noted, "like a specimen for a museum." [40] A succinct example of the brilliance and bite of these sketches is provided in the following paragraphs on an English colonel at a hotel in Boulogne:

He came down and seated himself at the breakfast-table, with a surly scowl on his salmon-coloured bloodshot face, strangling in a tight, cross-barred cravat; his linen and his appointments so perfectly stiff and spotless that everybody at once recognized him as a dear countryman. Only our port wine and other admirable institutions could have produced a figure so insolent, so stupid, so gentlemanlike. After a while our attention was called to him by his roaring out, in a voice of plethoric fury, "O!"

Everybody turned round at the O, conceiving the colonel to be, as his countenance denoted him, in intense pain; but the waiters knew better, and instead of being alarmed, brought the colonel the kettle. O, it appears, is the French for hot water. . . .

That brutal ignorant peevish bully of an Englishman is showing himself in every city of Europe. One of the dullest creatures under heaven, he goes trampling Europe under foot, shouldering his way into galleries and cathedrals, and bustling into palaces with his buckram uniform. At church or theatre, gala or picture-gallery, *his* face never varies. A thousand delightful sights pass before his bloodshot eyes, and don't affect him. Countless brilliant scenes of life and manners are shown him, but never move him. He goes to church, and calls the practices there degrading and superstitious, as if *his* altar was the only one that was acceptable. He goes to picture-galleries, and is more ignorant about art than a French shoeblack. Art, Nature pass, and there is no dot of admiration in his stupid eyes; nothing moves him except when a very great man comes his way, and then the rigid, proud, self-confident, inflexible British Snob can be as humble as a flunkey, and as supple as a harlequin.[41]

After this one can only regret the more profoundly that Thackeray nowhere provides a vignette of the often-mentioned Bishop of Bullocksmithy.[42]

In the early chapters of *The Book of Snobs* Thackeray returns to the vein of extravagant burlesque that he had learned from "Athanasius Gasker" and employed so entertainingly in *The Tremendous Adventures of Major Goliah Gahagan*. His prefatory remarks agreeably parody the ponderous treatises of the time, even to the mention in his first paragraph of "the French Revolution (which the reader will be pleased to have introduced so early)." [43] He makes an amusing pretence of being himself at the heart of fashionable life. As "the HISTORIAN OF SNOBS," the great "Snobonomer" or "Snobographer," he is "*répandu* in the world." [44] When the season ends, he is "tired of the town, where the sight of the closed shutters of the nobility, my friends, makes my heart sick." [45] His final paper includes the grandiose claim that "THE NATIONAL MIND IS AWAKENED TO THE SUBJECT OF SNOBS." [46] But quite apart from these passages, the reader is constantly amused by Thackeray's justness of phrase. Saintsbury has remarked the charm of one delightful sentence: "The most good-natured of women pardoned the error, and the butler removed the bird." [47] There are many others equally good: his reworking of an earlier "filler" for *Punch,* for example—

I read in the newspapers that the Right Reverend the Lord Charles James administered the rite of Confirmation to *a party of the juvenile nobility* at the Chapel Royal,—as if the Chapel Royal were a sort of ecclesiastical Almack's, and young people were to get ready for the next world in little exclusive genteel knots of the aristocracy—

or his characterization of the "usual English expression of subdued agony and intense gloom." [48] *The Book of Snobs* remains wonderfully readable, indeed; and we need not be surprised that George Henry Lewes thought Thackeray "the best writer in England" from the time that it began to appear.[49]

In Victorian literature *The Book of Snobs* deserves a place on the shelves between *Past and Present* and *Culture and Anarchy*. Despite the facetiousness, the extravagance, the carelessness of these papers, which first appeared, after all, in the columns of a comic journal, they show Thackeray to have been, as he jokingly claimed, "an eminent and profound moralist." [50] No doubt he is concerned with the surface of life rather than its depths; no doubt he limits himself to manners and social feeling rather than the struggle between good and evil; [51] no doubt he concentrates on the inconveniences and absurdities with which the abuses of the class system torment the prosperous, rather than on the miseries to which its inequities condemn the poor. Yet he shares with Carlyle an eloquent insistence on human solidarity. We are listening to the same gospel, though at very different levels, when Carlyle tells the grim story of the Edinburgh widow, denied help by her neighbours, who dies of typhus and thereby infects her lane so that seventeen other persons perish; and when Thackeray in a drawing used as the cover design for the 1848 *Book of Snobs* shows a footman accosting a startled grandee in court dress with the words, "Am I not a man and a brother?" [52] Thackeray anticipates Arnold by denouncing as snobbish the Victorian emphasis on money, position, and success, an emphasis which Arnold was later to deplore as the worship of "machinery." Both men were enabled to see clearly how their contemporaries were confusing means with ends, because both could draw upon what Arnold called "the inexhaustible indulgence proper to culture." [53] Different as their conceptions of "perfection" may have been, they were alike in their disinterestedness and flexibility, their knack of seeing all sides of a question, and their ability to make allowances for different points of view.

14

"Vanity Fair"

I

THOUGH LADY RITCHIE has suggested that Thackeray began *Vanity Fair* in 1841,[1] it seems almost certain that he did not embark upon the novel until after his return from Italy in February, 1845.[2] At this time he wrote half a dozen chapters or more in his earlier slanting hand, and by 28 March he was able to describe to his mother, as his chief current enterprises, his "Eastern book" and "another wh is projected and of prodigious importance. This is the scheme by wh I expect to make a great deal of money." [3] But though he "tried 3 or 4 publishers" [4] with his manuscript, none of them was interested. On 8 May he wrote to Henry Colburn, evidently the last in this series, asking for "the commencement of a novel wh I gave into your hands." [5] Meantime, pressure of work for the *Morning Chronicle* and *Punch* was building up, and Thackeray for some months put his novel aside.

By January of 1846 the manuscript, by this time entitled "The Novel without a Hero: Pen and Pencil Sketches of English Society," had been accepted by Bradbury and Evans for publication in monthly numbers beginning in May.[6] One, possibly two, monthly parts were put into type. But once more, "innumerable small jobs" intervened,[7] and the appearance of the first number was postponed. Settling his daughters in the Young Street household was a time-consuming business; and he had "The Snobs of

England" and *Mrs. Perkins's Ball* to occupy his working hours. Only towards the end of the year did he turn again to his novel. On 28 November Bradbury and Evans felt sufficient confidence in the proximate appearance of the first monthly part to announce in *Punch* a

NEW WORK BY MICHAEL ANGELO TITMARSH
VANITY FAIR
BY W. M. THACKERAY

The significant change in title will be noted; and thereby hangs an interesting tale.

In October or November Thackeray had sought the solitude afforded by Brighton's Ship Inn during the off season in order to work uninterruptedly on his novel. There he made the acquaintance of Kate Perry, daughter of a former editor of the *Morning Chronicle,* with whom he almost at once formed a close friendship. He later told this lady how he had "ransacked his brain" for a proper name for his novel, and "it came upon him unawares, in the middle of the night. (He said,) 'I jumped out of bed and ran three times round my room, uttering as I went, "Vanity Fair, Vanity Fair, Vanity Fair." ' "[8] Thackeray was delighted with this title, because it so perfectly summed up the changed perspective in which he had come to view his novel. His experiences in 1846, particularly the crucial one of re-establishing his home, had made him examine profoundly both the nature of the society in which he lived and his responsibility as a writer in describing this society.[9] He summed up his altered point of view in a letter to Mark Lemon of 24 February 1847, commenting on the final paragraph of "The Snobs of England":

> What I mean applies to my own case & that of all of us—who set up as Satirical-Moralists—and having such a vast multitude of readers whom we not only amuse but teach. And indeed, a solemn prayer to God Almighty was in my thoughts that we may never forget truth & Justice and kindness as the great ends of our profession. There's something of the same strain in Vanity Fair. A few years ago I should have sneered at the idea of setting up as a teacher at all, and perhaps at this pompous and pious way of talking about a few papers of jokes in Punch—but I have got to believe in the business, and in many

other things since then. And our profession seems to me to be as serious as the Parson's own.[10]

Inspired by these convictions, he set about revising his 1845 chapters to make them convey his vision of well-to-do England as Vanity Fair.

The alterations which he made at this time (they are readily identifiable, being entered in his later, upright hand) may be studied in the fragmentary manuscript of *Vanity Fair* in the Pierpont Morgan Library.[11] The chapters that Thackeray wrote in 1845 were very much in the vein of "The Luck of Barry Lyndon"; they form a detached, non-committal narrative in which the reader is told what happened, but rarely what to think about it. In revising his story Thackeray added a number of passages of moral commentary to supply this lack; and having fallen into this habit, he remained close at the reader's side during the rest of the book in his new capacity of "Manager of the Performance." The first of his additions, which occurs at the end of Chapter 8, will suffice to illustrate his procedure:

> And, as we bring our characters forward, I will ask leave, as a man and a brother, not only to introduce them, but occasionally to step down from the platform, and talk about them: if they are good and kindly, to love them and shake them by the hand; if they are silly, to laugh at them confidentially in the reader's sleeve: if they are wicked and heartless, to abuse them in the strongest terms which politeness admits of.
>
> Otherwise you might fancy it was I who was sneering at the practice of devotion, which Miss Sharp finds so ridiculous; that it was I who laughed good-humouredly at the reeling Old Silenus of a baronet—whereas the laughter comes from one who has no reverence except for prosperity, and no eye for anything beyond success. Such people there are living and flourishing in the world—Faithless, Hopeless, Charityless: let us have at them, dear friends, with might and main. Some there are, and very successful too, mere quacks and fools: and it was to combat and expose such as those, no doubt, that Laughter was made.[12]

With Chapters 12 and 13 Thackeray left his 1845 beginning entirely behind. His early chapters, despite their remarkable freshness and liveliness, had been blemished by occasional crudities, uncertainty of tone, and extravagant comicality. Such defects now vanished, for Thackeray's grand objective was clear, and his hand was fairly in. From January, 1847, until July, 1848, the yellow-wrappered parts of *Vanity Fair* appeared regularly each month. Often Thackeray could not provide copy, due according to his contract on the fifteenth, until two or three days before the end of the month; but his manuscript was always forthcoming in time for publication. No doubt some sections of the novel are more carefully executed than others,[13] but none falls below a very high level. The professional facility that Thackeray had acquired during his long years of literary apprenticeship enabled him to score a superb triumph when his opportunity finally came.

Thackeray's experiences during this period belong to the story of his years of prosperity, which will be chronicled in the sequel to this volume. It is only necessary to mention briefly here how his way of life in 1847–1848 contributed to his novel. These were busy and exciting months for him. As he achieved celebrity, he gained the entrée to many doors that had hitherto been closed to him; and curiosity joined with unimpaired health to make him indefatigable in exploring what lay within. Moreover, he came to see the accustomed sights of his established routine in a new and revealing light. Everywhere he went, he found illustrations of his conception of the world as a fair of vanities. One is reminded of the obsessive passion for his work displayed by the novelist in Chekov's *Seagull:*

> Here I am with you [Trigorin tells Nina in that play]; I am excited, yet every moment I remember that my unfinished novel is waiting for me. Here I see a cloud that looks like a grand piano. I think that I must put into a story somewhere that a cloud sailed by that looked like a grand piano. There is a scent of heliotrope. I hurriedly make a note: a sickly smell, a widow's flower, to be mentioned in the description of a summer's evening. I catch up myself and you at every sentence, every word, and make haste to put those sentences and words away into my literary treasure-house—it may come in useful!

The same passion may be discerned in Thackeray, with the important difference that for him such details were significant because they helped him to embody his moral vision. So it was that the second-floor arch of a London residence, a pile of letters, a family portrait, a public auction, a funeral, a glimpse of servants conversing, and a hundred other commonplaces of London existence stirred his imagination.[14] So it was that the smallest *trait de moeurs* seemed worth recording, if it could be used to exemplify one of his grand generalizations.[15] Since he was "always thinking of No IV or No V," [16] the real world around him formed a continuum with the imaginary world of his book, in that both alike were parts of Vanity Fair.[17] Thus the pressure of success induced in Thackeray a state of mind peculiarly conducive to creative work. He was alert, keyed up, constantly in thrall to what Dickens called "that wayward and unsettled feeling which is part (I suppose) of the tenure on which one holds an imaginative life." [18] When Thackeray's novel was completed, he told his mother: "It is as if the backbone of your stays were out." [19]

Under these auspicious conditions, Thackeray wrote his greatest book. Pausing in "the middle of the journey" to sum up what life had meant to him thus far, he gave to world literature one of those inexhaustible masterpieces which repay almost endless study. In this chapter attention will be directed to certain leading aspects of his novel: its establishment of realism as the dominant mode in English fiction, its assertion of the claims of the natural style, its demonstration of how fiction can be used for the comprehensive portrayal of society, its evaluation of the society thus portrayed, and its illumination of mankind's common moral experience. But it need hardly be said that a consideration even of these topics does not begin to cover the varied interests of *Vanity Fair*.

II

Vanity Fair was quite as revolutionary a book in the development of Victorian fiction as *Ulysses* has proved to be in the development of modern fiction; and Thackeray, like Joyce, intended that his novel should have a radically unsettling effect.

Through the subtitle, "A Novel without a Hero," he announced his break with the conventions of contemporary fiction. By discarding heroes and heroines,[1] villains and villainesses, he was enabled to dispense with the customary intrigue plot of the traditional novelist. By concerning himself chiefly with the experiences of Amelia and Becky after their marriages, he denied the common assumption that a novel should deal with the vicissitudes experienced by a young man and woman on their way to the altar.[2] Everywhere in *Vanity Fair,* indeed, he displays his awareness of how different his book is from what Victorian readers had come to expect, and his determination that they shall be brought to realize the superiority of what he has to offer. Perhaps these objectives are seen most clearly in the part-issue text of Chapter 6, which opens with burlesques of the Newgate and silver-fork styles of novel-writing.[3] These pages also serve as a reminder that Thackeray's series, "Punch's Prize Novelists," appeared in that periodical concurrently with the early numbers of *Vanity Fair*. Obviously he had planned his attack with care, bringing to bear at once the sixteen-inch guns of his great novel and the forty-millimeter artillery of his magazine parodies.

Of the seven "Novels by Eminent Hands," to give them their later title, six are clearly aimed at specific popular favourites of the day.[4] For the most part the books mimicked are now unread, and some of Thackeray's effects are consequently lost on the modern reader. But he has carried out his operation with great dexterity and wit, and one can readily imagine the hilarity with which the novel-fancier of 1847 must have greeted these exposures of the foibles of then celebrated authors. In "Codlingsby, by D. Shrewsberry, Esq," Thackeray captures Disraeli's very accent. Take, for example, his description of the London residence of Rafael, an omniscient, wealthy, and mysterious Jew, very like the Sidonia of *Coningsby* and *Tancred:*

They entered a moderate-sized apartment—indeed, Holywell Street is not above a hundred yards long, and this chamber was not more than half that length—and fitted up with the simple taste of its owner.

The carpet was of white velvet— (laid over several webs of Aubusson, Ispahan, and Axminster, so that your foot gave no more sound as it trod upon the yielding plain than the shadow did which followed you)—of white velvet, painted with flowers, arabesques, and classic figures, by Sir William Ross, J. M. W. Turner, R. A., Mrs. Mee, and Paul Delaroche. The edges were wrought with seed-pearls, and fringed with Valenciennes lace and bullion. The walls were hung with cloth of silver, embroidered with gold figures, over which were worked pomegranates, polyanthuses, and passion-flowers, in ruby, amethyst, and smaragd. The drops of dew which the artificer had sprinkled on the flowers were diamonds. The hangings were overhung by pictures yet more costly. Giorgione the gorgeous, Titian the golden, Rubens the ruddy and pulpy (the Pan of Painting), some of Murillo's beatified shepherdesses, who smile on you out of the darkness like a star; a few score first-class Leonardos, and fifty of the masterpieces of the patron of Julius and Leo, the Imperial genius of Urbino, covered the walls of the little chamber. Divans of carved amber covered with ermine went round the room, and in the midst was a fountain, pattering and babbling with jets of double-distilled otto of roses.[5]

"Lords and Liveries, by the Authoress of 'Dukes and Déjeuners,' 'Hearts and Diamonds,' 'Marchionesses and Milliners,' Etc., Etc." is a friendly imitation of the fashionable novels of Mrs. Gore. "Barbazure, by G. P. R. Jeames, Esq." retells the Bluebeard story in the manner of "that teeming parent of romance," G. P. R. James, the mildness of whose slow-moving, platitudinous narratives is nicely caught in Thackeray's neat, almost delicate, parody. Only one phrase of his opening sentence could not have been written by James himself: "It was upon one of those balmy evenings of November which are only known in the valleys of Languedoc and among the mountains of Alsace, that two cavaliers might have been perceived by the naked eye threading one of the rocky and romantic gorges that skirt the mountainland between the Marne and the Garonne." [6] "Phil Fogarty, a Tale of the Fighting Onety-Oneth, by Harry Rollicker," on the other hand, is the broadest conceivable burlesque of the boisterous high jinks that mark the military novels which Lever wrote over the pen-name of "Harry Lorrequer." Lever's customary mixture of sentiment and brutality is expertly hit off, and a diabolically clever parody of his efforts in verse is supplied:

You've all heard of Larry O'Toole,
Of the beautiful town of Drumgoole;
He had but one eye,
To ogle ye by—
Oh, murther, but that was a jew'l:
A Fool
He made of de girls, dis O'Toole.[7]

"The Stars and Stripes, by the Author of The Last of the Mulligans, 'Pilot,' &c." ridicules the assumptions of American superiority in James Fenimore Cooper's novels through an account of the behaviour at the court of Louis XVI of Benjamin Franklin, "Chief Tatua," and "Leatherlegs." In all these imitations Thackeray brilliantly achieves his objective of carrying to the absurd the kind of writing associated with each of his "Eminent Hands." What a pity it is that his intended parody of Dickens was never executed!

Only in the first and best of these "Prize Novels" does Thackeray depart from a predominantly playful tone which implies that he is grateful to these traditional story-tellers for the pleasure that they have given him, even while he makes good-natured fun of them. And no doubt it is a secondary aim of "George de Barnwell" by "Sir E. L. B. L. BB. LL. BBB. LLL., Bart." to provide a devastating parody of "Bulwerese." "In the Morning of Life the Truthful wooed the Beautiful, and their offspring was Love," is the characteristically high-flown beginning of Thackeray's preface, which ends with the assurance, borrowed from more than one of Bulwer's recent stories, that " 'Tis for the last time (probably) these fingers shall sweep the strings." Later Bulwer's supreme mastery of the *cliché* is suggested, as he is made to discuss "that happy period of life when the Boy is expanding into the Man. O Youth, Youth! Happy and Beautiful! O fresh and roseate dawn of life; when the dew yet lies on the flowers, ere they have been scorched and withered by Passion's fiery sun." [8] But Thackeray had a more serious purpose than stylistic imitation in writing "George de Barnwell."

In 1846 Bulwer had republished *Eugene Aram* as one of Bentley's "Standard Novels and Romances." When Thackeray reread this book, it rewakened all the revulsion that the Newgate novels had aroused in him during the 1830s. He found Aram depicted as a saintly figure of universal genius. His murder of Clark was not merely palliated by Bulwer but actually justified. Describing his crime, Aram observes:

I felt as if I and my intended victim had been left alone in the world. I had wrapped myself above fear into a high and preternatural madness of mind. *I looked on the deed I was about to commit as a great and solemn sacrifice to Knowledge, whose priest I was.* The very silence breathed to me of a stern and awful sanctity—the repose, not of the charnel house, but of the altar.[9]

Not only did Bulwer fail to repudiate this view; he even seemed to suggest that there was something to be said for it. At the end of the novel he relates of his hero, Walter Lester,

In every emergency, in every temptation, there rose to his eyes the fate of him so gifted, so noble in much, so formed for greatness in all things, blasted by one crime—self-sought, but self-denied; a crime, the offspring of bewildered reasonings—all the while speculating upon virtue. And that fate, revealing the darker secrets of our kind, in which the true science of morals is chiefly found, taught him the twofold lesson,—caution for himself, and charity for others. He knew henceforth that even the criminal is not all evil; the angel within us is not easily expelled; it survives sin, ay, and many sins, and leaves us sometimes in amaze and marvel at the good that lingers round the heart even of the hardiest offender.[10]

Intent on exposing this sophistical morality, Thackeray hit on the inspired device of parodying Bulwer's novel through the story of George Barnwell. This tale of a London apprentice, who is led by love of a lady of the town first to rob his employer and then to murder his uncle, already possessed notably comic overtones. It might be possible to conceive of a great scholar like Aram as a noble genius led astray by the inequitable distribution of wealth in society. But when the same regard was claimed for a London 'prentice boy, whose appearance and language closely resemble Aram's, the ludicrous aspects of the Newgate novel became sufficiently apparent. Nor did Thackeray fail to emphasize the dangerous implications in Bulwer's glorification of Aram's crime.

"And wherefore, sir, should I have sorrow," [George inquires of the chaplain just before his death], ". . . for ridding the world of a sordid worm; of a man whose very soul was dross, and who never had a feeling for the Truthful and the Beautiful? When I stood before my uncle in the moonlight, in the gardens of the ancestral halls of the De Barnwells, I felt that it was the Nemesis come to overthrow him. 'Dog,' I said to the trembling slave, 'tell me where thy Gold is. *Thou* hast no use for it. I can spend it in relieving the Poverty on which thou tramplest; in aiding Science, which thou knowest not; in uplifting Art, to which thou art blind. Give gold, and thou art free.' But he spake not, and I slew him."

To this the chaplain has to reply, despite his admiration for George: "I would not have this doctrine vulgarly promulgated, . . . for its general practice might chance to do harm." [11]

Thackeray's "Prize Novels" could not be ignored by the authors at whom they were aimed, however much they might be resented. In 1847 Bulwer published *A Word to the Public,* which he described as a "general defence of my writings" against such attacks as Thackeray's; and in 1849 he elaborately revised *Eugene Aram,* pruning his style of its worst excesses, making Aram no longer a killer but merely an accomplice in Clark's robbery, and excising the passage quoted above on the sacramental aspect of justified murder. Moreover, in the two novels that followed this revision, *The Caxtons. A Family Picture* and *My Novel . . . or Varieties of English Life,* he did his best to apply his essentially baroque imagination to the literal portrayal of contemporary social reality. Disraeli deserted fiction until seven years after Thackeray's death; and in *Endymion,* the second of the two novels that he wrote late in life, he included, as we have noted, a malicious portrait of Thackeray as the novelist St. Barbe. In the twenty-odd stories that G. P. R. James wrote after 1847, he abandoned his favourite gambit of the "two cavaliers," abandoned even his treasured alternative opening of the "solitary horseman," offering in 1851 an apology for his erstwhile fixation.[12] Lever's exasperation found vent in 1850, as has been pointed out, in a portrait of Thackeray as Elias Howle in *Roland Cashel;* but he too in *The Daltons* (1850–1852) and the novels that followed attempted to come to terms with the vogue for realism which

Thackeray had established.[13] Only Mrs. Gore and Cooper were apparently undisturbed, the former because she had no authorial vanity,[14] the latter because his long career was drawing to a close.

Thus it may be said that with *Vanity Fair* and "Punch's Prize Novelists" Victorian fiction came of age. When Arthur Hugh Clough met Thackeray a few years later, he remarked that his new acquaintance was "much farther into actual life than I am." [15] Thackeray was so far into life, indeed, that the substitute for it provided in popular fiction bored and irritated him; and in his own masterpiece he set out to demonstrate that the real is far more interesting than the imaginary. He stated his position most clearly, perhaps, in a letter to David Masson of 1851, commenting upon an article in which this critic had ranked Dickens, as a worker in the ideal, above Thackeray, a worker in the real:

> I think Mr. Dickens has in many things quite a divine genius so to speak, and certain notes in his song are so delightful and admirable, that I should never think of trying to imitate him, only hold my tongue and admire him. I quarrel with his Art in many respects: wh I don't think represents Nature duly; for instance Micawber appears to me an exaggeration of a man, as his name is of a name. It is delightful and makes me laugh: but it is no more a real man than my friend Punch is: and in so far I protest against him—and against the doctrine quoted by my Reviewer from Goethe too—holding that the Art of Novels *is* to represent Nature: to convey as strongly as possible the sentiment of reality—in a tragedy or a poem or a lofty drama you aim at producing different emotions; the figures moving, and their words sounding, heroically: but in a drawing-room drama a coat is a coat and a poker a poker; and must be nothing else according to my ethics, not an embroidered tunic, nor a great red-hot instrument like the Pantomime weapon.[16]

The fruit of Thackeray's preoccupation with the actual is seen most obviously, perhaps, in the abundance of authentic detail with which *Vanity Fair* is crammed. Thackeray's novel achieves for the first time in English the effects of massive realism; among the novelists of the world, indeed, only Stendhal and Balzac had earlier shown how to establish character in society by deluging the reader with information concerning the daily routine, the employments, the pleasures, and the manners of their figures. The English masters, even Fielding and Jane Austen, had been relatively sparing with this sort of data. The efforts of Thackeray's contemporaries to provide it had been vitiated, as he neatly demonstrates in "Punch's Prize Novelists," by a hopeless vagueness and indefiniteness. Their books can be described in the words which Beaumarchais applied to the works of his rivals: "Ces fades camaïeux où tout est bleu, où tout est rose, où tout est l'Auteur, quel qu'il soit." [17] Not so *Vanity Fair,* for Thackeray's varied existence had given him an intimate familiarity with many social groups. Whether his subject is the City or Russell Square, the artist world of Soho or Continental Bohemia, he knows accurately the life that he is describing. Nor does Thackeray fail to take time as well as social sphere into account in his picture of manners. Though *Vanity Fair* is not a historical novel, he none the less establishes with care the particulars in which Regency customs differ from those of the 1840s; an accurate period colouring is thus imparted to his story with ease and authority.[18] These things may seem small accomplishments today, when they are part of the equipment of many novelists, but for a pioneer like Thackeray to have displayed the meticulousness in such respects of Mr. Graham Greene or Mr. John O'Hara was a remarkable achievement.

Thackeray gauged his effective range very precisely. In narrating "this domestic comedy of Vanity Fair," he was content to confine himself to what he knew best, the histories of several interrelated family groups, mostly middle class (the Dobbins, Osbornes, and Sedleys), but in one case (the Crawleys) touching the fringes of the aristocracy. His central subject was thus early-nineteenth-century "ready-money society," [19] the same social group Galsworthy later described so expertly in *The Man of Property,* which beyond any other illustrated the failings of Vanity Fair. When the course of his story took him into territory with which he was unacquainted, he was not brought thereby to betray his realistic principles. In some cases he declined altogether to follow his character through these episodes. Of this expedient, his treatment of the battle of Waterloo is, of course, the classic example. When Rawdon Crawley, Dobbin, and

George Osborne march away from Brussels, Thackeray writes: "We do not claim to rank among the military novelists. Our place is with the non-combatants. When the decks are cleared for action we go below and wait meekly." [20] But he contrives to make his account of life among the camp-followers as absorbing as any narrative of battle-field action could have been. Sometimes it is essential, however, that he relate the adventures of his characters in what is for him *terra incognita.* Since he cannot desert Becky when she breaks into high society, he follows her course there by reporting what he has heard other people say about it. He confesses that all he has seen of Gaunt House is its exterior, but he has a friend, "little Tom Eaves, who knows everything," [21] to inform him about this great mansion. It matters not at all that Eaves is notoriously unreliable; Thackeray has disclaimed responsibility by presenting what he relates as hearsay; and in any event the great world's prestige derives from what people think of it, not from what it is in itself.

From this rich soil of vivid and authentic detail, Thackeray's imagined episodes spring up with the rapidity and naturalness of the beanstalk in the nursery tale. One example will suffice. To ingratiate herself with the Pitt Crawleys, Becky pretends to take seriously the pretensions to medical knowledge of Lady Southdown, Pitt's mother-in-law. One evening she allows herself to be outmanoeuvred by this formidable woman and has to swallow a particularly nauseous dose that has been prepared for her.

It did not much comfort Mrs. Rawdon [Thackeray continues]; her countenance was very queer when Rawdon came in and heard what had happened; and his explosions of laughter were as loud as usual, when Becky, with a fun which she could not disguise, even though it was at her own expense, described the occurrence, and how she had been victimized by Lady Southdown. Lord Steyne, and her son in London, had many a laugh over the story, when Rawdon and his wife returned to their quarters in May Fair. Becky acted the whole scene for them. She put on a nightcap and gown. She preached a great sermon in the true serious manner: she lectured on the virtue of the medicine which she pretended to administer, with a gravity of imitation so perfect, that you would have thought it was the countess's own Roman nose through which she snuffled. 'Give us Lady Southdown and the black dose,' was a constant cry amongst the folks in

Becky's little drawing-room in May Fair. And for the first time in her life the Dowager Countess of Southdown was made amusing.[22]

In *Vanity Fair* this sort of unforced comic invention is always at Thackeray's command. So comprehensively has he located his characters against their background that he is never at a loss for fresh and delightful developments in his narrative. Saturation in his subject has given him a marvellous fertility; yet, wonder of wonders, what he relates is always directly pertinent to his story. He is not yet distracted, as he sometimes is in his later novels, by "that tempting range of relevancies called the universe." [23]

Thackeray's realism is as exact in dialogue as in description and narrative. With the text of *Vanity Fair* before us, we hardly need Frederick Locker-Lampson's testimony to Thackeray's mastery of current slang and to the fidelity with which his conversations reproduce the speech of his day.[24] In the fiction of the 1840s it was common enough to find the dialogue of comic characters reported with some accuracy. Firkin's ungrammatical and exclamatory utterances, Sir Pitt's Hampshire crudities, and Mrs. O'Dowd's eccentric brogue can be readily paralleled in the novels of Bulwer, Surtees, and Lever, though none of these authors displays Thackeray's relative delicacy and restraint. His real triumph comes in his ability to differentiate the speech of educated characters who pretend to some degree of cultivation. His familiarity with the jargon of a score of professions helps him here, but still more useful is his sense of individual speech rhythms. Consider the three prominent maiden ladies of *Vanity Fair:* Miss Pinkerton, Miss Crawley, and Briggs. Even out of context, no saying of any one of these three could possibly be assigned to either of the others. As Mr. V. S. Pritchett has noted, *Vanity Fair* bears witness to "something of the modern ear's curiosity" in Thackeray.[25]

We have dealt thus far with the adjuncts of characterization, but the same realism is to be observed in Thackeray's completed portraits. Here too there is abundant contemporary testimony to the exactness with which he worked. Sir Algernon West asserts, for example, that "no one photographed like him the world I have known and seen." [26] To study the people who served as models for Thackeray's characters is to find a remarkable degree of harmony between what they were in life and what they have become in Thackeray's novels.[27] To examine the letters, diaries, and memoirs of the Victorian period is to come again and again upon figures who illustrate the truth of Thackeray's sketches. When Admiral Sir William James published *The Order of Release,* for example, the startling resemblance between that snobbish, low-brow parvenu, John Ruskin's father, and the older Osborne in *Vanity Fair,* must have struck many readers.[28] Even those figures in Thackeray's novel whose plausibility was sometimes questioned by his contemporaries are seen in retrospect to show how much wider was his experience than that of his critics. Trollope asked how Thackeray could bring himself to present "that crowning absurdity of Sir Pitt Crawley and his establishment . . . a stretch of audacity which I have [always] been unable to understand." [29] Yet, when Charles Kingsley urged, regarding Sir Pitt, that "it is impossible to find such coarseness in his rank of life," Thackeray replied that he was "almost the only exact portrait in the whole book." [30] There are at least two rival claimants, indeed, for the dubious honour of being his "original." [31]

The property of Thackeray's portraits that in the view of his contemporaries gave them a realism beyond that attained by any of his rivals was their embodiment of the mixed motives that operate in human nature, their illustration of the potentialities for good and for evil in all hearts. Accustomed as they were to the idealized simplifications of traditional fiction, Thackeray's first readers experienced a shock of recognition from such characterizations as that of Rawdon Crawley. In this heavy dragoon of the Life Guards Green, Thackeray initially sought to display a typical "buck" or "blood" of the Regency. Early in the novel Rawdon is presented almost entirely in terms of his pleasures, which are those of his class and period; gambling, duelling, womanizing, and sports like hunting, shooting, four-in-hand driving, and "fives" make up his whole existence.[32] Thackeray's principal aim seems to be to demonstrate that dandies were at this time admired simply because they were "so delightfully wicked." [33]

Only after Rawdon falls under Becky's spell does he become an individual. It is his unselfish love for her that brings him to life. In the last interview between the two before Waterloo, Rawdon rather than his wife is the centre of interest, as he notes down, "in his big schoolboy handwriting, the various items of his portable property which might be sold for his widow's advantage —as, for example, 'My double-barril by Manton, say 40 guineas; my driving-cloak, lined with sable fur, 50*l.;* my duelling pistols in rosewood case (same which I shot Captain Marker), 20*l.*' " [34] Later his devotion to little Rawdon, brought home in many inimitable episodes, fills out the portrait. Rawdon spends much time with his son in the nursery, Thackeray relates.

The room was a low room, and once, when the child was not five years old his father, who was tossing him wildly up in his arms, hit the poor little chap's skull so violently against the ceiling, that he almost dropped the child, so terrified was he at the disaster.

Rawdon minor had made up his face for a tremendous howl—the severity of the blow indeed authorized that indulgence: but just as he was going to begin, the father interposed.

'For God's sake, Rawdy, don't wake mama,' he cried. And the child looking in a very hard and piteous way at his father, bit his lips, clenched his hands, and didn't cry a bit. Rawdon told that story at the clubs, at the mess, to everybody in town. 'By Gad, sir,' he explained to the public in general, 'what a good plucked one that boy of mine is—what a trump he is! I half sent his head through the ceiling, by Gad, and he wouldn't cry for fear of disturbing his mother.' [35]

After a few such scenes, as a contemporary reviewer remarked, "the reader forgets the blackleg in the father," [36] for he has been shown in detail how "the bold and reckless young blood of ten years back was subjugated, and was turned into a torpid, submissive, middle-aged, stout gentleman." [37] But though Rawdon patiently endures the long boredom and humiliation of being "Mrs. Crawley's husband," we are conscious that he is moved by trust in his wife rather than complaisance in corruption. When the truth about Becky is revealed to him, not only does his decisive action give the reader immense satisfaction, but it also rounds out his portrait by allowing him to display both the manliness that he has always possessed and the integrity that over the years he has achieved.

Rawdon is certainly one of Thackeray's most masterly sketches, and no reader today finds any difficulty in accepting him. But to many of Thackeray's contemporaries his behaviour seemed hopelessly illogical. A reviewer in the *Dublin University Magazine,* for example, could not understand how a man who in one part of the novel is presented as a profligate and a scoundrel should later display "some of the finest and most beautiful qualities in our nature." This anomaly was only to be explained, so this reviewer argued, as an oversight occasioned by the haste of serial-writing.[38] Shrewder critics grasped the lesson of Thackeray's portrait, "that man is a mixture of qualities, and that it is the problem of genius to represent that mixture without inconsistency." Thackeray was to be praised, they contended, because he shows in *Vanity Fair* "a profound knowledge of that balance of opposite characteristics on which all truthfulness in the exhibition of human nature depends." [39]

Thackeray's conception of psychological realism, though it long continued to arouse protests from obtuse readers,[40] has been adopted by most subsequent English novelists of any stature. With ever-increasing subtlety and complexity, George Eliot, Henry James, and Joseph Conrad have used this method to enable readers through their fiction better to understand themselves and the lives that they are leading. But admirable as *Middlemarch, The Spoils of Poynton,* and *Nostromo* may be in this respect, it can be argued that they are marked by over-elaboration, just as the novels of Thackeray's contemporaries were marked by over-simplification, and that the classic moment of English realism occurs in Thackeray's masterpiece. This was the conviction of Edward FitzGerald, at any rate, who remarked to a correspondent about Disraeli's *Lothair,* which he read late in life: "the book is like a pleasant Magic Lantern: when it is over, I shall forget it: and shall want to return to what I do not forget, some of Thackeray's monumental figures of 'pauvre et triste Humanité,' as old Napoleon called it: Humanity in its Depths, not in its superficial Appearances!" [41]

III

If the mastery of reality to which Thackeray attained in *Vanity Fair* is sometimes underestimated today, still less is justice done by modern readers to his mastery of the art of writing. Yet with this novel he came into his own as a stylist. During his years of careless, hurried magazinery, he had neither the leisure nor the incentive to do his best, and, despite his great gifts, his prose was very unequal in quality. Yet he told Bedingfield that it was his ambition "*one day* to be ranked with 'classical writers,' " [1] and in *Vanity Fair* he achieved his goal.

When Thackeray's mature style is compared with that of his contemporaries, one sees at once that its distinctive features are naturalness and informality. His great achievement during the decade between *The Yellowplush Papers* and *Vanity Fair* was learning how to speak in his own voice.

> 'Tis an error, surely, to talk of the simplicity of youth [he makes Harry Esmond observe]. I think no persons are more hypocritical, and have a more affected behaviour to one another, than the young. They deceive themselves and each other with artifices that do not impose upon men of the world; and so we get to understand truth better, and grow simpler as we grow older.[2]

From the first words of Chapter 1 in *Vanity Fair*—"While the present century was in its teens"—the reader is taken with the unpretentious ease of Thackeray's writing. Yet each sentence has its personal stamp. Who else would have written of "the dismal precocity of poverty," or described the late Lord Southdown as "an epileptic and simple-minded nobleman"? [3] The turn of phrase in a longer passage, such as that in which we learn how Amelia is once again taken into favour by her jealous sister-in-law, is equally distinctive:

> One day the chariot, with the golden Bullocks emblazoned on the panels and the flaccid children within, drove to Amelia's house in Richmond; and the Bullock family made an irruption into the

garden, where Amelia was reading a book, Jos was in an arbour placidly dipping strawberries into wine, and the major in one of his Indian jackets was giving a back to Georgy, who chose to jump over him. He went over his head, and bounded into the little advance of Bullocks, with immense black bows in their hats, and huge black sashes, accompanying their mourning mamma.[4]

There could be no better illustration than *Vanity Fair* of the truth of Pascal's famous maxim: "Quand on voit le style naturel, on est tout étonné et ravi, car on s'attendait de voir un auteur et on trouve un homme." [5]

Though Thackeray's writing seems casual and unstudied, it is actually the product of that subtlest art which conceals art. Consider, for example, the range of effects that he employs to make *Vanity Fair* a "Comic History" [6] in the sense that Fielding used the term. First to be noted is the sheer wit of his writing. For sustained verbal brilliance, *Vanity Fair* can hardly be matched in nineteenth-century English fiction. Thackeray's most casual sentences have their satiric bite. "Miss Pinkerton did not understand French," he remarks early in the novel; "she only directed those who did." A little later he explains that Miss Crawley was "an object of great respect when she came to Queen's Crawley, for she had a balance at her banker's which would have made her beloved anywhere." In describing Pumpernickel, he observes that "there was a rich and numerous staff of officers, and I believe a few men." [7] When we are told that Becky and Lord Steyne are witty, we do not have to accept the statement on credit, for it is abundantly validated in the samples supplied of their conversation. Indeed, Thackeray introduces his great nobleman by a colloquy with Becky about the latter's need for "a *moral* shepherd's dog" which is as elegant and pointed as an exchange between Mirabell and Millamant in *The Way of the World*.[8]

The modern reader misses much of Thackeray's wit because of the wide range of allusion on which it relies. In a sense, the pleasure of reading Thackeray in *Vanity Fair* and his later novels is what Mark Pattison described as the pleasure of reading Milton, the last reward of scholarship, though for Thackeray the reader's scholarship should be, not so much in the classics, as in

English literature and social history. There is hardly a page of *Vanity Fair* without its echo of a phrase familiar to its first readers to which Thackeray contrives to give new pertinence through an ingenious application. In Chapter 4 Becky sings a pathetic song about an orphan boy wandering on the snowy moor to Jos Sedley, who is profoundly affected by it. "As she came to the last words," Thackeray remarks, "Miss Sharp's 'deep-toned voice faltered.' "[9] For contemporary readers the quoted phrase was not merely laughably unexpected; it also emphasized the factitious aspect of Becky's appeal, since it was drawn from T. H. Bayley's preposterous ditty, "We Met—'Twas in a Crowd":

> He spoke—his words were cold, and his smile was unalter'd;
> I knew how much he felt, for his deep-toned voice falter'd.[10]

Again in Chapter 53 Thackeray tells of Peggy O'Dowd

> performing a jig at Government House, where she danced down two aides de camp, a major of the Madras cavalry and two gentlemen of the Civil Service; and, persuaded by Major Dobbin, C. B., second in command of the —th, to retire to the supper-room, *lassata nondum satiata recessit.*[11]

The words thus applied to honest, hearty Lady O'Dowd and her innocent pleasures—"she withdrew, exhausted but not satiated"—are drawn from the terrible passage in Juvenal's *Satires* which tells of the departure of the Empress Messalina from the brothels of Rome after a night spent there as a common prostitute. If wit derives from startling incongruity, it surely attains a kind of ultimate reach here.

Perhaps Thackeray's perpetual allusiveness finds its best illustration, however, in what has been called his "science of names." Closely examined, nearly every name in *Vanity Fair* tells the reader something about the character who bears it. Yet Thackeray's nomenclature is neither gross and obvious like Ben Jonson's, nor frankly fantastic like Dickens's, but at once adroit and plausible. An obsequious and parasitical clergyman is my lord Trail, Bishop of Ealing. The ladies of easy virtue in Thackeray's *demi-monde* are Lady Crackenbury, Mme. de la Cruchecassée, Mrs. Firebrace, Mrs. Mantrap, and Mrs. Washington White. A notorious gossip is Tom Eaves; a country gentleman with a numerous family, Sir Lapin Warren. The dull and stodgy leaders of English fashion are Lady Fitz-Willis, Lady Grizzel Macbeth (formerly Lady G. Glowry), and Lady Slowbore. Lord Steyne's list of distinctions, a marvel of ingenuity, includes such titles as Viscount Hellborough and Baron Pitchley and Grillsby.[12] No wonder that a contemporary admirer of Thackeray wrote, "It is not everyone that could like him invent a humorous Court Guide, Peerage, and Baronetage, that to all appearances are as solemn and authentic as those interesting publications themselves." [13]

It is not only through allusiveness that Thackeray demands alertness from readers of *Vanity Fair;* his use of irony, burlesque, and the mock-heroic is equally challenging. His irony, indeed, is all-pervasive in the novel. It lurks in the simplest statement and is capable of the most elaborate development. When old Sir Pitt proposes to Becky at the end of Chapter 14, she is forced to reply, starting back in consternation, her eyes filled with tears of genuine regret: "Oh, Sir Pitt! . . . I'm *married already.*" The comment with which Thackeray begins his next chapter is characteristically sardonic:

> Every reader of a sentimental turn (and we desire no other) must have been pleased with the tableau with which the last act of our little drama concluded; for what can be prettier than an image of Love on his knees before Beauty? [14]

For a passage in which his ironic flair finds larger scope the reader may turn to the mock panegyric of George IV, which serves as a preamble to Chapter 48. Thackeray's gift for mimicry that shades into burlesque is exercised almost as freely in *Vanity Fair* as in "Punch's Prize Novelists." The various letters from boyish and female correspondents that he quotes are at once authentic and amusing; the songs that Becky sings—"Ah, bleak and barren was the moor!" and "The Rose upon My Balcony" [15] —are distillations of the sentimental ballads of the day; the titles given to the evangelical tracts distributed by the Southdown family are apposite and credible enough: "The Sailor's True Binnacle," "The Applewoman of Finchley Common," "A Voice from the Flames," "A Trumpet-warning to Jericho," even, at first glance, "Fleshpots Broken; or, The Converted Cannibal." [16] When Thackeray remarks that it is to Lady Emily, "I believe, we owe that beautiful poem—

> Lead us to some sunny isle,
> Yonder in the western deep;
> Where the skies forever smile,
> And the blacks for ever weep—" [17]

the reader assumes that this is one more inspired parody; to learn that Thackeray has here drawn upon his memory rather than his imagination [18] is to realize how complete is the author's spell in *Vanity Fair.* Thackeray drops into the mock-heroic vein many times in the novel—most successfully, perhaps, in his narrative of Dobbin's schoolboy victory over Cuff, in much of what he writes about Jos Sedley, and in his brilliant account of how Becky and Rawdon live on nothing a year.

But Thackeray's stylistic mastery is by no means limited to comedy. "Inside his fine sagacious common-sense understanding," James Hannay writes, "there was, so to speak, a pool of poetry,—like the *impluvium* in the hall of a Roman house, which gave an air of coolness and freshness and nature to the solid marble columns and tesselated floor." [19] When Thackeray ends his account of old Osborne's passing the night after George's marriage in going through his relics of his undutiful son and in preparing a new will, by noting, that "as he went up to bed: the whole house was alight with sunshine; and the birds were singing among the fresh green leaves in Russell Square"; when he describes Amelia as she appears to Dobbin just before Waterloo, her face white, wild, and despair-stricken, leaning against the wall and holding her "sash against her bosom, from which the heavy net of crimson dropped like a large stain of blood"; when he tells of Amelia's forcing herself to remain away from Georgy, whom she must shortly give up to his grandfather, "trying the separation:—as that poor gentle Lady Jane Grey felt the edge of the axe that was to come down and sever her slender life" [20]—in these and many other passages, the reader is conscious of this unexpected "pool of poetry" in *Vanity Fair,* which is all the more moving because it depends entirely upon quiet, simple, even homely effects. "Our novelist knows that great words do not always come at great moments," wrote a contemporary critic; "that, in a crisis of terrible suspense or frightful emotion, lesser impressions strike, smaller feelings and fancies intrude (by surprise as it were) than the wholesale passion-mongers can either understand or produce." [21]

Thus *Vanity Fair* commands admiration in part by its sheer stylistic authority. Recognizing the novelist's obligation to be amusing, Thackeray never fails in verbal resourcefulness throughout many hundred pages. Yet when he moves "from grave to gay, from lively to severe," the reader experiences no sense of disappointment. Mr. Pritchett has real warrant for insisting in his essay on *Vanity Fair* that "the pleasure of Thackeray is the sense of Style, the intimacy of an educated mind." [22]

IV

If *The Book of Snobs* presents English society analytically, *Vanity Fair* displays its workings imaginatively. That Thackeray should use fiction to convey a comprehensive vision of the social organism was itself a profound innovation; not since Fielding had an English novelist attempted such a feat. But in Thackeray's mind, as in Balzac's, there existed an imaginary world that paralleled the real world. All his stories were drawn from this source. Hence it was perfectly natural for him to introduce characters into *Vanity Fair* taken from his earlier books,[1] and in the novels that followed, these reappearances became even more frequent.[2] So eager was he to provide complete information about the world of his imagination, indeed, that he sometimes had to check his own enthusiasm. Having described the kindness displayed to Sedley after his bankruptcy by his clerk, Edward Dale, Thackeray goes on to relate that Dale

> married Miss Louisa Cutts (daughter of Higham and Cutts the eminent corn-factors), with a handsome fortune in 1820; and is now living in splendour, and with a numerous family, at his elegant villa, Muswell Hill. [Here, however, Thackeray brings himself up short.]

But we must not let the recollections of this good fellow cause us to diverge from the principal history.[3]

His constant generalizing about the society that he describes (his "science of names" is one means of suggesting such generalizations) is to be attributed to the same state of mind. He was always on the look-out for hints of the pattern which underlay his world.

Consequently, the contention that *Vanity Fair* is not only a "novel without a hero" but also a "novel without a plan" [4] is based upon a radical misconception of the book's real nature. *Vanity Fair* is designed to provide, as Mr. Percy Lubbock has noted, "the impression of a world, a society, a time—certain manners of life within a few square miles of London." Thackeray's novel is not primarily the story of any of his characters; "it is the story they unite to tell, a chapter in the notorious career of well-to-do London." "He is a painter of life, a novelist whose matter is all blended and harmonized together—people, actions, background—in a long retrospective vision." [5] With such an objective he was freed from the necessity of devising an elaborate plot, such as that of *Tom Jones,* which would through the person of its "ambulating hero" take him at each moment exactly where he wanted to be. Instead, he abandoned the picaresque formula, claiming the privilege of omniscience, and with it the ability to be wherever he pleased.[6] He had to know in advance only which of his characters were to figure as his principals,[7] and what the general pattern of their lives was to be.[8] More detailed planning [9] would have hampered the free and spontaneous invention which gives *Vanity Fair* its supreme naturalness and persuasiveness. Thackeray preferred to give his characters their heads, indeed, rather than to restrict them to a predetermined course. "I don't control my characters," he told Jeaffreson, ". . . I am in their hands, and they take me where they please." [10]

Thackeray's story emerged in his mind as he thought back over his experience and tried to comprehend it.[11] He understood with Kierkegaard that if life must be lived forward, it can only be understood backwards. All his major works of fiction, from *Vanity Fair* on, are explorations of "le temps retrouvé." It is this brooding scrutiny of life which gives his novels their special impress, which causes Chesterton to call Thackeray "the novelist of memory—of our memories as well as his own. . . . Thackeray is everybody's past—is everybody's youth." [12] For many persons, experience so judged acquires a quite particular value. Eugène Delacroix, who greatly admired *Vanity Fair,* remarks in his *Journal:*

Je crois que le plus grand attrait des choses est dans le souvenir qu'elles réveillent dans le coeur ou dans l'esprit, mais surtout dans le coeur. . . . Le regret du temps écoulé, le charme des jeunes années, la fraîcheur des premières impressions agissent plus sur moi que le spectacle même.[13]

This was the point of view, certainly, from which *Vanity Fair* was written.

Thackeray's perspective makes him particularly expert in bringing out the design of individual lives and of human life generally. Consider, for example, the career of old Mr. Sedley. Early in the novel he emerges for a time from Thackeray's vast panorama. We see a hearty, coarse-grained, jovial man, sure of himself and flushed with success, ordering about his wife and daughter and making his son uncomfortable with his rough jokes. He disappears for a dozen chapters. When we encounter him again, years have passed, his business has failed, and he has become the broken-down frequenter of a third-rate City coffeehouse,

Familiar as an old mistake
And futile as regret.

The assurance and high spirits of his halcyon days have departed; his mind is failing; but he still hopes to recoup his fortune and talks of millions, though he has in his pocket only the few pennies that his wife has doled out to him in the morning to get him through the day. The effectiveness of this characterization arises not so much from the contrasting portraits of Sedley in prosperity and in adversity, admirable as these are, as from their setting in the broad sweep of *Vanity Fair.* They are not "fine, isolated verisimilitudes," but parts of a coherent pattern.

Thackeray's point of view also enabled him to suggest the

passage of time with matchless ease. Covering the years 1812 to 1830,[14] *Vanity Fair* deals with the affairs of three generations. We follow the careers of Amelia and Becky, of Dobbin, George, and Rawdon throughout most of the book; but we also come to know well their fathers and mothers, their uncles and aunts, in the early pages; and their children claim our attention as the novel draws to a close. By a hundred unobtrusive touches Thackeray reminds us that, as time passes, the cycle of life repeats itself. One such occurs when Amelia returns to the Osborne house in Russell Square, after the death of her implacable father-in-law, and her son shows her his room, which had been his father's before him. " 'Look here, mother,' said Georgy, 'here's a G. O. scratched on the glass with a diamond; I never saw it before, *I* never did it.' "[15] The homily which begins this chapter, "in which two lights are put out," derives its effectiveness not only from Thackeray's eloquence but also from the aptness with which it sums up in a general statement the half-formed reflections to which passages such as this have given rise in the reader's mind throughout the book.

Yet, though a broad impression of life and its vicissitudes is the effect for which Thackeray has chiefly striven in *Vanity Fair*, Mr. Edwin Muir is not quite accurate when he asserts that "all the plot that remains is the series of incidents which widen and diversify the picture, and set the characters in different relations."[16] Both Becky's adventures and the quieter history of Amelia make an appeal to the reader's sense of drama, without which *Vanity Fair* would not be the complete and satisfying work of art that it is. This point can best be made by a consideration of the famous "discovery scene," in which Becky's career reaches its climax. After praising Thackeray's mastery of the pictorial art, "that fore-shadowing and generalizing, that fusion of detail, that subordination of the instance and the occasion to the broad effect,"[17] in the chapters leading up to this episode, Mr. Lubbock regretfully notes an abrupt change in Thackeray's method when Rawdon returns unexpectedly to the little house in Curzon Street to find his wife and Lord Steyne tête-à-tête. Rawdon is pale and dishevelled; Becky appears "in a brilliant full toilette," covered with diamonds; and Lord Steyne rises up, "grinding his teeth" and staring tremendous, for all the world "like some fierce tyrant in old tapestry." [18] The scene is over in a minute. "I am innocent," Becky unavailingly protests. If Steyne's words are brutal and direct, so are Rawdon's actions. When Steyne throws the taunt "bully" at Becky's supposedly complaisant husband, Rawdon slaps him, flings him to the floor, and throws at him one of his gifts to Becky, a diamond ornament which scars his bald forehead "to his dying day." For the moment Rawdon's boldness shakes even Becky out of her egoism. "She stood there trembling before him. She admired her husband, strong, brave, and victorious." [19]

A convinced disciple of Henry James, Mr. Lubbock holds that Thackeray has here missed his opportunity, that his climactic scene is spoiled by "the sudden heightening of the pitch, the thickening of the colour, the incongruous theatrical tone," which he employs.[20] No doubt many modern readers, trained as they are to rebel at any hint of melodrama, find Thackeray's treatment of this episode over-emphatic. (Certainly in dramatic and cinematic versions of *Vanity Fair,* adapters have used Thackeray's text for this scene almost verbatim.) But perhaps modern taste is here at fault. Strength is as desirable in art as subtlety. The finest fiction is that which strikes a balance between the two. "If Rawdon Crawley's blow were not delivered," Robert Louis Stevenson argues, "*Vanity Fair* would cease to be a work of art. That scene is the chief ganglion of the tale; and the discharge of energy from Rawdon's fist is the reward and consolation of the reader." [21] Conceivably that ripe judge of novels, George Saintsbury, was right after all when he asserted that the discovery scene is "beyond praise, . . . one of the greatest things in English." [22]

V

In *Vanity Fair,* as in *The Book of Snobs,* Thackeray not only displays but also passes judgment on English society. Nor does his point of observation change in the two books. If *The Book of Snobs* was written "by one of themselves," his novel is the work of "a philosophical frequenter of Vanity Fair," who addresses his fellows as "brother wearers of motley." [1] "The Manager of the Performance" has his booth in the Fair like the rest; and if he speaks harshly of "quacks," he is quick to add *"other* quacks, plague take them!" [2] His anecdotes are introduced by such formulas as "I remember one night being in the Fair myself, at an evening party," or "I knew once a gentleman, and very worthy practitioner in Vanity Fair." [3] And if the Fair is his subject, and he himself a "Vanity-Fairian," [4] the Fair also supplies his audience. Declining at one point to write further of Amelia's troubles, he explained, "it would be too dreary and stupid. I can see Vanity Fair yawning over it *d'avance."* [5] The advantage to a novelist of this sort of intimate association with his characters need hardly be emphasized. Few of us would seek out old Osborne as an acquaintance; yet it may be said of him, as of a recent American presidential candidate, that you have to know him well in order really to dislike him. To compare him with a similar personage in Dickens, Mr. Dombey of *Dombey and Son,* is to see how greatly Thackeray profited by his position as an insider in portraying upper-middle-class character.

The figure of old Osborne also illustrates the grand point of superiority of *Vanity Fair* over *The Book of Snobs* as an evaluation of English society. Thackeray's sketches in his *Punch* series were necessarily static and incomplete, while in his novel they emerge from a living picture of life and character. How inferior is his sketch of the angry English colonel quoted in the last chapter to such a glimpse of old Osborne as we get when he drives away furious from a dinner at the Bullocks:

So Russell Square is not good enough for Mrs. Maria, hey? . . . So she invites her father and sister to a second day's dinner (if those sides, or ontrys, as she calls 'em, weren't served yesterday, I'm d—d), and to meet City folks and littery men, and keeps the earls and the ladies, and the honourables to herself. Honourables? Damn honourables! I am a plain British merchant, I am: and could buy the beggarly hounds over and over. Lords, indeed!—why, at one of her swarreys I saw one of them speak to a dam fiddler—a fellar I despise. And they won't come to Russell Square, won't they? Why, I'll lay my life I've got a better glass of wine, and pay a better figure for it, and can show a handsomer service of silver, and can lay a better dinner on my mahogany, than ever they see on theirs—the cringing, sneaking, stuck-up fools. Drive on quick, James: I want to get back to Russell Square—ha, ha! [6]

As one would expect, the broad frame of his novel allows Thackeray to present his case against false gentlemanliness with much greater elaboration than in *The Book of Snobs*. He uses this opportunity to particular effect through the figures of George Osborne and of Dobbin, in whom he set out to portray the sham and the true gentleman. (It is worth noting that he made Dobbin an important figure in the novel only when he reworked his early chapters to bring them into harmony with his new conception of the world as Vanity Fair towards the end of 1846.) [7] In these companion portraits he epitomizes what he had learned in the years since he had himself entered upon the "education of a gentleman" as a boy of ten at Charterhouse. He firmly believed that a gentleman was essentially superior to "a low-minded man"; [8] to that extent he accepted class differences as part of the unarguable nature of things; but he was at war with the Regency conception of gentlemanliness, which still to a certain extent prevailed, and eager to see it replaced with a more reasonable ideal.

George Osborne (the given name is significant) is brought up to be the sort of dandy admired in the heyday of George IV. He is handsome, graceful, and self-assured. Throughout boyhood and youth he enjoys unvarying success and popularity, and in maturity he is the admired of all observers. Among the officers of his regiment he is known as "a regular Don Giovanni."

He was famous in field-sports [Thackeray continues], famous at a song, famous on parade; free with his money, which was bountifully supplied by his father. His coats were better made than any man's in the regiment, and he had more of them. He was adored by the men. He could drink more than any officer of the whole mess, including old Heavytop, the colonel. He could spar better than Knuckles, the private (who would have been a corporal but for his drunkenness, and who had been in the prize-ring); and was the best batter and bowler, out and out, of the regimental club. He rode his own horse, Greased Lightning, and won the Garrison cup at Quebec races.[9]

In his own mind these accomplishments make him superior to his origins, and he longs to be rid of "the whole pack of money-grubbing vulgarians" [10] of his own class and to establish himself as "a man of the world." Indeed, both in appearance and manner "Cupid," as Becky calls him, is admirably equipped to serve as the hero of a fashionable novel:

George had an air at once swaggering and melancholy, languid and fierce. He looked like a man who had passions; secrets, and private harrowing griefs and adventures. His voice was rich and deep. He would say it was a warm evening, or ask his partner to take an ice, with a tone as sad and confidential as if he were breaking her mother's death to her, or preluding a declaration of love. He trampled over all the young bucks of his father's circle, and was the hero among those third-rate men.[11]

The reader is not impressed by George's trivial accomplishments, nor dazzled by his surface glitter. If he is not a coward, if he is capable in his better moments of some affection and remorse, he is otherwise simply a spoiled and selfish snob, absorbed in his comforts and dissipations, incurably shallow and weak. Had Thackeray not elected to show Amelia's "scoundrel of a husband . . . well dead with a ball in his odious bowels," [12] he could have ended in only one other way. The story of his later career would then have added a further portrait to Thackeray's gallery of rakes and blacklegs, a portrait of a less patrician Deuceace, a less intelligent Brandon. Thackeray is saying, in effect, this is what a gentleman on the Regency pattern is really worth.

Dobbin, on the other hand, is almost ludicrously deficient in the personal advantages that make for success and popularity. He is splay-footed and long-legged, raw-boned and clumsy. Thackeray even makes him lisp. Since he cannot play games, is slow at his lessons, and has the misfortune to be the son of a retail grocer (a circumstance which earns him the nickname of "Figs"), his early years are a protracted misery. Yet even in this difficult time, he is honest, unaffected, gentle, and manly; and it is only his loyalty and simplicity which prevent him from seeing through George Osborne, to whom he is fanatically devoted.

With manhood there comes a change in the fortunes of this erstwhile ugly duckling. No doubt his appearance remains somewhat comical, but he makes a name for himself in the army and slowly gains the respect and affection of nearly everyone who meets him. When Amelia's son comes to know "our friend the major" after his return from India, the boy admires Dobbin's "simplicity, his good humour, his various learning quietly imparted, his general love of truth and justice. He had met no such man as yet in the course of his experience, and he had an instinctive liking for a gentleman." [13] Nor is Dobbin by this time any longer at a loss in society. "Swankey of the Body Guard," a later-day George Osborne who pays court to the widowed Amelia, speaks of him as "a d—d king's officer that's always hanging about the house,—a long, thin, queer-looking oldish fellow—a dry fellow though, that took the shine out of a man in the talking line." [14] His infinite superiority to George is clear to the reader long before Becky explains it to Amelia:

> You must have a husband, you fool; and one of the best gentlemen I ever saw has offered you a hundred times, and you have rejected him. . . . That selfish humbug, that low-bred Cockney dandy, that padded booby, who had neither wit, nor manners, nor heart . . . was no more to be compared to your friend with the bamboo-cane than you are to Queen Elizabeth.[15]

Thus, through Dobbin, Thackeray sought to complete the work of *The Book of Snobs* by establishing in the minds of his readers the true image of a middle-class gentleman.

> Perhaps these are rarer personages than some of us think for [he remarks]. Which of us can point out many such in his circle—men whose aims are generous, whose truth is constant, and not only constant in its kind, but elevated in its degree; whose want of meanness makes them simple: who can look the world honestly in the face with an equal manly sympathy for the great and the small? We all know a hundred whose coats are very well made, and a score who have excellent manners, and one or two happy beings who are what they call, in the inner circles, and have shot into the very centre and bull's-

eye of the fashion; but of gentlemen, how many? Let us take a little scrap of paper and each make out his list.[16]

It was Thackeray's hope, of course, that the list would lengthen, as the false conception of gentlemanliness was gradually replaced by the true.

No less central to Thackeray's evaluation of English life in *Vanity Fair* is the picture that he draws of its upper world. As I have pointed out elsewhere,[17] this is the best of all touchstones to his general attitude towards society. Professor Matthew Rosa, the historian of fashionable fiction, has shown how *Vanity Fair* became the silver-fork novel to end all silver-fork novels. "By its very success," he writes, ". . . [it] has so dwarfed its predecessors that they now no longer seem to occupy the position that is rightfully theirs." [18] How did Thackeray accomplish this feat?

When Thackeray began his novel, there were, broadly speaking, three ways of regarding fashionable life in fiction. To the "serious" it was quite simply immoral and reprehensible. In evangelical stories characters from the great world serve chiefly as terrible examples. Mrs. Sherwood writes of little Augusta Noble in *The History of the Fairchild Family* that she was "the darling of her mother, who brought her up in great pride, without fear of God or knowledge of religion; nay, Lady Noble would even mock religion and religious people in her presence." After this we know that there is no hope for little Augusta; and, indeed, she shortly plays with fire, in violation of the instructions of her doting mother and sycophantic governess, and burns to death in agony. Equally hostile and equally simple-minded was the view taken of fashionable life by extreme radicals. The penny "bloods" of the time, as well as the Surrey melodramas, drew their villains from the peerage and their heroes from the hardworking lower classes. This pattern survives almost intact in the scenes between Sir Mulberry Hawk and Lord Frederick Verisopht on the one hand and Nicholas on the other in *Nicholas Nickleby*.[19] Finally, there were the actual or would-be fashionables themselves. To this group "high life" offered the culminating pleasures of existence; its values and customs were accepted as part of the nature of things. *Pelham, Cecil,* and *Henrietta*

Temple, to name three emergent silver-fork novels, illustrate this point of view.

None of these attitudes satisfied Thackeray. His early surfeit of evangelicalism had made that narrow creed distasteful to him. When he was awakened to a new sense of responsibility in 1846, he became "earnest," in the sense that Dr. Thomas Arnold had given to that term, rather than "serious." [20] The naïve radicalism of the popular story-teller seemed absurd to him. His attitude is exactly that which Gilbert was later to hit off so neatly in *Iolanthe,* when his chorus of peers sings:

High rank involves no shame—
We boast an equal claim
With him of humble name
To be respected!

Nor could Thackeray accept the complacent satisfaction with high life which marked even such acute pictures of fashionable life as those provided by Bulwer, Mrs. Gore, and Disraeli.[21]

In *Vanity Fair* Thackeray accordingly contrives both to display the glamour of fashionable life within its own frame and to suggest the doubts which occur to the thoughtful onlooker once fashionable life is viewed in a larger context. Conceivably he succeeded so incomparably well in conveying the charms of high life in this novel because he was not yet familiar with it at first hand. "Never show a gifted novelist above the basement stairs," advises Frank Moore Colby, "if you wish him to retain an exciting sense of social altitudes." [22] Seen from a distance, at any rate, "the *theatrical show* of society" [23] entranced Thackeray. He communicates to the reader his own fascination with the details of genealogy, family history, and heraldry; [24] he makes us share his conviction that if Lord Steyne is a "worn-out old man," he is also a "great prince." [25] In his account of Becky's adventures in the great world (notably in Chapters 47, 49, and 51), he presents a wonderfully evocative picture, which displays the glories and miseries of the high life with an almost romantic appreciation. Even so good a democrat as Justice Oliver Wendell Holmes was constrained to remark after reading *Vanity Fair* that "there was splendor in Thackeray's time." [26]

Yet Thackeray concurrently applies the standards by which he judges life generally, with results that are hardly so favourable. His position is exactly that outlined by Walter Bagehot in commenting to his fiancée on a party given by Lady Palmerston:

It is all nonsense or morbidness, as you say, to call the world *all* hollow. It is an object of the greatest *intellectual* interest to those who have the mind and opportunity to study it. The mistake is to treat it as giving more than intellectual interest ever can. The deepest part of the soul after a little revolts at anything merely intellectual. Such things seem trivial and unworthy when forced on us as substitutes for what is deeper.[27]

So Thackeray constantly hints at reservations concerning the seemingly glamorous picture that he is drawing. One device, which we have noted, is to point out that he cannot vouch personally for the information that he provides. Another is to embark upon such flights of panegyric that the reader cannot but suspect irony. The two are employed together when he deals with Becky's presentation to George IV:

What were the circumstances of the interview between Rebecca Crawley, *née* Sharp, and her Imperial Master, it does not become such a feeble and inexperienced pen as mine to attempt to relate. The dazzled eyes close before that Magnificent Idea. Loyal respect and decency tell even the imagination not to look too keenly and audaciously about the sacred audience-chamber, but to back away rapidly, silently, and respectfully, making profound bows out of the August Presence.[28]

Occasionally, Thackeray is more direct in suggesting his verdict. He makes Becky reflect on her past history, after sinking to the company of "shabby dandies and fly-blown beauties" in a Parisian boarding-house kept by Mme. de St. Amour, in the following terms:

'The women here are as amusing as those in May Fair,' she told an old London friend who met her—'only, their dresses are not quite so fresh. The men wear cleaned gloves, and are sad rogues, certainly, but they are not worse than Jack This, and Tom That. The mistress of the house is a little vulgar, but I don't think she is so vulgar as Lady——' and here she named the name of a great leader of fashion that I would die rather than reveal.[29]

To many of its first readers in 1847 and 1848, a restive and uneasy period in English history, *Vanity Fair* seemed a dangerous manifestation of the levelling spirit of the times. Charlotte Brontë inquired:

Is the satirist of "Vanity Fair" admired in high places? I cannot tell; but think if some of those amongst whom he hurls the Greek fire of his sarcasm, and over whom he flashes the levin-brand of his denunciation, were to take his warnings in time—they or their seed might yet escape a fatal Ramoth-Gilead.[30]

Even fifteen years later a shrewd critic in *Fraser's Magazine* observed:

Vanity Fair admits of being explained as a representation of part of the world; but it may also be viewed, and that somewhat plausibly, as a general attack upon things as they are, and as a declaration of war upon the established order of society.[31]

Yet, as we have seen, *Vanity Fair,* like *The Book of Snobs,* is really conservative in spirit. In his comprehensive and impartial appraisal of English life Thackeray praised what was good while he attacked what was bad. If he was at war with the grossness and arrogance of the Regency, he was equally urgent in wishing to make the benign aspects of gentlemanliness part of the middle-class code that governed English behaviour in the 1840s. Considered in this light, *Vanity Fair* is the capital illustration in literature of the revolution in manners that occurred between the reigns of George IV and Queen Victoria.

VI

But interesting as *Vanity Fair* is as a description and evaluation of early nineteenth-century English society, it is far more than a historical document. Its claim to be regarded as one of the half-dozen great novels of the world derives most securely, not from any of the qualities thus far discussed, but from the illumination it provides of mankind's common moral experience. The sensitive and intelligent reader of fiction, as Edith Wharton has noted, is haunted by the "unconscious but insistent inner question: 'What am I being told this story for? What judgment on life does it contain for me?' "[1] Since *Vanity Fair* was written to communicate the vision of life that Thackeray sums up in his title, the answer to these questions is implicit in every line of his book.[2] What are the essentials of this vision, as he formulated them in his masterpiece?

We have seen how Thackeray began his literary career as the sworn enemy of humbug and cant. Persuaded, with Shaftesbury, that "impostors naturally speak the best of human nature, that they may the easier abuse it," he endeavoured to demonstrate his own sincerity by seeking out the selfish motives of even apparently disinterested actions. So far did he carry his search, indeed, that the epigraph of La Rochefoucauld's *Maximes morales* might also serve for *Vanity Fair:* "Nos vertus ne sont le plus souvent que des vices déguisés." The virtuosity which he acquired in analysing the devious ways in which interested motives manifest themselves is admirably illustrated in the following account of old Osborne after he has learned of George's death at Waterloo:

The news which that famous *Gazette* brought to the Osbornes gave a dreadful shock to the family and its chief. The girls indulged unrestrained in their grief. The gloom-stricken old father was still more borne down by his fate and sorrow. He strove to think that a judgment was on the boy for his disobedience. He dared not own that the severity of the sentence frightened him, and that its fulfilment had come too soon upon his curses. Sometimes a shuddering terror struck him, as if he had been the author of the doom which he had called down on his son. There was a chance before of reconciliation. The boy's wife might have died; or he might have come back and said, Father I have sinned. But there was no hope now. He stood on the other side of the gulf impassable, haunting his parent with sad eyes. He remembered them once before so in a fever, when every one thought the lad was dying, and he lay on his bed speechless, and gazing with a dreadful gloom. Good God! how the father clung to the doctor then; and with what a sickening anxiety he followed him: what a weight of grief was off his mind when, after the crisis of the fever, the lad recovered, and looked at his father once more with eyes that recognized him. But now there was no help or cure, or chance of reconcilement: above all, there were no humble words to soothe vanity outraged and furious, or bring to its natural flow the poisoned, angry blood. And it is hard to say which pang it was that tore the proud father's heart most keenly—that his son should have gone out of the reach of his forgiveness, or that the apology which his own pride expected should have escaped him.[3]

Yet it should be noted that Thackeray found most of the material for his cruel and penetrating analysis of universal egoism through self-examination. Though he addresses each member of his audience as *"Hypocrite lecteur,"* he is ready to add with Baudelaire, *"mon semblable, mon frère."* He makes no more ambitious claim than "Video meliora, deteriora sequor."

If Thackeray believed that such are the motives controlling conduct in the world, it follows that success in his eyes was an empty attainment indeed. When Becky visits Queen's Crawley after the younger Sir Pitt has come into his inheritance, she reflects:

'It isn't difficult to be a country gentleman's wife. . . . I think I could be a good woman if I had five thousand a year. I could dawdle about in the nursery, and count apricots on the wall. I could water plants in a greenhouse, and pick off dead leaves from the geraniums. I could ask old women about their rheumatisms, and order half a crown's worth of soup for the poor.'

Under such conditions, Becky concludes, virtue would be easy and natural.

And who knows but Rebecca was right in her speculations [Thackeray inquires]—and that it was only a question of money and fortune which made the difference between her and an honest woman? If you take temptations into account, who is to say that he is better than his neighbour? A comfortable career of prosperity, if it does not make people honest, at least keeps them so. An alderman coming from a turtle feast will not step out of his carriage to steal a leg of mutton; but put him to starve, and see if he will not purloin a loaf.[4]

Though his contemporaries protested against this line of argument as embodying the most dangerous sort of cynicism,[5] Thackeray was firmly persuaded of its justice. Success was a lottery, he held, quite unconnected with desert.

The hidden and awful Wisdom which apportions the destinies of mankind is pleased to humiliate and cast down the tender, good, and wise; and to set up the selfish, the foolish, or the wicked. Oh, be humble, my brother, in your prosperity! Be gentle with those who are less lucky, if not more deserving. Think, what right have you to be scornful, whose virtue is a deficiency of temptation, whose success may be a chance, whose rank may be an ancestor's accident, whose prosperity is very likely a satire.[6]

If those who flourish in the world gain their positions either through good fortune or by being "Faithless, Hopeless, Charityless," they surely deserve neither respect nor admiration. Thackeray reserves some of his bitterest irony for persons of "well-regulated minds," who have "no reverence except for prosperity, and no eye for anything beyond success." [7] "Pity the fallen gentleman," he urges his respectable readers after describing old Sedley's ruin; "you to whom money and fair repute are the chiefest good; and so, surely, are they in Vanity Fair." [8] Elsewhere, he continues:

You and I, my dear reader, may drop into this condition one day: for have not many of our friends attained it? Our luck may fail: our powers forsake us: our place on the boards be taken by better and younger mimes—the chance of life roll away and leave us shattered and stranded. Then men will walk across the road when they meet you—or, worse still, hold you out a couple of fingers and patronize you in a pitying way—then you will know, as soon as your back is turned, that your friend begins with a 'Poor devil, what imprudences he has committed, what chances *that* chap has thrown away!' Well, well—a carriage and three thousand a year is not the summit of the reward nor the end of God's judgment of men. If quacks prosper as often as they go to the wall—if zanies succeed and knaves arrive at fortune, and, vice versa, sharing ill luck and prosperity for all the world like the ablest and most honest amongst us—I say, brother, the gifts and pleasures of Vanity Fair cannot be held of any great account.[9]

Life is redeemed for Thackeray only by affection, by love, by loyalty to the promptings of the heart.

His writings mean, if they mean anything [observes Sir Leslie Stephen], that the love of a wife and child and friend is the one sacred element in our nature, of infinitely higher price than anything which can come into competition with it; and that Vanity Fair is what it is, precisely because it stimulates the pursuit of objects frivolous and unsatisfying just so far as they imply indifference to these emotions.[10]

Since a fair of vanities is a corrupting place, unspotted virtue is to be expected only in those who have entirely avoided "the contagion of the world's slow stain." Hence Thackeray's praise of the simple innocence that marks the "home-keeping hearts" of children and sheltered women. This exaltation of innocence seems strange today, but to Thackeray's contemporaries it was an *idée reçue*. From Amelia to Browning's Pompilia, the Victorian ideal was that summed up in *In Memoriam:*

> Thrice blest whose lives are faithful prayers,
>   Whose loves in higher love endure;
>   What souls possess themselves so pure,
> Or is there blessedness like theirs?

It was in order to communicate the view of life just outlined that Thackeray endeavoured to make *Vanity Fair* equally the story of Becky and of Amelia. The two were established in conscious contrast, like George Osborne and Dobbin, one accepting the usages of *Vanity Fair,* the other rejecting them. At first glance the life of well-to-do England that Thackeray describes might seem one of those "subjects too shallow to yield anything to the most searching gaze." But he learned, as Edith Wharton did many years later, "that a frivolous society can acquire dramatic significance only through what its frivolity destroys. Its tragic implication lies in its power of debasing people and ideals." [11] Becky's career is admirably suited to illustrate the destructive operation of the standards of Vanity Fair, but Thackeray desired through Amelia's history to show what he would put in their place, the life of personal relations, the loyalty and selflessness inspired by home affections. This recurring contrast was essential to his purpose. As one of the keenest of contemporary critics observed, "He could not have painted Vanity Fair as he has, unless Eden had been shining brightly in his inner eyes." [12]

Holding the balance even between Becky and Amelia offered almost insuperable difficulties, however, because Thackeray in

Becky created one of the great imaginative embodiments of energy and amoral enterprise.[13] He introduces her casually enough, in a postscript to a letter about Amelia, but by the end of the first chapter, as she throws Johnson's Dictionary back into Miss Pinkerton's garden, she has wholly captivated the reader. Even her situation calls for sympathy, since Thackeray has in effect cast the wicked sister in the role of Cinderella. Alone and unprotected, she begins the world in the difficult and anomalous position of governess; and at every step up the ladder, she must struggle against heavy odds. She is not a beauty.[14] "Green eyes, fair skin, pretty figure, famous frontal development," is the moderate summary of Dr. Squills. Mr. Clump, the apothecary, agrees; yet he is constrained to add that "there is something about her." [15] Becky works her spell, indeed, by sheer talent and vivacity. She is "an artist herself," "eminent and successful as a practitioner in the art of giving pleasure." [16] She sings with professional competence and is a notable mimic and actress. From the moment that she expresses her wish to see Miss Pinkerton "floating in the water yonder, turban and all, with her train streaming after her, and her nose like the beak of a wherry," [17] her wit is sharp and ready. Some of her sayings—like "I'm no angel"—have passed into common parlance. These qualities, together with her unfailing cheerfulness and contagious high spirits, win the reader in spite of himself, and he watches enchanted as Becky carves out her career.

Thackeray seems at first to conceive of Becky as a female Barry Lyndon, an adventuress who unconsciously reveals her own rascality; [18] indeed, Frank Chandler in his standard history of the rogue-tale views *Vanity Fair* as "the most powerful [story] in the range of picaresque fiction" and Becky as "the subtlest of antiheroines." [19] Certainly Becky's extraordinary social mobility is most useful to Thackeray in exploring the whole range of a rigid society in which the respectable and conventional individual could rise only slowly and painfully out of the rank in which he was born. Yet Thackeray soon saw that the Barry Lyndon formula was too narrow for his purpose, even though he allowed Becky to retain to the end something of the outlaw's point of view that she had learned from her clever and dissolute father.

Her sheer joy in playing the game of life becomes part of her hold on the reader; it is a pleasure to see such an expert competitor succeed. The reader grows annoyed when for a brief period she is duped by the dull and proper world in which she is building herself a position, but she soon recovers her sense of proportion, and he can say with relief, "Becky's herself again." No defeat daunts her long, and even after her catastrophe she contrives to enjoy herself as much in the depths of Continental Bohemia as when she "had the fee-simple of May Fair." [20]

Thackeray adroitly reveals the chink in Becky's armour to be her lack of the quality in which Amelia excels. She is unable to feel affection or love. Even towards Rawdon, whose picture she had dreamed about on her first night in the Crawleys' house,[21] and who had lavished upon her a devotion of which no one thought him capable, she displays merely a good-natured tolerance. This inability to feel cuts her off from normal people. By blinding her to what they expect, it infects her with a basic insincerity which gives her away at crucial moments, and is ultimately the cause of her downfall. So it is that by betraying the trust which her husband has placed in her, she brings about her exposure; and by neglecting her son, she makes an enemy of Lady Jane, who prevents Pitt from intervening to save her from ruin.

Even so, it must be granted that beside Thackeray's brilliant and varied picture of Becky, poor Amelia seems sufficiently pale and monotonous. During the course of *Vanity Fair's* serial publication, Thackeray had been hard put to defend Amelia from his readers; [22] and in "Before the Curtain" he thinks it necessary to observe that if

> the famous little Becky Puppet has been pronounced to be uncommonly flexible in the joints, and lively on the wire: the Amelia Doll, though it has had a smaller circle of admirers, has yet been carved and dressed with the greatest care by the artist.[23]

Amelia was particularly dear to her creator, as I have shown elsewhere,[24] because she was drawn in large part from his memories of his wife; and he reaches the height of his eloquence in the passages of his novel which are coloured by the pathos of her suffering.[25] But the handicap of Amelia's utter passivity is in the end insurmountable; she does nothing, she merely endures or enjoys as circumstances dictate. Thackeray himself is forced to admit that it "is not much of a life to describe. There is not much of what you call incident in it." [26]

Even if Amelia's inadequacy is granted, however, one must still insist that to regard *Vanity Fair* as primarily the story of Becky Sharp is to place the novel in a false and impoverishing perspective. D. H. Lawrence has observed that

> The artist usually sets out—or used to—to point a moral and adorn a tale. The tale, however, points the other way, as a rule. Two blankly opposing morals, the artist's and the tale's. Never trust the artist. Trust the tale. The proper function of a critic is to save the tale from the artist who created it.[27]

This missionary work has been attempted by many modern critics, who have held in effect (adapting Blake's phrase about Milton) that Thackeray was of Becky's party without knowing it. It must be emphasized that if the figure of Amelia does not suffice to discredit this contention, the whole structure and meaning of Thackeray's novel, as outlined in this chapter, surely do.

The final impression made by the view of life embodied in *Vanity Fair* is of a resigned and reasonably cheerful melancholy. No doubt Thackeray agreed with Swift that happiness is "the perpetual possession of being well deceived," but this persuasion did not drive him into misanthropy. His way of looking at things is one which those who wish to use literature as a means of changing society, rather than of understanding it, have always resented beyond any other. No doubt exasperated humanitarians will go on for ever thrusting aside Thackeray's "glasses of vintage sadness." [28] Writing of *Antony and Cleopatra,* Bernard Shaw has summed up their arguments with characteristic liveliness:

> The lot of the man who sees life truly and thinks about it romantically is Despair. How well we know the cries of that despair! Vanity of vanities, all is vanity! moans the Preacher, when life has at last taught him that Nature will not dance to his moralist-made tunes. Thackeray, scores of centuries later, was still baying the moon in the same

terms. . . . When your Shakespears and Thackerays huddle up the matter at the end by killing somebody and covering your eyes with the undertaker's handkerchief, duly onioned with some pathetic phrase, as The flight of angels sing thee to thy rest, or Adsum, or the like, I have no respect for them at all: such maudlin tricks may impose on tea-drunkards, not on me.[29]

But Ecclesiastes and Shakespeare are not bad company, and at the lowest estimate *Vanity Fair* is a powerful embodiment of one of the great recurrent responses to life. Most readers will continue to find behind Thackeray's concluding sentences a weight of deeply felt and pondered experience which renders them proof against all the verbal pyrotechnics of critics like Shaw:

Ah! *Vanitas Vanitatum!* Which of us is happy in this world? Which of us has his desire? or, having it, is satisfied?—Come, children, let us shut up the box and the puppets, for our play is played out.[30]

VII

Vanity Fair made Thackeray famous. When it began to appear, his name still meant little to the general public. If he had a few ardent admirers like George Henry Lewes, who thought that he was "the best writer in England," and Dr. John Brown, who had followed his career in *Punch* and elsewhere with mounting enthusiasm,[1] most informed observers would have agreed with Henry Kingsley's description of him as "a man known certainly to some extent, but who was thought to have had sufficient trial, and to have found his métier as a clever magazine writer." [2] When his first Christmas book, *Mrs. Perkins's Ball,* was published in December of 1846, he was quite satisfied with a sale of 1,500 copies, even though Dickens's *Battle of Life* sold 25,000.[3] Bradbury and Evans paid him only £60 a number for *Vanity Fair.* To his mind this was quite sufficient remuneration [4] for "two printed Sheets with two Etchings on Steel and as many drawings on Wood as may be thought necessary." [5]

The monthly numbers of *Vanity Fair* were praised by acute critics almost from the first. Peter Cunningham called attention to Thackeray's achievement in *Fraser's Magazine* for March, 1847. David Masson added his voice to the chorus in the *North British Review* for May. In July the *Sun* called Thackeray "the Fielding of the nineteenth century." Late in the year appeared the second edition of *Jane Eyre* with Charlotte Brontë's admiring dedication to "the satirist of 'Vanity Fair.'" And in January, 1848, Abraham Hayward ratified the popular opinion with a long and complimentary notice in the revered *Edinburgh Review*.[6]

Meanwhile, the novel had become increasingly the topic of literary conversation. In September, 1847, Mrs. Carlyle was exclaiming that *Vanity Fair* "beats Dickens out of the world"; and in December Leigh Hunt was assuring Forster that Thackeray "strikes me as another Fielding, not with the constant strength nor the masterly construction, but with the subtlety, the wit, & more tenderness. He is as sure, I think, to go down to posterity as Dickens; and you know what I think of *him*." [7] As this comparison with Dickens was repeated, Thackeray came to see himself as Dickens's conscious rival for pre-eminence among contemporary novelists. "He read 'Dombey and Son' each month with avidity," we learn.

> When the fifth number [for February, 1847] appeared, containing the death of little Dombey, Thackeray, with the part in his pocket, went down to the *Punch* office, and startled Mark Lemon by suddenly laying it before him and exclaiming, "There! read that. There is no writing against such power as this—no one has a chance. Read the description of young Paul's death; it is unsurpassed—it is stupendous." [8]

By the following January Thackeray was able to tell his mother: "I am become a sort of great man in my way—all but at the top of the tree: indeed there if the truth were known and having a great fight up there with Dickens." [9]

After *Vanity Fair* appeared in volume form at the end of June, the reviewers accepted the completed book as a masterpiece and Thackeray as a great writer. Their response is summed up by a critic in *Bentley's Miscellany:*

> When 'Vanity Fair' began, we saw, or fancied we saw, a strong man taking his ground patiently and quietly. . . . The book which at

first was scouted, yawned over, ignored, as merely dealing with bitternesses, follies, &c. &c., gradually as it went on, became more and more looked at, more and more listened for, its incidents more and more talked over as real things; its people more and more canvassed as well-known acquaintances, until the chorus swelled by a gradual *crescendo* (as the musicians say) into a full cry of admiration.[10]

Those who had earlier written off Thackeray as merely an agreeable journalist now hailed him as one of "the great and true observers of human nature." [11] It was generally held of Becky, that "as a creation or *character,* we know not where [she] can be matched in prose fiction." [12] The compliment that Thackeray had earlier regarded as the greatest of his life, that he was the "Fielding of the nineteenth century," [13] became a mere truism.

And with fame Thackeray at last attained financial security. For many months it had appeared that he might have to content himself with a *succès d'estime.* In October, 1847, he noted that *Vanity Fair* "does everything but sell"; in January of the following year he confessed that "the book doesn't pay with all its unquestionable success"; and as late as March he repeated this complaint.[14] But the novel went well in book form, and Thackeray eventually netted some £2,000 from it.[15] Its real professional service to him, however, was in multiplying the value of all his future work. Henceforth he was paid, not as a clever magazine writer, but as a great popular favourite.

With the triumph of *Vanity Fair,* Thackeray could fairly say, "my cup runneth over," even though he had to add, "Time finds a withered leaf in every laurel." And the book formed a watershed in his career. His life during and after 1847 assumed a new pattern, and his writing quickly came to reflect his changing preoccupations. But that is another story, which must be reserved for a second volume.

Appendix A

Richmond Thackeray's Will

(Calcutta March the third 1815.)

In order to save my friends trouble in the event of my decease I leave this will in order that my family may ascertain without difficulty the property which I possess and my intentions with regard to the disposal of it my wife my son my sister Augusta and my illegitimate Child I am naturally anxious to provide for in the first place but as my savings are now considerable I trust in a short time if it shall please God to prolong my life that I may be able at a future period to leave to my other Brothers and Sisters some token of the sincere affection which I feel for each of them 1st I leave in Company paper Sa R^{s} 26,000. r^{s} 400 of 1814–15 2^{d} I leave in the three Pr Cent Consols £3.300 standing in the joint names of my late venerable father William Makepeace Thackeray & in my name 3^{d} My lamented Brother Thomas has left me his sole heir he possessed exclusive of any little property appertaining to him in this Country £1000 in the 4 Pr Cents in England under the Will of my late venerable father. 4. I have paid into the hands of Alexander & Co at Calcutta various sums $amount^{g}$ in the Aggregate to S^{a} R^{s} [31,070 *lined out*] 41600 July 19 on account of the house in Chowringhee in which I reside 40.000 5th I possess a Service of plate and various articles of furniture et. which with my Carriage and horses may be reasonably estimated at SaRs 18000 and as my savings usually average about 2500 Rs per [month] my Executors on reference to the date of this paper will have no difficulty in ascertaining the probable amt of my future acquisitions I direct that my property may be disposed of as follows all my disposable property to be converted into Cash and invested either in landed property or in the public funds Indian or European as my Executors may determine if the purchase money of my house has not been liquidated it will be advisable in the first instance to complete the purchase Among my papers will be found the engagement of Alexander & Co to refund the amt with Interest if a proper title is not delivered within a given period and if the deeds are not delivered it will be just to settle the rent after deducting the sums which I have expended in giving the house a perfect repair which was indespensibly requisite the house not having been painted for four or five years & in various improvements amtg altogether to about Rs 3000 part of the marble in the Great hall belongs to me also the whole of that which is laid in the passage room leading to it the sums above specified will I trust afford a permanent annual income of £ eight hundred which I leave as follows to my wife an Annuity of £450 (two hundred) to my son £100 per Annum to my Sister Augusta £100 per Annum to my illegitimate Child £100 per Annum to the Mother of my illegitimate Child SaRs 16 sixteen per [month] for life to the wife of the old Syce who was killed by a horse in my Service Sa Rs 3 per [month] also for life should there be any deficiency a proportionate deduction must be made from each the whole of the above bequests are to be considered life Annuities and finally to devolve to my Son William Makepeace and if my wife marries again one half of her Annuity is to be deducted for the benefit of my said Son and such portion of it this moiety viz 225£ as may not be required for the purpose of providing for his Education and maintenance is to accumulate until he arrives at the age of twenty one years any sums which I may hereafter acquire if not specially provided for shall be after the above bequests are made good invested in the Public funds in Lands or houses at the discretion of my Executors and the Interest or rents arising divided into five shares one for my wife one for my Son one for my Brother William one for my Sister Augusta and one to be divided between my Brothers Francis and Charles the whole of which are to be life Annuities and finally to devolve to my Son William Makepeace if it shall please God to take my Son before he arrives at the age of 21 he being then unmarried the income provided for him is to devolve as follows one half to my wife for life and the remainder among each of my brothers and Sisters as may not possess £500 per Annum it will of course be an object with my Executors to provide my wife and Child with a passage to Europe and also my Sister Augusta and my illegitimate Child if it is considered adviseable for them to leave india my wife shall be the Guardian of my illegitimate Child I request my friends George Dowdeswell John Eliot and Henry Hodgson to be my Executors Jointly with my wife Major E. W. Butler and my brother in Law John Shakespear and to be the Guardians and protectors of my Son & in the event of the death of any of the above persons or in case they should not be able to act I request my brothers William St John Francis Charles to aid and assist in carrying into effect those injunctions. Richmond Thackeray—should my Son die without Children before my wife she may dispose of 225 per Annum as she thinks proper my Sister Augusta may also in that case dispose of her legacy.

In the supreme Court of Judicature at Fort William in Bengal in the Goods of Richmond Thackeray deceased Allen Graham of the Town of Calcutta a Captain of artillery in the Service of United Company of Merchants of England trading to the East Indies on their Bengal Establishment maketh oath & saith that he knew Richmond Thackeray late of Calcutta aforesaid a Senior Merchant in the Civil Service of the said United Company in his life time and is well acquainted with his hand writing he this deponent having frequently seen him write and this deponent further saith that the paper writing hereunto annexed marked & purporting to be the last will and testament of the said Richmond Thackeray deceased is all of the proper handwriting of the said Richmond Thackeray as this deponent verily believes. Allan Graham. Capn Lt Arty sworn this 29 day of September 1815 before me S. Royds.

On 5th February 1818. admon of the Goods of Richmond Thackeray late of Calcutta in the East Indies Esquire deceased was granted to John Ritchie the lawful Attorney of Anne Thackeray widow the Relict Edward William Butler and John Talbot Shakespear (in the will written John Shakespear) three of the Executors limited so far only as concerns all the Right Title and Interest of him the said deceased of in and to the sum of three thousand three hundred pounds three per Cent Consolidated Bank Annuities standing in the joint names of William Makepeace Thackeray and the said deceased and all the Interest & dividends due or to grow due thereon and all benefit and advantage to be had derived and taken therefrom for the use & benefit of the said Executors now residing in the East Indies being first sworn duly to admt George Dowdeswell John Eliot and Henry Hodgson the other Executors having been first only Cited to accept or refuse the probate & execution thereof with the usual Intimation but in no wise appeared.

Proved at London 7 Decr 1827 before the judge by the Oath of Anne Smyth formerly Thackeray (wife of Henry Carmichael Smyth) the Relict (one of the surviving Extors) to whom admon was granted being first sworn by Comon duly to administer Power reserved of making the like grant to George Dowdeswell Esquire the other Executor The Letters of admon (with the will annexed) of the Goods of the said deceased granted in the month of February 1818 under certain limitations to John Ritchie Esquire the lawful attorney of the said Anne Smyth and of Edward William Butler and John Talbot Shakespear three of the surviving Executors having been first voluntarily brought in & revoked by Jul 7 Decree.

Appendix B

Thackeray's Agreement with Bradbury and Evans for *Vanity Fair*

Memorandum of agreement made this Twenty fifth day of January 1847, between William Makepeace Thackeray Esqe of 13 Young Street Kensington, and William Bradbury and Frederick Mullett Evans, copartners, Printers & Publishers, Whitefriars—

The said William Makepeace Thackeray hereby agrees with the said William Bradbury and Frederick Mullett Evans, to publish a work in Monthly Parts to be called "Vanity Fair, Pen & Pencil Sketches of English Society"—

The said William Makepeace Thackeray undertakes to furnish by the 15th of every month sufficient matter for at least Two printed Sheets with two Etchings on Steel, and as many drawings on Wood as may be thought necessary—

The said William Bradbury and Frederick Mullett Evans agree to pay to the said William Makepeace Thackeray the sum of Sixty Pounds every month on the Publication of the Number—

It is then agreed that after the whole Expenses of the Work are paid (including the above named sum of£60—) that the said William Bradbury & Frederick Mullett Evans shall receive out of the first profits, the sum of £60, and that whatever further profits shall arise shall then be equally divided between the aforesaid William Makepeace Thackeray and William Bradbury and Frederick Mullett Evans—

That the Copyright of the said Work shall be the joint Property of the aforesaid William Makepeace Thackeray and William Bradbury and Frederick Mullett Evans—

[*signed*] W M Thackeray—

Notes

Much of this book is based on manuscript sources. With three exceptions, the name of the owner or depositary of each document cited is given briefly in parenthesis (a fuller identification being provided in the Preface), unless it has been supplied in an earlier note to the same chapter. The exceptions are documents frequently referred to throughout the notes. These are here located once for all:

Lady Ritchie's manuscript reminiscences, 1864–1865 and 1878. Two sets of recollections of Thackeray written by his older daughter, the first in the months following his death, the second many years later for her niece, Laura Stephen. Owned by the author.

Manuscript Silver diary. A diary kept by contributor Henry Silver, which records conversations at the *Punch* table between 4 August 1858 and 23 March 1870. Owned by the firm of Bradbury Agnew.

Certain printed sources have also been used so extensively that it is convenient to refer to them by cue-titles:

Bedingfield. Richard Bedingfield, "Recollections of Thackeray," *Cassell's Magazine,* II (1870), 12–14, 28–30, 72–75, 108–110, 134–136, 230–232, 296–299.

Biographical Introductions. Lady Ritchie, Biographical Introductions to *The Works of William Makepeace Thackeray,* 13 vols. (London, 1898–1899).

Buried Life. Gordon N. Ray, *The Buried Life: A Study of the Re-*

lation between Thackeray's Fiction and His Personal History (London, 1952).

Centenary Biographical Introductions. Lady Ritchie, Biographical Introductions to the "Centenary" edition of *The Works of William Makepeace Thackeray,* 26 vols. (London, 1910–1911).

Chapters. Lady Ritchie, *Chapters from Some Memoirs* (London, 1894).

Glances Back. Henry Vizetelly, *Glances Back through Seventy Years,* 2 vols. (London, 1893).

Gulliver. Harold Strong Gulliver, *Thackeray's Literary Apprenticeship* (Valdosta, 1934).

Hannay. James Hannay, *A Brief Memoir of the Late Mr. Thackeray* (Edinburgh, 1864).

Letters. The Letters and Private Papers of William Makepeace Thackeray, ed. Gordon N. Ray, 4 vols. (Cambridge, 1945–1946).

Letters, ed. Dexter. *The Letters of Charles Dickens,* ed. Walter Dexter, 3 vols. (London, 1938).

Letters and Literary Remains. Letters and Literary Remains of Edward FitzGerald, 7 vols. (London, 1903).

Memorials. Mrs. Richard Pryme and Mrs. William Bayne, *Memorials of the Thackeray Family* (privately printed, London, 1879).

Merivale and Marzials. Herman Merivale and Frank T. Marzials, *Life of W. M. Thackeray* (London, 1891).

Mrs. Brookfield. Charles and Frances Brookfield, *Mrs. Brookfield and Her Circle,* 2 vols. (New York, 1905).

Works. The Oxford Thackeray, ed. George Saintsbury, 17 vols. (London, 1908).

INTRODUCTION

I (pp. 1–9)

1. Manuscript diary, 20 November 1862.
2. Manuscript reminiscences, 1864–1865.
3. Manuscript letter (Fuller).
4. She objected principally to the illustrations that Fields had given of Thackeray's playfulness: "An anecdote I sh[d] like omitted is that one of my father attempting to put his legs out of the window (w[h] of course he would not have thought of really doing) another w[h] seemed to me not characteristic of him was his stopping in the street to make a quotation about the Edinbro' speech it seemed to me that altho' I of course understood that you meant to describe him as laughing at himself, it

would scarcely strike anyone who read it without knowing him, in that light" (undated manuscript letter, Huntington Library).

5. Manuscript letter from FitzGerald to Lady Ritchie, 17 May 1882 (Fuller).

6. *Works,* 24 vols. (London, 1878–1879), XXIV, 305–306.

7. Chap. 51.

8. "Discoveries concerning Thackeray," *Nation,* XXXII (1881), 56. Yates had not entirely abandoned his campaign against Thackeray even between 1863 and 1880. Stephen pointed out a disagreeable character modelled on Thackeray in Yates's *Dr. Wainwright's Patient,* when he noticed that novel for the *Saturday Review,* XXXI (4 February 1871), 154–155.

9. "An Old Club Scandal," *Time,* II (January, 1880), 385–392.

10. For a fuller account of Yates's campaign and its consequences, see my "Dickens vs. Thackeray: The Garrick Club Affair," *PMLA,* LXIX (September, 1954), 815–832.

11. William Ballantine, *Some Experiences of a Barrister's Life* (London, 1882); W. P. Frith, *My Autobiography and Reminiscences,* 3 vols. (London, 1887–1888); John Cordy Jeaffreson, *A Book of Recollections,* 2 vols. (London, 1894).

12. *The Table Talk of Shirley* (Edinburgh and London, 1895), p. 25.

13. *Biographical Introductions,* VII, xix.

14. *A Collection of Letters of Thackeray* (New York, 1887), p. vi.

15. Manuscript letter, 31 March 1887 (Fuller).

16. Manuscript letters from Stephen to Lady Ritchie, 15 January and 31 March 1887 (Fuller).

17. Manuscript letter of 23 October 1887 (Fuller).

18. See the *Standard's* correspondence columns and editorial page for 30 November 1887.

19. *Illustrated London News,* XCVIII (20 June 1891), 811.

20. *Temple Bar,* LXXXIII (1888), 193.

21. This decision explains why Stephen, who was editor of the *Dictionary of National Biography,* never attempted a life of his father-in-law. He declined such a commission in 1902, observing: "I could not ask [Lady Ritchie] to help me in producing a life for an edition competing with that in which her prefaces appear and which is issued by her and her father's old publishers" (Ifan Kyrle Fletcher catalogue 146, 1951).

22. *Private View* (London, 1953), p. 50.

23. Quoted by Mrs. Fuller, *Thackeray and His Daughter* (New York, 1924), p. 262.

24. *Mainly Victorian* (London, 1924), p. 68.

25. *Thackeray and His Daughter,* p. 263.

26. Darrell Figgis, *Studies and Appreciations* (London, 1909), p. 232.

27. *Thackeray and His Daughter,* pp. 298, 300.

28. Compare Mrs. Woolf's references

to Lady Ritchie in *A Writer's Diary* (London, 1953).

29. Melville's *Life of William Makepeace Thackeray,* 2 vols. (London, 1899), is almost worthless. His 1910 *Life* is an entirely new book.
30. See *Letters,* I, lxix–lxx.
31. *Bulwer and His Wife: A Panorama: 1803–1836* (London, 1933), p. 251.
32. "A Diffident Biographer," *New Statesman and Nation,* N. S., IV (24 September 1932), 347–348.
33. "In Defence of Thackeray," *Nineteenth Century,* CXIV (July, 1933), 103.
34. "William Makepeace Thackeray," the same, CXL (July, 1946), 50.
35. See my review of Prof. J. Y. T. Greig's *Thackeray: A Reconsideration* (London, 1950) in *Review of English Studies,* N. S., II (April, 1951), 196–198.

II (pp. 9–18)

1. "Thackeray," [London] *Bookman,* XXXVII (December, 1909), 144.
2. New York, 1948, p. 20.
3. Transcript of manuscript letter, 6 July 1856 (Fuller).
4. Arthur Bartlett Maurice, "Thackeray and Currer Bell," *Bookman,* LXII (December, 1925), 454–455, quoting a Victorian pamphlet.
5. See, for example, Jeaffreson, I, 261; Ballantine, I, 137; "A Long Awaited Story," *Bookman,* XXXIX (March, 1914), 1.
6. *New Statesman and Nation,* IV, 347.
7. *Axel's Castle* (New York, 1950), p. viii.
8. *Thackeray: A Critical Portrait* (New York, 1941).
9. *W. M. Thackeray, l'homme, le penseur, le romancier* (Paris, 1932).
10. [London] *Bookman,* LXXXIII (1932), 40.
11. *Jane Eyre: An Autobiography,* 2d ed., 3 vols. (London, 1848), I, x–xi.
12. *Review of English Studies,* XXIV (October, 1948), 342.
13. "From a Writer's Notebook," *Nation,* CLXXIX (14 August 1954), 135.
14. *Private View,* p. 43.
15. *The New Yorker,* 2 December 1945; 8 February 1947.
16. *Novels and Novelists from Elizabeth to Victoria,* 2 vols. (London, 1858), II, 28.
17. *The Victorian Age in Literature* (London, n. d.) pp. 28–29.
18. "Charles Dickens," *Works,* ed. Forrest Morgan, 5 vols. (Hartford, 1891), II, 271.
19. Ed. Kenneth Clark (London, 1949), pp. 213–214.
20. So Dorothy Van Ghent, for example, observes that Thackeray's creative perceptions are "more penetrating and profound" than Fielding's and "reach a good deal deeper into the difficulties, compromises, and darkness of the human estate" (*The English Novel: Form and Function,* New York, 1953, p. 140).

21. *Enemies of Promise* (London, 1949), p. 114.
22. *Masters of Literature—Thackeray* (London, 1909), p. xxxii.
23. *Mimesis,* translated by Willard R. Trask (Princeton, 1953), pp. 505–506.
24. Bedingfield, p. 28.
25. "Why Is Thackeray Neglected Now?" [London] *Sunday Times,* 13 September 1931.
26. *Lives of the English Poets,* ed. George Birkbeck Hill, 3 vols. (Oxford, 1905), I, 368.
27. *The Showman of Vanity Fair* (New York, 1947).
28. *Bookman,* XXXVII, 145.

CHAPTER *I*

The Three Generations That Made a Gentleman

I (pp. 19–23)

1. Hannay, p. 5.
2. Francis Henry Skrine, *Life of Sir William Wilson Hunter* (London, 1901), pp. 452–453.
3. *Correspondence of John Lothrop Motley,* ed. G. W. Curtis, 2 vols. (New York, 1889), I, 235.
4. Hannay, p. 5. See Horace, *Odes,* III, xix.
5. *Memorials,* pp. 5–6. See also "The Pedigree of Thackeray," *Herald and Genealogist,* II (1864), 315–328, 440–455, 557–558, and *Centenary Biographical Introductions,* XXV, xiii–xv.
6. *Letters,* IV, 285.
7. *Memorials,* p. 7.
8. *Biographical Introductions,* XIII, xxxvi. Yet Mrs. Bayne was some years later shown a "large, old-fashioned red-bricked house . . . in which the family had lived" (*Memorials,* p. 7). The edifice described to Thackeray may have been a smaller grey stone farm-house once belonging to the last of the Hampsthwaite Thackerays, which had disappeared long before Mrs. Bayne's visit.
9. *Memorials,* pp. 7–8.
10. The career of Archdeacon Thackeray is recounted in *Biographical Introductions, Herald and Genealogist, Memorials,* and Percy M. Thornton's *Harrow School and Its Surroundings* (London, 1885), pp. 121–143.
11. So writes the Rev. William Cole (quoted in *Herald and Genealogist,* II, 320). Wray's version is that "Chapman's friends refusing absolutely to concur with either of the two other parties, Thackeray's votes went over to George by agreement, and he was declared."
12. I have here followed *Memorials,* pp. 22–24. R. A. Austen-Leigh (*Eton College Register 1753–1790,* Eton, 1921), noting that from about 1771 until 1809 the widow of Thomas Thackeray "returned to her early home at

Eton and kept a fashionable boarding house," refers his readers to Chapter 24 of Lady Ritchie's *Miss Angel.*

II (pp. 24–37)

1. *Biographical Introductions,* XIII, xxxvi.
2. *Memorials,* p. 289.
3. Quoted by C. H. Philips, *The East India Company 1784–1834* (Manchester, 1940), p. 1.
4. *Speech in the House of Commons, 30th March, 1772* (London, 1772), p. 44.
5. Quoted by F. B. Bradley-Birt, *'Sylhet' Thackeray* (London, 1911), p. 14. It should be noted that the story of Thackeray's grandfather in Bengal has been traced by two scholars, each in his day a recognized authority on certain aspects of Indian history: Sir William Wilson Hunter in *The Thackerays in India and Some Calcutta Graves* (London, 1897) and Bradley-Birt. On these predecessors a biographer who is himself neither expert in Indian affairs nor inclined like Burke "by the research of years, to wind himself into the utmost recesses and labyrinths of the India detail," must necessarily lean heavily. But Hunter in particular is most inaccurate (see *Bengal Past and Present,* V, 368–369; XXXII, 69–70; XXXIX, 76), and both he and Bradley-Birt are exclusively counsels for the defence. W. K. Firminger does not exaggerate when he describes Hunter's book as "a most incomplete inquiry tricked out by the arts of a picturesque imagination and the fond beliefs of a hero worshipper"(*Bengal Past and Present,* VI, 406). Moreover, much information is available concerning Thackeray's transactions in Sylhet of which Hunter and Bradley-Birt either did not know or made only partial use. This information is embodied in two books, Henry Beveridge's *District of Bakaranj. Its History and Statistics* (London, 1876), and *The Farrington Diary,* ed. James Greig, 8 vols. (London, 1922–1928), III, 278–279; and in the following articles in *Bengal Past and Present:* W. K. Firminger, "Leaves from the Editor's Note-Book," V (1910), 183–194; W. K. Firminger, "Leaves from the Editor's Note-book," VII (1911), 228–231; H. E. A. Cotton, "The Farrington Diary," XXIV (1922), 45–46; R. B. Ramsbotham, "A Deal in Elephants," XXVIII (1924), 181–185; and Miss F. H. Sachse, "Thackeray's Apologia," XLI (1931), 41–50.
6. Quoted by Bradley-Birt, p. 16.
7. *Speech in the House of Commons,* pp. 44–45.
8. Log of the *Lord Camden,* cited in Manuscript Records of Bengal Civilians, p. 1868 (Commonwealth Relations Office).
9. Letter to his wife, 31 January 1766, quoted by Sir George Forrest, *Life of Lord Clive,* 2 vols. (London, 1918), II, 311.
10. *Narrative of the Life of a Gen-*

tleman Long Resident in India, ed. W. K. Firminger (London, 1910), p. 6.

11. *Oriental Memoirs,* 2 vols. (London, 1834), II, 479–480.
12. Quoted by Hunter, pp. 63–64.
13. *Speech in the House of Commons,* pp. 44–45.
14. Bradley-Birt.
15. See *Bengal Past and Present,* VI, 394, where this stanza from Tom Hood's parody of a song by J. H. Reynolds is also cited:

    Go where the maiden on a marriage plan goes,
    Consigned for wed-*lock* to Calcutta *quay,*
    Where woman *goes* for man, the same as *man goes,*
    And think of me.

16. *Works,* XI, 765.
17. *Biographical Introductions,* XIII, xxxviii.
18. *Memorials,* pp. 249–250.
19. The same, pp. 272–273.
20. *Bengal Past and Present,* IV, 297; Manuscript Records of Bengal Civilians, p. 853 (Commonwealth Relations Office).
21. *Bengal Past and Present,* IV, 499; XXVIII, 185. For an account of Rennell's career and achievements, see the *Dictionary of National Biography.*
22. Walter Hamilton, *The East India Gazetteer* (London, 1815), pp. 748–750.
23. Thackeray to the Governor and Council, 15 and 27 August 1775, *Bengal Past and Present,* XLI, 43–44, 49.
24. The same, V, 229.
25. Hunter and Bradley-Birt both assumed that the elephants marched nearly 1,000 miles to Belgaum in the Bombay Presidency, but it has been demonstrated that the nearby town of Belgram was their destination. See *Bengal Past and Present,* XXVIII, 183.
26. The same, V, 173–175.
27. See particularly "The Letters of Richard Barwell," printed in instalments by W. K. Firminger in *Bengal Past and Present,* vols. IX–XVIII; Hickey's *Memoirs;* and H. F. Thompson's *The Intrigues of a Nabob; or Bengal, the Fittest Soil for Lust* (1780), a *chronique scandaleuse,* which none the less seems to be accurate as far as it concerns Barwell (Firminger, *Bengal Past and Present,* V, 178–179).
28. Private memorandum of April, 1776, published by Joseph Parkes and Herman Merivale, *Memoirs of Sir Philip Francis, K.C.B.,* 2 vols. (London, 1867), II, 62.
29. *Bengal Past and Present,* XIII, 80; XIV, 233.
30. The same, V, 193.
31. *Letters,* ed. Mrs. Paget Toynbee, 16 vols. (Oxford, 1903–1905), VIII, 149. See also pp. 153, 157.
32. *Bengal Past and Present,* XIII, 77–78.
33. The same, p. 83.
34. The same, p. 96.
35. The same, XXIV, 46.
36. Manuscript Records of Bengal Civilians, p. 1868 (Commonwealth Relations Office); *Bengal Past and Present,* XXVIII, 182.
37. The same, XIV, 234.

38. Letter to the Council, 10 June 1776, cited by Bradley-Birt, p. 190.
39. *Bengal Past and Present,* XXVIII, 183.
40. Bradley-Birt, p. 201.
41. The same, p. 203.
42. The same, p. 206.
43. The same, p. 207.
44. *Bengal Past and Present,* XXVIII, 184.
45. The same, VII, 230.
46. *Works,* XIV, 685.
47. The same, XV, 784.
48. *Farrington Diary.*
49. Hunter, p. 99.
50. It may be noted that Thackeray continued to figure in the Company's lists until 1782 as a Senior Merchant "at home" (Manuscript Records of Bengal Civilians, p. 1868).

III (pp. 37–42)

1. For the Webb alliance and Thackeray's life after his return to England, see *Centenary Biographical Introductions,* XXV, xx–xxv; Bradley-Birt, pp. 216–257; Hunter, pp. 97–110; *Memorials,* pp. 289–296; and Lt.-Col. J. Shakespear, *John Shakespear of Shadwell and His Descendants 1619–1931* (privately printed, Newcastle upon Tyne, 1931), pp. 47–65.
2. *Bengal Past and Present,* IV, 502. Amelia had received permission from the Court of Directors to come out to India on 17 November 1773.
3. Shakespear, p. 60.
4. Charlotte's "sham marriage" and ensuing madness will be discussed in the sequel to this volume apropos of *Philip.* The marriage of Augusta on 20 November 1778 to a Mr. Evans had comic rather than tragic consequences. She later returned alone to England in ill health to visit her husband's people. According to family legend, as handed down by Charlotte to Emily Ritchie, she arrived one night after dark. "The next morning she woke early, as all Anglo-Indians do, and started to explore the house, the other inmates of which were still snoring. Opening a door she found herself confronted with canisters of tea, barrels of butter, bundles of tallow candles hanging from the ceiling, and realized that her Evans's father kept a grocer's shop." Charlotte Ritchie "used to describe graphically the dismay of the aristocratic little lady." She separated from her husband in 1792. (Shakespear, pp. 61–62).
5. *Letters,* III, 446.
6. *Biographical Introductions,* XIII, xxxvi, xlix.
7. *Letters,* I, 325.
8. The same, III, 447–448.
9. *Works,* XIV, 108.
10. *Memoirs of William Hickey,* ed. Alfred Spencer, 4 vols. (London, 1913–1925), II, 308–309.
11. *Bengal Past and Present,* XXXIII, 65.
12. *Memorials,* p. 294.
13. The same, p. 293.

14. The same, pp. 294–295.
15. See *Bengal Past and Present,* XXVI, 180–183.
16. *Memorials,* p. 318.
17. These letters were printed by Bradley-Birt, pp. 245–249.
18. *Memorials,* p. 290.
19. The same, pp. 318–319.
20. See Lady Ritchie's description of a book of his manuscript letters on business subjects in *Biographical Introductions,* XIII, xliii–xliv.
21. *Memorials,* p. 294.
22. There was a fifth daughter, who died in infancy.
23. Inglis endorsed the petitions of Webb (1805–1806) and St. John (1806–1807); and Bensley that of William (1795). Richmond Thackeray's petition (No. 5 for 1797) reads: "To the Honorable Court of Directors of the United East India Company. The humble Petition of Richmond Thackeray sheweth That your Petitioner has been educated in Writing and Merchants' Accounts and humbly hopes he is qualified to serve your Honors He therefore humbly prays that your Honors will be pleased to appoint him a Writer on the Bengal Establishment and should he be so fortunate as to succeed in this his prayer he promises to behave himself with the greatest diligence and fidelity, and is ready to give such security as your Honors may require
And your Petitioner will
ever pray
Richmond Thackeray
London 8 Feb[y] 1797
Geo: Woodford Thellusson."
Attached documents include a certificate of baptism, from the South Mims Register, dated 5 December 1781; and a certificate signed by "W. M. Thackeray, Hadley the 7th Feb[y] 1797," stating that he has taught his son writing and merchants' accounts (Manuscript Writers' Petitions, XIX, 9; XX, 13; XIV, 24; Commonwealth Relations Office).
24. Manuscript Records Bengal Civil Service (Commonwealth Relations Office).
25. Manuscript Records of the College of Fort William (Commonwealth Relations Office).
26. Austen-Leigh, *Eton College Register,* p. xxxi; H. E. C. Stapylton, *The Eton School Lists from 1791 to 1877* (Eton, 1885), pp. 9, 17, 24. In the Manuscript Records of the College of Fort William it is stated that Richmond Thackeray "Studied at Eton 7 Years."
27. *Madras Courier Extraordinary,* 29 September 1798; *Madras Courier,* 3 October 1798.
28. *Biographical Introductions,* XIII, xlvii–xlviii.

IV (pp. 42–52)

1. *Madras Courier Extraordinary,* 29 September 1798.
2. The same.
3. Manuscript journal (Ray).
4. Manuscript log of the Honourable Company's Ship *Thetis,* 18

September 1798 (Commonwealth Relations Office).

5. The same.

6. The same, 25 September 1798.

7. *Bengal Past and Present,* XLVIII, 26. For Richmond Thackeray's career in India, see Bradley-Birt; *Calcutta Gazette,* 1798–1815; *Centenary Biographical Introductions,* XXV, xxvii–xxxv; *East-India Registers,* 1803–1815; Hunter, pp. 141–175; Manuscript Records of Bengal Civilians and Manuscript Ecclesiastical Records, Bengal (Commonwealth Relations Office); H. W. B. Moreno, "The Birthplace of William Makepeace Thackeray," *Century Review,* I (1915), 4–14; W. F. Prideaux, "The Thackerays in India," *Athenaeum,* 20 January 1897, p. 149. Hunter's chapter is again more remarkable for narrative skill than exactness of detail. Calcutta life in Thackeray's time is described by Evan Cotton, "Calcutta in 1813. (A Contemporary Account)," *Bengal Past and Present,* XLVIII (1934), 23–31; Isaac Henry Townley Roberdeau, "A Young Civilian in Bengal in 1805," the same, XXIX (1925), 110–147; George, Viscount Valentia, *Voyages and Travels to India, Ceylon, the Red Sea, Abyssinia, and Egypt,* 3 vols. (London, 1809), I, 59–64, 235–262; and Capt. Thomas Williamson, *The East-India Vade Mecum,* 2 vols. (London, 1810).

8. *Voyages,* I, 236.

9. The same.

10. The same, p. 235.

11. *Memorials,* p. 319.

12. Three years, where the salary was over £500; six years, where over £1,500; nine years, where over £3,000; and twelve years, where over £4,000 (*East India Register,* 1803, p. xix).

13. Valentia, I, 242.

14. Sir Edward Blunt, *The Indian Civil Service* (London, 1937), p. 34.

15. Manuscripts European, D. 116, p. 55 (Commonwealth Relations Office).

16. Bradley-Birt, pp. 238, 240.

17. The same, p. 240.

18. Hunter attributes to Thackeray "a first class in Arabic, with distinction in Persian"; but the records show him thirty-seventh among forty-eight in Persian language, seventh among ten in Arabic language, and fourth among forty-two in Persian writing (Bradley-Birt, p. 239).

19. Manuscript Records of Bengal Civilians. The *East-India Registers* between July, 1803, and December, 1811, record only Thackeray's permanent offices at the Board of Trade, apart from a single description of him as "Officiating as Collector of Jessore" in the *Register* of 14 November 1805.

20. He estimates in a letter of 1801 that he will be making 800 rupees a month by the time his sister Emily reaches Calcutta (*Centenary Biographical Introductions,* XXV, xxix). The sicca rupee was worth 2*s.* 6*d.*

21. Bradley-Birt, p. 240.

22. *Centenary Biographical Introductions,* XXV, xxviii.

23. Bradley-Birt, pp. 242–243; Shakespear, pp. 135–136.

24. Henry Salt, *Twenty-four Views in St. Helena, the Cape, India, Ceylon, the Red Sea, Abyssinia, and Egypt* (London, 1809), letterpress to Plate III.

25. See Moreno, *Century Review,* I, 7–12.

26. *Calcutta Gazette,* 9 January 1806.

27. Roberdeau, *Bengal Past and Present,* XXIX, 145–146.

28. "It is a very general practice for Englishmen in India to entertain a *cara amica* of the country. This forms a complete and separate establishment, she dwells in a distinct but adjacent mansion and has her own establishment of female servants, &c. Like all other Women of India she seldom or never goes beyond the precincts of her own dwelling" (the same, p. 125).

29. *Centenary Biographical Introductions,* XXV, xxix.

30. Moreno, *Century Review,* I, 8. I correct Mrs. Blechynden's age from "55," following Manuscript Ecclesiastical Records, Bengal, LXII, 50.

31. "Radfield" in the entry concerning her marriage in Manuscript Bengal Records, XI, 276, and the notice of this marriage in the *East-India Register,* 1822, p. 464; "Redfield" in the entry registering her marriage at St. John's Church (*Bengal Past and Present,* XLIV, 97).

32. *Bengal Past and Present,* XLIV, 97, where the name "Rudd" is recorded.

33. Blechynden was one of the six natural children by two native mistresses of Richard Blechynden, an architect who had come out to India in the 1780s. His father sent him to Europe to be educated, and he applied for permission to return to Calcutta on 31 December 1811.

34. See Williamson, I, 412–416, 451–468.

35. Valentia (I, 241) remarks that "the most rapidly accumulating evil of Bengal is the increase of half-caste children," but his reasons for this judgment are political rather than moral.

36. Williamson, I, 412–413.

37. See Dennis Kincaid, *British Social Life in India 1608–1937* (London, 1938), p. 96.

38. *Voyages,* I, 242.

39. British Museum Add. MSS. 37,416, folio 10.

40. Roberdeau, *Bengal Past and Present,* XXIX, 120.

41. The same, p. 123.

42. Manuscript Ecclesiastical Records, Bengal.

43. The description which follows is condensed from the *Calcutta Gazette,* 17 December 1807, supp. p. 2.

44. Communicated to me by Mrs. Fuller, who had it from Lady Ritchie.

45. Manuscript Ecclesiastical Records, Bengal.

V (pp. 52–59)

1. The late Lt.-Col. Ley Becher of Inwood, Holybourne, Alton, Hampshire, in notes communicated to Mrs. Fuller on 9 January 1936, cites *Genesis* 46: 21; and tribal reference *I Chronicles* 7: 6 ff. Other information on the Bechers may be found in *The Bengal Obituary* (Calcutta, 1848); Maj. V. C. P. Hodson, *The Officers of the Bengal Army,* 4 vols. (London, 1927–1947); Hunter, pp. 159–169; Manuscript Ecclesiastical Records, Bengal; Manuscript Ecclesiastical Records (Wills), Bengal; Manuscript Records, Bengal Civilians; Manuscript Ships' Logs (Commonwealth Relations Office); and Lady Ritchie, "The Boyhood of Thackeray," *St. Nicholas,* XVII (December, 1889), 98–112.
2. According to the Register of Burials at Fareham, Anne Becher of Gosport was buried 28 June 1825, aged eighty-eight (Lt.-Col. Becher).
3. He describes himself in his will of 28 October 1799 as "Aged 35 years 7 months 2 days" (Manuscript Ecclesiastical Records, Wills, Bengal, 1801, no. 28).
4. From 1761 to 1767, during the period when Clive was in disfavour, he was in England without Company employment.
5. *Bengal Obituary,* p. 72.
6. Manuscript Ecclesiastical Records, Bengal.
7. Information communicated by Mrs. Fuller. See also Bedingfield, p. 136.
8. Manuscript reminiscences, 1878.
9. Manuscript Ecclesiastical Records, Bengal, IV, 58, 124, 156.
10. Manuscript Ecclesiastical Records (Wills), Bengal, 1801, no. 28.
11. Manuscript Ecclesiastical Records, Bengal, V, 356.
12. Information communicated by Mrs. Fuller.
13. Manuscript Ecclesiastical Records (Wills), Bengal, 1805, no. 57.
14. Hodson, I, 342.
15. Capt. John Williams, *An Historical Account of the Rise and Progress of the Bengal Native Infantry* (London, 1817), pp. 373–374.
16. Lt. John Pester, *War and Sport in India 1802–1806* (London, 1813), p. 419.
17. The same, p. 447.
18. Manuscript Ecclesiastical Records, Bengal, VII, 199.
19. Hodson.
20. Manuscript Ecclesiastical Records, Bengal, V, 95; VIII, 40; Manuscript Ecclesiastical Records (Wills), Bengal, 1819, pp. 865–872. The fourth child, Edward William Butler, was baptized 21 October 1797 at the age of three weeks. He was presumably dead when the boy born in 1806 was given his name. Caroline Butler married Lt. Isaac Pereira (1788–1847) of the Bengal Artillery. Her father cut her off with one rupee in his will because of her "ungrateful & unthankful conduct." She died

1 July 1845. Louisa Butler married Lt. James Nicolson (1788–1835) of the Bengal Army (Hodson; Manuscript Records, Wills, Bengal, 1819, pp. 865–872).

21. Hodson, I, 267.
22. *Calcutta Gazette,* 12 February 1807, supp. p. 2.
23. He is not mentioned, though the three daughters are, in John Harman Becher's will.
24. *St. Nicholas,* p. 102.
25. *Letters,* II, 551.
26. *St. Nicholas,* p. 102.
27. *Letters,* IV, 113.
28. The same, II, 798; IV, 7.
29. The history of the Carmichael-Smyths is summarized and the sources for it listed in *Buried Life,* pp. 98–101, 140. In what follows, the manuscript diary of Mrs. William Forrest, a transcript of which is owned by Mrs. Monroe, has also been used.
30. Hodson, IV, 143.
31. John Philippart, *The East India Military Calendar,* 3 vols. (London, 1823–1826), II, 337–340; Hodson, IV, 142–143.
32. *Works,* XVII, 606.
33. *Letters,* I, cxii–cxiii. I have substituted Lieutenant, Henry Carmichael-Smyth's correct title, for Ensign in this passage.
34. Manuscript Ships' Logs.
35. The same.
36. Manuscript Ecclesiastical Records, Bengal, VIII, 309.

CHAPTER 2

Calcutta and Home

1 (pp. 60–68)

1. Manuscript Ecclesiastical Records, Bengal (Commonwealth Relations Office).
2. Mrs. Fuller.
3. "I can't get rid of what has troubled me ever since my Billy Boy was born," she wrote to her mother in a manuscript letter of 4 October 1820 (Ray).
4. Moreno, *Century Review,* I, 7–12.
5. Manuscript Ecclesiastical Records, Bengal.
6. Alexander Macrabie's journal, quoted by Parkes and Merivale, *Sir Philip Francis,* II, 23.
7. By Hunter, p. 169; and Moreno, pp. 7, 12.
8. See Appendix A: Richmond Thackeray's will.
9. *Calcutta Gazette.*
10. See Julian James Cotton, "George Chinnery, Artist (1774–1852)," *Bengal Past and Present,* XXVII (1924), 113–126.
11. *Memorials,* p. 320.
12. Manuscript letter to Mrs. Butler, 9 July 1821 (Ray).
13. Roberdeau, *Bengal Past and Present,* XXIX, 124.
14. *Letters,* I, 4.
15. The same, III, 636.
16. *St. Nicholas,* XVII, 99.
17. Mrs. William Forrest's manuscript diary (Mrs. Monroe).
18. Cited from the *Government*

Gazette by Philippart, II, 337–340.

19. *Letters,* I, cxiv.
20. The same, II, 576.
21. Manuscript Ecclesiastical Records, Bengal.
22. 21 September 1815, supp., p. 2.
23. Moreno, pp. 5–6.
24. *St. Nicholas,* p. 107.
25. Manuscript diary, 1859–1864, under 18 December 1864 (Ray).
26. Printed verbatim in Appendix A.
27. Manuscript Ecclesiastical Records, Bengal, X, 28.
28. Manuscript Records, Bengal Civilians; *East-India Registers,* 1812–1815.
29. Manuscript Ecclesiastical Records (Wills), Bengal, 1818, pp. 29–32.
30. Manuscript letter to Mrs. Butler, 24 February 1821 (Ray). Elliot had died on 21 January 1818. His widow married Alexander Halliday, surgeon, 1 March 1820 (Manuscript Ecclesiastical Records, Bengal, X, 667; LIX, 143).
31. *Works,* XIV, 66.
32. Manuscript Records, Bengal Civilians.
33. *Works,* XVII, 553.
34. Manuscript Marine Miscellanies (Commonwealth Relations Office). The voyage home is recorded in the log of Honourable Company's Ship *Prince Regent,* 1816–1817 (Commonwealth Relations Office).
35. See *Memoirs,* IV, 357, 366, 376, 381, 410.
36. *Memoirs,* quoted by C. Northcote Parkinson, *Trade in the Eastern Seas 1793–1813* (Cambridge, 1937).
37. *Letters,* III, 97.
38. *Works,* XIII, 753.
39. *Letters,* III, 97; *Works,* XVII, 553.
40. See *Letters,* IV, 379.
41. *St. Nicholas,* p. 101.
42. "The Tomb of his Ancestors."
43. Sir William Hunter, as quoted by Lord Beveridge, *India Called Them* (London, 1948), p. 28; and in *The Thackerays in India,* p. 58.
44. The most notorious public manifestation of this prejudice was the conduct of Lord Cardigan in the so-called "black bottle affair" of 1840, which has been admirably described by Mrs. Cecil Woodham-Smith in Chapter 5 of *The Reason Why* (New York, 1954). Thackeray's comment on the case is significant: "I have been reading the Court Martial of poor Captain Reynolds, and that scoundrel Lord Cardigan. When are we to get rid of this insolent scum of lords altogether?" (*Letters,* I, 484).
45. *Harper's Weekly,* XLI (27 March 1897), 315.

II (pp. 68–78)

1. Gerald Ritchie, *The Ritchies in India* (London, 1920), p. 10.
2. Manuscript letter of 29 May 1821 (Ray).
3. Ritchie, p. 172.
4. Quoted from the text established by John Hammond Schacht, *A Critical Edition of Thackeray's*

"*Denis Duval,*" University of Illinois doctoral dissertation, 1947, pp. 252–253.

5. *Works,* XVII, 599.
6. The same, pp. 599–601.
7. Manuscript letters of [10?] July 1820, 7 February 1821 (Ray). This suggests that Thackeray's association of his reading of *The Scottish Chiefs* with the coronation of George IV (*Works,* XVII, 599) was owing to a lapse of memory, since George was crowned on 19 July 1821.
8. *Letters,* I, 5.
9. *Works,* XVII, 553–554.
10. The same, p. 495.
11. The same, p. 494.
12. Mrs. Irvine, quoted by Lady Ritchie, *St. Nicholas,* p. 105.
13. *Letters,* I, 8–9.
14. The same, p. 7.
15. Lady Ritchie, *St. Nicholas,* pp. 104–105; Bedingfield (p. 296) tells the same story.
16. *Works,* XIII, 30.
17. Manuscript letter to Mrs. Butler, 3 February 1820 (Ray).
18. *Centenary Biographical Introductions,* XII, xxi.
19. Manuscript Ecclesiastical Records, Bengal.
20. The same.
21. The same, IX, 183, 144. The Grahams had two other children: Henry Edward, born 26 December 1810 at Calcutta (VIII, 391), died 19 February 1812 at Calcutta; and another son whose name is not recorded, christened 15 April 1813 (IX, 179), died 9 July 1814 at Agra (IX, 389).
22. Manuscript Ecclesiastical Records (Wills), Bengal, 1816, pp. 301–304.
23. Manuscript letter, Maria Knox to Mrs. Butler, 3 September 1819 (Ray).
24. Manuscript Ecclesiastical Records, Bengal, X, 268.
25. Manuscript letter, Maria Knox to Mrs. Butler, 11 September 1819 (Ray).
26. Manuscript letter, Maria Knox to Mrs. Butler, 23 December 1821 (Ray).
27. Manuscript letter, Maria Knox to Mrs. Butler, 3 and 11 September 1819 (Ray).
28. Philippart, II, 202–209.
29. Manuscript Ecclesiastical Records, Bengal.
30. Manuscript letter of 17 August 1819 (Ray).
31. Manuscript Ecclesiastical Records (Wills), Bengal, 1819, pp. 865–872; manuscript letter from Mrs. Carmichael-Smyth to Mrs. Butler, 3 February 1820 (Ray).
32. Manuscript letter, Maria Knox to Mrs. Butler, 24 December 1820 (Ray).
33. Manuscript letter, Maria Knox to Mrs. Butler, 9 October 1821 (Ray).
34. Manuscript letter, Maria Knox to Mrs. Butler, 1 February 1822 (Ray).
35. Manuscript Ecclesiastical Records, Bengal, XII, 253.
36. Manuscript letter, Mrs. Carmichael-Smyth to Mrs. Butler, 4 October 1820 (Ray).
37. Manuscript letter (Ray).

38. Manuscript Ships' Logs (Commonwealth Relations Office).

39. On 6 April 1820 the Captain found the Mate asleep on deck after he had been ordered to go below. In the ensuing quarrel, the Captain noted in his log, the Mate said "that I treated him like a dog, and that my conduct to him was unmanly, cruel, ungentlemanlike and tyrannical," and, further, "that my conduct had been remarked by the Passengers on board the Ship, to be as he had stated it."

40. Manuscript letter from Mrs. Carmichael-Smyth to Mrs. Butler, [10?] July 1820 (Ray).

41. The same.

42. *Works,* XIII, 17, 70.

43. Manuscript letter to Mrs. Butler, 16 February 1821 (Ray).

44. Manuscript letter, Maria Knox to Mrs. Butler, 16 February 1821 (Ray).

45. Quoted in manuscript letter, Maria Knox to Mrs. Butler, 16 February 1821 (Ray).

46. Manuscript letter to Mrs. Butler, 25 August 1820 (Ray).

47. Quoted in manuscript letter, Maria Knox to Mrs. Butler, 9 May 1821 (Ray).

48. Manuscript letter of 7 February 1821 (Ray).

49. Manuscript letter of 4 October 1820 (Ray).

50. Manuscript letter to Maria Knox, 25 December 1821 (Ray).

51. Manuscript letter to Mrs. Butler, 26 October 1821 (Ray).

52. Manuscript letter to Mrs. Knox, 25 December 1821 (Ray).

53. Quoted by Lady Ritchie, *St. Nicholas,* pp. 108–109.

54. Manuscript letter of 25 December 1821 (Ray).

CHAPTER *3*

The Forest Life of a Public School

I (pp. 79–86)

1. "Public Schools," *Works of the Rev. Sydney Smith,* 3 vols. (London, 1848), I, 390. This article originally appeared in the *Edinburgh Review* in 1810.

2. D. D., "Some Few Thackerayana," *National Review,* XIII (1889), 794–803. Other studies of Charterhouse in Thackeray's time, which are useful in recreating his life there, include Charles Robert Baynes, "Horae Carthusianae," a manuscript poem in the Pierpont Morgan Library; John Frederick Boyes, "A Memorial of Thackeray's School Days," *Cornhill Magazine,* XI (1865), 118–128; Gerald S. Davies, *Charterhouse in London* (London, 1921), and "Thackeray as Carthusian," *Greyfriar,* II (1890–1895), 61–67; Thomas Mozley, *Reminiscences of Oriel College and the Oxford Movement,* 2 vols. (London, 1882), I, 63–64, 157–175; H. W. Phillott, "Some Charterhouse Reminiscences," *Greyfriar,* II

1890–1895), 75–79; Henry L. Thompson, *Henry George Liddell* (London, 1899), pp. 3–11; Martin Tupper, *My Life as an Author* (London, 1886), pp. 14–24; Edward Parry Eardley-Wilmot, *Charterhouse Old and New* (London, 1895).

3. Bower Marsh and Frederick Crisp *(Alumni Carthusiani,* privately printed, London, 1913, p. xiii) discovered among gown boys alone some ninety Charterhouse scholars who became writers or cadets of the East India Company.
4. Quoted by Davies, *Charterhouse in London,* p. 265.
5. Davies, *Greyfriar,* II, 64.
6. *Blue Books,* 1822–1825.
7. *Works,* XVII, 422.
8. So runs Davies's account of the system (*Greyfriar,* II, 62). Liddell (Thompson, p. 6) relates that the *praepositus* was selected from the form to be taught and elevated to the form above after six weeks of service. Phillott (p. 75) holds that all *praepositi* were taken from the fourth form.
9. Davies, *Charterhouse in London,* p. 265.
10. Anthony Trollope, *Thackeray* (London, 1879), p. 4.
11. *Works,* VIII, 36. Russell is alluded to in the last sentence. Thackeray used to refer to him as "the brute who drubbed τύπτω into me when I was a boy" (D. D., p. 794).
12. In my account of the ritual of flogging I have depended chiefly on Eardley-Wilmot (pp. 69–72). Though he knew Charterhouse only in the 1850s, the traditions of the school had been tenaciously maintained in the intervening period.
13. J. W. Irvine wrote to Lady Ritchie in an undated manuscript letter: "I remember his coming once (while I was a Master) & appearing outside school while a flogging was proceeding. He said playfully to Elwyn (Headmaster) 'I peeped thro' the Key-hole—& it brought back old times terribly!' " (Fuller).
14. Manuscript diary, 26 January 1859.
15. Eardley-Wilmot, p. 70.
16. Tupper, p. 16.
17. Eardley-Wilmot, p. 72.
18. The same, p. 71.
19. A conversation reported by Thackeray's fellow Carthusian Henry Silver further illustrates this preoccupation: "I went to Charterhouse the other day. Hadn't seen School come out since I left. Saw one little fellow with his hands behind him & a tear upon his cheek, & 2 little cronies with their arms r[d] his neck—& I knew what had happ[d] & how they'd take him to the bog & make him show his cuts" (manuscript diary, 2 March 1859).
20. *Works,* II, 706.
21. The same, IV, 319.
22. The same, XVII, 429. Thackeray, indeed, was a budding gourmet, who greatly enjoyed the primitive gastronomy that prevailed at Charterhouse. Many years later he recalled his taste

for "lollypops, hardbake, alicompayne, brandyballs!" "Turtle-soup is good," he continued; "but is it as good as open tarts? A cool glass of claret is not bad; but is it as pleasant as a half-penny-worth of liquorice, and brown sugar to the same amount, mixed with water in a twopenny vial, and kept hot in your pocket in the warm summer days? When you take it, or give it to a friend, you give the liquor a shake to make it froth, and take out the cork with your teeth, and bid your friend drink only to a certain place which you mark with your finger" (the same, III, 490).

23. Lady Ritchie's manuscript reminiscences, 1864–1865.
24. *Greyfriar,* II, 77.
25. Manuscript Silver diary, 5 July 1860.
26. On this point see Sir Frederick Pollock, *For My Grandson* (London, 1933), p. 18.
27. *Boswell's Life of Johnson,* eds. G. B. Hill and L. F. Powell, 6 vols. (Oxford, 1934–1950), I, 48.
28. D. D., p. 802.
29. *Works,* XI, 52.
30. *Tom Brown's School Days,* pt. II, chap. 5.
31. Compare *Works,* XIV, 137.
32. The same, IV, 317–323.
33. Davies, *Greyfriar,* II, 65.
34. *Letters,* II, 256.
35. *Works of the Rev. Sydney Smith,* I, 391–392.
36. Tupper, p. 17.
37. Thompson, p. 9.
38. Pp. 17, 21.
39. Manuscript Silver diary, 8 January 1862. A further detail from the same source may be relegated to the decent obscurity of a note: "Thackeray says one of the first orders he rec[d] [at Charterhouse] was 'Come & frig me'" (21 October 1858).
40. Quoted by Lytton Strachey, *Eminent Victorians* (London, 1918), p. 187.
41. Thompson, p. 5.

II (pp. 86–95)

1. What follows is taken from *Works,* XVII, 413–419.
2. The same, p. 419. The novel that Thackeray read was actually Mrs. Radcliffe's *The Italian, or the Confessional of the Black Penitents.* See *Letters,* II, 55n.
3. Manuscript Silver diary, 26 February 1862.
4. *Letters,* I, 12.
5. Col. H. M. Vibart, *Addiscombe: Its Heroes and Men of Note* (London, 1894).
6. *Letters,* II, 361.
7. In the Charterhouse *Blue Book* of May, 1824, he is listed as a resident of Penny's house; in that of May, 1825, he figures as a day boy.
8. *Letters,* I, 20–21.
9. What follows comes from pp. 126–127.
10. *Works,* IV, 52.
11. In a letter quoted by Rowland Grey, "Thackeray and France," *Englishwoman,* XXXVII (1918), 112.
12. *Works,* III, 328.
13. The same, XVII, 418–419, 429–432, 601–602, 608; *Letters,* I, 22.

14. *Works,* XVII, 608.
15. Boyes, p. 126.
16. Thackeray was none the less a close student of Hazlitt's writings. See his keen appreciation in *Works,* VI, 417–418.
17. Issue of 25 April 1825, p. 626.
18. *Poetical Works of Letitia Elizabeth Landon,* 4 vols. (London, 1831), I, 284.
19. Cited by Boyes, p. 125.
20. *Letters,* I, 17.
21. Thompson, p. 8.
22. D. D., p. 795.
23. *Works,* II, 416–417 and 415.
24. Orders governing Charterhouse, established 21 June 1627, and signed by Charles I (Samuel Herne, *Domus Carthusiana,* London, 1677, p. 132).
25. *Works,* XIV, 951–953.
26. The same, XI, 599.
27. Bedingfield, p. 296.
28. The same, p. 12.
29. Manuscript letter from Mrs. Carmichael-Smyth to Mrs. Knox, 25 December 1821 (Ray).
30. Ritchie, *Ritchies in India,* p. 12.
31. *Letters,* II, 609.
32. The same, p. 95; *Chapters,* p. 93.
33. Pp. 118–119.

III (pp. 95–100)

1. Davies, *Greyfriar,* II, 64.
2. Trollope, p. 4.
3. *Greyfriar,* II, 75.
4. P. 15.
5. *Reminiscences,* I, 63–64.
6. *Letters,* I, 24–25.
7. Pp. 75–76.
8. For Baynes's authorship of this poem, see Phillott, p. 76. Baynes was a gown boy in the first form with Thackeray. In later life he became an Indian judge.
9. Manuscript in the Pierpont Morgan Library. Necessary punctuation has been inserted.
10. *Letters,* I, 59.
11. *Works,* XVII, 400. In later life Thackeray contrived to look back on his experiences in the first form with something like equanimity. He gives Russell his due without malice, for example, in Chapter 2 of *Pendennis* (*Works,* XII, 19–23).
12. P. 15.
13. See *Letters,* I, 25–26.
14. Thompson, p. 11.
15. The same.
16. Davies, *Greyfriar,* II, 62–63.
17. William Harris Arnold, *Ventures in Book Collecting* (London, 1923), p. 76.
18. Venables, quoted by Trollope, p. 4.
19. P. 21. See also pp. 17–18.
20. *Works,* X, 210.
21. *Praeterita, Works,* XXXV, 210.
22. This was, of course, a general phenomenon in the England of Thackeray's time. "The upper, upper-middle and the professional classes were welded together in the Public Schools," G. M. Trevelyan points out, "and by the same token were further divided from the rest of the nation brought up under a different educational system" (*English Social History,* London, 1946, p. 520).
23. Trollope, p. 5.
24. *Morning Chronicle,* 3 June 1844.

CHAPTER 4

Devon Interludes

I (pp. 101–107)

1. *Letters,* I, 78.
2. Mrs. Forrest's manuscript diary (Monroe); *Memorials,* p. 330.
3. *Works,* XIII, 169.
4. *A New Guide to Exeter* (Exeter, 1824), p. 3.
5. *Letters,* I, 86.
6. Manuscript letter of 5 October 1883 to Lady Ritchie (Fuller).
7. This description has been assembled from Mrs. Brotherton's manuscript letters to Lady Ritchie of 14 December 1894 and 27 March 1895, neither of which is complete in itself (Fuller).
8. Manuscript letter of 25 August 1820 (Ray).
9. Manuscript letters of this period (Ray); *Letters,* I, 145.
10. Rev. Sidney W. Cornish, *Short Notes on the Church and Parish of Ottery St. Mary* (Exeter, 1869), p. 47.
11. Quoted by Ramsbotham, *Bengal Past and Present,* XXXII, 145. I have read *affliction* for *affection.*
12. Quoted by Cornish, p. 48.
13. The rectory was a family living worth £440 a year (*Liber Ecclesiasticus,* 1835).
14. It has usually been assumed that Dr. Cornish was the original of Dr. Portman. But Thackeray wrote on 4 February 1849 "of an old friend of ours in the country Dr Portman's daughter indeed who was a parson in our parts—who died of consumption the other day" (*Letters,* II, 501), and Lady Ritchie has noted that in 1856 "Dr. Portman . . . had already been gathered to his fathers" (*Biographical Introductions,* II, xl). Huyshe died in 1839; while Cornish, who was a young man without grown daughters when Thackeray knew him, was still alive in 1869.
15. In the volumes for 1831 (II, 487–488) and 1834 (I, 265–266).
16. *Letters,* I, 62.
17. The same, II, 310.
18. *Memorials,* p. 330.
19. The same, p. 332.
20. Gulliver, pp. 1–6. It seems to me most unlikely that Thackeray had a hand in the contributions assigned to him by Gulliver in the remaining pages of this chapter.
21. Mr. Coleridge's manuscript recollections, written for Lady Ritchie (Ray).
22. The same.
23. *Works,* eds. H. F. B. Brett-Smith and C. E. Jones, 10 vols. (London, 1934–1936), X, 268.
24. *Letters,* III, 15–16.
25. *New Guide to Exeter,* p. 89.
26. Manuscript letter, 19–25 June 1828 (Charterhouse).
27. *Biographical Introductions,* II, xl.
28. Bedingfield, p. 296.
29. Quoted in Sotheby catalogue, 15 June 1937.

30. W. W. Rouse Ball and J. A. Venn, *Admissions to Trinity College, Cambridge, 1801–1850* (London, 1911), p. 280.

31. *Biographical Introductions,* II, xix.

32. Quoted from letter to J. F. Boyes, Sotheby catalogue, 22 July 1909.

II (pp. 107–114)

1. *Works,* XVII, 424; see also II, 577–578.
2. *Letters,* I, 78. Thackeray's memories of these trips home are reflected in his recollections of stage-coach days in Chapter 7 of *Vanity Fair* (*Works,* XI, 85–87).
3. *Biographical Introductions,* II, xiii.
4. Speech at the London Tavern, 11 October 1855, quoted by George Hodder, *Memories of My Time* (London, 1870), pp. 263–264. Compare *Works,* XVII, 369–370.
5. *Chapters,* p. 15.
6. Whitwell Elwin, *Some XVIII Century Men of Letters,* 2 vols. (London, 1902), I, 17.
7. Bedingfield, p. 12.
8. *Letters,* II, 506.
9. Elwin, I, 17.
10. *Chapters,* p. 16.
11. Bedingfield, p. 30.
12. *Letters,* II, 506.
13. *Works,* XII, 13.
14. The observation in *Vanity Fair,* for example, that "Mother is the name for God in the hearts of little children" (*Works,* XI, 478).
15. Transcript of undated manuscript letter (Fuller).
16. The same, I, 163.
17. She published nothing. In 1857 Dickens refused a story which she had submitted for *Household Words* (*Letters,* ed. Dexter, II, 890).
18. *Letters,* II, 525.
19. The same, p. 207.
20. *Biographical Introductions,* VIII, xxxvii.
21. *Works,* XVII, 369.
22. *Letters,* III, 93–94.
23. Bedingfield, p. 136.
24. *Letters,* III, 13.
25. Lady Ritchie's manuscript reminiscences, 1878.
26. Manuscript letter to Mrs. Brookfield, 7 October 1848 (Rosenbach Estate).
27. John Forster, *The Life of Charles Dickens,* ed. J. W. T. Ley (London, 1928), p. 556.
28. *Letters,* II, 361.
29. *Prefaces* (London, 1934), p. 444.
30. Lady Ritchie's manuscript reminiscences, 1878.
31. The same. When Major Carmichael-Smyth was in India, so Mr. Evelyn Carmichael's father relates, "he went out to dinner one night with his sword on—they always went armed—when he was attacked by robbers. He killed one, wounded another and the third ran away" (manuscript notes, Mr. Evelyn Carmichael).
32. Lady Ritchie's manuscript reminiscences, 1878.
33. *Miss Williamson's Divagations* (London, 1882), pp. 150–151.

34. Information communicated to me by Mr. Evelyn Carmichael.
35. Manuscript letter from Maria Knox to Mrs. Butler, 29 May 1821 (Ray).
36. Manuscript letter of 6 December 1856 (Rosenbach Estate).
37. *Letters,* III, 17.
38. The same, II, 501.
39. Manuscript letter, 25 December 1821 (Ray).
40. *Letters,* II, 11.

CHAPTER 5
Cambridge

I (pp. 115–122)

1. Information concerning Cambridge of Thackeray's time will be found in Charles Astor Bristed, *Five Years in an English University* (New York, 1852); "Senior Wrangler," "Struggles of a Poor Student through Cambridge," *London Magazine,* April, 1825, pp. 491–510; Sir Leslie Stephen, *Sketches from Cambridge* (London, 1865); G. M. Trevelyan, *Trinity College: An Historical Sketch* (Cambridge, 1943); Denys A. Winstanley, *Early Victorian Cambridge* (Cambridge, 1940); [John F. M. Wright] *Alma Mater; or, Seven Years at the University of Cambridge,* 2 vols. (London, 1827). For Thackeray's career there, see *Biographical Introductions,* II, xix–xxxii; *The Gownsman;* Manuscript Minutes of the Debating Society (Ray); Manuscript Records of Terms Kept (Junior Bursar's Muniment Room, Trinity College); *Memorials,* pp. 347–348; *The Snob*. Chapters 17 to 20 of *Pendennis* indirectly reflect Thackeray's Cambridge experience.
2. *Letters,* I, 30.
3. The same, p. 35.
4. *Works,* XII, 200.
5. *Sketches from Cambridge,* p. 1. Compare Thackeray's remarks about the students at St. John's College, Trinity's traditional rival, *Letters,* I, 107.
6. Coleridge's manuscript recollections (Fuller).
7. Thackeray's sketch of Crump of St. Boniface (*Works,* IX, 319–320), includes traits of Whewell in later life.
8. John Willis Clark, *Old Friends at Cambridge and Elsewhere* (London, 1900), pp. 42–43.
9. *Letters,* I, 33.
10. Winstanley, p. 67.
11. *Letters,* I, 43.
12. The same, p. 115.
13. The same, p. 50.
14. *Works,* IX, 325.
15. *Letters,* I, 38.
16. The same, pp. 45–46.
17. Wright, I, 203.
18. *Letters,* I, 51, 70, 74.
19. Elwin, I, 180.
20. "Snob" at this time signified a person not belonging to the

University, and hence, by implication, low-born and vulgar. For the change which Thackeray brought about in the word's meaning, see p. 379 above.

21. *Works,* I, 2–3.
22. *Letters,* I, 76.
23. *The Snob,* 7 May 1829.
24. *Letters,* I, 79.
25. *Works,* I, 5.
26. Following Eyre Crowe's *Thackeray's Haunts and Homes* (London, 1897), p. 53, I stated in *Letters,* I, 79, that Lettsom was apparently editor of *The Snob.* I have since been able to examine John P. Wright's "The Light Blue: A Cambridge University Magazine" (*Christ's College Magazine,* XXVIII, 1913, pp. 7–13), which supplies a more authoritative account of *The Snob's* history. "A little before Christmas, 1860," Wright relates (pp. 7–8), "my uncle, the late Rev. W. Williams . . . told us that he had been Thackeray's first editor. When an undergraduate at Corpus, my uncle founded and edited a little magazine called *The Snob,* which was published by a bookseller in Rose Crescent. After the publication of the first or second number, he received a letter from another undergraduate, who wished to become a contributor to the magazine. An appointment was made; and one day, while the editor was sitting in the publishing office, there walked in a tall, thin young man, with an eye glass stuck in his left eye. This was my uncle's first introduction to Thackeray. . . . Thackeray never edited *The Snob.* . . . But he became a regular contributor to its pages. His first contribution . . . was a mock prize poem on *Timbuctoo.* . . . *The Snob* . . . was followed by *The Gownsman,* which had the same editor and to which Thackeray also contributed." FitzGerald confirms Williams's editorship of *The Gownsman* (*Letters and Literary Remains,* IV, 112).
27. *Letters,* I, 79.
28. The same, p. 81.
29. The same, p. 72.
30. The same, p. 68.
31. The same, p. 76.
32. The same, p. 83.
33. Quoted from William Hepworth Thompson, who sat next to Thackeray at the examination, in *Memorials,* p. 348.

II (pp. 122–126)

1. *Letters,* I, 44.
2. Williams was seventh Senior Optime in 1829.
3. *Works,* XVII, 439–440.
4. *Letters,* I, 85–86.
5. The same, p. 99.
6. The same, p. 90. Compare *Works,* II, 13.
7. *Letters,* I, 91.
8. *Works,* IV, 285.
9. *Letters,* I, 95.
10. The same, p. 88.
11. The same, pp. 90–91. Thackeray wrote "one or lost."
12. The same, p. 105.

13. Manuscript Minutes of Debating Society, 26 October 1829 (Ray).
14. *Works,* XVII, 618.
15. What follows is taken from "Shrove Tuesday in Paris," *Works,* III, 499–507.
16. *Works,* XVII, 617.

III (pp. 127–138)

1. "Senior Wrangler," p. 505; Wright, I, 208–209.
2. *Letters,* I, 104.
3. The same, p. 106.
4. The extent of Thackeray's contributions to *The Gownsman* is uncertain. Williams's son, H. Astley Williams, in a confused note written in old age (*Notes and Queries,* sixth series, X, 1884, p. 419), asserts that "Thackeray wrote over the signature 'ξ,' and my father over 'θ.'" But it seems reasonable to assume, since there exists a copy in Thackeray's hand of a contribution signed 'θ,' that this is his signature, and that Williams used 'ξ,' which occurs more frequently than any other signature.
5. *Biographical Introductions,* II, xxx.
6. *Letters,* I, 107.
7. Quoted in *Memorials,* pp. 347–348.
8. Manuscript Minutes of the Debating Society (Ray). The essay on duelling has not survived.
9. *Letters,* I, 495.
10. *Letters and Literary Remains,* IV, 111–112.
11. For the material in this paragraph, see *A House of Letters,* ed. Ernest Betham (London, n. d.), pp. 257–262.
12. *William B. Donne and His Friends,* ed. Catharine B. Johnson (London, 1905), p. 24.
13. *Letters and Literary Remains,* I, 265.
14. *Donne,* p. 24.
15. *Letters and Literary Remains,* I, 38–39.
16. The same.
17. *Sketches from Cambridge,* p. 131. The prizes for successful conformity were certainly very substantial. "The apparent openness of honours to all men," wrote Bulwer (*England and the English,* 2 vols., London, 1833, I, 27), "makes even the humblest shopkeeper grown rich, think of sending his son to College, not that he may become a wiser man or a better man, but that he may *perhaps* become my lord bishop or my lord chancellor."
18. London, 1851, p. 27.
19. See *Letters and Literary Remains,* IV, 112.
20. The same, I, 91.
21. *Letters,* I, 493–494.
22. Letter of 27 February 1854, quoted by Winstanley, p. 397.
23. See "Noctes Cantabrigienses" in no. 14 of *The Gownsman.*
24. *Gradus ad Cantabrigiam* (London, 1824), p. 50.
25. *Letters,* I, 78. See the Rev. W. Tuckwell, *A. W. Kinglake* (London, 1902), p. 21.
26. *Remarks on the Actual State of the University of Cambridge* (London, 1830), p. 23.
27. *Letters,* I, 137.

28. Sir Theodore Martin, quoted by Merivale and Marzials, pp. 235–236.
29. *Works,* XII, 61.
30. Mrs. Fuller, quoted in *Letters,* I, 506.
31. Merivale and Marzials, pp. 235–236.
32. Manuscript Records of Terms Kept (Junior Bursar's Muniment Room, Trinity College). The weeks were those ending 9 and 23 February and 9 March.
33. Manuscript diary, 15 February 1860. Charles Sloman was the little Jewish *improvisatore* of the Cider Cellars. Thackeray later sketched him as Nadab of the "Cave of Harmony" in Chapter 1 of *The Newcomes.*
34. *Works,* XII, 211.
35. On this topic see Bristed, pp. 339–354; Winstanley, pp. 375–382; and Wright, II, 142–145.
36. Bristed, p. 347.
37. Manuscript letter of November, 1848 (Rosenbach Estate). A translation of this letter appears in *Letters,* II, 453.
38. The same, pp. 541–542.
39. See J. A. Venn, *Alumni Cantabrigienses,* pt. II, IV (Cambridge, 1951), 361, for a brief summary of Matthew's career.
40. The same.
41. *Letters,* I, 151; II, 542.
42. See the same, pp. 190–191.
43. The same.
44. On 17 May 1849, just after Thackeray had finished the Oxbridge chapters of *Pendennis,* he visited Matthew, who since 1843 had been Vicar of Eversholt, Bedfordshire. Finding "a battered vulgar man," he reflected to Mrs. Brookfield: "I used to worship him for about six months—and now he points a moral and adorns a tale such as it is in Pendennis" (*Letters,* II, 541). Not only does Matthew's known career parallel Bloundell's with some closeness, but also the name Bloundell is practically identical with that of Matthew's school, Blundell's of Tiverton in Devon (*Alumni Cantabrigienses,* IV, 361). It was no doubt his painful interview with Matthew that led Thackeray to soften his portrait of Bloundell in revising *Pendennis* (see *Works,* XII, 994–995, for the passages that he cancelled). "He has had 15 years of a vulgar wife, much solitude, very much brandy & water I should think," Thackeray told Mrs. Brookfield. Furthermore, his legs had been paralysed since 1841, an affliction which he had to bear until 1861, when he died "after nearly twenty years of patient suffering" (*Gentleman's Magazine,* 1861, II, 213). So dreary a fate, Thackeray may have thought, was sufficient punishment without further chastisement in a novel.
45. My quotations come from the first edition of *Pendennis,* 2 vols. (London, 1850), I, 183–186. The same material will be found in *Works,* XII, 226–228, 994–995.
46. Manuscript Record of Terms Kept (Junior Bursar's Muniment Room, Trinity College).
47. *Remarks on the Actual State of the University of Cambridge,* p. 12.

48. Manuscript Records in the University Registry, Cambridge.
49. *Works,* III, 299.
50. See the famous passage in which Stephen develops this contrast, *Sketches from Cambridge,* pp. 4–5.
51. *Life of Henry Fawcett* (London, 1885), p. 95.
52. "William Makepeace Thackeray," *Chambers's Encyclopaedia* (London, 1930), X, 56.

CHAPTER 6
The Spirit of an Heir
I (pp. 139–147)

1. *Letters,* I, 138–139.
2. The same, p. 112.
3. Thackeray "expressly omitted" "Miss Lowe," the story in question, from the reprint of the *Fitz-Boodle Papers* in his *Miscellanies* (manuscript letter to F. M. Evans, 16 February 1857, Bradbury Agnew). Also dropped were "Dorothea" and "Ottilia," both of which are known to have autobiographical basis.
4. Manuscript letter from Thackeray to Mrs. Carmichael-Smyth, 14 December 1830 (Fuller).
5. *Letters,* I, 141.
6. The same, III, 442–445.
7. The same, I, 124.
8. See L. A. Willoughby, *Samuel Naylor and 'Reynard the Fox'* (London, 1914).
9. See *Letters,* I, 153–156 for a comprehensive list.
10. Walter Vulpius, "Thackeray in Weimar," *Century Magazine,* LIII (April, 1897), 920–928. See also two further articles by Vulpius: "Thackeray and Weimar," *Westermanns Monatshefte,* February, 1921, pp. 579–592; and "Thackerays Lehrlingzeit im Weimar," *Neuphilologische Monatschrift,* IX (1939), 111–114.
11. *Letters,* I, 126, 131.
12. The same, p. 130.
13. See Lily Braun, *Im Schatten der Titanen* (Stuttgart, 1910), p. 115.
14. *Letters,* I, 146–147. There is a heightened and exaggerated reflection of these harmless affairs in "Dorothea" and "Ottilia" of the *Fitz-Boodle Papers.*
15. What follows is taken from *Im Schatten der Titanen.*
16. *Poetry of the Anti-Jacobin,* ed. L. Rice-Oxley (Oxford, 1924), p. 131.
17. Donald MacLeod, *Memoir of Norman MacLeod,* 2 vols. (New York, 1877), I, 46–47.
18. Manuscript letter of 14 December 1830 (Fuller).
19. *Letters,* I, 136.
20. The same, III, 444.
21. The same, I, 147.
22. Manuscript letter of 14 December 1830 (Fuller).
23. See Gulliver, p. 23–26.
24. *Letters,* I, 147.
25. The same, III, 445.

26. See, for example, the same, I, 130, 136.
27. Quoted by Willoughby, p. 13.
28. *Letters,* III, 442.

II (pp. 147–149)

1. *Letters,* I, 137.
2. Some of Thackeray's biographers have assumed that he lived at 2 Brick Court and subsequently at 10 Crown Office Row while studying law. Actually he retained his chambers at 5 Essex Court until November, 1833, when he removed to France (John Hutchinson, *Catalogue of Notable Middle Templers,* London, 1902, p. 241). The Brick Court and Crown Office Row chambers were nominal addresses that Thackery used between 1849 and 1859 in order to accumulate seven years' standing at the bar and thereby qualify himself for appointment to a magistracy (Hugh H. L. Bellot, *The Inner and Middle Temple,* London, 1902, p. 80).
3. *Letters,* I, 182.
4. See the same, p. 245.
5. Walter Bagehot, "Bad Lawyers or Good?" *Works,* ed. Mrs. Russell Barrington, 10 vols. (London, 1915), V, 68. I have followed Bagehot (pp. 63–71) in this paragraph. Though his essay was written in 1870, it deals with the unreformed system of legal training, which was much the same in Thackeray's day as in Bagehot's.
6. The same, p. 70.
7. *Letters,* I, 238.
8. Tennyson, "Aylmer's Field," *Enoch Arden* (London, 1864), p. 73.
9. *Works,* XII, 366–367.
10. Thackeray was finally admitted to the bar in 1848, but he never practised.
11. See *Works,* XVI, 61.

III (pp. 150–153)

1. *Letters,* I, 292.
2. Sotheby catalogue, 15 June 1937, lot 364.
3. *Letters,* III, 29.
4. The same, p. 114.
5. See the same, I, 167–168.
6. The same, p. 275.
7. The same, p. 174.
8. "About Two Great Novelists," *Temple Bar,* LXXXIII (June, 1888), 193.
9. *Letters,* I, 160.
10. The same, p. 177.
11. The same, p. 198.
12. The same, p. 183.
13. This reproduction is taken from a plate in Sotheby catalogue, 28–30 May 1934, lot 559.
14. *Autobiography,* ed. Maria Weston Chapman, 3 vols. (Boston, 1877), II, 60.

IV (pp. 153–157)

1. *Cecil,* 3 vols. (London, 1841).
2. Bulwer, *England and the English,* II, 80.
3. For a detailed picture of the lives actually led by Carlyle's "Dandiacal Body" at this time,

see Michael Sadleir, *Blessington D'Orsay* (London, 1933), pp. 287–316.

4. FitzGerald and Henry Kemble had visited Paris together in 1830 (*Letters and Literary Remains,* III, 225).

5. *Records of a Girlhood,* 3 vols. (London, 1878), II, 200. The account of Henry Kemble's career which follows is drawn chiefly from this book.

6. The same, III, 149.

7. *Letters,* I, 172.

8. *Glances Back,* I, 171.

9. Compare *Works,* VIII, 223–231.

10. "The Cave of Harmony" in *The Newcomes* is usually supposed to have been drawn from Evans's in Covent Garden Piazza (see Wheatley, *London Past and Present,* II, 21), but this establishment did not become celebrated for its suppers and music-meetings until Paddy Green became its proprietor in 1844, nor did Sloman figure among its notable performers.

11. *Glances Back,* I, 171.

12. *Some Experiences of a Barrister's Life,* I, 31.

13. Manuscript Silver diary.

14. *Letters,* I, 209. See also pp. 195–196.

15. See the same, pp. 230n, 235.

16. Manuscript Silver diary, 23 October 1861; *Letters,* II, 112.

17. The same, I, 175.

18. Merivale and Marzials, pp. 235–236. See above, p. 134.

19. See *Letters,* I, 186, 187, 190, 191, 197, 199, 201, 202, 204, 205, 208.

20. The same, p. 504.

21. The same, p. 187.

22. The same, p. 202.

23. *Works,* II, 119.

24. See, for example, *Works,* VI, 128–130; X, 273–276.

V (pp. 157–161)

1. See, for example, *Letters,* I, 189, 210.

2. The same, p. 195.

3. The same, p. 199.

4. The same, p. 246.

5. The same, pp. 214–215.

6. The same, p. 220.

7. The same, p. 245.

8. The same, p. 229.

9. The same, p. 230.

10. The same, p. 255.

11. See the same, pp. 504–505.

12. *Fraser's Magazine,* April, 1843, p. 400.

13. See *Letters,* II, 103–105.

14. *Lambert Catalogue,* p. 88.

15. See above, pp. 194–196.

16. *Letters,* I, 197.

17. *Final Reliques of Father Prout,* ed. Blanchard Jerrold (London, 1876), pp. 141 ff.

18. *Mr. Thackeray's Writings in "The National Standard," and "The Constitutional"* (London, 1899), pp. 3–4. This compilation reprints only a small part of Thackeray's work for the *National Standard,* but enough to illustrate its general nature.

19. *Works,* XVII, 74.

20. *Letters,* I, 264.

21. See *Fraser's Magazine* of this date.
22. *Letters,* I, 270. It is true that the *Standard* was at this time edited by Maginn's friend Dr. Giffard.

VI (pp. 162–166)

1. See above, p. 64.
2. See *Letters,* I, 245.
3. The same, p. 271.
4. See W. H. Carey, *The Good Old Days of Honourable John Company,* 3 vols. (Simla, 1882–1887), I, 216. The failure of Cruttenden and Co. is dealt with in the *Englishman,* 13 January 1834, p. 3; and 14 January 1834, pp. 2–3.
5. *Letters,* I, 268–269.
6. The same, I, 267.
7. *Works,* XI, 761–762.
8. Manuscript draft of a letter to Charles Carmichael, [December?] 1845 (Fuller).
9. It is not clear why Mrs. Blechynden was at this time receiving only £52, instead of the £100 for which Richmond Thackeray's will provided.
10. *Letters,* I, 290–291.
11. *Letters Literary and Theological* (London, 1881), p. 93.
12. *Past and Present* (London, 1843), p. 197.
13. *Letters,* I, 152.
14. The same, p. 184.
15. The same, p. 190.
16. Frances Anne Kemble, *Records of a Girlhood,* III, 149.
17. Most of this information regarding Kemble's affair with Miss Thackeray (which furnished James with the *donnée* for *Washington Square*) comes from James's notes of a conversation with Fanny Kemble in 1880 (*The Notebooks of Henry James,* eds. F. O. Matthiessen and Kenneth B. Murdock, New York, 1947, pp. 12–13). For Miss Thackeray's income, see *Letters,* III, 279.
18. The same, p. 392.
19. Manuscript letter, Thackeray to Langslow, 9 February 1838 (Maggs).
20. Manuscript letter (Mrs. Edgcumbe).
21. *Works,* IX, 310.

CHAPTER 7
Golden Time

I (pp. 167–169)

1. *Letters,* I, 262.
2. The same, pp. 190, 260n.
3. The same, IV, 270.
4. *Works,* XIV, 302.
5. *Letters,* I, 262.
6. The same, p. 264. The date of Thackeray's election to the Garrick Club was supplied to Mrs. Fuller in 1937 by K. A. Plimpton, Secretary. Thackeray was proposed by Benjamin Robert Heath and seconded by William Reade.

7. *Letters,* I, 271.
8. It has been asserted that Thackeray as a young man attended the painting school of James Mathews Leigh (1808–1860). This can hardly be, since Leigh's school had not been established in 1834. It was a flourishing enterprise by the 1850s, however, and Thackeray may have come to know it when he refreshed his memories of the art-student world before embarking upon *The Newcomes.*
9. The most vivid description of the man and his school is to be found in Chapter 4 of W. P. Frith's *Autobiography* (New York, 1888). Lionel Cust, writing in the *Dictionary of National Biography* (L, 311), is of the opinion that Gandish was not drawn from Sass. Yet the resemblance between the two seems unmistakable, though it must be granted that Gandish is not "well-educated and a gentleman," as Frith asserts that Sass was.
10. Frith, p. 31.
11. The same, pp. 25–26.
12. See above, pp. 233–234.
13. Manuscript notes sent by Frank Stone's son Arthur to Lady Ritchie (Fuller). In *Works,* I, 592, Thackeray refers to Stone as "My friend Pebbler, himself a famous artist."
14. *Catalogue . . . of the Library of the Comte de Suzzanet* (Sotheby and Company, 26–27 March 1934), lot 206.

II (pp. 169–174)

1. See *Letters,* I, 266–267.
2. *Works,* II, 42–43.
3. *Letters,* I, 273.
4. Bedingfield, p. 30.
5. *Letters,* II, 503.
6. *Works,* II, 43.
7. *Letters,* I, 277.
8. J. K. Laughton, *Memoirs of the Life and Correspondence of Henry Reeve,* 2 vols. (London, 1898), I, 35.
9. *Mémoires des autres,* 6 vols. (Paris n. d.), V, 87–88. See *Letters,* II, 588.
10. Maunsell B. Field, quoted by James Grant Wilson, *Thackeray in the United States,* 2 vols. (London, 1904), I, 229.
11. *Letters,* I, 274.
12. The same, p. 279.
13. The same, p. 291.
14. *Memoirs and Experiences of Moncure Daniel Conway,* 2 vols. (London, 1904), II, 5–6.
15. *Letters,* I, 166.
16. See the same, p. 278. Though interesting for its anticipation of the bleakest naturalism, "A Gambler's Death" hardly rises as fiction above the level of unassimilated anecdote. But it is a capital autobiographical document. So strong is the impress of personal experience which it bears, indeed, that Thackeray's assurance that "the story is, for the chief part, a fact" (*Works,* II, 123) is superfluous.
17. *Works,* II, 117.
18. The same, p. 124.
19. The same, p. 125.

20. The same, p. 7.
21. *Letters,* I, 286.
22. Lady Ritchie's manuscript reminiscences, 1864–1865. Compare *Works,* XVI, 266.
23. *Letters,* I, 289–291.

III (pp. 174–176)

1. This catalogue of English motives for living in France is not exhaustive. There was a Duchess of Kingston, for example, who resided in Calais because she desired several husbands at once. "Such is her taste," the natives remarked indulgently. See R. Boutet de Monvel, *Les Anglais à Paris, 1800–1850* (Paris, 1911), Chapter 4.
2. *Works,* XVI, 298.
3. *Letters,* I, 296.
4. See Sir Joseph Crowe, *Reminiscences of Thirty-five Years of My Life* (London, 1895), p. 11.
5. See *Letters,* I, 509–511.
6. See Athol Mayhew, *A Jorum of "Punch"* (London, 1895), p. 16.
7. *Letters,* I, 295–296; but my text follows the manuscript, which I have seen since the publication of *Letters.*

IV (pp. 176–183)

1. See *Buried Life,* pp. 59–60.
2. Chapter 5 of *Buried Life* is largely devoted to a detailed account of Merrick Shawe's career.
3. Shawe's military career is outlined in the memoir of his services printed by Richard Cannon, *Historical Record of the Eighty-seventh Regiment, or the Royal Irish Fusiliers* (London, 1853), pp. 95–96.
4. Robert Shawe's influence in the army, like that of his nephew Merrick, was considerably greater than one would expect in an officer of his rank. Commenting on his decision to retire from the army on 19 December 1803, Merrick noted that Robert had failed to become a general only because of "the stoppage of all promotion which took place between the American & French wars." "You have the satisfaction to reflect," Merrick continued, "that you carry with you as high a reputation as any officer of your rank in the British Army has ever attained. It was only yesterday that an involuntary tribute was paid to your character in a large party at Lord Wellesley's table. Col. Nicolson (whom you will see in England) was speaking of your Colonel Lord Hutchinson and of the favors heaped upon him. He pronounced him the worst officer existing, 'notwithstanding which,' he said, 'they have made him a Lord, and to mend the matter they have given him the 74th Regiment over the head of Curnel Shawe the very best field officer by Ch–st in the whole *Brutish Ermy.*' There was more of true praise in old Nicolson's earnest manner and Scotch dialect than in a volume of fine words & flummery." (British Museum Add. MSS. 13,767, folios 103–108)

5. The same, folios 111–114.
6. Quoted by Richard Cannon, *Historical Record of the Seventy-fourth Regiment (Highlanders)* (London, 1850), p. 21.
7. The same, pp. 21, 28.
8. British Museum Add. MSS. 13, 767, folios 99 ff. Merrick had the news of Matthew's recovery from Maj.-Gen. Wellesley, who had written on 25 September: "Your brother's wound is doing well. He will not be obliged to quit the army" (*Despatches,* II, 232).
9. Cannon, *Seventy-fourth Regiment,* p. 46.
10. The same, p. 66.
11. Cannon, *Eighty-seventh Regiment,* p. 96.
12. War Office manuscript records 42/41/145: 3093; James Grove White, *Historical and Topographical Notes Etc. on Buttevant, Castletownroche, Doneraile, Mallow, and Places in Their Vicinity,* 4 vols. (Cork, 1905–1925), II, 11.
13. Rev. Patrick Woulfe, *Irish Names and Surnames* (Dublin, 1923), p. 239.
14. Sir Bernard Burke, *The Landed Gentry of Ireland* (London, 1912).
15. Woulfe, p. 239.
16. White, II, 11. Col. White reproduces a photograph of Laurentinum house in 1865, after its top storey had been removed (II, opposite p. 9).
17. Manuscript pedigree of Robert Shawe of Chester (Genealogical Office, Dublin Castle).
18. She was baptized in the Garrison of Fort William on 4 January 1817 (Manuscript Ecclesiastical Records, Bengal, X, 359, Commonwealth Relations Office).
19. He was born 29 September 1818, baptized at Barrackpore 9 October 1819 (War Office manuscript records 42/41/145; 3093–3097).
20. Baptized at Ghazeepore, 9 December 1823 (the same).
21. Cannon, *Eighty-seventh Regiment,* p. 27.
22. Manuscript Ecclesiastical Records (Wills), Bengal, IV, 226–227.
23. War Office manuscript records, Establishment of Widows' Pensions, 1828, 24/882, p. 86.
24. After the death of Arthur Creagh in 1833, his widow built Creagh House in Doneraile, and in 1838 removed there. "She found Laurentinum too lonely in the disturbed times," Col. White explains (II, 268; IV, 11), "and preferred living in Doneraile." Laurentinum House was the subject of a chancery suit and eventually passed out of the family.
25. Manuscript Records of Bengal Civilians, p. 1710 (Commonwealth Relations Office).
26. Col. H. G. Hart, *Army List* (London, 1863), pp. 291–292.
27. *Letters,* I, 433.
28. Laughton, I, 59.

V (pp. 183–188)

1. *Works,* XVI, 369–370.
2. See *Letters,* I, xc–xciii.
3. Thomas Adolphus Trollope, *What I Remember,* 3 vols. (London, 1887–1889), I, 288–289.
4. *Letters,* I, 268.
5. The same, p. 296.
6. Laughton, I, 59. He was perhaps employed by this paper, though not as its editor, as early as 7 October 1835. See *Letters,* I, 297.
7. It should be mentioned, however, that in a manuscript letter of 1858 Bowes wrote to Thackeray of *Flore et Zéphyr* (after remarking, "Let me tell you, Sir, you have done worse things since"): "That smiling little wretch M of B. Street did us most awfully I believe, & put a lot of money into his pocket" (Fuller).
8. The best source of information regarding the establishment of the *Constitutional* is the usually unreliable *Thackeray* of "Theodore Taylor," pp. 72–76. The author of this compilation appears to have had access to an authoritative source for this part of his narrative.
9. Henry Sayre Van Duzer, *A Thackeray Library* (New York, 1919), p. 21; *Letters,* I, 305.
10. *Letters,* I, 303–304.
11. The same, p. 309.
12. The same, p. 311.
13. Manuscript letter of 9 July 1861 (Fuller). Thackeray continues: "At least the portrait will be faithful."
14. *Letters,* I, 318–319.
15. Merivale and Marzials, pp. 107–108.
16. Manuscript letter of 25 August 1836 (Freshfield).

VI (pp. 188–190)

1. *Letters,* I, 322.
2. The same, p. 321.
3. The same, p. 325.
4. The same, p. 323.
5. *Works,* VII, 57–59.
6. *Letters,* I, 321.
7. See her letters to Mrs. Carmichael-Smyth (the same, p. 381 ff).
8. Speech at the Royal Academy Dinner, May, 1858, reprinted by Melville, *Thackeray* (1910), II, 115.
9. Manuscript letter from Ainsworth to Macrone, 13 July 1836 (Carnegie); *Letters,* I, 326–328.
10. The same, pp. 325, 328–329.

VII (pp. 190–193)

1. Manuscript letter from P. Forbes, Honorary Secretary of the Coffee and Eating House Keepers, to Maj. Carmichael-Smyth, 11 March 1837 (Ray).
2. *The Personal Life of George Grote* (London, 1873), pp. 111–113.
3. These contributions are reprinted in *Mr. Thackeray's Writings.* See *Works,* XVI, 269, for Thackeray's mature view of his letters to this paper.

4. *Mr. Thackeray's Writings,* p. 213.
5. The same, p. 212.
6. Fragmentary manuscript letter of the winter of 1836–1837 (Fuller).
7. *Mr. Thackeray's Writings,* p. 222.
8. The same, pp. 164–167, 203.
9. Fragmentary manuscript letter of the winter of 1836–1837 (Fuller).
10. *Letters,* I, 342.
11. *Mr. Thackeray's Writings,* p. 294.

CHAPTER *8*
Great Coram Street

I (pp. 194–201)

1. *Letters of Thomas Carlyle, 1826–1836,* ed. C. E. Norton, 2 vols. (London, 1888), I, 283.
2. Samuel Smiles, *Memoir and Correspondence of John Murray,* 2 vols. (London, 1891), II, 197.
3. *The Letters of Sir Walter Scott,* ed. H. J. C. Grierson, 12 vols. (London, 1932–1937), XI, 162.
4. "Hallam's Constitutional History."
5. *Journal,* ed. D. Douglas, 2 vols. (Edinburgh, 1890), II, 262.
6. *Letters of Thomas Carlyle, 1826–1836,* II, 309.
7. *Glances Back,* I, 110. An authoritative treatment of this topic will be found in A. Aspinall's "The Social Status of Journalists at the Beginning of the Nineteenth Century," *Review of English Studies,* XXI (1945), 216–232. See also what Dickens (*Letters,* ed. Dexter, I, 524) calls that "terrible paper on Theodore Hook . . . by Lockhart" in the *Quarterly Review,* CXLIII, 53–108.
8. *Works,* II, 44–45.
9. For example, in registering the birth of his daughter Jane in 1838 and her death in 1839.
10. He signed his own name to the prefaces of *The Irish Sketch Book* and *Notes of a Journey from Cornhill to Grand Cairo,* but both books are described as by "Mr. M. A. Titmarsh" on their title pages.
11. *Works,* I, 189. Professor Aspinall (p. 219) cites the following passage from an article published in the *London Review* of 1835: "That those who are regularly connected with the Newspaper Press are for the most part excluded from what is, in the widest extension of the term, called good society; or that, if admitted into good company, they are very rarely admitted on a footing of equality, is a lamentable truth familiar to everybody who has any knowledge of the world. . . . Men of birth, refinement and sensitive pride will not enter into an occupation which lowers their social position, and if any such engage in it, the illicit connection is carefully kept secret."

12. *Letters,* II, 137.
13. The best study of the tangled bibliography of Thackeray's early years is Gulliver's *Thackeray's Literary Apprenticeship.* This book summed up then existing evidence and speculation regarding Thackeray's unacknowledged periodical contributions, added much new information, and presented cautious and trustworthy conclusions regarding most points at issue. Few significant additions have been made to Gulliver's identifications for the 1830s; but those for the 1840s have been greatly extended by subsequent investigation. See my "[39] Articles Newly Identified as Thackeray's," *Letters,* II, 845–847; and "Thackeray and Punch: 44 Newly Identified Contributions," *Times Literary Supplement,* 1 January 1949.
14. "Fraser got instant circulation by bold slapdash" (manuscript letter from Francis Mahony to Thackeray, 15 December 1859, Fuller).
15. See Miriam M. H. Thrall, *Rebellious Fraser's* (New York, 1934).
16. *Letters of Thomas Carlyle, 1826–1836,* II, 25.
17. *Letters,* IV, 329.
18. Manuscript letter of May, 1838 (Maggs).
19. There was a final Yellowplush paper published in *Fraser's Magazine* for January, 1840, but it is critical rather than narrative.
20. *Works,* I, 167. Thackeray's conception would appear to hark back to an article in *Fraser's Magazine* of February, 1831, which describes Bulwer as a "Silver Fork Publisher" and the leader of the "Footman School of Novelists."
21. *Catalogue of the Library of W. M. Thackeray,* ed. J. H. Stonehouse (London, 1935), p. 168.
22. *Works,* II, 379.
23. H. Sutherland Edwards, *Personal Recollections* (London, 1900), p. 37.
24. *Letters,* ed. Dexter, I, 590.
25. *Letters,* I, 351.
26. Quoted from *Fraser's Magazine* by Derek Hudson, *Thomas Barnes of the Times* (Cambridge, 1943), p. 29.
27. The same, p. 114.
28. *Letters,* I, 375.
29. The same, p. 434.
30. See, for example, the same, pp. 377–378.
31. The same, III, 39.
32. John W. Irvine, "A Study for Colonel Newcome," *Nineteenth Century,* XXXIV (1893), 593–594.
33. *Letters,* I, 384.
34. The same, p. 400.
35. Manuscript letter (Cohen).
36. Quoted by Henry A. Beers, *Nathaniel Parker Willis* (Boston, 1885), p. 254.
37. *Letters,* II, 213. See Harold H. Scudder, "Thackeray and N. P. Willis," *PMLA,* LVII (1942), 589–592. Three further Thackerayan pieces appeared in the *Corsair* before it ceased publication in March, 1840, but these were all piracies of material published elsewhere.

38. John Brown and Henry Lancaster, "Thackeray," *North British Review,* LXXIX (February, 1864), 227.
39. *Letters,* I, 358.
40. Undated letter, American Art Association catalogue, 12 March 1936, lot 250.
41. *Works,* III, 388.
42. E. D. Cuming, *Robert Smith Surtees* (Edinburgh and London, 1924), p. 105.
43. *Journal,* I, 122.

II (pp. 201–206)

1. Manuscript Silver diary, 2 July 1862.
2. *Letters,* I, 376. At his trial for the murder of William Weare, Thurtell was described as "a most respectable man," "a man who kept a gig." Hence Carlyle's phrase for respectable society, "gigmanity."
3. *Works,* I, 509. Thackeray regarded Baker Street as the stronghold of rigid respectability. As the historian of Snobs, he later made it a subject of particular study, even assuring his readers that he was "engaged on a life of Baker, the founder of this celebrated Street" (the same, IX, 286).
4. Manuscript letter, Thackeray to Charles Carmichael, [December?] 1845 (Fuller).
5. *Letters,* II, 431.
6. The same, I, 352, 391, 412, 430; manuscript letter, Mrs. Thackeray to Mrs. Carmichael-Smyth, 22 November 1839 (Ray).
7. Mrs. Fuller's manuscript notes of a conversation with Mrs. Litchfield, daughter of Charles Darwin.
8. P. 13.
9. Lady Ritchie's manuscript reminiscences, 1864–1865, p. 7.
10. *Letters,* I, 368, 379, 367.
11. Entry in register of births, subdistrict of St. George's, Bloomsbury, borough of Holborn.
12. *Letters,* I, 366.
13. Entry in register of deaths, subdistrict of St. George's, Bloomsbury, borough of Holborn.
14. *Letters,* I, 379–380.
15. Manuscript letter to Mrs. Douglas Freshfield (Fuller).
16. Manuscript letter (Ray).
17. Manuscript letter from Mrs. Thackeray to Mrs. Carmichael-Smyth, 25 May 1839 (Ray).
18. *Letters,* I, 436.
19. Manuscript letter to Mrs. Carmichael-Smyth, 23 May 1839 (Ray).
20. Manuscript letter, 11 December 1839 (Ray).
21. *Letters,* I, 394.
22. The same, p. 400.
23. The same, pp. 394–395.
24. The same, p. 424. Lady Ritchie's earliest recollection of her father dated from this time; it was of her asking him to tell her the name of her doll, and his replying, "This is Miss Polly Perkins I think" (manuscript reminiscences, 1864–1865).
25. P. 232.

26. *Works,* II, 420; the phrase is repeated in III, 290.
27. *Letters,* II, 53.
28. P. 232.
29. *Letters,* I, 353–354.

III (pp. 207–212)

1. *Letters,* I, clxv.
2. The same, p. 435.
3. The same, II, 50.
4. Bedingfield, p. 13.
5. *Letters,* I, 398.
6. *Letters of Thomas Carlyle to His Youngest Sister,* ed. C. T. Copeland (Boston, 1899), p. 86.
7. Manuscript letter from Thackeray to Charles Carmichael, [December?] 1845 (Fuller).
8. *Works,* II, xxvii.
9. The same, III, 344.
10. *Letters,* I, 364.
11. The same, pp. 363–364.
12. The same, p. 444.
13. The same, p. 424.
14. The same, p. 398.
15. The same, p. 435.
16. The same, pp. 420–421.
17. Manuscript letter, Mrs. Thackeray to Mrs. Carmichael-Smyth, 31 December 1839 (Ray); *Letters,* I, 423.
18. On 31 December 1839, at a time when Thackeray was attacking *Jack Sheppard* and other Newgate novels in *Catherine,* we find Isabella writing loyally to Mrs. Carmichael-Smyth about the projected *Paris Sketch Book:* "If his book does not get sale and he popularity we can only say peoples taste must be very depraved since Mr Ainsworth has gained it by his unwholesome writing" (manuscript letter, Ray).
19. *Letters,* 467.
20. The same, p. 447.
21. The same, p. 424.
22. W. E. Church, *W. M. Thackeray as an Artist and Art Critic* (privately printed, n. p., n. d.), p. x.
23. In 1838 this was a supper club which met the last Saturday of each month. Its "Motion-Book" for the years 1837 to 1846 was discovered by the Rev. F. C. Clare, who has given it to the London Museum. The only direct reference to Thackeray in this interesting document is the following: "At the adjd 1/2 year general meeting 30. January 1846. William M. Thackeray Esqe of St James's Chambers St James's Street an old member & whose name was inadvertently omitted by Mr Banks from his list has been elected by ballot."
24. Manuscript letter, 11 January 1840 (Maggs); *Glances Back,* I, 140.
25. *Letters,* I, 388.
26. Bedingfield, p. 13.
27. Manuscript letter (Murray).
28. *Letters,* I, 357.
29. *Works,* XI, 532.
30. *Letters,* I, 399.
31. *Maxims of Sir Morgan O'Doherty, Bart.* (Edinburgh and London, 1849), pp. 48–49.
32. Manuscript letter, 23 May 1839 (Ray).
33. *Letters,* II, 431.
34. The same, I, 478.

IV (pp. 213–219)

1. *Letters,* I, 460.
2. *Works,* II, 412.
3. See, for example, *Letters,* I, 441.
4. Bedingfield, p. 29.
5. *Letters,* I, 458.
6. *Works,* I, 132.
7. Compare the same, III, 194–195.
8. *Letters,* I, 410.
9. *Works,* II, 314.
10. The same, I, 225–226.
11. The same, III, 41; compare III, 305.
12. The same, I, 191.
13. The same, III, 292.
14. In "A Caution to Travellers," for example, the silly little bagman Pogson, who pretends to be a gentleman, is read a humiliating lecture by Major British which leaves him whimpering abjectly, before the Major extricates him from the difficulties in which his folly has involved him. *Works,* II, 30–1.
15. *The Road to Wigan Pier* (London, 1937), p. 173.
16. *Works,* II, 411–412; compare II, 169.
17. See the same, pp. 172–175.
18. The same, III, 291.
19. Quoted from *Le Temps* by Brown and Lancaster, in the *North British Review,* LXXIX, 229.
20. *Letters,* I, 402.
21. *Works,* III, 56.
22. The same, p. 453.
23. The same, II, 412.
24. The same, pp. 323–325.
25. The same, III, 149.
26. The same, pp. 102–103. The whole of this passage, to the end of the paragraph, deserves close study by those who would penetrate to Thackeray's innermost mind. It anticipates by many years two better-known expressions of the same point of view in *Vanity Fair* (the same, XI, 532–533) and *Esmond* (the same, XIII, 15–16).
27. The same, II, 411.
28. *Letters,* I, 421.
29. The same, pp. 391–392.
30. The same, p. 397.

CHAPTER *9*
Apprentice Writer

I (pp. 220–222)

1. *Works,* II, 486.
2. Chap. 5.
3. Of these several types of fiction only the fashionable novel has been examined with any care. See Matthew Whiting Rosa, *The Silver-fork School* (New York, 1936), and Michael Sadleir, *Bulwer and His Wife* (London, 1933), pp. 115–117.
4. The popular poetry of the 1830s, like the popular fiction, remains largely unexplored. The only general survey of the field occurs in Thomas R. Lounsbury's vivacious but inaccurate *Life*

and Times of Tennyson (New Haven, 1915), pp. 98–204. For the annuals, see also the bibliographical note in Ralph Thompson's *American Literary Annuals and Gift Books: 1825–1865* (New York, 1936), pp. 165–166.

5. *Works,* II, 337–338.
6. Henry G. Hewlett, *Henry Fothergill Chorley: Autobiography, Memoir and Letters,* 2 vols. (London, 1873), I, 107–108, 120.
7. *Works,* II, 359–360.

(II pp. 223–226)

1. See Thrall, *Rebellious Fraser's,* who gives convincing reasons for rejecting (pp. 247–258) most of the articles claimed as Thackeray's by earlier students (among them "Elizabeth Brownrigge" of September, 1832), but adds (pp. 297–298) dubious lists of "works probably attributable to Thackeray alone" or "to Thackeray and Maginn in collaboration."
2. *Works,* II, 359.
3. *Maxims of Sir Morgan O'Doherty,* p. 51.
4. *Works,* II, 376.
5. *My Literary Life* (London, 1899), p. 86.
6. Manuscript diary of Kate Perry, 1849–1850, 22 January 1850 (Weber).
7. *Works,* I, 77; *Letters,* I, 396.
8. Quoted by Francis Espinasse, *Literary Recollections and Sketches* (London, 1893), p. 215.
9. For an account of Clarke and his pamphlet, see *Letters,* I, 373n.
10. See above, pp. 131, 236–237.
11. *Works,* I, 342, 552; II, 28, 33.
12. The pioneer account of Thackeray's relationship to Fielding was Frederick S. Dickson's "William Makepeace Thackeray and Henry Fielding," *North American Review,* CXCVII (1913), 522–537. Wilbur Cross's treatment of this topic in his *History of Henry Fielding,* 3 vols. (New Haven, 1918), III, 213–225, is largely based on Dickson's article. The most recent, as well as the most inclusive, study is Eva Beach Touster's "The Literary Relationship of Thackeray and Fielding," *Journal of English and Germanic Philology,* XLVI (1947), 383–394.
13. *Thackerayana,* pp. 74–77; *Catalogue of Library,* p. 169; *Memorials,* p. 348.
14. See, for example, *Mr. Thackeray's Writings,* pp. 166–167, 185.
15. In the issue of 2 September 1840 (*Works,* III, 383–393).
16. *Letters,* I, 412.
17. The same, III, 402.
18. *Works,* III, 383, 385.
19. The same, II, 182–184.
20. The same, p. 98.
21. The same, III, 385.
22. *The Works of Henry Fielding* (London, 1840).
23. *Works,* III, 384.
24. *Letters,* II, 462.
25. Quoted by Cross, *History of Henry Fielding,* III, 254.

III (pp. 226–238)

1. Gray, *Englishwoman,* XXXVII, 112–113; Bedingfield, p. 29.
2. *Works,* II, 46–47.
3. Balzac, *La Comédie humaine,* ed. Marcel Bouteron, 10 vols. (Paris, 1935–1937), II, 913.
4. *Horae Subsecivae, Third Series* (Edinburgh, 1884), p. 180.
5. *Works,* II, 188.
6. The same, p. 180.
7. *Letters,* I, 349.
8. *Works,* I, 168.
9. The same, p. xlix.
10. The same.
11. The same, pp. 179, 220.
12. The same, pp. 180, 212, 234, 245.
13. A foot-note (the same, p. 266) suggests that Thackeray himself came to regard them in this light.
14. "Miss Shum's Husband," the only other proper fiction in *The Yellowplush Papers,* is a mere anecdote, depending for its point on a surprise ending, almost in the manner of O. Henry.
15. *Works,* I, 190–191.
16. The same, p. 232.
17. Ellis, *Ainsworth,* I, 285, 362, 366. Compare *Letters,* I, 395.
18. Preface to 1840 edition of *Eugene Aram* (*Works,* Knebworth Edition, 40 vols., London, v. d.), p. xi. Bulwer had developed his theory at greater length in an essay of 1838 entitled "On Art in Fiction," which is reprinted in *Pamphlets and Sketches* in this edition of his *Works.*
19. *Works,* III, 46. "Biss Dadsy," of course, is "Miss Nancy." Thackeray develops this point of view further on pp. 3–4, 7–8, 31–32, 115–116, 165–166, 184–187.
20. The same, p. 184; *Letters,* I, 433.
21. See Andrew Knapp and William Baldwin, *The New Newgate Calendar,* 6 vols. (London, c. 1826), I, 347–364. It seems likely that Thackeray used this work, together with contemporary newspaper accounts of the crime, as the basis for his story, though there were competing summaries of the annals of English malefactors on which he might have drawn.
22. The same, p. 347.
23. In direct contradiction to his avowed intention in writing *Catherine,* Thackeray is led to reflect at one point "how dreadfully like a rascal is to an honest man" (*Works,* III, 78).
24. *Letters,* I, 433.
25. *Works,* III, 126, 140, 169.
26. The same, pp. 170–174, 182–183.
27. *Letters,* I, 421.
28. *Works,* III, 89–90, 127–129.
29. Manuscript Silver diary, 27 May 1863. Another bit of gossip from the same source (19 January 1859) adds a further detail: "Frank Stone is ill treating his wife, by whom he had several children before their marriage & ought therefore says Evans to have been more than commonly kind to her."
30. Manuscript letter of [?–3] March 1840 (Fuller), partially printed in *Letters,* I, 423–426. Compare the same, pp. 509–511.

31. Thackeray gives Caroline Isabella's appearance, even to her red hair (*Works,* III, 302), as well as many of her characteristics. It may also be noted that Caroline, "which he always pronounced Carolin', was his favourite woman's name" (*Centenary Biographical Introductions,* VI, xxi).
32. *Works,* III, 292, 313.
33. Saintsbury, who did share this attitude, ranks Andrea Fitch very high. See *Works,* III, xvii.
34. The same, p. 381.
35. *Letters,* I, 488. The four instalments of *A Shabby Genteel Story* printed in *Fraser's* required fifty-three magazine pages.
36. *Letters,* III, 146.
37. *Works,* III, 280.
38. The same, p. 311; manuscript Silver diary, 5 March 1862.
39. An anonymous writer in the *Calcutta Review,* XCIII (July, 1891), 20–36, claims that he has found "The Real Major Gahagan" in William Linnaeus Gardner (d. 1835): "Like his fictitious representative, our hero was a tall and brave wielder of the sabre, who raised and commanded a body of Irregular 'Horse.' Like Gahagan, he bearded the truculent Holkar in his durbar-tent, and won the love of a dusky Princess of Ind" (p. 20). But when this writer admits that Gardner was modest and retiring, one sees that the resemblance in careers does not extend to characteristics. Evan Cotton in *Bengal Past and Present,* XLI (1931), 77, notes that Thackeray took the costume of Gahagan's Ahmednuggar Irregulars from that of the regiment of Irregular Horse commanded by Colonel Skinner.
40. *Works,* I, 404.
41. The same, II, 471.
42. *Letters,* I, 365.
43. *Works,* II, 474. It may help to explain Thackeray's estimate of this tale to note that its inspiring idea derived from personal experience. "There was a story my father used to tell me," writes Lady Ritchie (*Centenary Biographical Introductions,* VI, xix), "of his own early youth, and of his passionate longing for a pair of Hessian boots; he ordered them to be sent home, but they were sternly sent back to the shop as unbefitting a schoolboy. It was a dreadful moment, he said, and one which he could never forget."
44. *Letters,* I, 433.
45. *Works,* II, 98–99.
46. The same, VI, 319–320.

IV (pp. 238–245)

1. *Works,* II, 362.
2. The same, p. 527.
3. The same, p. 393.
4. The same, pp. 57–58.
5. The same, p. 525.
6. Gulliver rescues some articles not printed in *Works.* See pp. 201–236.
7. See, for example, *Works,* II, 518.
8. Hannay, p. 13.

9. *Works,* VI, 386–387.
10. The Earl of Lytton, *Life of Edward Bulwer First Lord Lytton,* 2 vols. (London, 1913), I, 81.
11. *Nineteenth Century,* CXL, 53; *Bulwer and His Wife,* pp. 251–255.
12. Most recently Professor Greig in *Thackeray: A Reconsideration,* pp. 37–41.
13. See particularly *Bulwer and His Wife,* pp. 248–266.
14. *Rebellious Fraser's,* pp. 66–71.
15. *Letters,* I, 198.
16. See Gulliver, pp. 201–204, 214–217; *Stray Papers,* pp. 292–300.
17. Dr. Lardner is also presented as an intimate of Bulwer in "The History of Dionysius Diddler," a curious set of caricatures which Thackeray drew for the abortive "Foolscap Library" in April, 1840. See *Works,* I, 599–608; *Letters,* I, 438.
18. *Works,* I, 303.
19. The same, pp. 303–312.
20. The same, p. 308.
21. *The Garrick Club* (privately printed, n. p., 1896), p. 23.
22. Andrew Lang, *Life and Letters of John Gibson Lockhart,* 2 vols. (London, 1897), II, 37; Hewlett, *Chorley,* I, 194; *New Letters of Thomas Carlyle,* I, 188–189.
23. Manuscript letter of 12–15 December 1858 (Morgan).
24. *Letters,* II, 553–554. Compare *Works,* VI, 386–388.
25. *Mr. Brown's Letters to a Young Man about Town* (New York, 1853), pp. x–xi.
26. *Nineteenth Century,* CXL, 53. Professor Greig, whose book was written after the publication of *Letters,* remains of Mr. Sadleir's former opinion, which he cites (*Thackeray: A Reconsideration,* p. 39) without notifying the reader of its author's recantation.
27. *Flore et Zéphyr* (1836) is only a collection of lithographs; Thackeray had no hand in the piratical publication of *The Yellowplush Papers* which took place in Philadelphia in 1838.
28. *Works,* II, 94.
29. The same, IV, 163. This passage comes from a Fraserian paper of 1842, but it is characteristic of Thackeray's usual contempt for French physique.
30. The same, II, 252.

V (pp. 246–249)

1. *Works,* III, 330, 16.
2. The same, II, 19.
3. The same, III, 354–355; see also III, 345, 373.
4. The same, I, 311.
5. The same, II, 372–373.
6. The same, I, 490.
7. Espinasse, *Literary Recollections,* p. 215.
8. *Centenary Biographical Introductions,* VI, xix.
9. *Letters,* ed. Dexter, III, 393.
10. *Westminster Review,* 1853.
11. *Lettres sur l'Angleterre,* 2 vols. (Paris, 1866), II, 252.

CHAPTER 10
"A Year of Pain and Hope"

I (pp. 250–255)

1. *Letters,* I, 405–406.
2. The same, p. 438.
3. The same, p. 442.
4. The same, p. 443.
5. The same, p. 437.
6. The same, p. 447.
7. The same, p. 454.
8. Cunningham had apparently already succeeded John Macrone, under whose imprint the book appeared. See the same, p. 461.
9. The same, p. 453.
10. The same, p. 459.
11. The same, p. 462.
12. The same, p. 475.
13. The same, p. 463.
14. The same, pp. 462–469.
15. The same, II, 464–469.
16. Lady Ritchie's manuscript reminiscences, 1864–1865, where this event is described as having occurred "24 years ago."
17. *Letters,* IV, 271.
18. Manuscript reminiscences, 1864–1865.
19. *Letters,* I, 473.
20. The same, pp. 468–473.

II (pp. 255–260)

1. *Letters,* I, 474, 482–483; II, 429. For many years afterwards Thackeray noted the anniversary of Isabella's attempted suicide.
2. Thackeray's lodgings are described not only in *Letters* (I, 474, 481; II, 69), but also in *The Irish Sketch Book* (*Works,* VI, 87–92); for when he introduces in that book "a friend" on Grattan's Hill, "who lodged there with a sick wife and a couple of little children; one of whom was an infant in arms," he is clearly writing of himself in 1840.
3. *Works,* V, 87–91.
4. *Letters,* I, 472–476.
5. The same, p. 479.
6. The same, pp. 476, 478, 485.
7. The same, pp. 478–483.
8. The same, p. 484.
9. This manuscript has not survived. Thackeray once told Bedingfield (p. 28): "Ah, I haven't got hold of the trick that a dramatist wants. I sent a comedy to Charles Mathews, who, placing his hand on his heart assured me that anything of mine should have his most earnest attention; but, after six months, I knew he hadn't read my piece."
10. *Letters,* I, 478.
11. The same, p. 486.
12. *Biographical Introductions,* IV, xxix–xxxii. There is a briefer account of this journey in Lady Ritchie's manuscript reminiscences, 1864–1865, which agrees in its essentials with the passage quoted.

III (pp. 260–266)

1. *Letters,* II, 3–5.
2. The same, I, 488–489.
3. It has not previously been realized that *The Great Hoggarty Diamond* was written so early and in so short a period. Yet this is the inescapable conclusion from the available evidence. *The Second Funeral of Napoleon* and "The Chronicle of the Drum" occupied Thackeray during the latter half of December (the same, II, 6–7). He then began reading for "The Knights of Borsellen," but by 27 February he had some time since "put the novel aside . . . to get if poss: something ready agst April for Mrs T." (the same, II, 10). On 25 February he told Mrs. Carlyle that he had sent a "bundle" of manuscript to Bentley (manuscript letter, National Library of Scotland). And in an irate note received 1 June by that publisher, Thackeray wrote: "Have the goodness to give my M. S. of the Diamond to my friend Mr Cunningham. I can't get any answer about it from you good bad or indifferent, & next time your obedient Servant sends you an article you may set him down without fail to be you understand what [sketch of a donkey] yours & whatdyecallem W M Thackeray" (manuscript letter, Spencer).
4. Manuscript letter, 25 February 1841 (National Library of Scotland).
5. *Letters,* II, 4.
6. *Works,* III, 425–426.
7. *Letters,* II, 6–7.
8. *Works,* III, 399.
9. *Letters,* II, 136.
10. Manuscript letter, 20 March 1841 (Millar).
11. *Works,* IV, 132, 128.
12. *Letters,* II, 440.
13. See *Works,* IV, 125–126.
14. See the same, p. 113.
15. *Letters,* II, 440, 795.
16. The same, p. 7. Of particular interest are the occasional departures from this new mood, notably the vindictiveness with which Sam repels the advances of would-be rakes towards his wife (*Works,* IV, 82, 139) and the profound resentment that he feels towards the attorney Smithers for suggesting, even as a well-intentioned stratagem, that Mary is unduly interested in his friend Gus Hoskins. These passages possibly point to some unrecorded episode in Isabella's history, a fuller knowledge of which might help to explain her mental break-down. See *Letters,* II, 237.
17. *Works,* IV, 3.
18. See the same, I, 234; III, 300.
19. Yet Sir Frederick Pollock (*Personal Remembrances,* London, 1887, 2 vols., I, 189) relates that Thackeray was directed by "the conductors of *Fraser's Magazine*" to "cut short and bring to a speedy conclusion his story of 'The Great Hoggarty Diamond'. . . . The Public did not like it." After more than forty years Pollock may have confused this

tale with *A Shabby Genteel Story.*

20. Carlyle, *The Life of John Sterling, Works,* 30 vols. (London, 1899–1902), XI, 223. The missing name is presumably Bulwer's. The letter which Sterling wrote to Thackeray about *The Great Hoggarty Diamond* (*Works,* IV, 3) has not survived.

IV (pp. 266–273)

1. *Letters,* II, 10; manuscript letter to Mrs. Carlyle, 20 March 1841 (Millar).
2. Quoted in an introductory note to "The Second Funeral of Napoleon," *Cornhill Magazine,* XIII (January, 1866), 48. Thackeray's correspondent is not identified, nor has this letter survived.
3. Manuscript letter to Mrs. Carlyle, 20 March 1841 (Millar); *Letters,* II, 25. At this time Thackeray thought that O'Donnell was "a noble high principled fellow of a sumptuous generosity of disposition that I value more than brains"; but he had to change this estimate two years later when his friend, hard pressed by poverty, persuaded him to have printed in *Fraser's Magazine* papers that turned out to be plagiarisms. Taxed with this offence, O'Donnell treated his exposure as "a capital joke," and Thackeray regretfully washed his hands of him (the same, pp. 130–131).
4. The same, p. 5.
5. The same, p. 11; compare *Works,* III, 504–505.
6. *Letters,* II, 431.
7. The same, pp. 5n, 18, 21; manuscript letter to Mrs. Carlyle, 20 March 1841 (Millar). "The Knights of Borsellen" is printed, together with Thackeray's surviving notes concerning it, in *Centenary Biographical Works,* XXV, 3–46.
8. *Works,* IX, 166.
9. *Letters,* II, 795.
10. "The Fashionable Authoress," also written at this time, has the same abrasive texture and reflects the same cynicism regarding the current literary scene.
11. *Letters,* II, 14, 29, 30.
12. The same, p. 20.
13. The same, pp. 14–15.
14. The same, p. 18.
15. The same, p. 23.
16. Manuscript letter (Fuller). On the basis of his *Fraser* paper it would appear that Thackeray's role in the campaign was that of an observer rather than a participant. Still, we know that he wrote at least one election squib (*Letters,* II, 33), and both the reference to the "famous Firebrand Correspondence" and the presence in the *Fraser* article of a journalist brought down specially from London for the election suggest that he may have been very active indeed in Bowes's campaign.
17. Bowes represented South Durham for four successive Parliaments, after which he lost the dissenting vote by supporting Whig educational measures and failed of re-election (*The Larch-*

field Diary. Extracts from the Diary of the Late Mr. Mewburn, First Railway Solicitor, London, 1876, p. 85).

18. *Personal Remembrances,* I, 177.
19. *Letters,* II, 31.
20. The same, p. 36.
21. The same, pp. 36, 38. When questioned about the water-cure in later life, Thackeray's comment was: "The system had been discovered in Germany by an inspired peasant, and was administered in England by peasants not so inspired" (Charles Gavan Duffy, *Conversations with Carlyle,* New York, 1892), p. 200.
22. *Letters,* II, 34.

V (pp. 273–277)

1. *Letters,* II, 12.
2. The same, pp. 30–31.
3. The same, pp. 22, 39.
4. The same, p. 429.
5. The same, IV, 145–146.
6. *Works,* XV, 28.
7. *Dramatis Personae* (London, 1864), p. 157.
8. *Letters,* II, 36.
9. Quoted by Hannay, p. 19.
10. *Heretics* (London, 1905), p. 129.
11. This view of Thackeray's character and work is developed further in *Buried Life, passim.*
12. See *Boswell's Life of Johnson,* eds. Hill and Powell, II, 247.
13. *Letters,* I, 464.
14. The same, p. 438.
15. *Works,* II, 421.
16. See, for example, the same, III, 490, 511.

CHAPTER *II*
Bachelor Life

I (pp. 278–283)

1. *Letters,* II, 43, 215.
2. The same, p. 43.
3. *Letters and Literary Remains,* III, 228.
4. *Letters,* II, 166.
5. *Glances Back,* I, 249–250.
6. *Letters,* II, 189.
7. See *Works,* VII, 48–50.
8. Bedingfield, p. 108; *Works,* VI, 39.
9. P. 108.
10. The same, p. 29.
11. *Letters,* II, 49.
12. The same, p. 134.
13. The same, p. 138.
14. The same, p. 101.
15. The same, p. 97.
16. The same, p. 148.
17. *Letters and Literary Remains,* I, 223.
18. *Works,* III, 513, 535.
19. Manuscript diary, 10 February 1859.
20. P. 74.
21. Advertisement in the 1841 edition of *The Second Funeral of Napoleon;* manuscript Silver diary, 11 April 1860.
22. *Letters,* II, 109, 112.

II (pp. 283–292)

1. *Letters,* II, 94, 97, 109, 166.
2. The same, p. 726.
3. One comes closest to Morton, perhaps, in the fragments from his letters to FitzGerald, which the latter gave to Trinity College, Cambridge.
4. *Letters,* II, 26.
5. The same, p. 114.
6. *Mrs. Brookfield,* pp. 155–174.
7. *Letters,* II, 308.
8. See *Letters of Elizabeth Barrett Browning Addressed to Richard Hengist Horne,* ed. S. B. T. Mayer, 2 vols. (London, 1877), I, 124–127.
9. *Letters,* II, 110.
10. The only book available concerning Forster, a sound biography of whom remains a major desideratum of Victorian scholarship, is Richard Renton's exasperating and inaccurate compilation *John Forster and His Friends* (London, 1912).
11. *The Garrick Club,* p. 30.
12. Manuscript Silver diary, 12 March 1862.
13. Sir Frederick Pollock, *Personal Remembrances,* I, 294.
14. Espinasse, *Literary Recollections,* p. 116.
15. *Alfred Lord Tennyson: A Memoir,* by his son, 2 vols. (London, 1897), I, 347.
16. *Letters,* II, 252–253.
17. Renton, p. 100; Espinasse, pp. 115–116.
18. Forster, *Dickens,* ed. Ley, p. 463.
19. *Letters,* II, 252–253.
20. The same, p. 296.
21. Bedingfield, p. 29.
22. Fields, *Yesterdays with Authors,* p. 20.
23. *Works,* XVII, 513; *Letters,* II, 593.
24. *Works,* VI, 393, 412–416.
25. *Library of the Late Major Wm. H. Lambert. Part II. Thackerayana* (New York, 1914), p. 76.
26. *Works,* II, 640.
27. *Letters and Literary Remains,* I, 222–223.
28. *Works,* VI, 554.
29. Hesketh Pearson, *Dickens: His Character, Comedy, and Career* (New York, 1949), p. 256.
30. *Letters to Her Family,* p. 171.
31. See, for example, *Letters,* II, 229, 231.

III (pp. 292–301)

1. *Letters,* II, 80.
2. *Works,* V, 117.
3. W. J. Fitzpatrick, *The Life of Charles Lever,* 2 vols. (London, 1879), II, 405–410.
4. Manuscript letter, 15 October 1860 (Houghton Library).
5. See *Letters,* II, 68–69, 73–74; *Works,* V, 86–92.
6. *Letters and Literary Remains,* I, 142.
7. *Letters,* II, 69; *Works,* V, 31–38.
8. Undated manuscript letter (Fuller).

9. *Letters,* II, 78.
10. *Works,* V, 286.
11. *Letters,* II, 120. Thackeray wrote "jolly good man of the sea."
12. Manuscript letter to Mrs. Procter, August, 1843 (Murray-Smith).
13. *Works,* VII, 31–33.
14. The same, IX, 82.
15. *Letters,* II, 150; *Works,* IX, 81.
16. *Letters,* II, 152–155.
17. The same, p. 157.
18. *Sand and Canvas: A Narrative of Adventures in Egypt, with a Sojourn among the Artists in Rome* (London, 1849), pp. 336–337.
19. The same, pp. 340–342.
20. Manuscript letter (Bradbury Agnew).
21. Manuscript letter of 10 January 1845 (Bradbury Agnew).
22. Duffy, *Conversations with Carlyle,* pp. 76–77.
23. XIII (March, 1846), 199.
24. *Works,* IX, xv–xvii.

IV (pp. 301–308)

1. *Letters,* II, 139; manuscript letter to Tom Fraser, 11 March 1844 (Cohen).
2. *Letters,* II, 78.
3. The same, p. 172.
4. The same, p. 102.
5. The same, p. 240.
6. Margaret Thackeray (later Mrs. Gerald Ritchie), Anne Thackeray, and their mother Mrs. Edward Talbot Thackeray, at this time Amy Crowe.
7. "Felix Summerly" was the penname of Sir Henry Cole, whose daughters were afterwards the intimate friends of Anny and Minny.
8. Manuscript reminiscences, 1878.
9. *Letters,* II, 91.
10. Manuscript reminiscences, 1878.
11. *Letters,* II, 217.
12. Manuscript reminiscences, 1878.
13. *Letters,* II, 194.
14. The same, pp. 197, 210, 240–241.
15. The same, p. 225; manuscript letter from Thackeray to Charles Carmichael, [December?] 1845 (Fuller).
16. *Letters,* II, 238–240.
17. The same, p. 250.
18. *Biographical Introductions,* I, xxvii–xxviii.
19. *Letters,* II, 255–256.

CHAPTER *12*

Free-lance

I (pp. 309–317)

1. The *Punch* contributions will be discussed in the next chapter. To *Fraser's Magazine* for May and October, 1844, and January, 1845, Thackeray contributed "Little Travels and Roadside Sketches," which are interesting chiefly as an illustration of his determination to make each of his excursions yield its return of

publishable manuscript. From his trip to Belgium in August, 1840, Thackeray returned with some pages of impressions which he had no leisure to work into final form. When he visited Belgium and Holland in August, 1843, he again came back with scattered notes. But the following year he thriftily made the two fragments into one narrative and sold it to Nickisson. Thus "Little Travels and Roadside Sketches" deal only in appearance with a single trip. *Works,* VI, 469–476 and 490–506 date from 1840, the rest from 1843. Further 1843 fragments are printed in *Letters,* II, 831–839.

2. *Works,* V, 327.
3. The same, p. 319.
4. *Letters,* II, 106.
5. *Works,* IX, 228.
6. The same, V, 47.
7. *Letters,* II, 78.
8. The same, p. 70.
9. The same, p. 88.
10. *Works,* V, 364.
11. See Thackeray's review of Venedey's *Irland, Morning Chronicle,* 16 March 1844.
12. *Works,* V, 86.
13. The same, p. 76.
14. The same, p. 57.
15. The same, p. 339.
16. The same, pp. 68, 250.
17. The same, pp. 65, 110, 91–92.
18. Manuscript letter of 1843 (Fuller). This document, like all matter quoted from manuscript sources, is printed as it was written. It may be mentioned that Thackeray's French was typically fluent but capricious.
19. *Works,* V, 30, 161, 338, 7, 296.
20. *Ainsworth's Magazine,* III (May, 1843), 435–438; "Titmarsh's Travels in Ireland," *Fraser's Magazine,* XXVII (June, 1843), 678–686.
21. See, for example, *Athenaeum,* 13 May 1843, pp. 455–457; *Literary Gazette,* 13, 20, 27 May 1843, pp. 315–316, 334–335, 350–351; *Morning Chronicle,* 23 May 1843; *Spectator,* XVI (20 May 1843), 471–472.
22. CXXVI (June, 1843), 647–656.
23. So the *Tablet* reviewer admits, "At bottom, the man is as good-natured, cant-hating, humanity-loving a creature, as any cockney that ever got smoke-dried by the atmosphere of Bow-bells," 13 May 1843, p. 292. And Prof. B. G. MacCarthy, writing nearly a hundred years later comes to much the same conclusion in an acute article on "Thackeray in Ireland," *Studies: An Irish Quarterly Review,* XL (March, 1951), 55–68.
24. *Works,* V, 150.
25. The same, X, 122.
26. *Letters,* II, 152; *Works,* IX, 142.
27. The same, pp. xii–xiii.
28. The same, pp. 130–131, 174–175.
29. The same, pp. 88, 144, 253.
30. The same, pp. 170, 173.
31. The same, p. 83.
32. *Guardian,* 18 February 1846, pp. 76–79; *Tablet,* VII (7 February 1846), 88–89.
33. *Morning Chronicle,* 29 January 1846, pp. 5–6; *Morning Post,* 9 February 1846, p. 6.

34. *Morning Post,* 9 February 1846, p. 6.

35. *Daily News,* 14 February 1846, p. 7.

II (pp. 318–332)

1. See above, pp. 238–245.
2. *Works,* VI, 387.
3. The same, p. 540. See the same, II, 337–378, for his three papers on the annuals: two for *Fraser's Magazine,* one for the *Times.*
4. *Works,* VI, 590. See the same, pp. 386–416, 538–547, and 581–609, for Thackeray's papers on Christmas books.
5. The same, p. 580.
6. The same, pp. 539–540.
7. The same, II, 607.
8. The same, pp. 630–631.
9. See *Letters,* II, 829n, 50–51.
10. *Lambert Catalogue,* lot 358.
11. Thackeray's connexion with the *Foreign Quarterly Review* was first explored by Richard Garnett in *The New Sketch Book* (London, 1906), in which he collected the articles in that magazine that he believed to be by Thackeray and stated the reasons for his attributions. Garnett assigned twelve articles to Thackeray. Lewis Melville, reviewing Garnett's work in the London *Bookman,* XXX (April, 1906), 32–33, presented a somewhat different list, deriving from a memorandum in the hand of Whitwell Elwin, the friend of both Thackeray and Forster. In *Thackeray's Literary Apprenticeship,* pp. 133–137, Gulliver re-examined Thackeray's connexion with the magazine, and arrived at still other conclusions. Each of these writers depended chiefly on stylistic evidences for his attributions.

    The publication of *Letters* in 1945–1946 provided external evidence for assigning certain articles to Thackeray; and since that time other documents have come to light which afford reason for regarding further articles as his. A list of the articles in these two categories follows:

    "The Rhine, by Victor Hugo," XXIX (April, 1842), 139–167 (see *Letters,* II, 42, 44, 830).

    "The German in England," XXIX (July, 1842), 370–383 (see the same, II, 70).

    "The Last Fifteen Years of the Bourbons," XXIX (July, 1842), 384–421 (see the same, II, 42, 50–51, 70, 830).

    "Travelling Romancers. M. Dumas on the Rhine," XXX (October, 1842), 105–124 (an undated manuscript letter from Thackeray in the possession of Maggs Brothers forwards this article to Forster and asks him to make certain alterations in it).

    "George Herwegh's Poems," XXXI (April, 1843), 58–72.

    "English History and Character on the French Stage," XXXI (April, 1843).

    "Balzac on the Newspapers of Paris," XXXI (April, 1843), 140–168.

    "The Mysteries of Paris. By Eugène Sue," XXXI (April, 1843), 231–249.

(Forster wrote to Thackeray in a manuscript letter of 14 March 1842 owned by Maggs Brothers: "I'll send you the French Order in the course of the day. Did you think of Janin? The bearer will bring you Herwegh." In another manuscript note, evidently written later in the month and also owned by Maggs, Thackeray offers an unrhymed English version of the second stanza of Herwegh's "Zuruf"—see *New Sketch Book,* p. 119—and continues: "I will go to the Garrick to day for the paper and have kept your boy to alter a stanza on page 8." The only article in this issue of the magazine which is based on a long list of French books for which Thackeray would have needed an "order" is "English History and Character on the French Stage." The reference to Janin establishes Thackeray's authorship of "Balzac on the Newspapers of Paris," which deals with Janin's assault on Balzac as well as Balzac's attack on the Parisian press. The two notes also afford proof positive that Thackeray wrote "George Herwegh's Poems.")

"New Accounts of Paris," XXXII (January, 1844), 470–490 (see *Letters,* II, 126, 135).

"The Problematic Invasion of British India," XXXIII (April, 1844), 213–229 (see the same, II, 161).

For two other articles the stylistic evidence is so strong that I am inclined to join Garnett, Melville, and Gulliver (supported by Saintsbury, *Works,* V, xiii–xviii) in assigning them to Thackeray:

"French Romancers on England," XXXII (October, 1843), 226–246.

"Angleterre (by Alfred Michiels)," XXXIII (July, 1844), 433–442.

No doubt even this list fails to exhaust Thackeray's contributions to the *Foreign Quarterly Review.*

12. Undated manuscript letter (Fuller). The manuscript of Thackeray's unfinished article on the July Monarchy is at Harvard.

13. *Letters,* II, 50–51; *New Letters and Memorials of Jane Welsh Carlyle,* I, 121.

14. *Letters,* II, 64.

15. The same, p. 164; Charles Mackay, *Forty Years' Recollections of Life, Literature, and Public Affairs, from 1830 to 1870* (London, 1877), p. 83.

16. *Letters,* II, 362, 364, 373, 442, 459.

17. The same, pp. 171, 172, 216, 225, 229.

18. The same, p. 252.

19. My edition of *Thackeray's Contributions to the "Morning Chronicle,"* which is to be published in 1955 by the University of Illinois Press, will contain all of the articles listed in *Letters,* II, 845–846.

20. "Christmas Books—No. 2," 26 December 1845.

21. "Christmas Books—No. 1," 24 December 1845.

22. "Diary and Letters of Madame

d'Arblay. Vol. 6," 25 September 1846.

23. *Works,* XVI, 446–447.
24. 16 March 1846.
25. 21 April 1846; 27 August 1846; 19 June 1846; 2 April 1844; 4 July 1846.
26. See particularly Thackeray's reviews of 3 April 1845; 13 May 1845; and 31 December 1845.
27. 3 April 1845.
28. 13 May 1845.
29. 13 May 1845.
30. 26 December 1845.
31. 24 December 1845.
32. 13 May 1844.
33. 13 May 1845.
34. 6 May 1844.
35. 4 May 1846.
36. 24 December 1845.
37. 29 April 1844; 7 May 1846.
38. 2 April 1844.
39. *Letters,* II, 97, 139, 142, 147–148, 166, 175, 840–842.
40. See the same, pp. 142, 144, 158–159; and W. C. Desmond Pacey, "A Probable Addition to the Thackeray Canon," *PMLA,* LX (June 1945), 606–611.
41. *Letters,* II, 189, 190, 203; compare *Works,* VI, 452.
42. *Letters,* II, 65.
43. The same, p. 76.
44. *Works,* II, 622.
45. Compare the same, VI, 315–317; Bedingfield, p. 231.
46. *Letters,* II, 190–191.
47. *A Selection from the Correspondence of Abraham Hayward from 1834 to 1884, with an Account of His Early Life,* ed. H. E. Carlisle, 2 vols. (London, 1886), I, 106.
48. *Letters,* II, 212.
49. The same, pp. 214–215.

III (pp. 332–339)

1. He also published unimportant stories in *Ainsworth's Magazine* and the *New Monthly Magazine.*
2. *Letters,* II, 54.
3. See *Works,* IV, 201–253, *passim.*
4. The same, pp. 235–236.
5. The same, pp. 239–253.
6. A manuscript letter to F. M. Evans, 16 February 1857 (Bradbury Agnew), suggests this explanation, though it is conceivable that Thackeray omitted these stories simply because he found them "stupid." See *Works,* IV, 282–283.
7. The same, p. 265.
8. See the same, pp. xxi–xxii.
9. Fitz-Boodle's assertion in his concluding letter to Oliver Yorke, dated 10 July 1843, that "the story of the Ravenswing was written a long time since" (the same, p. 461), is simply a device to enable him plausibly to relate the subsequent history of his characters. Many passages (for example, pp. 390, 400–401, 427, 435) suggest that the story was begun in the winter of 1842–1843 and continued, instalment by instalment, the following year.
10. The same, pp. 356, 358, 354, 425.
11. The same, IV, xxii.
12. See, for example, *Letters,* II, 41–42.

13. *Works,* XI, 229.
14. The same, IV, 463.
15. See above, p. 209.
16. *Works,* IV, 472, 482.
17. See *Letters,* II, 141–144, 160, 840–841.
18. "Othon l'Archer," *Les Frères Corses* (Paris, 1867), pp. 247–274.

IV (pp. 339–347)

1. *Letters,* II, 29.
2. London, n. d., but 1810 or shortly thereafter.
3. This volume is still preserved at the Bowes Museum, Barnard Castle.
4. What follows is taken from my own copy of Foot's *Lives,* also annotated in a contemporary hand; *The Confessions of the Countess of Strathmore Written by Herself* (London, 1793); and the entry on the Strathmore family in G. E. C., *The Complete Peerage,* ed. Vicary Gibbs, 13 vols. (London, 1910–1953), XII, 400.
5. Quoted by Foot, p. 8.
6. The same, p. 35.
7. The same, pp. 28, 112.
8. The same, pp. 120–121.
9. The same, p. 114.
10. The same, p. 186.
11. Ed. Roger Ingpen, 2 vols. (New York, 1903), I, 17.
12. P. 111.
13. *Letters,* II, 38, 125.
14. The same, pp. 141, 149, 180, 156.
15. See above, p. 314.
16. See *Works,* VI, 134–177; *L'Empire,* 2 vols. (Paris, 1836), I, 220–245. Before this source was identified, critics assumed with some confidence that Thackeray in the Princess's Tragedy was retelling the story of Königsmark. His sources in general are discussed by Brander Matthews, "My Favorite Novelist and His Best Book," *Munsey's Magazine,* XVII (May, 1897), 230–234; Frank T. Marzials, introduction to *The Luck of Barry Lyndon* (London, n. d.), pp. xv–xxix; and Lewis Melville, "The Real Barry Lyndon," *Fortnightly Review,* July, 1911, pp. 44–55.
17. See Frank Wadleigh Chandler, *The Literature of Roguery,* 2 vols. (Boston and New York, 1907), II, 454–462.
18. *Munsey's Magazine,* p. 233.
19. *Works,* V, 164–169.
20. The formulation of Saintsbury (*Works,* VI, xi), who objects to this transition as implausible. On Thackeray's motives for writing Barry Lyndon, see *Buried Life,* pp. 27–29; 131, n. 62.
21. *Mr. Thackeray's Writings in "The National Standard" and "Constitutional,"* p. 85.
22. *Works,* V, 191.
23. The same, VI, ix.
24. See the same, pp. 234, 245, 252, 278–279, 309–311. This editorial comment was largely excised when Thackeray revised *Barry Lyndon* for his *Miscellanies.* See *Buried Life,* p. 131, n. 60.
25. P. 14.
26. *Letters,* II, 29.
27. The same, p. 76.

28. The same, p. 29.
29. See the same, I, 456–457; II, 24–25; *Works,* IV, 215; VI, 400, 402, 425–427.
30. *Letters,* II, 193.
31. *Cornhill Magazine,* XIII, 48.
32. *Works,* V, 78–79. Compare the same, V, 34, 91–92, 129; VI, 384, 551.
33. Pp. 297–298.

CHAPTER *13*
The "Punch" Connexion

I (pp. 348–354)

1. The chief source for the account of *Punch's* early years which follows is M. H. Spielmann, *The History of "Punch"* (London, 1895), but I have also drawn on a number of subsidiary sources, including the manuscript Silver diary.
2. Manuscript Silver diary, 7 March 1866.
3. The same.
4. The same, 23 July 1862.
5. Quoted by Spielmann, p. 308.
6. *Letters,* II, 54.
7. The same, p. 82.
8. Manuscript Silver diary, 28 June 1860; compare Spielmann, p. 306.
9. *Letters,* II, 135.
10. The same, pp. 169, 172.
11. Spielmann, p. 260.
12. The same, p. 253.
13. The same, pp. 103–104.
14. "A Legend of Jawbrahim-Heraudee," II (18 June 1842), 254.
15. VI (11 May 1844), 209.
16. *Letters,* II, 455.
17. *Works,* VIII, 1.
18. The same, pp. 37, 38.
19. The same, p. 45.
20. *Studies on Thackeray,* p. 48.
21. *Works,* VIII, 36–37.
22. The same, VII, 413.

II (pp. 354–361)

1. Manuscript Silver diary, 30 July, 1862.
2. "ML says when he first came to B & E John Forster ruled the roost—& bought ar article [for *Punch*] from Fonblanque which ML altered, thinking it libellous. JF indignant. Bought another on Lord Brougham—worse—ML refused it, & Fonblanque wrote no more." "ML again talks to P[ercival] L[eigh] and H[enry] S[ilver] of his rejection of Fonblanque's libellous articles to the disgust of Forster & affright of B & E" (the same, 12 March and 22 October, 1862).
3. *Glances Back,* I, 138. Dickens hit off this last feature once for all when he had Mrs. Gamp describe Jerrold "tossing back his iron-grey mop of a head of hair with the other [hand], as if it was so much shavings" (Forster, *Dickens,* ed. Ley, p. 462).
4. *Glances Back,* I, 139.
5. Walter Jerrold, *Douglas Jerrold.*

Dramatist and Wit (London, n. d.), p. 17. This work and the same author's *Douglas Jerrold and "Punch"* (London, 1910) are the chief sources of information concerning their subject.

6. Preface to *Collected Works,* quoted in the same, p. 561.

7. Quoted in the same, p. 526. In later life Jerrold was quick to defend his early radical mentors. When Thomas Holcroft was abused as an atheist in 1847, Jerrold defended him by describing the repressive atmosphere of Holcroft's time, when the term was applied indiscriminately to all reformers by "the wicked old hag, Old Toryism [who] spat the foul word at him as at others who openly and manfully exposed her wickedness" (*Douglas Jerrold and "Punch,"* p. 116).

8. So in *Thomas à Becket* (1829), as the contemporary critic George Daniel noted, "every opportunity is seized to exaggerate the pride, luxury and lasciviousness of the Church." In *The Mutiny of the Nore* (1830) the grievances of the mutineers are eloquently developed. In *The Rent Day* (1832) Jerrold attacks absentee landlords who squander in London gambling "hells" money wrung from their tenants. *The Golden Calf* (1832) satirizes excessive deference to wealth and position. And *The Factory Girl* (1832) attacks the practice of overworking children in the weaving industry. Yet, no more than Dickens's early novels, to which they afford an interesting parallel, can these plays be regarded as serious commentaries on pressing social problems. Jerrold's usual solution to the knots that he ties, as a critic of *The Factory Girl* pointed out, is simply "to have an extensive relationship discovered among the principal characters" (quoted in *Douglas Jerrold,* p. 212).

9. The same, p. 189. During the mounting agitation for reform in 1831, Jerrold "is reported to have written a very violent political pamphlet which was suppressed" (the same).

10. *Heads of the People: Portraits of the English,* 2 vols. (London, 1840), I, iv–v.

11. Spielmann, pp. 141–142, 268–270.

12. See Arthur William à Beckett, *The à Becketts of "Punch"* (London, 1903), the only substantial source, but a very unsatisfactory one.

13. Manuscript Silver diary, 9 December 1858.

14. *Glances Back,* I, 218.

15. P. 301.

16. The same, p. 328.

17. Manuscript Silver diary, 8 August 1866.

18. The same, 28 October 1868.

19. See particularly F. G. Kitton, *John Leech: Artist and Humourist* (London, 1884). William Powell Frith's confused and incoherent *John Leech: His Life and Work,* 2 vols. (London, 1891), is useful only for its illustrations.

20. Manuscript Silver diary, 21 October 1858.

21. Kitton, p. 6.

22. Spielmann, p. 436.

23. "Then we revert to poor Leech —his Voluntas was stronger than his arbitrium says P. L.—he could deny no one, not excepting himself. . . . P. L. tells of ye old father calling on him this morng & bowwowing about the article in the Times which implied that family money matters had injured Leech's health—'You must write & contradict this Mr Leigh' 'I shall be most happy to do so Sir, if you will supply me with some facts on which I may refute this statement.'—Old Leech was keeper of the London Coffee House. And ML says he knows that Leech accepted bills for the old man & his daughters for £3000 or so: which swept away the sum he received for his first 100 paintings. While JL was at Homburg [in 1864] the father called to borrow £50 of old Joyce & then of ML—& hearing this made JL very indignant & angry—& ML seeing how agitated he was said 'Your duty is to work for your wife & children, & not to let your mind be harassed—& if buttoning up your pockets leads to a quarrel with your father, I still should advise you to button them up'" (manuscript Silver diary, 26 October 1864).

24. P. 79.

25. Manuscript Silver diary, 26 October 1864.

26. Kitton, p. 70; confirmed in *Glances Back,* I, 136.

27. Manuscript Silver diary, 2 March 1859.

28. *Works,* II, 626–627.

29. 26 December 1845.

30. Manuscript Silver diary, 27 June 1866.

31. Spielmann, p. 74.

32. An account of representative evenings at the *Punch* table is given by Spielmann, pp. 68–73.

III (pp. 362–373)

1. "Thackeray was the only man upon the *Punch* staff," writes Joseph Hatton *(Critic,* 17 January 1885, pp. 34–35), "with whom Mark Lemon was not upon thoroughly easy terms. 'I never felt quite at home with him,' he said to me during one of our numerous gossips, 'he was always so infernally wise. He was genial; but whatever you talked about, you felt he would have the wisest views upon the subject. He seemed too great for ordinary conversation.'"

2. Compare *Letters,* II, 389.

3. Manuscript Silver diary.

4. *Glances Back,* I, 292.

5. Manuscript Silver diary, 9 April 1862. For further illustration of this class feeling, see Thackeray's condescending account of a *Punch* river-excursion, *Letters,* II, 247.

6. *Glances Back,* I, 290.

7. P. 13.

8. Spielmann, p. 296.

9. See *Douglas Jerrold and "Punch,"* pp. 26–29.

10. The same, p. 29.

11. See *Letters,* III, 342.

12. Spielmann, p. 74.
13. *Douglas Jerrold and "Punch,"* p. 26.
14. *Works,* IX, 307.
15. Spielmann, p. 101.
16. Christmas issue, 1844.
17. IV (27 May 1843), 216.
18. Quoted in *Douglas Jerrold and "Punch,"* p. 50.
19. IX (20 September 1845), 133; *Works,* VII, 362.
20. V (27 January 1844), 52.
21. VIII (5 April 1845), 153.
22. X (31 January 1846), 61.
23. Quoted in *Douglas Jerrold,* p. 540.
24. Quoted in the same, pp. 480–481. "Benjamin Sidonia," of course, was Disraeli.
25. XV (4 November 1848), 198; *Works,* VIII, 610.
26. J. A. Hamilton in *Dictionary of National Biography.*
27. "Gossip at Reculver," quoted in *Douglas Jerrold,* pp. 352–353.
28. Quoted by Spielmann, p. 230.
29. *Letters,* II, 681.
30. Quoted in *Douglas Jerrold,* pp. 529–530.
31. IX (23 August 1845), 94; *Works,* VII, 231.
32. XVIII (9 March 1850), 92–93; *Works,* VIII, 256–257.
33. Quoted in *Douglas Jerrold and "Punch,"* pp. 124–125.
34. "JL used to do battle with DJ. about the People, & their rights" (manuscript Silver diary, 27 May 1863).
35. "I remember him mentioning to me," Vizetelly goes on (*Glances Back,* I, 292), "his having noticed at the Earl of Carlisle's a presentation copy of one of Jerrold's books, the inscription in which ran: 'To the Right Honourable the Earl of Carlisle. K. G., K. C. B., &c., &c.' 'Ah!' said Thackeray, 'this is the sort of style in which your rigid, uncompromising radical always toadies the great.' "
36. *Letters,* II, 274.
37. The same, p. 281.
38. *Works,* IX, 308–309.
39. Thackeray's phrase about Leech, *Times,* 21 June 1862.
40. *The Man in the Moon,* III, 241.
41. Thackeray himself remarked on the way in which *Punch* had "raised his eyes from Bloomsbury to Belgravia" (Spielmann, p. 422) in his 1862 article on Leech for the *Times:* "Mr. Leech surveys society from the gentleman's point of view. In old days, when Mr. Jerrold lived and wrote for that famous periodical, he took the other side; he looked up at the rich and great with a fierce, a sarcastic aspect, and a threatening posture, and his outcry, or challenge was: 'Ye rich and great, look out! We, the people, are as good as you. Have a care, ye priests, wallowing on a tithe pig and rolling in carriages and four; ye landlords grinding the poor; ye vulgar fine ladies, bullying innocent governesses, and what not —we will expose your vulgarity; we will put down your oppression; we will vindicate the nobility of our common nature,' and so forth. A great deal was to be said on the Jerrold side, a

great deal was said—perhaps, even a great deal too much."

42. Quoted by Spielmann, p. 197.

43. Manuscript Silver diary. The earlier relation of Jerrold's political and social views to Dickens's is worth noting. In 1843 Jerrold contributed an article to the new *Illuminated Magazine* called "Elizabeth and Victoria" in which he expressed his abhorrence of old institutions and opinions and held the dead hand of the past responsible for most of the abuses and inequities of the present. On 3 May 1843 Dickens (*Letters,* ed. Dexter, I, 517) wrote to express his enthusiastic approval of these views: "It is very wise, and capital; written with the finest end of that iron pen of yours; witty, much needed, and full of truth. I vow to God that I think the parrots of society more intolerable and mischievous than its birds of prey. If ever I destroy myself, it will be in the bitterness of hearing those infernal and damnably good old times extolled. . . . I am writing a little history of England for my boy. . . . I have tried to impress upon him (writing, I daresay, at the same moment with you) the exact spirit of your paper. For I don't know what I should do if he were to get hold of any Conservative or High Church notions; and the best way of guarding against any such horrible result, is, I take it to wring the parrots' necks in his very cradle." Dickens was equally enthusiastic about Jerrold's other writings. He remarked, for example, in a letter of 16 November 1844: "I have so steadily read you, and so selfishly gratified myself in always expressing the admiration with which your gallant truths inspired me that I must not call it time lost" (the same, I, 638). When Dickens on 1 December 1844 read *The Chimes,* his first important public pronouncement on the "Condition-of-England Question," Jerrold was among the select group of invited guests.

44. Quoted in *Douglas Jerrold,* p. 445. How foreign this "new spirit" was to Jerrold's may be gauged by his announcement in a prospectus for *Douglas Jerrold's Shilling Magazine* the previous year that the great question of the day was "the social wants and rightful claims of the people"; that a "social contest" was beginning which must end in more equitable distribution of wealth, now that mankind had awakened "from a long, vain dream, that showed the many created only to minister to the few"; and that fiction should "breathe with a PURPOSE" and was admissible only *"if illuminating and working out some wholesome purpose"* (quoted in *Douglas Jerrold,* pp. 379–380).

45. *Letters,* ed. Dexter, I, 804.

IV (pp. 373–383)

1. It should be noted that "The Snobs of England" was rigorously revised before its publication as *The Book of Snobs* at two and sixpence in a little green-wrappered volume during 1848. Thackeray entirely omitted the political chapters (17 to 23), explaining in a note: "On re-perusing these papers, I found them so stupid, so personal, so snobbish—in a word, that I have withdrawn them from this collection" (*The Book of Snobs,* London, 1848, p. 66).
2. None the less, Jerrold thought well enough of the Snob papers, even in the period of the "Snob-Parson" controversy, to defend Thackeray by ironically attacking them in *Punch* in a letter signed "Slaverly Fitz-Toady." See X (6 June 1846), 249; *Douglas Jerrold and "Punch,"* p. 103.
3. *William Makepeace Thackeray,* p. 86.
4. *Works,* VII, xix; IX, xix.
5. A. W. Kinglake, *The Invasion of the Crimea,* chap. 14.
6. *English Traits* (London, 1903), p. 110.
7. *Reflections on the Revolution in France.*
8. *England and the English.*
9. *The English Constitution, Works,* ed. Forrest Morgan, 5 vols. (Hartford, 1891), IV, 124–125.
10. *Conversations with Northcote,* Works, ed. P. P. Howe, 21 vols. (London, 1930–1934), XI, 293.
11. Quoted by G. M. Young, "The Age of Tennyson," *Proceedings of the British Academy,* XXV (1939), 128.
12. London, 1866, p. 148.
13. Chap. 8.
14. See Stephen's sketch of "the true theory of snobbishness," "The Writings of W. M. Thackeray," pp. 332–336.
15. *British Novelists and Their Styles* (Cambridge, 1859), p. 245.
16. "The Writings of W. M. Thackeray," p. 333.
17. "Thackeray," *Westminster Review,* LI (July, 1864), 181.
18. Picking up Thackeray's whimsical observation in his introductory chapter, that it is his mission "to track Snobs through history, as certain little dogs in Hampshire hunt out truffles" (*Works,* IX, 261), Trollope remarks: "But we can imagine that a dog, very energetic at producing truffles, and not finding them as plentiful as his heart desired, might occasionally produce roots which were not genuine,—might be carried on in his energies till to his senses every fungus-root became a truffle" (*Thackeray,* p. 82).
19. *William Makepeace Thackeray,* pp. 84–85.
20. *Works,* IX, 297.
21. See the same, IX, 272–276.
22. Introduction to *The Book of Snobs* (London, 1911), p. ix.
23. These passages were too much even for Saintsbury, who owns that he would rather have liked

to examine Thackeray "for half an hour or so on his knowledge of the 'brutal un-Christian blundering feudal system'" (*Works*, IX, xxi).

24. The same, p. 301.
25. The same, p. 337.
26. The same, pp. 272–273, 375, 491.
27. The same, pp. 425, 355.
28. The same, p. 265.
29. *Studies on Thackeray*, p. 51.
30. Stephen, "The Writings of W. M. Thackeray," p. 335.
31. *Gradus ad Cantabrigiam* (London, 1824), p. 101. See *Works*, IX, 324.
32. The same, p. 261. Thackeray's use of the word "snob" has been surveyed by Margaret Moore Goodell, *Three Satirists of Snobbery: Thackeray, Meredith, Proust*, in *Britannica*, XVII (Hamburg, 1939), 9–22.
33. *Works*, IX, 269.
34. The same, p. 271.
35. The same, p. 429.
36. The same, p. 493.
37. *Correspondence of John Lothrop Motley*, ed. Curtis, I, 235.
38. Though one would use terms somewhat differently weighted, it is possible to agree with Whibley (*William Makepeace Thackeray*, p. 84), when he writes of *The Book of Snobs:* "[Thackeray] never shook himself free from its bondage. It is not uncommon, this spectacle of an author enslaved by his own book."
39. *Works*, IX, 316–317, 355.
40. *Studies on Thackeray*, p. 46.
41. *Works*, IX, 382–383.
42. Thackeray picked up this name from Hood's "Our Village."'
43. *Works*, IX, 259.
44. The same, pp. 408, 385, 409, 368.
45. The same, p. 389.
46. The same, p. 489.
47. The same, pp. xxi, 265.
48. The same, pp. 312, 364.
49. Edwards, *Personal Recollections*, p. 150.
50. *Works*, IX, 417.
51. Only once in *The Book of Snobs* does Thackeray go beyond his self-imposed restrictions. This is in his brief account of old Fawney (the same, p. 460), who has the sinister aura of a figure out of Graham Greene.
52. The same, pp. 258, 341.
53. *Culture and Anarchy*, ed. J. Dover Wilson (Cambridge, 1946), p. 68.

CHAPTER *14*

"Vanity Fair"

I (pp. 384–388)

1. *Biographical Introductions*, XIII, xvii. "Some years before the publication of *Vanity Fair*," Thackeray told J. F. Boyes (*Cornhill Magazine*, p. 121) "that he had a novel in his desk which, if published, would sell, he thought, to about seven hun-

dred copies." Boyes surmises that this might have been *Vanity Fair;* but it was probably "The Knights of Borsellen."

2. Here is the principal evidence against the 1841 date, apart from the absence of any certain reference to *Vanity Fair* until 1845: (1) A cancelled passage in the manuscript of Chap. 6 includes references to Hugo's *Le Rhin* and Sue's *Mystères de Paris,* which Thackeray mentions having read on 25 February 1842 and 18 January 1843 respectively (*Letters,* II, 42, 92). (2) Thackeray derived the character of Jos Sedley, who figures prominently in the novel's early chapters, from his friend George Trant Shakespear (see *Buried Life,* pp. 42–47). Shakespear was in India from 1829 until 1843, when he returned to Europe on furlough. Thackeray does not seem to have met him until shortly before 12 June 1844, when he wrote that he had seen him twice, adding, "we have besides exchanged cards genteelly" (*Letters,* II, 173). (3) In Chap. 4 there is what appears to be an unmistakable reference to Jerrold's *Mrs. Caudle's Curtain Lectures,* which began its course in *Punch* in January, 1845 (see Lambert Ennis, *Thackeray: The Sentimental Cynic,* Evanston, 1950, p. 137n). It may also be noted that Thackeray was out of England from August, 1844, until February, 1845, and had no leisure to embark upon new projects.
3. *Letters,* II, 190.
4. Undated manuscript letter (Fuller).
5. *Letters,* II, 198n. In 1847 Thackeray noted that "Colburn refused the present 'Novel without a Hero' " (the same, p. 262).
6. The same, p. 225.
7. The same, p. 232.
8. *Reminiscences of a London Drawing Room,* pp. 2–3.
9. This subject is considered at length in my *"Vanity Fair:* One Version of the Novelist's Responsibility," *Essays by Divers Hands,* N. S. XXV (London, 1950), 87–101.
10. *Letters,* II, 282.
11. The manuscript consists of Chaps. 1–6 and 8–13, two drafts being preserved of Chap. 6. Chaps. 1–4 and the first draft of 6 are in Thackeray's slanting hand, with unimportant corrections in his upright hand. Chap. 5 is entirely in upright; the second version of 6 in upright pieced out by blocks of page proof; 8 largely in slanting, but the final pages in upright; 9–11 alternately in slanting and upright; and 12 and 13 entirely in upright.
12. *Works,* XI, 96.
13. An example of the difficulties in which Thackeray's casual methods of work sometimes involved him may be cited from Chap. 59 (first published in No. 17 for May, 1848). Because of the pressure of time, he evidently did not see proof for this chapter; and two long paragraphs ("However, when" to "Mrs. George Osborne," *Works,* XI, 754–755)

were printed out of their proper order. They should appear after the paragraph ending "the arrival of his son" earlier in the chapter, p. 750. But Thackeray suffered no inconvenience from this gross mistake. "One or 2 people have found out how careless the last no of V.F. is," he told his mother (early in June, it is true, yet evidently referring to the May number), "but the cue is to admire it and consider the author a prodigy. O you donkies!" (*Letters,* II, 383). To this day no edition of the novel has printed these paragraphs in their proper sequence.

14. *Works,* XI, 768–770, 227–229 and 440, 282, 200–201, 530, 562.
15. See, for example, the same, pp. 186, 267, 275–276.
16. *Letters,* II, 286.
17. It should be noted that, though *Vanity Fair* is set in the early years of the century, Thackeray everywhere assumes that "the manners of the very polite world were not [then], I take it, essentially different from those of the present day" (*Works,* XI, 643). In his illustrations, indeed, he dresses his characters in the modes of the 1840s, on the ground that he does not have "the heart to disfigure my heroes and heroines by costumes so hideous" as those of the Regency (p. 884).
18. Quoted by Forster, *Dickens,* ed. Ley, p. 640.
19. *Letters,* II, 408.

II (pp. 388–400)

1. His remark concerning Becky at Brussels, "If this is a novel without a hero, at least let us lay claim to a heroine" (*Works,* XI, 369), is of course ironical.
2. See the same, pp. 318–319.
3. These paragraphs were much abbreviated when Thackeray revised the text of *Vanity Fair* in 1853. See *Works,* XI, 882–884, 60–61.
4. The seventh "novel," entitled "Crinoline," is different in nature from the rest. In part it is a parody of Thackeray's own excursions into footman-English; in part it is a study of the absurd behaviour of French dandies in England.
5. *Works,* VIII, 108.
6. The same, p. 126.
7. The same, p. 140. The admonition to "give his old sowl/ A howl" in the last stanza of this poem was apparently responsible for the name "Elias Howle" under which Thackeray appears in *Roland Cashel.* "Elias" may have been chosen in allusion to Thackeray's Irish uncle, Elias Thackeray.
8. *Works,* VIII, 84–86.
9. London, 1846, p. 408.
10. The same, pp. 430–431.
11. *Works,* VIII, 97. In a foot-note Thackeray admits that George's speech is a "gross plagiarism," citing *Eugene Aram* (pp. 418, 416) as his source.
12. See S. M. Ellis, *The Solitary Horseman* (London, 1927), pp. 253–259.

13. See Lever's preface to *The Fortunes of Glencore,* 3 vols. (London, 1857), for his own account of this change in his work.
14. See my article, "The Bentley Papers," *The Library,* fifth series, VII (September, 1952), 190–192.
15. *Letters and Remains* (London, 1865), p. 241.
16. *Letters,* II, 772–773.
17. Preface to *Le Mariage de Figaro, Théâtre Complet,* ed. Maurice Allem (Paris, 1934), p. 257.
18. Most of Thackeray's information of this kind had come to him over the years through conversation and general reading. But as he wrote, he was in touch with acquaintances who possessed expert knowledge of special subjects (see, for example, *Letters,* II, 327), and certain specific sources can be noted. Tom Moore's *Letters and Journals of Lord Byron* was useful in filling out his conception of the lives led by Regency dandies (*Works,* XI, 885). His portrait of Lord Steyne owes something to the newspaper accounts of the litigation that followed the death of the third Marquess of Hertford. He had worked up the background for the French chapters of his novel during the course of his labours on "The Last Fifteen Years of the Bourbons" for the *Foreign Quarterly Review.* For the Waterloo episode he consulted George Robert Gleig's *Story of the Battle of Waterloo* (*Letters,* II, 294); and he may also have read in manuscript Lady De Lancey's *A Week at Waterloo in 1815,* which offers some interesting parallels to Thackeray's Brussels chapters. This work was first published in the present century by Maj. B. R. Ward (London, 1906); but Thackeray could have seen it through Dickens (*Letters,* ed. Dexter, I, 305–306) or through Sir James Carmichael-Smyth, his stepfather's older brother, who was present at the death of Sir William De Lancey (Ward, pp. 110–111).
19. *Works,* XI, 219, 246.
20. The same, p. 361.
21. The same, p. 589.
22. The same, p. 528.
23. George Eliot, *Middlemarch,* book I, chap. 15.
24. *My Confidences* (London, 1896), p. 302.
25. *In My Good Books,* p. 126.
26. *Recollections, 1832 to 1886,* 2 vols. (London, 1899), I, 99.
27. See *Buried Life, passim. Vanity Fair* is discussed in Chap. 3.
28. See particularly *John Ruskin and Effie Gray* (New York, 1947), pp. 102, 131–133.
29. *Thackeray,* p. 97.
30. *Yeast* (New York, 1909), p. 19.
31. Surtees asserts that he was taken from Sir William Chaytor of Witton Castle, from whom he himself drew Lord Scamperdale in *Mr. Sponge's Sporting Tour* (Cuming, *Surtees,* p. 264). Saintsbury identifies him with Lord Rolle, the owner of Stevenstone and Bicton in Devonshire (*Works,* XI, xvii).
32. The same, pp. 112–113, 121–128, 884–885.

33. The same, p. 128.
34. The same, p. 367.
35. The same, pp. 476–477.
36. *Athenaeum,* 12 August 1848, p. 797.
37. *Works,* XI, 578.
38. "Contemporary Writers—Mr. Thackeray," XXXII (October, 1848), 447.
39. "Vanity Fair," *Times,* 10 July 1848.
40. So George Eliot remarked to a friend, after the publication of *Adam Bede* in 1859: "We see the great public so accustomed to be delighted with *mis*-representations of life and character, which they accept as representations, that they are scandalized when art makes a nearer approach to truth" (*The George Eliot Letters,* ed. Gordon S. Haight, 3 vols., New Haven, 1954, III, 176–177).
41. *Letters and Literary Remains,* III, 16–17.

III (pp. 401–406)

1. P. 29.
2. *Works,* XIII, 90–91.
3. The same, XI, 17, 414.
4. The same, p. 781.
5. *Pensées, L'Oeuvre de Pascal,* ed. Jacques Chevalier (Paris, 1936), p. 831.
6. *Works,* XI, 621. This phrase is of course intended to echo Fielding's "comic epic in prose," and Thackeray meant by it something far subtler and more civilized than his earlier magazine "comicalities." When Bedingfield (p. 30) asked him, "just before 'Vanity Fair' was published, whether it was 'funny,' he replied, 'It will be humorous.' "
7. *Works,* XI, 9, 103, 804.
8. See the same, pp. 472–475.
9. The same, p. 42.
10. *Songs, Ballads, and Other Poems,* ed. by his widow, 2 vols. (London, 1844), I, 234.
11. *Works,* XI, 544.
12. See the same, p. 829. A most piquant example of Thackeray's practice is cited by Saintsbury. In Chap. 51 the guests at Becky's Curzon Street assembly are all of the utmost fashion, "quite the cheese," in fact. They are accordingly named: "The Duchess (Dowager) of Stilton, Duc de la Gruyere, Marchioness of Cheshire, Marchese Alessandro Strachino, Comte de Brie, Baron Schapzuger, [and] Chevalier Tosti" (the same, XI, 639).
13. "Thackeray's Novels," *Bombay Quarterly Review,* I (January, 1855), 82–83.
14. *Works,* XI, 178–179.
15. The same, pp. 42, 651.
16. The same, pp. 100, 416.
17. The same, p. 412.
18. See the same, V, 263.
19. *Brief Memoir,* p. 12.
20. *Works,* XI, 284, 371–372, 628.
21. *Bentley's Miscellany,* 1848, p. 254.
22. *New Statesman and Nation,* 22 March 1941, p. 302.

IV (pp. 406–410)

1. For example, Deuceace from *The Yellowplush Papers,* Captain Rook from "Captain Rook and Mr. Pigeon," Captain Walker and Mr. Woolsey from "The Ravenswing," the Bareacres family from "The Diary of C. Jeames de la Pluche," the Perkins family from *Mrs. Perkins's Ball,* and Major Ponto from *The Book of Snobs.*
2. See Isadore Gilbert Mudge and M. Earl Sears, *A Thackeray Dictionary* (London, 1910), *passim.*
3. *Works,* XI, 207.
4. Robert Bell, "Vanity Fair," *Fraser's Magazine,* XXXVIII (September, 1848), 332.
5. *The Craft of Fiction* (London, 1921), pp. 95–96.
6. Edwin Muir, *The Structure of the Novel* (London, 1928), pp. 38–40.
7. The novel was planned from the first around Amelia and Becky, with George Osborne and Rawdon Crawley as the other main figures. Dobbin appears only very briefly as "Tawney" in the first draft of 1845; he was given his present name and raised to a prominent position in the story when Thackeray added Chap. 5 to his manuscript late in 1846.
8. So Thackeray has Becky buy Jos's picture at auction in Chap. 17 and preserve George's note to her in Chap. 29, events which turn out to be of crucial importance in the final chapter of the novel.
9. Close and careful planning was necessary, of course, within the monthly numbers. In each a situation was presented and brought to a climax, which in turn gave rise to curiosity as to what would follow. Part One deals with Becky's campaign to capture Jos's affections, in which she appears to have every reason to expect success; and the number ends with Jos's assuring himself, "Gad, I'll pop the question at Vauxhall." Part Two relates the failure of this campaign, but also tells of Becky's departure for the novel scene of Queen's Crawley. Part Three is taken up with her conquest of Rawdon Crawley; and Part Four describes her affecting discovery that, with a little patience, she could have had his father. And so it goes. Throughout the novel, moreover, Thackeray saves his most telling strokes for the conclusions of his monthly numbers: George's reconciliation with Amelia, the departure of the regiment for Belgium, George's "lying on his face, dead, with a bullet through his heart," Amelia's giving up her son to his grandfather, and the famous discovery scene.
10. *Book of Recollections,* I, 196.
11. The first hint for *Vanity Fair* came to him, so he relates, in the winter of 1830–1831 at Weimar (*Works,* XI, 793, 849).
12. *The Victorian Age in Literature* (London, n. d.), p. 126.
13. Delacroix wrote in 1849, after reading a French abridgement of

Vanity Fair: "Cela m'a intéressé au dernier point" (*Journal,* ed. André Joubin, 3 vols., Paris, 1932, I, 269).

14. See *Works,* XI, 63–64, 865.
15. The same, p. 780.
16. *Structure of the Novel,* p. 39.
17. *Craft of Fiction,* p. 100.
18. Pope, *An Essay on Criticism,* pt. III, l. 28.
19. *Works,* XI, 676. " 'When I wrote the [latter] sentence," Thackeray told Hannay (pp. 20–21), "I slapped my fist on the table and said *'that* is a touch of genius.' "
20. *Craft of Fiction,* p. 104.
21. "A Gossip on Romance," *Works,* 26 vols. (London, 1922–1923), XII, 194.
22. *Works,* XI, xx.

V (pp. 410–418)

1. *Works,* XI, 342, 227.
2. The same, p. 1.
3. The same, pp. 186, 267.
4. The same, p. 200.
5. The same, p. 721.
6. The same, pp. 537–538.
7. See above, pp. 385–386.
8. *Works,* XI, 258.
9. The same, p. 143.
10. The same, p. 246.
11. The same, p. 252.
12. *Letters,* II, 309.
13. *Works,* XI, 763.
14. The same, p. 767.
15. The same, p. 866.
16. The same, p. 792.
17. *Essays by Divers Hands,* pp. 96–100.
18. *The Silver-fork School,* p. vii.
19. This leaves out of account a later development, the radicalism that informs Dickens's novels after *David Copperfield,* in which the world of high life is seen as a monstrous ceremonial, ridiculous yet terrible in itself, and infecting with its poison the lower classes that imitate it. See *Essays by Divers Hands,* pp. 98–99.
20. See Thomas Hughes's introduction to *Tom Brown's School Days* (London, 1869), p. xiii.
21. In the last hundred years the point of view of Bulwer and Disraeli has been defended not so much by the aristocracy itself, which has experienced a failure of nerve, but by middle-class critics, intoxicated with aristocratic sentiment. So H. J. C. Grierson criticizes Thackeray for being deficient in "ease and naturalness" in his description of fashionable life, when *Vanity Fair* is compared with, of all books, Swinburne's *A Year's Letters.*
22. Quoted by Van Wyck Brooks, *The Confident Years, 1885–1915* (New York, 1952), p. 297.
23. The phrase is Walter Bagehot's, whose development of this conception in Chap. 9 of *The English Constitution* owes a good deal, it may be suggested, to *The Book of Snobs* and *Vanity Fair.*
24. See *Works,* XI, 77, 411, 829.
25. The same, pp. 828, 597.

26. The whole passage, which occurs in a letter of 1931, deserves quotation: "I have given *Vanity Fair* my first adequate reading. It seems to me to be a great novel—very great. The greatest drawback to me in this and *The Newcomes* is that mundane motives and interests seem to be Thackeray's own ultimates, *non obstant* pious ejaculations when he talks of Amelia. Of course I am not talking religion but of the scale of intellectual preoccupations. I admit that the bias is more natural in London than elsewhere. The prizes are greater—and there was splendor in Thackeray's time—and even in ours." (*The Pollock-Holmes Letters,* ed. M. De W. Howe, 2 vols., Cambridge, 1942, II, 294)
27. *The Love Letters of Walter Bagehot and Eliza Wilson,* ed. Mrs. Russell Barrington (London, 1933), p. 185.
28. *Works,* XI, 604.
29. The same, p. 820.
30. *Jane Eyre,* 2d ed., I, x.
31. LXIX (April, 1864), 415.

VI (pp. 418–426)

1. *The Writing of Fiction* (New York, 1925), p. 27.
2. Continental critics have perhaps seen this more clearly than English, since the English tradition has always encouraged the view that an artist is also a moralist. Hence, though Thackeray is quite legitimately regarded as a classic realist within the frame of English literary history, French and German commentators have sometimes declined to call him a realist at all. Taine nearly a hundred years ago devoted the whole of a long article on Thackeray, later incorporated in his *Histoire de la littérature anglaise,* to showing that he was primarily a satirist. And Auerbach in *Mimesis* (pp. 32, 492) has recently passed over *Vanity Fair* in his survey of realism through the ages, holding that in this "great novel" the "method of elaboration remains ethical rather than historical," since Thackeray "on the whole preserves the moralistic, half-satirical, half-sentimental viewpoint very much as it was handed down by the eighteenth century."
3. *Works,* XI, 438–439.
4. The same, pp. 532–533.
5. See particularly George Henry Lewes, *Morning Chronicle,* 6 March 1848.
6. *Works,* XI, 725.
7. The same, pp. 96, 274.
8. The same, p. 243.
9. The same, p. 484.
10. "The Writings of W. M. Thackeray," p. 352.
11. *A Backward Glance* (New York, 1934), pp. 206–207.
12. George Brimley, *Essays,* ed. William George Clark (London, 1882), p. 256.
13. How Thackeray conceived of Becky remains a mystery. He assures the reader that he first heard her story at Weimar in 1830–1831 (*Works,* XI, 849). Yet it is probable that the Pauline of

his surreptitious Paris trip the previous spring counted for something in his picture of Becky during her vagabond years; Theresa Reviss, the illegitimate daughter of Charles Buller, gave him hints for her character in girlhood (*Letters,* I, clvii–clx); and he may have added other details from the notorious histories of such public figures as Lady Morgan (see Lionel Stevenson, "*Vanity Fair* and Lady Morgan," *PMLA,* XLVIII, 547–551) and the governess in the household of the Duc and Duchesse de Praslin (see William Roughead, *The Seamy Side,* London, 1938, p. 282). One is inclined to look for a more specific model, but if such a person existed, she no doubt belonged to the Bohemian side of Thackeray's life, of which in the nature of the case we are granted only occasional and fleeting glimpses.

14. Thackeray skirts the topic of Becky's sexual attractiveness, as he does that of her presumed infidelity. Yet within the limits imposed by Victorian conventions, he contrives to make his meaning clear enough. Had Waterloo not intervened, she would have granted George Osborne an assignation. (Thackeray writes of an "elopement," but this was obviously impracticable with a major battle impending, and he wants the reader to understand that an assignation is meant.) Except for Rawdon's timely return, Lord Steyne would at last have received the favours for which he had paid so heavily. If accident thus preserves Becky in technical virtue until her spectacular downfall, Thackeray leaves no doubt that even this shred of rectitude is lost (see *Works,* XI, 812–813) after she becomes a raffish outcast on the Continent.
15. See the same, p. 233.
16. The same, pp. 638, 856.
17. The same, p. 14.
18. See, for example, her long letter to Amelia in Chap. 8.
19. *Literature of Roguery,* II, 462.
20. *Works,* XI, 662.
21. "The mantelpiece cast up a great black shadow . . . over two little family pictures of young lads, one in a college gown, and the other in a red jacket like a soldier. When she went to sleep, Rebecca chose that one to dream about" (the same, pp. 84–85).
22. See the same, p. 131.
23. The same, p. 2.
24. See *Buried Life,* pp. 31–37.
25. See, for example, *Works,* XI, 217, 371–373, 406, and above all the whole of Chap. 50, which to many Victorian readers was the high point of the novel.
26. The same, p. 134.
27. *Studies in Classic American Litterature* (New York, 1923), p. 3.
28. The phrase is Pritchett's.
29. *Prefaces,* pp. 716–717.
30. *Works,* XI, 878.

VII (pp. 426–428)

1. *North British Review,* LXXIX, 223.
2. "Thackeray," *Macmillan's Magazine,* LX (February, 1864), 356.
3. *Letters,* II, 258.
4. *Glances Back,* I, 284.
5. See Appendix B: Thackeray's Agreement with Bradbury and Evans for *Vanity Fair.*
6. See *Letters,* II, 283n, 772, 312n; "Thackeray's Writings," *Edinburgh Review,* LXXXII (January, 1848), 46–67.
7. Quoted by William Harris Arnold, *Ventures in Book Collecting* (New York and London, 1923), pp. 221, 223.
8. Hatton, *Critic,* 17 January 1885, pp. 34–35.
9. *Letters,* II, 333.
10. XXIV (1848), 252.
11. *Tablet,* 1 July 1848, p. 426.
12. "Vanity Fair," 22 July 1848, p. 709.
13. *Letters,* II, 311–312.
14. The same, pp. 318, 334, 365.
15. The same, IV, 155.

Genealogies of the Thackeray, Becher, and Shawe Families

Entries in the genealogies that follow have been restricted to persons figuring in this book. More complete genealogies of the Thackerays and the Shawes will be found respectively in *The Letters and Private Papers of William Makepeace Thackeray* and *The Buried Life*. The Becher genealogy has been compiled from information furnished by Lieutenant-Colonel Ley Becher, Mr. M. L. Dix-Hamilton, and Major V. C. P. Hodson, and from data in the Commonwealth Relations Office and the War Office.

I. THACKERAYS

(*1*) Archdeacon Thomas Thackeray (1693–1760)
m. (1729)
(2) Ann Woodward (1709–1797)

(*3*) Thomas (1736–1806)
m. (1763)
(*4*) Lydia Whish (1737–1830)

(*5*) Frederic (1736–1832)
m. (1767)
(*6*) Elizabeth Aldridge (1736–1816)

(*7*) Jane (1739–1810)
m. (1772)
(*8*) Major James Rennell (1742–1830)

(*9*) William Makepeace (1749–1813)
m. (1776)
(*10*) Amelia Richmond Webb (1757–1810)

(*11*) Henrietta (1746–1807)
m. (1771)
(*12*) James Harris (*d.* 1790)

(*20*) George (1777–1850)
m. (1816)
(*21*) Mary Ann Cottin (*d.* 1818)

(*22*) William (*b.* 1778)

(*23*) Emily (1790–1824)
m. (1803)
(*24*) John Talbot Shakespear (*d.* 1825)

(*25*) Richmond (1781–1815)
m. (1810)
(*26*) Anne Becher[1] (1792–1864)

(*27*) Augusta (1785–1849)
m. first
(*28*) John Elliot
m. second
(*29*) Alexander Halliday (*d.* 1849)

(*41*) Mary Ann (1817–1879)

(*42*) George Trant (1809–1844)

(*43*) Colonel Sir Richmond (1812–1861)

(*44*) WILLIAM MAKEPEACE THACKERAY (1811–1863)
m. (1836)
(*45*) Isabella Shawe (1820–1893)

(47) Anne Isabella ("Anny") (1837–1919)
m. (1877)
(48) Sir Richmond Ritchie (*d.* 1913)

(49) Jane (1838–1839)

(50) Harriet Marian ("Minny") (1840–1875)
m. (1867)
(51) Sir Leslie Stephen [2] (1832–1904)

(52) Hester Thackeray
m.
(53) Richard Fuller

(54) William

(55) Laura

(30) Charlotte Sarah (1786–1854)
m.
(31) John Ritchie (*d.* 1849)

(46) William

(32) Webb (*b.* 1788)

(33) St. John (*b.* 1791)

(34) Francis (1793–1842)
m. (1829)
(35) Anne Shakespear

(36) Charles (1794–1846?)

(37) Sarah Jane Henrietta ("Selina")
m.
(38) Robert Langslow

(13) Elias (1771–1854)
m. (c. 1802)
(14) Rebecca Hill (*d.* 1846)

(15) Dr. Frederic (1774–1852)

(16) Martin (1783–1864)
m. (1834)
(17) Augusta Yenn (*d.* 1869)

(18) Jane Townley (1788–1871)
m. (1813)
(19) George Pryme (1781–1868)

(39) Alicia
m. (1837)
(40) William Joseph Bayne (*d.* 1844)

[1] Mrs. Thackeray remarried in 1817, her second husband being Major Carmichael-Smyth ("GP").

[2] Stephen remarried in 1878, his second wife being Mrs. Herbert Duckworth. Virginia Woolf was a child of this marriage.

II. BECHERS

(*1*) Captain John Becher, R. N. (b. 1736)
m.
(*2*) Anne Fleyeham (1737–1825)

(*3*) John Harman (1764–1800)
m. (1786)
(*4*) Harriet Cowper [1] ("GM") (1770?–1847)

(*5*) Captain Alexander, R. N.
m.
(*6*) Frances Scott

(*7*) Anne

Children of (*3*) and (*4*):

(*8*) John (*b.* 1788?)

(*9*) Harriet (1790–1820?)
m. (1810)
(*10*) Captain Allan Graham (1786–1816)

(*10*) Anne (1792–1864)
m. (1810)
Richmond Thackeray
(*See Genealogy I*)

(*11*) Maria (1795–1822)
m. (1817)
(*12*) Colonel Alexander Knox
(1759–1834)

Child of (*9*) and (*10*):

(*13*) Mary ("Polly") (1815–1871)
m. (1841)
(*14*) Colonel Charles Carmichael (*b.* 1790)

[1] Mrs. Becher, then called Mrs. Christie, married Lieutenant-Colonel Edward William Butler in 1806.

III. SHAWES

(*1*) Rev. Merrick Shawe (*b.* 1692)
m.
(2) Catherine Browne

(*3*) Matthew (1736?–1796)
m. first
(*4*) Jane Fersse
m. second
(*5*) Mary Moore

(*6*) Brigadier General Robert (*d.* 1811)

(*7*) Lieutenant-Colonel Merrick
(*d.* 1843)

(*8*) Lieutenant-Colonel Matthew
(*d.* 1826)
m. (1813)
(*9*) Isabella Creagh

(*10*) Jane
m.
(*11*) George Corsellis

(*12*) Merrick Arthur Gethin
(*b.* 1814)
m. (1853)
(*13*) Ellen Cattell

(*14*) Isabella Gethin
(1816–1893)
m. 1836
WILLIAM MAKEPEACE THACKERAY
(*See Genealogy I.*)

(*15*) Captain Arthur George (*b.* 1818)

(*16*) Jane Bagwell Corsellis

(*17*) Henry Robert (*b.* 1823)

Index

Two abbreviations are employed in this index: T. for Thackeray and G. for the Genealogies immediately preceding. Titles are listed under authors, and characters in books under titles.

OPINIONS AND ATTITUDES

WORKS

ABOUT THE AUTHOR

Gordon N. Ray was born on September 8, 1915, in New York City and grew up in Winnetka, Illinois. He graduated in 1936 from Indiana University and received his doctorate from Harvard in 1940. He has taught at Harvard, the University of Oregon, and New York University. Since 1946 he has been Professor of English at the University of Illinois and Head of the Department of English there since 1950. He has been awarded two Guggenheim Fellowships and a Rockefeller Grant, and in 1948 was elected a Fellow of the Royal Society of Literature. That same year, he served as a member of the original U.S. Educational Commission which established the Fulbright program in the United Kingdom. During the war he was an officer on the aircraft carriers *Belleau Wood* and *Boxer* in the Pacific.

Professor Ray is a well-known authority on Victorian literature, who has long specialized in Thackeray and has written and edited several books on aspects of the novelist's work. These include *The Buried Life: A Study of the Relation between Thackeray's Fiction and His Experience* (1952), four volumes of *The Letters and Private Papers of William Makepeace Thackeray* (1945–1946) as well as editions of *The Rose and the Ring* and *Esmond.*

Thackeray: The Uses of Adversity, 1811–1846, with its companion volume *Thackeray: The Age of Wisdom, 1847–1863,* which will appear later, is the first full-scale biography of the novelist. It was written with the complete cooperation of the Thackeray family, who released to Professor Ray Thackeray's private papers—material which had been hitherto unavailable to a biographer.

Professor Ray's next undertaking will be a comprehensive biography of H. G. Wells, a work which has been authorized by the Wells family and which will be based on the large collection of Wells papers recently acquired by the University of Illinois.